IVAN THE TERRIBLE

Ivan the Terrible.

IVAN THE TERRIBLE

BY

K. WALISZEWSKI

Translated from the French by

LADY MARY LOYD

ARCHON BOOKS
HAMDEN, CONNECTICUT
1966

FIRST PUBLISHED 1904

REPRINTED 1966 BY ARRANGEMENT WITH
WILLIAM HEINEMANN, LTD.
IN AN UNALTERED AND UNABRIDGED EDITION

LIBRARY OF CONGRESS CATALOG CARD NUMBER: 66-16088
PRINTED IN THE UNITED STATES OF AMERICA

INTRODUCTION

THE work of Peter the Great and Catherine the Great show us modern Russia, armed already, *cap-à-pie*, for all the conquests, moral or material, gained then or since. But this work, as all men know, possessed certain antecedents, and Peter gave himself out to be a follower—of whom ? His immediate predecessors we know—the earliest Romanoffs, obscure sovereigns of an Empire cut off from all European contact, closed to all external influence, and incapable of evolving even a rudimentary civilization from its own elements. Going back further, to the closing years of the sixteenth century, we see the *sinoutnoié vrénica* ('the troublous times')— that is to say, disorder, anarchy, barbarism, darkness. Yet, looking closely, the sudden brightness of the eighteenth century was no dawn. For a rising sun the light was all too brilliant. Peter the Great was not mistaken. The darkness out of which his vivid genius flashed was only an eclipse.

The internal and external development of the great Northern Empire seems to partake of the nature of the avalanche. At widely-parted intervals we have a sudden displacement of the centre of gravity, resulting in a swift movement forward, followed by a more or less lengthy period of immobility. This phenomenon has occurred several times already, and appearances are all in favour of its reproduction. The reason and the explanation are both very simple. The nation, in the performance of the mighty task laid upon it, was bound to meet with formidable obstacles, and consequently to make successive efforts. At this moment, and for the past twenty years, its progress has been apparently suspended internally, and checked on the lines it had previously pursued externally.

This is because Russia's activity has been absorbed and diverted by the conquest of a new territory, destined to widen the field of her efforts yet further—to the Chinese Seas on one side, to the Persian Gulf on the other. But the problems momentarily put aside are ripening all the same, slowly but surely, and beware of the avalanche !

The predecessor whom Peter the Great invoked was a contemporary of the last Valois Kings, and to this period we must go back, indeed, to discover the reformer's political and intellectual origins. The task is a heavy one, but it is the price which must be paid for our comprehension of the final result, and it is the *raison d'être* of the volume I now place in my readers' hands. I shall be told, no doubt, that I ought to have begun with it ; but in history, as in anatomy, it would be foolhardy to go, in the first place, to the very beginnings, to the embryo, to the cell—and in reality I am only following the regular order and method of every study.

From the sixteenth to the eighteenth centuries, then, Russia dwelt apart, or almost apart, from the European community and from civilization. But she had made a previous effort to enter both, and the work to which Voltaire lent his aid and gave his praise was begun when Charles IX. and Henri III. reigned over France. At that moment Muscovy, huge and barbarous, set forth to enter into contact with her Western neighbours. She found the road barred. Poland, with Sweden, threw herself athwart it, and the removal of the obstacle was the work of more than a hundred years. But, if it had not been for Batory, the hands of the clock which marks the hours of all great historical evolutions might have whirled round the dial a century before. Externally, the acquisition of the Baltic seaboard, the destruction of the last vestiges of the Tartar power, the conquest of Siberia, the opening up of political and commercial relations with all the European countries ; internally, the introduction of the elements of foreign culture, the reorganization of the State on the very basis we see at the present day — all this, accomplished by Peter and Catherine, was undertaken, outlined, even partly realized, in the course of that first morning on which an all too speedy evening fell.

Who did it ?   The man of whom Custine wrote that he had,
' so to speak, outrun the limits of the sphere within which God
permits His creature to work harm,' the tortures, whose figure
is a nightmare, whose name is a terror, the emulation of Nero
and Caligula—the Terrible !

Here we have one of the most curious instances of aberration
to be found in legend, and even in critical history.

To begin with the name ' the Terrible,' with which, to
insure the recognition of my personage, I have been forced to
head my volume—the name is, I say, a misinterpretation.   The
Russians of the present day, deceived by a translation imposed on them by foreigners, do not recognise this themselves.
The Germans hesitate between *der Schreckliche* (the Terrible)
and *der Grausame* (the Cruel), and while both versions are
incorrect, the second is the worst.   Never did the Muscovites
of his time call Ivan thus.   He was the *groznyï*.   Now hearken :
In the course of an epistolary dispute which is one of the
curiosities of the period, Batory having reproached his
adversary with surrounding himself with battle-axe-men
(*ryndy*) when he received the King's envoys, Ivan replies,
' Eto tchine gossoudarskii, da i GROZA ' ' Thus it must be,
for my rank and the respect I must inspire ').

The Groza has never meant any other thing.   Consult the
'Domostroï,' the famous Muscovite household book of that
epoch, as to the duties imposed on the father of the family ;
he is expected to be *groznyï*—that is to say, respected and
worthy of respect.   But what, then, of the tortures, the
scaffolds, the hecatombs of human lives, whereof the chroniclers
speak ?   That is another matter.   Do you know, in any European country, a chapter of sixteenth-century history that
reads like an idyll ?   In Poland, perhaps, where the *szlachta*,
with the last of the Jagellons, was inaugurating the perilous
experiment of the *noli me tangere*.   And there, again. Batory
set things in order for a time.   But from this point of view
Poland and Russia were the very antipodes. and if the latter
has succeeded where the former failed it is just because she
has not been too dainty as to her methods.   Look into the
huge crucible in which this people has laboured, from the Ural
to the Carpathians, the White Sea to the Black ; it is not

gentleness, politeness, consideration, that made it possible to mingle, and bray, and melt twenty diverse races into the compact block which is the Russia of to-day ! That Ivan IV., in the course of his work, may have gone somewhat beyond the atrocity usual in his century, may be. We will go back to that. But both in legendary and in critical history the surname of ' the Terrible ' has become synonymous with an unreasonable and inexcusable ferocity, purely barbarous in its origin, and carried to madness in its manifestations. To anybody who knows the power there is in words the consequence cannot be doubted : the word has set its false hallmark on the thing.

The evocation of the man and his surroundings cannot, indeed, be parted from some hideous sights and my readers must brace their nerves to meet some severe shocks. Yet athwart these gloomy visions they will perceive that of which I have spoken—the sunrise. The *bright* sun, the *red* sun, of the rhapsodists : in their tongue the two adjectives are one and the same. A blood-stained sun, lighting up a gloomy landscape. That, again, is another matter. The ideal here sought and gained is not, perhaps, the most seductive in the world's history ; but an ideal it is, and it gave, and still gives, the law to a great nation.

In the last Rurikovitchy who ruled—for Feodor was a mere shadow—Kaveline, one of the leaders of the Slavophil school, has already recognised ' the central figure ' of his country's history. Since then attempts at posthumous rehabilitation and apotheosis have so multiplied as to reach a not less evidently excessive point in the other direction. I shall endeavour to determine, between these opposing currents, what is truth and what justice.

It has not appeared to me possible to begin this study without preceding it by a general view of the geography, political, social, and intellectual condition, and habits and customs of a country into which, even nowadays, the historian must penetrate in the guise of an explorer. To these subjects the first four chapters of the book are devoted. Their length and detail must be excused ; without them I should have run the risk of failing to make myself understood, and of talking in perpetual riddles. To most of my readers, I believe, this *key* will be indispensable.

My authorities this time include few unpublished sources. Of the documents I might have utilized most have either been printed or continue inaccessible. The literature of the subject is exceedingly abundant, so much so that, to avoid overloading my pages, I have abstained, with very few exceptions, from direct references. I may add that this literature exists, as a whole, in the form of unworked materials, collections of documents, or monographs. The historical edifice has yet to be built up.

I beg my friend, I. Stchoukine, whose rich library and unwearying kindness have alone enabled me to begin and accomplish my task, to accept the expression of my deep gratitude.

CONTENTS

PART I

RUSSIA IN THE SIXTEENTH CENTURY

CHAPTER I

THE COUNTRY AND THE PEOPLE

PAGES

I.—RUSSIA, NEW AND OLD. II. — THE TERRITORY. III.—
SOCIAL MATTERS : THE ARISTOCRACY. IV.—POLITICAL
AND SOCIAL ORGANIZATION : THE ORIGIN OF ABSOLUTISM.
V.—THE PEASANTS. VI.—THE SERFS. VII.—THE TOWNS-
FOLK. VIII.—THE CHURCH - - - - 1-34

CHAPTER II

POLITICAL AND SOCIAL LIFE

I.—THE CENTRAL POWER. II.—PROVINCIAL ORGANIZATION.
III.—THE MIÉSTNITCHESTVO. IV.—THE COMMUNE. V.—
JUDICIAL ORGANIZATION AND LEGISLATION. VI.—THE
ECONOMIC SYSTEM. VII.—THE FINANCES - - 35-61

CHAPTER III

INTELLECTUAL LIFE

I.—CAUSES OF ITS WEAKNESS. II.—INTELLECTUAL CURRENTS.
III. — LITERATURE. IV. — ART. V. — THE RENOVATING
MOVEMENT - - - - - - 62-90

CHAPTER IV

HABITS AND CUSTOMS

I.—THEIR ASPECT, PHYSICAL AND MORAL. II.—THE WOMEN.
III.—THE FAMILY. IV.—SOCIETY - - - 91-115

xi

PART II

THE YOUTH OF IVAN

CHAPTER I

THE FIRST RUSSIAN TSAR

PAGES

I.—THE BIRTH OF THE TERRIBLE. II.—THE GOVERNMENT OF
THE BOÏARS. III.—MARRIAGE AND CORONATION. IV.—
SYLVESTER AND ADACHEV. V.—THE FIRST ASSEMBLY :
RUSSIAN PARLIAMENTARIANISM - - - 116–138

CHAPTER II

THE FIRST REFORMS

I.—THE REFORMING CURRENTS. II.—THE NEW CODE. III.—
THE REORGANIZATION OF THE 'SERVICE.' IV.—THE RE-
LIGIOUS REFORM - - - - - 138–156

CHAPTER III

THE EXPANSION EASTWARDS—THE TAKING OF KAZAN

I.—THE REMNANTS OF THE MONGOL EMPIRE. II.—IVAN'S
ARMY. III.—THE CAPTURE OF KAZAN IV.—THE CONSE-
QUENCES. V.—THE CAPTURE OF ASTRAKAN. VI.—THE
COSSACKS. VII.—THE CRIMEA AND LIVONIA - 156–172

CHAPTER IV

THE CONQUEST OF LIVONIA

I.—HISTORICAL ANTECEDENTS. II.—THE LIVONIA OF THE SIX-
TEENTH CENTURY. III. — THE MUSCOVITE CONQUEST.
IV.—THE EUROPEAN INTERVENTION - - - 172–187

CHAPTER V

THE STRUGGLE FOR THE EMPIRE OF THE BALTIC

I.—SWEDEN AND POLAND. II.—THE COALITIONS. III.—THE
COLLAPSE OF THE ALLIANCES : MAGNUS. IV.—IVAN'S
CANDIDATURE FOR THE POLISH THRONE. V.—THE ELEC-
TION OF BATORY - - - - - 187–215

PART III

THE CRISIS

CHAPTER I

THE POLITICAL AND INTELLECTUAL EVOLUTION

PAGES

I.—THE CONFLICT OF IDEAS AND PRINCIPLES. II.—THE DIS-
GRACE OF SYLVESTER AND ADACHEV. III.—THE FLIGHT OF
KOURBSKI - - - - - - 216–236

CHAPTER II

THE OPRITCHNINA

I.—THE FICTIONS AND REALITIES OF THE DRAMA. II.—THE
TERROR. III.—THE TSAR SIMEON. IV.—THE OPRITCHNINA
AT THE BAR OF HISTORY - - - - 237–273

CHAPTER III

THE ANGLOMANIA OF IVAN THE TERRIBLE: IVAN AND ELIZABETH

I.—THE FIRST ENGLISHMEN IN RUSSIA. II.—PROJECTS OF
ALLIANCE. III. — A PROJECTED MARRIAGE. IV. — MARY
HASTINGS. V.—THE DUTCH COMPETITION AND THE RUP-
TURE - - - - - - 273–297

PART IV

THE END

CHAPTER I

THE POLISH INVASION : BATORY

I.—BATORY. II.—THE STRUGGLE. III.—THE POLISH ARMY.
IV.—THE RUSSIAN ARMY. V.—THE CAPTURE OF POLOTSK.
VI.—THE POLES IN MUSCOVY. VII.—THE DIPLOMATIC
INTERLUDE. VIII.—THE SIEGE OF PSKOV - - 298–326

CHAPTER II

THE LOSS OF LIVONIA—ROME AND MOSCOW

I.—CHÉVRIGUINE'S MISSION. II.—THE PAPAL MEDIATION. III.
—THE TRUCE OF IAM-ZAPOLSKI. IV.—POSSEVINO AT
MOSCOW. V.—THE DAY AFTER THE TRUCE - - 326–349

CONTENTS

CHAPTER III

THE CONQUEST OF SIBERIA : ERMAK

PAGES
I.—CONQUEST AND COLONIZATION. II. — THE STROGANOVS.
III.—THE COSSACKS. IV.—ERMAK IN SIBERIA - 350-357

CHAPTER IV

THE COURT OF IVAN THE TERRIBLE—HIS PRIVATE LIFE

I.—THE COURT. II.—THE SLOBODA OF ALEXANDROV. III.—
IVAN'S DOMESTIC LIFE. IV.—THE TSAR'S FAMILY - 357-377

CHAPTER V

THE MAN AND HIS WORK

I.—HIS DEATH. II.—CHARACTER AND TEMPERAMENT. III.—
KNOWLEDGE AND INTELLIGENCE. IV.—IDEAS AND FEEL-
INGS. V.—THE RESULTS OF HIS REIGN - - 377-399

BIBLIOGRAPHY - - - - - - 400

INDEX - - - - - - - 417

PART I

RUSSIA IN THE SIXTEENTH CENTURY

CHAPTER I

THE COUNTRY AND THE PEOPLE

I.—RUSSIA, NEW AND OLD. II.—THE TERRITORY. III.—SOCIAL
MATTERS : THE ARISTOCRACY. IV.—POLITICAL AND SOCIAL
ORGANIZATION : THE ORIGIN OF ABSOLUTISM. V. — THE
PEASANTS. VI.—THE SERFS. VII.—THE TOWNSFOLK. VIII.—
THE CHURCH.

I.—OLD AND NEW RUSSIA.

' AN eagle, many-winged, with lion's claws, has fallen upon me.
He has robbed me of three Cedars of Lebanon : my beauty,
my wealth, my children. Our country is deserted, our city
is in ruins, our markets are destroyed. My brothers have been
carried to a place where neither our fathers, nor our grand-
fathers, nor our forefathers have dwelt. . . .'
Thus, by the mouth of one of her chroniclers, did Pskov, a free
and republican town, absorbed, in the year 1510, into the new
Muscovite Empire, lament her lost independence, her broken
privileges, and her exiled sons. The father of Ivan the Terrible,
Vassili Ivanovitch, had just passed by, had carried off the great
bell which for centuries had called the townsmen to the
viétchié—the popular meetings of the place—deported
hundreds of families—quickly replaced by Muscovite immigrants—to the interior of his territories, and proclaimed the
incorporation of the Republic with his State.
And this, in a then unknown corner of the European world,
was the repetition, at short notice, of a chapter of European
history. Thus, at Liége, in 1467, Charles the Bold had over-
thrown the famous *perron*, the ancient bronze column, at the
foot of which, for centuries past, the people had been wont to

I

make its laws and accomplish all the acts of its public life.
Thus, too, at the same time, and hard by, Louis XI., striving
with his vassals of Burgundy, Brittany, and Guyenne, was
labouring to ' *réunir les fleurons* ' of the crown of France.

From one end of the European continent to the other, this
was the decisive hour of great political formations, everywhere
attended by the same painful crises. But here, in the far
North-East, the task of the ' gatherers of the Russian land,'
as they have been called, was especially difficult and arduous.
This was, in fact, no matter of welding together provinces already
bound by numerous affinities, common traditions, an evident
solidarity of interests. Conceive the France of the fifteenth century conquered by the English, and some Burgundian Prince
founding, not at Dijon even, but in Germany, in Switzerland,
or in Italy, the nucleus of a new monarchy, destined to gather
into one whole the rsmnants of the French fatherland, dismembered, broken into pieces. There you have the equivalent
of the obscure and laborious process of gestation which gave
birth, in the early days of the sixteenth century, to that new
world, the Russia of the Ivans and the Vassilis.

What was that Russia ? Not the country you now traverse
in your sleeping-car from Kiev to St. Petersburg, from Warsaw
to Irkutsk. The Russia of Kiev had passed away ; as yet the
Russia of St. Petersburg was not. Of the lands which in the
tenth and eleventh centuries had made up the Empire of the
Jaroslavs and the Vladimirs, the Sovereign seated at Moscow
held not an inch. He called himself Duke, or Tsar, ' of All the
Russias ' indeed, but his right to assume the title was much on
a par with that of the English kings, his contemporaries, to
reckon the crown and arms of France in their own patrimony.
The Russia of Kiev was now part of the Polish territory ; the
Russia of Mokhilev belonged to Lithuania. Red Russia, White
Russia, Little Russia, were all held by neighbours. Moscow
was but a Russian colony in a foreign—a Finnish—country.

Between the eleventh and thirteenth centuries, the Empire
of Kiev had melted away in the fratricidal struggle waged by
the sons of Vladimir Monomachus. In the thirteenth century, it
underwent a Tartar invasion, in the next, a Polish-Lithuanian
conquest, and naught remained. At the height of the tempest,
George Dolgorouki, one of Monomachus' heirs, put himself at
the head of a band of Russian colonists in quest of a new home.
Crossing the huge forests which at that time parted the plain
of the Dnieper from that of the Volga, he pushed north-
westward, subjugating the tribes of Finnish origin he found on
his way. And this led to Moscow, founded in 1147—a town
set in a conquered country, an emigrant station. And here,
again, the Mongol invasion had overtaken the scarcely settled

colony, and imposed foreign laws and foreign customs. For two centuries, reckoning from the disaster of the Kalka (1224), it bowed the country down under all the weight of an Eastern tornado. It was only towards the close of the fifteenth century that the Muscovite princes, taking advantage of the slow crumbling of the Mongol Empire, felt strong enough to cast off the yoke. They had laboured, meanwhile, to bring together some neighbouring colonies, first, and then some other remnants, relatively near, of the ancient Russian fatherland, and thus had gathered them up a new empire, and endowed Russia with a new home. Novgorod had been theirs since 1478 ; Tver, Rostov, Jaroslav, soon joined them. Ivan III.— the Great, as he has been justly called—added more territory, which had not been included within the boundaries of Ancient Russia, pushing the frontiers of New Russia as far as Finland, the White Sea, and the frozen seas to the north, and towards the Ural on the east. His son Vassili added Riazan and Novgorod Siéverskiï, to the south. Did all this constitute a country in the historical meaning of that word ? Not yet !

II.—THE TERRITORY.

When he succeeded to the throne, in 1533, Ivan IV.—the Terrible—inherited a territory already extensive, but which, geographically speaking, lacked unity and harmony. The tumult of battle, the confusion of conquest, were apparent everywhere. It was a scene of spoils scattered broadcast. Around the Muscovite nucleus in the centre had been grouped, in constantly broadening eccentric circles, territories which, for the most part, had no resemblance, even, to provinces, and can only be designated by topographical indications : the Governments of Arkhangelsk, Vologda, and Olonetz to the north-east ; those of Novgorod and Pskov to the north-west ; to the west and south-west, the region of the Dnieper, and the present Government of Smolensk, the western portion of the present Government of Kaluga, part of that of Tchernigov, and the western parts of those of Orel and Kursk ; north-east lay the Steppe country, without any definite southern frontier, and for its northern limit the 55th parallel—the northern boundary, in other words, of the present Governments of Kaluga, Tula, Riazan, Tambov, Penza, and Simbirsk ; and, lastly, to the east, the basin of the Kama and its tributaries, the Viatka, the Tshoussova, and the Biela.

A singularity which in itself paints the nature of this settlement is that its most recent and distant conquests, Novgorod and Pskov, with their dependencies, were its most important constituents ; for these included the industrial and commercial regions of the country, and on these, economically speaking, the new Empire subsisted and depended.

Industries were trifling, trade brisker, but still confined to very modest proportions. The population of this land of desolate marsh and moor, living mostly by fishing and only quite exceptionally by husbandry, drew its chief subsistence from a certain flow of merchandise passing to and fro between the Baltic seaboard and the interior of the country. But on an area of 282,127 square versts there were but fourteen towns. Most of these, too, were no more than tiny forts (*ostrojki*), and in the districts (*piatiny*) of Biéjets and Olonetz, a huge country covering 171,119 square versts, there were no towns at all; their place was taken by villages (*possiélki*), with markets and small bazaars.

Up to near the second half of the sixteenth century, Novgorod, with its 5,300 dwelling-houses, was the most important of all the towns in the Empire, save Moscow; and at Pskov the inventories of the period enumerate 1,300 shops or trading-houses within the town alone, apart from the suburbs. But these documents everywhere point to a phenomenon which looms large in the sixteenth-century history of this particular sphere—the swift extinction of the civilian citizen, properly so called, eliminated by the military element which takes his place. At Gdov, which boasts the largest number of inhabitants belonging to this class, the lists for 1580-1585 only give fourteen! And this is the work of the Muscovite conquest, which, with its system of general confiscation and its bestowal of the confiscated properties on men of its own choice, has rapidly succeeded in changing the face of the country, even as to its social elements. Now, these newcomers are all warriors, and Moscow, in her invading march, her overflowing expansion, still preserves the primitive characteristic of her first settlement—a military colony in a conquered country.

And it could not be otherwise, for this, like all the other provinces of the new Empire, remains a battlefield, with frontiers ill-defined on one side, and constantly disputed elsewhere. Amongst the fortresses protecting it on the north-west, Smolensk, only conquered in 1514, is still the nominal capital of a Lithuanian-Polish Palatinate, and Viélikié-Louki will soon be snatched by Batory from Ivan IV. North-eastward colonization creeps gradually along the White Sea, from the Onega and the Northern Dvina to the Ural; but possession is limited along this coast—*pomorié*, as it is called—to the seashore and the river-banks, and even from the economic point of view, monasteries—strategically-occupied points more than pious foundations—take first rank here. That of Solovki, on the White Sea, possesses, with valuable salt-works and fisheries, a police force and a little army of its own. Further on, east of the Dvina, the conquest is barely outlined : the only rallying-point of the poor fishing population is a half-yearly fair at Lampojnia, on the Mezen, and, the Mezen once crossed, there is a desert country.

A further singularity is that Moscow, girdled by a ring of fortified posts, remained an open town, with all the appearances of a temporary settlement. The city proper, indeed—the *Kreml* —was surrounded by battlemented walls studded with towers. But this enclosure, which included the Sovereign's palace, some boïars' houses, a few churches and monasteries, did not in any sense encircle the life of the capital. The town, with its wooden dwelling-houses, its shops, its markets, its *gostinnyï dvor*, a stone-built bazaar on the Levantine model, and all its busy trade, escaped outwards in huge suburbs, some open, some protected by mere wooden palisades, and all stretching out into the country, till its meadows and tilled fields mingled with the houses and shops. Industrial life was scattered still further afield, in spacious *slobodas*, perfect villages, which neighboured it, still amongst fields and woods and gardens, with more monasteries, whose white enclosures and gilded church domes carried the landscape, half urban, half rustic, far out to the horizon. And a fitting capital it was for this Empire on its outward march, moving to a future that still lay obscure, hidden in a perpetual beyond.

The designations of the hastily-formed provinces of the new Empire corresponded with the migratory nature of their constitution. Men said ' The towns beyond the Oka,' ' beyond the Kama,' the word town (*gorod*) meaning, to them, the territory with its chief town. For the central region itself, the nucleus of the Empire in process of formation, the expression was ' The towns beyond the Moskva, *zamoskovnyié gorody*.' Nijni-Novgorod, recently conquered by the rulers of Moscow from another group of the descendants of Monomachus, was sometimes looked on as belonging to this central region, and sometimes relegated, with Arzamas and Mourom, to the outer zone. And yet here the Russia of the North-West, just beginning her new life, possessed another Kiev, as it were, on the very marches of the annexed territories. The situation, the beauty of the site, were both the same. Jenkinson, the Englishman, starting thence. in 1558, with his flotilla of galleys, for the Far East, was to see a renewal of the period of the floating caravans despatched by the Princes of Kiev on the ' Voyage to Greece.' But all around, even to the neighbouring river basin of the Kliazma, save for Vladimir, where some remnants of vanished splendours still remained, the conquest had laid the country waste and scattered it with ruins. The population in the country parts still clung to the soil. In the towns no one was left, save the soldiers, who were everywhere. This is the general hall-mark of the new settlement. The populated centres of the province of Moscow, beyond a radius of some 60 to 100 miles, themselves bore this mark. Northward, at the distance thus indicated, stretched an essentially military zone, wherein military considerations were constantly mingled with peaceful occupations, and the urban districts—Tver, Rjev, Zoubstov, Staritsa—were all strategic points. South-ward, the towns of Serpoukhov, Kashira, and Kolomna, on the Upper Moskva, and the Oka, guarded the passage of the two rivers against an ever-threatening invasion. Beyond these lay another desert, the *dikoïë pole* (wild field), not to be colonized till in the second half of the century.

Such was the territory to which the rule of Ivan IV. was to annex, with Kazan, Astrakan, and their dependencies, the low-lying lands along the Middle and Lower Volga, the Kama, the Viatka, and the Caspian seaboard, and to which, as a field for future hope, was to be added, from the banks of the Volga to those of the Don, the Northern Doniêts, and the Lower Dnieper, the enigmatic sphere of the *Kozatchina*, that huge reservoir into which, from the furthest depths of Poland and Muscovy alike, a whole population of willing exiles per-petually flowed; upon which, from either side, the same action of laws, political and social, poured forth, in one continuous stream, the same quota of diverse elements, driven out of their natural centres by those three eternal instruments of the formation and disaggregation of societies—the spirit of revolt, the spirit of enterprise, and the spirit of liberty.

As to the total numbers of the population within these borders we have no clue, not even approximate. Touching the capital itself, information varies to an extent which defies all certainty. The number of houses set down for the year 1520—41,500—would give us a population of at least 100,000 souls. But thirty years later the Pope's Envoy, Possevino, gives 30,000 as a more likely number. True it is, indeed, that the town, during the interval, had undergone a Tartar invasion which had laid it in utter ruin. But the same thing is true of most of the towns of this Empire, in which war still raged almost everywhere, and, between any two given periods —often in the space of a year—changed the whole face of a country.

From the ethnographical point of view, the Russian element in nine-tenths of this country was that exceedingly slight one arising out of a very recent colonization. There is no necessity, at this period, for scratching the Muscovite to discover the Tartar, or, above all, the Finn. The bulk of the population everywhere is of this latter race. Yet, in this respect, the conquests of the Terrible and his successors have been the chief instruments of the introduction into the composition of the Empire of that great diversity, the existence of which Keppen's map even now demonstrates. We have no documents, indeed, on which to found any exact opinion as to the part played by the various races. This scarcely appears, except in the moral and intellectual life of the country, and these I shall set forth later. Politically it is almost non-existent ; whether by elimination or absorption, the Muscovite hegemony has put down all resistance. Socially, the difference of origin does not appear, for another reason. It is hardly possible to assert that this Muscovite centre contained two, or several, distinct societies, in mutual but antagonistic contact. Was there, in fact, any society at all ?

III.—Social Classes : The Aristocracy.

Amidst the divergencies on which a certain school of history and politics has been fond of dilating, even to exaggeration—divergencies greatly diminished at a later date, which then separated this growing world from Western Europe—the absence of all social classes holds the front rank. Other features of dissimilarity may easily be noted. There was no feudal organization, nor any of its modern offshoots ; no chivalry, nor survivals from it ; no Church armed with secular powers, and using them to battle with the State. But all these features are easily traced back to one common denominator—no social classes.

The phenomenon is genuine, but most complex, both as to its causes and its manifestations. In this country, of course, as in every other, there are rich men and poor, labourers and tradesmen, townsfolk and country folk, and a variety, therefore, of social elements. But these elements have no real organic value here. Let me explain myself.

Ivan IV. was to spend his whole life warring against the boïars. The boïars certainly formed an aristocracy, and the country, indeed, recognised several of these. Along with the boïars, the descendants of the old appanaged Princes—who traced back their origin in some cases to Rurik, the first Russian, in others to Guédymin, the first Lithuanian, Prince, and who all held governmental powers in that country—claimed a predominant position. Some members of the elder branch of the family of the founder of the dynasty—the ruling house of Moscow was of the younger branch—and still holding remnants of their ancient patrimony, had just claims to high pretensions, and did not fail to put them forward. They enjoyed certain rights and privileges, clearly denoting their former quality as independent Sovereigns, and fought for them fiercely.

But read the Code drawn up by the grandfather of the Terrible, the *Soudiébnik* of 1497 : not a trace does it bear of all these rights and privileges and pretensions! The clergy once set apart, it divides all the remaining dwellers in the country into two categories, which have no social quality about them, and in which the diverse conditions history creates count not at all : ' men who serve ' on one side, ' men who do not serve ' on the other—*sloojilyié* and *niésloojilyié*, nothing more. What does this mean ? It means that the legislator wiped out all historical precedents, and, dealing despotically with the mass of beings at his disposal, divided it up according to the constitution of the existing settlement at Moscow— that, as I have endeavoured to show, of a campaigning army.

In a regiment, there are neither princes nor churls, neither merchants nor labourers—there are soldiers, corporals, officers. And here we have a regiment. In a prison, the prisoners are only known by their numbers. And this is, or is to be, a prison. The *sloojilyié* are soldiers, who are to help their chief to ' gather up the soil of Russia.' The *niésloojilyié* are the labourers, the fatigue-parties, who feed the army on its march. Neither class has any place, or dignity, or function, save that allotted to it by the regulation. Every man to serve in the ranks —that is the general order. No sign of any hierarchy of birth. In the first category, with the boïars, the Princes, the great officers of the Crown, the chief functionaries, and hardly distinguished from them by a subordination of a purely administrative character, we see the humble workers, civil and military, blacksmiths and gunners, carpenters and private soldiers. Merchants and agriculturists, again, in the other category, are mingled together under the common law of the taxation imposed on them. The *sloojilyié* of the highest rank do, indeed, enjoy certain privileges—they perform the higher functions, they own the land. In the eye of the law their testimony carries greater weight, and the indemnity rightfully paid them for an offence is three times that a mere *diak* (clerk) can claim. But this tariff of honour, varying according to grades and occu- pations, affects every rank. There is nothing social about it, as yet. It forms part of the emoluments assigned to each post.

I have yet to explain how it became possible to carry out this artificial grouping and despotic classification of the social forces. It was inevitable, in the first place, that elements so torn apart and cast into new and arbitrary moulds should have but little coherence at the outset. As regards the aristocratic element this was assuredly the case. Here, as in the West, the higher stratum of society found its first nucleus in the Prince's immediate following. Etymologists disagree as to the origin of the word *boïar*. Whether it comes from *boï* (fight), or from *bol, bolïi, bolchyï* (greater), it was used, in the first instance, to designate the comrades of the leader of the primitive band, his *droojinniki* (*droojina*, suite, company), who played, at his side, the part played by the *anthrustions* of the first Frankish chiefs, the Anglo-Saxon *thanes*, the *ministeriales* in the heart of feudal Germany. But whereas in the West the relations thus formed between the Princes and their vassals were solidified by the establishment of each and all on domains, in political and social functions, clear, fixed, hallowed by law, by custom, and by habit, the same relations here continued vague, and shared thegenera mobility of all things. For a long time the Prince was a nomad, and his *droojina* followed, or did not follow, him. There was no rule nor any obligation in this matter. The chief could dismiss his comrades, and they could leave him if they chose. They frequently used their right. When the Prince of Volhynia undertook a campaign against the Prince of Kiev, in 1149, his *droojina* failed him, and exposed him to disaster. No constraint was recognised. When Russia was all cut up amongst a number of Sovereigns, the boïars had no scruple about going over from one ruler to another, according to their own interest or fancy, and these desertions were no disgrace whatever. They were not regarded as felonious acts. The deserters continued to hold their lands, and carried them into the pale of the authority of the new chief, chosen of their own free will.

When Moscow began to play her part in history, she did not hesitate to take advantage of these habits, which she recognised as a wonderful instrument to serve her policy of unification —a means of ruining the neighbouring States by their dis-aggregation, and strengthening her own sovereignty at their expense. She had become an unrivalled centre of attraction, so the game held no risk for her ; everything came to her, none dreamed of leaving her. Thus, from one neighbour to another, she gathered up the remnants of the lesser planets absorbed into her own sun—all the wreckage from scattered Courts and disbanded troops—and found in them an eminently plastic substance, easily shaped in her own chosen mould.

The Sovereign had fresh companions—not even the com-rades who had shared his perils and his triumphs, but beaten men, captives, rooted up from their own soil. Further, the whole aristocracy in the heart of this North-Eastern Russia, even that which had remained on its hereditary domains,

lacked any sufficient consistency. Its descent was not over
ancient, and it had no solid foundation. Under the feudal
régime, the relations between the Sovereign and the great lords
had their counterpart, on a lower scale, in those between the
nobles and their churls. Serfdom completed vassalage. Here,
as we shall see, amidst a free agricultural population, which
only gave the great landed proprietors a sorely-bargained and
disputed, and always most precarious, forced service, the
counterpart was non-existent. And to use these floating elements at will and solidify them, under another form, into a
military organization, the power of Moscow must have been
strongly constituted indeed.

IV.—POLITICAL AND SOCIAL ORGANIZATION : THE ORIGIN
OF ABSOLUTISM.

The origin and nature of this power have given rise to much
conjecture. The school of history at the teaching of which I
have already hinted has chosen to recognise it as an organic
phenomenon, arising out of the temperament of the Slav
race, domiciled, by the chances of destiny, in a land far distant
from its ancient home. It has also taken it to be the only
régime that has proved capable of supplying the special
needs of this race, politically speaking, and of insuring the
living existence of the settlements founded by it. After careers
occasionally very brilliant, but always short, all the Slav States
founded on other principles have proved themselves insufficiently protected against an abnormal development of the aristocratic element, and weakening of the central power.

But whence came the special inclination of the Slav colony
in the north-east to adopt this régime, and its adaptability
to it ? Monsieur Zabiéline has ascribed the phenomenon to
the principle of domestic absolutism developed by the teaching of the Eastern Church. Monsieur Kostomarov holds
that it proceeds from the Tartar conquest, and others have
attributed it to the influence of the Finnish element. These
three explanations are of small value. The Eastern Church
wielded quite as great an influence, or greater, óver Southern
Russia during the Kiev period, and during that very period
the application of a personal and absolute power, as realized
in Moscow towards the close of the fifteenth century, was
unknown. The most ancient information we have as to the
Slav peoples—Byzantine chronicles, Procopius' historical
works, those of the Emperor Leon, of Dithmar, of Merseburg
—shows us popular assemblies wielding supreme power, or
sharing it, and the Slavonic tribes settled in Russia form no
exception to this rule. As Nestor testifies, they even did

without Princes. Later, in the eleventh century, we find the same democratic institutions at Kiev and Novgorod, at Smolensk and Polotsk. From one end of the country to the other the *viétchie* (from *viéstchat*, to announce), as the popular gatherings were called, are doing their work with varying privileges : here a full exercise of sovereign power, there a right to choose the ruler, and everywhere a more or less complete share in every authority, guaranteed by regular contracts and formal charters.

Autocracy itself, in its first form, was not synonymous, here, with absolute power. Certainly the Muscovite *samodiérjets* is the counterpart of the Byzantine *autocrator*, but the absolutism of the Byzantine Emperors admitted the clergy to a share of power. And for a lengthened period the Muscovite clergy recognised the *samodiérjavié* merely as a symbol of the national independence in dealing with the foreigner. It reserved the rights of the Church, at all events, if not those of the people, too. The word, nevertheless, favoured a dangerous misunderstanding, and, as a matter of fact, even long before the coming of the Tartars, the rival principle of popular sovereignty, compromised first in the North-Eastern regions, where the Princes of Souzdal and Riazan succeeded in establishing their dynasties on a firm basis of heredity and primogeniture, only maintained itself in exceptional cases. At Pskov and Novgorod it was preserved in all its integrity till the close of the fifteenth century. Elsewhere, from the beginning of the thirteenth, it had been eliminated or visibly weakened.

The phenomenon does not find its explanation in the Mongol hegemony any more than in the Byzantine influence. The former did, indeed, introduce a radical change into the relations between governments and the governed. For the traditional source of supreme power, the popular favour, it substituted the caprice of the new sovereign masters. A journey towards the banks of the Volga and gifts offered to the Khan were better than any election. The pilgrim hied him homewards with an *iarlik* which made any other investiture superfluous. The Florentine Union and the fall of Constantinople also worked, to some extent, in the same direction. Up to the end of the fourteenth century, the Church recognised but one *Tsar* in Russia —the Emperor of Constantinople—called ' Emperor of the Russians ' and ' Sovereign of the Universe,' even in the prayers of the Muscovite clergy. After that date it became necessary to carry the same homage elsewhere, and the ruler of Moscow rose according to the measure of the Byzantine Sovereign's fall.

Yet all these incidences, we must admit, played but a

secondary part; their action decided nothing. As to the influence of the Finnish element on the evolution in question, if the fact that a conquered people has imposed its ways, its ideas, its customs on its conquerors is not altogether undiscoverable in history, we must at least conclude, in every example known to us, that this triumph was accounted for by some superiority of culture. In this case no such hypothesis can be entertained. The Russian colonists of the thirteenth and fourteenth century were certainly barbarians, but those they had to deal with were more barbarous still, and it was not force of numbers which gave them the victory.

The key to the riddle lies, as it seems to me, in the combined action and mutual reaction of two phenomena to which I have previously referred : the absence of any organic development in the heart of Russian society, and the military form imposed on that society by the circumstances attending the constitution or reconstitution of its new settlement in the north-east. Here Russian colonization found itself, for many years, in a hostile country, hemmed in by foes. Thus the Sovereign became the leader of an army. In this quality he naturally acted as a dissolvent on social elements which possessed no sufficient coherence, and, as they crumbled to atoms, his power fed on their weakness.

The origins of most States have witnessed the reproduction of these phenomena. The curious thing, in the case of this eccentric community, is that after long tarrying on the outer borders of European life, it was suddenly initiated into certain of Europe's noblest conquests, and into the refinements of a culture according but ill with the backwardness of its organization, social and political. Everything in it was done all at once, and the normal course of progress was often reversed. In a certain sense, the civilizing current, coming from without, has favoured the development of absolutism in this country, by endowing the personal power with resources and means of action it could never have drawn from the heart of a barbarous society. Ivan IV. was an 'intellectual,' and as such a far more redoubtable despot than Louis XI., who professed scorn for literature, science, and the arts. He only took men's bodies, but Ivan was to take their souls, and shut them up in that iron cage of his, within which all Russia was to live, bent double, for centuries to come.

It is easy to show how this cage was built. When a sufficient tale of ' comrades,' tempted from neighbouring Princes, had been enticed away, and Moscow was overflowing with men fit for service, the lord of the city grew eager to put down the system of free enlistment which had enabled him to fill up his fighting corps. His neighbours, indeed, had begun the work for him. Their own interest had impelled them to impose some restrictions in the matter, but it was a Republican and so-called Liberal Government which had taken the decisive step. Republics are responsible for a good many misdeeds of this nature, and nobody can accuse me of dealing with present events—the fact occurred in the year 1368 ! At that date the Republic of Novgorod decreed that any citizen quitting her territory forfeited all right to hold any property within it. All Moscow had to do was to follow suit. For some time yet the principle was respected, but even under Ivan III. any ' man who served ' who seemed inclined to leave the Prince was cast into prison ; and to get out, he had not only to renounce his right, still nominally respected, but to undertake not to use it, and sometimes to furnish security as well.

I dwell on these details because they are indispensable to any comprehension of the interior development of the nation. Ivan IV. was to apply the precedents thus created in the broadest fashion, going so far as to establish a sort of mutual insurance against the infidelity of his *sloojilyié*.

Yet princes and boïars, even thus enlisted and settled in the ranks, preserved a certain autonomy, political and social, rooted in their illustrious origin and their possession of the ancient domains, or the remains of them—appanages and freehold lands—over which they still held certain sovereign rights and numerous privileges. To this the Muscovite Government applied a twofold remedy—first, by placing at the head of its new military hierarchy, not the descendants of Rurik and Guédymin, natural peers and rivals of the new master, but his own ' comrades '—those who had been his first helpers in the task of ' gathering up the soil of Russia,' even if their ancestors had been no more than humble stable-grooms. The absence of any corporate spirit, any caste feeling, in this aristocracy in embryo made the operation all the easier.

To this the Muscovite policy added another and a yet more efficacious expedient. A system of confiscation, energetically applied, amidst the destruction of the ancient principalities annexed to the Empire, placed a huge area of land at the Government's disposal. This Moscow parcelled out afresh, but, when she bestowed them on her ' servants,' she carefully avoided preserving the peculiar rights attending the possession of these lands by the old proprietors. They were no longer called appanages or freeholds (*vottchiny*) : they were mere *pomiéstia*— in other words, as their name denotes (*miésto*, place), allotments, corresponding to the posts held by their occupiers in the ' service,' and intended as remuneration for their work. They were thus life interests, or hereditary only in so far as the *pomiéshtchik's* heir showed himself fit to succeed him in his functions too. They were free from taxes, like the *vottchiny*, but burdened with the heaviest impost of all, that of forced service. They bore some analogy to the feudal holdings of the West, but differed from them in that, far from the service being a freely accepted condition and charge on the fief, the fief, in this case, was the consequence, the reward, of an arbitrarily' imposed service. To sum it up, there was no aristocratic or corporative position here. There was pay, emolument in kind. And, further, there was a deliberate intention to gradually assimilate the ancient appanages and freehold lands to this new type of property, and the *vottchinniki* to the *pomiéshtchiki* of the new régime.

The new territorial holdings, uncertain both by their mode of constitution and their slight chance of permanence, remained within very small proportions. Some did not cover more than 30 *diéssiatines* (about equal to a French *hectare*, or 2½ acres, English), and even within these limits their bestowal was often delayed, or purely fictitious. Towards 1570, out of 168 ' children of boïars '—the term used to describe the fallen descendants of those high functionaries who had been unable to transmit the titles of the posts they had held to their heirs— out of 168 of these young men, borne on the ' service ' lists at Pootivl and Rylsk, 99 had been given nothing, because there was no post to give. And at the same time, and for the same reason, a certain *pomiéshtchiki*, very well provided for on paper, had not received 74 *diéssiatines* out of the 80 conferred on him !

Hence, in matters of household life, lodging, food, clothing, the mass of the *sloojilyié lioodi* were scarcely distinguishable from the common peasantry. Their condition sometimes appears even lower. The dwellings of a few great men, holding high posts, and well paid accordingly, were the only ones which, though invariably built of wood, presented an imposing appearance, with their many pavilions clustered against a central block, their covered outer staircases, their projecting galleries, their elaborate roofs, and huge outbuildings. In most cases these palaces were replaced by *isbas*, which, with their wooden floor, daily washed, scraped, and swept, the truss of hay by the entry to wipe the visitors' feet, and a certain display of plate, more often pewter than silver, in the first room, had no lordly quality about them.

The difference between the boïar and the peasant was more especially marked by the number of servants the former thought himself obliged to keep—cooks, bakers, gardeners, tailors, workmen of every kind. Other daily guests he had, higher in degree, but rather less important, whose only function was to follow the master, on foot or horseback, whithersoever he went, and keep him company on his travels, in his business,

and his pleasures. I had forgotten the steward, but he was
the most indispensable man of all. Even if he only held a few
trifling acres, the *pomiéshtchik* could not do without this *alter
ego*, nor himself cultivate the soil on which he was to live.
Had he possessed the desire, he would not have had the time.
His time belonged to his Sovereign, who, from infancy to
extreme old age, disposed of it at will. Campaigning service,
service at the desk—the *sloojily* is a man of all work. We see
him called out to fight. He takes a small bag of millet, a few
pounds of salted pork, a little salt and pepper mixed (if his
means allow of his indulging in this last much-appreciated
condiment, already regarded as a luxury). To these supplies
he adds a hatchet, some tinder, and a cooking vessel, and therein
consists his whole equipment. On campaign he will dispense
with the services of a military commissariat, non-existent here.
When he comes back to his property, to find it devastated,
perhaps, and pillaged, certainly, by that same steward, he will
pick up the orange-skins and scraps of pumpkin thrown from
the passing traveller's vehicle—see Herberstein—but he will
not even knock at his neighbour's door except on horseback
and attended by a serving-man.

Such are his fortunes. And it not unfrequently happens
that his desires tend towards quitting them, and losing himself
in that other category of ' non-servers ' who, not having the
same burdens to bear, are often more comfortably circum-
stanced. The only thing that holds him back is the chain that
binds him to his post. Of *esprit de corps* he has no trace. In
fact, the line of demarcation between the two classes is marked
by the official registers only. The son of a boïar, borne on
them, has brothers who, having escaped enrolment by some
chance, are plain peasants, and are glad of it. Another
sloojily may have become a tailor in some boïar's house.

Even in the highest places the solidarity of this hierarchy—
a legacy of ancient aristocratic affinities, or the product of
a new community of functions and positions—is constantly
weakened and destroyed by the perpetual despotism and
never-ceasing changes which break up every position attained,
and carry men of every grade from the foot of the ladder to the
top, from the lowest rank to the highest, making a dog-boy, on
the shortest notice, the equal of the proudest boïar. Feeling
themselves thus swallowed up in the mob of low-born 'servants,'
with no link of blood, tradition, nor even interest, between
themselves and many of them, the descendants of Rurik and
Guédymin soon lost, if not the memory of their own origin and
their pride in it, their eagerness, at all events, to defend and
establish and illustrate the new dignity they shared with
comrades such as these.

Thus, voluntary abdication followed on enforced humiliation, and this shadowy aristocracy, constrained at first, and then submissive, surrendered itself to a victorious absolutism, till a power which knew how to turn it to account and use it, to serve the needs and higher ends of Russia, had thus been consolidated, and even rendered indispensable.

And the same evolution repeats itself through every stratum of this society which is no society. Its progress is even more evident, perhaps, in the destiny of other classes, and notably in that of the peasant class.

V.—THE PEASANTS.

The story I must here tell is a sad one. As a child, I saw the closing days of a régime which, in this humble sphere, only died out of Russia a little less than half a century ago, and the Emancipation of 1861 was then looked on as a belated act of justice and political wisdom. But, as a matter of fact, it was a premature and hasty measure, for the state of things it ended had only lasted two centuries and a half. Contrary to what had happened in every other European country, the serfdom of modern Russia was not the painful legacy of a barbarous age, but a new fact, coinciding with the country's entrance on the path of European civilization, and the contradictory consequence, in a certain measure, of that new phase of the national existence.

This is an unquestionable paradox. Towards the close of the sixteenth century, when in every European country, and even close by, in Poland, the personal bond between the agricultural population and the landowners was breaking, or slackening, at all events, under the action of the new social and economic laws which were reforming the old feudal world, Russia contrives to forge, all complete, the very chains which have hitherto been non-existent within her borders!

Up to this period most of the peasants dwelling on the land conquered or recovered by Russian colonies in the north-west had been free—in theory, at all events—and the social condition of the class had even undergone some improvement. These peasants, once called *smerdi*—a name indicating scorn, if not infamy—(*smerdit*, to smell nasty), were now known by another generic title, which, while testifying to the lack of corporative differentiation always to be a peculiarity of the social elements of their country, clearly indicated a rise in the social scale. Whether town or country dwellers, tilling the soil or following other avocations, they were all simply called *Khrestianié* (Christians).

They made up the contingent of agricultural or industrial

labourers. As agriculturists, whether working their own land or land belonging to another, their time and their labour were their own. In the first case, they had the free disposal of their property, so long as they paid the taxes imposed by the State or by their own commune. In the second, whether as tenant farmers or metayers, they paid for the use of the ground according to the very varying provisions of their agreements with the owners. These depended on local custom, on the value of the land, and especially on the nature of its judicial tenure.

The land was said to be ' white '—free from State taxation— or ' black '—that is, taxed. The former category belonged to the *vottchiny* and the *pomiéstia*, the latter either to the Court or to the peasants themselves. Church lands might belong to either category, according to the concessions conferred on the clergy or the acquisitions made by them.

Leases on the metayage system for the period of crop rotation —three years—or even longer, were common, especially in the north and centre of the country, and those who held them were generally better off than their neighbours.

Other agreements imposed obligations on the farmer, resembling those of the English *sveman*, such as to cut wood and bring it to the manor-house, and pay certain fines, much like the French *formariage*, when his daughters married.

It was customary also, at Christmas and Easter, and on some other solemn feast days, for the tenant to make his landlord certain presents. These special dues bore the name of *barchtchina* (the lord's work), or *izdiélié* (work), or *boïarskoié diélo* (the lord's work). They foreshadow the forced service, soon, alas ! to be the law of serfdom. But at this period their definite and common reason is to be found in the supplies of money, implements, and seeds frequently received by the farmer from his landlord, and the interest on which he thus returned.

The relative importance of these dues varies greatly, and it is rather difficult to fix their value. In the central provinces, towards the middle of the sixteenth century, the rent of an obja or a *vyt*—five to six *diéssiatines*—reached two or three roubles. But very often the charge was paid in labour, the tenant of an obja, for instance, being bound to till a diéssiatine, or one and a half, for the landlord's benefit. And, further, we should have to settle the value of the rouble at that period. It has been reckoned, according to the price of corn, at nearly 100 roubles of our coinage, but this seems a doubtful calculation.

On the ' black ' lands belonging to the State these taxes were replaced by imposts and forced service, which occasionally reached a similar value, but were, generally speaking, less

2

heavy. On lands, ' black ' or ' white,' belonging to the Church, the expenses connected with working the soil were also much lighter, as a rule.

The tenant, wherever he was, could give up his tenancy when he had settled accounts with his landlord, and the landlord had power to put in a new tenant as soon as the old one's lease had expired. The extreme mobility of the popular existence —a universal feature, hereditary, and accentuated at this period—made these migrations matters of frequent occurrence. From the fifteenth century, however, economic necessities had brought about a certain modification of this freedom on both sides. First of all arose a custom according to which no landlord exercised his rights in harvest-time, a moment at which no peasant could dream of using his. This led Ivan III. to fix a period of fourteen days, just after St. George's Day (November 24), for the relinquishment of tenancies and the winding up of accounts with landlords ; and in his time the outgoing tenant further paid for his right of habitation (*pojiloïé*) a sum varying, according to the value of the land occupied, between fifty-six kopecks and one rouble six kopecks.

Such was the law. In practice, as may be imagined, many evasions were possible. Labour being scarce and universally sought after, proprietors enticed farmers from one property to another, just like the Sovereigns, on the look-out for ' servants.' Often there were forcible abductions. These were called *svoz*. Often, too, on divers pretexts, outgoing tenants were called on to pay more than they owed, and thus detained. Yet, liberty, even so fettered and curtailed, was liberty still. What with the dues to his landlord and his commune, the extra charges for judicial proceedings, and the constantly increasing taxes laid upon him, the peasant had a heavy burden. Monsieur Rojkov, in his book on ' Russian Agriculture in the Sixteenth Century ' (1899, p. 244), has calculated that the peasant in the northern provinces gave the landlord back one-half of the cereal produce of his holding, and that the other half hardly fed himself and his family for six months. Cattle-raising and some small industries enabled him to make two ends meet, but barely that. Very poor he was, but, like the old Anglo-Saxon *ceorl*, or the German *Markgenosse*, he continued to some degree the equal, from the judicial and administrative point of view, of the boïar, the merchant, and the Churchman. The courts of justice were open to him as to others, and such was the equality in this respect, that in a dispute between men of different ranks, amenable, by virtue of their condition, to different jurisdictions, the peasant, like any other subject of the Empire, had a right to choose his judges.

Within his own commune, too, whether rural or urban, he enjoyed a certain administrative autonomy which has taxed the sagacity of quite recent historians, and the nature of which I shall have to indicate more precisely when I reach a more detailed study of the organization of the country.

Finally, as I have just reminded my readers, these peasants were not all husbandmen. The documents of the period frequently divide them into two classes : labourers (*pakhatnyié*) and villagers (*dereviénskiié*). What are these villagers who do not dig ? In this category we find men registered as millers, tailors, shoemakers. Here again is manifested, once again, that lack of the corporative spirit, that confusion of social atoms, which, save in the Church—and even there we shall soon have to go back to the subject—keeps the national organization in the outline stage. If many country peasants do not till the soil, the towns hold many who are husbandmen. In country places the peasants of this first-named category often, though the fact is disputed (see Monsieur Diakhonov's ' View of the History of the Rural Populations in Russia,' 1889, p. 209, and Serguiéiévitch's ' Judicial Antiquities,' 1903, iii., 133, etc.), belonged to the mysterious class of the *bobyli*, landless peasants, occasionally tillers, but not on their own account, and in that case agricultural labourers, but trade labourers often, and, oftenest of all, vagabonds pure and simple, lost in the mass of *outlaws* of every kind—Cossacks, wandering jugglers, beggars, and thieves. Those who would differentiate them from the *tiaglyié*—qualified peasants—are mistaken. Except in the case of lands enjoying a temporary or perpetual, but always an exceptional, freedom by virtue of special charters, the *tiaglo* (from *tianout*, to draw, to drag a load) is the universal rule of the period. Everybody pays in some fashion, everywhere, and on everything, and the *bobyli*, who pay taxes or imposts on the houses they inhabit or the trades they follow, are no exception. They owe nothing for the soil they till, because they till for others, and in this lies the sole difference between them and the ordinary husbandman.

Whether imposed on them by some misfortune or voluntarily accepted, nothing binds them to this comparatively humiliating condition in life. They can always leave it as soon as they find means to do so, and share the common rights once more. In the sixteenth century the proportion of *bobyli* in the country parts was from 4·2 to 41·6 per cent., the lowest percentage occurring on the lands held by monastic establishments. In the following century, and under the influence of the tumult into which the disputes over the inheritance of the Terrible cast the country, these figures will be quite upset.

In a more and more floating population the monasteries

alone, or almost alone, will preserve a regular supply of labour,
settling most of these *bobyli*, together with another class of
unqualified peasants, the ' children of the monasteries ' (*mon-
astyrskiïé diétiénychy*), in their own villages and hamlets. These
last were peasants of an inferior class, but free in their own
persons, and not serfs at all. Were there no serfs, then, in
this country, which, till the middle of the nineteenth century,
was the last stronghold of European serfdom ? Yes, indeed.
But in the sixteenth century they formed an almost im-
perceptible element in the mass of the population.

VI.—The Serfs.

Even at a later period, the conversion of war captives into
slaves was considered a natural law, and there were other
causes of slavery besides, such as marriage with a slave,
slave birth, bankruptcy, certain domestic functions, and
even the deliberate laying down of his own liberty by any
man. Down to the fifteenth century the man who performed the duties of a *tivoune* (turnkey) was necessarily a
slave, and until the seventeenth, an insolvent debtor was
made over to his creditor, and remained his slave until the
debt was paid.

To these constituting causes of serfdom the sixteenth century added a new custom—the *kabala*, or, after an Arab word,
the contract made by a man who borrows a sum of money
and undertakes to pay the interest with his labour. This
transaction did not in itself involve loss of liberty, and
in Germany and Southern Italy similar contracts did not
produce this consequence. The *kabalnyï* could free himself
by paying his debt. In Germany and Italy the man thus con-
ditionally permitted to recover the power of his own person
generally made use of the possibility. In Russia, as a rule, the
fulfilment of the conditions was impossible, and the whole
history of serfdom, as finally established in the country, rests
on this fact.

Ivan IV.'s Code noted four classes of slaves : full slaves
(*polnyié*)—that is to say, those whose slavery, like that of their
offspring, was unconditional—senior slaves, whose slavery,
no doubt, was limited, according to a fashion unknown to us ;
slaves called *kabalynié ;* and slaves known as *dokladnyié*, enslaved by virtue of a *doklad*, another form of free contract.
But the legislator, while thus noting a state of things created
by the action of the past, sought to reduce the proportions
of this legacy from barbarous times, to restrict the causes
constituting a state of slavery, and to encircle their application with formalities which in many cases became prohibitive.

Russia, now brought into contact with the Western world, showed her inclination to follow in the path of freedom, as well as on other roads to civilization ; and besides, though lack of documentary evidence prevents us from offering any exact figures on the subject, the question, according to the agreement of many authorities, affected only a very small proportion of the labouring population.

Yet this period it was which led up to the general serfdom of the whole people. How ? By what strange reversal of the natural development of corresponding relations ?

Up to a comparatively recent date, the Russian Government of the close of the sixteenth century has borne the heaviest and most terrible responsibility in this matter. Alone, according to the very general belief, on its own initiative, by its own action, it worked this ruinous and far-reaching change in the judicial and social position of the classes affected by it. At the present day this view is generally cast aside. In Russia, as elsewhere, serfdom has been the outcome of time, and of a particular stage in the political and economic history of the country, and there is no necessity for seeking an explanation of the phenomenon in the misty conceptions of the Slavophile doctrine.

According to Kaveline (see his ' Works,' vol. i., p. 630), this phenomenon was the natural, necessary, logical result of the general organization of the country, itself based on the principle of domestic authority, and, as such, was rather beneficial than otherwise in its nature. This power of one man over another, used cruelly sometimes, because the habits and customs of the time were rough, but not really abused on the whole, was limited, in his view, to a sort of guardianship, founded, not on the strength of the guardian who had thus found means to impose his will, but on the feebleness of the ward, whose consciousness of weakness led him to accept an indispensable authority, guidance, and protection.

Granting this hypothesis, we should still have to account for the sudden discovery of a condition of social incapacity which had in no wise been previously revealed, and the coincidence of this new state of things with a period of growth which should rather have prevented or diminished it. The truth, as it appears from historical data, would seem to be very different. In the records of the populations in question during the sixteenth century, two facts rule. One is the rapid disappearance of the peasant proprietor, the other the equally rapid impoverishment of the peasant in general. And behold the results : On one side a mass of men, agricultural labourers and others, who, finding they cannot support themselves in any other way, agree to sell their liberty, so that they may not

die of hunger ; on the other a mass of tenants, who, being
unable to pay their landlords' dues, lose the essential right
on which their liberty depends—that of leaving their tenancy
at the end of their term. The first-named, having lost the
scrap of land on which they lived, are forced either to beg or
to give service ; the others, who have received a subvention,
in some form, from their landlords, find its repayment an impossibility. In the most ordinary circumstances a peasant
entering into possession of his farm received an advance of
three roubles. In ten years he had thirty roubles to pay,
besides either fifty-six kopecks or one rouble fifty-six kopecks
for the *pojiloié*—say, about 300 roubles in all, in our money.

In most cases the finding of such a sum was a pure impossibility. Therefore there was difficulty at the very start : the
conversion of the debt that kept rolling up, the *serebro*, as
it was called (*serebro*, money), into a sort of obligation which
bound the debtor to the soil ; the habitual assimilation of
the *serebrianiki* to the serfs in common law, Kholopy *dokladnyié*, or *kabalnyié*. Here we have the history of the insolvent
farmers of the *ager publicus* at Rome, as set forth by Fustel de
Coulanges.

In fact, from the second half of the sixteenth century,
liberty, while it was the theoretical right of most peasants,
had practically become the privilege of a constantly decreasing
number of proprietors and solvent tenants.

But what had caused this general impoverishment of the
agricultural class ? Easily guessed ! A state of war is a most
expensive condition. The Muscovite Government, when it
adopted the fighting organization to which I have already
referred, and perpetually increased its army, was forced to
increase its expenditure and pay the ' service men,' whose
numbers grew from day to day. Then, when it placed its
establishment in some degree on a European footing, it had
to pay for the necessary plant, for the arms imported from
foreign parts, and the *employés* recruited in every European
country. And wherewithal ? The only funds it could command, the only real wealth of the country, lay in the soil.
The land, then, had to bear all these new charges. To find
pomiéstia for the *sloojilyié* the peasants were dispossessed,
and to pay the foreign handicraftsmen the Government taxed
the *pomiéchtchiki*, who, themselves hard pressed, ground down
their tenants.

The land answered for everything, paid for everything,
became a sort of State coin, convertible into labour, military
and civil service, obligations of every kind. It made no fight.
It had never, even in the hands of the *vottchinniki*, been subjected to any complete, tangible appropriation. The con-

ception of a very early date made it a thing belonging essentially to the State, which could only be private property
within certain limits, and subject to higher rights. The
proprietors, on their side, were all in the master hand, and,
lacking, as I have already shown, any cohesion or corporate
organization, were incapable of making any serious resistance. Their weakness and docility only hastened the development of the system under which they suffered. The
most recalcitrant could only hit on one expedient—flight.
This has always been a feature in the Russian character. The
Russian who finds himself in an unendurable position will
always slip out rather than resist. We shall have to follow
the historical manifestation of this phenomenon. The
peasants, but in far greater numbers, acted on the example
thus set them. In their case flight was easier. The *vottchinniki* and *pomiéchtchiki* who sought fresh employment in
the neighbouring country of Poland were more closely watched
and less easily satisfied, and they ran serious risks and chances.
But all the peasant had to do was to slip across the south-
west frontier, ill-guarded and constantly pushed further
afield, and there, in endless spaces, find hospitality on a virgin
and untaxed soil.

Therefore, from the earliest years of the sixteenth century,
the exodus of the agriculrural population and the abandonment of the soil, left to lie untilled, became the great contemporary fact, a national peril. Then the State, whose
pocket was threatened, resolved to interfere. It began with
that which seemed most pressing. It would seem—though
the assertion is debatable—that in the middle of this century
a series of administrative measures and judicial decisions,
if not of legislative arrangements, established a fixed system
of rating, and thence it resulted that the ratepayers on the
'black' lands belonging to the Court were unable to leave
them. For though the tenant was still free to give up his
tenancy, he had to pay the same *tiaglo*, or a higher one,
elsewhere. Then came the turn of the 'white' lands held
by the 'service men.'

The peasants' flight ruined the *pomiéchtchik*, and a ruined
pomiéchtchik brought poverty on the State. Wherefore the
State, without having recourse, as yet, to any general measure,
laboured to insure the continuity and yield of its 'service'
by means of individual and local arrangements, which, in
exceptional cases, authorized certain owners to keep the
peasants settled on their land, or force the fugitives back
to it.

The policy of Moscow always leaned to this marking out,
in the first instance, of a regulation ultimately to become

general and definite. Towards the middle of the century
two charters, granted to the brothers Stroganov, marked a
decisive step forward on this road. They stipulated that
the concessionnaires should seize and send back such peasants
as might seek refuge, in their flight, on the huge domains
they proposed to colonize in that far-away land of uncultivated
steppes to which the current which was sapping the economic
prosperity and military organization of the country had turned
its course.

It has been further supposed that a general law, passed in
the middle of the sixteenth century, suppressed the right of
free exodus in the case of a certain class of peasants, the
starojiltsy, or husbandmen settled for many years on the
land they worked. But Monsieur Serguiéiévitch, disagreeing
with Monsieur Diakonov and several other historians ('Antiq.
Jur.,' iii., p. 460, etc.), has finally refuted this hypothesis.
The questions of labour and rating were the only ones which
played a decisive part in the matter, and prepared the birth
of the monster called *Kriépostnoïé pravo*, the law of serfdom.
One slavery involved another, and the 'service man,' shut
up in his iron cage, forced it on the peasant, soon to be followed
by the merchant and even the Churchman. We have seen
that there was no distinction, in this country, between the
urban and the rural populations. Here, again, is an abyss
which parts the Russia of the sixteenth century from the rest
of Europe.

VII.—THE TOWNSFOLK.

In the West, the progress of trade and industry led to the
organization of the townsfolk into corporations, which armed
themselves to withstand feudalism. In the bosom of these
associations, in the mutual relations of their members, was
elaborated that spirit of liberty from which the institutions
of communal autonomy sprang, and that material and intellectual activity which evolved the higher forms of economic
existence—the creation of capital, the establishment of credit,
and the most elevated forms of cultured life, science, art, and
society.

Russia has known nothing of this kind, and the absence of
these centres of social life and resistance has contributed,
more than any other reason, perhaps, to the maintenance
and confirmation of the despotic organization imposed upon
the country. Trade was restricted, manufactures hardly
existed, and consequently the Russian town was not the
natural outcome of their development. For long, as their
name shows us—*gorody* means places that are *ogorojennyié*,

fortified—the urban settlements performed a very different function. As a matter of fact, industrial life, as we have seen in the case of Moscow, escaped beyond their enclosures into the *possady* and *slobody*, in which most of the artisans, sharing their destinies and habits with the equal or larger number of husbandmen who likewise dwelt there, made their homes.   It was only in the sixteenth century that the State was moved to draw a line, not even between the two classes of inhabitants, but between the places in which they lived. And this distinction was of a purely fiscal nature, inasmuch as the townsmen had to pay more than the rustics, the reform, of course, not going so far as to create any organic tie between the taxpayers. The only anxiety of the Government was to obtain the highest possible yield from the taxable body, and insure a fixed taxation.   And its ideas of political economy being misty and generally false, it succeeded in paralyzing this source of revenue, instead of increasing it, by multiplying the taxes and the places where they were paid, setting a Custom-house officer at every cross-road and a collector at every street corner, and monopolizing for its own benefit every branch of industry and commerce, from the sale of rye, oats, and every cereal, to the making of beer, *kvass*, and every drink.

No resistance here, as in other countries—no trace of any struggle against this creeping system of monopoly. For the cases of Pskov and Novgorod are purely political. Yet elements of resistance are not lacking. From the very earliest times commerce had been honoured in the country, and held to be a noble occupation. The enterprises of the Varegians and of the ancient Slav Princes had been both military and commercial in their character, and the heroes of the national legends, Sadko, Soloviéï Boudomirovitch, Tchourila Plenkovitch, Vaska Bouslaiév, all personified this twofold type of adventurous activity and courage. What was lacking was *esprit de corps*. The retail trader (*koupiéts*) and the wholesale merchant (*gost*) were both of them in trade, indeed, but they were also capable of turning to other avocations, and very frequently did so turn. On the other hand, the professional speciality to which they owed their designations was by no means confined to their persons. Everybody was in trade : peasants, monks, soldiers, high functionaries, all dabbled in it as they chose, till the time came when the Empire, still spurred by the same anxiety, separated the functions, so as to be better able to apportion and settle the charges they were to bear. That was to be the work of the seventeenth century. But even then there was only to be one regiment more in the great army, more prisoners in the great cage, and no corporation as yet. That was to be set up, by virtue of *ukases*, in Peter the Great's time, and Catherine the Second's —the march of history never evolved it.

Thus these elements, as separate as all their fellows, and bereft—after the ruin of Pskov and Novgorod, consequent on their absorption into the great Empire—of the only centres in which they could have attained to efficacious association, shared in the general servitude, and were utterly incapable of playing the part in the rise and progress of civilization so brilliantly borne by the town communities of the West.

The Church remained. I shall now show how she, too, failed, partly on account of the same causes, to follow the path of her Western rivals in this matter.

VIII.—THE CHURCH.

By the prestige attaching to her functions in this land of a robust faith, by her position as the depositary of all knowledge and the sole imparter of instruction, and even by her material resources, the Church was a mighty power. Comprising, from early in the sixteenth century, the ten eparchies of Moscow, Novgorod, Rostov, Vologda, Souzdal, Riazan, Smolensk, Kolomna, Saraïsk, and Perm, she exercised, within their borders, a far-reaching authority, at once spiritual and civil, alike over her clerical servants and her lay administrators, episcopal boïars and *diaks*, lieutenants and bailies. To exercise justice meant, in those days, to levy taxes on those amenable to it, and this order of things, copied from the civil organization of the country, and borrowing therefrom a system of imposition based on private rights, while it added to the strength of the institution which took advantage of it, was not calculated to increase its moral authority. It was destined, indeed, to feel the reform which tended, in the course of the sixteenth century, to the erection of several administrative centres into autonomous communes. On the model of what then happened in the matter of civil administration, representative persons, *starosts*, duly elected and sworn in, were introduced in every jurisdiction, and the civil and spiritual jurisdictions were separated. But this arrangement was ephemeral. The State, which had outlined it by a mere accident, under the influence of the liberal tendencies reaching it from the West, very soon returned, as we shall see, to its original despotism, and the Church followed this second current as she had followed the first.

It was her destiny to be identified, all through the course of time, with that other power, the rival of her own, till an almost complete confusion of organs, functions, and prerogatives was reached.

Yet means whereby the Church might have maintained and safeguarded her independence were not lacking. Even to the administration of her property her prerogatives were equal to the Sovereign's. The Church lands, like the Sovereign's, were, from the judicial and administrative point of view, save in the case of certain criminal affairs—theft, murder, brigandage—quite independent of the local authorities. And these lands were vast. The wealth of the clergy—secular and regular, but regular especially—most unequally divided, but constantly increasing, exceeded that of all the other classes. The properties owned by the Metropolite at the close of the sixteenth century brought in as much as 3,000 roubles a year, and the archbishopric of Novgorod, with 10,000 or 12,000 roubles a year, was richer still. The other bishoprics were more or less well dowered, but all of them richly. The parochial clergy, with their modest allotments, sometimes not exceeding three diéssiatines, and seldom attaining, thirty or their sub-ventions (*rougi*) varying from nineteen roubles to twelve kopecks, could not hope much from the liberality of the faithful, generally bestowed on the monastic establishments, and were less well provided.

Four times a year at least the priest, bearing cross and holy water, passed round his parish with outstretched hand, but even on the results of this quarterly begging expedition the Bishops took their tithes.

The greater part of the public wealth was in the hands of the 'black' clergy. Not only was their landed property much larger, but their revenues were increased by the tribute of the national piety, which frequently produced enormous sums. From Ivan IV. alone the monastery of the Troïtsa must have received, in less than thirty years, the sum of 25,000 roubles, averaging, according to some calculations, about a million roubles of our money. The monastery of St. Cyril at Biéloo-ziéro, less highly favoured, received 18,493 roubles in the same space of time, without reckoning gifts in kind—a hundred pounds of honey, for instance, in 1570, ten horses the next year, and from time to time *ikons* and sacred objects of great value, one single gift of sacerdotal vestments being reckoned at 6,000 roubles.

On these huge lands of theirs, generally free from all imposts, on which they levied their own taxes, to which they attracted and on which they kept an abundant supply of labour, the monks added to the harvests of a soil that was better farmed than any other in the country, and to the perpetual aggran-dizement of their properties resulting from increased colonization, a variety of other industries. They gathered up all the money in the country and turned it over in advantageous investments ; they were big capitalists, almost the only ones in Russia—very big merchants, and far the largest of all the landed proprietors. The domains of the monastery of the Troïtsa, which comprised all the best land in the twenty-five districts, bore, at the close of this century, 106,600 peasants, and its revenue was calculated at 100,000 roubles, about 2,400,000 roubles of our money. Monsieur Ikonnikov (' Essay on the Byzantine Influence on the History of Russia,' 1869, Part I.) reckons the revenues of the monastic communities in South Russia at 824,593 roubles, drawn from 3,858,396 diéssiatines of land, tilled by 660,185 peasants ; to these figures should be added the sums produced by the lands cultivated by the monasteries themselves.

These valuations, we may be sure, are only approximate. But the whole of the documents at our disposal give us an impression of considerable wealth, quite out of proportion with the general resources of the country.

It would be absolutely unjust to assert, as it was asserted even at that period, that the clergy, secular or regular, only used their material wealth for their own advantage. For long years here, as elsewhere, the moral consciousness of the people had no refuge save in the bosom of the Church, and no expression save in her teaching. Up to the middle of the sixteenth century the spiritual power of its chiefs, and notably of its Metropolitan, acted as a precious counterpoise to the omnipotence of the State. Among the rights claimed by the upper clergy, that of intervening in favour of the victims of arbitrary power and violence is written in letters of gold in the country's history.

And much more. The Church and her secular clergy were active co-operators, and, to a certain point, even the chief workers, in the great labour of national unification pursued at Moscow. This calls for explanation. Amongst the first ' gatherers of the soil of Russia ' the idea of unity only appears in the half-conscious stage. The will of Simon the Superb, son of Kalita (1341-1353) does, indeed, enjoin on his son to march in the pafh he has traced out for him, ' so that the memory of our fathers and our own may not die out, and *that the torch may not be extinguished.*' Yet an anxiety very different from any ambitious dream of a great fatherland seems to have inspired these obscure Princes in their centuries of effort. When they bought village after village, added land to land, heaped their coffers with gold, silver, precious stones, and pearls ; when they cheated their Tartar master of his tribute; when they misused and stripped their brother Kings, if any of them ever went so far as to reveal his inner thought, and hint at the reason of this unflagging toil, he was simply heard to speak of the time when ' God shall deliver us from the Horde.' What they sought was liberty first and foremost, power to live without bending their backs under the conqueror's foot, and licking up the drops of fermented milk dropped on his horse's mane from the goblet they themselves had handed to the master. For they were still as low as that. And from that state of humiliation they longed to be delivered. Which done, they will amass more riches, commit more violence and more acts of spoliation, simply, as it would seem, for the sake of gaining a few more acres or filling a few more coffers to the brim.

Yet slowly the idea of a national unity works its way into the obstinate brains of these hungry spoilers. But it had sprung into being, and grown already, close at their very side. Long before any Prince of Moscow thought of making himself the political representative of a united Russia, the Metropolitan of Moscow had become its religious representative. The force of circumstance had brought this about. Eastern Slavdom could only conceive an eparchy dependent on the Patriarchate of Constantinople. Here, then, it found a first centre of unity, a common hearth. This centre, like all the rest, was nomadic for a considerable time. But a contemporary of Kalita's (1325-1341), the Metropolitan Peter, took upon him, even at that period, the title of ' Metropolitan of All the Russias,' and then among all the Princes, each claiming the primacy for Moscow, Riazan, Souzdal, Tver, arose a competition for the presence of the Primate in his capital, and, with it, a visible sign of his own pre-eminence. Michael Iaroslavitch of Tver gained the first advantage by forthwith dubbing himself ' of All the Russias ' too. But Kalita soon retaliated triumphantly, and the Muscovite hegemony was founded a century and a half before the days of Ivan IV.

A hundred and fifty years later, religious unity was to disappear, owing to the constitution, close beside it, of a new religious focus—that of the Polish-Lithuanian Empire. The Florentine union completed the severance of the two centres. But by that time political unity, as maintained and fortified at Moscow, had acquired a fair chance of integrity and duration.

The monasteries, on their side, contributed their share to that simultaneous work of colonization, of which all modern Russia is the issue. The forward progress of the monastic establishments, generally speaking, took a direction contrary to that pursued by the ordinary colonists, who were impelled by exclusively practical motives. While these last turned towards the fertile southern lands, the monks, many of them ascetics, inspired by a higher ideal, preferred the north-eastern countries, deserts and pathless forests, which but for them would long have checked the enterprise of their lay rivals. There they came into touch with the Finnish inhabitants, still sunk in idolatry; and labouring on their twofold task, breaking up the barren steppes and instructing pagan souls, they pushed onwards, ever onwards. Such a man was Phéodonite, a contemporary of Ivan the Terrible. On the banks of the Piétchenga, aided by his comrade Triphonius, he taught agriculture and the truths of the Faith, at once, to bands of Lapps, who, hostile at first, threatening and ill-treating the pious hermits, ended by hearkening to their voice.

To the east, on the Tartar frontier, the religious apostolate marched abreast of the military conquest. Monastic establishments were pushed across the Soura as early as in the fourteenth century, long before the fall of Kazan, and from that time they followed, aided, and sometimes protected, the progress of the expansion of the nation. These monasteries, which everywhere commanded great resources, and were often strongly fortified, served as points of support for the campaigning armies. That of St. Cyril, with its ramparts garnished with artillery and its eight-and-thirty great towers, was more important, strategically speaking, than Novgorod.

And even if the affluence of the faithful towards favourite places of pilgrimage resulted in some unjustifiable trafficking at the fairs held on the various saints' days, if the legality of the money advances made by the monks to private individuals at interest generally reckoned at between 10 and 100 per cent. gave rise to painful controversies, a tradition which subsisted even down to the eighteenth century likewise held the wealth accumulated in these monasteries to be a sort of reserve fund, on which the country was entitled to draw in days of trouble. These treasures, like those laid up by the Egyptian priests, were not so jealously guarded as to prevent their forming part, in certain circumstances, of the common patrimony. Custom further demanded that no monastery should ever refuse food or temporary hospitality to any person. Even Princes and boïars took advantage of this rule, halted as they passed by these houses of God, and, having refreshed themselves, departed, laden with provisions for their journey. As to the poor, they looked on these establishments as being, in a sense, their own property. And the monasteries justified the pretension. On one single day, in a year of famine, 7,000 starving creatures were given bread at the monastery of Volokolamsk, and for months from 400 to 500 received their daily food. That was under Vassili Ivanovitch, father of the Terrible, and in the course of that year the prior Joseph sold the cattle and

even the wearing apparel of his community, and the monks did
without *kvass*, and reduced their own food to the barest neces-
saries. The establishment of permanent refuges and hospitals
within the monasteries dates from this period.

What was wanting to these priests, whose lives were so often
heroic, who went from door to door begging the sustenance of
thousands of unhappy beings, braved the elements in wild
northern countries, or—and that was worse—faced, on the
steps of the throne, the rage of Princes ? What did they lack
to raise them up yet more, to make their churches and their
hermitages, like those of Western lands, centres of higher
culture or of elementary teaching, to enable them to be, not
only the religious teachers, but the educators and civilizers of
their people ?

History has long since answered this question. They were
uneducated.

Up to the Mongol invasion, out of twenty-three Metropolitans
holding Russian sees, seventeen were Greeks, and long after
that the Greek or Bulgarian element predominated in the
composition of the two clergies. Even after Constantinople
had ceased to appoint them—that is to say, after the Florentine
Union—the Metropolitans were still confirmed in their titles
there, and the constant advent of Eastern monks, who came to
collect alms in Russia, and the journeys, just as frequent, of
Russian pilgrims to the shrines of Mount Athos and other
neighbouring sanctuaries, kept up a constant stream of intercourse between the two Churches. Thus the religious life of
the country was in perpetual touch with its original source.
Now history has taught us what that spring, from which the
Europe of the West herself had drunk in former times, had now
become. I shall presently have to show what the Russia of
the sixteenth century was able to draw from it, what elements
of moral and intellectual culture it could supply. I will confine
myself, at present, to one fact.

Between 1420 and 1500, the country had seen the rise of
150 new monastic establishments, between 1500 and 1588,
of 65 more. Although the English traveller Fletcher exaggerated when he described sixteenth-century Russia as
‘ a land of monasteries,’ it is certain that foundations of that
nature did then increase to a relatively considerable extent.
To this the extreme liberty in connection with such establishments largely conduced. Any hermit who found means to
build a little wooden church or oratory could, if it so pleased
him, become a prior, or head of a community. He applied
to the Sovereign, to the boïars, or simply to wealthy persons,
for a gift of land, and the piety of the faithful, the value generally attributed to monkish intercession, did the rest.

But all these communities accepted the rule of St. Basil, as the Western communities for many years accepted that of St. Benedict ; and this feature, perpetuated and continued even to our own day, is surely a proof that the religious life, thus hardened in a single mould, was anything but intense !

Life means movement, and, besides, the motives ruling these communities had no connection, in many cases, with any longing for pious edification or for an ideal culture of the soul. Having exposed the face of the phenomenon, I must now turn to the reverse side. The facts to which I must refer are of universal notoriety, and have stirred a disapproval and caused a reaction even in the very bosom of the Church, the nature and origin of which I must describe, but which, in its results, has been powerless and wellnigh barren.

The ascetic idealists of this period, such as Maximus the Greek, Vassiane Kossoï, or Nil Sorski, closed their lives in a solitude other than that which they had chosen. All of them, like the heroic Phéodonite himself, to whose exploits I have already referred, and who expiated in a prison the crime of having set his contemporaries an example too sublime for them to follow, were attainted, anathematized, and driven beyond the pale of religion. Though the great majority of their fellow-monks wore the same garb, they were very far from reaching the same heights. Though not content with eating the fruits of their pious trade in idleness, if not in debauchery ; though, as I have already shown, willing to give the poor their share, their horizon, none the less, was circumscribed within the limits of a narrow-minded devotion, confined to most material practices. Many archimandrites and priors followed still less worthy leanings, using the monastic possessions for purposes of fruitful speculation, and adapting the rule of their order to habits of sybaritic idleness. Life in common was quite an exception to the general rule. The common table only fed a few brothers with the remnants of the sumptuous repasts shared by the higher authorities, who swallowed up the common wealth, with their numerous guests—relations, friends, and wealthy gentlemen who elected to inhabit these luxurious solitudes. They led a gay life there, and drank deep. From the sixteenth century to the seventeenth, as Monsieur Prijov shows us in his ' History of Taverns ' (1868, p. 53), the monasteries were the chief manufacturers and depositaries of beverages of every kind. The company frequenting them was numerous and gay. Ladies were frequent visitors in the monks' cells. Occasionally other visitors, too, were seen—little boys. In certain conventual establishments monks and nuns lived cheek by jowl.

The reforming current of the sixteenth century was destined

to reach these communities, infected, like the Western communities of the same period, by the general corruption of morals. But here, where it did not find elements strong enough to support it and insure its victory, the reforming effort missed its aim, and the authority of the Church was irremediably damaged.

At the same time, and as the result of yet another cause, her social power was reduced and partly forfeited. Up to the period of the Tartar invasion, the subdivision of the country into petty principalities, and the maintenance of the Church under the ultimate authority of Constantinople, had guaranteed an independent position to her chiefs. But at this moment they thought it wise to place themselves under the protection of another power, and the Metropolitan Cyril established his seat at the very Court of the Khans. This attitude was rewarded by a charter graciously bestowed by Mengou-Timour, and numerous *iarliks*, freely distributed by his successors. But the obtaining of such favours involved a complete abdication of the old independence, and by the time Moscow took over the inheritance of the Asiatic despots the habit was formed. *Ukases*, following on the *iarliks*, claimed the same obedience.

Further, the Church, having co-operated, as I have shown, in the constitution of the national unity, did not hesitate to join in the work of destroying the appanages. The division of the country, as a fact, interfered with the exercise of her power. But the political enterprise thus pursued in common inevitably resulted in a confusion of the two allied elements, and then to the subjection of the weaker to the stronger. The omnipotence acquired by Moscow perpetuated this result, and the rupture with Constantinople deprived the gradually subjugated Church of that national character and external support which made the fortune of Catholicism, and continued its best defence against the enterprises of civil despotism. When, after the close of the sixteenth century, the collation of ecclesiastical dignitaries and of church benefices in Russia became matters entirely at the Sovereign's discretion, this state of things was not the outcome of any kind of *concordat*. It was the natural evolution of the country's institutions, which had wedded, and inseparably mingled, the two orders of interest and power.

Even in the fifteenth century the Sovereign, as the chief protector of orthodoxy, summoned the *Conciles*, and in these assemblies affairs of State were discussed, as well as questions touching faith or religious rites. On the other hand, the high ecclesiastical dignitaries were frequently called to sit on the Sovereign's Lay Council, the *Douma*, and shared all its deliberations. Between such a position and that of being enrolled with everybody else in the great army of the *sloojilyié*, under the

3

common law of 'service,' there was but a step. Even the regular clergy did not escape it. While the archimandrites and priors of certain monasteries had their seats both at the lay and the religious council boards, the Russian monks, after the example of their Western brethren, were moved, at a very early date, to appeal to their Sovereign against the episcopal authority, just as the others appealed to the Pope ; and the Sovereign lent a willing ear, until the time arrived when he felt himself strong enough to simplify all these relations by centralizing their jurisdiction in his own civil government.

Both orders of the clergy might certainly, by virtue of their ministry alone, have lifted themselves out of the downfall entailed on them by their common fate. But to that end, the intellectual dignity and moral value of their leaders, at all events, should have been on a par with the prestige of their sacred functions, and the light and heat shed by the flame of their august vocation should have kindled and burned as brightly in the centres of this autocephalous Church as in those of the West, where, even in Rome's worst disorders, such men as Leo X. and Pius V. shed a brilliance that fell on every side. Alack ! our Cyrils and Ionas failed to discover any divine spark under the ashes of Byzantium !

Under Ivan III. the upper secular clergy still held out. A quarrel on some liturgical point set the Grand Duke and the Metropolitan by the ears. The latter abandoned his diocesan seat, left his churches unconsecrated, and thus forced the Sovereign to 'beat his forehead' in repentance. But when, under the successors of this Sovereign, himself not sufficiently strongly entrenched, as yet, in his omnipotence, it took more than a consciousness of outraged dignity to withstand a victorious despotism,—when St. Philip, the story of whose martyrdom I shall have to tell, sealed his lonely profession of independence and faith in disowned traditions with his blood, his voice found no echo, his example no followers. The Church, like all the rest of the nation, passed into the silence and the darkness, and there was another wheel in the great machine that ground up the intelligence and the wills of men.

CHAPTER II

POLITICAL AND SOCIAL LIFE

I.—THE CENTRAL POWER.   II.—PROVINCIAL ORGANIZATION.   III.—
THE MIÉSTNITCHESTVO.   IV.—THE COMMUNE.   V.—JUDICIAL
ORGANIZATION AND LEGISLATION.   VI.—THE ECONOMIC SYSTEM.
VII.—THE FINANCES.

I.—The Central Power.

THE machine was not built and set in motion in a day. When Ivan the Terrible came to the throne it already boasted a very complicated mechanism and a multiplicity of machinery— the result, it may be, of the ancient organization, domestic in some sort, adapted to the modest existence of the ap- panaged Princes, as admitted by Monsieur Klioutchevski (' The Council of the Boyards in Ancient Russia,' 1883, 2nd edition, p. 19, etc.), or possibly, as Monsieur Serguiéiévitch asserts, distinct political organs. I cannot here enter into this discussion. There were offices, or rather departments, the numbers of which were perpetually on the increase, and the duties of which were divided in most irregular fashion. This was because their creation and activity corresponded with the progress of conquest and colonization. A certain depart ment—one of the older ones—would have to deal with affairs in a great many provinces. Such was the War Office (*razriadnyi prikaz*). Another, again, was responsible for the whole of the business of one recently-acquired province. This was the case of the Kazan office, after the capture of that town (*Kasanskii dvorets*); the Office of Foreign Affairs (*possolskii prikaz*), naturally served the whole Empire. The powers of certain provincial bureaus—those of Moscow, Vladimir, Dmitriév, and Riazan—were restricted to certain fields within the limits of their provinces, and thus combined the distinguishing features of the institutions belonging to the two first categories.

Here, as elsewhere, the disorder of battle was apparent.

To work and control this varied machinery a central spring was needed. Where was it ? In the Sovereign's hand ? Not so, apparently. At the head of the departments was the Council of Boïars (*Boïarskaïa*) which bore a pretty close analogy to the ' Council ' of the first Capet Kings, or to the *curia regia* of the Norman Kings of England. Here, as there, it was the product of history, springing from the national association organized in the fifteenth century on the banks of the Oka and the Upper Volga, and consequent on the military formation then adopted. Head of this band, the Prince of Moscow, like

3—2

every other General, was bound to consult his lieutenants about
any operations of importance, and the *Boïarskaïa Douma*, in its
first form, was a mere Council of War, transformed, in later
times, by the complication of interests it was called on to discuss. Head of his patrimony, the Sovereign had to reckon, too,
with the descendants of his former comrades, now settled, like
himself, on hereditary domains, over which they exercised a
partial authority. Thus, the competence of the Council of War
took on a political character, and in its composition an aristocratic tincture became strongly marked.

In the sixteenth century sixty-two families, forty of which
held princely rank, seem to have sat on it by right. But was
it really a right ? No; an eligibility rather, utilized at the
Sovereign's will and pleasure. And here, already, appears
the powerlessness of an institution which might have
been regarded as a restriction on the absolute power. The
lack of corporative organization prevented it from attaining
any sufficient power of resistance. Many boïars and Princes
habitually appear at these councils, but with them we note a
still more numerous company of functionaries who are neither
boïars nor Princes—high officers of the Crown (*okolnitchyié*,
from *okolo*, around, men who are about the Prince), courtiers,
(*dvorianié*), and even mere clerks (*diaki*). As a fact, it did not
suffice to be of great family in order to be summoned on this
Council. On a list for the year 1527 we do not see a single
Galitzine, nor Kourakine, nor Vorotynski, nor Pronski, nor
Khovanski, nor Prozorovski, nor Repnine, nor Soltykov.
The names I have quoted are some of the greatest of that
century. Nor did it follow that because a man had been
called on one council he was to be summoned again. For
one piece of business, twenty out of the hundred men on the
list might be warned, and for another, only eight. There was
no rule, and no usual course of things to take its place. The
function of councillor, like the rank, depended on the Sovereign's will, and, in a sense, the function always continued something apart from the rank. In this we have the germ of the
future organization of the *tchine*.

The competence of this body was extensive, and, in a way,
unlimited. It was not confined to the enlightenment of the
Sovereign. In concert with him, the Council wielded every
power—legislative, judicial, and administrative. It governed,
in the widest meaning of the word, and that whether collec-
tively or individually. A *doumnyi dvorianine* who had just
been taking his share in some debate on a question of foreign
policy might be sent as provincial governor to Viatka, and
then to command a regiment at Siévsk, or, between two similar
appointments, he might be delegated to represent his Prince as

cross-bearer in some solemn procession, or carry the dishes sent from the Sovereign's table to some distinguished personage. And after all that, going back to his Council sittings, he might have to decide a lawsuit for which the Council had resolved itself into a Court of Appeal. It would seem, at all events, that an article of the Code of 1497 mentions a jurisdiction of this nature conferred on the *Douma*.

To get through all this work, the Council must have found the two daily sittings mentioned by the chroniclers all too short. It sat, in summertime, from seven in the morning till one or two o'clock in the afternoon ; and then again, after an obligatory attendance on the Sovereign at Mass, dinner, and a siesta, from sunset till late at night. But, in practice, this heavy work only fell on a certain number of councillors at a time, and their intervals of service were widely spaced. As a general rule, the institution did no work at all. And was it really so much as a regular institution ? It was the fiction, rather, of a division of power which, from the sixteenth century onwards, especially, had but a shadowy and deceptive appearance of reality. Whether they really acted together or separately, the fiction still united every act of the Sovereign and his *Douma*. The master, even if absent, was supposed to be invariably present at the deliberations of the assembly, and even if he acted independently, he was held to be acting in concert with it. Monsieur Serguiéiévitch is wrong, as it appears to me, when he pronounces against the theory of this mystic union ; it survived the *Douma*, and was perpetuated in Peter the Great's relations with his Senate. But it was an idea, and nothing more. The fact—from the sixteenth century onward, more especially—is the existence of a personal and absolute power, exercised by the Sovereign assisted by another deliberative assembly, the composition of which was still more arbitrarily settled, while its more restricted membership left a yet wider margin for absolutism ; a private council, generally held in the Sovereign's bedroom, and only consisting of two or three boïars or confidential men of any rank—a reproduction of the *commune consilium* noticed, concurrently with the *magnum consilium*, in the organization of all the European monarchies, but vaguer and more uncertain in its nature, in this particular place, and more completely subject to the master's will or caprice.

And in certain provinces the master's authority is undivided, even in appearance. In certain districts, as we shall presently see, jurisdiction, either as a special right belonging to the Sovereign or as a privilege claimed by those amenable to justice, by virtue of special charters (*tarkhany*), is in the hands of his direct agents. In similar fashion, he alone has the right to consider the petitions addressed, by ancient usage, to the Prince,

and which became so numerous as to necessitate the establishment, in the sixteenth century, of a special office—the *Tchelo-
bitnyï prikaz*, the germ of the future ' secret chancery '—to deal
with them.

Consequently, the Sovereign was, in actual fact, the real and
only government, and his councillors, like his ' service men,'
were only so many soldiers whom he ordered about—pawns
pushed hither and thither on the chess-board, without any
possible resistance or control of theirs. In an army, the Council
of War attains importance, makes itself heard, even imposes
its decisions, as long as the campaign goes ill ; but when victory
comes, the General-in-Chief, successful and conscious of his
power, soon sends his staff to the right-about. A Napoleon's
plans are not subject to discussion. Moscow was victorious ;
she passed from triumph to triumph, and the heirs of Kalita,
having no account to render for the past, claimed the privilege
of rendering none in future.

Such was the central situation, and a similar type of military
organization was repeated round it.

II.—PROVINCIAL ORGANIZATION.

It essentially depended on the possession of the land. The
possession of land entailed two kinds of obligations on its
proprietors. If they were peasants, they owed taxes ; if they
held freeholds (*vottchiny*) or fiefs (*pomiéstia*), they owed service, they were *sloojilyié*—that is to say, besides the civil
functions with which they might be invested, they constituted the Sovereign's army, quartered on their territorial
possessions in time of peace, and instantly mobilized in time
of war. Service began when a boy was fifteen. At that age
the son of a *pomiéchtchik* received a portion of the paternal
domain, or, if the family was too numerous to permit of that,
a fresh allotment. When the *pomiéchtchik* died, his lands
were divided up among his sons, the girls, too, receiving shares
in which they had a life-interest only, and which they had to
relinguish if they married. If the land did not suffice, an
additional allotment could be claimed. The exchange of
pomiéstia was allowed, on condition the State suffered no
damage ; for its service, every man must be replaced by
another. In the case of the *vottchiny*, the State nominally
did not intervene in matters of inheritance, but it took
care that each lot of land should be represented by a man
capable of service.

The system was evidently more easily applied in the case
of the *pomiéchtchiki*. The Sovereign, who was master of their
fortunes, had them much more completely in hand. Where-

fore the policy of Moscow invariably tended to replacing freeholds by fiefs, putting life grants in the place of hereditary
domains. On the lands annexed to the Empire by force of
arms this process of substitution was far easier, and was rapidly
accomplished. The laws of war, admitting, as they did, of
wholesale confiscation and the distribution of the confiscated
lands, provided for it. Twenty years after the annexation of
Novgorod we find, in a document dated 1500, that in the
two districts of Ladoga and Oriéchek 106 *pomiéchtchiki* held
half the arable land between them ; most of these were of
the humbler class, artisans and servants, and consequently
all the more docile. The judicial ancestor of the ordinary
type of landed proprietor of that country in the sixteenth
century is the dog-boy of the appanaged Prince of the fourteenth—obedience is in his blood.

Elsewhere, in countries where the work of unification had
been done with a gentle hand, the *vottchiny* were still in the
majority. They were much less manageable, and against them
the furious onslaught to which the Terrible owes his title was
to be launched.

The *pomiéstia* class, which spread still more generally as the
result of this struggle, laboured under another drawback.
Owing to that insufficiency of land at the Sovereign's disposal,
to which I have already alluded, a landed proletariat came
into existence. One *pomiéchtchik* called out for military
service complains that he has not the means to provide himself
with a horse. Another, who, while he awaits the promised
allotment of land, performs the functions of a church chorister,
does not even possess the wherewithal to serve on foot. Yet
the numbers are kept up, after all, and the Sovereign's army
costs him nothing.

But he must have an administration besides, and this
costs nobody but the governed anything at all. To administer
meant, in those days, to exercise justice and keep criminals in
order—nothing more—and those who did it were fed. Here,
too, the general system was the same. By virtue of ancient
privilege on most allodial properties, by virtue of special
charters on other lands, the owners, soldiers, or even Churchmen, sat in judgment—in other words, they traded, on their own
account, on the rights of justice, which they turned to their
personal profit. They pocketed the proceeds of pettifoggery,
minted into taxes and charges of various kinds, and the proceeds of public prosecutions, in the shape of fines paid by
convicted persons, or, failing them, by their communes. On
lands which escaped this jurisdiction the trade in judicial
matters was divided between the direct agents of the State,
acting for it, and other 'service men,' to whom the State de-

legated its rights and profits, and who represented it in the guise of lieutenants (*namiéstniki*), bailies (*volostniéli*), and governors. To govern a town or province was to live on that town or province by means of charges levied on the dispensation of justice. This was called *kormlénié*, from *kormit*, to feed, and the governors were the *kormlenchtchiki, par excellence.* When, at a later period, the economic life of the country called for administrative agents in the true sense of the word, the thought of using the governors for this purpose never occurred to anybody. New needs brought new organs into being, and the old ones stayed on to be fed, and with no other *raison d'être.*

The *kormlénié*, which was in perfect harmony with the territorial rights of the *vottchiny*, and much more a privilege than a function, was connected with civil rather than with political rights. A boïar's widow might claim it, or his other heirs if there was no widow—any of the deceased man's family, in fact. In the same way, while the governor turned his province to account, the bailie, within his own bailiwick, was not the governor's subordinate, but his competitor. He kept certain classes of business and people in his own jurisdiction—he had legal power over the ' black ' lands, for instance, whereas the 'white' lands were ruled by his neighbour.

The abuses to which this system lent itself may be imagined. In theory, indeed, the expenses of judicial proceedings were defined, and profits limited to what they ought to bring. But there were extras, bribes which must be paid, the result of the wholesale trickery rampant in an organization over which no effectual control existed. This was the plague-spot on the whole system.

There was no rule—no rule laid down, at all events—for the recruiting of this double set of State servants. The Sovereign chose whom he would. Yet, practically, his choice was limited by the difficulty of finding, outside a certain social class, men fit to do the work. The Moscow policy strove to widen these borders and take in fresh blood, drawn from every class of society, even the humblest. These democratic tendencies were checked by the lack of sufficient intellectual development. Dog-boys whose training permitted them to cut a decent figure in the guise of *namiéstniki* were not common. And thus it came about that the social element, the hereditary principle, and the aristocratic spirit all blended with the political element and the principle of co-optation, and produced in the result a phenomenon the like of which has never been seen in any other European country : the *miéstnitchestvo.* The very name is hardly known outside Russia. I will endeavour to explain the thing.

III.—THE MIÉSTNITCHESTVO.

It means, theoretically, the right, not established by any code, but recognised by custom, whereby no *sloojilyi* ordered to serve with another of his class could be given a place (*miésto*) inferior to any held by himself or his ancestors with relation to the said comrade or his forefathers. Take two men appointed to command two battalions of the same regiment. Both are sons of boïars, but the grandfather of one, being a General, has had the father or grandfather of the other under his orders. Here is a case of *miéstnitchestvo* : the General's grandson has an absolute right to refuse to serve with the comrade suggested to him. There is no reason why his Sovereign, if such were his goodwill and pleasure, should not turn him into a stableman, and he would not dare to object, unless, sweeping the dung out of the same stable, he were to meet some other stableman whose father had been a scullion when his own progenitor was handling the saucepans. But he cannot be turned into a General willing to share his rank and command with that scullion's son.

Now consider that the calculation of precedence thus claimed affected ancestry in every degree and branch, and conceive the complication and frequency of the disputes thus engendered. The political life of the Muscovite State has been full of them, and they have constituted the sole restriction, but a serious one, on the Sovereign's absolute power.

Pogodine has sought the origin of the *miéstnitchestvo* in the relations between the appanaged Princes. But this theory has few partisans now. In the first disputes of this nature of which we have cognisance, and which, indeed, coincide with the appearance of the earliest books on genealogy (*rodoslovnyia knigi*), the family principle is more generally and strongly marked. The Muscovite Government, in its own interest, respected and cultivated this principle, on which its dynastic establishment was based, and out of its endeavour to combine it with its contradictory system of a hierarchy based on 'service' came the *miéstnitchestvo*. The Government welcomed it at first. The disputes it stirred, all directly and solely concerned with places conferred by the Sovereign, ran absolutely counter to the corporative spirit : they excluded all idea of an aristocracy, properly so-called, and strengthened that of 'service.' And at first they were mere private matters, and affected trifles only. One boïar claimed another boïar's seat at a friend's table ; the wives of two high functionaries fought over their places in church ; a Bishop— for the clergy were interested in the matter, too—refused to eat out of the same dish with another and less well-connected prelate. In the ' black ' clergy, indeed, there was a hierarchy of monasteries, and monks within the communities quarrelled over their places in the processions that followed the holy *ikons*. Merchants obeyed the general lead, and the great dramatist Ostrovski has demonstrated the survivance even to our own day of the habits then contracted in that class of life.

But a time came when, on a day of battle, in the very face of the enemy, two Generals began a squabble of this sort. This was at Orcha, in 1514, and the battle was a failure. A change was indispensable. The Government tried every-thing—the suspension of precedence for a fixed period during a campaign, for instance, and severe penalties in the case of any unjustified claim—but did not dare to lay its hand on the unwritten, but all the more strongly rooted, privilege. The aristocracy used all its powers, fired its last shots, set all its last haughty hopes upon the die, and forgot, while thus plunged in its calculations of nobility, that power was slipping from its hands. For many years, indeed, the highest places were given to the nobles, because at first the State could not fill them up otherwise. But when other candidates were to be had, the *miéstnitchestvo* was powerless to resist a democratic levelling process harmonizing with the State's own principles. By putting forward the posts bestowed by the Sovereign's free-will as a factor in family calculations, it destroyed the generic element of its own social and corporate value; it elaborated, as a reinvestment, a collective body of another kind, more docile, more pliable, and but for which the Russia of the sixteenth century might perhaps have failed in her tremendous task; but it was not a class—it was a crew rather, a regiment, a convict gang.

This system, by setting up individual qualification against birth, certainly succeeded, in some measure, and on a final analysis, in bringing out another fruitful principle—personality ; and it would thus be most unjust to regard the *miéstnitchestvo*, with Valouiév and some other historians, as an instance of Chinese immobility. The system itself was not unchange-able. It altered in the course of time : it developed ; it felt and exercised divers reactions. But though, by its passive resistance, it raised serious obstacles in the path of absolutism, it did not bring any such social or political force to bear as might, by paralyzing its action, have supplied its place, directed or controlled it.

Another force of this nature existed, in embryo at least, in the communal organization to which I have already referred.

IV.—THE COMMUNE.

The appearance of Baron von Haxthausen's studies of the Russian commune as it now exists, with its autonomous administration and its collective proprietorship, was a revelation, even a joyful surprise, to Russia. It was like the discovery of a new world, proving the originality and excellence of a primordial institution, in which the nation felt it might glory in the face of astonished Europe. This proud conviction had a fall. Further inquiry proved a pre-existence of similar institutions in all countries, European and others—from Ireland to Java, from Egypt to India. The difference, then, between Russia and her Western neighbours was narrowed to one of age and civilization. But the pursuit of truth and the disappointments resulting therefrom did not end here. Students began to think they perceived that the Russian commune, which had been taken to be identical with primitive forms of organization, delayed and kept in the rudimentary form by a slower development of social and economic life, was really a thing of recent growth. Far from being the outcome of the patriarchal communism of prehistoric times, was it not rather the result of a collective responsibility for the payment of taxes—a responsibility unknown to the free peasants of the sixteenth century, and imposed on the rural communities of a later date by the law of serfdom ? A fossil formation ? Not a bit ! A product of the political system which triumphed in Russia under Ivan IV. ? A national trait ? No, again ! A State institution.

Thus, according to the point of view set forth by Monsieur Tchitcherine ('Essays on the History of Russian Law,' 1858, p. 4, etc.), and still more recently by Monsieur Milioukov ('Essays on the History of Russian Culture,' i., p. 186, etc.), we here have an instance, and a most striking one, of that reversed progress which, in some things, appears a peculiarity of the economic and social development of this country.

But is it a well-chosen instance ?

During the first half of the sixteenth century serfdom, as we have seen, was only an occasional condition in Russia. But the commune, with its association of free peasants, already existed. Every peasant, in fact, was bound to belong to one of these associations. Those who lived outside their borders were mere vagabonds. These associations were autonomous organizations, within which a democratic and communistic form of existence reigned. The assembly which discussed the common interests was composed of the elders of every household in a certain district, which included several of these associations, and was called a *volost*. This in no way resembled the institution now known by this name. The ancient *volost*, which was something between the canton and the commune in France, and somewhat approached the American *township*, possessed far more extensive privileges. The assembly which represented it at this period had power to issue decrees (*by-laws*); it chose the mayors (*golovy*) and the elders (*starosty*) of the commune; it allocated the direct taxes imposed by Government on trade and agriculture; it appointed the members of each commune who were to help the judges to exercise their functions, or play the part allotted to the *schöffen* in ancient Germany, and to the *nemd* in Sweden; and finally, through freely-elected magistrates, it kept order and defended the common interests before the judges.

Such, at least, is the state of things of which traces are discoverable on the 'black' lands, owned by free peasants. But it is impossible to assert that the same condition existed on lands of the other class, concurrently with that judicial and police organization amidst which the privileged magistrates wielded their authority. On the other hand, and on these very lands, even in the fifteenth and sixteenth centuries, signs and rudiments of collective possession or holdings have been detected. In the centre of the country more especially, the documents of the period make frequent reference to husbandmen, called *sossiédy* (neighbours), *skladniki* (from *skladat*, to put together), or *siabry*, who seem to have been peasants associated together to work a certain stretch of land. Monsieur Serguiéiévitch, though he interprets the name and manner of life of these husbandmen in a different sense, believing them to have bound themselves together for the payment of their obligations only, grants, in his 'Judicial Antiquities' (1903, vol. iii., p. 61, etc., and 119, etc.), the existence of other agrarian communities. On the lands held by the higher clergy and by the monasteries, the history of which is much better known, the enjoyment of certain hired areas seems to have been common to all the tenants, inasmuch as the lot given to one family, the *vit*, or *sokha*, as in the case of the English *virgate*, did not constitute a right to occupy one particular space, enclosed within certain limits, but that to occupy and till five diéssiatines, for instance, in each of the three fields belonging to the manor. On one property belonging to the Troïtsa monastery (Serguiéiévitch, *ibid.*, p. 440) we note, quite as an exception, the tillage in common of parcels of ground made over to associations of peasants. And on the lands confiscated by the father of Ivan the Terrible after the annexation of Novgorod, lands taken from boïars and given to qualified peasants, a common ownership in meadows, lakes, and forests certainly sprang up, and showed a tendency to develop. But all this was local, rudimentary, or recent, a far cry from the full and general collectivity of the Russian *mir* of our days, with its periodical redivision of allotments, like the run-rig on certain modern manor lands in England and Ireland. In those days the *mir* only existed in the most embryonic form, and no possibility offers, so far, for tracing either its origin or its mode of development.

This development occurred in the fifteenth century. At that period the Russian commune was assuredly not a relic of the patriarchal organization of the old times, wiped out by the Norman invasion, or even before that, as some historians have admitted, by the admixture of foreign and Finnish elements with the Slav race. But were there any Finns in ancient Southern Russia ? The fact is not clear. Was this renovated commune a resurrection of the ancient communistic régime, called forth by the permanence of certain social habits ? Or was it the entirely new product of a spontaneous generative process, to be explained, as the Slavophils are inclined to explain it, by a special aptitude of the national temperament for a communistic life ? These are knotty questions, and the demands of the national vanity do not facilitate their solution. That such an aptitude may exist is undeniable. Of that the *artels* are a standing proof. But in Germany, and more especially in England, as in the case of those guilds which have held out against the whole force of modern centralization, the spirit of association has proved infinitely more energetic.

I am disposed to opine that the two principles of historic atavism and congenital predisposition, working on a popula· tion in the case of which the inorganic stage had been exceedingly prolonged, combined to determine the production of this rudimentary organization on the very threshold of the modern epoch. The Russian commune of the fifteenth century has no family quality about it. It is open to all comers. Any peasant who pays his share of the common obligations can enter it. It is purely conventional, and this characteristic distinguishes it from the antique formations preserved, in their primitive peculiarities, amongst some other Slav peoples. Yet a certain administrative autonomy brings it back to this ancestral type. The nature and character of this autonomy are likewise open to discussion. Did the commune of the fourteenth century bear any part, and, if so, what part, in the exercise of justice ? This is still an open question. But it is certain, nevertheless, that the judicial organization of that period, and the system, already described, of the *kormlénié*, left little room for the exercise of any rival

power. This domain belonged to the 'service men.' It was
a private preserve. For in those days any man amenable to
justice was still fair game.

But with the following century the scene changes. Communal autonomy suddenly widens its borders. It tends
towards the absorption of the whole of the provincial administration, and of all the powers thereto attached. What has
happened ? This—that the 'service men' have failed in
their task. They have worked the land so hard that they
have ruined it. By their exactions and extravagance they
have not only done serious damage to private interests, for
which the State cares little, but they have compromised the
interests for which the State does care—they have destroyed
or diminished its taxable property. And the State, wavering
between the two poles of its own political theory, then in course
of evolution, between the current of absolutism and the current
of liberty, resolves to break down privileges it has itself conferred, and which have not borne their expected fruit, and with-
draws functions the bestowal of which it now regrets. For the
discharge of these, it calls on the elements of that communal
organization it has long scorned and even misused. Charters,
bestowed by a more and more liberal hand, place the communal
starosts and wardens in possession of a power tending first to
the diminution and then to the suppression of that once held
by the lieutenants and bailiffs of the Crown. But for all that,
the State does not drop its fundamental programme ; it does
not quite abdicate its despotism. Between this last, and the
spirit of the institutions thus called to play a new part, it seeks
a compromise, and finds it in the separation of the authority
it concedes from the independence it refuses. These magistrates, whose powers it has increased, will still be functionaries, men of its own, and the commune, thus widened and glorified, will be a State institution—we shall watch this phase—
until, under the law of serfdom, the approaching evolution
gives it yet another form—the autonomy of the galleys, the
association of the chain that binds one pair of legs to another.

To comprehend these successive changes we must devote a
closer, though still a cursory, examination to the working of
the particular parts of the machine affected by them.

V.—JUDICIAL ORGANIZATION AND LEGISLATION.

Till towards the middle of the sixteenth century this sphere
is wholly ruled by the idea that the administration of justice
is a privilege, a valuable asset. Fiscal agents and Crown
officers on the ' black lands,' property-owners on the ' white,'
all feed or are fed at the same manger. Decrees are pretexts,

first and foremost, for levying taxes; the repression of crime is, above all things, a financial operation. Even though cognizance of certain crimes, such as murder and brigandage, is reserved to the State, it is all a question of cash, even there. These affairs bring in more money, and the State keeps the best morsels for itself.

Wherefore, in the Code of 1497—after the *Rousskaïa Pravda*, the earliest copy of which dates from 955 or 962, legislation has come to a standstill—the provisions for criminal cases rank first. In civil cases the legislator generally defers to custom. He hardly mentions the relations and obligations arising out of family ties or contracts, and is absolutely silent concerning all other judicial relations. As regards public rights, he gives nothing, or hardly anything. There is some dim conception of a right of guardianship over the common people, vested in the State, evidenced by an injunction that no man must be deprived of his liberty without the Sovereign's consent. The legislator's chief anxiety has been to organize the work of justice, and organization, in his view, consists in the reckoning up and allotment of expenses and taxation. The *Soudiébnik* is a penal code and a book of profits, very little else.

In the number and severity of the penalties suggested, the Tartar influence is clearly seen. The *Rousskaïa Pravda* was a far gentler Code, and a more liberal one, too; it gave the culprit power in many cases to buy himself off. The new Code ignores this privilege. The words *bity knouty, biti batogy*, recur in almost every line. In the application of these penalties, and in the whole of its legislation, the idea of equality, which is very apparent and accords with the democratic tendencies of the Code, is at war with the contrary principle of vested rights claimed by the Byzantine spirit of the Church. Judicial practice itself was thus drawn from the civil sources of the Greek legislation—from the laws of Constantine the Great, Justinian, and Leo the Philosopher, from the Eclogues of Leo the Isaurian and Constantine Copronymus; so that if these tribunals are responsible for the peasant as well as for everybody else, the peasant will be hanged, and the boïar only whipped or put in prison. In most cases, too, he will be tortured to make him confess his crime. The accused person is always put to slow torture : his ribs are broken in, nails driven into his flesh. This is the sixteenth century !

Up till the seventeenth, this same Code, lingering far behind the rest of Europe, will accept the judicial combat, also part of the habits of the country. At Novgorod the law even permitted such combats between two women who accused each other, while at Pskov a more gallant statute allowed the fair

sex to find male substitutes, the same privilege being extended
to old men, infirm persons, and monks.

Ivan IV.'s Code was to provide for a similar equalization of
the combatants' strength. But at that moment the judicial
combat was beginning to change its nature. It had long been
looked on as a merely human expedient, held in scant respect,
and ranking lower than confession and testimony among the
means available for demonstrating the truth. As a mark
of distrust and scorn, the oath and the casting of lots were added
to it. Before proceeding to the combat the oath was taken,
and the oath was deferred till after the casting of lots. The
idea of Divine intervention did not present itself save in a
latent condition; but now it began to rear its head and gather
strength. The judicial combat was taking on the form of a
Divine judgment.

In this fact some people will recognise another instance of
Russia's reversed march in the path of progress; it will be
recollected, in any case, that the *ordalie* proscribed in France
by the edict of Louis le Débonnaire, in 829, was forbidden,
and forbidden afresh by the French Parliament in 1400.
And, indeed, this *ordalie* was not quite the same thing. It
essentially depended on the idea of a celestial arbitrament,
which was not associated with such encounters, in Russia, till
a late period. It was a mere legacy, in her case, of a barbarous
past, when each man did justice for himself, and when the
decision of every quarrel depended on the personal valour of
the disputants. Thus, far from favouring its maintenance and
application as she favoured the various appeals to the Divine
judgment in other places, the Church, even while labouring to
endue the custom with a religious meaning, opposed its practice.
She succeeded by this means in withdrawing its two accessories
—the oath and the casting of lots—which were finally made
independent forms of proof. At a fairly early date, this last
was currently employed in ecclesiastical business. The
sentence was drawn like a lottery-ticket. Before the common
law tribunals similar judicial methods were pursued, down to
the close of the sixteenth century, according to a procedure
of which Henry Lane, an English commercial agent, gives a
curious account in connection with a lawsuit in which he was
interested, in the year 1560.

It was connected with a sum of 600 roubles claimed from him
by a Kostroma merchant. The matter was to have been
decided, in the first instance, by a single combat, for the purposes of which Lane had provided himself with a redoubtable
champion in the person of a fellow-countryman of his own,
employed, like himself, by the English trading company settled
in Russia. This man, whose name was Romanus Best, was

destined to become the founder of an illustrious Russian family, the Bestoujev. But the Kostroma man, thinking his opponent too dangerous, no doubt objected to him, and recourse was then had to the casting of lots. In the presence of two high officials, who acted as judges, and a numerous audience, the two parties were first of all invited to come to terms. Then, neither being willing to yield, the judges, turning up their sleeves, exhibited two balls of wax, and one of them hailed a member of the crowd. ' You there, with such a coat and such a cap, come here !' The man advanced, held out his cap, into which the two balls were put, and then another man, chosen in the same way, drew them out, one after the other. The first drawn won the battle, and as it turned out, the English-man got his verdict; whereupon the audience applauded, quite convinced of the excellence of the cause thus gained, and of the uprightness of English merchants in general (' Hakluyt Collection,' ii., p. 209).

The reasons which prevented the State from putting the same confidence in ordeals of this nature in cases affecting itself are easily divined. It therefore devised others, and amongst them the *povalnyï obysk*, a sort of inquiry into morals, in high favour in the days of Ivan the Terrible. In this the voice of the people—*vox Dei*—was supposed to intervene, and to that end a great mass of testimony was indispensable. False witness was severely punished, knouted without mercy. But the effect of this penalty was that most men would not open their lips. As for documentary proof, that did not make its appearance till the end of the sixteenth century. The carrying out of the sentence, in civil matters, often involved very peculiar practices. The condemned party, if a bankrupt, was delivered over to his creditor ' with his head ' (*golovoiou*) ; in other words, the debtor became his creditor's thing, his slave, till the debt was paid. The solvent debtor who refused to pay was subjected to the *praviéje*. This means that the recalcitrant was led out in front of the house in which the court sat, and there whipped on the fleshy parts of his legs from morning till night. The severity and efficacy of this display of force were both very un-certain, and depended on the fees given the executioners by the two parties. One debtor would get off without great damage, another might be maimed. The duration of this punishment, undetermined at first, was fixed, between 1555 and 1628, at one month for a sum of 100 roubles ; at the expiration of that time the debtor was to be made over to the creditor. But men of mark possessed the privilege of always being able to escape the *praviéje*, either by finding substitutes or simply by default.

The extreme venality of the judges was another and a more serious obstacle in the way of an equal-handed administration

4

of justice ; over this abuse custom spread a generous cloak of tolerance.   In theory, bribes (*viatki*) were severely forbidden, but in practice, parties presenting themselves at the bar of justice had to lay an offering 'for tapers' before the holy pictures, and at Easter, magistrates of every degree had a right to receive 'red eggs,' accompanied by several ducats each. Vassili, father of the Terrible, heard that a judge, having accepted a sum of money from one of the parties to a suit, and another and smaller sum from the other party, had then given his verdict in favour of the man who had paid him most.   The magistrate, summoned before his sovereign, admitted his act, and thought to justify it by saying, 'When I have to deal between a rich and a poor man, I never hesitate about believing the rich man's word, for his interest in deceiving me is smaller.'   Vassili smiled, and was merciful.

Let us, in our turn, shew mercy to a society in which the struggle for life was embittered, in every class, by the uncertainty affecting every condition, and let us try to realize the nature of an economic régime under which the inception and maintenance of the *praviêje* were possible.

VI.—The Economic System.

Apart from the industrial and commercial centres to which reference has already been made, the Russia of the sixteenth century, like the Russia of the present day, was an essentially agricultural country.   Yet the art of cultivation tarried in its earliest stages of development, and was limited to the most elementary of methods.   The province of Jaroslavl, to the north of Moscow, and the banks of the Oka, from Riazan to Nijni-Novgorod, on the south-east, were reckoned amongst the most productive parts of the country.   According to Herberstein, indeed, the lands along the Oka yielded something between twenty and thirty fold.   Northward, again, in spite of the severity of the climate, the land along the banks of the Northern Dvina, fertilized by spring floods, produced very large harvests. But little wheat was grown there.   The most usual crops were rye, oats, and buckwheat, consumed for the most part in the country.   There was a certain amount of exportation to the west, by the seaport of Narva, and at a later date by Arkhangel, and overland into Poland.   But this trade could not attain any great volume, for the needs of Europe were not then what they are now.   The State paralyzed this, like every other traffic, by its monopolies, and, finally, any large exportation of corn was discouraged as likely to impoverish the country. Prices, too, were so ruled by the yield of each harvest, and by the relative remoteness of the places where it was grown, by war and other troubles affecting the country, that they varied by ten degrees, and all dealings with foreign markets were affected by this fact. On the whole, however, prices ruled very low.

Here I must parenthetically explain the monetary system of the country. The unit then, as now, was the rouble (from *roubit*, to cut), and each rouble consisted of 100 kopecks. Now, this rouble was supposed to weigh 16 silver *zolotniki*, weighed, therefore, in precious metal, almost seven times as much as the rouble of the present day, and was reckoned by the English merchants to be worth 16s. 8d. of English money. But after the fifteenth century especially this value suffered a gradual depreciation, resulting from the Muscovite policy, which was even then inaugurating a system the consequence of which now appears to us in a rouble which has fallen to the value of two shillings and a few odd pence. The kopiéïki were originally called diéngi (from the Tartar word *ding*, money), the present name not having been adopted till towards the middle of the sixteenth century, when these small coins were stamped with the figure of a warrior with a lance (*kopié*). Even under the father of Ivan the Terrible, the idea of cutting up the rouble into 250 diéngi had been adopted, and, under the pressure of financial necessity, during Ivan's minority, this number was increased to 300. There were two sorts of roubles at that period, for the Novgorod rouble still retained its original weight, and was worth twice as much as the Moscow rouble. This makes it very difficult to calculate the price of food-stuffs from any document of the period.

The small change of the country also included *altiny* (from the Tartar word *alt*, six), six-kopeck pieces ; *grivny*, twenty-kopeck pieces ; *poltiny*, or half-roubles (*poltiny*, half) ; and copper coins called *poloudiéngi* or *pouli* (half-kopecks). The silver *diénga*, an irregularly-shaped, rather oval coin, borrowed from the Tartars, was so small that it was easily lost. Shopkeepers settling their accounts generally put them in their mouths, fifty at a time. According to several foreign travellers, such as Herberstein and Fletcher and the chroniclers of the period, and according, too, to the calculations of Monsieur Rojkov (*loc. cit.*, p. 202, etc.), the average price of the *tchetviért* of rye (25 bushels—the *tchetviért* of those days was half that size) varied, at the beginning of the sixteenth century, between 10 kopecks, the lowest, and 69 kopecks, a high, price. And all other produce was subject to the same fluctuations. This, as compared with present prices, makes an average of 93·9, and we may conclude the purchasing power of the rouble of that day to have been ninety-four times greater, and its value therefore ninety-four times higher, than that of the rouble of ours,

But at the close of the century the proportion drops to about 20 to 24, and it is impossible to fix it with any precision.

The price of labour naturally depended on the price of corn. In 1598, we find peasants binding themselves to furnish sawing-wood, to be cut and carried for the building of a bridge, for an agreed price of a *diénga* and a half. In 1573, an *obja*, a piece of ground which one man could till with a horse, was to be bought for between 8 and 10 roubles. A house cost 3 roubles. Four cows and twenty sheep were to be had for 4 roubles 16 *altines*, and a horse for from 1 to 3 roubles.

Crops were taken in a three-years' rotation—rye, oats, and fallow. The peasant who settled on an *obja* sowed two and a half to three and a half *tchetviérti* of rye and as much barley, and, if his harvests were good, made as much as 3 roubles a year. His keep having been taken out of this income, he still had to dress himself. A full suit cost him half a rouble, without the belt and gloves, indispensable in cold weather, and for which he had to give 24 kopecks and 6 kopecks. Then he had his taxes, some 75 kopecks to 1 rouble, as it seems, by a reckon-ing taken in 1555.

But all this only relates to the ' black ' lands, on which the free peasants lived. On the ' white ' lands the advances given by proprietors towards the farmers' preliminary expenses, and the succour they distributed in times of famine or murrain, made the husbandman's life easier, but endangered his freedom. The peasants settling on communal lands generally obtained a remission of taxes for the first four or even eight years of their tenancy, but they could not reckon on any other advan-tage. The monastery lands were looked on as an El Dorado, and I have already explained why. Yet, though the monks, less heavily burdened themselves, were in a position to be more lenient with others, the name *strada* (*stradat*, to suffer), com-monly applied to the forced labour demanded by these land-lords, would seem to prove their El Dorado was no paradise.

I have already mentioned one of the causes which acted as an obstacle to the development of the agricultural industry. That celebrated household book, the ' Domostroï,' composed by Pope Sylvester in the reign of Ivan the Terrible, to which I shall make further reference, sheds a curious light on this point. According to this book, all industrial activity seems to have been essentially domesticated. Under the roof of every boïar of that period we see a cluster of workshops, which supply all the home needs of the establishment, and make any external development of the same trades a matter of impossibility.

Yet carpentering, joinery, boat-building, that fashioning of small wooden utensils and objects which has attained such ex-tensive proportions in the particular form of industrial activity now known as *koustar*, had existed and been general in the country from a very early date. At Kosmodiémiansk, near Nijni-Novgorod, there was a celebrated industry in chests, and there were others, famous for their red-leather and seal-skin appointments, at Kholmogory. The sledges made at Viazma and the wooden spoons produced at Kalouga were also highly renowned, but none of this was exceedingly profitable merchandise. The Kholmogory chests were used to carry wares to Moscow, and then sold there at very low prices. A hundred Kalouga spoons were worth 20 altines, and a Viazma sleigh was to be had for a *poltina*.

Trade, though comparatively stronger, was still starved. In the matter of exports it was almost exclusively confined to raw materials. The first place was held by furs, and 500,000 roubles' worth were sold in Europe and Asia every year. The finest sables came from Obdorsk, in the present Government of Tobolsk. White bearskins came from the banks of the Piétchora, and sealskins from the Kola Peninsula. A fine sable skin cost as much as thirty gold florins ; a boïar's cap trimming, in black fox, was worth fifteen. But ermine was little sought after in those days, and an ermine skin could be bought for 3 or 4 diéngi. Wax held the second place in the external trade of the country ; about 50,000 pounds were exported every year. Tallow came next, a considerable quantity, some 30,000 or 40,000 pounds, being sent annually out of the provinces of Smolensk, Jaroslavl, Ouglitch, Novgorod, Vologda, and Tver. Within the boundaries of Russia this commodity was not very largely consumed, for the rich used wax candles, and the poor burnt torches made of resinous wood. The honey so abundantly produced in the provinces of Riazan and Mourom, and, later, round Kazan, was principally employed in brewing the favourite beverage of the country, but a certain quantity was also sent abroad, Pskov and Novgorod, Jaroslavl and Vologda, exporting as much as 10,000 pounds a year. For elk-skins, too, much praised by Fletcher, there was a foreign demand. The finest elks were to be found in the forests near Rostov, Vytchegda, Novgorod, Mourom, and Perm. The oxen were too small to be of much mercantile value. The neighbourhood of Arkhangel sent seal-oil to the foreign markets, and the fisheries of Jaroslavl, Nijni-Novgorod, Biélooziéro, and Astrakhan—after the conquest of that country—furnished abundance of fish and fish-roes, already much sought after by English, Dutch, and French merchants. These were sold even in Italy and Spain. In his ' Treatise on the Sarmatians,' published in 1521, Matthew Miechovski speaks of the whale-fisheries in the White Sea. But it seems strange that efforts which have so frequently failed in later times should have been successful at this period. Most probably, as Monsieur Zamy-slovski opines, all that was then done was to turn a few stranded whales to account (see his study in the *Revue du Min. de l'Istr. Publ.*, published May, 1882, p. 67). Certain varieties of birds had a constant sale abroad—gerfalcons, especially, brought very high prices. Flax from Pskov, and hemp from Smolensk, Dorokho-bouje, and Viazma, all found foreign purchasers, and so did the salt from the Staraïa-Roussa salt-works, and the tar from Smolensk and Dvinsk. Persia took all the walrus teeth, using them both for industrial purposes and in the preparation of much vaunted remedies and antidotes against poison. Mica, found in great quantities on the banks of the Dvina and in Carelia, was used instead of glass all over the country, and was also exported with other mineral products, such as saltpetre, prepared at Ouglitch, Jaroslavl, and Oustioug; sulphur, taken out of the lakes of Samara; and iron from the mines of Carelia and those near Kargopol and Oustioujna.

Some manufactured articles, though principally consumed at home, found a certain number of purchasers abroad. Tartary took saddles, bridles, linens, cloths, and garments, and sent back Asiatic horses in their stead. The European merchants brought ingot silver, gold thread, copper, cloth, looking-glasses, lace, cutlery, needles, purses, wines, and fruits. Their Asiatic comrades sold silk stuffs, gold tissues, carpets, pearls, and gems. Both were bound to bring all their merchandise to Moscow, where the Sovereign, having made his own selection in the first place, gave them leave to offer the rest for public sale. Peter the Great's daughter was to claim this privilege, with regard to the merchants who brought fashions from France, in later days.

The meeting-place of all the merchants was at the confluence of the Mologa and the Volga. Here, in ancient days, had stood a little town, called the 'town of the slaves' (*Kholopii gorodok*), of which a church was the only remaining vestige. This town had been founded, according to tradition, by Novgorod slaves, who had fled from the rage of their masters, whose honour they had cruelly outraged during an abˉence which had proved too long for the virtue of the wives they behind them. The fair held on this spot was the most famous in all Russia. It lasted four months, and filled the huge estuary with such an army of boats, packed close together, that men passed dryfoot from one shore to the other. German, Polish, Lithuanian, Greek, Italian, Persian merchants, crowded along the shores, and exposed their wares in a huge meadow, circled with temporary inns and wineshops. These last establishments numbered as many as seventy, and the bartering round about them was so extensive as to be worth 180 pounds of silver to the

Sovereign, year in and year out. These operations, indeed, were nearly all carried out in kind, and no coin passed. Coined money was an uncommon thing, as a rule, monopolized by a few rare capitalists, and especially by the Sovereign, the greatest hoarder in the country.

The only rival of this fair, as regards business and extent, was that held at Lampojnia, to which I have already referred, and which did a special and considerable trade in furs bought from the Samoyedes. For an axe, these savages would give as many sable skins as could be passed, all bound together, through the hole into which the wooden haft fitted. The Lithuanian merchants had their own special meeting-place, close to a monastery of the Trinity—not the celebrated abbey of that name in the province of Moscow—on the banks of the Dnieper, in the province of Smolensk.

These exchanges with foreign countries were detestably one-sided, for the Russian products were generally sold at very low prices, and foreign merchandise was very dear. An archine ($27\frac{33}{100}$ inches) of velvet, damask, or satin, cost a rouble, a piece of fine English cloth 30 roubles, a barrel of French wine 4 roubles. Gold crowns were also imported merchandise, the coinage of the country not sufficing for its needs, and these paid duty like any other commodity.

The Russian merchants of that period, though their clever-ness and spirit of enterprise were much admired, otherwise enjoyed a sufficiently evil reputation. Foreigners were never tired of complaining of their cunning and bad faith, and this without exception, save as to the men of Pskov and Novgorod, though, even in their case, the fame of their ancient honesty was tarnished. The local proverb, 'Merchandise is made for the eyes,' was freely applied, and so was the habit of raising the price asked for a thing tenfold if the would-be purchaser happened to appear rich and simple-minded. Wholesale merchants generally employed experts, but these very frequently tried to get money out of both parties to the bargain. Foreigners noticed that the more a merchant called on God, and took Him to witness as to his own honesty, the more he was likely to cheat them. Dishonest dealings as to the quality, origin, and weight of merchandise, the sale of imitations, the substitution of one article for another, just before it was delivered—these were common practices.

The success of foreign traders—the sort of privilege over the Muscovite markets, won as early as in the fifteenth century, by various importing and exporting houses, German, Flemish, and Dutch, previous to the real monopoly of the English com-pany—are in great measure explained by these odious proceed-ings. Not, indeed, that the foreigners did not end by imitating them to some extent. Herberstein admits that it was no uncommon thing to see them selling an article not worth more than one or two ducats, for twelve.

The Russian, ignorant, and cheated himself as often as he cheated others, fleeced by the State, which did not give him proper protection, deceived by the very foreigners who complained of his dishonest dealings and themselves did likewise, looked on trade as a warfare, in which stratagem of every kind was legitimate and almost necessary. The bonds and burdens laid on his industry by the greed and clumsiness of those who ruled him were endless. The Empire was cut up into little commercial provinces, each covering a radius of from 10 to 20 versts round its central town or village. Within the limits of each province no exchange was allowed, except at the central point. This was to prevent any shirking of taxation. The taxes, huge and innumerable already, were aggravated by a system of farming which opened the door wide to abuse and exaction. The merchandise, before it reached its market, had to pass under the Caudine Forks of an exaggerated fiscal system. There were toll-bars on the roads, there were dues for crossing rivers, there were Custom-houses at the gate of every town. If the town was a river-town, there were charges on the embarkation and landing of goods. If it contained a *gostinnyi dvor*, the merchant must take up his quarters there, and pay the regulation tax. Dues for going in, dues for coming out, storage dues, and dues on the sale of everything that went out of the warehouse. If a horse was sold, there were dues on the brand and the written contract ; if it was a pound of salt, there were dues on the weight.

Imagine a peasant coming into the market with the results of his humble toil. There must be a great deal of that to make up a rouble's worth. A horse, or two cows, or twenty geese, or ten sheep, or some ten *tchetviérti* of rye, or four sleighs. And he has already spent eight or ten *diéngi* on his way in—more than the value of one day's work. By the time he has sold his horse he will have spent another fifteen.

The system, indeed, was by no means peculiar to the country. It was the common rule at a period when France still preserved the remnants of a not less irksome and oppressive feudal system, under which the ancient *telonium*, converted into the *tonlieu*, and the antique *vinagrum*, now called the *vientrage*, fleeced merchants as they passed through each territory ; and in the year 1567 there were between 100 and 150 crossing-places on the Loire alone at which fees were paid ; while (see Lavisse and Rambaud, *Hist. Générale*, iv., p. 201) a case of mercery goods, sent from Paris to Rouen, paid pedlar's fees before it left the city, paid again at Neuilly, at St. Denis, at Chatou, at Le Pecq, at Maisons, at Conflans, at Poissy, at Triél, at Meulan, at Mantes, at La Roche-Guyon, at Vernon, at Les Andelys, at Pont-de-l'Arche, on Rouen Bridge, and, if it was to be sent to England, paid again, at Rouen itself, the *droits de vicomté, de rêve et de haut passage*, not to mention the Admiralty shipping license, freight, pilot's fees, and all the rest.

Yet in France Louis XI. had endeavoured to reduce the number of these dues, which had enormously increased during the anarchy of the Hundred Years' War. They were largely the outcome of anarchy. In Russia, on the contrary, they were the result of a system which grew worse and worse as the needs and demands of the State increased, and which was complicated and encumbered by a mass of minor regulations suggested by economic ideas, of which I have already pointed out the dangerous tendency. A Lithuanian merchant who had brought a quantity of cloth-stuffs to Moscow, and there taken over a corresponding quantity of beeswax, added a few trifling silver articles, and saw the whole of his merchandise seized, because the exportation of the precious metals was forbidden.

Trade still had to suffer from the general poverty of the urban centres. The towns were built of wood as a rule, and paved, when they were paved at all, with the same material. And once in ten years, for the most part, they were burnt down. After the fire of 1541, which consumed the whole of the Slav quarter at Novgorod—some 908 houses—another, in 1554, devoured over 1500 dwellings. One of the chronicles of the city—the second—is hardly more than a calendar of these periodical misfortunes. No precautions were taken to prevent a recurrence of the disaster. It was not till 1560 that it occurred to anybody to establish, near the dwellings, some of those troughs filled with water and those hooks shaped like huge brooms which may be seen to this day in the country parts of Russia at the entrances of the *isbas*, which are in constant danger of destruction. In 1570, the Government issued an order that no bath was to be heated in summer, and no bread baked, even, except in outdoor ovens.

To this may be added the condition of the roads in a country which, for want of the necessary materials, has to do without metalled highroads even now. From the port of St. Nicholas, on the White Sea, when the English landed there, to Vologda, where they opened their first counting-house, they had to travel fourteen times twenty-four hours by water, and eight days by road in winter; in summer-time the land road was impracticable for a long period. The journey from Vologda to Jaroslavl was reckoned at two days, that from Jaroslavl to Arkhangel at twenty, all by water. Between Novgorod and Narva, a most important line for foreign exports, the land road consisted of mere paths running through forests and over marshes. There were no inns, and very few villages. The country between Novgorod and Moscow was a desert, and summer travellers had the greatest difficulty in getting from Moscow to Vilna. The only tolerably convenient and pretty nearly practicable road at every season of the year was that between Pskov and Riga, on the western frontier. Thus, in summer-time heavy merchandise was transported exclusively by water, and in winter over the frozen snow. It was no uncommon thing, in the winter season, to meet 700 or 800 sledges, all laden with grain or fish. They travelled in large bands, as a rule, fearing the armed attacks so frequent in those days.

This state of insecurity was general. On the east, Tartars made perpetual incursions into the country, stripping and murdering travellers. In the south, there were Cossacks and robbers everywhere. On the Volga, pirate bands even defied the military expeditions sent out year after year to put them down.

Foreign travellers have noted one feature which, in connection with those to which I have just referred, strikes us as surprising—excellent posting arrangements. When the roads were good—in winter, that is to say—the 524 versts between Novgorod and Moscow could be covered in seventy-two hours, at a very moderate charge—6 kopecks for a stage of 20 versts— and the traveller could get as many relays of horses as he wanted. A tired horse was quickly replaced—left behind, and a fresh one taken in its stead, in the nearest village, or from the first passer-by. This was the Tsar's service, and the traveller only had to show a way-bill signed by the proper authority to insure his being served in this fashion. In summer, indeed, the scene changed. The horses were out at pasture, or working in the fields, and hours would slip by before the necessary team could be collected. But at that season travellers preferred the water-ways, on which there were boats and rowers, also belonging to the State.

This was a legacy from the Tartar conquest, which partly owed its startling successes to the extreme rapidity and clever handling of its transport. It must not be forgotten that France had no posting system till Louis XI. established one by edict in 1464, and then with an exclusively political object, to convey the King's couriers. Russia has ever been a country of surprises.

But this single advantage did not compensate, in the sixteenth century, for the other causes of inferiority which paralyzed her economic life. In the year 1553, 25,000 corpses were buried in the cemeteries at Pskov, without reckoning the unknown number left to rot in the open country. This was the plague, a scourge as periodic in its visitations as fire. In the spring of 1565 it was raging at Louki, at Toropiéts, and at Smolensk ; in the autumn it was at Polotsk. The following year it was to ravage Novgorod, Staraïa-Roussa, Pskov again, Mojaïsk, and even Moscow itself. Before the plague, or behind it, or with it, as in 1570, came famine. And the means devised to stamp out the disease were as fierce as the pest itself. In 1551 the Pskov merchants suspected of being infected were driven out of Novgorod, and those who resisted were burnt alive. So were any priests who dared to visit the sick.

As a matter of fact, famine was endemic, the normal condition of the country. The Englishman Jenkinson, a clever business man and a sagacious observer, mentions eighty-four persons as having perished under his eyes, within a very short period of time, for lack of sustenance—of a little straw, in other words, for dried and pounded straw was the ordinary winter food of many of the natives, who lived in summer on grass, roots, and the bark of trees (Hakluyt, i., p. 323). The foreign observer complains, in this connection, of the inhumanity of the inhabitants of the country, who were unmoved by the sight of their fellow-creatures falling down and dying of hunger in the streets. This trait occurs whenever the general poverty induces a general hardening of the human heart. In sixteenth-century Russia, wealth, even ease, was an exceptional pheno-menon.

Apart from the monasteries, hardly any family, except the Stroganovs, owned any considerable fortune. Fletcher reckons that this house, besides its landed properties, which were huge, its farming establishments, which ran from the banks of the Vytchegda to the Siberian frontier, and its industrial establish-ments, in which it employed 10,000 free labourers and 5,000 serfs, owned 300,000 roubles in hard cash. It paid 23,000 roubles of taxes to the State, but the State was ruining it by its perpetually increasing demands, and to the State system must be ascribed the fact that the Stroganovs were such an exception to the general rule.

The State and the Church, a Baal with two faces, devoured everything, sucked the national riches, and dried up their fount—the State by its exactions, the Church by the usurious interest on her loans. Everybody was in debt, and the poorest paid the interest on what they owed in labour, thus rendered valueless to the general economy, and contributing nothing towards the building up of the public wealth. The formula whereby the man, the woman, and sometimes the whole family, children included, undertook to labour ' for the in-terest ' (za rost sloujiti ve dvoïé po vsiadni) occurred more and

more frequently in the constantly increasing number of contracts between borrower and lender.

The scarcity of coinage, to which I have already referred,
was in itself a symptom of the general distress. Until the close
of this century, according to Guagnino, squirrel skins were used
as currency, and, indeed, Peter the Great paid his functionaries
their salaries in the same fashion. Yet there was a free coinage
in the sixteenth century, the State only intervening to verify
weights and designations. Some artisans, indeed, were given
the right to stamp their own names on their coins. A great
deal of ingot silver was also used, and the ancient Novgorod
coins, of which Chaudoir gives us facsimiles in his book (*Aperçu
sur les Monnaies Russes*, 1836), were nothing but ingots, either.
The habit of regarding gold and silver as merchandise was long
to linger in the Russian mind. But there was a shortage in
the supply of raw material. Though the mines, contrary to
the assertions of Paulus Jovius (*Pauli Jovii Descriptiones*, i.,
1571), were not entirely unproductive, though even in 1482
Ivan III. was asking the Hungarian King Matthius Korvinus
to send him engineers to work fresh ones, and though argen-
tiferous soil had been discovered in 1491 on the banks of the
Tsylma, an affluent of the Piétchora, the supply of metals
was trifling, and Russia depended, in this respect, on foreign
countries. As to gold, the only coins in circulation were
foreign—Hungarian, Dutch, Polish, and Florentine ducats, and
English shiff-nobles and rose-nobles. And amongst the silver
currency, numbers of Dutch florins, German thalers, generally
known as *efimki* (Joachim's Thaler), and English shillings
figured. Gold pieces were so rare that any event which brought
about a larger demand for them, such as a marriage or baptism
in the Sovereign's family, or the despatch of a foreign mission,
resulted in a sudden rise in value, sometimes amounting to
doubling the value of each gold coin. On such occasions as
marriages and christenings the Sovereign received gifts of
ducats from the boïars and the representatives of the various
constituted bodies ; and Ambassadors, even in Poland, needed
gold pieces if they were to make any decent show.

The Sovereign always had all he needed in his cellars. He
was the very wealthy master of a very poor country. He
dazzled everybody, even the Western world, by his riches ; but
it is impossible to come to an absolutely clear understanding of
the amount of these, nor of the manner in which they were
acquired. I shall consequently limit myself to a very few
brief remarks upon this subject.

VII.—THE FINANCES.

We have no information touching the Muscovite Budget until the close of the sixteenth century. In the last years of that century, under the son of Ivan IV., Fletcher calculated the revenue of the Empire at 1,400,000 roubles, of which 400,000 were supplied by direct and 800,000 by indirect taxation. Taken in connection with such documents concerning the reign of Alexis as we possess, these figures seem near the truth, and lead us to suppose the receipts under the Terrible to have been about 1,200,000 roubles. In England, at that period,' there was no direct taxation at all, and consumers' taxes only brought in 140,000 crowns, Henry VIII.'s whole revenue not exceeding a million of crowns. Taking the rouble of those days at 16s. 8d., Ivan IV. asked four times as much from his subjects as Henry VIII. demanded of his (see Philippson, *Westeuropa im Zeitalter von Philipp II.*, 1882, p. 59).

In reality he got a great deal more out of them. The great resource of the Muscovite Sovereign was the land, which was parcelled out among his ' service men,' and supplied all the essential needs of the State, the upkeep of the army and administration. Thus it was that the Sovereign was able to hoard up riches. War material and the pay of the few troops who formed the nucleus of the regular army did, indeed, involve a fairly heavy outlay. Three-quarters of his revenue, according to some authorities, were swallowed up by it. But, at all events, he was able to put by the remaining quarter, for to keep up his Court the Grand Duke, like every other European Sovereign, had his own patrimony—thirty-six towns, with the villages and hamlets depending on them, and these, besides a money payment, sent him corn, cattle, fish, honey, and forage, which not only supplied the necessities of the Court, large as it was, but were sold in considerable quantities. Ivan IV. thus made an additional income of 60,000 roubles a year, and his successor, a more economical man, increased the sum to 230,000 roubles.

These features have come down, in a measure, to our own times. They formed an integral part of a régime which has stood the brunt of centuries, and has insured the country which had the docility to submit to it material greatness and strength at all events, if not prosperity, together with an enormous power of concentration and expansion. The secret of this docility remains to be discovered. We may discover it, perhaps, in the course of our endeavour to understand the mind of a people which, with such means, has accomplished so great things.

CHAPTER III

INTELLECTUAL LIFE

I.—CAUSES OF ITS WEAKNESS. II.—INTELLECTUAL CURRENTS. III.—LITERATURE. VI.—ART. V.—THE RENOVATING MOVEMENT.

I.—THE CAUSES OF ITS WEAKNESS.

THE Mongols who overwhelmed Russia in the thirteenth century are generally regarded as the authors of a crime against civilization. The rupture between Muscovy and the western countries, the sudden check in the development of the national culture, are taken to be their work. For many years I shared the common error, and I confess it without shame ; appearances all pointed that way, and the history of the invasion is still exceedingly obscure. The first testimony against this view which attracted my attention was all the more conclusive in that it was borne by one of the Princes of the national Church ; and it is a well-known fact that, until the eighteenth century at all events, the whole intellectual life of the country was almost entirely concentrated in that Church.

' Judging by the state of her knowledge and the progress of her development during the two centuries which preceded the Mongol invasion,' writes Monsignor Macarius in his ' History of the Russian Church ' (v. 285), ' we do not believe her progress during the two following centuries would have been any more rapid even if the Mongols had not come among us. . . . These Asiatics did nothing to prevent the clergy, especially the cloistered clergy, from pursuing their learned studies. But the Russians of that period do not seem to have felt any need of a higher culture. They followed in the path of their ancestors, and their longings were confined to being able to read easily, and understand the sacred texts. . . .'

Recent inquiry, too, has destroyed the illusion according to which a flood of Eastern barbarism was supposed to have swept, with the invaders, over all the elements of European culture. The comrades of Batou, and of the great head of his staff, Soubatoï, were not, as Monsieur Léon Cahun has most excellently set forth in a book which is a revelation (*Introduction à l'Histoire de l'Asie*, 1896, p. 343, etc.), such desperate barbarians as all that. They were first-rate strategians and wonderful organizers, worthy representatives of a civilization which was to astonish Henry of Castile's Ambassadors to Samarkand a century later (1405), and spread the use of Ouloug-Beg's astronomical tables all over

Europe. They were no deliberate wreckers, either, except in cases of military exigency; nor oppressors, beyond the taxation they imposed; and their very numbers precluded them from submerging others. The legend of the overwhelming flood is a melodramatic invention : Soubatoï won his victories, in every case, with very small, but exceedingly well-equipped, mobile, and splendidly commanded bodies of troops.

The truth appears to be that he found nought but ruins everywhere—a rotting Empire, a country parted from Europe already, and cast, both from the political and intellectual point of view, into an almost utter isolation. Since Jaroslav (1016-1054) had married one of his sisters to Casimir of Poland, another to the King of Norway, and a third to Henry I. of France, no similar alliance had carried the tradition down to the heirs who fought over the great Kiovian Prince's legacy ; and even as early as 1169, Kiev had been sacked by barbarians who did not come out of Asia. All the small Russian Princes strove for the possession of the old capital, carrying fire and sword with them. And the truth is this— that, by reason of her spiritual alliance with Byzantium, Russia, thus devastated and dismembered by her own children, was bound to a corpse, held in vassalage by the learning of the Greeks at a moment when doom had fallen on the antique culture, when the ancient schools were closed, when the introduction of the Oriental view had stifled that free inquiry essential to all progress. The contemporaries of Photius ascribed (A.D. 891) the patriarch's knowledge to the spells of a Jewish page-boy, and the learning of Archbishop Theodore (Santabaren) was confused by Leo the Grammarian with evocations of the spirits of the dead. Historiography was reduced to the collecting of legends, the teaching of philosophy was forbidden, intellectual activity was circumscribed within the sphere of religious polemics—marked phases, all these, of an irreparable decay. Even in the twelfth century the eastern monasteries proved themselves incapable of utilizing the scientific materials at their disposal.

The intellectual isolation of orthodox Russia was the direct outcome of her affiliation to her Byzantine almamater. Out of the 240 writers who appeared in Russia up till the close of the seventeenth century (without reckoning the Catholics of the south-west), 190 were monks, 20 belonged to the secular clergy, and the remaining 30 dealt chiefly with religious subjects. Thus literature and science were almost exclusively Church property. And this Church, even in the thirteenth century, was a closed body, shut up in itself. Orthodoxy forbade all contact with unbelievers to such a degree as to impose on Russian Sovereigns that custom of washing their hands after giving audience to foreign Ambassadors which so sorely offended Possevino at the Court of Ivan the Terrible. This isolation was aggravated by the adhesion of the Metropolitan Isidore, the elect of Byzantium, to the Florentine Union, and by the capture of Constantinople by the Turks, which last, though the triumph of Islam was taken to be a well-deserved chastisement, cast suspicion on the East itself. And at that period the legend of St. Andrew's sojourn in Russia, and consequently of the antiquity and indepnedence of local orthodoxy, sprang into life, and spread with great rapidity. The idea of a national religion expressive of the original features of the Slav spirit became general in every mind.

And yet the national Church, instead of beaming with an ever-brightening light, relapsed into constantly deepening darkness. We do not find a trace, at the close of the fifteenth century, of the monastery schools, the previous existence of which is proved by numerous witnesses. At the beginning of the next century St. Gennadius, Archbishop of Novgorod, notes with sorrow that the men presented to him for ordination can neither read nor write. Even oral instruction had disappeared, the pulpits were dumb, and, according to foreign travellers, hardly one native out of ten could say his *Pater*. A century later, in 1620, a learned Swede, John Botvid, seriously discussed the question of whether the Muscovites were Christians at all, or not.

The monasteries, to be sure, did go on collecting books : some of them even possessed librarians. But reading became the speciality of a small and select group. It rose to be a science, and more and more the only science in existence. To read all he could, and even learn the things he read by heart—was not that as much as any man might do ? The learned man was called a *knijnik*, a man of many books (*kniga*, book). But what books ? In the monastic libraries a place, and even the place of honour, was given to the Apocrypha— 'Adam's Manuscript, confided to the Devil,' 'The Last Will of Moses,' 'The Vision of Isaac,' . . ., these enjoyed the same credit as the canonical books. Maximus the Greek, the corrector of the sacred texts summoned from the East at the beginning of the sixteenth century, was the first who dared to protest against the belief that the sun did not set for a week after our Lord's resurrection, and that, somewhere on the banks of the Jordan, a viper still guarded Adam's last will and testament. The catalogue of the library of the Troïtsa in the seventeenth century is still in our hands. Ancient literature is therein represented by 411 manuscripts.

This is very much the total reached by the Glastonbury library in the thirteenth century. But how different the composition! At Glastonbury the first rank is held by the Roman classics, historians, and poets. At the Troïtsa we find 101 Bibles, 46 liturgical works, 58 collections of the Fathers of the Church, 17 books on ecclesiastical law, and one solitary book on philosophy. The works on asceticism are the most numerous of all. Until the seventeenth century the ancient Greek and Latin authors were unknown to Russian readers. In profane literature chronicles were the favourite reading. But what chronicles! Those of Malala (or Maleles), with his quotations from Orpheus! The still more popular chronicle of George the Hamartolian, with its detailed description of the garment of a certain Jewish priest who went to Judæa to meet Alexander the Great! The authorities on geography and cosmography were George Pissides, and, above all, Cosmas Indicopleustes, whose conclusions as to the dimensions of the earth, founded on the form of Moses' tabernacle, were undoubtingly accepted, and whose teaching, a mixture of the Apocrypha, Ptolemy, Aristotle, and the dreams of the Manichæans and Gnostics, disseminated conceptions of the most preposterous nature. In philosophy, students held by John the Damascene and his theory of the reduction of science to the love of God. But the book of all, read, up till the eighteenth century, with the works of the contemplative school, of Basil the Great and Denis the Areopagite, was the ' Bee,' an incoherent compilation of Scripture quotations, extracts from the Fathers of the Church, and a medley of detached thoughts from Aristotle, Socrates, Epicurus, Diodorus, and Cato—a literary *omnium gatherum*.

Under the influence of the notions thus acquired, the prediction of an eclipse was held to be sorcery; books on mathematics —and arithmetic and astronomy, geography and music, were all confused together under this title—were proscribed as impious, and the *knijnik* was shut up within a narrow horizon, above which the light of European science could not rise, and forced to trample the same ground, ever and always, far from the current on which his Western neighbours were being borne onward.

During the sixteenth century, indeed, a beam of light, a breath of air, entered this dungeon. Maximus the Greek, an Albanian monk who had studied in Greece and Italy, was in some sense a European. Though his literary activity was confined to religious and moral questions, he brought to Russia, on the soles of his shoes, a little of the dust gathered at Milan, Florence, Venice, Ferrara, and especially at Padua, where the mighty struggle between the partisans of Plato

5

and Aristotle, the current which had impelled intellectual circles to copy pagan customs and attack the theology of the Middle Ages, had not failed to affect him. At Venice he had known the famous typographer, Alde Manuce ; at Florence he had stirred the still smoking ashes of the pile on which Savonarola had met his fate ; he had realized something of the great scientific importance of Paris. None of which prevented him from being absolutely devoid of that critical instinct which is the great lever of the Western world of intellect, and deeply tinctured with an absolute scepticism as to profane learning, which led him to condemn a Russian translation, then just appearing, of the celebrated Lucidarius,— a twelfth-century work, ascribed to St. Anselm of Canterbury, or to Honoré d'Autun—and wherein certain problems in cosmography and physics were treated in a comparatively sensible spirit. He forbade its inclusion in the libraries, from which the Greek and Latin classics were banished.

A legend has grown up around a collection of these same classics, supposed to have existed, with a great number of other profane works and some Hebrew manuscripts, at the Moscow Kremlin, as early as the fifteenth century. The presumed existence of this library, revealed by the researches of two foreign savants, Klossius (1834) and Tremer (1891), has provoked, in more recent times (1894), a controversy in the press, and even a search in the subterranean chambers of the ancient palace. This has brought no result. Whether it was that the Livonian chronicler Nyenstaedt, who wrote the first book in which the library is mentioned, and Professor Dubiélov, of the University of Derpt, who, in the year 1820, invented a catalogue which nobody has ever been able to discover since, were imposed on themselves, or imposed on others, the story, it seems pretty certain, has no foundation in fact. At a much earlier period, indeed, a similar legend had ascribed the possession of a quantity of Byzantine manuscripts—made over to their safe keeping, by the Emperor John, just before the Siege of Constantinople— to the Muscovite Sovereigns. Wherefore, in the year 1600, Cardinal San Giorgio sent Peter Arcudius the Greek in the train of a Polish Embassy to verify the story, which he discovered to be false—a pure invention. Ivan IV. and his predecessors did certainly own some books and manuscripts ; but up till the close of the fourteenth century, we only hear of the authentic existence of one single work in a foreign language, a German herbal, in the whole of their collection of liturgical books, instructions, chronicles, and astrological treatises.

Under the twofold influence of the original Byzantinism and the inherent materialism pervading every class of society, intellectual life, still in the earliest phases of its development, was destined to waver, for long years yet, between two opposite tendencies, which, nevertheless, occasionally combined, as we shall see, after a very curious fashion. These, an asceticism void of all ideal and a coarse sensuality, were the twin roads that led to general nothingness.

II.—INTELLECTUAL CURRENTS.

From the elementary and barren independence—the independence of savagery—in which it had lived till Christianity was introduced, the country had suddenly fallen under the yoke of an austere morality—as savage after its own fashion—which forbade liberty to know, liberty to create, and even to exist, in every quarter. Under this rule, all those living forces which have ennobled the human race were condemned, and even accursed. The world of free knowledge was accursed, as a centre of heresy and corruption ; the world of free creation was accursed, as an element of corruption ; and accursed, too, as an element of scandal, was free life, with its joys, its merriment, its profane delights. The bards have disappeared from the courts of Princes ; the lively tone and poetic turn of thought of the chroniclers of the eleventh and twelfth centuries give place to dry didactic narrative, that disfigures and even proscribes the very documents on which it is founded ; even any conversation that does not turn on religious subjects is anathema. Abstinence in every form has become the essential rule of life. In certain families, the very young children are made to do without milk, and by the time they are two years old they are expected to observe all the fasts. Meat is only allowed three times a week, and conjugal relations are likewise forbidden on three days in each week, on feast days, and during the whole of Lent. The Russian com-pilers from Byzantine writers were well acquainted with Cato's dictum, ' We rule the world, and the women rule us.' It occupied a prominent position in the ' Bee,' as also did the saying of Democritus, married to a tiny wife, ' I have chosen the smallest evil.' The Church, guided by these principles, looked on woman as the devil's chief instrument in his work of destruction, and therefore woman, too, was accursed, and accursed, with her, all forms of art, of which she has everywhere and always been the chief inspirer.

In the religious life, this tendency led directly to the stupid formalism of the ecclesiastical doctors, who perceived eternal truths and immutable doctrines in the trimming of a beard or the cut of a garment. After the Florentine Union and the erection of the national Church into the sole guardian

of the sacred traditions, form became the tabernacle, the holy
ark which sheltered the true faith. Outside it, nothing save
rationalism, Latin, Catholic or Protestant—all sources of
heresy and impiety. Argument, reasoning, were forbidden,
and by this elimination of the essential leaven of all progress
Moscow placed itself on a lower intellectual basis than that of
Byzantium, where the right of dogmatic controversy was
always preserved. Here, from the twelfth century onwards,
the only problems discussed are such as these : ' Can a priest
who has not slept since he has eaten food celebrate the holy
sacrifice ? Can he do so if he finds a woman's handkerchief
sewed to his garment ? . . .' The very sermons, such as
are preached, only deal with ritual questions : ' Must
the celebrant move with or against the sun ? Should the
sign of the cross be made with two or three fingers ?' The
first *Concile* called by Ivan IV. considered this question, and
pronounced sentence of excommunication on those who crossed
themselves with two fingers.

The identification of faith with rite reduced piety to the
accomplishment of certain external practices, the keeping of
fasts, long prayers in church. Confession, which implied an
act of internal religion, was relegated to the second rank.
The most devout did not present themselves at the tribunal
of repentance oftener than once a year ; the most scrupulous
did not make it a case of conscience to keep back none of their
sins. Ceremonial took the place of everything else. It
grew more and more extensive, and was attended by a more
and more theatrical display. On Palm Sunday the Metropolitan, riding upon an ass, went in procession to all the
churches, bestowing his blessing on the crowd that cast its
garments under the hoofs of his symbolic steed ; and on the
feast in memory of the three Hebrews cast into the fiery
furnace, the place of the pulpit was filled by a huge stove,
into which three white-robed youths were thrust with many
a complicated rite. The performance stopped short here,
and they were not actually burned.

Religious feeling continued very intense ; it wandered into
muddy paths, and floundered into sloughs. While the
Domostroï enjoined the repetition, six hundred times every
day, of a certain prayer, the effect of which, after a per-
severance of three years in the process, was to be a triple
incarnation of the Father, the Son, and the Holy Ghost in
the person of the individual using it, the question whether
it was not a sin to cross the threshold of the house inhabited
by a woman lately brought to bed, or whether the milk of a
cow that had just calved was unclean or not, was much debated.
While sensualism thus lay in wait for pious souls and overtook

them at the corners of bye-ways, superstition laid other snares for them. The Finnish element, still half pagan, came to the front in the constantly-increasing ceremonial of the Church, openly ruled by the pagan spirit. In the north, up till the eighteenth century, the beliefs and customs, and all the structure of the ancient worship, were to preserve their authority over a population which its ethnographical peculiarities rendered less amenable to the Slav conquest, and less easily influenced by Christianity. In this zone, for many years, the progress of the two powers was only marked by islets here and there, colonies scattered hither and thither over the huge territory. Even quite recently, Keppen's map has shown us how the characteristic traits of the Tchoud race predominate in the case of quite half the population ; and this race was superstitious above all others. In this part of the world Nature has always laid a heavy hand on man. Trackless forests, rocks that pierce the clouds, deserts heaped with stones, an endless succession of lakes and bogs—there is something terrifying about the landscape. Our ears are deafened by the roaring of cataracts or the perpetual howl of the angry winds ; aurora borealis cast their lurid light around ; Will-o'-the-wisps, flickering over the faces of the stagnant pools, startle the imagination ; fierce or venomous creatures, bears and vipers, threaten man with death at every step. Out of all these the Finn had built himself up a religion that was nothing but one long shuddering terror. His gods were the sons of Ahriman, rather than of Ormuzd. Every stone, every tree, was the home of some evil spirit. And only one weapon availed against them—sorcery. His priest was priest and sorcerer in one. An artificial imitation of the noises of hostile Nature calmed the spirits' never-ceasing irritation. This was the very essence of the faith spread over the huge continent that stretches from the Ural Mountains to the seas of China and Japan, from the dreary shores of the Frozen Sea to the lonely heights of the Himalaya, and it is the secret of a liturgy which, within those geographical limits, was a mere tempest of unchained elements, of noise and movement. The sorcerer-priest, the *Chamane* of the Ostiaks, danced round the fire beating a drum, and his audience did their best to drown his noise with that they made themselves, till the pontiff, faint and giddy, was seized by two men and half-strangled by the cord they twisted round his neck. The deafening noise, the leaping flames, the convulsions of the priest's body, and the compression of his throttle, threw him into a trance, in the course of which the spirit was supposed to reveal itself to the medium.

No doubt these rites, the unconscious aim of which was a

dominating power over Nature, had something to do with the great tide of freedom on which the human instinct, everywhere, has swept to claim its just superiority, and conquer its noblest privileges; but in this time and place the process of evolution was in its earliest phase, and Northern Russia was content for many a year to stammer its religious feeling, to con the alphabet of freedom, to practise with it in the most rudimentary of forms. In the middle of the sixteenth century the Finnish tribes of the *Vodskaïa-Piatina*—the present Government of St. Petersburg—worshipped trees and stones, and made their offerings to them. To these folk the world was still peopled with fantastic beings : a winged viper with a bird's head and a proboscis that could blow destruction over the face of the whole earth ; a ten-headed dragon ; a plant that looked like a sheep, and produced lambs. The Russians of that period showed caps trimmed with the fur of these monsters to their foreign visitors.

The orthodox clergy, while generally opposing these superstitions, favoured them occasionally. Some of its members themselves composed books of spells, contrived to introduce them into the ecclesiastical literature, and made a great deal out of them. Men who called up spirits were to be found in the very monasteries. Ivan the Terrible, at the close of this century, had sorcerers in his household. In the most pious Christian families, certain pagan deities still held their ground— the *rod* and the *rojanitsy*, amongst others, which presided over birth and death, must receive offerings; and amongst these offerings was the *koutia*, the funeral dish, adopted by the Church.

Under the influence of these superstitious beliefs, the most trifling incidents of life took on mysterious and prophetic meanings. The cracking of a wall, a buzzing in the ears, an itching finger, presaged a journey ; the quacking of ducks, a quiver of the eyelashes, betokened the approach of fire. The generic name of *Rafli* was given to a whole literature devoted to the interpretation of these portents and to the meanings of dreams, which were considered of great importance. Pregnant women gave bread to the bears led about in troops by wandering jugglers (*skomorokhy*), and judged the sex of the unborn child according to the creatures' growls. These *skomorokhy*, generally sorcerers themselves, and magicians, too, —priests of the half-Christian, half-pagan faith held by the inhabitants of the country—enjoyed a prestige which all the thunders of the Church could not destroy. They armed a man against his Sovereign's displeasure by making him carry an eagle's eye wrapped in a handkerchief under his left armpit. They took up a little earth under the feet of one who was to be got rid of, and the man was surely doomed to death. For when that same earth was cast into the fire, he dried up with it. This did not involve any oblivion of the angels, who were invoked at the beginning of every piece of work, and St. Nikita had a special power of driving the demons out of a house where his help was sought. Paganism and Christianity, religion and superstition, were all mingled and confused together. At the midnight festivals held on certain feasts, on St. John's Eve, Christmas Eve, Twelfth Night, and St. Basil's Day, both God and the devil had their dues. On the Saturday before Pentecost, the people danced in the graveyards, howling dolorously. On Holy Thursday they burnt straw to call up the dead, and going to the churches, fetched, from behind the altar, a pinch of salt, an infallible cure for certain ailments.

In the sixteenth century remnants of superstition lingered in the best-managed Courts all over Europe, and even at the Vatican. Apart from the astrologers whom Paul II. consulted on every important occasion—but these were held to represent a science—was it not the settling of an owl that warned Alexander VI. of his approaching end ? But in Russia the same century witnessed the fullest blossoming of such beliefs, the sole basis of an intellectual life which possessed no other substantial aliment. On it, till the very threshold of the modern epoch, literature largely subsisted, and what remained was not calculated to stay its readers' appetites.

III.—LITERATURE.

The writers of the fourteenth and fifteenth centuries confined themselves, as a rule, to mechanical works of compilation. Stillborn works, these ! Not a living touch concerning manners and customs, even in the lives of the native saints ; mere chronicles, with the style and contents of an official journal. The most remarkable of these collections—the *Stiépiénnaïa-Kniga*, or ' Book of Degrees,' written by the Metropolitan Macarius, only rises a little above the average, because its author has endeavoured to establish some agreement between the acts and genealogies of the various Sovereigns. It is a work with a political tendency, and, as such, less commonplace than its fellows. It inspired the Terrible with the idea of tracing his descent from Cæsar Augustus ! A work of religious edification, too, which strove to show the Divine intervention in all things. Yet the Churchman who composed it, as we shall soon perceive, was nothing but a compiler in the broader sense.

Both in matter and in form, the literature of this period is inferior to that of Kiev. All poetry, all naturalness and sim-

plicity, all freshness and charm, have disappeared.   No spon-
taneity is left.   Inspiration is replaced by calculation, and the
search after the beautiful, when it occurs—and this is very rare—
fails to reach art, and only attains to artifice.   Not a line revealing
a touch of emotion, or that depth of feeling which might atone
for superficiality of thought.   No poem at all—and yet this is
the epoch of Chaucer and Villon, of Petrarch and Boccaccio.
Not an attempt at scientific or philosophical inquiry, though in
Italy the birth of Galileo is near, and the coming of Bacon, in
England, of Montaigne, in France.   And the epoch of Shake-
speare and Cervantes, of Giordano Bruno and Descartes, of Robert
Estienne and Du Cange, is just about to open.   Even close by, in
Poland—though that neighbour country is nearing the downward
slope of an irreparable decadence—the sixteenth century can
show a pleiad of artists and thinkers, a political literature which
is prodigiously fertile, at all events, and one writer of genius,
Rej.   The language is formed, style is shortly to reach perfec-
tion in the sermons of Skarga.   Batory is soon to carry
about his printing-press even on his campaigns in the heart of
Muscovy.   In Russia the art of typography, like every other
art, is as yet unborn.   Printing in the Russian language does
exist, indeed, or shortly will, but the printers are at Cracow, at
Venice, at Cettigné, at Tübingen, at Prague, at Vilna.   When
they come to Moscow the people will try to kill them, and their
house will be burnt down.   And what could they print if they
were here ?   Books of hours, psalters, Bibles.   Up to the end
of the sixteenth century there will   scarcely be any change
in the repertory ; the only works proving some independent thought will be called ' The Articles of the True Faith '
(Tübingen, 1562), ' Short Tales for Sundays and Feast-days '
(Tübingen, 1562), ' Of the Justification of Man before God '
(Niéswiéz, in Lithuania, 1562).

There is the popular poetry, indeed, but except in the field of
history, soon to reflect the mighty personality of the Terrible,
and bear witness to the new impulse the national genius received
from him, even this poetry subsists on the legacy of the ancient
Russia of the days of Kiev.

Literary activity posterior to the destruction of the old
Russian Empire was manifested, in the first half of the sixteenth
century, in two works, which between them summed up all
the acquired knowledge and current ideas of the nation, the
whole of its intellectual possessions.   One of these, finished in
1552, but begun in 1529, is an encyclopædia ; the other, which,
by its conception and its composition, hails from an already
remote past, takes the form of a household book.   This is the
celebrated *Domostroi*, which is balanced, on the other side, by
the 'Tcheti-Minei' of the Metropolitan Macarius.   These ' Tcheti-

Mineï,' or readings for every month (from μήν, month, and *tchitat*, to read), are a collection of instructions, a sort of composition very common in the fifteenth century, but which in this case takes a singularly extended form. As a rule, these instructions only aimed at supplying edifying reading for every day in the month, appropriate to the memory of the saint mentioned in the calendar for that day. Macarius set himself the task of gathering the whole literature of his country into twelve huge volumes. Sacred books, with the commentaries on them, lives of the Russian saints (*pateriki*) and of the Greek saints (*sinaksary*), the works of the Fathers of the Church, earlier encyclopædic works, such as the 'Bee,' travels—he used them all. He did not exhaust the whole of his material. Either by deliberate omission or by a copyist's error, several books of the Bible are not present. In the case of the Song of Solomon, the former conjecture seems the most probable. The work, as it stands, is an unrivalled authority on the intellectual history of that period, and the hagiographic portions of the book bear curious testimony to the process then in course of accomplishment in the national mind. The saints of the ancient instructions had been local heroes and wonder-workers. Those of Novgorod were unknown at Moscow, and *vice versâ*. Macarius shows them all united in a glory and a worship shared by every corner of the Empire. Here we have the triumph of the Moscow policy, asserted in the Christian Olympus which invaded the churches of the Kremlin, and shared the secular glories of the united monarchy.

The Metropolitan, as may be imagined, was not able to do more than oversee the preparation of his work. Surrounding himself with a carefully chosen band of fellow-workers, he founded the first literary circle ever known in Russia, and gave the initial impulse to a movement which grew around him and survived him. He ascribed great importance to style, and insured the predominance of his own tongue—the ecclesiastical Slavonic—in the national literature, instead of that popular form of speech in which the lives of the saints had been originally written. But the critical spirit must not be looked for in his works, any more than in those of Maximus the Greek. He never troubled himself to verify the authenticity of the texts he piled up in his book, and side by side with the most silly inventions he introduced biographies of absolutely imaginary saints, including those of forty canonized, all in a lump, at the *Conciles* of 1547 and 1549. But in this matter, again, the Moscow policy gave the law; it must have a heaven to suit itself, blazing with a glory suddenly widened by the huge area of the provinces lately added to the common stock.

Macarius, in his own person, was a writer of many books.

Besides the *Stépiénnaïa-Kniga*, which I have already mentioned, and a great number of epistles and instructions, the authorship of the *Kormtchaïa Kniga* (*kormtchyi*, pilot) — a collection of Russian canons, of all canonical or reputedly canonical works, a book of monastic regulations, another compilation, in fact, is attributed to him. But the writer was an orator too. He unsealed the lips of the Church, which had been silent so long, and two or three of the sermons which have come down to us—well composed, and written with a simplicity at war with every literary precedent of that time, so much so as to lead one to think they must have been extemporary—usher in the coming of a new literary world. His third sermon, preached in the presence of Ivan the Terrible after the taking of Kazan, is the most laborious and least successful of them all—a regrettable return to the worst practices of the past. His general lack of culture forbade any attempt at art, properly so-called, on the part of this really gifted man, and on this occasion, when, in his desire to be worthy of the great historical event he was to celebrate, he aimed too high, he missed sublimity, and his fall was heavy and clumsy.

The *Domostroï* has been likened to many other and apparently similar works in Italian, French, and even Hindu. I am inclined to assert that it escapes all comparison. It is unique. In the first place, the book possesses this peculiarity—that it does not correspond with any precise epoch or settled sphere. It is, as I have already indicated, a work of compilation and a work of retrospection, and this is what makes it so widely representative. Its groundwork was probably borrowed by Pope Sylvester from yet older works, composed at Novgorod, the habits of which place the book pretty faithfully reflects. The domestic life it reproduces is just that of the local aristocracy, a little world of boïars, half-landowners, half-merchants. To this secular portion of the work is added an appendix devoted to religion and morals, and there, amongst other borrowings from ecclesiastical literature, and from a didactic literature held in high honour in the monasteries— which comprised, notably, a set of Lenten bills of fare—the Moscow spirit inspires and rules the whole of the contents. The last chapter only—an instruction addressed by the Pope of the Church of the Intercession of the Blessed Virgin to his son Anselm—is believed, and rightly, to have been Sylvester's personal work. And even in it, the author only sums up the teachings contained in the preceding chapters. These teachings deal with a good Christian's duties to God and to his neighbour, his Sovereign and his servants. Some, such as that of holding the breath when kissing the sacred pictures, are rather quaint ; and others cast a peculiar light on the part played by the female sex in the Muscovite household—the woman is not to go to church unless her avocations permit it.

We shall see they left her very little leisure ! The head of the family is expected to show greater assiduity, but the recital of his duties and functions unpleasantly recalls the national legislation. It reads like another penal code. The husband, father, master, is commanded to use discernment in the matter of punishment, but without any undue weakness. He must avoid striking guilty persons on the head or ' beneath the heart ' ; he must not use his feet nor any instrument likely to break the skin. Certain contradictions appear amidst these precepts. Thus, in one place the use of the stick is forbidden, while in another we are told, ' If thou strikest thine unruly son with a stick, it will not kill him.' This is the drawback to all compilations. The family relations between the beater and the beaten seem to have been limited, in any case, to an allotment of the blows to be inflicted or endured. Some consideration is allowed in the wife's case. The husband is to take her apart, far from curious eyes, and, having stripped her of her shift—this point is insisted on, and is of capital importance, indeed, in a book in which the idea of order and economy holds so large a place—without any anger, holding her hands kindly, but using all the requisite strength, he is to toy upon her shoulders with his whip, and is bound, the correction once administered, to behave affably and affectionately, so that conjugal relations may not suffer by these interludes !

Their tolerably frequent recurrence seems highly probable. For if the functions of the man who beat the woman seem to have been practically restricted to performances of this kind, those of the woman he trounced were numerous and sufficiently severe. Having risen earlier than anybody else, she was bound, after her morning devotions were accomplished, to assign and overlook the tasks of all the servants, and set them a good example by being constantly at work herself. She must be skilful in all manual occupations, an expert dressmaker, laundress, and cook. Neither her husband nor her visitors must ever find her sitting with her hands before her. She must not joke with the women about her, nor exchange idle talk with them, and she must never open her door to the gossips of the neighbourhood, to fortune-tellers, nor even to female pedlars.

This is but an ideal rule, evidently, a picture turned upside down, as it were, which must be twisted round again if we are to obtain any clear view of the realities corresponding to it. This remark applies to more than one page of the book, to the paragraph which counsels women to drink nothing but *kvass*,

and to that which enjoins that servants shall be treated with
humanity and gentleness, well dressed and well fed. But at
the same time the outline of the servant sent out to deliver a
message rises up before us like a cinematographic picture. This
model messenger, when he reaches the door of the house to
which he has been sent, wipes his feet, blows his nose—most
probably with his fingers—coughs, spits, and finally observes
' May our Saviour be praised !' If nobody says ' Amen,' he
will repeat the remark thrice, raising his voice each time,
and will then knock gently. Once inside, he will deliver his
message, without blowing his nose, coughing, or putting his
fingers in his nose, and then hie him home as quickly as he may.

The most salient feature of all these pictures, as of the commentaries attached to them, is the materialism pervading
the domestic and social life they represent. The education of
children is restricted to teaching them to dread their God and
to perform manual tasks, and an extraordinary importance is
attached to small household details, to the making of garments,
the using up of scraps of material, the arrangement of trusses
of hay and straw mats. The same tone marks every reference
to social intercourse. Guests invited to a banquet must be care-
ful not to drink too much, or sit too long at table. These are
the essential points to be observed.

The book improves at the end, on which Sylvester has set
his personal seal. But even here its radical dualism—asceticism on one side, sensualism on the other—comes to the front.
Is the son to whom the author suggests a model of Christian
existence a worldly man, a layman ? At first sight one might
be deceived. Not to sleep over the time for matins, never to
forget the hour for going to Mass, to sing matins, complines, and
nones every day, and never get drunk when he ought to be
going to vespers—these are all things which may be very
properly expected of a monk, as monks were in the sixteenth
century. But no ! The man of whom these things are asked
has a house of his own, to which he is desired to bring priests
who will celebrate *molebni* (services) ; he goes to market, and
is admonished to give abundant alms there, not forgetting
his own interests meanwhile. And this mixture of the Divine
and the profane, of a virtue carried to extreme austerity and
a practical wisdom verging on the cynical, runs from one
end of the book to the other. To love one's fellow-creatures
sincerely; to judge no man; not to do to others what we would
not have them do to us; to open the door of one's house wide to
the poor, the sick, and all who are distressed ; to bear ill-
treatment uncomplainingly; to succour one's very enemies;
and to keep one's body pure by dint of necessary mortifications
—all this, indeed! But also, if disputes arise, to lay the blame

on one's own servants, though they are in the right, and strike them, even, to avoid a quarrel; to try to please everybody; and above all things, not to neglect recipes for good Lenten dishes.

The author of this book understood nothing, it is quite clear, of the spirit of Christianity, devoted as he was to its forms. His great idea was to compose a manual of opportunist philosophy, and with all his assiduous study of the Scriptures he got no further, in some matters, than the Old Testament. There was more of the Pharisee than of a disciple of Christ about him, for the Christian life he suggests as an example is his own. And this is not merely hinted. He takes care it shall be known that he has freed his serfs and brought up many orphans, and that the well-merited floggings he has inflicted on his servants have won him their universal love and esteem. This chapter, in Sylvester's own hand, is an Imitation of Sylvester. We shall see its author did not invariably succeed in pleasing everybody.

Taking the book as a whole, it combines the evangelical ideal, that of humility and love, with the Biblical ideal, that of the power of the family, which it makes the motive principle of every relation, social or domestic. And in this respect the *Domostroï* gives us an exact conception of a society in which the family is not the centre only, but the sole rallying-point of social life, ruled by a head in whose person that family is summed up and absorbed. The head of the family is not only the master, to whom everyone owes obedience, but the being to whom everything is referred and on whom everything depends. And this was precisely the state of things existing, not only at Novgorod, but at Moscow, in the sixteenth century. The *Domostroï*, though partly an exposition of manners and customs, is also a code of laws. It imposes certain restrictions on the all-powerful will of paterfamilias. We have seen, alas! how frail and inconsistent these restrictions were. The absolutist spirit of Moscow made short work of them.

The book, in spite of its Novgorodian origin, is essentially Muscovite. Similar features may have been noted in Vladimir Monomachus' 'Instruction' (twelfth century); in the *Dottrine dello Schiavo di Bari* (thirteenth century); in the *Treatise* drawn up by Egidio Colonna for Philippe le Bel, in Francesco Barberini's *Regimento delle Donne*' (fourteenth century); in the Paris *Ménagier* (*circa* 1393); in certain Tchek writings of the fourteenth and fifteenth centuries; and even in the *Indische Hausregeln* published by Fr. Stengler. The human race is very much the same through all the ages, whatever the degree of its civilization or the latitudes it inhabits. But all this notwithstanding, we are in presence, here, of a society of a very special kind, in which we look in vain for the delicate and sentimental relations between husband and wife depicted by the Italian writers, or the luxurious living so fully described by the French chronicler. Baldassare Castiglione's *Cortegiano*, which stands nearest, chronologically speaking, to the *Domostroï*, introduces us to a society in which life, even among artisans, and in the close quarters of the workshop, takes on a certain elegance and artistic distinction ; and an abyss instantly yawns between the two pictures on which we gaze. As Monsieur Pypine has justly observed (' Hist. of Russian Literature,' ii., p. 211), one direct link only is discoverable between the Muscovite work and the literary productions of other countries, and this connects it with that Greek literature which has left its mark on all the Russian thought of that period, and which supplied most of the writers who were Sylvester's contemporaries and fellow-countrymen with materials, or inspired them.

The impression produced by this book, which had dropped into oblivion, and was only disinterred, in 1849, by one of the leaders of the Slavophil school, was most curious. Ivan Akssakov began by rising in revolt. How could a work so absolutely contrary to the national spirit have been conceived and written on Russian soil ? ' I would hunt a teacher who dared to suggest such lessons to me to the other end of the world !' But, thinking it over, he recollected habits and customs he had himself noticed among the Moscow merchants. What ! did the *Domostroï* still live on among them ? And forthwith, one discovery leading to another, Akssakov remembered certain chapters of Tatichtchev's book on ' Rural Administration ' (1742), and his own indignation at the idea that they constituted a proof of the influence of Germany on the national habits and customs. ' How deep it went !' he had said to himself. And then the *Domostroï* opened his eyes ; in its pages he found, identically reproduced, the very features which had so offended him (' Works,' p. 270, etc. ; ' Letters,' 1850).

I have said nothing concerning the style of Sylvester's book. There is nothing to be said about it. The author had no artistic quality at all. But was there such a thing as art in the Russia of those days ?

IV.—ART.

Secular literature was scarcely known there till the writings of Ivan IV. and Kourbski appeared. And until that period, art, too, remained essentially religious in character. Its chief exemplifications were churches, the ornamentation of religious books, and *ikons*. What was the value of these productions, and in what measure did they constitute an expression of the national genius ?

The artistic aptitudes of the Russian people cannot be

denied ; later years have proved them. Though I do not attach the importance ascribed by most Russian, and even many foreign writers, to local folklore and rustic handicrafts, as proofs of a special vocation in this respect, I am willing to accept them as presumptive evidence. Yet a close consideration of this popular poetry and decoration, which many would fain have us take to be original, leads us to note that their chief characteristic is a complete absence of all originality and a perpetual imitation ; they are poor, if not absolutely lacking, in subjects drawn from life or from surrounding nature. We see a handkerchief embroidered by a peasant woman from the neighbourhood of Tver. A delicate design, indeed, but the design has come from Persia. We see a wooden goblet of graceful form, but we read India in the bottom of it ; and Monsieur Stassov, in spite of all his opponents (*Messager de l'Europe*, 1868), seems to me to have triumphantly proved the exotic descent of most of the bylines. Yet art has many degrees, and even imitation is an upward step. At the present day the signs of an absolutely spontaneous inspiration are discoverable in Sylvester's native country ; but do any of them date from the sixteenth century or its predecessors ?

The national architecture, from the eleventh to the sixteenth century, presents two distinct types. Both proceed directly from Byzantium, but in one, that of the south, the Byzantine influence rules continuously and almost exclusively, while in the other, all over the north, from Novgorod to Vladimir and Souzdal, a Germanic or Lombardian current wars against it. And everywhere a confused medley of features, borrowed from every corner of the European and Asiatic horizon—from India and Persia chiefly, until the fifteenth century, from the Italian Renaissance, after it—are introduced into the details of these buildings, the general form and plan and construction of which are governed by these two component factors.

As to the nature and mode of propagation of these factors, the existence of which is uncontested, and their relative importance, opinions are much divided. The hypothesis of a direct importation of Oriental and Central Asiatic types has met with passionate opposition. Whether from the national or the religious point of view, the theory of an artistic initiation of Slav or Servo-Bulgarian origin has appeared far more palatable. Some German writers—Schnaase, among others, in his ' History of the Arts ' (iii., p. 351)—have supported the theory of the Eastern connection, and regarded it as a sign of inferiority and almost of disgrace. One French writer, Viollet-le-Duc, has asserted it, and claimed it as a glory. The time, no doubt, is drawing near when it will be possible to discuss the problem without any regard to sentiment, but I fear it will continue

insoluble. Russia has been, in a most special sense, one of
those laboratories in which currents of art, flowing from the
most opposite points, have met and mingled, to produce an
intermediate form between those of the Western and the
Eastern worlds.

Every civilization, indeed, has been the fruit of some such
fusion, and circumstance has served the artistic development
of this particular country better than its intellectual progress.
The isolation, in this matter, has been less complete. The first
church-builders, and those most generally employed from the
eleventh to the thirteenth century, were Greeks. But at a
later period, heartily as the Westerners were hated or scorned,
their skill was often used, and even in 1150 Andrew, grandson
of Monomachus, sent for Lombard architects to build the
Church of the Assumption at Vladimir, while his son George,
who had married a Georgian Princess, employed Armenian
workmen at Souzdal. The intervention of Persian workers elsewhere, at the same epoch, seems proved by the style of certain
decorations, and from the fifteenth century onwards the appearance of Italian art, with Pietro Solario, the Milanese, Aristote
Fioraventi, the Florentine, Mario, Alevisio, and many more,
has become a matter of history.

How these elements combined, and in what proportions, is a
question which cannot now, and probably never will be, precisely answered. In architecture Byzantium, though main-
taining her supremacy, was forced to yield somewhat to the
advancing wave, Mongol or Scandinavian, Romanesque or
Turanian. And Byzantine art, itself composite, owing tribute
to the Farthest East, to Persia, Asia Minor, and even Rome,
rather led its Russian imitators back to the sources of its own
inspiration. The most ancient of the religious edifices in
Southern Russia possess a slimness of outline and elegance of
proportion which differentiates them from the purely Byzantine form, or even the architectural type adopted at the same
epoch in France and Italy and Germany. They seem to have
been inspired by some other model, or partly, perhaps, by some
original idea. Who can tell ? When St. Louis sent an envoy
to the Court of the Khan, he found a Russian architect there,
as well as a French goldsmith !

During the thirteenth century the influence of Indo-Tartar
art makes itself clearly felt. Curves which seem to have
been borrowed from Thibetan monuments, rounded columns
crowned with bulging capitals, appear upon the scene. The
primitive plan of the churches, as regards its chief outlines,
is not changed, but to the central dome, which has existed from
the earliest times, others are added, raised up like towers, and
crowned with bulbous roofs covered with metal, curiously

worked, and often painted or gilt, which recall the Temple of
Ellora. Within, the great curves of the Byzantine vaults
are broken up into sharp angles. Presently corbelled pyramids are added to the cupolas. These, quite foreign to Byzantine taste, are exceedingly frequent in Hindu architecture.
The military buildings of the period follow the same lines.
The towers of the Kremlin, built in a square, their ramparts
crowned with narrow merlons, are a deviation from the more
ancient models.

But was it Asia that triumphed in all these changes ? Is
it to Asiatic influences that, as Viollet-le-Duc believes, the door
of the fourteenth-century church at Rostov, owes its niches,
with their centres formed by the arcs of a circle, and a sharp
rectilinear top, and its wall-space so rich in decoration that
the groundwork cannot be seen ? Does not the Romanesque
style delight in the multiplication of such ecclesiological
details, as Father Martynax has proved ? Was not Byzantium
the connecting-link between Russia and Asia, just as the Slav
countries of the south-west were the connecting-link between
Europe and the Russian provinces that lay nearest her ? Hard
by some instance of Russian foliage decoration, connected by
Viollet-le-Duc with a Hindu design, Darcel has succeeded in
detecting a Byzantine ornament that holds a place between
the two types. But the transmission of ideas and forms may
have followed other paths and other byways. A curious
example of this is to be noticed in the case of a literary work.
' Bova, the King's Son' (*Korolevitch Bova*), a very popular
Russian tale, is certainly of Hindu origin. It belongs to the
cycle of Somadeva, the *Kathá-sarit-sàgara*, or ' Ocean of Tales.'
And yet Bova is not one of Somadeva's heroes ; he is the
knight Beuves d'Antone, a hero of the Carlovingian period.
India has thus travelled across Western Europe to reach
Russia, and the Western inspiration has accidentally found
its way into this other department of the national existence,
isolated though it has been, and jealously guarded against
external influences.

Some mention must also be made of other forms of art,
though they were but slightly apparent in Russia at this time.
At Souzdal, and more especially at Novgorod, iconography,
influenced by one of the many Greco-Oriental schools existing
in the twelfth century at Byzantium, in Italy, and in the Slav
countries of the south-west, Servia and Bulgaria, reached
a considerable development between the thirteenth and the
fifteenth centuries. The specimens of the work of the latter
town—that done at Souzdal has entirely disappeared—
probably give us the exact measure of the originality attainable by the artists of the period. Observers have noticed, and

very rightly, the existence of certain types quite absent from
the Byzantine iconography, such as pictures of the Intercession of the Blessed Virgin (*Pokrov*), of St. Nicholas, called
the Warrior, of St. Cyril and St. Methodius, St. Boris and
St. Gleb ; also a special interpretation of certain mysteries
or religious subjects, and the softened expression of some other
types.   And this, most assuredly, is something.   In form, too,
these pictures differ from their Eastern models, but in the
sense in which a bad copy differs from the original.   Some
Russian critics have endeavoured to discover, in their much
simpler drawing, a tendency to a closer approach to Nature.
But it strikes me as being only a lack of knowledge.   There is
no reason why nature should be interpreted clumsily, after the
manner of schoolboys who scribble on their copybooks.   The
same process of simplification, even to the giving up of the
gold backgrounds, probably necessitated by the poverty of
the monasteries, rules manuscript decoration down to the
end of the thirteenth century.   But in the fourteenth a much
more visible change takes place, and carries the Russian
school, in this particular, far from the Byzantine tradition and
its hieratic forms.   We see a sudden introduction of the in-
finite forms of human and animal life, together with a pro-
fusion of designs recalling the scrolls and interlacing patterns
carved on the wood of ancient Scandinavian churches, or,
yet farther back, on the belt-plates and chiselled clasps
of the Merovingian epoch, and sometimes traceable to Iranian
types, by no means foreign to the Romanesque and Byzantine
styles of early ages.   This is like a return to the original
sources, for such fantastic representations of men, animals,
birds, and insects were known in Herodotus' time, among the
peoples then dwelling on Russian soil.   But even as regards
the Iranian inspiration, it would seem as though this renaissance had come through the West, for the manuscript literature of Novgorod, in which it was more specially exemplified,
and which almost entirely escaped the Tartar influence,
underwent a very strong current of European influences,
which travelled by way of Riga and the Hanseatic towns.
    In the fifteenth century these abnormal forms of fancy made
way for combinations of single lines, the symmetrical inter-
lacements of which terminated in long cusped foliage.   Then
another current, to which no Oriental or Asiatic origin can be
assigned, swept over the national art ; and finally, in the
fifteenth century, there was a backward eddy.   Under the
pressure, probably, of religious feeling, of the spirit of orthodoxy, alarmed by the struggle between the Papacy and the
Reformation, the Byzantine tradition got the upper hand again,
linked this time with a certain infusion of German and Protes-

tant taste, to be recognised in the long, deeply-serrated leaf—
that of a sort of wild fig-tree—which spreads or curls in its
cold black tints in the midst of the warm Oriental colouring.

All this is thoroughly and incontestably Russian, but is
it an artistic expression adequate to the genius of the nation ?
Is it, in other words, capable of stirring the admiration and
the imitative faculties of other nations, as did the Greek and
even the French and Italian art of certain periods ?   Did it
even constitute a private fund susceptible of any independent
development ?   If the Russian borrowers, when they turned
to foreign models, had added anything to them beyond
failures in executive skill—more or less successful alterations,
and combinations the results of which were unsuccessful as a
rule ; if they had introduced anything of their own—the fauna
and flora of their own country, any reflection of their own sky ;
if, amidst their perpetual assimilation of exotic types, they had
known how to enter into direct communion with Nature, that
first condition and starting-point of any original art, we might
have answered, Yes !   But all they did was to copy, to fit in,
to disfigure.   Look at the carved balcony of an *isba*.   There
you will see, so coarsely reproduced as to be almost, though
not wholly, unrecognisable, faces of lions and panthers, and
representations of fig-trees and palm-trees, invariably.   We
have to come down to the most recent exemplifications of
an art that is still feeling its way, the timid effort of some
ultra-modern draughtsman, before we discover, under the
pencil or brush, the outline of a fir-tree, the white fur of any
Northern creature.

Under what conditions, after what plan, by whose hands,
these thirteenth and fourteenth century churches, the style
of which is now thought worthy of praise, were built, we cannot
tell.   As to the buildings, secular and religious, of the fifteenth
and sixteenth centuries, which attract the eye for the same
reason—the Church of the Assumption at Moscow, the doorway of St. Nicholas at Mojaïsk, the famous ' palace of the
facets' (*Granovitaïa palata*)—we have an historical certainty :
Italian artists have left their mark upon them.   Until quite
lately the disconcerting and bewildering Church of the Blessed
St. Basil (*Vassili Blajennoï*), built between 1553 and 1559,
which Karamzine calls ' a masterpiece of Gothic architecture,'
Father Martynov ' an evocation of the *Erectheion* of the
Athenian Acropolis,' Theophile Gauthier ' a huge crouching
dragon,' Kugler ' an enormous heap of mushrooms,' and
Custine ' a jam-pot,' has also been taken to be of Italian
workmanship.   This mistake has now been recognised.   The
architects' accounts have been unearthed, and have revealed
two Russian names, Barma and Postnikov.   We must render

the Russia of the sixteenth century the honour which is her
due, and rid the philosophy of art of one of its most baffling
riddles.   And we must acknowledge, too, that, contrary to
long-received assertion, this strange edifice was not an isolated
phenomenon of its period, the ' only proof that was ever drawn.'
It is connected with a whole system of architecture, the origin
of which is probably to be discerned in the wooden buildings
so common in this country, and the type of which may be
noticed at various places within its boundaries, as at Novomoskovsk, in the present Government of Ekatièrinoslav, and
at Diakovo, quite close to Moscow.   The lack of other material,
or, at all events, the difficulty of getting stone, which paralyzed the development both of architecture and of the statuary's
art, necessitated this mode of structure, some impressions
of which may have been drawn from India, and the essential
characteristic of which is a grouping and confused mingling
of a number of incongruous blocks of buildings.   The Novomoskovsk church consists of three buildings close together,
forming nine distinct compartments.   The architects of the
Vassili Blajennoï succeeded in producing twice as many, in
a mighty jumble of styles, Byzantine, Persian, Hindu, Italian—
a wild dance of cupolas and pyramids and campanile. . . .

It would be rash, perhaps, to judge this building according
to notions of art which, though hallowed by the approval
of centuries, can hardly be asserted to be an eternal and universal criterion.   Gothic architecture stirred quite as bitter
a criticism, at one moment, as that our present æsthetic taste
might be disposed to apply to the masterpiece of Barma and
Postnikov.   From the artistic point of view, it may fairly
be noted, the type thus originated has never been developed.
The architects' eyes were not torn out, indeed, when their
work was finished, as the story goes, to prevent their producing
another like it.   This is a mere reproduction of the legend
concerning the maker of the famous Strasburg clock in this
same century.   But no fresh start, or hardly any, was made,
and the legend, like many another, has its meaning.   The
inspiration of the two Russian artists, thus left to its own
devices, evolved nothing but this one architectural fancy ; none
of their successors cared to renew so strange and barren an attempt, and the solitary proof once drawn, the plate was cast aside.

It would be a grief to me to grieve my Russian friends, but
they are beginning to ask too much.   Towards the middle of
last century, so their most authoritative exponents, such as
Tchadaiév and Herzen, averred, they possessed nothing of
their own, neither a national art nor any national literature
or science.   Now they claim everything at once, and even
to have had it all since the twelfth century !   Messrs. Tolstoi

and Kondakov, two learned historians of art, felt, while they were travelling through the province of Vladimir, as though they were in one of the Lombard provinces of Italy ! This is a pious illusion. In Russia nature and history alike have set their faces against any rapid progress in this path. They have denied the artist his rough materials, and assigned him, as the chief well-spring of his inspiration, Byzantium, with her dried-up or stagnant waters. The Russian genius is rooted in patience, and this the apologists of the national art seem to forget. At the period now under consideration Russian art is beginning to drink at other springs ; the living stream will soon flow fast, no doubt, but the rise of the river is not yet, and we are at the very beginning of things.

In the bosom of the Orthodox Church, too, within which, until a recent epoch, every form of intellectual activity has been circumscribed, the national art has felt the action of the twofold current, ascetic and sensualist. A dark medley of monkish cells, blossoming out into a profligate luxuriance of form—that is the Church of the Blessed Basil, and the true image of the Russian spirit of the sixteenth century.

Yet it was in this ecclesiastical and specially monastic sphere that feelings and ideas destined to cast a leaven of revival into the stagnation of a people on which age was laying a cold hand, even in the heyday of its youth, first sprang to life.

V.—The Renovating Movement.

The Russia of the fifteenth and sixteenth centuries had a reform of its own. Isolated though the country was, and closed against any action from foreign sources, it could not remain absolutely unaffected; and, besides, it was itself, though in a different way and in a much more limited degree, passing through certain revolutionary phases, and consequently under-going a certain process of upheaval. A renovating movement, either spontaneously developed in the national mind or induced by some foreign influence, began to show itself as early as in the fourteenth century, chiefly in the province of Novgorod, the cradle and the last refuge of the traditions of freedom. The original date of this movement may be assigned to the year 1376. At that period three heretics, founders of the sect of the *strigolniki*, or cloth-shearers (one of the leaders thus put to death belonged to this trade), were cast from the summit of the bridge in that republican city. This sect repudiated all idea of an ecclesiastical hierarchy, as being based on simony. The Church, whose supremacy extended at Novgorod to the sphere of economic interests, soon put down the revolt ; but even in the second half of the fifteenth century the *strigolniki* attracted attention, and their doctrine then found fresh food in the shape of additions to the ecclesiastical literature—fresh writings, still of Byzantine origin, but conceived in a more independent spirit, which indicated various defects in the religious life, declaimed against an excess of ascetic practices, which was animalizing faith and piety at the expense of their spiritual qualities, and denounced the corruption of the monastic rule.   Meanwhile the teachings of certain Byzantine heresiarchs, Pauliciens and Bogomiles, drawn from those of the Gnostics, the Manichæans and the Messalians, began to creep into the country.

On this groundwork a mass of local heresies sprang up, and these were soon generalized under the name of ' judaizing heresies ' (*jidovstvouiouchtchyié*), because certain of their external features were borrowed from some anti-Talmudic Jews or Caraïtes, who took refuge at Novgorod towards the year 1471.   Some of these heresiarchs went so far as to adopt the Jewish Easter, the Jewish calendar, and the rite of circumcision.   But the general tendency of all these sects was towards rationalism, a common denial of the Trinity, of our Lord's Divinity, of the future life, and of all the external trappings of Christianity.   Their appearance certainly did the Orthodox Church a great service.   It forced her, in the first place, to a certain exegetical labour, imposed by the necessity for making a fight against her adversaries, and also to some amount of self-examination and an endeavour at internal reform.   Thus one religious movement stirred another.   The last took two different directions.   The correction of the sacred books, on which Maximus the Greek was employed, indicates a desire to parry certain doctrinal criticisms.   But monastic life deserved a yet severer censure.   I have already endeavoured to set forth this twofold aspect of the religious life, which is set down in letters of fire and branded with a hot iron in Ivan the Terrible's famous writings.   Here is a passage from his celebrated letter to the Monastery of St. Cyril, written in 1575 :

' Bred up in abstinence from your very childhood, you kill yourselves with privations : loving God, you flee from men ; dwelling in solitude and silence, you put away all earthly enjoyments ; you mortify your flesh with a cruel hair-shirt, you bind your loins with a harsh belt that wrings all your limbs, and thus you have weakened your very backbones ; you have sent all succulent dishes far from your table, so that your dried-up skin clings to your poor bones ; you have cast off every earthly thought ; the lack of nourishment has dried up the marrow in your bones ; your protruding ribs have strangled your stomachs ; all your nights have been spent in prayer, and you have wetted your beards with your tears.'

And alongside this ironical piece of oratory we find the reverse of the medal, in one of the proposals laid by the Sovereign before the *conciliable* of 1551.

' Monks and nuns take the habit and the veil, not to save their souls, but to spend idle, pleasant lives, wandering hither and thither, and perpetually moving from one village to another in search of amusement. . . . In all the monasteries monks and abbots drink to excess. . . . At Moscow and in all the other towns they may be seen sharing their dwellings and their wealth with worldly men and women. . . . Archimandrites and abbots forsake the common board and hold revel in their own cells with their invited guests. . . . Women—even loose women—have free access to them; monks and hermits go about the country shamelessly, taking young boys with them. . . .'

The evil was not confined to the ' black ' clergy. In that very *conciliable* of the year 1551, mention was made of priests who only celebrated Mass every six or seven years, came to church drunk, quarrelled amongst themselves, and said the prayers all wrong. Lasicius (*De Russorem . . . Religione*, 1582, p. 210) mentions popes who had been seen lying dead drunk in the public squares, and Herberstein (*Commentarii*, Startchevski, i. 21) saw priests publicly flogged on this account. Instead of being houses of prayer, the sacred edifices, thus profaned by their own priests, became places of meeting, clubs, markets. Men entered them, even when Mass was going on, without baring their heads, talked and laughed at the top of their voices, discussed and settled their business affairs, and often broke in upon the chanting with coarse words. Though an analogy may be traced between these features and those pointed out by Rabelais, Calvin, and Luther in the religious habits of the West, their testimony cannot detract from the example set and the work performed at that same period, by St. François de Paul and the Benedictines of St. Maur. In Russia, up till the early years of the sixteenth century, at all events, no such counterpoise existed. But at that moment the necessity for amendment forced itself on the best minds within the bosom of the monastic communities themselves. As to ways and means, opinions differed. Ivan Sanine, the son of a Lithuanian deserter—in religion Joseph, called Volotski—who founded the monastery of Volok-Lamskoii (now Volokolamsk) in 1479, thought he had found them in a return to the strict application of the old rule. By education he belonged to the old type of Russian *Knijniki*, with their utter lack of the critical instinct, and their absolute respect for everything *that has been*. But this could not suffice for everybody. From the depths of those hermitages, to the appearance and multiplication of which in the northern deserts I have already referred, another wind began to blow. Nil Sorski, born in 1433, of an ancient boïar family, the Maïkov, having first spent several years at the monastery of Mount Athos, then lived near Biélooziéro and the monastery of St. Cyril, and finally founded a hermitage, the name of which he took for himself, on the banks of the little Sorka River, suddenly came forward as the representative of a new religious world. His travels and his reading, fuller and better chosen than that of his fellows, had, to a certain point, turned the *knijnik* in him into a theologian. He had learnt to admit and assert that 'all written things were not holy things.' He ventured to reject the authority of the *document*, in the sense in which it was accepted by most of his contemporaries—that is to say, apart from the origin and value of the testimony it bore. Finally, he had looked for something more than texts in the sacred writings : he had sought inspiration. On these lines, and independently of his views concerning the religious life, novel, in Russia, and occasionally very deep, he was destined to conceive a new ideal of monastic existence, to consist, not in the exact observance of external discipline, but in an internal transformation of the soul. Hence his choice of the isolated life, already adopted by a certain number of monks in that country, but destined, under his influence, to attain a much greater development.

Nil Sorski had soon gathered several hundreds of followers round him, and to these the generic title of ' monks from beyond the Volga ' (*Zavolojskiié startsy*) was given. Their example and teaching were to play an important part in the religious life of the sixteenth century. They had no rule, so to speak ; they enjoyed an almost complete independence ; they were free to choose their own material conditions and means of existence ; one principle only ruled these—poverty. Here was where the split came with Joseph Volotski and his school, and the clamour of the quarrel thus begun filled the first years of the reign of the Terrible, and lasted on after he himself was dead.

The problem of monastic proprietorship divided the two camps. Nil Sorski's solution of it will be easily guessed, and it brought the *niéstiajatiéli* and the *lioubostiajatiéli*, the adversaries and partisans of the property in question (*stiajatiel*, an acquirer ; *lioubit*, to love), face to face. Nil, though condemned by the *conciliable* of 1503, was allowed to go back to his desert. But the question continued to fill the literature of the day, and the hermit's ideas were adopted and brilliantly set forth by another monk, the least qualified of all his comrades, seemingly, for such a task. Even under his *klobouk*, Vassiane Kossoï, otherwise Prince Vassili Ivanovitch Patrikiév-Kossoï, who traced his descent from Guedymin, a near kinsman of the reigning house, continued a man of the world. A statesman and diplomatist, it was only after a most brilliant career, and even then by *force majeure*, and in consequence of a sudden loss of favour, that he assumed the monkish garb in 1499. Old ties bound him to a circle in which freedom of thought prevailed, almost to the point of heresy, and his forced stay at Biélooziéro brought him into contact with Nil Sorski. Summoned to Moscow for the *conciliable* of 1503, he boldly espoused the cause of the *niést-jatiéli*, placing at its service a skill and energy which the hermit of Volok lacked, and a literary talent which, though he was no more than a popularizer of other men's ideas, gave him a high rank among the few writers Russia then possessed. After Sorski's death, Vassiane found a fighting comrade in the person of Maximus the Greek, whose labours as a corrector had led him to seek out other elements of moral corruption, and who, in the heat of his discussions with local and foreign heretics, had gone so far as to echo the Hussite view as to Church property. Joseph Volotski had followed Nil to the grave in 1515, but his partizans, the *Iosiflianić*, as they were called, still held firm, and at the *conciliable* of 1523 Maximus, in his turn, received a sentence, the imposition of which was rendered easier by some translating blunders due to the weakness of his scientific methods and his ignorance of the Russian language. Then it was that he met Vassiane Patrikiév, himself exiled and under sentence, at the monastery of Volok (1531), and the rest of his life was dragged out in prison cloisters. 'We kiss your bonds, but we can do nothing for you,' wrote the Metropolitan Macarius, a more wily diplomatist than even Vassaine himself, whose skill enabled him to play a dubious part between the two camps.

But the struggle continued and its borders widened. Among the men sentenced by the *conciliable* of 1531 there was a prior of the Troïtsa called Artemi, who, like all professors of the doctrine of the *Iosiflianié*, objected to the putting to death of heretics, and in this resembled the ' monks from beyond the Volga,' who held the same view. ' We have no right to judge these unhappy beings,' wrote one of these hermits ; ' all we can do is to pray for them.' A development of liberal thought, surprising at such a period, occurred in this circle, and Artemi and his disciples simultaneously came into contact with the anti-Catholic movement, which reached them through Poland, where Protestantism was then in full progress, while other opponents of the official Church, soon to be smitten by her thunderbolts, though accepting certain features of the teaching of the hermit of Volok, followed a line of thought that ran parallel with the rationalist movement of the day.

Thus the Russian reforms spread out in several directions, the *Zavolojskiié startsy* and the *Iosiflianie* only differing as to the means to be employed for the reconstruction of the religious edifice, while the sectarians of Artemi's type pursued an altogether revolutionary and destructive work. A political element also intervened in the quarrel. Volotski was conservative even in his conception of the proper relations between Church and State—the State to serve the interests of the Church, and the Church, in return, to yield the State full obedience. According to this organization, the monastery, the material existence of which was based on a privileged land tenure, took on the character of a State institution, the centre and nursery of an ecclesiastical aristocracy, and the triumphant assertion of this doctrine certainly contributed to the establishment of autocratic power at Moscow. The views of the *Zavolojskiié startsy* on this subject were very different. Nil Sorski put the question aside altogether. It possessed no interest for him, and, from his essentially Christian point of view, had no existence at all. The moral principles he extolled were compatible with every form of political life. But Vassiane Patrikiév was affected in a different way. He could not forget his own origin and parentage, and his patrician soul recoiled from submission to any unlimited and uncontrolled political power. Thus he spent all his personal authority and all the prestige of his party to strengthen an opposition with which Moscow had to wrestle till its professors were crushed under the iron hand of Ivan the Terrible.

All the elements I have indicated had their share in this struggle, and for that reason I have dwelt somewhat fully on their precise nature. The noble seed, the existence of which, in a dim corner of the national history, is revealed to us through the dark and painful fate of some scarce known heroes, was trodden into the soil and drowned in blood by the victory of the official Church and the absolute power. That seed lies in the earth yet, and even now is scarcely rising above the ground. The harvest is still a long way off. But grains of wheat have slumbered in Egyptian tombs for centuries without mouldering away, and it is good to know, it is a consoling thought, that in Russia, too, beneath the dust of centuries, the past has sown such fruitful atoms, which yet bide their time.

I have still to elucidate the conditions under which the great drama to which I have just referred was played out—a drama which will constitute the greater part of the subject of this work—by an evocation of a part of the national life on which the preceding pages have frequently touched, but which must now be more completely sketched.

CHAPTER IV

HABITS AND CUSTOMS

I.—THEIR ASPECT, PHYSICAL AND MORAL.   II.—THE WOMEN.   III.—
THE FAMILY.   IV.—SOCIETY.

I.—Their Aspect, Physical and Moral.

The thirteenth-century invaders did not prevent all civilization in Russia ; in fact, they imposed their own civilization on the country, and, to judge by the consequences, this side of their conquest was far-reaching.   Look at the Muscovite of the sixteenth century.   To begin with, he is dressed from head to foot after the fashions of Samarkand.   *Bachmak, iazam, armiak, zipoune, tchebygi, kaftane, outchkour, chlyk, bachlyk, kolpak, klobouk, taflia, temlak*—all these are the Tartar names he applies to the various items of his attire.   If he falls out with his comrades, and begins to use rough language, the word *dourak* invariably occurs in his vocabulary ; if he comes to blows, the *koulak* straightway appears.   When he metes out justice, he binds the culprit with *kandaly* (chains), and appeals to the *kate* (executioner) to give the condemned man the *knout*. If he is an official he gathers the taxes into a *kazna* (treasury), protected by a *karaoul* (guard-house), or organizes relays which he calls *iamy* on roads served by *iamchtchiki*.   When he gets out of his posting-sleigh, he is seen going into a *kabak* (tavern), which has taken the place of the old Russian *kortchma*. And all these words belong to the same Asiatic dictionary. The meaning of all this, though it affects external matters only, is surely very significant.   A more serious thing is that a certain infusion of Mongol blood seems to have accompanied this prompt and docile assimilation.   What was its extent ?   It is difficult to decide.   Russian documents dealing with the subject are non-existent, and the observations of foreign travellers contradict each other.   ' The real Muscovite natives,' wrote Vigenerius (' Description of the Kingdom of Poland and the Neighbouring Countries,' 1573), ' are short, as a rule, with good constitutions, strong and hardy, with very white skins, green eyes, long beards, short legs, and well-proportioned bellies.'   Except for this last feature, noted by the majority of witnesses, this portrait is rather like that of the famous red-headed tavern wench.   Peer Persson, or Petreus (*Travels*, in *Rerum Rossicorum Scriptores Exterii*, 1851, vol. i.), had the good luck, when he was in the same country, to see nothing but men who stood six feet high, and women whose *black* eyes, slight figures, dainty bosoms, delicate hands, and taper fingers

filled him with admiration.   These same eyes, as black as jet,
were also noticed by Jenkinson.   But the item of complexion
continues to be discussed, Petreus declaring it to be naturally
fair, and only spoilt by the abuse of paint and cosmetics, which
the fair Muscovites used with singular want of taste, not only
on their faces and necks, but on their eyes and teeth, while
Fletcher ascribes their addiction to these artifices to a desire
to conceal natural defects of colouring.

As an excuse for one and all of these observers, it should be
added that they could not see clearly, because the persons they
sought to behold hardly showed themselves at all, the women
being hidden in their own special quarters, and even the men—
of the aristocratic class, at all events—concealed beneath the
mass of garments they wore.   The list of these, as given
by Fletcher, is amazing.   To begin with the men.   There
was first of all the *taflia*, a little cap which covered the
head, itself completely shaved.   No man let his hair grow,
except as a sign of mourning or disgrace.   The *taflia*,
in the case of great nobles, was made of cloth of gold,
and embroidered with pearls and precious stones.   Over this
came a great tiara-shaped cap, in the Persian style, trimmed
with black fox, the most valuable of all furs.   The collarless
shirt left the neck bare, but this was adorned with a richly-
worked necklace, some three or four fingers deep.   This shirt,
made of fine material and loaded with embroideries, was worn
in summer as the indoor garment.   In winter it was hidden by a
light silk overgarment, buttoned down the front, and reaching
to the knee, and over this came the *kaftane*, a long narrow gown,
sometimes made of cloth of gold, and reaching the instep ; a
girdle, knotted very low, below the waist, with a dagger and
a spoon thrust into it ; the *odnoriadka*, a silken garment, still
longer and wider, edged with fur, and embroidered all down
the front ; and then, for outdoor use, the *okhabene*. . . .

I will spare my readers the other variations of the costume,
the *feriaz* and the *kontouche*, all completed by the high morocco-
leather boots, worn instead of hose, and also embroidered
with pearls and gems.

The feminine wardrobe, as may well be imagined, was no
less complicated ; the features common to both were opulence
and the superposition of many garments.   The hair was confined by silken nets, red or black, covered in summer with a fine
cambric or lawn kerchief embroidered with pearls, and fastened
under the chin.   This was replaced in winter by a cloth of gold
cap, edged with some valuable fur, and likewise sprinkled with
pearls and precious stones.   The first loose gown—the *opachnia*
—was generally scarlet in colour, and its long sleeves reached
the ground.   Over it came an incredible series of garments,

some of them wide and some of them narrow, some of silk and some of cloth of gold, some fur-lined, others sewn with gems, and whole coffers full of necklaces and bracelets and ornaments of every kind. The noble Muscovite lady, in her white or blue or yellow leather buskins, also pearl-embroidered, could scarcely stand under her heaped-up glories. She was like a shrine.

This was the wardrobe of the aristocrats. That of the common folk was simpler, as may be well imagined. A shirt and a pair of long boots—two chemises, one over the other, for decency's sake, in the woman's case—in summer-time; in the winter a coarse blue or black cloth gown, reaching nearly to the feet, and a sheepskin pelisse, were its invariable and chief constituents. For the woman, a metal cross and earrings of some kind were also indispensable. Under the ascetic influence, religion and modesty played a foremost part in the constitution of the female toilet. Even the excessive use of cosmetics seems to have had its origin in this quarter, these being employed to hide charms which had better be concealed. But if God was served by this device, the devil lost nothing by it, and some modes of dressing the hair, and the choice of certain stones, like the emerald and the ruby, considered to heighten the brilliance and expression of the wearer's face, were certainly not dictated solely by the precepts of the *Domostroï*.

Did the dresses and customs bearing these Tartar names really come out of Tartary ? It is a curious thing that Fletcher should never have suspected this origin. According to him, the Russians of his day were dressed *à la Grecque*. The garb of the Muscovite Sovereigns, identical with that worn by all European monarchs at a much more ancient epoch, certainly came from Byzantium rather than from Samarkand. And the Byzantine origin of the cosmetics so dear to the coquettes of the country is not less certain. They were a legacy from Olga, the wife of Igor. This Princess was attended, when she travelled to Constantinople in 955, by a numerous female suite, and the ladies did not waste the time they spent on the shores of the Bosphorus. In the Europe of the Middle Ages, Constantinople held the place now occupied by Paris, as the metropolis of luxury. The Russian women of the sixteenth century, when they covered their teeth with a black varnish, and even succeeded, by some now unknown process, in dyeing the whites of their eyes black, would seem to have drawn their inspiration from some primitive system of tattooing rather than from the delicate processes of the Greco-Roman belles. But we must take this to be a consequence of that clumsy deformation undergone by every form of art in a country where feminine vanity strove to realize the ideal of beauty set forth in the

popular song, ' A face as white as the white snow, and eyes as
red as poppies.'

From the shores of the Bosphorus, Olga's ladies brought back,
if not the *kila* itself, one form of that head-dress, at all events—
that adopted by the ancient Muscovite Sovereigns, with the
viazy, long strings of pearls falling down to the shoulders on each
side. This head-dress occurs among the ancient Greek
colonists on the Black Sea, and in a tenth-century evangelistary
preserved in the Gotha Library, Theophania, Empress of Germany, and her son Otho III., are represented with costumes
strongly resembling those of the boïars and boïarines of the
sixteenth century.

In this case, then, names and things do not exactly correspond, and a peculiarity of all conquests is the creation of
appearances frequently rendered illusory by an appropriative
action as ephemeral as it is shallow. As regards the Russian
women of the period now under consideration, it is at Byzantium that we must look for the secret of their ways and their
outward appearance. Byzantine asceticism ruled them and
wrapped them round. Though, during the woman's growing
years, it allowed a certain development of her body and blossoming of her physical charms, it commanded, once she was
married, that these charms should be hidden from all eyes save
her husband's. The wife's hair must be concealed, her form
must disappear under her load of wide and floating garments,
worn one above the other. She must not wear a belt, save
with her *sorotchka*, an indoor dress in which she would never
show herself before strangers. But, by an inversion common
in the case of ideas of this sort, the belt must always be worn
with the *sorotchka*, and any neglect of this duty would cause a
scandal.

In habits thus constituted, secular convenience was often
mixed up with religious conventions. The full garments corresponded with the prevailing habit of body. The idleness
and lack of exercise common to both sexes in the upper classes
made the men stout and full-bellied and the women fat, at a
very early age ; and the peculiarity thus associated with an
ideal life of luxury ended by becoming an element of beauty—
one still valued in the case of the St. Petersburg coachmen and
amongst middle-class women in Russia.

Let not my readers scorn, on this account, the female charms
which tempted the Russian contemporaries of Ivan the
Terrible ! The Muscovite lady of the sixteenth century, in
spite of her excessive embonpoint and her thick and ungraceful
accoutrements, was assigned a place of honour in Jost Amman's
' Gynæceum ; or, Theatrum Mulierum ' (1586). ' *Qualem vix
similem Gallia culta dabit !* . . .' The taste for dress, the

worship and care of personal beauty, were, indeed, one of the
features under which the æsthetic feeling of a still barbarous
people, and its aspirations towards the superior forms of civilized life, were then revealed.   For it must not be forgotten that
the very men who wore these gorgeous garments lived in hovels,
and I will not deny that, having used the spoon they carried in
their belts for their soup, they eat the rest of their meals with
their fingers !   Very coarse they still were, in life and morals,
under their splendid toggery.   But here we note the usual march
of civilization, proceeding from the individual, thus cultivated
and ennobled in the simplest and narrowest sense, to idealiza-
tions of a more and more general and complex kind.

Let us pass on to their moral condition.   As to this, all testimony is agreed, and it is not complimentary.   Anything else
would have been surprising.   A high standard of morality
concurrent with a low state of culture is a fiction which history
constantly contradicts.   It is well, nevertheless, to recollect
that the testimony, in this case, is of foreign origin, and that
a certain amount of ill-nature must be allowed for.   The
features on which it lays special stress are pride, roguery, in-
credulity, and bad faith.   The Muscovites, in their simplicity,
thought themselves superior to all other men.   They were
liberal with promises which they never dreamt of performing.
No mutual confidence at all existed among them.   The father
doubted his son, the son believed nothing his mother said, and
nobody would lend a halfpenny without security.   These are the
terms of the witness borne by two Germans, Buchau and Ulfeld,
by Persson, a Swede, and Michalon, a Lithuanian.   The worst
of it is that the Englishmen, Fletcher and Jenkinson, echo these
sentiments.   ' It may be most truthfully said . . . that from
the highest to the lowest, except in some rare cases, very difficult to discover, no Russian believes anything that is said to
him, or says anything that is worthy of belief.'   Now, these
last witnesses, belonging to a race which at that period enjoyed
a privileged position in the country, may be taken to be less
dubious than their fellows.   And they outdo them, adding
another feature to the list, one to which I have already had
occasion to refer—cruelty.   Fletcher, it is true, excuses this by
the following explanation : ' Harshly and cruelly used by the
magistrates and the upper classes, the nation has grown harsh
and cruel to its equals, and especially to its inferiors.'

This is the history of barbarism everywhere, and it was
aggravated, in this particular country, by a climate which is not
calculated to make men tender.   The national historians have
vainly striven to lay the blame in this particular, too, on the
Mongol invasion, which, so they assert, corrupted the vanquished people's habits, and taught it cunning and violence.

But two centuries before the Tartars came, the ancient Russia
of Kiev was a scene of blood and rapine, plunged in that state
of warfare which was to last till the very threshold of the modern
epoch was reached, and which was in itself a deteriorating
agent. Ferocity is the very essence of war. It has its own
laws, which contravene every code and every gospel, and it
excludes all honesty. In war, cunning is a merit, and violence
a virtue. In this land, where anarchy reigned for centuries,
it was not the Tartars who replaced the phenomenon known in
Western Europe as 'chivalry' by another, which, though
certainly not its equivalent, was, historically speaking, co-
incident with it—'brigandage'—a brigandage enshrined in
legend, sung by the national bards, personified by the popular
heroes. In one of the *bylines*, which brings Ivan IV. upon the
scene, we find a robber tale which is a specimen of the ideas
elaborated under the influence of these peculiar historical
precedents. A young man, haled before the justice-seat,
is subjected to the *praviéje*. The Sovereign passes by, and
inquires into the matter. It concerns a theft of treasure by
the culprit. The young man gives his explanation. The
treasure had been in the hands of a robber band. The bold
fellow had fallen upon it, laid hands on the booty, and then
gone from tavern to tavern, sharing his plunder with all the
vagabonds in the country. The Sovereign does not hesitate :
the hero of the adventure deserves not punishment, but
reward, for his bravery and open-handedness. The judges are
commanded to make him large amends, and all the people
rejoice with him.

The attitude of mind here exemplified is not the specific
characteristic of any Asiatic or European race, but the acci-
dental result of a certainly abnormal evolution, during a
transition period of development.

During the sixteenth century, under the coating, very superficial, as we have already seen it to be, of the Mongol alluvion,
the strongest visible mark on Muscovite habits is that left by
the nearest, the Byzantine, East. But this influence, just at
that moment, was giving rise to fierce reaction. Under the
excessive weight and pressure of the ascetic yoke, Nature,
physical and moral, was revolting and rebelling, breaking her
bonds, casting them off, and rushing, under the reflex action
of unbridled instincts, into wild flights in a quite opposite
direction—extravagant debauchery, monstrous vices, the
oblivion of all modesty even amongst the women, once they
contrived to break down the barriers of the *terem*. These phenomena naturally stand out against the ordinary background
of social and domestic life. They strike the attention of
observers, and thus elicit severe judgments, which should be

carefully weighed. These more particularly affect and condemn the Russian woman. As foreign witnesses saw her, she
is a monster. Into this closer inquiry must be made.

II.—THE RUSSIAN WOMAN.

The position imposed on man's partner by Muscovite
customs and legislation was certainly not affected by racial
influences. The *terem*, as all men know nowadays, was not of
Eastern origin. In it we recognise, under a Tartar name, the
Greco-Roman *gynæceum*, dressed up Byzantine fashion. Nor
can the general tendencies of the Slav race be blamed; they
rather leant towards giving women a privileged position.
Most of the Slav laws, unlike those of Rome, Germany, or
Scandinavia, reject the idea that woman is an inferior being,
placed under the permanent guardianship of her male relations,
or assimilated to things of which they have the arbitrary
disposal. In Russia, according to the code of Jaroslav,
the indemnity due for murder (the *glovchtchizna*, price of the
head) was higher when the murdered person was a woman,
and even according to Ivan IV.'s code, both sexes were equal
before the law. It was not till 1557 that it occurred to the
Terrible to attack this principle by deciding that any clause
whereby a wife willed the management of her property away
to her husband was invalid. ' What the husband orders, the
wife writes '—so runs the preamble of the new law. But this
is a mere acknowledgment of a fact, and a precaution taken in
the wife's interest, rather than a decree of forfeiture.

Whether or not it should be attributed, as the learned historian of Slav law, Maciejowski, holds, to her participation in
the duties of the priesthood in ancient Slav communities, or
to some other and more authentic cause (for the equality in
priestly matters itself looks like a result), Eve's comparative
triumph, even on Russian soil, is not open to any doubt. But
in Russia Byzantium set on this primordial fact the seal of
her own very different conceptions, largely borrowed from
pagan teachings. The Constantinopolitan compilers had
carefully noted the aphorism ascribed to Solon—' The wise
man thanks the gods daily for having made him a Greek and
not a barbarian, a man and not a beast, a male and not a
female.' They had further noted that Aristotle gave the
citizen full power over children, slaves, and women, and they
industriously amalgamated these precepts with their Christian
notions as to damnation and the origin of sin.

' What is a woman ?' we read in an ancient religious instruction imported into Russia from the East. ' A net to tempt
men ! with her clear face and her high-set eyes, she works

7

spells ! . . . What is a woman?   A viper's nest !'   The Eve
of the Byzantine world is a being ' twelve times impure,' and
always dangerous.   On certain days no man must sit at table
with her, and the meat she has killed is poison.   Wherefore,
in the country parts of Russia, in the sixteenth century, house-
keepers might have been seen running through the village to
find a man to wring the neck of the chicken they wanted to
boil.   The younger and fairer the woman was, the more she
was pernicious and accursed.   And only old women were
allowed to prepare the sacred wafers.

To lessen the mischief and diminish the peril, the woman
must be shut up.   ' She sits behind twenty-seven locks—she
sits locked in with twenty-seven keys, so that the wind
may not blow on her, so that the sun may not burn her,
so that bold comrades may not see her. . . .'   In the case of
women of high rank, the precautions thus enumerated in the
popular song are literally applied.   The boïarina's apartments,
at the back of the house, with a special entrance of their own,
constitute a prison of which the boïarine keeps the key.
No other man, not even a near relation, can enter.   The windows all look on to an inner court, protected from indiscreet
curiosity by a tall fence.   This is the gaol-yard, where the
prisoners take their exercise.   Generally there is a chapel or
oratory, where the woman is allowed to perform her devotions,
only going to church on great occasions, and surrounded then
by the various precautions which attend all her rare excursions
out of doors.   The carriage which transports her, when this
happens, is a sort of cellular vehicle, with bladder-skins
instead of glass in its windows, so that the occupant can see
out without being seen, and it is attended by a whole escort of
serving-men, half-spies, half-guards.   Most of these will spend
the whole of their lives without ever beholding their closely-
watched mistress, and even their master's own friends may not
be more highly favoured.   As a matter of principle, the wife
does not appear before her husband's guests.   But an exception
is made on the occasion of banquets given to persons to whom
the entertainer desires to do special honour.   In the course of
such repasts, a ceremony is performed which would seem to
show some glimmer of the chivalrous ideas of the West.   At
a signal given by her lord, the boïarina descends the staircase
of the *gynæceum*, dressed in her most gorgeous attire, and
bearing in her hand a golden cup.   Having touched this with her
lips, she offers it to every guest, and then, standing upright at the
place of honour, permits each to greet her with a respectful kiss.

All this was possible, evidently, in the aristocratic class ;
but outside it, such cloistered retirement seemed less indispensable, and the danger slighter.   The woman of humble

birth was a beast of burden, who might very well be left to the free exercise of her household duties, to carry the linen to the public washing-place, and labour in the fields. Even in the middle class, the *terem* admitted of some modifications. When the great festivals drew near, the women of the lesser nobility, and those of the merchant and poorer classes, crowded round the seesaws and roundabouts set up in the streets, the chief entertainment of the female public of that period. The great ladies had them in the inner courts of their houses. When the ladies got off their seesaws, they went to dance in some meadow. The dancing of that period seems to have been a simple and somewhat monotonous business. The dancers kept stamping their feet on the same spot of ground, twirling round and round, moving their shoulders, swaying their hips, nodding their heads about, raising and lowering their eyebrows, waving handkerchiefs—all to the accompaniment of their own singing and of the shrill music of a *skomorokh*. But Peerson noticed a less innocent aspect of these gambols, a dubious habit of standing back to back, and rubbing the more fleshy parts of their bodies against their partners', not to mention extempore songs on most improper subjects.

Here, again, we have to note the inevitable consequence of a too severe religious law. Dancing, however decent, was forbidden by the Church, with games and pastimes of every kind. This was shutting the door in the devil's face, so that he might climb in by the window. The public baths gave rise to much more serious disorders. In them the sexes were nominally separated, but men and women came out of their respective hot rooms, stripped, streaming with sweat, and their blood heated by smart rubbing, met at the entrance, fell without any embarrassment into eager conversation, and cast themselves pell-mell into the river, or rolled in the snow, amidst shouts and jests and jokes the nature of which will be easily divined.

This was the filthy outlet of the ascetic system. Only one woman almost entirely escaped this system—the widowed mother of sons. From the domestic and social, even from the political, point of view, she attained complete independence, and enjoyed rights equal to a man's. But if the widow had no son, she dropped into the class of orphans and infirm persons, of whom the Church had the care and trouble, for society would have none of them. Thus the exception was a confirmation of the rule. Unless, again, the Eve on whom the ascetic ideal had laid its curse lifted herself, whether mother or maid, above the malediction, and, rising, by some prodigy of virtue, to the level of that ideal, became a saint according to its canons. But such an elevation seems to have been particularly

7—2

laborious, for the ' Tcheti Mineï ' of Macarius only chronicle the lives of two female saints in all. Russian hagiographers, indeed, appear to have professed a certain scorn for these scarce beings, even when recognised and adopted by the Church. St. Olga and St. Euphrosyne of Polotsk, who lived, one in the tenth and the other in the twelfth century, found no biographers till the fifteenth—and both of them were Princesses !

One other opening there was for women who could not reach such heights as these—that world of supernatural forces to which the popular imagination ascribed so mighty a power over human life. Woman, banned out of society, scorned as a wife and mother, was dreaded as a sorceress and courted as a soothsayer. She could be queen of the magic kingdom of superstition. And in the *raskol*, where superstition played so great a part, the power of woman was to recover all its privileges and retake first rank. In ordinary life, at all events, was the wife and mother permitted to taste the joys of domestic existence ?

III.—THE FAMILY.

Here an initial fact presents itself. In the upper class, the education of the children was generally taken out of the mother's hands. In this quarter, therefore, we find nothing at all. Maternal love and filial love both lay under the interdict of the Church. The only thing left was marriage. But marriage, in a young girl's case, did not mean that she had found a young man for whom she cared, or was even likely to care. Except in the case of second marriages, the matching of couples concerned the parents only, and they, as a rule, never thought of consulting the young people's inclinations ; all the more, as the persons married were very frequently mere children. Twelve years old for a girl, fourteen for a boy, were considered quite marriageable ages. And before they went to the altar, even up to the very threshold of the nuptial chamber, the young couple might be, and, strictly speaking, ought to be, strangers. The bride, especially, must not be seen by her bridegroom until the supreme moment. To avoid surprises of a too painful nature, some lady relation of the man's assumed the delicate duties of the *smotritiélnitsa*, or looker (*smotrit*, to look). She was brought into a room decorated for the purpose, and caught a glimpse of the betrothed behind a curtain which was drawn aside for a moment. Substitutions, facilitated by such prearranged presentations, were not uncommon. The husband thus deceived had a right to make a complaint, demand an inquiry, and demand the revocation of the contract. As a rule, he preferred to solve the difficulty by treating the woman so ill that he drove her to take the veil. In exceptional cases, and if his suit was greatly desired, the young man was allowed to accomplish the ceremony of the *smotr* in person ; but if he drew back afterwards, it was an affront which carried heavy penalties with it.

After the *smotr* came the *sgovor*, or espousals, on which occasion long speeches were made on each side, the contract was drawn up, and the dowry (always, until the sixteenth century, furnished by the bridegroom) sometimes immediately paid over, in fulfilment of the proverb, ' The money on the table, the young girl behind the table.' But the betrothed bride was never present. It was not till after the signatures had been exchanged that one of her female relatives brought the bridegroom a few trifling gifts from her.

The marriage itself was attended by very complicated rites, symbolizing the entrance into a new life, and very closely reproducing those customary on the accession of a Prince. They were presided over by two personages—one called *tyssiatski*, a name corresponding with important functions under the appanage system and the *viétchié*—a sort of chiliarch, appointed to command the crowd of groomsmen and bridesmaids ; the other, the *iassiélnik* (equerry), whose duty was to protect the ceremony and all who took part in it from evil spells of every kind ; for such occasions were supposed to be particularly auspicious for evil spirits and sorcerers.

The evening before the wedding the guests gathered in the bridegroom's house, where he received their congratulations, gave them a banquet, and sent his bride, who was still invisible, more or less splendid presents—a casket with rings and cosmetics and dainties, and a symbolic whip. At the same moment the matchmaker was busying herself about preparing the nuptial couch. She began by walking all round the house with a rowan-branch in her hand, to drive away spells. The bridal chamber was generally arranged in a loft, so that, being as far as possible above the ground, it might evoke fewer thoughts of the tomb. It was hung with carpets and marten furs, an essential sign of wealth and comfort ; in the four corners four pewter vessels filled with hydromel were set, and the necessary adjuncts of the sleeping-chamber were brought in procession, the pictures of Christ and the Virgin carried first. The bed was generally made on wooden benches set side by side. On these, sheaves of wheat were first laid, the quantity, which always had a meaning, differing according to the rank of the newly-married couple. The wheat was covered with carpets, on which eiderdown coverlets were laid, and close to the bed open barrels full of wheat, rye, barley, and oats were placed.

The next morning there was a second banquet in the same

house, for which the *korovaï* (wedding-cake) was baked, and
this time the bride occupied her own place at the head of the
table beside the bridegroom.   In front of her were three cloths,
laid one on the top of the other, and on them a salt-cellar, a small
loaf of white bread (*kalatch*), and a cheese.   The bridegroom
went to fetch his bride with a great following, *korovaï*-bearers
and taper-bearers—two of them, sometimes, to each taper,
some of which weighed as much as ninety-six pounds.   A
groomsman followed with the *ossypalo*, a great dish of hops,
(typical of joy and plenty), marten furs, gold-embroidered handkerchiefs, and coins, to be distributed among the company.   A
similar procession formed up behind the bride, who was invisible, shrouded in a thick veil.   Two bridesmaids carried two
dishes, on which might be seen the bride's head-dress, a goblet
filled with a mixture of wine and honey, the use of which will
shortly be detailed, and handkerchiefs, also intended for the
guests.

The two processions took their way to the young couple's
residence, and the banquet was opened by long prayers recited
by the pope.   According to custom, the guests hardly touched
the first course, until the matchmaker, rising, requested the
bride's parents' leave to dress her hair.   Tapers were lighted,
and a strip of silk with a great cross embroidered on each
side was stretched between the couple.   The matchmaker
took off the bride's veil, dipped a comb into the symbolic
goblet, and passed it through her hair before covering it with
the net and the *kika*.   At this moment, while the bridesmaids
fanned the couple with marten-skins, the habit, in the middle
classes, was that the betrothed persons should bring their
cheeks close to the silk that was being held between them.   A
mirror was held in front of them, and thus for the first time
they could see each other's features.   At that moment, too,
one of the wedding-guests approached them, wearing a *touloupe*
with the fur outside, and wished them as many children as there
were hairs in the fur.

Then came the distribution of the kerchiefs and other objects
on the *ossypalo*, the exchange of rings before the pope, and the
handing to the bridegroom by the bride's father of the emblem
of his paternal authority.   My readers will have guessed it
was a whip !   ' I hope I shall never need it,' quoth the bridegroom gallantly.   But he stuck it in his belt.   Here there
was a break in the feasting, and everybody went to church.
On the way there was singing and dancing, in spite of the pope's
presence, and, under his angry eyes, the *skomorokhy* delighted
the party with their tricks.   After the benediction the bride
sometimes prostrated herself and touched her husband's boot
with her forehead, in sign of submission, while he, with a pro-

tecting gesture, sheltered his chosen partner with a corner of his garment. Sometimes, too, the pope held out a cup, at which the couple wetted their lips three times. Then it was cast upon the ground, and each tried to set his or her foot upon it. If the woman proved the most active of the two, it was taken as an omen that she would have the upper hand in the household. And as they left the church there were more symbolic ceremonies and make-believe endeavours to separate the couple, who clung together. Then everybody went back to the wedding-feast. The bride was expected to weep freely, and her companions egged her on, singing sad songs to her. Neither she nor the bridegroom were allowed to touch any of the dishes till, a swan having been served to all the other guests, a roast fowl was set before the newly-married pair.

This was the signal for their retirement, and here, even more clearly than in the details already related, the spirit of local mysticism, in its most coarsely sensual and naïvely cynical form, was manifested. The symbolic fowl led the way to the nuptial chamber, escorted by the taper-bearers, the *korovaï*-bearers, and all the rest of the company. The tapers were thrust into the barrels of corn, the married pair were conducted into the room with much further ceremony, and the guests went back to the feast, while the matchmaker and her assistants helped the young people to undress. When this process began, the wife, in token of humility, had to pull off her husband's boots. In one of them a coin was hidden, and if she pulled this boot off first, it was looked on as a lucky omen. Meanwhile the husband enacted his part by drawing the symbolic whip out of his belt and applying it with the discretion the occasion demanded ! The couple were left alone at last, still guarded by an *iassiélnik*, who went on a protective round outside the house, on foot or horseback, and the feasting continued merrily for an hour. At the end of that time a girl was sent to ask for news of the married pair. If the husband answered through the closed door that he was well, it meant that ' good had been accomplished between them,' and forthwith the guests went back to the loft to carry food to the husband and wife. The fowl constituted the chief portion of this ritual feast, but other dishes were habitually added to it. There was an exchange of toasts and compliments, then the newly-married folk were put to bed again, and the guests, departing, sat down once more to make merry.

The next morning the ceremonies followed their course. First came the indispensable bath, after which the wife presented her husband's mother with the proofs of her virginity, in the shape of the shift worn on the wedding night, which was carefully preserved.   When the Tsar married, it was not till this stage of the business that the Court beheld the new Sovereign, a boïarine of high rank lifting the corner of her veil on the point of an arrow.   On this day it was the bride's parents who entertained the wedding guests.   But on certain occasions they were exposed to a terrible humiliation.   The husband's father might offer them a cup with a hole bored in it, stopped by the pressure of his finger.   The finger removed, the contents of the goblet, wine or brandy, escaped, and the audience knew the young wife ' had not been what she should have been. . . .'

All through these festivities, except to pronounce certain sacramental words, the bride never spoke.   Her silence, apart from these, was considered a proof of her being well brought up.   Her companions, on the other hand, enjoyed a quite unusual freedom, of which they took liberal advantage, a joyous slackening of the bonds, sometimes degenerating into a sort of madness, which carried the most chaste and modest of creatures into sudden shamelessness and the wildest excess. And after all that, the heavy doors of the *terem* closed once more on the short snatch of gaiety, and on the fate of the newly-married wife.

The probable nature of that fate may be easily imagined. The *Domostroï* has no doubt exaggerated the austerity of domestic life, but it must have been very like a cloistered existence, all the same.   Several times a day the denizens of every house of any size gathered in the *krestovaïa komnata*, a room intended as a place of prayer, and covered with *ikons* from its ceiling to its floor.   All the events of life, small or great, involved the invocation of the sacred pictures, with which relics and other similarly precious objects—such as tapers that had been lighted at the celestial fire of Jerusalem, or fragments of a stone on which our Lord had set His foot—were venerated.   Even outside the *krestovaïa* a woman's rosary was never out of her grasp, and in the hands of the recluses of the *terem* these instruments of supplication, which must needs be of artistic workmanship and blessed at some special centre of devotion, such as the Troïtsa or the monasteries of Solovki or Bielooziéro, were a faithful image of the monotonous and empty lives that slipped through their fingers with their *Paters* and their *Aves*.

Everybody, whether of high or humble rank, rose early : with the sun in summer-time, several hours before it in the winter.   Even in the sixteenth century, time was still reckoned on the Oriental system, twelve hours in the day and twelve in the night, the equinox being taken to be the normal reckoning, and the first hour of the day corresponding with the seventh, according to our present calculations. The services of the Church were regulated on this system of timing, and all other occupations were based on these. These, in the aristocratic class, beyond that of passing from one orison to another till dinner-time came, were very few After dinner a siesta was absolutely indispensable. The very tradesmen shut up their shops, and nobody worked but the barbers, who removed overluxuriant tresses on one of the Moscow spaces, known as the 'Square of Lice.' There was a good reason for this period of repose. People ate a great deal ; they loaded their stomachs with a huge quantity of food, often of a most indigestible nature, and Dimitri the impostor betrayed his true origin by neglecting this national habit.

For the wife of a rich boïar, the whole of life consisted in praying, eating, and sleeping. Other women had their household duties, but their life was one of toil, of convict labour. The boïarina, born to idleness and stupefied by it, would not even take the trouble to embroider some church ornament, except to lighten her own unbearable ennui. And boredom was not the most dangerous guest in a conjugal existence constituted after the fashion we have noted. How many ill-assorted unions did it create ! How great the risk of consequent conflict ! Did not the law provide a special penalty for the wife who poisoned her husband ? And what a hideous penalty ! She was to be buried alive, her head above ground, so that her torture might be long. It sometimes lasted many days. Some culprits escaped this fate by taking the veil, but they were forced to live in separate cells and wear chains.

But in most cases the woman, ill-treated, outraged, and not unfrequently forsaken, avenged herself on these unions, in which love was so seldom her portion, through love. Closely watched as she was, she generally succeeded in ' putting her husband under the bench,' as the common expression went. Even the repulsion with which the ' non-Christians,' as all foreigners were called, inspired her, did not prevent her committing adultery with them, if we are to believe the travellers of that time ; and the chapter of the *Domostroï* which forbids the admission of gossips of doubtful reputation into the *terem* certainly points to the not uncommon infraction of an over-stringent law. Some of these women, who acted as go-betweens, were always to be found about the places frequented by the poorer class—wash-houses, markets, fountains—and they were also to be seen in the most respectable houses—where they generally performed a double duty, and so insured the master's favour. There was no necessity for his concealing his mistresses, for custom permitted him to take them even in his own house, and by force, without incurring any serious reproach.

Amongst the lower orders, laxity of morals as to this matter was extreme, and the neglect of all reserve and decency almost general. Women would issue stark naked from the public bath-houses, and brush against the passers-by in the open street. In the following century, Oléarius recounts a scene he himself witnessed at Novgorod. A great crowd had gathered for some religious ceremony. A woman came out of a tavern where she had got drunk, and, dazed by the open air, fell down in an indecent posture. A drunken peasant saw her, threw himself like a wild beast on the naked form, while the crowd, men, women, and children, gathered, shouting with laughter, round the horrid sight. . . .

Even when the wife became a mother her miserable fate was hardly bettered. Maternity, for her, was reduced to the material cares and duties of the child's earliest years, and the essential element—affection—was always to be lacking. Respect for parents was, indeed, believed to insure a long and happy life. It was said of a man who spoke evil of the authors of his being, ' The ravens will tear him with their beaks, the eagles will devour him. . . .' ' A father's curse dries up,' runs another proverb ; ' a mother's curse roots up.' But the family law, while it ascribed a much greater authority to the father, ' Look on thy father as on God, and on thy mother as on thyself,' seems to have had its roots in fear. The father thus commended, not to the love, but to the respect of his children, was the august bearer (*groznyï*) of the whip. It was a law of slavery still, devoid of all moral strength, the fitting counterpart of the political system which it completed, which it partly inspired, and which it made acceptable. And here again, as quoted by Karamzine (' History of Russia,' ix. 156), is the testimony of a Russian moralist who has much to say and conceals nothing as to those family relations, the sad truths concerning which no historian of the epoch can overlook or hide. They have lain like a curse on ten centuries of the past history of a people which thereby, more than by any other cause, has been prevented from entering into earlier and fuller dealings and community of thought with other civilized nations. ' Better it is to have an unsheathed dagger at one's side than an unmarried son in one's house. . . . Better it is to have a goat in the house than a girl who has grown up ; the goat runs about the meadow and will bring home milk, the girl runs about the village '— here there is an untranslatable play on words—' she will bring home her father's shame.'

Under the domestic roof, which so often sheltered a very

hell, the one event crowned with an aureole of sincere and
august morality was death.   In that hour the religious law,
which claimed more than any life could render, obtained full
and utter satisfaction.   To die surrounded by one's family,
and in full possession of one's faculties, was accounted a
heavenly benediction.   So great was the power of faith that
the moment did not terrify.   It was prepared for long before
it came, the last will duly made, and as many good actions
as possible introduced into it—alms, the freeing of slaves, the
remission of debts, or merely their discharge.   The keeping
of engagements was accounted a merit, and the whole process
was graced with an expressive name, ' to build one's soul '
(*stroït douchou*).   It often happened that the dying man
desired to put on a monkish habit, and in the Tsar's case this
was generally done.   If a man who had put on the *skhima*
recovered his health he was obliged to enter a monastery.
But even on the brink of eternity, and in spite of the part
played by Christian beliefs, pagan traditions still claimed
their rights, and the scenic effect produced was instinct with
materialism of the grossest sort.   There was a funeral banquet,
as a prelude to which a preparation of flour or of *kacha*—perhaps the *koutia* already known to us—was laid on a window-
sill, and there were lamentations in which the profane or
profaning spirit ruled : ' Oh, my darling,' the widow would
begin, ' why hast thou forsaken me ? . . .   Was I not pleasant
to thee ? . . .   Did I not know how to dress and adorn myself
to please thy taste ? . . .'   And the rest would cry : ' Why
didst thou die ? . . .   Hadst thou not thy fill of meat and
drink ? . . .   Was not thy wife fair ? . . .'
    The family was not so much a moral entity as an association
of interests.   And it was capable of extension in the form of
certain communistic groups, of which the principle, on an
equally low level of culture, may be found in Iceland, in Servia,
and even in America—elementary communities of from ten
to fifty persons, living under the same roof, eating at the same
table, and recognising the authority of a leader, instead of
any bond of relationship.   The Servian *zadrouga* is the most
perfect type of this description.   These communities, which
were mentioned by Nestor and in the *Pravda* (code) of Jaroslav,
continued to exist in Russia down to the seventeenth century,
both in the north-west provinces, towards Pskov, and those
in the south-west lying near Lithuania.   This method of
association, while, as its apologists have pointed out, it suppressed the bitterness of economic rivalries, contributed yet
more to the paralysis of the spirit of individual enterprise,
and certainly did not render family or sexual relations purer or
tenderer.

That family life, properly so called, as practised amongst the Muscovites of the sixteenth century, did not admit of the progressive development of certain domestic virtues cannot be affirmed, and this the unfavourable testimony of all contemporary observers notwithstanding. Their observation was limited to the most apparent phenomena, and virtue is a plant which usually flourishes in the shade. One characteristic trait in this respect is the solidarity of feeling so powerful in the numerous class of serving-men and daily guests who surrounded the heads of families of the period. These men, whether slaves or freemen, really constituted a sort of court (*dvornia*), surrounded by which the boïar loved to play the king, aping the ceremonial and the conferring of places practised in the Grand Ducal household, save that in his bedroom he was apt to replace the *spalnik* by a *postiélnitsa*. Badly fed, as a rule, for the turnkey (*klioutchnik*) did not fail to levy an unconscionable tithe on the food destined for the servants' support ; ill-clothed, too, for, as in the Grand Duke's palace, fine liveries and rich clothes were only worn on great occasions, the members of the *dvornia* frequently sought compensation out of doors. They wandered about the streets, fraternized with vagabonds and beggars, asked charity like them, and helped them, when darkness fell, to strip the passers-by. Reward and punishment alike were bestowed on their master's whim, and their idea of justice was one in which morality had no part. ' The master,' they said, ' will find a fault if he wants to strike.' But they were ready to die for him. When a quarrel arose between two boïars their servants always intervened, and made this intervention a point of honour identical with that observable in the relations between the *sloojilyié lioodi* and the Sovereign. The boïar, habitually robbed and even betrayed by his servants, just as he often ill-used them, both in their persons and in their dearest interests, felt no scruple as to his own master, whom he deceived and whose property he stole, whenever and however he could, and whom he was quite capable, too, of betraying on occasion, though he would serve him, on some other, with an unchangeable devotion. Ivan the Terrible was to spend his whole life in denouncing and chastising his servants' disloyalty, and yet he always found men to carry out all his undertakings : men with a moral system of their own, in which the sense of right and wrong had no place, and conscience played no part, but in which a single directing instinct asserted itself in prodigies of complete and absolute self-sacrifice—that one principle of ' service.' This imperative absolute, the basis of the social and political organization of the country, triumphantly forced on the docile mind of a robust and patient race, has been the secret of its triumphs and its glories. The whole of Russia's greatness reposes on this foundation.

We have crossed the threshold of the family dwelling ; let us now follow the boïar on his walks abroad.

IV.—SOCIETY.

We know already that he never goes out except in a carriage or on horseback. The horse's trappings are as splendid as his master's clothes. The rider and his mount are all of a piece. The saddle is covered with morocco leather or velvet, embroidered with gold ; the housings are of the same precious material, the frontlet silver-mounted, and chains and necklets and bells jingle down to the creature's very hoofs. A perfect peal, in fact, giving warning, even from the distance, of the great man's coming, and bidding passers-by get themselves out of the way. The carriage, generally, was a sledge, for even in summer-time wheeled vehicles were despised, being considered much less dignified. This sledge, long and very narrow, usually held only one person. But two servants, as a rule, crouched on it at their master's feet, hidden, like him, in winter-time, by a mass of furs. The horse, another peal of bells, adorned according to the season of the year with feathers or fox and marten tails, was bestridden by the coachman. Thus our boïar fared forth a-visiting, but as he neared the house he proposed to honour with his presence, a question of etiquette arose. Where should he dismount or get out of his sledge ? This, if the house to which the visit was paid belonged to a person of the highest rank, must be done at the courtyard gate. At the Kremlin, a few dignitaries had the *entrée* to the courtyard, but they would have been knouted if they had dared to cross it altogether. Amongst equals, the visitor could drive or ride to the steps of the house. Here he was received, according to circumstances and to the rules of a most scrupulous ceremonial, by the master of the house or some attendant. Once within doors, he began by saluting the holy pictures, crossing himself before them, and then touching the ground with his right hand. Then he proceeded to salute his host, exchanging civilities ruled by the equality or differences of the respective ranks, and ranging from handshakings to genuflections. Everything, down to the tiniest detail, was carefully regulated. The opening remarks, too, followed certain stereotyped formulas, very ceremonious and hypocritically humble. ' I strike my forehead like a slave in the presence of my benefactor ! . . . Pardon the poverty of my intelligence ! . . .' Speaking to a Churchman, it was absolutely necessary to declare one's self ' a great and impious sinner,' and

to address him as 'Orthodox doctor' and 'Guardian of the
great light.' After these and similar grimaces, refreshments
were accepted—these were offered at every hour of the day—
and when the guest departed, he began, as when he arrived, by
paying his duty to the holy pictures.

Meetings in public places involved less etiquette and constraint, but they were not of common occurrence. The bathing
establishments were not much frequented by people of condition, though the habit of taking baths daily, or several times
in the week at all events, was shared by every class. But the
humblest of gentlemen had his own *bania*. The moment a
Muscovite felt out of sorts he drank a glass of brandy seasoned
with pepper or garlic, ate a slice of onion, and took a douche.
This was the usual course of treatment for every complaint ;
none but a few great lords bestowed any confidence—and in
their case it was limited—on doctors, who were not numerous
in those days, and all of them of foreign origin. The first, who
came into the country with Sophia Paleologus, wife of Ivan III.,
had been sentenced to death because he failed to cure one of
his patients. This precedent had not produced an encouraging
effect. Yet under Ivan IV. a medical body was to be formed,
in which a quartette of Englishmen, Standish, Elmes, Roberts,
and Frensham the apothecary, were to compete with Elysius
Bomelius the German. But not the whole of them together
could have induced any native-born Russian to swallow a pill
or accept any similar remedy.

Apart from the bath-houses, social life found its expression
in banquets, which occurred pretty frequently and took two
forms : they were either private or collective—arranged, in
this latter case, by associations, communities, and called
brattchiny (*brat*, brother). Friends and relations feasted
among themselves on the great festivals, and important family
gatherings, marriages, christenings, and funerals. Court banquets were given on such occasions as a coronation, the
installation of a new Metropolitan, or the reception of a foreign
Ambassador. The question of the places to be assigned to
the guests at these feasts was hugely important, and often gave
rise to quarrels, and even to bloody scuffles, although it was
the correct thing for a guest to make difficulties about taking
his rightful seat at the high table. Two persons generally
ate out of the same dish, helping themselves with their fingers,
and putting the bones on their plates, which were not intended
to serve any other purpose, and were not changed during the
meal. The amphitryon distributed the bread and salt, and
sent delicate morsels to his guests. The number of the courses
passes all imagination, and the duration of these repasts,
together with the peculiar taste of most of the dishes and the

smell of garlic, onions, and rotten fish that soon filled the air, the excess to which the guests carried their libations, and the disgusting conduct in which most of them indulged, made them unendurable to foreigners. It was not an uncommon thing even for ladies, who took their meals apart from the men, to be carried home unconscious, and when their hostess sent to inquire for them the next day, the correct answer, their tribute to the hospitable entertainment they had received, was, ' I was so merry yesterday that I do not know how I got home !'

Amongst devout folk, religious observances were strangely mingled with all this carousing. The clergy were invited and set in the place of honour ; they paid their score in prayers and ceremonies of various kinds, blessed the food and drink, and burned incense in every room in the house. Sometimes, in imitation of the practice in the monasteries, a monstrance containing ' the host of the Blessed Virgin ' was placed upon the table. The meal was stopped now and then, and psalms were sung. Beggars were fed in the antechamber, and some were even made to sit down among the other guests. The seclusion of the *terem* was broken, and the two sexes met. Players on instruments and jugglers fanned the general merriment, and filthy songs rang on the air.

Amongst the peasants, the feast took the name of ' private beer,' because it presupposed the permission, only occasionally granted, to brew strong drinks, beer, fermented liquors, or hydromel, all of which were monopolies. This authorization could be had for three days, or even for a week, at the great festivals, and when the period closed, the fiscal authorities sealed up the various drinks until the next feast-day came.

The *brattchiny* were also called *ssypnyié* (from *ssypat*, to pour together). In ancient days the shares were probably paid in wheat, poured on to the same heap. These collective banquets, which were presided over by an elected *staroste*, enjoyed a judicial autonomy, of which some remnants existed down to the seventeenth century. The quarrels between persons present at them were not amenable to the ordinary tribunais. The proverb, ' We will brew no beer with that man,' indicates the nature of these feasts, symbolic of an alliance, an action taken in common. At them peasants and nobles met in perfect equality. But disorderly scenes, scuffles, even murders, were of more frequent occurrence here than at private gatherings. Wherefore pious folk generally avoided them. The drinking was excessive. Vladimir had already written, ' *Roussi vésselé piti : nié mojet bez tavo byti* ' (' The joy of Russia is to drink : she could not do without it '). Joy, tenderness, sympathy, a whole gamut of feeling, found its expression in the bowl. A man got dead drunk to express his friendship for his guest or for a cheery comrade. And he ate, too, till he was ready to burst—pikes' heads dressed with garlic, fish soups with saffron in them, hares' kidneys stewed in milk and ginger, strongly flavoured cookery all of it, highly spiced, that burnt the mouth and necessitated copious libations. The wines most commonly consumed came from Hungary and the Rhine, and are not always easy to recognise under their corrupted names. For *Petersemen* we must read *Peter Simon's wein*, a Rhenish vintage imported by Peter Simon, a Dutch merchant. There were French wines, red and white burgundies—amongst which the Romanée vintage no doubt figured under that name of *Romaneïa* now applied in Russian taverns to corn-brandy and alcohol distilled from fruits, malmsey, alicant, and other Spanish wines. French wines were more especially used by the Church. Brandy was also imported in large quantities, and so were German and French white wine vinegars. The usual drink of the common people was *kvass :* but Tetaldi the Italian mentions another preparation, frequently used, called *tolokno*, into the composition of which dry oatmeal entered. But Russian authorities only speak of this as a food.

As to the extent of the habits of intemperance thus revealed, witnesses disagree as much as on every other matter. According to Jenkinson, the English traveller, Russia would have been a drunken country whether Ivan IV. had been sober or not, whereas a memorandum drawn up at Lubeck in 1567, on the occasion of a projected embassy from Germany to Ivan's Court, points quite in the opposite direction. The Ambassadors are charged to keep perfectly sober, because drunkenness is considered the greatest of vices in Muscovy. And the author of this memorandum is a merchant who made a considerable stay in Moscow (Forsten, 'The Baltic Question,' i. 475). Michalon the Lithuanian, certainly an impartial witness, speaks in the same sense, adding, it must be confessed, a statement, thoroughly untrue, that there were no taverns in the country. Towards the close of Ivan IV.'s reign, according to Tetaldi, the sale of spirituous liquors was only allowed in one suburb of Moscow, which is also mentioned by Herberstein, Guagnino, and Olearius, though each, according to his own fashion, maims the word, the etymology of which they derive from *nalivat*, to pour. The real word was *Nalivki*, and the spot, which is within the boundaries of the present city, is marked by a Church of the Transfiguration, still called *na Nalivkakh* (at the *Nalivki*). The trade in strong drinks seems, in fact, to have been centralized, at a certain moment, in this outlying corner of the ancient capital. At the same time, however, the other towns and villages of the country were completely free in this respect, thanks to the innumerable taverns, the existence of which the fiscal authority favoured in its own interests.   In this matter, as in so many others, secular interests were at variance with the principles of a vexatious system of morals, and the result was a series of compromises which have led observers astray.

The Church, as may be imagined, warred against the *kabaks* ; but from a general point of view, if the Church's own witness is to be believed, her commands and anathemas did very little good.   The *conciliable* of the year 1551 has left us a picture of contemporary morals which reveals a condition, in the popular classes, at all events, of extreme profligacy.   In the course of certain nocturnal gatherings, which combined the commemoration of a Christian festival with the worship of a heathen tradition—the feast of St. John and the festival of Iarilo, the Slav *Priapus*—drunkenness favoured every other form of debauchery.   Men and women, girls and boys, spent the night in some out of the way spot, dancing, singing, indulging in every kind of excess ; and, so we read in the report of this illustrious assembly, 'when dawn came, they ran shouting like mad folk down to the river, where they all bathed together, and when the bell rang for matins they went back to their houses, and there fell down, like dead people, of sheer exhaustion.'   The stress laid by the members of this council, and by all Church writers of that time, on the sin of sodomy, is equally significant.

But the Church, as we know, exacted much—too much. She confounded and condemned every form of sociability with a quite excessive severity.   Secular art, like pleasure, fell under her interdict.   She waged war, too, against the *skomorokhy*.   According to a popular legend, which had a religious basis, the devil took on the form of these wandering jugglers and musicians, so that he might lead honest folk to their perdition.   Without this special action on the devil's part, the *skomorokhy* frequently played the part of burglars—nay, even of highway robbers.   Considered outlaws, and treated as such, they moved about, to insure their own safety, in bands numbering from thirty to sixty persons, and sometimes they grew dangerous.   They were artists in their way, and the forerunners of the entertainers who form an integral part of every civilized life.   They supplied the comic note, and the national theatre is the outcome of their coarse and burlesque performances.   They had rivals, too, pursued, like them, by the thunders of the Church—other comedians, these, bearleaders.

The bear held an important position in the Muscovite life of this epoch.   He, too, was an artist after a fashion ; and not

8

only had he been taught to perform every kind of trick, but
he figured as the chief character, and under divers aspects,
in a comic repertory dear to the common herd. Sometimes
he was a judge, who took bribes and delivered grotesque
sentences ; sometimes he was a husband, fooled first of all,
and then thrashed. He was the Punch, the *Snagarelle*, of
the country. Now and then, indeed, he was promoted to
play some tragic part. Physical exercises and effort of every
kind, races on foot or on horseback, archery competitions,
tournaments, at which the riders picked up rings on their
lance-points, and fights, whether with fists or cudgels, were
all much enjoyed. But the most favourite sport of all was a
match between the bear and hounds, or other animals, or,
above all, between the bear and a man. The man, armed with
a spear, strove to strike his terrible adversary in the breast
just when the creature stood up on its hind legs. If he missed
his aim, he ran the risk of being torn to pieces, and this often
occurred. The bear's antagonists were generally selected from
amongst the Sovereign's dog-boys ; but on the lists of the most
famous champions we find such aristocratic names as that of
Prince Goundorov, who, in 1628, was rewarded with a piece of
blue damask for having killed a bear in single combat and of
Feodor Sytine, the son of a boïar, torn to pieces, in the course
of a less successful struggle, in 1632.

Affairs of honour were also decided with fists or cudgels.
It was not considered necessary to unsheath the sword on
such accounts, and the fact suffices to show how rustic and
savage this half-complete society still was, how far removed
from the elegant forms of life already existing in the West.
It was a far cry, indeed, to those French and Italian palaces
where the guests already talked, after they had laughed and
danced ; where the man who could tell a story pleasantly,
or ' say the word,' was welcomed ; where things of beauty were
admired, at all events, if comfort was not generally sought ;
where love was full of poetry, and there was wit even in hatred ;
where, if a quarrel arose, men slew each other—after they had
taken their leave—nobly, as they had delighted to live. To the
models of beauty and grace there blossoming in the flush of a
new art summer, the spirit of Russia opposed a very different
type, personified by another order of vagabonds, one which
enjoyed the favour of the populace and the indulgence of the
clergy — the *iourodivyié* or *blajennyié*, coarse seers and magicians, who turned the people's credulity to account, and
skilfully concealed their real trade under professions of extreme
austerity and appearances of miraculous power. They stalked
naked in the bitterest cold, they let their neglected tresses
float on the breeze, they pretended to need neither food nor

clothing, but they went into any shop and took what they wanted without paying for it. To be robbed by them was an earnest of prosperity, a certainty of blessing. They were accounted saints. They had the privilege of telling the truth, even to the Sovereign himself, and we shall see the Terrible, when brought to close quarters with one of them, yield to his bold words. The Church tolerated them, and even admitted them to paradise, and at the splendid funeral of the *blajennyi* Basil, to whom the masterpiece of Barma and Postnikov on the Kremlin Square is dedicated, the holy man's coffin rested on Ivan's own shoulder.

I have said enough to enable the reader to measure the abyss which parted Europe from this corner of the European world, at the moment when Russia was about to enter into contact with the civilizations lying nearest her, and thus to render the story of this evolution, which I am now about to commence, intelligible.

PART II

THE YOUTH OF IVAN

CHAPTER I

THE FIRST RUSSIAN TSAR

I.—THE BIRTH OF THE TERRIBLE. II.—THE GOVERNMENT OF THE
BOÏARS. III.—MARRIAGE AND CORONATION. IV.—SYLVESTER
AND ADACHEV. V.—THE FIRST ASSEMBLY: RUSSIAN PAR-
LIAMENTARIANISM.

I.—THE BIRTH OF THE TERRIBLE.

ON Ivan the Terrible's birthday, August 25 (September 4),
1530, the whole country was filled with the noise of thunder,
and with awful flashes of lightning. Even when the child
began to stir in his mother's womb, the Muscovite armies
fighting before Kazan had felt a flush of eagerness and
valour such as they had never known before. More genuine
than the prodigies of which popular legend has thus preserved the memory were the shocks which at that moment
were staggering all Europe. Luther and Calvin, Wycliff and
Huss, had made their entry on the world's stage, and from
one end of Western Christendom to the other, on battlefields
where brother fought against brother, and on public squares
that bristled with scaffolds, in churches torn with distress
and courts shaken by revolution, Catholics and Protestants,
soldiers and priests, Princes and varlets, were striving
to turn the great shout of liberty that had rung from the
battlements of the Wartburg into a war-cry, an instrument of
massacre and oppression. Shaken to her foundations, the
Church, from her begging friars to her Pope, was arming to
fight for her privileges; but within the walls of Rome,
shattered by the assault of the German troops, the Holy
Empire and France were disputing the empire of the world.

116

In the North, the religious reform was serving as a stepping-stone for the new dynasty that was climbing to the Norwegian and Swedish thrones, and Muscovy, wrapped in centuries of isolation, had no part in these events—was not aware of them, or scarcely felt their distant consequences. Yet Time was labouring to reknot the bonds Time had himself untied. Western Europe was beginning, in some quarters at all events, to take an interest in the mysterious neighbour by whom she herself was scorned and disowned. As early as the fifteenth century, when the leaven which was to destroy her internal unity and harmony was already working within her, she had watched the rising of yet another peril above her horizon. Answering the tempest against the Papacy that roared within her boundaries, she had heard the mighty clamour of Islam, making ready to assault the Christian world. Stirred by the twofold threat, Rome and Vienna, Genoa and Venice, had looked about them for some new support, and had discovered Russia. Ever since that day, Italian diplomats and Levantine agents had been labouring to bridge the gulf. By his marriage with the daughter of the Paleologus, Ivan IV.'s grandfather had entered the family of the European Princes, under the auspices of the Holy See. In 1473, the Venetian Senate reminded the Muscovite monarch of his claim to the Byzantine inheritance. In 1480 and 1490, the direct heir, Andrew Paleologus, tried to strike a bargain as to his rights, at Moscow. He failed, and began to treat with Charles VIII. of France. But Rome was still supposed to hold the key of this treasure, and Rome, so men fancied, would dispose of it to secure a Russian army to fight the Turks. In 1484, Sixtus IV. found it necessary to reassure Casimir, King of Poland, who imagined his own rights, as an elder member of the Slav family, threatened.

Ivan III., who cared more for realities than for imaginary titles, sent one scornful refusal after another. Yet the matter of the Russian provinces, claimed alike by Muscovy and Poland, was dependent on the hypothesis of a great Slav empire, strengthened by the investiture of Rome. The new diplomatic combinations which arose in this sphere of rival influences and dominations themselves endued the Pan-Russian idea with body and strength.

Though the Grand Duke dismissed Andrew Paleologus to seek other buyers, he gave a far better reception to the Emperor's envoy, Von Turn. He avowed himself ready to make an alliance with Maximilian, with the eventual object of opposing Islam, but to settle historic accounts with his Polish neighbour, in the first place. Without waiting for any Papal bulls, he allowed his subjects to call him by the name of

Tsar, which corresponded, in the imagination of the orthodox, with the Imperial dignity and the claim to the inheritance of Byzantium. And to this, in 1483, he added, by his own authority, the title of Sovereign of all the Russias, which amounted to an assertion of his rights over Kiev and Vilna.

This autonomous solution of the great Oriental problem had been long since prepared. The south-western Slavs had been the first to perceive it. In the fourteenth century Douchan, a Servian, and Alexander, a Bulgarian, had both suggested it, when each dreamt a conquest of Constantinople, and began by proclaiming himself Emperor. A reference to the building of a new *tsargrad* (imperial city) at Tyrnov appears in the manuscripts of that date. But, as Monsieur Milioukov has justly observed, before the Russia of the sixteenth century could appropriate this programme of national greatness, she had to await an impulse that was to come from Europe, just as the Russia of the seventeenth century was to feel a similar external impetus before she could conceive and accept the reform of Peter the Great.

When Ivan III. died, in 1505, he left five sons, and divided his inheritance among them. But to Vassili, the eldest, he gave not one-third, according to precedent, but two-thirds—seventy-six towns and provinces, including the capital. Vassili had married, as his first wife, the daughter of a boïar, Salome-louriévna Sabourov. He had no children, and mourned the fact. ' The birds are happy !' he would say when he looked into a nest. The spells to which the barren wife had recourse produced no effect. A council of boïars, summoned in 1525, proposed another expedient, coinciding, no doubt, with the husband's secret desires. ' A barren fig-tree must be cast out of the field !' One councillor alone, the bearer of a name soon to win lustre in the camp of the aristocratic opposition, Simon Kourbski, dared raise his voice in defence of the sacred bond about to be broken, and his protest was supported by the members of the clergy who represented the reform party, Vassiane Patrikiév and Maximus the Greek. They were overruled. Salome was thrown into a cloister, and Vassili led Helen Glinski, the daughter of a Lithuanian refugee, to the altar. He was desperately in love with her, and the barrenness of his repudiated wife was probably a mere pretext. Since the Muscovite Sovereigns had given up taking their wives from foreign Courts, a habit had come in of opening a sort of beauty competition among the native ladies, from whom the master made his choice. Hundreds were brought together from every corner of the country. Now, on this occasion nothing of the kind seems to have been attempted.

A beautiful woman, who, thanks to her origin, had enjoyed

a comparatively superior education, Helen Glinski possessed
charms which Vassili could not have found in any Muscovite.
Her father, Vassili Lvovitch, had died when she was very
young, and she had grown up under the guardianship of her
uncle Michael, a former comrade-in-arms of Albert of Saxony
and the Emperor Maximilian, a wandering knight, whose
adventures had led him to Italy, where he had even become
a Catholic. Thus did Western Europe find her way back into
the Kremlin. According to Herberstein, Vassili went so far
as to shave off his beard to please his new partner, and this in
itself was almost a revolution.

This second marriage, called adulterous by the ' monks from
beyond the Volga,' did not promise, however, to be more
blessed by Heaven than the first. There was talk already of
a son born to Salome in her convent. But at last the prayers
of a more indulgent monk, Paphnucius Borovski—afterwards
declared a worker of miracles and canonized, as a reward for this
one—were granted. Helen brought the longed-for heir into
the world. Three years later, on October 15, 1533, she bore
a second son, George, and immediately afterwards she was left
a widow. Ivan III. had altered the succession, according to
which the throne, in former times, had passed to the dead
Sovereign's brothers. The regency, at all events, should have
been theirs. That Ivan left any other order seems uncertain.
But Helen, the scion of a race of adventurers, energetic and
ambitious, had a strong party behind her, and knew how to
use it so as to grasp power, and keep it.

She made a twofold blunder by refusing to share it with her
uncle, a gifted man, and giving the lion's share to her lover,
Prince Telepniév-Obolenski, a mere muddler. Trouble soon
began. Helen, having thrust her own uncle and one of
Vassili's brothers, George, into prison, found herself in difficulties with another brother-in-law, Andrew, who had received
Staritsa as his appanage, and avowed himself discontented
with his share. She reached the brink of civil war, and
only escaped it by laying an ambush into which the Prince
fell. He departed, in his turn, into one of those Muscovite
dungeons which so seldom yielded up their prey. Hunger and
the weight of the chains with which he was loaded hastened his
end, and his adherents, to the number of about thirty, garnished gibbets set at stated intervals along the road from
Moscow to Novgorod. Novgorod had seemed inclined to send
the vanquished man armed help.

Thus for several years Helen struggled on, forced, as well, to
hold her own against enemies beyond the border, Tartars and
Poles, who joined hands to take advantage of the weakness of
her Government. In 1538, her foes at home had recourse to

poison, it is thought, and Ivan was orphaned. Then the power fell into the hands of the boïars, and oligarchy was soon expressed in anarchy.

II.—THE GOVERNMENT OF THE BOÏARS.

Left to himself, Obolenski at once lost his footing in the tempest. Rivals whom the Regent had been able to hold in check now rushed upon an easy revenge. Above the ruins of a decimated party the Chouïski raised their heads. By their origin they stood very near the throne, and their pretensions aimed at something more than a mere temporary supremacy. They belonged, like Vassili and Ivan, to the line of Alexander Nevski, the elder branch of a family of which the reigning house was only a younger one, and the height to which their dreams of ambition soared may be conceived. Within a week they had got rid of the favourite, who disappeared into an *oubliette*, in which Ivan lost his natural guardian and even his foster-mother, Obolenski's sister, Agraféna, who shared her brother's fate. But Vassili Vassilévitch Chouïski and his cousin Andrew, who came out of prison at this juncture, found themselves face to face with another apparition. The opening of the dungeons had brought a whole army of competitors into the lists, and among them Prince Ivan Biélski, who had no intention of giving way to any other person. He advanced the claims of his own ancestor, Guédymin, as against those of the descendants of Rurik. His father, Feodor, had married a Princess of Riazan, niece of Ivan III. His brother Simon, molested by Helen, had fled, and found in Poland, in the Crimea, and even at Constantinople, something better than a refuge—an alliance that enabled him to claim his hereditary possessions, Biélsk and Riazan, annexed to the Muscovite Empire.

Thus, in the struggle which, from 1538 to 1543, filled Moscow with violence and carnage, and from which Ivan's own person and the integrity of his inheritance found no protection save in the antagonism of the rival families and their eagerness to destroy each other, the whole existence of the work accomplished by the younger branch of the Rurikovitchy was threatened. But the child had to pass through cruel trials. In their triumph, the Chouïski lost all moderation, sacked the Tsar's treasury, and made themselves absolute masters. Ivan Chouïski, who had become head of the family on the death of Vassili Vassilévitch, forgot all respect. ' In my presence,' wrote Ivan IV. at a later date ' he stretched out his booted feet on my father's bed.' And he remembered, too, that the victor of the hour, who had been covered by a shabby pelisse, ended by eating off gold plate. 'He certainly did not inherit that from his father. If he had, he would have begun by getting himself a better coat. And meanwhile I was suffering privations, lacking everything, even to food and clothing.' The young Sovereign suffered in his affections too. First his foster-mother had been taken from him, then, in 1543, he was deprived of his earliest friend, Feodor Siémiénovitch Vorontsov. This unhappy man, whom the Chouïski hunted into a room in the Kremlin, beat, and threatened with death, owed his bare life to the intervention of the Metropolitan ; but even this could not prevent him from being exiled to Kostroma. The Metropolitan throne itself, indeed, had to suffer attack. Whenever a *coup d'état* placed one family or the other in power, the holder of the see changed too. In 1539, the Biélski put Jehosaphat in the place of Daniel. In 1542, when the Chouïski got the upper hand and sent Ivan Biélski to Bielooziéro, the Metropolitan shared his disgrace. The provinces received no better treatment. Under the Chouïski's rule especially, barbarity and confusion were rife. Except at Novgorod, in which town they had supporters and favoured friends, their representatives, as the chroniclers tell us, behaved 'like wild beasts.' Everybody who could took to his heels, and the towns stood empty. The Italian architect Friasini, who had been summoned to Russia, and permanently established there by Vassili, escaped and got across the frontier just when he was being sent to Siebiéje to direct the construction of the fortifications there. He told the Bishop of Derpt the boïars were making everybody's life impossible. The Biélski were more humane, and likewise more intelligent. It was during their short tenure of power that the first charters—forerunners of the autonomous communal system—were granted. But none of these men had any idea of government save by an abuse of power.

While subjecting their country to a most intolerable tyranny, they were teaching its future master the most odious of lessons. Thanks to them, violence in every form took hold of the boy's feelings and imagination, and inspired him, body and soul. Violent he was to be, like them, growing up as he did in an atmosphere of perpetual battle, ready to give back blow for blow, desperately nervous, cruel, irritable. His earliest pleasures, shared with the companions chosen for him, were hideous, like everything about him. Seeing men tortured under his eyes, he tortured beasts till he should be able to do likewise. His great amusement was to throw dogs down from the top of one of the castle terraces and enjoy their anguish. He was given his way, he was even encouraged in it. The men's turn was soon to come.

It was a rash undertaking for the Chouïski and the Biélski, who brought the boy up in this fashion, to claim any lengthy control over an autocrat who would soon have a beard on his chin, and was already old enough to realize his own position. He beheld the very men who offended and ill-used him in private, who quarrelled over his patrimony, and used it, one after the other for, their own convenience, go back to their real rank when there was any official function—Court festivity or reception of a foreign Ambassador—bend lowly before his throne, become crawling slaves. He was soon to turn this lesson to account. In September, 1543, he had allowed himself to be parted from Vorontsov. In the December of that year, having previously put the docility of his dog-boys to the test, he had Andrew Chouïski carried off by them. The rogues obeyed, and even went beyond their orders, for they strangled the boïar, whom they had been told to hale to prison. Ivan held it well done, and everybody understood that Russia's master, at all events, if not her government, was changed.

The boïars he had spared went on governing in their own way, but they did not venture to cross their Sovereign, who, before Louis XIV., had, after his own fashion, spoken the words, *L'état, c'est moi!* He began to go about the streets now, thrashing the men he met, violating the women, and always applauded by those about him. Feodor Vorontsov, whom he had recalled from exile, was one of these ; but the master's favour was already veering towards more docile comrades, whose names and parentage shielded them less from his caprice.

Ivan preferred his dog-boys to members of the aristocracy, whom he was apt to suspect and dread as being fresh Chouïski. In May, 1546, while he was hunting near Kolomna, he found himself face to face with a troop of armed men who barred his way. They were the Novgorod musketeers, coming to complain of their governor. Ivan, who understood nothing about their business, ordered them to be put aside. There was a scuffle, in the course of which several shots were exchanged. The young Prince was not hurt, but he was very much frightened. His physical courage was always to fail him. In addition to a very probable hereditary predisposition, the terrors of his childhood had made him nervous in the extreme, his body shivered and his soul was troubled at the slightest alarm. He took to his heels, imagined a plot, and ordered an inquiry. A candidate for his favour, Vassili Zakharov, at that moment a plain *diak*, had no difficulty in obtaining a hearing for his accusation of Vorontsov and his family, already under suspicion and in semi-disgrace. The pupil at once went far beyond his teachers. The Terrible came upon the scene.

There was work for the executioner and his scaffold.   He was not to enjoy many idle hours in future.   Feodor Vorontsov and one of his cousins lost their heads.   Other presumed accomplices took their way into exile.

Zakharov may not have been the sole author of this catastrophe.   In the Sovereign's intimate surroundings a man had already appeared, whose character and career a whole school of history has delighted to idealize, associating therewith a brilliant period in the new reign, which, thanks to his influence, according to its view, was freed from bloody excess, and stuffed with noble effort and glorious exploits.   Alexis Adachev, a man of humble origin, who had been in the Sovereign's household since the year 1543, was borne on the Court registers as one of the officers of the bedchamber, 'makers of the bed.'   I shall endeavour, later, to define this man's character and the part he played.

Towards the end of this same year, 1546, Ivan was to affirm his emancipation in yet more decisive fashion.   On December 17 the news ran through Moscow that the Grand Duke had resolved to marry, and to marry a daughter of the soil.

III.—MARRIAGE AND CORONATION.

This resolution was probably not so sudden as it has generally been taken to have been.   As early as 1543 an embassy had been sent into Poland ; Feodor Ivanovitch Soukine and Istoma Stoianov, the envoys, were desired to let it be understood that the Prince was old enough to look about for a wife (Bantich-Kamiénski, *Correspondance Diplomatique, Lectures de la Société d'Histoire*, 1860, p. 72).   Other attempts of the same nature would appear to have been made, and it was only after many failures that Ivan's pride bowed to the necessity of an alliance that would not revive the tradition of Jaroslav.   He was resolved, at all events, to make up for his discomfiture to some extent.   The day after that on which his decision had been announced, a *Te Deum* was sung in the Cathedral of the Assumption, and after it, Ivan, calling his boïars together, announced that he intended to be crowned likewise, and this, not like his predecessors, as Grand Duke, but under the title of Tsar, to which they had hitherto made no formal claim.

Tsar, Emperor—the two titles were synonymous in the language of the country, though the first, indeed, had lost caste owing to the discredit brought on it, amidst the dismemberment of the Mongol power, by the crowd of Tartar princelets— some of them tributaries to Moscow, or mere heads of provinces in her pay—who had assumed it.   Yet the lords of ancient

Byzantium had borne it, too, and it was the Empire of the East that Ivan dreamt of raising up once more in the new capital of the Orthodox world. Church literature had long been labouring towards this resurrection. In all books written in the Slav tongue the word *tsar* was used indifferently to denote the Kings of Judæa, the rulers of Assyria, Egypt, and Babylon, the Emperors of Constantinople and of Rome. At the same time, by perpetual insinuation, by cunningly-suggested freaks of fancy, the illusion of an historical descent connecting the rulers of Moscow with these predecessors filled the readers' imaginations, and slowly permeated the national mind. Was not Muscovy the 'Sixth Empire' mentioned in the Apocalypse? And had not the house of Rurik, before the days of Sophia Paleologus, won a right to the inheritance of the *Porphyrogenetes*, to that of Constantine the Great, and even to that of the Roman Cæsars themselves? We have seen that for centuries the idea of a 'third Rome' had been floating like a dream in the Slavonic world, and perpetually seeking some more definite form. After the fall of the Slav Empires in Bulgaria and Servia, after the conquest of the Balkan Peninsula by the Turks, this dream was naturally driven northward. Cyprian the Bulgarian, sent in 1382 from Constantinople to Moscow to fill the Metropolitan see, brought with him the phraseology elaborated by Ephimus at Tyrnov, and found it was received by willing ears. Immediately after the fall of Constantinople, all those who had escaped the shipwreck of Southern Slavdom turned their final hopes in this direction. Pakhomii the Servian, in his turn, revealed a solemn recognition of the imperial title of the Moscow Sovereigns by the Emperor John Paleologus. Other writers set to work to bring the investiture into harmony with the sacred texts. They had already succeeded in applying these prophecies to Alexander of Bulgaria. It required less effort to transfer them from one Slav Prince to another. According to the Greek tradition, Ishmael was to be vanquished by a 'fair' people, and the word for 'fair' in Russian is *roussyii*. One of the best-known of the legends of Byzantine origin current among the Slav peoples—one which travelled westward in the German poem of Apollonius of Tyre, and the old French romances dealing with Oberon and Huon of Bordeaux, relates that the imperial Insignia of the *Porphyrogenetes* came from Babylon, whither the Eastern Emperor Leo had sent to fetch them. Other legends referred to the acquisition of these insignia by Vladimir Monomachus, or St. Vladimir. In the *Stépiénnaia Kniga* Macarius learnedly explains that Vladimir, when he was dying, confided this sacred treasure to his sixth son, George, so that he and his descendants might keep watch and ward over it till a Prince capable of making use of it should arise in Russia. As early as in the eleventh and twelfth centuries, on the other hand, Slav genealogists had contrived to trace the descent of the Bulgarian Assanids from an illustrious Roman house, and in the fourteenth they likewise discovered a relationship between the Servian Nemanitch and the Emperor Constantine—nay, even with Augustus himself. Thus, when Macarius introduced a *Prouss*, brother of Augustus, whose descendant Rurik was supposed to be, into his life of St. Olga, a Russian Princess, he was only following former precedents.

The title now claimed by the son of Vassili was all this: a whole world of myths and symbols, of glorious memories and ambitious dreams, made flesh in living and tangible reality.

The coronation took place on January 16, 1547, and nothing which might heighten its glories was forgotten. In presence of a mighty concourse, amidst the joyous pealing of bells and all the mustered pomp of Church and Throne, Bishops, priests, and monks prayed God to grant the new Tsar the light of justice and of truth, while all around him his boïars scattered handfuls of gold pieces, emblems of the prosperity which was his promised lot. Yet the heir of the Greek and Roman Emperors did not venture to make known his pretensions to the foreign Sovereigns. He knew both his father and his grandfather had met with a rebuff. Vassili had succeeded, in 1514, in slipping the title of Cæsar into a treaty with the Emperor Maximilian. But Vienna, disowning her own plenipotentiary, Snitzpanner, had refused to sign until the text was altered. Poland, too, was irreconcilable as to this matter. Some of the small German States and the Patriarch of Constantinople were the only powers that showed any disposition to oblige, now they themselves offered the sole hope of dignity left to the professors of the Orthodox faith. And even in this quarter Ivan thought it well to delay his application till the morrow of his greatest victories in the year 1561, and offered with it, then, a liberal donation. He met with very moderate success. The Patriarch Jehosaphat did indeed acknowledge the son of Vassili as Tsar, and as the descendant of Princess Anne, the Emperor Basil's sister. He even went so far as to offer, superfluously, to renew the coronation ceremony by the intervention of a Metropolitan despatched for that purpose. But out of the thirty-seven signatures which adorned the charter sent from Constantinople to Moscow, five-and-thirty were later to be recognised as forgeries (Pierling, ' Russia and the Holy See,' i. 319 ; Milioukov, ' Essays on the History of Russian Culture,' iii. 71, founded on Regel, *Analecta Byzantino Rossica*, 1891).

Even the Orthodox Church held aloof, though the Patriarchs
of Alexandria and Antioch vied with each other in their zealous
acceptance of the accomplished fact, and the Patriarch of
Jerusalem went still farther, and proclaimed the new Tsar
'the head of Christendom.' The great body of the Eastern
clergy refused to follow this lead, and the *Tsarate* was fain to
enter this community, wherein it claimed the highest place of
all, by a low-browed door, and to stumble on the threshold.
But the Muscovite people knew naught of these details.   In
the poetry of the *bylines*, wherein facts and dates were hope-
lessly confused, the national pride and the popular fancy
worked in unison, casting a veil of fascinating fiction over
humble beginnings and early discomfitures.   In these the bearer
of the Imperial insignia, passing from Babylon to Constantinople, where he found the Empire laid in ruins and the Orthodox faith endangered, travelled from the shores of the Bosphorus
to the banks of the Volga, never halting till he reached the
camp before Kazan, and there fell in with the true Defender
of the Church, the conqueror of Islam.   On the panels of the
symbolic throne still shown in the Cathedral of the Assumption,
the native artists spent their skill on representations of other
and similar myths, and, within the limits of his huge dominions
at all events, Ivan felt himself girdled by a radiance of power
and glory such as no ancestor of his had ever known.

His marriage was to bring him a happiness such as few of
them, we may be sure, had tasted, either.   The bride had
been chosen, this time, according to the accepted rule.   All the
marriageable girls in the Empire belonging to the class of the
'men who serve' had been ordered to repair to Moscow.   A
huge building containing many rooms, each with twelve beds
in it, had been prepared for their reception.   On the occasion of Vassili's first marriage, 500 beauties, according to
Francesco da Collo, or 1,500, according to Herberstein,
had thus been brought together.   These figures probably
apply to two successive choices out of the general mass of
competitors, and a preliminary selection had no doubt been
made in the various provinces.   At Byzantium, where the
same practice was in vogue, the provincial governors received
detailed instructions for the purpose, with directions as to the
height and other qualifications required.   When the seraglio
had received all its inmates, the Sovereign, accompanied by
one man, chosen among his oldest courtiers, took his way
there.   He walked through all the rooms, and presented each
fair lady with a kerchief embroidered with gold and gems,
which he threw upon her bosom.   His choice once made,
gifts were bestowed on the companions of the bride, and they
were sent back to their own homes.

After this fashion, in the year 1547, the Tsar's choice fell on Anastasia, the fatherless daughter of Iouriévitch Zakharine-Kochkine, of an ancient boïar family, which, amidst the ruin of the princely families, had contrived, thanks to an avoidance of those perilous rivalries from which the young Sovereign had suffered so bitterly, to retain its place close to the throne. It is not impossible, indeed, that even on this occasion the customary competition was a mere matter of form. The Zakharine-Kochkine were favourites of Fortune. Like the Chérémétiev, the Kolytchev, and the Kobyline, they were said to be the descendants of a certain Andrew Kobyla, a Prussian fugitive, so the chroniclers assert. But the national vanity, at a later date, turned 'Prussia' into 'Novgorod'—there was a quarter of that city the denizens of which were commonly called Prussians. Kobyla's Slav origin cannot be contested. His very name proves it. *Kobyla* stands for 'mare' both in Russian and Polish, and it is a well-known fact that the present capital of the Germanic nation stands on Slav soil.

We have no details concerning Ivan's marriage, but those given in the preceding chapter of this work are applicable to the occasion. The young Tsar was as much in love with his wife as his father had been before him, and long years afterwards he was to call up, with bitter regret, the joys, all too soon cut down, of a union in which he seems to have found every satisfaction and pleasure known to body, heart, and mind. But his honeymoon was soon and cruelly disturbed. He was married on February 3, 1547. Less than three months after that date, a whole quarter of his capital was de stroyed by fire. Ivan was torn from the sweet peace in which he had seemed to revel, and which those about him had rejoicingly accepted as the guerdon of a happier future. The fair and gracious Anastasia was already looked on as the good angel destined to dispel the Sovereign's fits of fury, and insure his subjects' peace. But this was but a dream, and it may well be, in a country which is the home of legend, that an influence the visible effects of which are not attributable to any permanent cause was somewhat magnified. Ivan's irritable nature, which had slumbered for a time, woke suddenly to life. When the inhabitants of Pskov came, in their turn, on June 30, 1547, to make a complaint against their governor, the Tsar gave them a worse reception than that he had bestowed on their fellows of Novgorod. Returning to the cruel pastime of his boyish days, he poured lighted brandy all over them, and then, having had them stripped, would have proceeded, no doubt, to put them to death, had not a lucky diversion turned his mind from this particular form of entertainment.

The scene had taken place in the village of Ostrovka, close to the capital, and just at this crisis a messenger arrived bearing bad news : the great bell of the Kremlin had fallen down. It was a gloomy portent, the presage, according to the spirit of those days, of other and more terrible catastrophes.· And this time, indeed, the omen was to come true, amidst events destined to bring fresh characters on the scene, and change the face of the lately-opened reign. Ivan forgot all about his victims. Calling for a horse, he galloped to the scene of the accident.

IV.—Sylvester and Adachev.

Once again, on June 21, fire devoured Moscow, and this time its ravages exceeded anything ever seen within the memory of man. The Kremlin itself suffered. The cupola of the Cathedral of the Assumption, the Tsar's palace and the Metropolitan's, the treasury, the arsenal, two monasteries, and several churches, with all the wealth within them, were consumed by the flames. The Metropolitan Macarius was nearly suffocated, tumbled down in his flight, and hurt himself severely. Seventeen hundred victims, men, women, and children, were burnt alive. Every shop in the mercantile quarter was destroyed. Ivan was left without a roof over his head. He took refuge in the village of Vorobiévo, on that 'mountain of the sparrows' whence Napoleon was to catch his first glimpse of the city which was to be the tomb of his glory, and there the Tsar held a council. His confessor, Feodor Barmine, talked about witchcraft, to which, according to him, the disaster was due. In this connection, indeed, there was a legend. The sorcerers were supposed to take human hearts, torn out of corpses, to dip them in a pail of water, and then kindle the fire by watering the streets with the contents of the pail. A few boïars backed the accusation, and the search for the culprits began. Swayed by a treacherous suggestion, the crowd gathered on a Sunday, some few days later, before the blackened ruins of the cathedral, mentioned names. Helen's regency had left some bitter grudges behind it. Undying hate pursued her mother and her brothers. Witnesses were found who had seen them drench the streets and walls with the maleficent liquid. The Tsar's uncle, Prince Michael Vassilévitch Glinski, was living with his mother on a distant property near Rjevo, but his brother George was close at hand. He sought refuge in the very church the firing of which was laid at his door. The mob pursued him inside it, dragged his corpse to the spot where condemned criminals were executed, hunted his servants. Three days later the murderers pre-

sented themselves at Vorobiévo, clamouring for fresh victims.
Andrew Chouïski's relations and adherents, who had been
exiled after his execution, and subsequently recalled and
restored to the Sovereign's household and favour, urged
him on to bloody reprisals.

But Ivan was soon to reveal himself. It was a tragic and
decisive hour. If the son of Vassili had yielded to this criminal
pressure he would have entered on a course which would have
made his only mark on history a mark of blood. To yield
was not in his nature. A merciless judge he was—too merciless very often—but he was always to hold full mastery over
his own judicial acts. Whatever he thought of the accusation—and at his age, especially, and superstitious as he was,
like all his contemporaries, he may very well have thought it
plausible—accusers who were bold enough to encroach on his
own rights by dictating or even forestalling his decisions struck
him, no doubt, as being more guilty than any incendiary,
genuine or supposed. He rose up, showed himself as he was,
established his reputation. Behind the tyrant the Russians
knew already, they perceived the Sovereign they were about
to know. Michael Glinski, who had fled towards the Lithuanian frontier, had been caught by one of the Chouïski, Peter
by name. Ivan had set him free, and he would not have the
mother touched. The executioner had work to do, but the
heads he took off belonged to the abettors of disturbance, who
had hoped to build their own fortunes, or gratify their own
resentments, on the ashes of the ruined capital.

Ivan's earliest biographer, Kourbski, has introduced an
episode into his history of these events which must have misled
the imagination of many of his successors. Just when Ivan
was in full dispute with the half-tipsy murderers, a man, an
unknown priest, whose aspect resembled that given, in local
iconography, to prophets, appeared in the Tsar's presence. His
finger was uplifted, his expression at once threatening and
inspired. With all the authority of a Divine messenger, we
are told, and quoting many a Scripture text, he boldly asserted
that what was happening was a manifest sign of God's wrath.
He is even declared to have supported his claim by revelations
and miracles. This last feature would suffice to edify us as
to the nature of the story, even if we did not possess other
information enabling us to reconstitute the historical truth.
Sylvester, the author of the *Domostroï*, to whom Kourbski
has chosen to attribute this curious intervention, could not
have been a stranger to Ivan, seeing that for several years he
had served the Church of the Assumption, the priest or proto-
pope of which was, by virtue of his position, the Sovereign's
own confessor. He was on friendly terms with Prince Vladimir

9

Andréiévitch, one of the Tsar's uncles, for whom he had already successfully interceded in 1541, and thus his influence, though still circumscribed within the narrow limits imposed by the humble priest's worldly position and intellectual quality, was evidently of much older standing, and had been exercised in a far more natural manner.

Kourbski, no doubt, remembered Nathan's coming into the presence of David; but there was nothing prophetic about the language of the *Domostroï*. A moment was certainly approaching at which, without any question of miraculous intervention, other and quite as humble persons in the Tsar's household were to rise to foremost rank. Ivan, as he realized the necessity for a change in his methods of government, was to look about for new men to fit new positions. Unconsciously, we may be sure, he was to imitate Louis XI. ' Distrusting, and not without good cause, highly-placed men, and honest men, he was fain to discover in the unknown herd some bold fellow or other—one of those who, without having learnt anything, succeed by their own instinct.'

Like that other terrible monarch, and in closely analogous circumstances, Ivan, too, was ' to love none but those he made himself, and who, but for him, would have been nothing at all ' (Michelet, *Histoire de France*, vii. 262). Nothing is more probable than that the catastrophe of 1547 may have led up to this moment, and that Sylvester may have risen into prominence amidst the troubles which attended it. But nothing, on the other hand, proves that the influence over his young Sovereign ascribed to him by Kourbski and other historians was acquired at that particular juncture.

And, further, was he a man whose gifts would ever have enabled him to enact such a part in connection with a man of Ivan's calibre ? The *Domostroï* does not give us the idea of a very far-seeing politician, nor a moral teacher of a particularly high order. Apart from this book, the only three epistles from the pen of its author preserved to us are mere twaddle and nonsense. And that addressed to Ivan—its authenticity, indeed, is doubtful—is by no means the least foolish of the three. Its only injunctions as regards morals are connected with the avoidance of the sin of sodomy. But as an inculcator of virtue, Ivan already possessed Macarius. Sylvester, much inferior to this prelate in acquirements, and with an intellectual outlook far below that of the chosen circle gathered around Maximus the Greek, neither embodied nor represented anything striking or seductive. Subsequent to the year 1547 he is said to have performed the duties of a teacher—duties of a kind calculated to produce some impression on his young master's mind. It

had become necessary to redecorate the rooms of the Grand
Duke's ruined palace.   In every country and at every period,
mural paintings have been a faithful expression of the feeling
of the century producing them.   In Russia, during the sixteenth
century, no difference existed, in this respect, between secular
and religious edifices.   In every building, the style and subjects
of the decoration were almost identical, and chiefly drawn
from Scripture or from ecclesiastical tradition.   Sylvester
seems to have been appointed to overlook the work of the
artists at the Kremlin.   The paintings then executed were
preserved till the end of the seventeenth century, and Monsieur
Zabiéline ('Private Life of the Tsars,' p. 149) has been able
to give us an exact account of them.   The only conclusion
at all flattering to the pope to be drawn therefrom is his possession of certain courtly aptitudes already brought into relief
in the *Domostroï*.   Whether as a repentant sinner or—and
this more especially—as a triumphant conqueror, as Joshua
entering a vanquished city or Solomon pouring forth a flood
of beneficent wisdom, Ivan's is the figure perpetually limned
in the huge apotheosis that typified and idealized all the
great facts and glories of his reign.   And though the young
Sovereign may have found some means to edification in these
pictures, he must have discovered still more, and more per-
suasive, temptations to pride, while the scenes of carnage
connected with the triumphs of the Biblical conqueror, the
'cutting off of every living soul' represented on the broken
walls of these ravaged Jerichoes, were not calculated to soften
the inherent ferocity of his instincts.

Sylvester's apologists have further credited him with a
somewhat novel piece of daring, to which the work of the
unknown artists he is said to have inspired bears witness.   The
figure of a woman 'with her sleeves dropped as if she was
dancing' close beside the hieratic presentment of the Christ,
gave rise to scandal and to an ecclesiastical prosecution.   But
Macarius himself appeared as the champion of art, and defended the artist's right thus to symbolize debauchery amidst
the other vices confounded and put to shame by the word of
the Divine Master.   The introduction of a certain flow of
innovation into the plastic art of Russia unquestionably dates
from this epoch, and this was due to a current of foreign
influences with which Sylvester certainly had nothing to do.
In two *ikons* simultaneously painted by Pskovian artists for
the Church of the Annunciation, Rovinski has recognised an
undoubted imitation of Cimabue and Perugino.

But the reforming period of Ivan's reign only began with the
convocation of an assembly of which the date and precise
nature cannot, so far, be clearly settled, but which certainly did

not meet till at least two years after the disaster of 1547. At that moment, too, Alexis Adachev appears upon the scene, and joins hands with Sylvester. Yet during the whole course of this assembly, it is Macarius who plays the leading part. Sylvester hardly appears at all, and it is only thanks to a false and subsequent interpretation of the information at disposal that a part, which closer observation convinces us neither was capable of playing, has been ascribed to the two comrades. Round Adachev particularly a legend has grown up, so wide and full that in most historians' eyes the Terrible himself has been almost eclipsed by his own servant. Deceived by the self-interested assertions of a political ally—I refer to Kourbski—and by the Sovereign's own, they have, as it were, put the henchman in his master's place ; they have made him think and act instead of his lord, and, taking him in conjunction with Sylvester, they have imagined a bicephalous government, which they suppose to have endowed Russia, for the space of ten years, with every imaginable kind of prosperity.

I shall endeavour, further on, to set forth the elements of a very different state of matters, and give men and things their proper values. Kourbski's testimony, like that of the monarch himself, was borne after the two favourites had fallen. At that moment Kourbski, himself a voluntary exile, was endeavouring to avenge his own disappointed ambition by means of more or less ingenious inventions, and Ivan was always a proficient in that sort of fiction which enabled him to divest himself of his personal responsibility by casting it on his enemies. During the struggle into which the Sovereign's reforming policy was soon to draw him, and in which he was doomed to strive till the close of his long and stormy career, it would be difficult indeed to discover the party at the head of which the pope and his comrade put themselves, or which they even joined. Parvenus, both of them, they have been taken to represent the new blood brought in by Ivan to oppose the old boïar oligarchy. But to this oligarchy Kourbski belonged heart and soul, and he was the friend and accomplice of Sylvester and Adachev. Other contradictions, just as inexplicable, can only be avoided by taking the two partners for what they were—mere dummies. Ivan used them against the boïars, but they preferred to use the boïars, and even to make common cause with those they used. Then Ivan crushed them, and called other utility actors to his aid. Let us come to facts.

V.—The First Assembly : Russian Parliamentarianism.

In 1547, Ivan had held his own against the mob and the mob-leaders who had egged him on to crime. He had done justice, and several heads had fallen. But after that time, as before it, the boïars held the reins of government, and the tumult of which Moscow had been the scene was as nothing compared with the more permanent disturbances which continued to torture and mangle the whole country. Two or three more years elapsed before Ivan could persuade himself that this intolerable system must be suppressed, or that he himself was strong enough to suppress it. It was in 1549 or 1550—this latter date seems the most probable—that he finally made up his mind. At that time, according to the chroniclers, he convoked an assembly of all classes from every province, at Moscow. The sitting and the palaver were held in the open air, on the Red Square in front of the Kremlin. The Tsar spoke first, and brought his accusation against his untrustworthy boïars. He set forth a long list of their misdeeds, and announced that they were about to come to an end, and to be replaced by ' the triumph of virtue—and of love.' In conclusion, he turned towards the Metropolitan : ' I beseech thee, holy master, to be my help and mainstay in this work, which, as I know, obtains thy favour. Thou knowest that when my father died I was but four years old. My other kinsmen took no care of me, and my powerful boïars thought of nothing but abusing their own strength . . . and while they multiplied their rapines and their excesses, I, because of my youth, was deaf and dumb. They ruled as masters. Oh, peculators, depredators, and dishonest judges, how will you answer now for the blood and the tears that have been shed through you ? My hands are clean from that blood ! But you, make you ready for the chastisement you have deserved !' Then, bowing on every side, the Sovereign begged his audience to forget ' for a space ' the misdeeds from which they might have suffered, because ' it was not possible to repair them all.' But thenceforward he himself, as far as might be, would be their judge and their defender.

That very day Adachev was raised to the rank of okolnitchyï. and appointed to attend to all petitions. Ivan ordered him to look with most particular care into those presented by the humblest of his subjects, and to have no fear of the resentment of the great lords, ' the monopolizers of the great posts, and the oppressors of the poor and weak.'

This story requires some explanation. Ivan was always a great lover of scenic effect, and though he may not have

indulged to the very letter in the lyric effusions the chroniclers
have put into his mouth, and of which he himself has given
us several versions, he may very well have discoursed on the
Red Square in similar terms and under similar circumstances,
for he was always a great talker.   But what was the object
of the scenic effect and of his speech ?   In the young
monarch's appearance before his assembled subjects the Slavo-
philes hail a striking example, an ideal relationship between
the ruler and the ruled—a relationship rooted in love, a
characteristic trait of the Slav race, the only one capable of
conceiving such a basis.   Many historians, on the other hand,
have taken the whole thing to be an appeal to the popular
imagination against the boïar domination.   These are all
fancies.

We have no sure information as to the composition of the
assembly of 1550, but if we judge by those convoked on later
occasions, the representation of the popular element in it
seems more than doubtful.   We have nothing to prove that
the representative principle existed in it in any form or to
any extent whatever.   A passage in the chronicle known as
the ' Chronicle of Khrouchtchov,' a manuscript of doubtful
origin preserved in the archives of the Moscow Foreign Office,
has been interpreted in this sense.   This work, like the ' Collection ' by Macarius, to which I have already referred, is a
' book of degrees ' (Stépiénnaia Kniga), a form of compilation
very usual at that period.   But at the very place in question,
Monsieur Platonov (' Studies of Russian History,' 1903, p. 223)
has detected an interpolation, probably dating from the second
half of the seventeenth century, and which was most likely
made under the influence of ideas which had only then come
into vogue.   It should be taken, therefore, to reflect the constitution of assemblies convened at a much later date, and
under quite different conditions, by Ivan's successors.   As to
the assembly of 1550, Ivan himself has given us a piece of
information which tends in quite a contrary direction.   Speaking at a conciliable called in the following year, and referring
to his speech on the Red Square, he gives us a glimpse of the
reality hidden by a deceptive mise-en-scène and under the
flowers of a fallacious rhetoric.   At Moscow, people were
very easily satisfied with words, or rather some people there
had a marvellous faculty for using coin of this sort in payment of certain intricate scores.   No other race ever had so
pronounced a taste for face values, fiction, circumlocution ;
and this time, again, Ivan took good care not to speak quite
clearly.   ' I have urged,' he said, ' all my boïars, officials,
and provincial governors to reconcile themselves with all the
Christians in the Empire.'   If we compare and condense the

texts we arrive at a plausible conjecture : the assembly of 1550 was no more than a gathering of officials, an incident in the administrative life of that system the features of which I have already sketched, and the nature of which Ivan never dreamt of altering.

He had so little thought, at this juncture, of appealing to his people against his boïars—that is, against his officials— that, though he abused them roundly, his reproaches were addressed to themselves, and to themselves only. His discourse on the Red Square was an apostrophe *ad homines*, combined with a use of the third person. What could he have made out of the people ? And how would he have got hold of it, to begin with—I mean men of that class who would have been capable of understanding anything about problems of this nature ? And still less could he have found men fit to make any better hand of the work the others had done so ill.

But what was he driving at, then ? At this : Without laying his hand on the system of ' service ' nor on the *sloojilyié lioodi*, who had been abusing it so long and so hideously, Ivan hoped to improve the working of the machine by taking the command of the machinery into his own hands, and confiding it, in part, to creatures chosen by himself. Hence his announcement that he would do justice in his own person, and hence his appeal to Adachev's services. So much for the future. For the past, as ' everything could not be repaired,' it was necessary to pass a wet sponge over the face of an overcrowded slate. Thousands of complaints were waiting their turn, piles of papers were accumulating, in the hope of a settlement which, by the ordinary methods of the slowest and most complicated procedure ever known, was utterly impossible. Wherefore ' the triumph of virtue and of love,' like the ' reconciliation of all the Christians in the Empire,' simply meant, in the phraseology of that period, the substitution of a friendly arrangement for that interminable procedure. A tolerably short interval had been assigned for this purpose, no doubt, for in 1551 Ivan, found himself in a position to announce that the settlement of all the matters in suspense had been carried through.

The convoking of popular assemblies, in the strict meaning of that term, did not enter into the plan of the political edifice which Ivan had inherited, and the destruction of which he by no means contemplated, except in so far as to alter its internal arrangements at a future date, and thus adapt it to more modern needs. There was no place here for any Parliamentary institution, and so little idea was there of its introduction that the representatives of the aristocratic oligarchy, with Kourbski at their head, made not the slightest objection to the principle of periodical meetings, modelled on that of 1550, which they appear to have taken as a purely administrative and judicial expedient, and nothing more. Some of them, such as the author of a political pamphlet much talked of at that time, and to which I shall make further reference—'The Conversation of the Wonder-workers of Valaam'—even suggested the permanent institution of this particular form of council.

Yet there was no fresh attempt at convocation until 1566, and then, as before, it was for one special object—to look into the disputes with Poland. The official list of the members of this second assembly has come down to us. It comprises thirty-two members of the upper clergy, two hundred and fifty-eight boïars or sons of boïars, officials of various ranks, nine landed proprietors, fifty-three Moscow merchants, and twenty-three belonging to Smolensk, or who had business interests there, called by the generic title of *smolianié*. There is no trace as yet of any popular element. It is a council of 'men who serve,' with whom some men of special competence are associated, because the national relations with Poland affect trade, and more particularly those engaged in the frontier trade. There is no sign, either, of any return to the traditions of the ancient *viétchié* nor of any appeal to those of the representative assemblies of the West. It was probably the *osviastchennyï sobor*, the *conciliable* or council of the high ecclesiastical dignitaries, summoned regularly, since the most remote times, to discuss affairs affecting the Church and even the State, which suggested the idea, and provided the type of these other meetings, which ultimately received an analogous title, *ziémskiié sobory*—land *conciliables* or councils—in the administrative sense now conferred on that appellation. The correct meaning of the word *sobor* is *conciliable*.

The ancient *viétchié* were very unlike these. Neither the political nor the social organization of the Empire could supply any material for a process similar to that which, amongst other Slav races, and among the Germanic peoples, evolved representative institutions out of the primitive national assemblies. All the intermediate forms—the 'diets of nobles,' *magna consilia, Herrentage*—were lacking here. The *ziémskiié sobor*, like the *boïarskaïa douma*, was the simple outcome of the habit, common to all Russian Princes, of calling their comrades, whom they afterwards turned into their 'servants,' into council. With the extension of the administrative service, a necessity for representation arose. It was not possible to summon all the *sloojilyié loodi* to Moscow. And, on the other hand, when the Government thought proper to appeal to the elective system for the bestowal of certain functions, the persons thus elected found themselves in possession of a sort of representative authority. It became the established custom, for certain deliberative purposes and the settlement of certain reckonings, to summon to the capital, at arbitrary intervals of time, a selection of officials, some of whom held an electoral mandate, not as members of an assembly, but as performers of their administrative functions. The admission to this assembly depended on a different system. In what did this consist ? Was the choice made by election, and, if so, what form did that election take ? We know nothing of all this. However it may have been, the officials summoned to the assembly only appeared as, and because they were, *officials*. They did not represent social, they represented administrative, interests. They raised their voices, not as the advocates of certain corporate groups, but as Government organs, called to furnish information to the central administration, and take their orders from it. Here was all that underlay the fictitious appearance of this deliberative assembly, from which the Government occasionally made believe to take advice, but to which, in sober truth, it simply gave its orders.

Of any such thing as political rights pertaining to these phantom representatives, or to those who elected them—in spite of the wily endeavours of the Muscovite policy to cultivate an illusion, favoured by the uncertain form to which the institution was always restricted—there never was a question. As a matter of fact, once more, there is no trace of any legislative work accomplished by any of these assemblies nor even of any spontaneous decision come to by them. The nomad character of the first Russian settlements had prevented any development of corporative elements, or the formation of any strongly-constituted classes. The task of grouping the scattered forces of society had thus fallen to the central power, which, in performing it, had naturally applied itself more to imposing duties on the associations it called into being than to acknowledging that they possessed rights of their own. As a consequence, the political edifice, both in its general structure and as to its inner details, was entirely founded on the principle of ' dues,' the *tiaglo ;* and even the introduction of the elective system into this architecture did not modify its fundamental features. In the absence of any sufficiently developed social interests, or any adequate consciousness of them, electors and elected saw nothing in this concession beyond another burden to be added to its predecessors. Even if it possessed an elective basis, which is by no means clearly proved, the institution of the *ziémskiié sobory*—the result of a State need, and not a victory won by the emancipated forces of freedom ; the outcome of a Government extemporization, and not of the long travail of a nation's life, a superstructure mechanically adjusted on the exterior of a huge archaic building, and not the fruit of any internal development at all—was no more than an incident and an ephemeral phenomenon in the country's history. Between 1550 and 1653, sixteen of these assemblies were called, and the memories and regrets left by the last are neither very sharp nor over deep. As an arbitrary act on the part of the only real power had called them into life, so did another arbitrary act send them back into the darkness, and neither their existence nor their exit made much mark upon the destinies of the Russian race. If the constitutional inaptitude of this particular branch of the Slav family for the free forms of political existence, acknowledged by some historians, be an antiphrasis, and its vocation for perpetual absolutism a blasphemy, it is quite certain that no serious attempt at a Parliamentary system was appropriate to the shadow of the Kremlin in the sixteenth century.

The whole historical importance of the assembly of 1550 lies in the troubles which paved the way to the expedient. and in the other and more efficacious measures of which it was the starting-point. The Tsar had proved that he realized the painful sores from which the body of society was suffering. He had stripped them boldly. He was about to show his anxiety to do more than dress them with the panacea thus supplied. The following year was to inaugurate the era of reform.

CHAPTER II

THE FIRST REFORMS

I.—THE REFORMING CURRENTS. II.—THE NEW CODE. III.—THE REORGANIZATION OF THE 'SERVICE.' IV.—THE RELIGIOUS REFORM.

I.—THE REFORMING CURRENTS.

FROM the heart of the intelligent class—a very small one, numerically speaking, in the days of Ivan's rule, but eager, nevertheless, to study certain political and social problems— and out of the focus formed by the men who thought and discussed and wrote, a twofold current of reform passed at this moment, converging, in spite of its exceedingly diverse points of departure, on analogous, if not identical, objects. In both cases the ideas and calculations advanced dealt with the burning question of the day; that of the possession of the land. My readers are already acquainted with the position assumed, as to this delicate matter, by Nil Sorski and Vassiane Patrikiév. Towards 1550, a pamphlet, couched in a form so strange as occasionally to render the author's thoughts unintelligible, but full of a striking fervour of expression, gave a fresh impulse to the views of the *Niéstia-jatiéli* (non-acquirers). The pamphleteer borrows his characters—the wonder-workers of Valaam, Sergius and Hermann—from the world of fiction. His own personality is wrapped in mystery. Some people have chosen to identify him with Patrikiév, but the author's denunciations of the excess of wealth accumulated in the hands of the ' black ' clergy, and the abuses resulting therefrom, are too vehemently irreverent to proceed from a wearer of the *klobouk*. There is something monkish, indeed, about the curious artlessness of his political ideas ; the permanent assembly he longs to see established is to apply its chief anxiety and care to insuring the strict keeping of fasts ! But would Patrikiév, monk as he was, have ventured to claim, as the sole property of the laity, the place his brother priests had usurped in the Sovereign's councils ? The lot of the cenobite, according to the author of this pamphlet, is poverty and prayer. Patrikiév's ambitions tended in quite a different direction.

The problem thus set was widening its borders, threatening other joint interests, inciting other claims. If the excessive expansion of monastic property was an evil, were not the distributions of land, now so numerous, to the ' men who serve,' and the gradual monopoly of the soil by the privileged class, whose conduct Ivan had just branded with dishonour, evils too ? And behold, a second pamphlet, published under the form of an epistle or petition to the Tsar, from Ivan or Ivachka Peresviétov—whether this was the author's real name or a pseudonym has never been thoroughly settled—formulated an accusation against this rival class of landholders. By their spells and their intrigues they were said to have won the Sovereign's heart, and imposed their will on him in every particular. Enriched beyond all measure, as much so as the monks, by their expropriation and merciless squeezing of the dispossessed husbandmen, they lived in idleness and debauchery. As cowardly as they were greedy, they jeopardized the safety of the Tsar's armies in time of war, and in time of peace they levied a huge tithe on the taxes extorted from his subjects, and became the responsible agents of all the public woes.

But what then ? The secularization of the monastic properties had been an item in the Muscovite policy for many years. Ivan III. had turned his attention to the matter, and made some slight attempts in that direction. How did Ivacha

Peresviétov propose to solve the other portion of the problem ? By an equally radical measure : by the suppression of the *kormlénié*, by returning all the lands allotted to the *sloojilyié-loodi* to the State, and the substitution, for this mode of reward, of a money payment, which would insure obedient officials to the Sovereign, restore the land to its natural uses and legitimate owners, and relieve the mass of the people from the pressure of an unendurable tyranny.

From the literary point of view, the two pamphlets would seem to possess some bond of relationship. The imaginary characters in the first are replaced, in the second, by a Palatine of Wallachia, with whom the author has made a sojourn. The style of both is equally uncouth. But enigmatic as is the form of the work, with its strange circumlocutions, uncertain and obscure as all the phraseology of the period, never, in any country, was a more revolutionary process of reform suggested. The modern Nihilism of Russia can claim ancient parentage! In those days, as in ours, the space that parted theory from practice was wide. The question here was nothing less than a thorough reconstruction of the edifice, social and political. But the two programmes of the reformers, though they affected two different classes of land tenures, did not clash, as has been supposed. They were in a very natural agreement, and one supplied what the other lacked. They constituted two expressions of one and the same solution, revolutionary and democratic.

What was the state of Ivan's mind ? How did he stand as to this twofold current of thought ? That he was disposed, as far as Church property was concerned, to follow in his forefather's footsteps, we cannot doubt. On this point, through every vicissitude, from reign to reign, even from dynasty to dynasty, the Muscovite policy was never to be changed. But the grandson, like his grandfather, had to reckon with an opposition which nothing but the long-drawn complicity of time could wear down and overcome. The reorganization of the lay tenure was more difficult still. When Ivacha Peresviétov— I care not whence he came or what the source of his inspiration may have been—spoke such bold words, he must have felt a strong hand behind him. Parts of his pamphlet, indeed, seem no more than an echo of the young Tsar's speech on the Red Square. When we take him to have been a semi-official writer, we are probably not far from the truth. But unworthy as the ' men who served,' whom he would have dispossessed and reduced to their legitimate portion, may have been, and severely as the Sovereign might be resolved to treat them, they constituted the army and the administration, the very pillars of the temple ! How were they to be replaced ? Ivan meant to do it. But while he was finding thousands of Alexis Adachevs, he had to live ; and for that purpose it would be better, instead of modifying the political status of the ' men who served ' to their detriment, to think of insuring them a livelihood. Though no reform had shaken their legal position as yet, the privileges of the *sloojilyié*, now so bitterly attacked, had been severely damaged already. To the more or less just complaints brought against them they could reply with others, quite as legitimate. If they applied excessive pressure to the peasants who tilled the soil, the peasants themselves, by forsaking the cultivated areas, were ruining their masters. The Government, having begun by welcoming and favouring the agricultural exodus, which had so powerfully aided the process of colonization, now perceived this exodus to be a source of immediate peril, far more to be dreaded than the abuse of power, or even the insubordination, rife amongst its *kormlénchtchiki*. The executioner could always deal with insubordination. But supposing the material to fill the ranks of the 'service' were to fail ? Supposing the holders of the *pomiéstia*, already so poorly supported by their scanty allotments, came short of food ? The State would find itself disabled at once.

Further, Ivacha Peresviétov, when he brought all the landholders, small and great, the owners of stingily-proportioned life allotments, and the holders of huge hereditary domains, under his anathemas and his plans for dispossession, went astray, and missed the only mark then attainable, because he went beyond the facts as they existed at that date. Seeing that the land in Russia was still the only capital at the State's command, it was perfectly natural that it should be used to remunerate the State's servants, there being no other form of payment at the State's disposal. But the servants of the State were of various kinds. The land tenure of the ordinary *pomiéchtchiki*, precarious in its nature and extremely restricted in its proportions, was not an abuse from the social point of view, nor any peril from that of politics. The people who were really privileged and really dangerous were the holders of the ancient appanages, who alone, amidst the gradual ruin of their weaker neighbours, continued to enjoy a certain amount of wealth, and, thanks to the social and economic crisis which was swallowing up the fortunes of their feebler rivals, even increased their possessions ; for they attracted all the available labour by offering hope of better pay, if not by sheer force, and on the freehold lands thus populated and enlarged they kept or created a following, and maintained or strengthened their independence. These, too, were servants of the State, but often only as their pleasure, their leisure, or their con-

venience willed it. They were undisciplined, carping, as unaccustomed to obey as they were difficult to punish.

To protect the interest of the State in this dual system, and,
instead of destroying both these elements, without knowing how
to replace them, to set one against the other, weakening the
stronger—the only one he had to fear—and strengthening the
weaker and inoffensive ; then, that first result attained, to
strike hard, and rid himself of the standing menace ; to keep
the building intact, to preserve its good pillars, and pull down
those that were in the way ; to work out that historic evolution
which, with slow but resistless force, was putting the Russia of
the autocrat and the *pomiéstia* in the place of the ancient
Russia of the appanaged Princes and the *vottchiny*—this was
the plan on which Ivan, on a day yet to come, was to decide ;
and it was the only one that harmonized with the traditions
and present necessities of his Empire.

This is the story which has hitherto been so ill understood,
and the whole story of the *opritchnina*.

Ivan did not arrive at it suddenly. At the period which we
have now reached he had probably allowed himself to drift
astray between the two currents of thought, the novelty and
boldness of which attracted his own open and enterprising mind.
He lent an ear to the *niéstiajatiéli*, and probably encouraged
Ivacha Peresviétov. He was feeling his way, and was destined to begin with experiments, attempts, and compromises.
These form the history of 1550-1551, and the events which fill
them ;. the drawing up of a new Code and the assembling of an
ecclesiastical council, which, thanks to that habit we have
noticed of introducing lay representatives and discussing secular
questions, marked an epoch in the political life of the country.

II.—THE NEW CODE.

That collection into one volume of the laws and customs of
France which had been the dream of the dying Louis XI. was
not realized, as my readers know, until the days of Henri III.
And was it not a mere codification, then ? In Russia the
codifiers of 1550-1551 had to amend the *Soudiébnik* of 1497,
which had already endeavoured, under an exaggerated system
of unification, to establish a uniform procedure and a unique
judicial organization. This advance on Western legislation
was, indeed, less real than apparent. The legislator of 1497
had hardly touched the ideas and judicial conceptions of the
Rousskaïa pravda of the eleventh century, except where, as in
one or two places, he adapted it to the point of view of his
own period. Save as to procedure and matters of organization,
he was content to transcribe the old Customary. His work

had been inspired, above all things, by the centralizing policy
he was carrying on.   That of his grandson was the outcome of
two tendencies which, at first sight, appear inconsistent and
contradictory.   It marks, in a sense, a backward step—a
return to the old local jurisdictions, expressive of the autonomous movement of the period.   But at the same time, and in
much more timid fashion, it marks, from the purely judicial
point of view, an advance on the path of progress.

The first of these two aspects of the new Code was far the
most important.   The administration of justice at that time
was practically the only administration in existence, and this
was the beginning, in the vaguest fashion and under the form
of a mere indication, of a general organic reform.   No great
exactness must ever be expected of the literary productions
of that period.   Even when they are prolix they tell very little,
express what they do tell very ill, leave a great deal more to be
understood, and are content with a hasty sketch, the features
of which it is by no means easy to catch.   But the outline
exists, and it has been fairly claimed to have been the deter-
minative argument of the Code, and of the assembly to which
the Code was submitted.

This reform did not spring spontaneously from Ivan's brain,
nor from the mind of his councillors.   In spite of his centralizing views, the legislator of 1497 had accepted the principle
of a certain share in the exercise of justice on the part
of those amenable to it, through their elected representatives,
starosts, hundreders, *prud'hommes*.   This was rendered imperative by the toughness of certain local traditions.   But these
assessors' duty, limited to a right of examination, was
merely optional.   Starosts, hundreders, and prud'hommes did
not exist everywhere, and in some places nobody cared to
have them.   The new Code announced that the principle was
to be generally applied, and made its application obligatory.
Elected and sworn assessors were to be established in every
bailiwick.   And more.   During Ivan's minority, in the midst of
the disorder into which the incoherence of the central Government had cast the provinces, the force of circumstances had
evolved other judicial authorities, intended to replace the
official magistrates, who had forgotten all their essential duties.
Somebody there had to be, to arrest, and try, and punish, the
brigands and malefactors of all sorts who swarmed in every
place.   Thus, in many parts of the country, rural and urban
communes had sought and obtained leave, by special charters,
to supply this need, by choosing judges of their own.   The
magistrates of this new type were generally known as *goobnyié
starosty*.   The *gooba* was the generic title applied, in some parts
of the country, to the ward.   The districts of Pskov and Novo-

torjok were divided up into *gooby*. But these wards were not originally connected with the criminal jurisdiction in any way. To this acquired fact the Code of 1550 gave an official confirmation. By a stroke of the pen, it placed all this department of jurisdiction under the charge of the communes. And this was only a preliminary step. The outbreak of war soon necessitated a general mobilization of the ' service men,' and the expediency of appealing to the new magistracy for the discharge of all the administrative duties left unperformed by the *sloojilyié*, absent on military duty, shortly became apparent. By a series of charters, which grew more and more numerous after the year 1555, the very financial organization, and the assessment and collection of the taxes were included in the same system.

This was neither more nor less than the adoption of Ivacha Peresviétov's plan, the cutting off of the *kormlénié* at the root, by the elimination of the *kormlenchtchiki*. At one moment, and as early as 1552, Ivan made no secret of his determination to reorganize his administration to the exclusion of these officials, who would thus have lost, if not every title—for they would still have been soldiers—the most essential of their rights to the possession of the land. And a remarkable feature is that the persons affected made no protest, and expressed no complaint. They would willingly have sacrificed their privileged possession of the land to obtain a pecuniary compensation, which, even if trifling, would have been more certain than the revenues of their ruined properties. But the reform, which had thus reached a point at which it seemed on the brink of realizing a complete communal autonomy, and, simultaneously, a profound alteration in the social, economic, and political constitution of the country, suddenly stopped short. As might have been foreseen, the men to carry out the ideas were not to be found. The benefit of the autonomy thus offered to populations quite insufficiently prepared for the duties they were expected to assume, was far beyond their powers of assimilation. The right of jurisdiction involved heavy responsibilities. The great distance between the various dwellings, which, though these were placed in the midst of elements naturally inclined to sociability in every form, enforced a necessity of a very opposite nature, was in many cases a quite insuperable obstacle to any organization of communal groups. And, further, the State did not bestow this benefit—which the people did not know how to use, and the responsibility of which it dreaded—as a free gift. It was a privilege, and the tradition in Russia, as elsewhere, was that privileges must be paid for. The· charters conferring autonomy were therefore burdened with a ransom ; in other words, the commune had to buy out the judicial rights of the persons who had previously held them.

Many refused to incur this pecuniary sacrifice ; others were too poor to make it. In this respect, the course of the Upper and Lower Oka seems to have divided the country into two distinct regions. On the northern side, the population, thicker and more industrious, showed an inclination to accept the reform. On the southern, the resources of the people, material and moral, were too poor to permit of their welcoming it. A more general application of the principle might, indeed, have resulted from a development of prosperity, and coincided with the progress of communal existence ; but this progress was soon to be compromised and stifled by the law of serfdom, while the Government, impelled by the bureaucratic system maintained in certain provinces, and strongest of all at the central point, was itself to intervene, and warp the working of the new institutions. In fact, from the close of the sixteenth century onwards, the *goobnyié starosty*, in the very places where they had been called into active existence, were to find themselves converted into mere officials appointed by Government, and dependent on its offices at Moscow.

Ivan's abortive attempt, as I have just sketched it, bears a pretty close resemblance to the reform which called the urban communes of France into life, under Philippe-Auguste and St. Louis, in the twelfth and thirteenth centuries, and a yet closer one to that movement in the tenth and eleventh centuries which, through the charters granted to certain associations of serfs belonging to a feudal lord, resulted in the formation of the rural communes. The difference between the general processes of evolution, tending in one case to the complete enfranchisement of the classes, and in the other to their more and more complete servitude, differentiates the two phenomena. The Russian peasants, already, when Ivan claimed to use their instincts of independence for his projected scheme of reorganization, more or less deeply plunged into servitude, turned their backs on this ideal. Between the *kriépostnoié pravo* and *self-government* no compromise was possible.

Ivan also imitated Edward I. of England by putting the administration of justice and police matters into the hands of the *gentry*. But while in England, both in theory and in practice, the responsibility and the privilege were bound together, in Russia the two terms were to be practically separated. Whether it was that the peasant class failed to supply candidates for the pseudo-autonomous functions offered, or that the Government did not care to find them in that class, the privilege fell to the ' men who served,' in that the choice of the electors found nobody else on whom it might fall. Thus, the peasants' share ended by being all duty and no rights. And the *sloojilyié* themselves soon found theirs too heavy.

10

It lacked one essential charm—independence. For—and here we have the most characteristic feature of the Muscovite experiment, and it was also one, and no doubt, the strongest, of the reasons which induced Ivan to undertake it—this tentative reform, far from being the fruit of a decentralizing tendency, was really the outcome of an anxiety of a quite different nature.

In connection with this matter, the part played by appearances and fictions in the political life of Moscow stands out in striking relief. One durable effect, and one of the objects, of this experiment, was the dissolution of the comparatively independent political organisms still present in the composition of the Muscovite State. The programme of unification, the execution of which Ivan was now pursuing in his turn, was hampered by the hereditary rights of a number of petty provincial potentates, who held certain regal rights within their own dominions. These remnants of the past the young Tsar had in view, and these he expected to wipe out, when he set up a rival organization—an organization of which he, who had created it, root and branch, was to be the regulator and master. In the West, the centralizing movement found a weapon to its hand in that emancipation of the classes which broke up the old feudal moulds, and in the particularism of the old local institutions. In Russia, where these classes did not exist—for there the town, the monastery, the village with its lord, the bailiwick with its free peasants, were only so many separate units—the State evolved the idea of creating these elements artificially, by a system of forced service imposed on the communities it undertook to constitute. But ukases cannot impart life, and the reform thus devised was stillborn, save in the sense I have just indicated—that of an agent which destroyed the past and paved the way to a system of universal servitude.

The Code of 1551 laid only the lightest of fingers on the great question of the land. Contrary to the reforming tendency, and conformably with the desire of the conservative party, it converted a custom which had fixed and consolidated the tenure of the land into a law—the right to buy back patrimonial properties. In other words, the vendor of such a property, or, failing him, his relatives, were allowed to take back the lands sold at any period, so long as the price that had been given for them was repaid. The future exercise of this right was limited, indeed, to a period of forty years, and given to collateral relations only, but, notwithstanding this, it constituted a recognition, on the legislator's part, of a most detestable archaism, opposed to all freedom of exchange and economic progress.

On yet another point his work is marked by a capitulation in the struggle between the two antagonistic elements and principles. As I have already remarked (p. 20), the causes constituting slavery, as recognised by custom and by the Code of 1497, were restricted by that of 1550. Thus, children born before their parents became slaves were to be free ; enslaved parents were forbidden to sell their children born out of slavery ; all contracts of servitude were to be signed in the presence of certain high officials, and that only in the towns of Moscow, Pskov, and Novgorod, etc. But at the same time, and with a quite opposite tendency, the Code gave the peasants power to leave the lands they worked *at every season,* if they desired to barter their own freedom and sell themselves as serfs; and, further, the new law, by increasing the dues on his dwelling-house, tightened the rope that was already strangling him round the husbandman's neck.

The personal inclinations of the Sovereign probably did not affect these last provisions in any way. A series of proposals, drawn up for presentation to the assembly in his name, prove his own leanings to have been very different. But the man who was some day to jeer at Batory's limited power did not venture, as yet, to make use of his own omnipotence. He was too young, and too uncertain of his ideas and convictions.

As regards civil rights, the new Code left the order of succession untouched. It was not till 1562 that an important change was to mark the triumph of the political programme sketched above : the hereditary domains of Princes, in the absence of male heirs, and the hereditary properties of boïars, failing immediate heirs or testamentary dispositions, were to go back to the State. Ten years later, the right of succession was limited to *vottchiny* in the original deed of concession of which this power had been specially stipulated for, and only direct heirs and collaterals to the second degree were allowed to enjoy even these truncated rights.

The Code of 1550, indeed, like that of 1497, was above all things a rule of procedure, and in this respect it constitutes a distinct advance on its predecessor. Measures for insuring greater regularity in the course of justice, severe penalties for careless or dishonest judges, the putting down of bribery, the regulation of the use of torture and of the judicial combat—nothing calculated to correct vices unfortunately all too inveterate and obstinate, was overlooked. In another order of things it may be credited with a capital innovation—the establishment of a fixed and graduated rate of fines for offences. But taking it all in all, the conservative party came out victorious, and Ivan was left face to face with the triumphant army of his unruly boïars, who had kept all their rights and privileges, and were as ready as ever to abuse them.

Yet Ivacha Peresviétov had not spoken in vain. In the course of that same year (1550) Ivan, though he still hesitated, scarce knowing what end he should pursue, or how he should attain it, took one decisive step on the only path open to him, if he was to enter on the inevitable struggle with any hope of victory, and reconcile a reform which had become indispensable with the maintenance of a political system of the destruction of which he could not dream. On October 10, he published a ukase for the reorganization of the upper class of the 'men who served.'

III.—THE REORGANIZATION OF THE 'SERVICE.'

Notice the expression. It embodies the germ of the entire system of the *opritchnina* and of the whole internal history of Ivan's reign.

Orders were issued to collect a thousand sons of boïars, chosen among the best, and give them *pomiéstia* in the Moscow district and those nearest it. This elect body was to form the nobility of the capital, the nucleus of a contingent which was to be available for service of every kind, and for military service more especially. The oldest aristocratic families established in the region were included in the group, and provided, if they did not already possess them, with allotments of landed property in the immediate neighbourhood. The whole body of this aristocracy was divided into three classes, or *stati*, acording to seniority in the service. In this fashion, the legislator without suppressing the *miéstnitchestvo*, determined and limited the field of his future labours. The service to be paid for each allotment was also carefully defined and fixed : for every hundred acres (about fifty diéssiatines, or as many hectares) the holder was to supply one mounted man, and a second horse if the expedition was to be a long one. A money payment might be substituted for the man and the horse, and the Sovereign, on his part, guaranteed an indemnity for extra men supplied, in addition to the campaigning pay every man received.

Hence the theory of 'service,' which upset all positions and ruled all questions of rank and precedence, was destined, even more than in past days, to hold the foremost place in the hierarchy thus constituted. And here is an indication of the result obtained. No Princes appear on the lists of the great personages summoned to the assembly of 1566. In the course of the evolution which had carried the official class into the front rank, they had disappeared, or, officially speaking at all events, they were as though they did not exist, for their titles still appear in their signatures, and they thus maintained and affirmed their rights. But the law ignored them, and they sometimes ended by forgetting their own identity. Even in 1554, we find Michael Ivanovitch, the descendant of the ancient appanaged Princes of Vorotynsk, claiming no more than the title of *dvorianine* (courtier), higher, now, than any other ; and the trend of the Muscovite policy itself always tended to eliminate the hereditary element in the higher sphere, for in 1566, out of ninety-four *dvorianié* of the first class, only thirty belonged to the princely families.

This was the work wrought by the ukase of 1550, and a few years later the system was further and largely extended by a service, reorganized in 1571, for the protection of the southern and south-western frontiers, and confided to the landed proprietors of those regions. A fort had been built, during Ivan's minority, at Temnikov, on the Mokcha, a tributary of the Oka, and a number of posts established along the natural lines of defence rendered it possible to keep a watch on the Tartars' movements. In 1555 a regular guard of *Striéltsy* and Cossacks was organized, all along the Volga, and one Cossack regiment, the *khoperskii polk*, still preserves the remnants of a standard presented to it by Ivan IV. He did more than this. By his care, another contingent of boïars' sons in search of an establishment was assigned *pomiéstia* in the territory threatened by invasion. The holders of these lands were thus interested in the defence of the frontier, and bound, in return for the landed properties bestowed upon them, to keep up a permanent guard. A double chain of fortified townlets thus arose, from Alatyr and Temnikov to Poutivl, and from Nijni-Novgorod to Zvenigorod. And after this, the system, which had proved its value, was successively extended to the eastern and western frontiers, and made up one huge whole, ensuring the Empire the tranquillity it had hitherto lacked.

This work alone, so wide in its conception and so vigorously carried out, in spite of the painful struggles through which he was then passing, should suffice to clear Ivan of the too general and most insufficiently justified opprobrium cast on this portion of his reign. The Terrible did not spend it in doing nothing but cutting off men's heads. It was no fault of his that the assembly of 1551, to which his Code was presented, did not itself inscribe a far more brilliant page in the nation's history.

IV.—THE RELIGIOUS REFORM.

In history this assembly bears the name of *Stoglavnyĭ-sobor*, or the ' *Conciliable* of the Hundred Chapters,' which it owes to an arbitrary division of the report of its deliberations. My readers will remember, in this connection, the ' Hundred and One Griefs ' of the Diet of Worms. It was the fashion of those times. As usual, the *conciliable* included the Metropolitan, the Archbishops of Novgorod and Rostov, and many Bishops, archimandrites, and priors. The lay element was represented by the great Court dignitaries, and by the whole body of the *boïarskaïa douma*. Ivan did not fail to make speeches of his own. He multiplied his rhetorical efforts, made an act of contrition, and appealed to the counsels and prayers of his whole audience. All this was his usual course of scenic effect. Then the new Code was considered and approved. This was a mere matter of form. The questions affecting the work of legislation had been previously cleared up between the Sovereign and his lay counsellors, the only persons concerned in them. All that Ivan expected from the composite gathering now assembled, and representing the highest moral authority in the country, was a recognition of his reforms, whether accomplished or proclaimed. This was the ordinary procedure, and an invariable feature of every successive avatar of the Parliamentary existence of the country. By the way, however, the Sovereign was pleased to call on the assistance of the *conciliable* as to certain fresh legal proposals, in connection with which he sought, not its adhesion, but its advice. These were the suppression of the *miéstnitchestvo* in time of war ; a revision of the Crown grants of land, with the object of bringing them into proportion with the amount of service rendered ; the means to be employed for fixing the level of taxation by remedying the present fluctuations of the taxable population ; the putting down of taverns ; the bestowal of landed properties on the widows and orphan daughters of boïars ; and the establishment of an official cadastral survey. . . .

We must not expect method any more than we must expect perspicuity, from the legislators of this epoch. Their procedure was one of riddles and of jerks. The assembly made some attempt to fulfil the task imposed upon it. A remedy for the fluctuation of the population was by no means easy to find, and the gathering suggested none. The plan for putting down the taverns, which had been inspired by the religious party, ran counter to the fiscal interest, and did not advance beyond a pious wish. But it was decided that in war-time ' places ' were not to count ; the cadastral survey and the revision of the landed properties were undertaken,

and as to the widows and orphan girls, a system of life allotments was adopted, the lands to be given up if the holders
married or took the veil. All this, however, was but an introduction to the feast, and the ' Hundred Chapters ' bear
no trace of these labours. In this assembly, in which the
Church predominated, the anxieties filling men's minds were
of a quite different order. Ivachka Peresviétov's programme
had been put aside or reduced to a minimum, the scope of which
was probably not even understood, but that of the wonder-
workers of Valaam remained upon the scene. The reform
claimed by the *Niéstiajatiéli* had still to be dealt with.

In this matter Ivan seemed disposed, at first, to give proofs
of a more lively originating power. He certainly was influenced by Nil Sorski's disciples. Artemi, the declared
enemy of the *Iosiflianié*, and soon to be appointed Prior of
the Troïtsa, was allowed to present the Sovereign with a
memorandum which boldly demanded the secularization of
the monastic properties. So, at least, we are led to think by
a letter from the monk which has come down to our own times.
Among the members of the *sobor* was Kassiane, Bishop of
Riazan, supposed author of a vigorous denunciation of the
corruption of thought and morals rampant in both orders
of the clergy. Isolated though she was, Russia was not
entirely untouched by the revolutionary currents which were
convulsing the Western world of that period. But the Metropolitan Macarius, a worthy pupil of his alma-mater, the monastery of Volok-Lamski, spoke, not less vigorously, against
the radical proposals. In a famous epistle, which has been
guessed to be a reply to some new law proposed by the young
Tsar, he appealed to the example of the Greek Emperors,
the Russian Sovereigns, and even the Tartar Khans, who had
all shown equal respect for Church property. The *Iosoflianié*
had a huge majority in the *sobor*. And Ivan gave in again,
agreed to present the question in a very modified form, and
contented himself with calling the assembly's attention to
the faulty administration of the monastic properties, and to
the monks' excessive greed.

In theory, the *sobor* pronounced for the suppression of these
abuses, and ended, though not without sharp resistance, by
accepting some practical measures to that end—the restitution
of freehold lands (*vottchiny*) ceded to the monasteries by
boïars without the Sovereign's consent, and a similar restitution of all lands of every kind illegally acquired by the Church ;
the annulling of all gifts to the Church during Ivan's minority ;
the monasteries to be forbidden to acquire the patrimonial
estates of the ancient appanaged Princes, and the clergy in
general to be forbidden to acquire *vottchiny* without the

Sovereign's leave. Although she laid great stress on the value of the service she already paid by furnishing a certain number of military recruits and contributing to the repair of the fortifications of certain towns, the Church was forced to accept fresh burdens. She had to pay her share towards a fund for ransoming prisoners, and the concessions she made led on to others. In 1573 a *conciliable* was absolutely to forbid, *by the Tsar's order*, any donations of freehold land to the rich monasteries, already well provided in this respect ; and another, held in 1580, was to apply the principle still further, by forbidding all future acquisition of any lands whatsoever by any member of either clergy, whether by gift or purchase.

Thus the growth of the landed property of the Church was checked.

In 1551 Ivan sought to give more complete satisfaction to the ideas of the reformers in another matter. His intentions were made manifest in a series of questions addressed to the assembly, so sharp and searching that they sound like an echo of the English ' Black Book ' of 1534—that accusation drawn up by the agents of Thomas Cromwell against the monks of his day, their dubious morals, their pride, their coarseness—or else of the scandalous tales which enlivened Layton's correspondence with his master. This somewhat insulting interrogatory, the answers given by the assembly, and the Sovereign's further remarks, enter into the composition of the 'Book of the Hundred Chapters ' (*Stoglav*), and constitute the most essential portion of it. The dialogue we are thus enabled to follow is most curious. We observe that the *sobor* at first tried every means of avoiding the discussion. In the first forty chapters, the Tsar's indiscreet queries are all brought together. Then follows a general reply, which altogether begs the question, slipping into side issues, and stealing away into the uncertain regions of the *qui pro quo*. Ivan finds sharp fault with the bad use made of the wealth piled up in the monasteries. The assembly pretends it does not know what he means, and replies by putting forward divers liturgical problems. This part of the book most likely adheres to the order and procedure first adopted in the debate. After the forty-first chapter these are altered, probably because the Tsar thought a change of method advisable. Questions and answers now follow in regular alternation, though the fathers of the Church still do their best to quibble and avoid any too definite response. A return is made, but with no better success, to some of the points already discussed. When the morals of the clergy are called in question, the *sobor*, not without a touch of spite, drops into lamentations over the increase of sodomy amongst the laity, and solemnly passes on to some such problem of ascetic morality as this : Can a sick nun make her confession to a member of the secular clergy ? Sometimes the dialogue warms into a quarrel, and descends to personalities. Ivan has made a remark as to the bad painting of the *ikons*. The *sobor* replies, ' Look at what is going on in the Kremlin !' This is a hit at an *ikon* of doubtful orthodoxy lately substituted for a famous one painted by Roublev, a fifteenth-century artist. Thus, through it all, amidst all the shuffling and straying hither and thither, the general idea of the reform is lost—evaporates, as it were, never attains solidity on any point. Some few amendments as to details : the institution of ecclesiastical *starosts* and tithing-men to overlook the morals of the clergy ; a rigorous separation of the sexes within all monasteries ; a stricter observance of the rules of the various communities, were accepted in principle, but in practice they were destined to remain a dead letter. The assembly, thus forced to acknowledge the reality of certain disorders which had brought shame on the National Church and compromised her future, did not fail to recognise their essential cause—the state of ignorance in which both clergy, the regular and the secular, continued to wallow. And it decided on opening a great number of schools for the education of priests. But it did nothing to insure the carrying out of this decision. It imagined, or feigned to imagine, that it could reckon, for this purpose, on the zeal and devotion of the poor popes, who were most of them forced to beg, and did not themselves possess the requisite learning ; and the wealthy Bishops and archimandrites refused any personal contributions, and refused, too, in this case, to admit the necessity of beginning at the beginning —in other words, of raising the intellectual standard of the upper ecclesiastical hierarchy in the first place. Macarius himself was apt to commit the grossest errors in the interpretation and selection of his texts !

Under the influence, as we may suppose, of Maximus the Greek, the *sobor* turned its attention to the corruptions of the sacred books, and ordered the establishment of a printing-press —the first that ever existed at Moscow—to reprint them according to the most correct copies to be had. Alas ! as my readers already know, the existence of this printing-press was of the shortest, thanks to a local tumult. All that remained were the interdicts pronounced by the assembly at the same time on certain impious and heretical works. But, alas, again ! these works—the *Secreta Secretorum*, a repertory of the science of the Middle Ages, here called *Aristotel*, and ascribed to Aristoteles, and the astronomical tables of Emmanuel Ben Jacob, known under the title of the *Chestokryl*—constituted the whole profane literature of the country. And to save its face, reply to the accusations of immorality, and flatter the ascetic tendencies of the epoch by giving itself an appearance of rigorous austerity, the assembly took good care to renew all the Church's anathemas against profane amusements.

Quite as empty was the shadow of administrative reform embodied in the autonomous institutions the new Code had proposed to call into life. The ecclesiastical jurisdiction, as exercised by the Bishops' delegates, whether boïars, clerks, or tithing-men, gave lively cause for complaint. The suppression of these magistrates did not seem feasible ; they had existed under the great Metropolitans Peter and Alexis ! The popes were given leave to have themselves represented, for judicial purposes, by elected *starosts* and hundreders, but the assembly forgot to define the part these representatives were to play !

And yet, in spite of its weaknesses and failures, the labours of the assembly of 1551 do not seem to me to deserve the scorn which has fallen upon them in their own day, seeing that the very anathema with which it was smitten at a later date, by the *conciliable* of 1667, attests the scope and comparative boldness of its endeavour. Is not the fact, in a society so depraved and generally devoid of knowledge—a society in which no ideal existed, and given over to the rule of the coarsest instincts—that a handful of men attained so much, and asked a great deal more, a sufficient title to our indulgence and even to our respect ? Attempts have been made to minimize and even to deny Ivan's share in the result obtained. Silvester or Adachev, Maximus the Greek or Macarius, we are told, did it all, even to inspiring or formulating the famous set of questions on which the deliberations of the assembly were based. Most assuredly, the young Tsar neither acted nor thought alone. Even during the progress of the debate, the earlier decisions of the *conciliable* were sent to the Troïtsa, where Jehosaphat, the former Metropolitan, Alexis, a former Bishop of Rostov, and a few other ecclesiastics, had to pronounce upon them. It was in consequence, indeed, of this consultation, as it would appear, that the question of the monastic properties, first put aside, and then brought back under discussion, was solved in the sense I have just indicated. But Jehosaphat and his comrades, all of them former ecclesiastical dignitaries in disgrace, and avowed partisans of Nil Sorski's, could only have been called into consultation in this way by virtue of some act of high authority, which certainly did not proceed from the council itself. Silvester is mentioned as having been one of the monks who brought back Jehosaphat's views from the Troïtsa. He would not have applied for them on his own account, and we may even doubt whether he would have had any desire to serve the cause of the ascetics ' beyond the Volga ' in this fashion. The coarse asceticism of the *Domostroï* was also invoked by the

Iosiflianié.   It was the standard of the official Church.   Among
the materials which served for the composition of the *Stoglav*
some people have included the epistle addressed to Ivan by the
pope of the Church of the Annunciation.   I have already said
that the authorship of this epistle is doubtful, and only one of
the subjects of which it treats was touched by the *conciliable*—
the question of wearing beards, which Silvester connects with
that struggle against the sin of sodomy, which seems to have
been the great anxiety of the author of the *Domostroï*.   And
his point of view is the one generally taken up by the moralists
of this school, their idea being that ' beardless men, by making
themselves look more like women, were more liable to stir
sinful desire in others.'

Young as Ivan was, his intelligence and education both
raised him to a higher level than this.   The set of questions the
conciliable had to consider was not only presented to it in the
Sovereign's name, but partly written by his own hand ; and
a comparison with other and later writings by the same author
reveals his personal mark as strongly apparent in it—not his
thought only, but his forms of speech, his way of putting things,
cutting like a knife, vigorous and biting, rugged and blunt.
Nothing here recalls Silvester, with his inferior composition
and poverty of thought.   Even on questions of liturgy, as to
which Macarius may well have directed him, Ivan was always
to give proof of very wide information.

Further, no study of the ' Book of the Hundred Chapters '
was attempted till at a comparatively recent period, and the
text available was incomplete, and gave rise to a great deal of
uncertainty.   The *Stoglav*, which fell under interdict in the
year 1667, escaped the curiosity of historians for two whole
centuries.   Macarius may probably be considered as the author
of the relative failure of the work of 1551, and the chief organizer of the assembly's opposition to the reforming tendencies
of Nil Sorski and Jehosaphat, and the personal inclinations of
the Sovereign.   The Metropolitan did advocate a reform, but
one which would have operated in a different direction.   He
turned his back on all progress, and saw no salvation save in
a return to the past and its traditions, which had been scorned
and violated, and to the old arbitrary ideal of the primitive
Christians.   This ideal consisted in a piety based on a scrupulous performance of rite ; a Church with a mighty hierarchy
entrenched in the very heart of the aristocracy, and rolling
up more wealth, ' which came to her from God,' from year to
year ; an understanding with the State, on the basis of mutual
support ; the merciless putting down of heresy ; and no schools
at all.   As for Jehosaphat's opinions, they would certainly never
have been either received or sought for but for the inter-

vention of the only omnipotent will able to hurl such a defiance at the majority. Their insertion in the *Stoglav* has given rise to some natural confusion, producing an impression that the assembly had adopted them, and even gone the length of adopting the views of the *Niéstiajatiéli*. As a matter of fact, the *sobor* only made a partial capitulation, and the honour of this cannot be denied to Ivan.

His victory, modest as it was, was still further diminished by the later efforts of the vanquished party. In some localities the decisions of the assembly long continued a dead letter. Everywhere the official Church endeavoured to hamper their application, and when the clergy were once more called together in 1554, to judge the heresies of Matthew Rachkine and his followers, they revenged themselves by dragging several of the most prominent of the reformers into the trial. Soon, too, certain of the ecclesiastical conservatives, wounded or threatened in their dearest interests, were to meet with other malcontents. Ivan's pursuance of his plan of reform was to rally every element of opposition against him : religious and political interests were to join hands, and with them all he was to enter on a fearful struggle, from which he did indeed emerge victorious, but leaving a terrifying name, and a memory that makes men shiver, even now, to his descendants.

The religious reform had failed. The political reform, more resolutely imposed, was to bring a reign of terror with it.

But Ivan had to solve other problems first. In his case, as in that of his predecessors, the territorial expansion of the huge and growing Empire called him to the frontier. The legislator was to be transformed into the conqueror.

CHAPTER III

THE EXPANSION EASTWARDS—THE TAKING OF KAZAN

I.—THE REMNANTS OF THE MONGOL EMPIRE. II.—IVAN'S ARMY. III.—THE CAPTURE OF KAZAN. IV.—THE CONSEQUENCES. V.—THE CAPTURE OF ASTRAKAN. VI.—THE COSSACKS. VII.— THE CRIMEA AND LIVONIA.

I.—THE REMNANTS OF THE MONGOL EMPIRE.

WHEN Ivan ascended the throne, the Tartar conquest was nothing but an ugly memory. The Empire of Gengiz and Timour had crumbled in the conquerors' hands. On the east and south, the remnants of the Golden Horde, which had set up almost independent khanates or tsarates at Kazan and Astrakan, and on the Crimean steppes, still lay along the frontiers of Muscovy. The Mongol tide, as it drew back to the high Asiatic plateaus, had left little pools on which waves were still rough and eddies threatening, but their onset was steadily weakening. Not an inch of Russian soil was now covered by the flood, which in these countries, as I have said, had never reached the proportions of an ocean. Russian conquest and Russian colonists had taken the offensive, were marching in the track of the old invaders, and penetrating further every year, almost every day, into the huge Finn-Tartar continent. Slowly but surely the Sovereigns of Moscow were widening their borders, and adding more and more vast spheres of influence to their possessions. Vassals once, they had now made themselves the suzerains of the nearest Khans, and Sàfa Ghireï, Khan of Kazan, paid them tribute.

In the Crimea, however, a new centre of Tartar domination had been established. This power, thanks to a political and military organization, modelled, on much stronger lines, after the old ones, had succeeded in recovering the fealty of the neighbouring khanates, and breaking the bonds which bound them in vassalage to Moscow. This began by being an annoyance, but it soon became a danger. In 1539, Khan Saïp-Ghireï, who had succeeded in getting a footing at Kazan, and had even garrisoned the place, attracted or welcomed Simon Biélski, then a fugitive, to his Court, and sent a message to Moscow which sounded like an echo of the imperious summons of the old days : ' I am going to march, and I do not march in secret. . . . I shall take thy lands, and if thou followest me, thou wilt not reach mine !' And an undertaking not to lay a finger on Kazan did not suffice the insolent aggressor ; he demanded a promise of annual tribute—a return to the shame of the past. From 1539 to 1552, then, there was a struggle, the anguish of which tinctured the boyhood and youth of Ivan, and the details of which my readers will thank me for sparing them. At Kazan the partisans of Safa, and, later, of his son Outémich, a minor, strove with the Muscovite party, which, helped by the most famous warrior of that country, Boulat, succeeded in replacing Saïp's *protégé* by one of Ivan's, Schah-Ali, or Schig-Aleï. But Saïp, dragging Biélski in his train, and strengthening his forces with a Turkish contingent, and with muskets and heavy ordnance sent him by the Porte, ended by threatening Moscow itself. At that moment the question as to whether the young Tsar was to stay in his capital and bear his share in defending it, or not, was seriously discussed, and it was only thanks to the interference of the Metropolitan Jehosaphat that manly counsels prevailed. On such occasions Ivan's ancestors, even when they had reached a fighting age,

had always insured the safety of their own persons. But
Moscow, as Jehosaphat pointed out, had now become something
more than a mere capital city. It was a metropolis, a holy
town, wherein the whole of Russia had deposited all that she
held most sacred—her faith and her relics, her hopes and her
pride.

So Ivan held his ground, and his very presence made Saïp
retire. Behind the Tsar, the crowned boy who would not flee,
the Khan's fancy beheld an army strong enough to beat his
Tartars, no longer what they had been in Baty's time, plun-
derers rather than soldiers, now, lovers of easy victories. As
Ivan grew older, he did better still. Twice over, in 1548 and
1549, he exposed his own person, and led expeditions—unsuccessful ones indeed—up to the very walls of Kazan. He
started too late each time, and the winter overtook him. His
regiments melted in the snow, and the Volga swallowed up his
artillery. In their desperate quarrels about precedence, the
'men who served' forgot all their duties. Twice over the
Tsar, weeping tears of fury, was forced to beat a retreat, while
the Crimeans and *Kazantsy*, plucking up their courage, ravaged
his fairest provinces.

But the second expedition did bring some result ; a town
was founded on the enemy's territory, and quite near Kazan,
at the confluence of the Sviaga and the Volga. This town was
Sviajsk, and the neighbouring mountaineers, Tchouvaches and
Mordvians, soon found it a centre of attraction, while the Kazan
Tartars recognised it as an establishment with which they
would have to reckon. The Khanate was dismembered, in
fact. The Kazan Tartars, forsaken by the Crimeans, who
quitted the town to the number of 300 fighting men,
leaving their women and children behind them, but sacking
everything before they went, displeased with Outémich, whom
they betrayed to the Russians, and just as ill-pleased, soon
afterwards, with Schah-Ali, ended by asking the Tsar to choose
them a ruler, and Ivan fancied himself on the brink of a blood-
less triumph. The selected governor, Prince Simon Ivanovitch Mikoulinski, had almost reached the gates of the city in
February, 1552, when the intrigues of Schah-Ali, who had
quietly retired to Sviajsk, and the intervention, no doubt, of
some of Saïp's emissaries, operated a sudden change. The
gates remained closely shut. An appeal to arms ensued.
Couriers hurried into the Crimea to ask for reinforcements, and
the adventure threatened to become a disaster.

At Sviajsk, on which place Mikoulinski had to fall back—for
he had but few troops with him—he narrowly escaped being
surrounded and destroyed. The plague, and mutiny, which
came with the sickness, entered his camp. Debauchery was

added to material distress. ' The men shaved off their beards,' so the chronicler tells us, ' . . . and debauched their younger comrades.' The boïars, sitting in council at Moscow, devised none but the most frivolous expedients ; they had the sacred relics carried in procession from the Cathedral of the Annunciation to the Cathedral of the Assumption ; they sent water consecrated by these same relics to Sviajsk, together with an edifying instruction drawn up by the new Metropolitan, Macarius. Ivan and his closest counsellors felt something else must be done. The prestige of Moscow, the whole future of the Muscovite policy in the countries affected, were at stake. A blow must be dealt, this time, that would win the day, or else all hope of conquest must be relinquished, and the ancient yoke, maybe, assumed once more. Saïp, once grown bolder, would not yield again. The experience of past years proved the necessity for haste. On June 16, 1552, having made over a sort of regency to the Tsarina Anastasia, ordered the liberation of a great number of prisoners, and performed various other pious acts, in the hope of bringing down the heavenly benediction on his undertaking, Ivan set out with all the available forces remaining to him. Of the importance, composition, and quality of these forces, I shall now endeavour to give some approximate idea.

II.—IVAN'S ARMY.

In this country, where the feudal system was unknown, the military organization of the period was, nevertheless, essentially feudal in all its features. In France, naught of such an organization remained, save the *ban et l'arrière-ban*—a small matter, some 2,000 or 3,000 men, little or nothing in presence of the regular and permanent forces, the real army of modern times. In Russia, Ivan was only beginning to form this new type of contingent, by giving it a nucleus in the shape of the corps called the *Striéltsy*, a name which appears for the first time in the course of the decisive campaign of 1552 against Kazan. The *Striéltsy* were arquebus-men (*striélat*, to fire), recruited from the free class, on a life engagement. Most of them were married men, and they ultimately formed a separate body in which the profession of arms was hereditary. They were armed and equipped in the European fashion, and each received a rouble to build himself a house, another rouble of yearly pay, uniform, powder, and some measures of flour and *kacha*. These arrangements having proved insufficient, the Government ended by giving land, and allowing the *Striéltsy* to pursue divers trades, subject to the performance of their military duties. This led to their being confused with the 'men who served.' At the close of Ivan's reign they numbered 12,000 men, 7,500 of whom garrisoned Moscow, and formed, with the town Cossacks, the first body of infantry the Russian Tsars ever possessed. A permanent corps of artillerymen, divided into gunners (*pouchkari*), fort artillery-men (*zatinchtchiki*), grenadiers (*granattchiki*), and artificers, and a special corps of arquebus-men (*pistchalniki*), was organized at the same time.

All this did not constitute an army. The bulk of the force consisted of the 'men who served,' and of what was called the *rat*, the germ of another regular force. In war-time two things were done. All or part of the 'men who served' were called out, on the one hand, and on the other, levies were ordered, such and such a town or diocese being obliged to furnish so many foot soldiers or mounted men, recruited outside the military class. This constituted the *rat* or *possokha;* and for one campaign alone—that undertaken to recover Polotsk from the Poles—Ivan was to collect 80,000 of these *possochniki*. They were not disciplined troops, as may well be imagined, nor calculated to cut any very brilliant figure on a battle-field. As a rule, therefore, they were employed in digging earthworks or preparing war material. The Muscovite Government, indeed, permitted its taxpayers to pay a money indemnity of two roubles instead of each man due, and even preferred this plan. It was simply a form of taxation.

Mobilized by circulars sent by the War Office, or *Razriad*, to the provincial *voiévodes*, and specifying the number of men to be called out, the points on which they were to be concentrated, and the nature of their armament, the 'men who served,' boïars, boïars' sons, and courtiers (*dvorianié*), were divided, from Ivan IV.'s time onward, into five regiments—the great regiment, the vanguard, the right hand, the left hand, and the rearguard. When the Tsar was present, a sixth regiment, called 'the Sovereign's regiment,' was added. The first regiment consisted of three, and the others of two divisions, subdivided into 'hundreds' (*sotnias*). Each regiment was commanded by a *voiévode*, each division by a lieutenant who ranked as a *voiévode*, and each *sotnia* by a *dvorianine* of the first class. In the Tsar's absence, the whole body was under the orders of a Court *voiévode*, the *magister militarum* of the Romans, the *generalissimo* of the present day, who was surrounded by a numerous staff, which included *sborchtchiki*, whose business was to bring the troops together; *okladtchiki*, who had to divide them; *possylnyié, lioodi*, or aides-de-camp; *stanovchtchiki*, or engineers; foreign artisans, employed in siege works, provosts, medical men, and priests.

How many men did all this come to? We have no data

for the year 1552, but in 1556 the full numbers of the vanguard regiment did not bring it up to 1,500 horsemen. In 1578, in the campaign against Lithuania, the army, though increased by the presence of a Tartar contingent, only numbered 39,681 fighting men in all, made up as follows :

Russian and Circassian Princes	212
Moscow boïars and boïars' sons	9,200
' Men who served ' from Novgorod and Iouriev	1,109
Tartars and Mordvians	6,461
Court *Striéltsy*	2,000
Striéltsy and Cossacks from the provinces	13,119
Possokha from the northern provinces	7,580
	39,681

Part of the available forces had probably been left to guard the frontier, while every boïar, on the other hand, took at least two *ratniki*, or fatigue men, with him, and some brought fifty or more.

One traveller of this period, Clement Adams, mentions 90,000 as the total number of men available for the Tsar's service, but adds that he only called out a third of these on his campaigns, being obliged to leave the other two-thirds to guard the fortified places. There is a striking agreement between this calculation and that furnished by the rosters for the year 1578.

Apart from the *Striéltsy* of the special corps and the *possokha*, all these troops were mounted. Their armament was of the most varied description. In Ivan's time, the curved Turkish sword and the bow were the favourite arms with most Russians. Only a few substituted pistols or long muskets. An axe hanging at the warrior's saddle-bow, a dagger, and now and then a lance, made up the campaigning equipment. Cuirasses were very little patronized. A few great lords wore them, and of very splendid make, out of vanity, and covered their heads with ' sallets ' or ' morions.' There were no spurs—the whip supplied their place. The horseman held his bridle and his bow in his left hand, and clasped his sword and whip with his right. When he shot he dropped the sword and whip, both of which were fastened to a strap. The moment the enemy came within range every arrow flew at once, and, however much or little the adversary's onslaught were checked, the whole body of troops beat a retreat without awaiting the shock of battle. Thus it came about that this cavalry never learnt to stand in the open country against the Polish squadrons, which had been taught to charge right home. Its chief merits were its endurance and its extreme mobility. On

their unshod horses, most of them undersized, and all clumsily
accoutred, these Russian soldiers covered huge distances, and
unflinchingly endured the greatest fatigues and the most
extreme privations. Clement Adams and Chancellor show
them camping out in the snow, lighting a tiny fire, content
with such poor nourishment as a handful of flour mixed with
boiling water, and lying down to sleep with no covering but
their cloaks, and without even a stone for a pillow. The
second of these two English travellers wonders how many of
the warriors of his own country, prouder than most men of
their valour, would have been able to hold out, even for a
month, against these troops, and comes to the conclusion that
if these men realized their own strength nobody in the world
would be able to stand against them.

But endurance is not everything in war. Ivan's undrilled
and undisciplined soldiers did not possess the very elements
of their art. The only tactics they knew consisted in surprising the enemy, overwhelming him with a force two or
three times larger than his own, and deafening him with their
yells and the discordant clangour of their trumpets and
cymbals. Brave in their own way—as brave as they were
temperate—they were seldom known to sue for mercy, even
if they were worn out and on the brink of giving way. But
they broke up very easily. They were useless in the service
of any skilled strategy, and they were just as useless for
siege operations, such as those which awaited Ivan under the
walls of Kazan. In cases of defence their superiority was
evident. Once shut up and cut off from all chance of taking
to their heels in flight, they were extraordinarily tenacious,
bore cold and hunger without a murmur, died in their thousands on the earthworks and wooden defences they perpetually
repaired, and never gave in till the very last extremity. Hence
the constant use in the Muscovite armies of portable defences,
shields made of planks, with holes bored for the musket-
barrels—these were called *khoulaï gorody* ('towns on the
march')—and hence, also, the precocious development of a
very powerful artillery service.

The first cannon the country had ever possessed were of
foreign make, but even in Ivan III.'s time, foreign workmen
were casting them in Russia. A gun produced by this home
factory, and bearing the date of the year 1485, is still preserved in the St. Petersburg arsenal. Under Ivan IV., the
war material thus collected included all the European improvements in ballistics—serpentines (here called *zmeï*), falconets
(*sokolniki*), and mortars of various calibres, amongst which
were classed the *haufnizy* (from the German word *haufnitz*),
the *haubitzen* of a more modern type, and the *volkomiétki*

(from *volk*, wolf, and *miétat*, to launch). No Christian Prince of the period, according to Fletcher, possessed such a quantity of ordnance, and in 1557, Jenkinson speaks with wonder of the Russian gunners' drill, in which he saw them vie with each other, laying their guns with extraordinary swiftness and skill.

The chronicles speak of 150 pieces of ordnance as having been brought under the walls of Kazan in 1552. This figure is probably as much of an exaggeration as that of 150,000 men given as the total effective of the troops which accompanied the guns. But certain it is that the Tsar entered on this campaign with a very considerable force. And yet he must have made a great effort of will to start at all. Apart from that dislike of the risks of war, which he shared with all the Rurikovitchy, other motives must have held him back. His wife was expecting the birth of her first child, and the appeal of the *Kazantsy* to their Crimean brethren had not been in vain—the bands of the new Khan, Devlet-Ghireï, had already made their appearance before Toula. But the young Tsar would not be turned from his resolve. Toula held out, on August 13 he was at Sviajsk, where the effect produced by his presence was more salutary than that of the holy water and admonitions despatched from Moscow, and on the 23rd he was encamped before Kazan.

III.—THE CAPTURE OF KAZAN.

The ramparts of the town were only built of wood and earth, but from the very outset the garrison, which the chroniclers reckon at 30,000 men, seemed determined on a most obstinate resistance. Judging, and rightly, that it could expect no pardon, it also realized, no doubt, that this meeting was destined to decide a struggle, now centuries old, between two races, two powers, and two religions. Until now, apart from the foundation of a few outposts, such as the new establishment at Sviajsk, Moscow had done no more than exercise reprisals. In Kazan she was to take possession of one of the bulwarks of ancient Islam. Supported by a chief sent from the Crimea, Tsar Indiger-Mohammed, and strengthened by the picked warriors who had come with him, the Tartars revived the memory of their ancient valour, victoriously repulsed the first assaults, and drove Ivan to fear the merciless winter would again overtake him.

In September a fearful storm overthrew quantities of tents in the Russian camp and destroyed a number of storehouses on the Volga, and from the top of their ramparts, in which his artillery failed to make any breach, the besieged began to jeer at the White Tsar. Making obscene gestures, so the

chroniclers tell us, turning their backs and lifting up their
garments, they cast defiance at him : ' Look, my Lord Tsar,
this is how thou wilt take Kazan. . . .' And with strange
yells and contortions, which passed for sorcerers' spells, they
terrified their adversaries' superstitious minds.

Ivan did not flinch. To fight the spells, which had called
down torrents of rain, he sent to Moscow for a miraculous
cross, which brought back the fine weather, and against the
fortifications, which the Tartars so industriously repaired, he
appealed to the skill of his foreign engineers, who constructed
works of approach which doubled the effect of the Russian
fire and hastened the end of the business. In the popular
poetry this siege, which really lasted a few weeks, attains the
proportions of the Siege of Troy. Ivan is described as having
spent *eight*, or even *thirty*, years at it. By the end of September,
in reality, the artillery had battered a sufficient breach, and
a general assault was arranged. This was delivered on
October 2, 1552. The result, a complete victory for the besiegers,
was a foregone conclusion. But on this occasion Ivan, who
had hitherto proved his tenacity and courage, did not dis-
tinguish himself. His followers had already grown accustomed
to see him take active command. By making them fear, he
had taught them to obey him. They looked for him at the
head of the columns that moved out to the attack. He was
not there. The leader had disappeared ; all that was left was
the Rurikovitch, who fled before danger, shrank from the
bloody struggle, and lingered in prayer before the altars. At
dawn, while Prince Michael Vorotynski was blowing up the
last works, a solemn office had been said in the chapel erected
in the middle of the Muscovite camp, and the legend tells us
that the mining operations corresponded with the solemn
course of the Orthodox liturgy. The Slav version of the *ponem
inimicos tuos scabellum pedum tuorum*, chanted by the deacons,
was followed by the first explosion, and a yet louder one greeted
the Gospel verse, ' There shall be but one fold and one Shepherd.'
But deacons and sappers alike had done their work ; the thing,
now, was to mount the breach. Appeals to the God of the
Christian and the God of Mahomet were already mingling in
the air with the hail of arrows and bullets. A breathless
boïar ran in : ' Sire, it is time to start !' he cried ; ' your men
are at close quarters with the Tartars, and your regiment is
waiting for you !' Gravely Ivan replied, in the words of a
Scripture text, of which the men of his period and his intellectual calibre carried an inexhaustible supply in their memories.
This one conveniently indicated the value of long prayers, and
the Tsar did not budge an inch. Then came a second and
more pressing summons. The Tartars were recovering their

lost ground, and the Sovereign's presence at the head of his troops was absolutely indispensable. . . . Ivan heaved a deep sigh, shed copious tears, and once more set himself, aloud, this time, to invoke the Divine help.

The whole spirit of his race was expressed in the young Prince's behaviour, and some allowance, too, must be made for his personal temperament and the particularly nervous nature we know him to have possessed.

Was he a coward ? No ! The man who was soon to face the fury of others, impose his indomitable will by fire and sword, and maintain it, in spite of the hatred, the weak-heartedness, and the defeated conspiracies of his closest comrades, for twenty years, the coming champion of the *Opritchnina*, could not be a coward. He was the heir of the Russian Princes who had made Russia great, not by prodigies of valour performed on battlefields, but by the dim paths of intrigue, bargain-making, and economy, by miracles of patience, cunning, humiliation, stoically borne ; and he was the pupil of the ancient Eastern teachers of his country, who had imparted to him their own Asiatic habits of indifference, scorn of physical effort, and haughty calm. The act of fighting, of dealing blows and running the risk of receiving them, did not enter into their conception of a Sovereign's duty. The master had slaves for all that work. His part was to give his orders, send his men out to die, and say prayers himself.

But the boïars about Ivan did not take this view. One of them, very likely, offered his Sovereign some violence, for at last the Tsar, having exhausted every shift, kissed the miraculous picture of St. Sergius, drank a little holy water, swallowed a morsel of the host, received his chaplain's blessing, harangued the clergy, praying for their pardon, and claiming their blessing too, now he was going 'forth to suffer for the true faith,' mounted his horse, and galloped off to join his regiment. But even then, Kourbski tells us (and it did not occur to the Terrible himself to contradict this eye-witness's assertion), though the battle was nearly over, and there was no reason to fear any fresh onslaught on the part of the besieged forces, some difficulty was experienced in getting the horse and his rider to the front—the boïars had to lay their own hands on the bridle.

The Muscovite standards were already floating over the ramparts, and the leading columns of the assault had entered the town. The carnage began. Six thousand Tartars vainly tried to reach the open country by fording the river Kazanka. Ivan never thought of putting a stop to the bloodshed. Even in the West, a town taken by assault was a town condemned to death. The women and children alone were spared, and they

were carried into captivity.   After all was done, the Tsar
ordered a *Te Deum* to be sung, and with his own hands planted
a great cross on the very spot over which the standard of the
last Khan of Kazan had waved during the fight.   A church
was to be built there, and within two days it was ready and
consecrated.   By the end of the week two governors, Prince
Vassili Siémiénovitch Serebrianyï and Prince Alexander Borissovitch Gorbatyï, were installed in the conquered city, and the
victor was hurrying back to Moscow, and to Anastasia.

On his way home, at Vladimir, joyful news awaited him.   The
Tsarina had borne a son, who received the name of Dmitri.
At Taïninskoïé, one of the oldest villages in the vicinity of
Moscow, whither Ivan was one day to retire, during the trials
which were to follow on this triumph, his brother George and
his chief boïars came to offer him their first congratulations.
At Moscow the Metropolitan, attended by all his clergy, met
him, and compared him to Dmitri Donskoï, to Alexander
Nevski, and to Constantine the Great; then, casting himself
at the Sovereign's feet, he thanked him for having won this
triumph for the country and the Church.

A great triumph it was, indeed,—greater, both in its immediate and its more distant consequences, than Henry II.'s
acquisition, that same year, and at the other end of Europe, of
the Three Bishoprics.

IV.—THE CONSEQUENCES.

In 1555, Gourii, first Archbishop of Kazan and Sviajsk,
went forth to take up his new post, with a whole following
of priests, and his departure was the counterpart of that
migration of the Greek clergy which, in Vladimir's time, had
brought the true faith from Byzantium to Korsoun.   After
officiating at the consecration of a Church of the Intercession of
the Blessed Virgin, built within the Kremlin, in memory of the
new conquest, Gourii took ship, the chants and prayers continuing even on board, and all along the course of the Moskva
and the Volga a huge concourse of enthusiasts greeted the
representative of the true faith.   Russia was beginning an
apostolate of her own.   The blow delivered on the walls of
Kazan had struck the whole of Islam, and the budding prestige of the Crimean Khans had been irreparably shaken.   There
was to be no more of that talk of ' beating his forehead ' in
their presence, which had previously appeared in Ivan's correspondence with his redoubtable neighbours, even though he
claimed to be on equal terms with the Emperor of Germany
and the Sultan of the Turks !   From the material point of
view alone, Kazan was a most precious prize.   This remnant

of the Mongol power, set on the middle course of the Volga, and barring the way eastward, had been an obstacle in the way of Russian development, if not an actual menace to Moscow. At Kazan the first collision between Islam and Christianity had occurred, long before this time, when the Mahometan Bulgars, the earliest inhabitants of the place, had fought with the first Princes of the new Russia of the north-east. To Asia, Kazan had been a commercial and industrial centre, to the Mongol Empire, the only solid footing left it in Europe ; for, once reduced to the Khanate of the Crimea, it became a mere nomad camp, floating hither and thither over the southern steppes. Astrakan still remained, but once Kazan had fallen, the breaking of the other dyke that barred the onward course of the Muscovite flood became inevitable, and the conquest and process of colonization thus begun were to rush with resistless force towards the rich lands watered by the western tributaries of the Volga, and the eastern affluents of the Don.

Kazan, in short, was the natural rallying-point of all the numerous savage tribes—Tcheremisses, Mordvians, Tchou-vaches, Votisks, Bachkirs—dwelling in the mountains and on the plains along both sides of the Volga. The mountaineers, already attracted by the shelter of Sviajsk, were creeping into the bosom of Muscovy; the men of the plains were soon to follow them.

But, in his eagerness to return to the joys of home, and taste the glories prepared for him at Moscow, Ivan had been in too great a hurry to leave the country. The boïars, Kourbski tells us, had pressed him to wait till the spring. Yet they themselves, it may be, had furnished him with good reasons for a contrary decision. Though they had had to drag him by his bridle under the walls of Kazan, at the last moment, his ' men who served ' had threatened to forsake him several times before he got there at all, declaring they were worn out, and their strength and resources alike exhausted. A silent struggle was already going on between him and them. He felt he could not hold them, and they saw he was not the man to be long content with a grudging, capricious, and uncertain obedience. The reforms he had accomplished or prepared had evoked a discontent which never lost an opportunity of showing itself, among the higher aristocracy, and Ivan probably felt none too safe in the midst of the warriors who had taken upon themselves to show him his proper place in battle, and put him into it by force.

None the less, as early as in the month of December, the benefits of the victory seemed likely to slip through the victors' fingers. At Kazan and in its neighbourhood alarming symptoms appeared. Open revolt soon followed. The Cossacks and *Striéltsy* of the occupying force lost 1,000 men in a fight with the tribes of the *gornaïa storona* (mountainside), and the rebel mountaineers actually founded a new town on the Mecha, some seventy versts from Kazan. In 1554, it became necessary to undertake a regular campaign against these insubordinate hillmen, and five years were to elapse before the peaceable possession of the country was insured. But Moscow had already taken a new and important step in another direction.

V.—THE CAPTURE OF ASTRAKAN.

In the spring of this same year 1554, 30,000 Muscovites embarked on the Volga, under the orders of Prince George Ivanovitch Pronski, and on August 29, while Ivan was keeping his fête-day at Kolomna, a courier brought him the news of the taking of Astrakan. This was not a final conquest ; Pronski contented himself with setting up a Tsar of his own choosing in the town, Derbich-Ali by name, who was obliged to pay a yearly tribute, and guarantee the Muscovites free navigation of the Volga between Kazan and Astrakan. The Muscovite policy was following the game which had worked so well with Schah-Ali at Kazan. The results in this case were similar. Derbich's task, between the new protectors, the native Tartars, who were very impatient of their authority, the Khan of the Crimea, who claimed to exercise his, and the Turks, who seemed inclined to have a finger in the quarrel, was a very difficult one. He soon entered into communication with the Tartar-Nogaïs, a neighbouring tribe, the headship of which was in dispute between two brothers at war with each other, Ismaïl and Iousouf, and, supported by one of these competitors, he sought to make himself independent. A fresh expedition became necessary. Derbich having made a pact with Iousouf, who was afterwards killed by his brother, and then, with the dead man's children, Moscow treated with Ismaïl, who, as the reward of his assistance, claimed certain modest gifts—three hawks, a falcon, a gerfalcon, and a sparrow-hawk, a great deal of lead, a great deal of saffron, a large quantity of colouring matter and paper, and 500,000 nails. . . . Derbich was driven out. His place was taken by Ismaïl, who in his turn grew unruly, and had to give way to his nephews. Moscow had trouble for many years with all these turbulent vassals ; but her acquisition of the mouths of the Volga was definite and final, and the little principalities round the Caucasus, which brought Russia into their own disputes, begged her to arbitrate between them, or craved her support, gradually drew her—unconsciously, or almost against her will—further and further eastward, to new fields of action, which, one by one, perpetually widened the frontiers of her all-absorbing hegemony.

The emigrant colonists followed the progress of this policy, step by step, and now and then even outstripped it. From the banks of the Don and the Terek, where they had already taken root, they spread to the Crimea, to the very gates of Azov, in never-ending enlargement of the sphere called the *kazatchina*—the Fatherland of the whole floating population of the Empire, a Fatherland of indefinite limits and continually changing borders. The power of the system of territorial aggrandizement thus set in motion was tremendous. But it contained an element of danger.

VI.—THE COSSACKS.

The authority wielded by the metropolis over this element, so variable and turbulent in its nature, was purely nominal, and destined long so to remain. It was not till 1570 that Novossiltsov, one of Ivan's lieutenants, was to endue it with a little more coherence on the banks of the Don, and it was the third centenary of this event which the present army of the Don celebrated some thirty-four years since. But even in 1577, Ivan was obliged to send Mourachkine with a whole army corps to put down the brigandage and violence of his unruly subjects, and it was then, as it is believed, that Ermak and his comrades, the future conquerors of Siberia, to escape just reprisals, took refuge with the Stroganovs, other colonists of a different type, whose huge possessions touched the borders of Asia.

This led the way to a fresh, and still greater conquest ; but meanwhile, the behaviour of these Cossacks and their arbitrary enterprises forced Moscow into an inevitable struggle with the last remnants of the Tartar power. Unable to make Ermak and his armed thousands on the Crimean border bend to his will, Ivan was fain to take the initiative in a duel which was not to end till Catherine II. sat on the Russian throne. As early as 1555—a prelude to the expeditions led by Galitzine and Münnich—he sent out 13,000 men under Chérémétiev. As always happened in such circumstances, the Khan, the swifter and bolder of the two, forestalled his opponent, beat a retreat before the Tsar, but inflicted a serious defeat on his lieutenant. This did not prevent a Cossack detachment, under the *diak* Rjevski, from making a reconnaissance as far as Otchakov, and stirring lively emotion and an outbreak of warlike feeling among the Little Russians along the banks of the Dnieper. Then came the turn of a subject of the Polish King's,

Prince Dmitri Wisniowięcki, who occupied and fortified an island in the Dnieper—the Khortitsa—and tried to brave the neighbouring Khan by dint of an alliance with the Tsar.   He was driven out in 1557, but took his revenge the next year, under the very walls of Azov ; while the commander of the Muscovite forces, Daniel Adachev, reached the estuary of the Dnieper, captured two Turkish vessels, landed in the Crimea, and spread terror through that country.

The moment seemed to have arrived when a mighty effort promised to end it all, and the men about Ivan eagerly pressed him to act.   But the young and glorious Sovereign had wheeled round already.   His enterprising spirit, its back turned on the east, was travelling westward, whither it was drawn by stronger intellectual affinities and more seductive prospects.   Livonian affairs held him tight, and were to absorb him for many a year. It was the story of Peter the Great already.

VII.—The Crimea and Livonia.

The two undertakings were irreconcilable, and however he may have been criticised then or since, the determination at which the Tsar arrived seems fully justified.   To go to the Crimea was not the same thing as to go to Kazan or Astrakan. The transport of troops and stores from the banks of the Moskva to those of the Volga was insured by a network of navigable rivers, running, partly at all events, through a comparatively populous country.   The other road, once Toula and Pronsk were left behind, was over the desert, through resourceless and shelterless wastes, in which, till the end of the eighteenth century, the ceaseless efforts of Russia's best military leaders were to meet with shipwreck.   And behind the Crimea, it must be remembered, lay the risk of having to face Turkey—the Turkey of the sixteenth century, the Turkey of Solyman the Magnificent.

Further, Ivan was not absolutely free to choose.   Since 1554, he had been at war with Sweden on account of this same province of Livonia, and on its account, too, but for a succession of truces, always on the point of being broken, he would have been at permanent war with Poland.   Thus the solution of the one problem was not so urgent as that of the other. Anxious as the Crimean business was, it could wait.   But in Livonia neither Poles nor Swedes would wait, for they could not afford to delay an intervention in which Moscow must forestall them if she was not to be cut off for ever from all access to the Baltic.   The ancient colony of the Teutonic knights was reaching that condition with which Poland was one day to become acquainted, and which constitutes, in a sense, a strain on all neighbouring greeds ; the house was on fire, and everybody was trying to be the first to put it out. Give the whole thing up ? Ivan could not dream of that ! Even at Kazan he had only won his victory thanks to Western help, aided by the European engineers and workmen whom he laboured to gather from Germany, Hungary, and Italy. But if in Italy, and to some extent in Germany, a disposition was shown to second his efforts, other European countries, and those his nearest neighbours, kept up a suspicious and hostile attitude, stopping his recruits on the border, forbidding the sale of the most modern war material, and striving to maintain the wall built by centuries of isolation between themselves and their too enterprising neighbour. Livonia was a door—the door which Peter the Great was one day to beat down with mighty strokes. The chance of opening it at once, and that, as it seemed, without any excessive effort, offered now.

Might not Ivan have used the shores of the Gulf of Finland between the mouth of the Siestra and that of the Narova, which were already his, to the same end ? This objection has been advanced, but it is not conclusive. The foundation of St. Petersburg had not occurred to the young Tsar. Even if he had possessed the genius of Peter the Great, he would probably have found it impossible to force the huge and unreasonable labour involved in such an undertaking on his subjects. To make that other effort, the value of which is open to discussion, possible, a century and a half later, the century and a half of labour, which insured the triumph of the absolute power and gave the son of Alexis a weapon the son of Vassili never wielded, was indispensable. Peter the Great himself was not to be content with his marshy port on an inhospitable coast, and it seemed, at this time, as if all Ivan had to do was to put out his hand.

In fact, though his undertaking failed, its failure was solely due to a surprise which nothing led him to foresee. This surprise, this miracle, was the ephemeral career of Batory, a real King, in a country which for years had known mock Kings only —a Hungarian cavalier, who broke in the Polish mare, and drove her full gallop to stop the Russian horseman's way. Only ten years this wild ride lasted, but they sufficed to work an utter change in the chances and positions of the two parties : to transform the Poland of the Jagellons, which Moscow knew, and which she could defy, into another Poland, of which she had not dreamt and whose strength she could not gauge ; to make the triumph on which the victor of Kazan and Astrakan had so surely reckoned a disaster, and convert the match on which every appearance had encouraged him to stake his fortunes into a most disastrous wager.

He brought the prestige of his recent exploits to it—a glory the splendour of which one only of his successors was to increase, and a popularity none of them attained. The conquests and reforms of Peter the Great, less understood, have consequently been less appreciated. Ivan, the conqueror of Islam, the lawgiver who cared for the humblest, and wrought terrible justice on the ' great ' only, forced admiration even from foreigners. No Prince in Christendom, thought Jenkinson in 1557, was so feared by his subjects, and so loved. At the same epoch, Foscarini, the Venetian envoy, eulogizing the justice meted out by this peerless Sovereign through his simple and appropriate laws, and praising his affability, his humanity, the variety of his information, the splendour of his Court, and the strength of his armies, places Batory's future opponent among the foremost Princes of his time. He enumerates, with evident pleasure, his *gens d'armes*, equipped in the French fashion, his artillery-men, drilled on the Italian system, and his splendidly taught arquebus-men, and affirms that no other European power possessed so formidable a war machine. In a mirage of victory, his fancy beholds two armies, each numbering 100,000 men, ready to march at a sign from the great Tsar—' which seems almost improbable,' he adds, ' but it is absolutely true.'

The truth, which I have endeavoured to follow strictly, certainly warranted Ivan's momentary belief in the certainty of his superiority over his Polish and Swedish neighbours. He had a numerous army, a well-filled treasury, the advantage of a strongly-constituted power, the assurance which is born of success. All these—power, glory, and popularity, were to be swallowed up in a gulf, the dangers and the depth of which neither he nor any other man could recognise or plumb.

CHAPTER IV

THE CONQUEST OF LIVONIA

I.—HISTORICAL ANTECEDENTS. II.—THE LIVONIA OF THE SIX-
TEENTH CENTURY. III.—THE MUSCOVITE CONQUEST. IV.—
THE EUROPEAN INTERVENTION.

I.—HISTORICAL ANTECEDENTS.

THE sixteenth-century struggle for the possession of the Baltic was a dispute over an inheritance. This inheritance had been left by the Hansa, that great political and commercial con-federation which the discovery of the New World ruined and left defenceless in the hands of its greedy neighbours. It was a formidable struggle, both as to the competitors—Sweden and Denmark, Muscovy and Poland—whose enmity it stirred, and as to the interests—industry and commerce, religion and culture—it involved. Up till about 1540, Moscow's part in the matter was quite a small one—that of an auxiliary of the two Scandinavian Powers. But at that period the common adversary, the Hanseatic Towns, was almost worn out, and as an inevitable consequence, the quondam allies fell out over the division of the spoils.

Historically speaking, the claims of the Muscovite competitor were the most ancient. Even such early works as Nestor's have been argued to contain proof that Livonia and Esthonia formed an integral part of the ancient Russian Empire. When the old chronicler enumerates the peoples under the yoke of the Varegian Princes, he speaks of *Liv* and *Tchoud*, settled on the Baltic coasts. But such proofs as these are rather dubious in their nature. The first undoubted attempt by the Russians to get a footing on the Livonian coast dates from the year 1030, when the town of Iouriev was founded on Tchoud territory, under Jaroslav the Great. But the existence of this establishment, which received a serious check at the hands of the Semigalian inhabitants of that neighbourhood, soon became most precarious, and it was threatened, in the following century, by a still more redoubtable competitor—the Germans were close at hand

The history of the German colony in Livonia goes back to the foundation of Lubeck by Henry the Lion, about the year 1158. The merchants of the new city, seeking an opening in the direction of the Scandinavian countries and the Far East, played the part of Columbus to that other America. A struggle then arose between Germans, Russians, and Scandinavians, each seeking to get first possession of the course of the Eastern Dvina, already connected with the whole river system of Russia, and even with the basin of the Dnieper. Livonia was the key of this situation, and here, as in many places, then and even nowadays, German colonization was backed up by German missionaries. During the latter half of the twelfth century—the exact date is not settled—Meinhard, a canon of the Augustine Order, built a church near the town of Uexkull, which became the seat of a bishopric and the nucleus of a fortified town. Meinhard's successor, a Cistercian, Bishop Berthold, was a prelate after the manner of Barbarossa, who wore a sword on his hip, and used it oftener than his crozier. In the year 1198, backed by a crusading Bull from the Pope, he appeared with an army and a fleet at the mouth of the Dvina. A series of successes and reverses ensued, and it was not till the days of the third Livonian Bishop, Albert, a descendant of a noble Bremen family, who founded Riga, and

the Order of the Brothers of the Sword, that a final conquest
was effected. The new confraternity was modelled on that of
the Templars, though less directly ruled by the Pope. It had
a Grand Master, who resided at Riga, and a Chapter, including
five chief Masters, and all the members of the Order were bound
in equal submission to the episcopal authority. It thus constituted a strongly centralized power. But the regular and the
secular element soon fell out of harmony, and in the course of
the struggle that swiftly ensued, the Order was led to develop
the material and political side of its organization, to the detriment of its spiritual calling. This brought it face to face with
fresh rivals, and involved it in ruin.

In Prussia, and hard by these knights with red crosses on
their white mantles, dwelt the Black Cross Knights of Hermann
von Salza, created an Order of Hospitallers by the Pope in
1191, converted into a religious Order by German Princes in
1198, and endowed with an establishment on Slav territory by
Conrad, Duke of Mazovia and Cujavia, who, as ill-luck would
have it, appealed to these knights, in 1225, to put down and
convert the Prussian idolaters. In the following century
St. Bridget was to denounce, and prophesy terrible chastisement for, the misdeeds of these false apostles, ' who only fight
to feed their own pride and gratify their covetousness.' Greedy
and overbearing, they felt hampered within their own dominions,
and the neighbouring country of Livonia struck them as a
desirable prize. In 1236 an unhoped-for chance favoured their
ambition—the almost total destruction of the Brothers of the
Sword in a fight with the Lithuanians at the Saula. Rome,
solicited by both Orders, decided on their fusion, and the Red
Cross Knights disappeared.

But in this new arrangement the neighbours had to be considered. In 1238, Denmark received Revel, Harrien, and
Wirland. In 1242, after a desperate encounter with Alexander Nevski's Russians on the Peipus, the Black Cross Knights,
who had begun to spread along the Finnish coasts, were forced
to retire, and give up their most recent conquests. At the
close of the thirteenth century the Order had to reckon with
yet another hostile element—the burgher class in the towns,
which was growing very powerful, and which made common
cause with the Bishops against the knights. The knights won
the day, and towards the middle of the fourteenth century
they celebrated a greater triumph still : Courland, Livonia,
and Esthonia fell under their exclusive rule, Denmark only
preserving a nominal claim, to be put forward at a later date,
to her ancient conquests.

It was but a short-lived triumph. In the next century, Poland
came upon the scene, and on September 1, 1435, the troops of

the Order and the Russian-Lithuanian bands under Svidrigaïlo, which had been artfully drawn into a fratricidal struggle, suffered a crushing defeat at the famous Battle of the Swięta. At that moment the Knights of the Black Cross were in jeopardy even in Prussia. On July 15, 1410, a quarrel, then two centuries old, renewed since then, and perpetuated under various forms, was fought out in a memorable combat, for the commemoration of which preparations are now being made at Cracow and Moscow. More appropriately divided, this time, into two hostile camps, the world of Germany and the budding world of Slavdom had set their picked warriors face to face, and at Grünwald, on that great day, the flower of German chivalry fell before the onslaught of the Polish-Lithuanian army under Iagiello and Witold, and the power of the great Order bit the red dust of that historic battlefield.

Into the balance of that fight Poland had cast her own fate. The Order, ready to join hands against her even with the Slavs, while, in its hate of their very name, it called her, to whom it owed everything, the ' hereditary foe,' had plotted her ruin, and would have shrunk from nothing that might insure it.   In the previous century it had laboured to induce Sweden, Hungary, and Austria to accept a plan of partition, the earliest of them all (Treitschke, *Historische und Politische Aufsätze,* 1867, p. 35 ; compare Martens, *Recueil des Traités,* v., *Introd.,* p. vi). From that same period, too, while striving to obstruct the understanding between Poland and Lithuania which was to be its ruin, it had shown an inclination to adopt the future watchword of secularized Prussia—an alliance with Moscow and against the benefactors thus rewarded.

The Battle of Grünwald settled all these accounts for a time. The knights, obliged, in the following year, to accept a peace at Thorn, which diminished their Prussian dominions, felt their Livonian interests threatened by the Polish-Lithuanian agreement, which they vainly strove to break, and the Muscovite alliance was still a far-off dream. Meanwhile the reflux of Muscovite expansion in Livonia itself had to be faced. In 1483 the belligerents were fain to make a truce, and before this had expired, the Russians had built Ivangorod, their own Narva— a standing threat to the Teutonic Narva on the opposite bank —on the eastern side of the mouth of the Narova River.

At the same time, the Order was undergoing a process of internal decomposition, soon to be hastened by the appearance of the Reformation, and the conversion of Albert of Brandenburg, appointed Grand Master in 1510. In 1525, when, at the Landtag of Wolmar, Albert, after an unsuccessful war, accepted the suzerainty of Poland over his secularized States, Livonia seemed inclined to follow the same course. The courage of

Walter von Plettenberg, who led the Livonian party in the Order, failed him; but from the towns Protestantism was pouring forth with resistless strength, shaking the knights' fortresses to their foundations, finding its way even into the Bishops' courts, leaving nothing of the Catholic establishment standing, save its external trappings, and casting the whole country into a state of anarchy which, whencesoever it came, rendered the final catastrophe inevitable. In 1554, Plettenberg's successor, Fürstenberg, began to treat with Moscow; but in 1557, having shown an inclination to defy Poland, he was forced to appear before King Sigismund-Augustus at Pozwol, and accept an offensive and defensive alliance against Russia. It became clear, then, that Livonia was to be the lists on which that country's own fate was to be fought out between its neighbours, and for their benefit. She was to save nothing for herself, not even her honour.

II.—THE LIVONIA OF THE SIXTEENTH CENTURY.

The Muscovite invasion, to which all this was the prelude, and all the horrors that came in its train, have been represented in the German literature, and even in the popular poetry of that epoch, as a Divine chastisement. Truly, the spectacle the country then presented was both sad and repulsive. The Order was fast nearing its end. The warlike spirit of the old knights had died out; there was no civic spirit to take its place. The vow of celibacy had given rise to a state of unbridled and filthy debauchery. Immoral women swarmed round the knights' castles, and the perpetual orgies in which they lived and the luxury they displayed reduced the poor to a state of hideous misery. Sebastian Münster, in his 'Cosmography,' published in 1550 (French translation, dated 1575, p. 1618), has given us a dark and revolting picture of this revelry, and the distress which was the reverse of the medal; and a preacher of that period—Tilman Brakel, of Antwerp—has not left us a more favourable account of the lives of the upper clergy, greedy and dissolute, living in the midst of concubines and bastards.

But morals were corrupt at that time all over Europe, and this feature would not in itself suffice to explain the weakened condition of every local institution. To this other causes contributed. Ever since the twelfth century, the country had been offering the contradictory spectacle of a German colony, engaged, after the fashion of the Greek settlements on the coasts of Sicily and Asia Minor, in forming an independent State, without any national basis at all. The local population, of Finnish or Lettonian race, though it submitted to the foreign masters who thus imposed their yoke, had nothing in common with them—neither tongue, nor customs, nor religion. Forced into Catholicism, and now driven towards Protestantism, it continued equally indifferent and hostile. Hence there was no solid foundation, no real link with any metropolitan or central religious power. The Emperor's power over the Order and the Pope's power over the Church were both of them purely nominal. There was no real centralization and no real unity, only a perpetual fight between the secular and regular elements, in spheres the frontiers of which were ill-defined, and perpetually altering. The general tendency of all towns was indifferently to repudiate the authority of both the rival powers. Anarchy reigned everywhere. As Droysen has justly observed (*Geschichte der Gegenreformation*, 1893, p. 204), in that hour, when the seven provinces of the Low Countries were evolving a new European State out of a great war, *viribus unitis*, the State of Livonia was crumbling, *viribus unitis*, under the centrifugal action of its own dissociated elements.

Against the fourfold threat of invasion—Polish, Muscovite, Swedish, and Danish—there were no home resources at all. As a military power, the Order had disappeared, and there was no money, or no inclination to give it, for recruiting an army— no hope of outside help. The Order did indeed reckon on appealing to the German Fatherland in the hour of danger, but for two centuries it had never failed to claim from that same Fatherland every right and license dear to a haughty and suspicious particularism. Poland was offering support, and even insisting on its acceptance ; but Poland, torn by intestine quarrels, weakened by the vices of her own Government, and absorbed by the great work of her union with Lithuania, was more to be feared as an enemy than welcomed as an ally. In 1554, Gustavus I., King of Sweden, would fain have taken advantage of the difficulties besetting Ivan, then busy with his Eastern conquests ; but the league in which he invited Livonia, Poland, and Lithuania to join him fell to the ground, and, left alone to cope with Moscow, he was forced, in 1557, to agree to a forty years' truce. Thus the unhappy Livonia was left face to face with the fourth rogue, who found plenty of reasons or pretexts for attacking her.

What reasons ? In the tacit agreement entered into by a portion of Western Europe to keep the door shut between herself and her powerful neighbour in the North-West, the Baltic provinces were fond of assuming the watchdog's part. At this very moment the famous business of Hans Schlitte gave proof of their zeal in this matter. This Saxon adventurer, who, in 1548, had received the Emperor Charles V.'s permission to recruit artisans and men of learning in Germany for the Tsar's service, was stopped by the Livonians, with his troop of followers, cast into prison, and kept there until all his men, some 100, or even 300—the authorities contradict each other as to the exact figure—had dispersed. Another reason. Once Novgorod had been incorporated into the Russian Empire, the conquest of Livonia became necessary to that Empire. The new masters of the city had begun by destroying the German counting-house, or *niémiétskii-dvor ;* but the trade thus taken from the Hansa at once passed to the Livonian towns, Riga and Narva, fresh centres of operations by which Moscow suffered—hostile cities where foreigners were forbidden to learn Russian, and all credit given to Russian merchants was punished with fines (Richter, *Geschichte der Ostsee Provinzen,* 1857, ii., p. 422).

What pretexts ? In old days, between the Livonian town of Neuhausen and Pskov, there had lain a belt of wild country, over which, after many years of contest, the Russians had obtained a sort of suzerainty, based on an annual tribute of 10 pounds of honey, paid by the Livonian husbandmen living on the land. When the bee-swarms disappeared, together with the forests in which they had lived, this tribute had first of all been converted into a money payment—fixed, according to some authorities, at six crowns a year—and had finally fallen into disuse. In 1503, Moscow revived the ancient memory, and endeavoured to confuse the issue with her pretensions on Derpt, the Iouriév of the old Russians. In 1554, just after the taking of Astrakan, Ivan added more recent griefs : violations of his frontiers and confiscations of orthodox churches by Protestant fanatics. In 1556, having insured the safety of his new possessions in the East, he began to use sterner language. One of his predecessors had already sent the Livonians a whip as an admonitory hint. The Tsar's Ambassador seems to have borne this precedent in mind. The tribute of 10 pounds of honey or six crowns was transformed, in his mouth, into a tax of one mark for every member of the population, and he claimed arrears amounting to 50,000 crowns.

The Bishop of Derpt flattered himself he would get out of the difficulty by a diplomatic quibble ; he promised full payment, but made the execution of his engagement dependent on the Emperor's approbation. And to the Emperor the Livonians forthwith wrote, in what sense my readers will easily imagine. Terpigorev, the Ambassador, pretended he did not understand all these artifices. The Emperor ? What had the Emperor to do with it ?

' Yes or no—will you pay the money ?' Instead of the coin, they brought him an explanatory letter for Ivan.

' Ho, ho !' said he, as he carefully put the paper into a silken bag, ' here's a beast that promises to grow big and fat !' And, ordering refreshments to be served to the astonished magistrates, he gambolled joyously about, jumping on the tables. Terrified, the city fathers dilated on the impossibility of getting so large a sum of money together in a few days.

' Come, come, there are twelve barrels full of money in the cellars of your Town Hall !'

' Maybe so, but we are not the only people who have the keys. Revel has one, and Riga has another.'

' Very good, very good ! If you don't choose to give the money, the Tsar will come and fetch it !'

And the Tsar really was coming. Had not Macarius likened him to Alexander Nevski after the Siege of Kazan ? Ivan was to pin his pride on justifying the flattery by following in the national hero's wake, and going back to the road out of which, since the thirteenth century, the necessities of her defence against the Tartars of the East had forced Russia. But the times were changed. Poland, Sweden, Denmark, and the whole of Europe were to take part in the struggle now ; even Spain herself, to serve her dream of extending her universal monarchy to the distant North, aimed at seizing the Sound, disputed the Danish alliance with Mary Stuart, and claimed an interest in the fray.

III.—THE MUSCOVITE CONQUEST.

In February, 1557, a Livonian deputation made its appearance at Moscow, begged for further delay, and was dismissed. Ivan refused to see the envoys himself, desired Adachev to pack them off, and organized a punitive expedition. It was swift and cruel. Towards the close of the year, an army, largely made up of Tartars, and commanded by Schah-Ali, the late Tsar of Kazan, invaded Livonia, and ravaged the country in a frightful manner. Not a feature was lacking. Women were abused till they died, children were torn from their mother's wombs, houses were burnt down, crops were destroyed. There may be a certain exaggeration in the chronicles of the country, but at that period war was hideously barbarous everywhere, and Schah-Ali's Tcheremisses were probably no whit inferior to the Duke of Alva's more disciplined bandits. Having chosen out the most beautiful of their female captives, and satisfied their lust on them, they tied them to trees, and exercised their skill as marksmen on their living targets. This may have occurred, though the presence of two Russian commanders—Prince Michael Vassilévitch Glinski and Daniel Romanovitch Zakharine, brother of the Tsarina Anastasia— probably laid some restraint on these savage performances.

But the expedition was not so much a conquest as a summons, *manu militari*. As Terpigorev had said, the Russians had come to fetch the money ; thus some amount of terrorism may have appeared necessary.

Scarcely any resistance was offered. Over a distance of some 200 versts the invaders only met a few weak detachments, easily put to flight or cut to pieces. But as yet no result was apparent. Most probably Ivan had not settled on any definite plan. He was working a little at random. In January, 1558, Schah-Ali, having amassed a huge amount of booty, agreed to a truce, and more delegates travelled to Moscow. They brought an instalment of the sum claimed, and they obtained a hearing. Thanks to the intervention of the Russian merchants concerned in the trade with Derpt and the neighbouring towns, and thanks, too, it may be, to certain other gold pieces prudently bestowed, unhoped-for concessions seemed within view. Ivan had already consented to treat, and to waive his claim to tribute, on account of the exhaustion of the country. But all the negotiations were upset by an unexpected piece of news. Narva, refusing to accept the truce, had continued to exchange cannon-shots with Ivangorod ; the town had surrendered in April, 1558, but the fortress had continued to hold out ; now (May 11) it had been carried by assault. Instantly Adachev, who was in charge of the negotiations, changed his tone. Hitherto the question had been, in somewhat nebulous and confusing terms, that of a tribute to be paid by the Bishopric of Derpt. Now a quite different claim was put forward ; the whole of Livonia was called upon to accept, not only a similar obligation, but the suzerainty of Moscow, ' on the same terms as the territories of Kazan and Astrakan.' Fürstenberg, Grand Master of the Order, and the bishops of Derpt and Riga, were to proceed to Moscow, and there do homage, and Narva and the other lately-conquered towns were to be simply annexed to the Empire.

This method of proceeding by stages, and as it were by a succession of forward leaps, has always been the traditional policy of Russia. But Ivan certainly did not expect his new conditions to be instantly accepted. He was drawing a bow at a venture. Punishment had been wreaked, and he was now broaching conquest. The war went on, and the unhappy Livonia was no more fit to face it than before. The towns alone checked the invasion for a time. In his despair, Fürstenberg, who could only get 8,000 men together, made over his command to his coadjutor, Gotthard Kettler, who did no better. The fortresses yielded in their turn : first Neuhausen fell, then Marienburg. Cowardice and treachery were in every corner ; the German chroniclers themselves admit it.

' Marienburg, das edle Schloss
War uebergeben ohne Schoss,'

sang Taube, the Livonian.

In July, 1558, the Siege of Derpt began, and the Bishop and his immediate circle seem to have hastened the surrender so as to insure certain personal benefits for themselves. In the wars of the sixteenth century this capitulation constitutes an exceptional case, and one which does honour to Moscow. The Russian Commander-in-Chief, Prince Peter Ivanovitch Chouïski, granted the natives of the town a full amnesty, the free exercise of their religion, the maintenance of their ancient municipal laws, judicial autonomy, and liberty to carry on a free trade with Russia. And at first these conditions were scrupulously observed. Moscow's tactics altered with her plans. After the assault at Narva, a regular system of pillage had been arranged, the traces of which are still apparent in the St. Petersburg *Künstkamera*. The country was rich, though it could find no money for defensive purposes. In the house of one citizen, Fabian von Tisenhausen, 80,000 marks in gold were found. But the very graves were ransacked, we are told. In those day the laws of war permitted or authorized even worse profanations. Once they had sacked everything, the victors grew less fierce, and even showed great moderation. The privileges granted at Derpt were extended to Narva. Steps were at once taken to restore the town, and the husbandmen round about it were liberally encouraged and helped.

Ivan, indeed, thought things had gone too far in this direction. He only ratified Chouïski's charter subject to certain restrictions : a Russian member to be admitted to the municipal tribunal ; the appeal to the Riga court to be replaced by an appeal to the Muscovite *Voiévode* or to the Tsar ; and trade with all Russian towns, save Novgorod, Pskov, Ivangorod, and Narva, to be taxed. As an offset, the natives of Derpt were to be allowed to settle in any part of the Empire that suited them. These advantages must have been sufficiently alluring. for before autumn came, twenty other towns had offered their submission.

Yet the war was not nearly over. Revel still held out, and in September, when Chouïski, after the invariable habit of Russian Generals, retired before the approach of winter, Kettler seized the opportunity and took the offensive. Gathering 10,000 men, he recovered Ringen, after an attack which was said to have cost him 2,000 men, and pushed on as far as Siebiéje and Pskov, the suburbs of which town he burnt. Ivan, threatened by the Crimean Tartars, was fain to gulp down his wrath and agree to a truce in May, 1559. But the next year the Crimean danger had passed away, and he had his revenge.

On August 20, under the walls of Fellin, Kourbski met the flower of the Livonian nobility, gathered for one mighty effort, and crushed it at a blow. The fall of Fellin very soon afterwards gave him possession of the person of Fürstenberg, who had already resigned in Kettler's favour. The former Grand Master, with other prisoners of high rank—the Landmarschall Philip Schal von Bell, his brother, Werner Schal von Bell, Comtor of Goldringen, and Heinrich von Galen, Bailiff of Bauschenburg—was sent to Moscow, and treated, according to the Livonian chronicles, with great barbarity. The prisoners, we are told, after being led through the streets and beaten with iron rods, were put to further tortures, massacred, and their bodies left to be devoured by birds of prey. As regards Fürstenburg, this assertion is certainly disproved. He was not killed ; he was given a landed property in the Government of Iaroslavl, and as late as 1575 he declared, in a letter to his brother, that he had no reason to complain. Some Danish Ambassadors happened to be at Moscow when he arrived there. They ascertained that the ex-Grand Master was being well treated, and on their return journey they testified to this effect before the magistrates of Revel. But they added that the other prisoners had been put to death.

These executions, we must admit, were logical, according to Ivan's view of the situation. As the progress of his arms in Livonia woke ancient memories, flattering to the national pride, the Tsar, not unnaturally, ended by looking on the possession of the country as his vested right, and its inhabitants as rebellious subjects of their legitimate lord. When the King of Denmark insisted on his own claim to Esthonia, did not Ivan reply that Iaroslav had established a far more valid claim 500 years before, when he built Iouriév, and covered the face of the country with Orthodox churches ? Livonian and German authorities are unreliable, and Russian authorities, unfortunately, non-existent, as far as this war is concerned. It finds no echo even in the national poetry of the country. The fall of Kazan, the conquest of Siberia, and the interests, religious and economic, they involved, produced a far deeper effect on the imagination of a race which then, as now, was both realistic and mystic to a high degree. The realities to which the Livonian massacres, void of all brilliant feats of arms, led up, were nothing to it ; they spoke neither to its mind nor to its heart.

Yet they were beginning to be clear enough in Ivan's brain. Three parts of the work of conquest were accomplished. Kettler and his comrades, reduced to a few strongholds in Livonia and threatened in Esthonia as well, applied, turn about, to the Emperor, to Denmark, Sweden, and Poland. Any chance of intervention seemed most problematical.

IV.—The European Intervention.

All over Europe, in truth, the impression produced was very deep. From the very outset of the war, the Protestant writers, always ready to denounce Spanish intrigue, had asserted that Philip II., who, as a Catholic monarch and as King of England, had a double interest in taking advantage of the quarrel, would strike at Protestantism in Livonia, and gain a footing on the Baltic seaboard. The Pope, no doubt, was playing this game with him. The Emperor was called on to act. But Ferdinand I. was Emperor now—a bureaucratic Sovereign, eager to apply quietism to politics. He called for reports, opened a correspondence with Ivan, exchanged views with the Kings of Denmark, Sweden, and Poland, and did not budge an inch.

Ivan, indeed, took pains to humour this high authority. The relations between the House of Hapsburg and the Moscow Government, which had begun in the fifteenth century, could only be kept up, on the Russian side, by dint of a constant and deliberate sacrifice of the susceptibilities and pretensions it reserved for its other neighbours. This time, therefore, with many an evasion and recantation, the Tsar went so far as to impute the misfortunes of Livonia to her having forsaken the Catholic faith !

The seaboard towns and the German Electoral Princes offered a better hope, for all of them expressed a desire to come to their Livonian brothers' assistance, and recognised the urgency of the necessity. Yet at the Augsburg Reichstag in 1559, this fine zeal ended in a vote of 100,000 florins subsidy ! The Deputationstag of Spire took the matter more seriously, declared the whole of Germany threatened and Mecklenburg in imminent peril ; but here, too, the result was trivial— another subsidy of 400,000 florins, an interdict on Russian trade, and some talk of a solemn embassy to Moscow. The prohibition, simultaneously imposed, of any intercourse between Livonia and Poland, or other neighbouring Powers, betrayed the real anxieties of the gathering, and none of its decisions were carried into effect. As Droysen puts it, all the Germany of those days knew how to do was *queruliren, protestiren, dupliciren, und tripliciren.* Ferdinand did something on November 26, 1561, by publishing the celebrated manifesto which forbade the navigation of the Narova. This amounted to forbidding the introduction of Western merchandise, and especially of war material, into Russia. But England had already discovered other roads, and was using them, in spite of the denials which fell from the lips of the astute Elizabeth, who had just (1558) succeeded her sister Mary Tudor. And,

on the other hand, in spite of a more or less sincere feeling in
favour of the Livonian cause, the Hansa itself was betraying an
inclination to compete with the English traders in this matter,
and also to take advantage of the catastrophe which had rid it
of dangerous rivals at Riga, Revel, and Derpt.

Livonia was forsaken, neither more nor less, and in her
despair she was driven to knock at those foreign doors which
her natural defenders, even while they themselves betrayed her,
had sought to shut in her face. In January, 1559, an envoy
from the Order made his appearance before the Polish Diet at
Piotrkow. He found it absorbed in home affairs, and appealed
to the King. This King was Sigismund-Augustus, the last of
the Jagellons, the representative of a worn-out race. Indolent,
debauched, weak, careless of the morrow as he was, the best
blood of the great Italian politicians ran in his veins. His
mother was that Bona Sforza who, with the culture and habits
of her native land, had brought the intriguing spirit and violent
instincts of her own family to Cracow. To all external questions, as a rule, her son brought a clear conception of the interests at stake, and a deep conviction of his own proper course.
He listened to the envoy, and some two months later he began
to parley with Kettler, and formulated his conditions. Poland
would defend Livonia, even if that involved a war with Russia,
but she must have Kokenhausen, Uexkull, Dunaburg, and Riga
—the keys of the burning house. The risk was a heavy one
indeed, and Bona's pupil could not renew the mistake, the
folly, into which his father Sigismund I. had fallen, letting the
proffered friendship of Prussia slip, and helping, for the benefit
of the House of Brandenburg, to build up a power that was
crumbling away. The acquisition of a northern frontier and
of the Baltic seaboard was becoming a question of life or death
for Poland, and the present opportunity, though less favourable than the last, was tempting enough.

For some time Kettler hesitated. He travelled to Vienna to
seek a better bargain, made an attempt to get a hearing from
the Augsburg Diet, but ended by going back to Vilna, while
the King parleyed with his unruly senators, and at last the
merciless logic of facts overcame all resistance. Between
August 31 and September 15, two treaties were signed, whereby,
in return for a promise of help against Ivan and an undertaking
to respect the religion, rights, and privileges of the inhabitants,
about a sixth of the Livonian territory was made over to Poland.
This frontier strip ran from Drujen to Ascherade. As to the
places which might be recovered from Russia, they were to
return to Livonia after payment of an indemnity of 700,000
florins, which Sigismund-Augustus was confident never would
be found. But how about the Emperor's authority? The King

declared he would insure its being respected. And the truce he had just signed with the Tsar ? Sigismund would intervene as the legitimate Sovereign of the country in dispute, and would thus break none of his engagements.

He was in no hurry, indeed, to put this complicated and somewhat ambiguous programme into execution, and the repugnance manifested by the Polish *Szlachta* to the effort required of it does not suffice to explain his inaction. The game was a risky one, and it was wise to make suitable preparation, and await the best possible opportunities. Livonia was begging for help, but she was not quite open in her dealings yet. The Polish army, valiant but undisciplined, might not be equal to the task. To have Riga would be a good thing ; but what was the use of Riga without ships, without a fighting and a merchant navy ? Sigismund, a born diplomat, dreamt of a league which would unite the Scandinavian Powers and the Hanse towns under his own direction ; a cunning politician, he sought to provide himself with the weapons he lacked—regular troops, ports, and a fleet.

Time, alas ! was to fail him, and so was the complaisance of his fancied allies. The Hansa had other views, and the Scandinavian Powers had not the remotest intention of playing Poland's game. As soon as Derpt had fallen, the nobility of Revel had appealed to the King of Sweden. Gustavus Vasa, a dying man, remembered the humiliation imposed on him when Livonia had stolen away and left him to accept the peace of 1557, which the Tsar had refused to negotiate in person. The *voiévodes* of Novgorod had been good enough then to treat with ' the little King of Stockholm.' The habit of using these intermediaries dated back to the days when Novgorod had been independent. ' What,' said Ivan, when objections were made—' what is *Stekolna* (*sic*) and its master ?' A shabby little town that had turned a merchant's son into its Sovereign ! He was doing it too much honour already ! The Livonian envoys waited for the accession of Gustavus' son, the impetuous and ambitious Erik XIV., who received them more graciously. In May, 1561, in spite of all Kettler's opposition, a fresh treaty stipulated that Revel, with the territories of Harrien, Wirland, and Ierwen, should be made over to Sweden. There was a Polish garrison in Revel, it is true, but Erik's fleet and his German mercenaries made short work of that. On June 15 the garrison laid down its arms, and thus began a duel which lasted for a century, and which, by the exhaustion of the two adversaries, was to end in the ruin of the Republic and the triumph of Russia.

Then Denmark entered the lists. As early as in 1558, King Christian II., even while sending an embassy to Moscow to conclude a treaty of peace and claim the return of Esthonia to its legitimate owner, had opened negotiations with the Bishop of Oesel, Johann von Münchausen. This was his answer to the supplications of the unhappy Livonians, who had not failed to knock at that particular door on their own account. Christian died, and an understanding with his successor was all the more easily arranged. Frederic II. had a brother, Magnus, a lad of twenty, and old enough to claim his share of the inheritance, Schleswig-Holstein. Either spontaneously or incited by Christopher von Münchausen, the Bishop of Oesel's brother, a most enterprising man, the King was inspired with the idea of offering the following compensation to his younger brother. Johann von Münchausen, who had no right whatever to do it, sold his bishopric for the sum of 30,000 thalers ; the Dowager Queen of Denmark, Dorothea, advanced the money, and in April, 1560, Magnus landed at Arensburg, the castle of which place was made over to him by the episcopal bailiff, and a certain number of Livonians joined him there. Christopher von Münchausen had already, and on his own authority, assumed the title of the King of Denmark's lieutenant in Esthonia, Garria, Oesel, and so forth. Magnus, whose career was to be a most extraordinary one, and who was the finished type of the adventurer of those days, was soon to call himself King of Livonia.

Thus was prepared the confused and mighty conflict which was to hold the future of the countries affected, and the chances of the various competitors, in suspense for over twenty years. And thus, too, Sigismund-Augustus' hand was forced, and he himself driven to act sooner than his natural wisdom would have dictated. In August, 1560, Nicholas Radziwill, ' the Black,' appeared at Riga with a Polish army, and, tearing off every veil, demanded the cession of the whole of Livonia, with the secularization of all the territories on the right bank of the Dvina and their direct annexation to Poland.

Kettler's fellow-countrymen have looked on him as a traitor. In all probability he was only an unlucky player of the game. He had striven to find an ally ; but, as a certain writer has asserted, in justification of Sigismund-Augustus, nobody can ally himself with a corpse. And Fürstenberg's unlucky successor certainly exhausted every means of resistance and every form of delay. It was not till Poland appealed, at the close of this fateful year, to the altered circumstances and the necessity of fighting three enemies instead of one, that he was forced to give in. On March 5, 1562, having, in his quality of Master of the Teutonic Order, recognised, by a document dated November 21, 1561, the union of Lithuania and Livonia, and accepted the possession of Courland and some neighbouring districts, with the title of Duke, in vassalage to Poland, for himself and his heirs, he resigned his cross, his mantle, and the keys of the castle of Riga, into Radziwill's hands.

The spectacle offered by the Baltic provinces at that moment was an extraordinary one, even for that period of incessant territorial rivalries. It surpassed that presented at Milan or in Flanders. The new Duke of Courland, a feeble copy of the first Duke of Prussia, was beginning his reign south of the Dviña. In the north the King of Poland was installing himself as lord and master on part of the ancient possessions of the Order, and proclaiming himself suzerain of them all. Riga, while submitting to the same authority, remained in theory a free city of the Empire, and so preserved a shadow of independence. The Swedes kept Revel and Harrien. Oesel, Wiek, and Pielten were subject to Magnus. And the Muscovites, established in the Bishopric of Derpt, in Wirland, and along the Lettonian frontier, were preparing to dispute the ownership of the whole country with all its other occupants.

'At present,' wrote a gazetteer of that period, ' Livonia is like a young lady round whom everybody dances.' One important fact had already passed into history—the close of the period of the Crusades and of the Orders of Chivalry. Modern Europe, even while she still hesitated to receive Russia into her bosom, had joined with Muscovy in wiping out the past, and laying the foundations of a new order of politics. But this new order had yet to evolve itself out of a mighty and chaotic struggle, the incidents of which I must now briefly relate.

CHAPTER V

THE STRUGGLE FOR THE EMPIRE OF THE BALTIC

I.— SWEDEN AND POLAND. II.—THE COALITIONS. III. — THE COLLAPSE OF THE ALLIANCES : MAGNUS. IV. — IVAN'S CANDIDATURE FOR THE POLISH THRONE. V.—THE ELECTION OF BATORY.

I.—SWEDEN AND POLAND.

Is the question of the possession of the Baltic provinces definitely settled even now ? Such an assertion would certainly be rash. It may very possibly become one of the objects, at all events, if not the cause, of a fresh struggle—a conflict of powers far more formidable than those whose onslaught and fierce strife the sixteenth century saw. The elements of the problem have modified, to be sure ; yet, great as the change has been, a certain amount of reality, living, or capable of second

birth, may well linger amidst the memories I must now evoke.
Herein lies the chief interest of this particular page of history.
In some of the episodes I shall endeavour to set forth, Ivan's
physiognomy stands out clearly, and this will be their only
charm. For the sake of clearness, I shall point out, in the first
place, the phases apparent in a succession of events so complicated and intervowen that a guiding thread of some sort is
absolutely necessary. And beforehand, too, I claim my
readers' patience ; the thought of a possibly not far distant
future will lead them to regard this return to an instructive past
as interesting, or, at least, useful.

The first phase brings us down to the year 1564. Ivan,
wavering between a Swedish and a Polish alliance, humours
Denmark, and triumphantly holds his own against Poland. In
the second phase, from 1564 to 1568, Sigismund-Augustus, by
allying himself with Frederick II., drives Sweden and Muscovy
into an agreement, and brings about a land war between
Sweden and Denmark. The Tsar preserves the upper hand on
land in Livonia ; but while Poland is absorbed and paralyzed
by her internal affairs, Ivan's struggle with his boïars and the
old régime also tends to distract his attention from the Livonian
problem : this is the period of the *Opritchnina*. Third phase :
The dethronement of Erik XIV. in 1568, and the accession of
John III., brother-in-law of Sigismund-Augustus, bring about
a reconciliation between Sweden and Denmark, thanks to the
good offices of Poland. The fear of a coalition carries Magnus
over to Ivan's side. Fourth phase : The death of Sigismund-
Augustus, in 1572, places Poland temporarily out of action.
Ivan puts forward his own candidature for the inheritance of
the Jagellons. Fifth phase : The election of Batory ends in
the triumphant reappearance of Poland on the scene, and the
decision of the struggle in her favour, almost exclusively.

Germany, it will be observed, does not appear in the conflict,
though the soil concerned was German, or, at all events,
Germanized. Yet we shall catch a glimpse of her playing the
part and wearing the expression, both of them neutral, which
devolved on her at that time, not without making some ineffectual attempts at intervention. She stood by, and awaited the
favourable moment, but of her rights, her ambitions, and her
hopes she did not abdicate a jot.

For half a century, as I have said, ever since 1514, when
Russia had snatched Smolensk from Poland, the relations
between the two countries had been in a condition which
could not be described either as war or peace. Now fighting,
then negotiating, doing both at once sometimes, they disputed, theoretically, over the possession of that one town and
the territory round it, but the quarrel really covered a much

wider area. The negotiations, perpetually renewed, had ended by constituting a sort of protocol, in virtue of which every fresh parley began with the claim, on one side, not to Smolensk only, but also to Novgorod and Pskov, as the ancient patrimony of the Lithuanian Princes, and, on the other, with a demand for the cession of those three towns, and also of Kiev and all the Russian territories then under Polish rule, after which the parties separated, the envoys, Russian and Polish, declared the negotiations broken off, and took their leave, departing, in some cases, without further ceremony, but always allowed themselves to be brought back, and always, failing some final understanding, accepted a provisional arrangement of some kind. The question of the *patrimonies* was left to stand over ; Poland would not recognise the Tsar's new title, and the Tsar, by way of reprisal, refused to give Sigismund-Augustus the title of King, so the difficulty was eluded by drawing up the terms agreed on in duplicate—one Russian copy and the other Polish—and signing a truce.

Into relations already most difficult Livonia had introduced a fresh subject of dispute, and one which seemed to admit of no compromise whatever. Yet in 1560, at the very moment when the treaty imposed on Kettler had imparted a decisive form to the King of Poland's intervention, Ivan took upon himself to despatch an important Ambassador, bearing very conciliatory proposals, to Warsaw. An event had occurred, the consequences of which have been exaggerated, but the influence of which on the Sovereign's mind, on the development of his character, and, to a certain extent, on the trend of his policy, cannot be denied. The Tsar had just lost his wife, that Anastasia whose beneficent influence as his guardian angel forms part and parcel of a legend I am sincerely sorry to weaken. Ivan loved the mother of his elder children dearly, and the delights of home life, which she alone seems to have taught him to enjoy, probably did something to soften his fierce and violent instincts, just as the grief the loss of his companion caused him may have produced a contrary effect. More than this cannot be asserted with any certainty. And neither his love nor his sorrow, indeed, can have been so very deep, for the monarch's first care, on the morrow of the disaster, was to seek another bride.

Sigismund had two unmarried sisters, and the chief object of the mission confided to Ivan's Ambassador, *Vokolnitchyï* Feodor Ivanovitch Soukine, was to obtain the hand of one of these ladies for his master. Somewhat ungraciously, and after much delay, the King allowed the Ambassador a sight of the two Princesses at church. Whether by accident or on purpose, the younger of the two, Catherine, turned round, and this was the prologue to one of the darkest tragedies of a period most fertile in dramatic episodes. Besides the personal charms which Soukine set himself to press on his Sovereign, the betrothed thus suggested had the advantage, in Ivan's eyes, of representing, with a brother who had no sons, a race which had reigned, and reigned by hereditary right, at Vilna. In her the Tsar of all the Russias would possess yet another right, newly acquired and most incontestable, to claim *his Lithuanian patrimony*. Fed, no doubt, by his passionate and stubborn temperament, this idea was to root itself so deeply in the monarch's mind as to become, in the course of the following years, the directing element of his whole policy.

But very probably Sigismund-Augustus sought nothing more on this occasion than to save appearances, and so gain time. From the Polish point of view, this question of the Lithuanian inheritance, quite apart from the difference of faith, was in itself an obstacle in the way of a marriage which would have threatened the integrity of the national possessions, and might compromise the success of that other union between the two Slav races of Poland and Lithuania which the last of the Jagellons was then labouring to complete. Besides all this, Catherine had already been almost promised to John, Duke of Finland, brother of the King of Sweden. In 1562, this promise became a reality, and immediately afterwards, hostilities between Russia and Poland began.

Just as in past days, they fought while they negotiated, and negotiated while they fought. Ivan wrote abusive letters to Sigismund-Augustus, and Sigismund-Augustus avenged himself by inciting the Khan of the Crimea to invade Russia. In February, 1563, the Tsar, in command of a numerous army, and carrying with him a coffin which, he declared, was to serve either for the Polish King's corpse or for his own, won a signal advantage. First Smolensk and then Polotsk, the chief town of a Polish-Lithuanian palatinate, and an important commercial centre, carrying on relations with Riga, fell into the hands of the Muscovites. Until Batory's time, their powerful artillery was always to tell in a war of sieges. Ivan talked more than ever of taking back Kiev ; with his usual vehemence, he jeered his unlucky adversary, who had appealed to the King of Sweden in support of his claim to Livonia, and called him his ' brother.' ' What King ? What brother ? . . . He might as well fraternize with a water-carrier !' But the next year, on a battlefield which, in 1508 and in 1514, had already proved fatal to the Russian arms, on the banks of the Oula near Orcha, the Poles had their revenge. Nicholas Radziwill, ' the Red,' cut the troops led by Prince Peter Ivanovitch to pieces, and the Prince himself fell in the fray.

Instantly the Tsar, forgetting all his recent scorn, attempted to come to an understanding with Sweden. Erik XIV. had lost no time about sending an embassy to Moscow when he ascended the throne in 1561, and since that time, in spite of the rude treatment showered on him from that quarter, and against the advice of his recognised counsellor, Philip de Mornay, who urged him to prefer an agreement with Poland, he had persevered in his course, extending his own possessions in Livonia meanwhile. To these, in the year 1563, and thanks to the self-interested assistance of Christopher, coadjutor of the Bishop of Riga, who sought the hand of the King's sister Elizabeth, were added a number of towns—Wolmar, Wenden, Kezholm, Pernau, and Padis. Now that the Tsar was making him these unhoped-for overtures, Erik fancied his cause was won, and that they were to go halves. He had to lower his pretensions. Ivan began by claiming the lion's share, and would only give up Revel, Pernau, and Wittenstein. Then, quite suddenly, he tried to bring the Polish Princess, now Duchess of Finland, whom he had hoped to call his own, and whom even now he would not give up, into the negotiations. He wanted almost the whole of Livonia, and he wanted Catherine, too. She was married, but that was of no consequence to him. A Duke of Finland was nothing at all. He had married a wife himself, but that, too, was nothing ; she was only one of his own subjects—a mere slave, therefore. At a later date he declared he had never intended to interfere with the freedom of the lady he coveted, nor tamper with the sanctity of the bonds into which she and he had both entered. He had believed Duke John to be dead. . . . He had not thought of marrying Catherine or making her his mistress. . . . He only wanted to hold her as a hostage . . . His explanations are multifarious and most improbable. The brutal fact remains : his claim, impudently manifested and obstinately maintained, to get possession, with no honest intention assuredly, of this modern Helen, on whose account nations were making themselves ready to fight. As to the motive of his obstinacy, little doubt can be felt : far less than on the lady—though he thought of her too, no doubt—it was on Lithuania that the fiery despot's fierce desire was set.

Erik XIV. began by assuming an heroic attitude. He would not give up his sister-in-law any more than he would give up Livonia, and he was already talking of allying himself with Poland, with the Emperor, with all the German Princes, to bring this barbarous Russian to reason, when his threatening dreams were confronted by another and far more threatening reality. Negotiations had been going on since 1561 between Poland and Denmark ; they had just been brought to a conclusion. On a treaty of alliance, offensive and defensive, signed at Stettin on October 5, 1563, had followed an agreement with Lubeck, whereby the Hanseatic League joined the coalition. Ivan, on his side, had also negotiated, and signed at Mojaïsk, on August 7, 1562, a treaty with Denmark, which bound the two Powers to act against Poland and Sweden, the Tsar recognising the Danish rights over Esthonia, Oesel, and Pilten. Sweden found herself alone ; she was fain to capitulate. It may be that her sacrifice was too eagerly and too complaisantly made. Erik's envoys went to Derpt, agreed to negotiate with the Governor of Novgorod and Russian Livonia, Michael Iakovlevitch Morozov, only, and accepted almost all the conditions Ivan had previously demanded : they gave up Livonia, except for Revel, Pernau, Wittenstein, and Karkhus, and by a secret clause they undertook to give up Catherine's person. The Tsar, at all events, never ceased to claim the execution of this last engagement, concerning which, it must be confessed, we have no precise and absolutely reliable testimony. Erik had always been opposed to a marriage which carried his brother into the Polish camp, and the presence of Danish envoys in Poland at the moment of the wedding would seem to indicate that diplomatic arrangements, the vexatious effects of which Sweden was now called on to endure, were not unconnected with it. The question of the independence of Finland seems to have been put forward at the same time, and Erik, without waiting for any confirmation of his suspicions as to that matter, lost no time in making it impossible for his rebellious brother to realize them. After a shortlived struggle, he captured him, and shut him up in the Castle of Gripsholm. Catherine shared her husband's imprisonment. The King, therefore, was in a position to dispose of her according to his redoubtable partner's will.

Was this ever his intention ? Or did his plenipotentiaries exceed their powers ? The problem has never been solved. The one undoubted fact is that the Treaty of Derpt was not ratified at Stockholm. Fresh negotiations only resulted in the conclusion of a truce. However all this may have been, Erik, engaged in a double war against Poland and Denmark, was forced, whether he would or no, to become Ivan's ally, and this position set his foot on a dangerous declivity, to the bottom of which he was destined to slip. From this time forward two coalitions stood face to face, while Magnus, now reduced to Oesel, Dago, and a few strongholds, fought for his own hand in the general *mêlée*, and watched his opportunity to join whichever side promised him most.

II.—THE COALITIONS.

Sigismund-Augustus tried to draw in even the Low Countries, but he only succeeded in vexing the States by the measures he took to cut off the Narva trade. In 1565, while success and reverse were pretty evenly balanced in Livonia, the Poles taking Pernau and the Swedes harrying Oesel, two successive disasters overtook Sweden : in January, Frederick II. closed the Sound, and so cut her off from Europe ; and in November, the Emperor Maximilian, yielding to the remonstrances of Frederick of Saxony—the real Agamemnon of this war between the nations—published a manifesto which laid the Swedes under a ban, as breakers of the peace, allied with a barbarous monarch. This paralyzed Erik's progress in Livonia, and his brother's party began to lift its head. Yet Maximilian was being constantly worked on in an opposite sense by the representatives of certain German trading-houses which had interests at Moscow. Their agents were busily employed in turning public opinion. One of them, Veit Zenge by name, the Duke of Bavaria's commercial envoy at Lubeck, went further than his fellows. Did not Ivan glory in his own German origin ? This was, in fact, one of the Tsar's manias. Veit Zenge even felt sure he had Bavarian blood in his veins ! In return for the honour of entering into closer relations with the Emperor, and receiving one of his orders, the Muscovite Sovereign would give 30,000 of his best cavalry to fight against the Turks, and a large sum of money into the bargain ; he would even relinquish his claims to Livonia, and place his Church under the Pope's authority ! Matrimonial arrangements might set a convenient seal on this agreement, so desirable in the interests of Christendom in general. Ivan had a son and daughter, both of marriageable age, and in the Moscow *terems* there were beauties who might well set all the Princes in Germany a-dreaming. These conceits, discussed at all the German *Tagen*, did not fail to produce their effect on the decisions of the Empire and its ruler, both of them already inclined to an indolent and prudent neutrality.

In 1566, Magnus, hard pressed by the Swedes, sought a reconciliation with Poland. His pretensions were high : he asked the hand of Sigismund-Augustus' second sister, with Livonia as her dowry. The last of the Jagellons did not take the proposal seriously, and set himself, in 1567, to strike a mighty blow, and personally lead a campaign against Livonia. There was a stir at Dantzig. This sea-coast town, which had scant taste for the Polish domination, and was discontented with its own lot, had shown a preference, from the very outset, for the

hostile camp. The agents it employed at Warsaw soon calmed
the agitation. 'The King had the gout in his right arm and
his left leg, and that was the greater part of his equipment.'
The campaign, indeed, turned out a miserable failure. The
royal army, reckoned beforehand at 200,000 Poles and 170,000
Lithuanians, did not bring a tenth part of these numbers
into the field. Nevertheless the Russians, after an unsuccessful engagement with some of these troops at Runnafer, manifested a desire to treat. Ivan's home difficulties were heavy on
him ; the *Opritchnina* was beginning. In Poland, the union
with Lithuania, which, though an accomplished fact, had still
to be finally organized, the strained relations with the Prussian
towns, and internecine quarrels, combined to make peace
earnestly desired. But Ivan laid claim to Revel and Riga,
and began an epistolary argument with the Lithuanian nobles,
which was not calculated to prepare the ground for pacific
agreement.

Kourbski, after fighting bravely and winning brilliant successes with the Tsar's armies in Livonia, had allowed himself
to be surprised under the walls of Nevel in 1562—an event
apparently prepared, to some extent, by his previous and
dubious relations with Poland. Since that time he had
been kept in a sort of semi-disgrace, and the irascible boïar,
thus all the more incited to rebel against his master's despotic
tendencies, had ended by raising the standard of revolt after
the Russian fashion — *i.e.*, by crossing the frontier. The
conclusion drawn in Poland was that the *Opritchnina* would
shortly furnish more rebels of the same kidney, with whom
it would be well to enter into relations, and thus Ivan became
aware of a number of letters addressed to certain of his subjects
by Gregory Chodkiewicz, Grand Hetman of Lithuania, by some
other Lithuanian noblemen, and by the King himself. Angry
and disturbed, his first idea was to convoke, in the year 1566,
the assembly to which I have already referred (p. 136), and
which unanimously pronounced against any concessions at all
in Livonia, while the landed proprietors on the Lithuanian
frontier declared themselves ready to die rather than give up
an inch of ground. The Tsar, thus comforted and strengthened, undertook to dictate answers to the Polish corre-
spondents. It would have been better, perhaps, to treat them
with silent scorn ; but Ivan was always sorely afflicted with
the letter-writing itch. Wherefore Sigismund-Augustus, who
had offered the Prince Ivan Dmitriévitch Biélski a splendid
appanage in Lithuania, learnt what it meant to propose such
bargains to the Tsar's subjects. 'I am fairly well provided,'
wrote the Prince to the King, and addressing him as his brother,
'but you might do a wiser thing—give up Lithuania to my

master, by which means you might make sure of keeping
Poland as his vassal, and becoming, like myself, the subject of
the best of masters !' The text of the other answers may
easily be divined. They are curious specimens of the learning
the Terrible knew how to apply to the service of his spite, calling his adversaries *Sennaherim* and *Navkhodonosor* (*sic*), and
of that Oriental infatuation by which he was occasionally
inspired.

At that moment the Tsar felt the wind was veering round in
his favour ; and, indeed, Erik had come back to the charge,
and seemed inclined to give in altogether, provided Ivan left
him free to settle his own account with Poland. He was even
ready, if we may rely on Dahlman (*Dissertatio de occasione
fœderum regis Erici XIV. cum Russia*, Upsala, 1783), who had
access to the original diplomatic documents, to give up
Catherine herself.

As early as in 1566, the King, we are told, invited deliberation
as to the granting of this concession to the Tsar ; and when his
counsellors refused to agree to it, he instructed his envoy,
Gyllenstjerna, to hold out till the very last, but yield the
point if the alliance could not be had on any other terms.
This information appears all the more likely to be true because
it seems less possible, considering the circumstances, that
Gyllenstjerna can have dared, this time, to exceed his powers.
Now, on February 16, 1567, at the *sloboda* of Alexandrov, where
the *Opritchnina* began its bloody orgies, the Swedish plenipotentiary certainly did sign a treaty of alliance, all the clauses
of which were explicitly made to depend on this condition.
Ivan joined his fate with that of Sweden, on the basis of
the *uti possidetis* in Livonia and freedom of the contracting
parties as regards future conquests (except Riga, which the
Tsar reserved for himself) ; he promised his intervention in
favour of a reconciliation between Sweden and Denmark and
the Hanseatic League, and his armed assistance if his intervention failed. But all this only if Catherine's person was given
up to him. The whole treaty was to be annulled if the Princess
were to die, and the execution of the final clause thus to become
impossible.

The admiration with which this diplomatic document has
inspired certain Russian historians is not very easily justified.
Ivan provided liberally for himself ; the retention of Riga in
Russian hands was the death-blow of the Swedish Revel, and
deprived Poland of her best reason for disputing the possession
of Livonia with her two rivals. The eventual support of the
Russo-Swedish coalition by the Hanse towns also insured the
undoubted inferiority of the Polish-Danish alliance. But Ivan,
not content with these advantages, made them all depend on

the performance of a condition which might prove impossible, and which was certainly disgraceful. Besides his share of Livonia, he demanded, not a wife indeed, nor merely a woman, but the heiress of the Jagellons, a part of Poland! And on this he insisted, against all reason and against all apparent possibility, for the lady was married, and even if she became a widow, was not very likely to consent to marry the man who had carried her off. Unmoved, he followed up his idea, and this proves that the mighty crisis in which he was then involved within the borders of his Empire did not disturb his mind so much as has been supposed ; but he developed and applied his idea in a way which points to a certain weakening of the intellectual faculties corresponding with a simultaneous exasperation of the worst instincts of his nature. In the case of men of robust temperament, drunkenness produces this partial derangement, and Ivan, in the fierceness of his conflict, in the constant use and abuse of his strength, and the hideous stupefaction of the sufferings inflicted under his direction, was drunk for several years—drunk with rage, with pride, with blood—though he went his way, all the same, stumbling, and contrived, in spite of some falls and many extravagances, to maintain a marvellously complete sense of what he had to do, of his interests and his duties.

Fortune, which may be said to have favoured him on this occasion, forbade the execution of the treaty of the *sloboda* of Alexandrov. In May, 1567, a Muscovite embassy proceeded to Upsala to claim its ratification and the surrender of Catherine's person. Ivan, meanwhile, had bethought him of asking the hand of one of Erik's sisters for his son, now eighteen years of age. The girl was sixteen, and her beauty was already renowned. But the Tsar demanded Revel with her as her dowry. This was asking too much, and, further, the Russian envoys found an *Opritchnina*, in Erik's country, which, as to misconduct and excesses, quite rivalled their own. Wrestling with an aristocracy which could not forgive him his origin, and was disgusted by his violence, ' the son of the crowned merchant,' as Ivan had dubbed him, was raving too, and at the Castle of Gripsholm the scenes of a distressing drama were being enacted, one by one. For some time the ex-Duke of Finland, imprisoned within its walls, had been expecting death. A verdict pronounced in 1563 had condemned him, and the King's favourite, Persson, himself doomed to a terrible end, was pressing the execution of the sentence. Erik, though blood had flowed in torrents at his command, ever since 1562, had some scruples of conscience. To satisfy Ivan, he had endeavoured to separate Catherine from her husband, but the intrepid daughter of the Jagellons, proof alike against the most awful threats and the most tempting promises, showed the King's emissaries a ring engraved with the words ' Death only. . . .' The miserable monarch, at the end of his arguments and his resources, threatened himself by the rising rebellion around him, and, dreaming of a safe refuge in Russia, ended, as his most determined apologists admit (Celsius, ' History of Erik,' xiv., French translation, 1777, ii. 139)—though Persson denied it, even on the scaffold—by thinking the advice of his gloomy counsellor the best that offered. John's death would settle everything. The Muscovite envoys were actually making ready to receive their prey, when Erik's reason, already trembling on the steep abyss of his meditated crime, gave way completely. Confusing their mutual positions, he fancied himself the prisoner, restored the captive of Gripsholm to freedom, and besought his pardon. The attack lasted till towards the close of the following year, and Ivan's envoys still hoped to turn it to account for the attainment of their ends. But the Swedish Council continued its opposition, and in a lucid interval, Erik, instead of granting the Tsarevitch his sister's hand, thought he was doing quite enough when he offered him that of Virginia Persdotter, the daughter of one of his many concubines ! Ivan was deeply angered, and in 1568, the last scenes of the drama approached : Catherine's husband ascended the Swedish throne, threw the brother who had so nearly been his executioner into a dungeon, and thus inaugurated a new era in the more and more complicated struggle of which Livonia continued to be the object. In this struggle, Magnus was about to claim a leading part.

III.—THE COLLAPSE OF THE ALLIANCES : MAGNUS.

The new King of Sweden, married to a Jagellon, was the natural ally of Sigismund-Augustus and the chosen instrument of the Catholic reaction against Protestantism. The treaty of 1563 between Sweden and Russia was practically annulled, and the Swede passed over to the enemy's camp. A gifted politician, well trained in matters of war, though more of a theorist than a fighting soldier, John, by the struggle he was soon to begin with Moscow, by the heroic defence of Revel in 1570-1571, and the brilliant victory of Wenden in 1577, was to endow his country with a military glory which was to endure a century and more, until the disastrous day of Poltava. In November, 1568, at Roeskilde, he believed himself on the point of obtaining peace with Denmark and Lubeck, but he was unable to ratify the concessions his plenipotentiaries had allowed their opponents to wring from them. In the mediating hands of the Emperor and the King of Poland, the negotiations dragged on till 1570, and then the Danish cause was compromised by an understanding between Magnus and the Muscovites, while Sigismund-Augustus, who interfered with the preparation of the treaty, and demanded that Sweden should give up all her conquests in Livonia and make common cause against Russia, still further complicated the problem.   For had not the Polish King just signed a three years' truce with Ivan, thus leaving the Tsar free to support Magnus against the Swedes ?

I am tempted to fear my readers' heads must be beginning to swim, but I am helpless.   I am simplifying and abridging to the best of my ability, though my efforts, no doubt, make little show.   Was Magnus acting as the representative of Denmark in Livonia ?   This point, which is still disputed, was unendingly discussed in those days.   There were perpetual diplomatic gatherings and congresses, the litigious question of the *dominium maris Baltici*, and the quite as thorny one of the navigation of the Narova, were both called up, and the end of it all was a treaty, signed at Stettin in February, 1571, in which almost the whole of Europe, the Empire, and, through the Emperor's agency, France, Spain, England, Scotland, and even the Hanse towns—though they were not overpleased— figure alongside of the contracting parties, and express their agreement —which treaty was not put into execution any more than its fellows had been.

Theoretically, this arrangement, which reconciled Sweden and Denmark, left Ivan at war with the Swedes and the Poles, who would now be free to join all their forces against him.   But, in exchange for the free passage of the Sound granted by Denmark, and that country's proffered mediation with the Tsar and Magnus, Sweden had undertaken to respect the traffic on the Narova ; now the King of Poland was to interfere, and Sweden was soon to break her promise.   The Emperor had undertaken, on his side, to buy back the territories Sweden had been holding in Livonia ; neither he nor his successors ever thought of doing this, any more than Livonia ever thought of acknowledging the Emperor's suzerainty.   Denmark emerged triumphant from the struggle, and kept an apparent supremacy over the Baltic ; but the key to the *dominium maris Baltici* remained in Livonia, and through Magnus, whom he was soon to convert into his tool, Ivan still held the dominant position there.

Neither Poles nor Swedes could contrive to check him. Sigismund-Augustus' dreamt-of fleet continued a dream, and the German and Flemish corsairs the Emperor managed to equip were always fought by others, sent out by the Tsar under a famous leader, Kersten Rhode, who pushed on as far as Dantzig.   Thereupon Denmark intervened, and seized the bold pirate's person ; but Denmark's attempts to gain a footing on the Livonian coast were fruitless, likewise. Ivan exchanged artillery fire with Erik's successor in Finland, whither he sent an army and Ambassadors ; but the Swedish envoys found themselves checked by the Tsar's claim for the execution of the 1567 treaty in its integrity. First of all they were kept at Novgorod, and then dragged from Moscow to Mourom, and from Mourom to Kline, in a state of genuine captivity, embittered, according to their own reports, by the most odious acts of violence. Under the twofold pretext of the Swedish failure in keeping the undertaking, and of some affront of which the Russian envoys would seem to have had to complain when they reached Stockholm, the unlucky messengers of peace were treated as if they had been captives of war. Their hands were tied behind their backs, they were marched through the streets amidst a hooting mob, and threatened with the bastinado if they did not give the Tsar satisfaction on every point, including the surrender of Catherine's person. The ex-Duke of Finland was not dead, since he was a reigning Sovereign, and Catherine had become Queen of Sweden ; but Ivan pretended to know nothing about that. So many stories were going about the world !

In the midst of his struggle with the internal crisis his reforms had evoked, the Tsar had just had to endure another and a terrible trial. From 1563 to 1570, he had vainly striven to stem the Tartar invasion with which Poland threatened him. In vain had his envoys, Nagoï and Revski, carried conciliatory messages and splendid gifts to the Khan. Poland did as much, and more, and the Sultan, irritated by the conquest of Kazan and Astrakn, supported Poland. In 1569, a combined Tartar and Turkish expedition threatened Astrakan, and Simon Maltsev, the Tsar's envoy to the Tartars, who had been taken captive by the Cossacks, was a rower on one of the Moslem galleys. In 1570, Ivan agreed to pull down a fort he had lately built on the Terek, but Selim II. instantly claimed Kazan and Astrakan, and the Tsar's acceptance of his suzerainty. Naturally enough, the negotiations were broken off, and in May, 1571, the Tartars, having crossed the Oka unopposed, appeared before Moscow. This time Ivan followed the tradition of his ancestors, and took refuge first at the *sloboda* of Alexandrov, and finally at Rostov. The capital, thus left to its fate, was put to fire and sword. According to testimony which is probably exaggerated, 800,000 men perished in the flames, while the Metropolitan, shut up with part of his clergy in the Cathedral of the Assumption, waited for death ; and Prince Ivan Dmitriévitch Biélski, who had been left in charge of the defence, was stifled in the cellar in which he had sought refuge.

The Tartars, as was their wont, shrank from the assault on the Kremlin, and retired with 150,000 prisoners ; this figure, again, seems improbable. but allowance must be made for the fact that on such occasions as these the whole of the neighbouring population would flow into the capital.

In any case, the disaster was tremendous and the humiliation extreme. On his homeward march the Khan wrote to the Tsar : ' I have ravaged your land and burnt your capital for Kazan and Astrakan, and you, who call yourself the Muscovite Sovereign, have not appeared in their defence ! If you had possessed any valour or any decency, you would have shown yourself ! I want no more of your riches now, I want Kazan and Astrakan, and I have seen and known every road in your Empire !' Ivan swallowed the insult. It was not only as a fugitive that he remembered his ancestors, and his madness, as I have already said, admitted of a great deal of method between his fits of extravagance. His reply was both humble and cunning : he begged a truce, and offered to give up Astrakan ; but his instructions to Nagoï, who still remained in the Crimea, imparted a doubtful meaning to this concession. Astrakan was to be ruled by one of the Khan's sons, who was to receive a resident boïar chosen by the Tsar, just as in the case of Kassimov. Kassimov was one of the small Tartar khanates which had acknowledged the Moscow suzerainty in this manner, and was being slowly absorbed into Russia. These overtures were accompanied by an offer of money ; Ivan went so far as to accept the shame of an annual tribute !

Both sides began to treat. The Khan would listen to nothing unless he was given Kazan and Astrakan, without any conditions whatever. As the negotiations dragged, he demanded an instalment of the tribute—2,000 roubles—which he needed, so he said, to buy plate and other merchandise for some family festival. But Ivan had already taken his measures, had swiftly mobilized all his forces, and, on pretext of the exhaustion of his finances resulting from the recent campaign, sent ' all he had in hand '—200 roubles. Mehemed-Ghireï realized at last that the Tsar was only trying to gain time, and in 1572, he recrossed the Oka. But on the Lopasna, 50 versts from Moscow, he came into collision with the troops commanded by Prince Michael Ivanovitch Vorotynski, and was forced to beat a retreat. Whereupon Ivan forthwith changed his tone, withdrew all previous concessions, and sent jeering messages instead of his former humble missives. ' The Khan still wanted money ? What ? Had he not professed his scorn for riches ?' The Tsar's whole soul is revealed in this trait.

Yet the frightful turmoil had thrown him into a state of irritation which he was quite unable to control. He ascribed the catastrophe to his boïars, who had been guilty of connivance with the enemy, and one of them, at least—Mstislavski—was to acknowledge his guilt ; he multiplied executions, and vented his rage, incidentally, on the unlucky Swedish envoys. Yet in 1571, on his way to Novgorod, whither we shall have to follow him, and where we shall see him presiding over hideous hecatombs, he did consent to see the Ambassadors—in the street— and have an explanation with them as to Catherine. 'If she had been sent to him, everything would have been arranged. It was John's marriage with that Polish woman which had spoilt the whole business in Livonia. Since that time, the Tsar had persuaded himself she was a widow ; otherwise he would never have dreamt of parting a wife from her husband and a mother from her children. But the mischief was done, now, and either he must have the whole of Livonia or the war must go on.' When the Tsar came back from Novgorod he was calmer, as if the shedding of blood had appeased him. He invited the Ambassadors to his own table, and very suddenly caused his representatives to question them as to King John's daughter. She was said to be fair, and he desired her portrait.

The Tsar was not thinking of his son, this time. He had married again, several times over, since Anastasia's death, and to the end of his life he was to interest himself in matters of this kind, much after the fashion of Henry VIII. and the tale of Bluebeard ; and the report of this Swedish embassy, drawn up by its chief, Paul Junsten (*Beiträge zur Kentniss Russland's*, Derpt, 1816), abounds in details of a not less singular nature. Though the inclination he now manifested towards Sweden was so particularly friendly, Ivan resorted, at the same time, to his favourite system of epistolary polemics, and threw himself into them with all his usual spirit.

'You ought to tell us whose son your father was, and what was his grandfather's name ! Was he a King ? What Sovereigns were his friends and allies ? The Emperor of the Romans is our brother, and other great Sovereigns are our brothers likewise. Can you say as much ?'

Then came fresh explanations about Catherine. 'If he had known John was alive, Ivan would never have dreamt of taking his wife from him. He had always intended, indeed, to give her back to the King of Poland in exchange for Livonia. Unhappily, blood had now been shed in torrents, in consequence of this misunderstanding, and the Tsar's envoys had been illtreated at Stockholm. Now they were great lords, not peasants, like John's envoys !' John himself, much addicted to correspondence, wrote back in his best ink, but Ivan insisted.

' Yet it is an absolute truth that you come of a family of churls !'   And once again he began his cross-examination.

' Your father, Gustavus, whose son was he ? . . . When our merchants used to go to Sweden, in your father's reign, with wax and tallow, did they not see him put on his gloves and go as far as to Wiborg to turn the merchandise over, and haggle about the prices ? . . .   And you talk of the Kings who were your predecessors ! . . .   What Kings ?   Where did you find them ? In your larder ?'

The Tsar declared himself ready, indeed, to treat with the tallow-merchant's son, but on condition he begged his pardon, humbled himself, and submitted.   He would then be treated as a relative.   If not, he would find out what happened to the Khan of the Crimea without the Tsar's having even condescended to draw his sword to chastise him as he deserved. His boïars had quite sufficed for that business.   And so letter followed letter, some described as ' severe orders,' others as ' comminatory warnings,' till Ivan, tired, or possibly put out of countenance by some particularly sharp reply, suddenly declared he did not intend to enter into any epistolary dispute.

' You have taken a dog's throat to bark at me.   It does not suit me to fight with you in this fashion !   If your taste leans to that sort of conflict, take another peasant like yourself for your adversary !'

These letters have been published (*Drevnaïa Rousskaïa Vivliofika*, vol. i., part i., p. 23, etc. ; part ii., p. 52, etc.). They cannot have inspired King John with any desire to continue the negotiation they accompanied, nor given him much hope of its success.   All the more so as the Tsar, to his certain knowledge, was meanwhile entering into a correspondence with Erik in his prison, and favouring an arrangement with Magnus.

This arrangement was the work of two Livonian renegades, Taube and Kruse, the first a former councillor to the Bishopric of Derpt, and the second a member of the Livonian deputation sent to Moscow in 1557.   These two men, who had been the Tsar's captives, and had been won over to his side, had become active agents of his propaganda.   In 1568, they had raked up an old attempt at an agreement between Albert of Prussia and Ivan's father, and made it the basis of a new arrangement, to which the King of Poland's present vassal seemed favourably inclined.   In 1570, again, having been rewarded, in spite of their failure—one with the title of Prince and the other with the rank of boïar—they hit upon their right road and found their man.   Ever since 1567, Ivan had been desirous of placing a member of the late Order as Governor in Livonia. Fürstenberg and Kettler both refused, and the name of Magnus occurred to the renegade pair.

Driven out of Revel in 1560, recalled the following year by his brother, who hoped to get him elected coadjutor in the rich Bishopric of Hildesheim, again dismissed, and sent back to Livonia, where he was to see the Swedes and Poles dividing up the territories he longed to possess, this Prince-adventurer—missshapen, one-eyed, and club-footed, according to the not very reliable report of the Catholic writers—having vainly essayed to ally himself with one side or the other, now found himself at the end of all his resources and expedients. His joy may be imagined when Taube and Kruse offered him no less than the sovereignty of Livonia, as the Tsar's vassal. As a matter of form, he applied for Frederick II.'s consent, assuring him his new kingdom would remain dependent on Denmark — an untruth and a piece of nonsense. As a matter of form, too, his elder brother made a few objections, and the matter was settled. Magnus' plenipotentiaries brought back unhoped-for and magnificent conditions from Moscow. The throne, together with that of Denmark, if male heirs failed in that kingdom, was to be hereditary in the new King's family ; all conquests in Livonia hitherto made or to be made by Russia were to be given over to him, and the Tsar promised to help him to retake Riga, Revel, and other towns —all in return for a simple undertaking to serve with the Russian armies in time of war. In May, 1570, Magnus proceeded, with a suite of 400 persons, to Moscow, and there received, not his crown only, but a bride—Ivan's own niece, Euphemia, on whom the Sovereign bestowed a dowry of five hogsheads of gold ! Livonia was to preserve her religion and her institutions, and the Tsar undertook not to introduce any Russian officials into the country.

It was a dream ! But it was nothing more ! When Germany and the whole of Europe expressed a certain emotion, the King of Denmark disclaimed all responsibility—Magnus, he said, had acted without consulting him. Nevertheless, Frederick II.'s agents laboured, underhand, to turn the course of opinion ; it was the Emperor's fault if Livonia was a prey for anybody to take ; and besides, there was the precedent of Albert of Prussia ! When Magnus sent his brother an official announcement of his accession, Frederick replied by a letter of congratulation. But the new King of Livonia made a bad beginning ; he attempted, at the head of a body of mercenaries and Russian auxiliaries, to take Revel from the Swedes, but after a siege lasting thirty weeks—from August 21, 1570, till March 16, 1571—he was forced to beat a retreat, burn his camp, and dismiss his troops, while Taube and Kruse fled to Derpt, and there laid plans with the Poles for an attempt, which very nearly proved successful, against the Russian garrison.

The career of these two rogues is instructive : after intrigues, desertions, and treacheries innumerable, they were one day to find grace in the eyes of Batory himself. Taube, having been forced with a high hand on the Livonian *landtag*, which had refused to receive him, passed away in peace on his own country property, and Kruse was on the point of performing a mission to Prussia for the King when death overtook him. Such was the morality of those days !

During the siege of Revel, Magnus had vainly expected help from Denmark. Just at that moment, as my readers will remember (*vide* p. 198), the Treaty of Stettin was in course of preparation. After the signatures had been exchanged, Sigismund-Augustus once more claimed the aid of Denmark against Muscovy. On September 17, 1571, he published a manifesto, according to the terms of which he undertook to cut off the trade of Narva, blockading the town, and giving more scope and means of action to his privateers than formerly, and thus seemed on the eve of that great effort which had so long been expected from him. Taube and Kruse, no doubt, had already discounted the effect produced. But their calculations were upset, for a time, by an unexpected incident. On July 7, 1572, the last of the Jagellons died of a chill. The extinction of the dynasty and the inauguration of the system of an elective monarchy in Poland were once more to alter the conditions of the fight, and the positions of the adversaries in the long struggle.

IV.—IVAN'S CANDIDATURE FOR THE POLISH THRONE.

In Livonia, as in Poland, the inheritance left by Sigismund-Augustus was not an easy one to take up. With Kettler, with the Scandinavian Powers, with the Khan, his diplomacy had been a brilliant success. But his natural indolence, alas ! had conspired with the idle and anarchical tendencies of his subjects to turn his successes into mere illusions, for there never was any sufficient display of material strength to enforce them. The union with Lithuania had likewise been a triumph over Moscow, but the struggle begun in the heart of Catholic Poland at that very time against Protestantism, and incidentally against every dissident form of faith, had evoked a feeling of resistance amongst the Orthodox populations of the annexed provinces, which drove them towards Russia's outstretched arms. The eager proselytism of the Jesuits, already installed in the Bishopric of Wilna, only quickened the current, and the extension of its sphere of action to Livonia introduced a fresh element of complication. In the absence of a fleet, the blockade of Narva, though it raised difficulties with all the neighbouring maritime Powers, even with Dantzig, threatened to become a farce ; and there being no regular army, any chance of checking Ivan's far superior forces on land appeared most doubtful. Wherefore Sigismund Augustus had hardly closed his eyes in death ere in Lithuania, and even more especially in Poland, a current of opinion began to flow in favour of a solution likely to insure the heirless kingdom something more than the benefits of the most advantageous peace. F. Voropaï, the Polish-Lithu-anian envoy, was deputed to announce the vacancy of the throne to Ivan, and to inform him at the same time of the desire felt to see his son Feodor appear as a candidate for the late King's succession.

The desire was by no means unanimous, nor were those who expressed it entirely sincere. The choice of Feodor was only a compromise, accepted by the mass of the influential electors because they could not agree as to Ivan's own can-didature, which was strongly supported in some quarters, and as vehemently opposed in others. This, in Poland, as in Lithuania, was absolutely repugnant to the great nobles, who were persuaded, and rightly so, that the accession of such a ruler was incompatible with the maintenance of their oligarchy. The Radziwills are even said to have plotted to poison the Tsar's Ambassador to the Diet of Stezyça ; but the only authority the Russian historian who has espoused this story (Oumaniéts, *La Pologne dégénérée*, 1872, p. 71) can put forward to support it, is the copy of a letter of doubtful authenticity. The lesser nobles could not be swayed by these reasons, or rather those very reasons led them to prefer the Muscovite candidate. In Poland, at least, the *Szlachta* was enthusiastically in his favour. Did the *Szlachta* know nothing of the Terrible's temperament and character ? That is not likely. We have proof to the contrary, indeed, in the electoral manifestoes published at the time. In these the faults and virtues of the wished-for Sovereign were laid in the balance, and the excesses of the *Opritchnina* were appropriately re-marked on and discussed. Yes ! Ivan was a severe and pitiless ruler, but in Muscovy he had to deal with subjects whose treason justified the treatment he meted out to them. Things would be quite different in Poland, where his electors' loyalty would disarm his wrath, while his contact with their superior culture would soften his manners. And in him they would have a firm and energetic Prince, one who would be bold and enterprising. They went crazy about him, in short,

and, as Ivan's Ambassadors were to perceive, everything in
Warsaw—dress, carriages, harness, and so forth—rushed before-
hand into the Russian fashion ('Collections of the Imperial
Historical Society of Russia,' lxxi. 763, etc.).

In Lithuania opinion seemed more divided. The country
gentlemen, who had only lately been initiated into the immuni-
ties, liberties, and privileges of the Polish system, and found
them much to their liking, were still more alarmed at the
idea of losing their benefits. But they had not shaken off
the impression produced by the recent and easy capture of
Polotsk, and between the two terrors—of having Ivan for their
master or their adversary—the great nobles themselves,
though they hated him, and reckoned on defeating his hopes,
accepted the Muscovite candidate. Taking it all in all, Ivan
had the advantage of numbers, and it must be admitted that
in this particular crisis the balance of political wisdom and
breadth of view was heaviest in the ranks of the small nobility,
of which Voropaï had constituted himself spokesman. It had
already resolutely undertaken, single-handed, a reform of the
national institutions, and now, single-handed again, it had
conceived the hope of insuring the success of this reform by
the assistance of the dreaded but powerful monarch to whom
it appealed, and of creating, under his ægis and on a Polish
basis, a great Slavonic Empire, strong enough to fulfil a mission
in history which neither Poland nor Russia could undertake
alone.

The idea of this last *union* was not a new one. As early as
in 1506, when, after the death of Alexander Jagellon, a shadowy
election had taken place in Poland, Ivan's father, Vassili, had
come forward. The son remembered this fact, and gave
Voropaï a hearty reception. But why was there any talk
of Feodor? That would only perpetuate the antagonism
between the two countries! Lengthily, with many an argument and metaphor, the Tsar set forth his theory and pleaded
his own cause. 'He had only two sons,' he said, 'and they
were the two eyes in his head. Was he to be robbed of one?
He had been given an evil reputation for severity in Poland and
Lithuania. He did not propose to deny it. Severe he was,
in good sooth, but to whom?' Voropaï had to listen to the
detailed story of all the misdeeds of which the Tsar had reason
to complain on the part of his boïars. Were the Poles likely
to treat him and betray him in the same way? No, indeed!
and he would treat them accordingly. The Tsar-King would
respect their privileges and liberties, would even increase
them. He knew how to treat good men well. 'Look,' he
said to the envoy, 'to a good man I would give the jewelled
collar about my neck and the gown on my back. . . :' And

as he spoke he made as though he would take them off. 'Even if Poland would not have him to reign over her,' he went on, ' he was still ready to sign a peace, and give back Polotsk and all the lands belonging to that place, in return for the cession of Livonia up to the banks of the Dvina. Peace, and the settlement of the questions in dispute between the two countries, were the only really important matters, and Feodor's election could not serve them in any way.'

The Polish and Lithuanian oligarchs knew that well enough, and for that very reason, too, they had adopted this bastard solution, which, as it presented no serious advantage, was less likely to come to anything. As the mass of the electors held to their original idea, and made their preference for Ivan more clearly felt, the nobles went further still. Within a few months, a fresh Polish-Lithuanian envoy, Michael Haraburda, appeared at Moscow, and offered Ivan his choice between his own candidature and that of his son, but burdened it with conditions which Voropaï had not mentioned. The auction mart at Warsaw was open by this time, and the Ambassador of Henri de Valois, Montluc, was soon to defy all other competitors, ' If they ask me to induce the future King to throw a golden bridge across the Vistula, I shall reply, " In what kind of gold would you like it—red or green ?" ' Haraburda was less exacting, and only claimed such a rectification of the frontier as would give Poland possession of Polotsk, with Smolensk, Ousviat, and Oziérichtché as well.

Instantly a misunderstanding, destined to be of long duration, and in itself an obstacle to the success of the Muscovite candidature, arose between the parties. Ivan had no idea of soliciting the Polish vote, much less paying for it. Did he want Poland ? No ; it was Poland who wanted a King to suit her. If he was the King she wanted, she must behave in a proper manner, be humble and suppliant, like all the other folk who came to beg favours of the Tsar. On this point he was quite immovable. Never would he consent to exchange his part for that appropriate to Poland, and he spoke quite clearly to Haraburda, though he mingled his refusal, reasonable enough in itself, with observations which were less so. ' If the Emperor and the King of France laid themselves out to please the electors, that was no reason why he should imitate the example of Sovereigns none of whose ancestors had reigned in their respective countries for as much as two hundred years. He was descended from the Roman Cæsars of the very earliest centuries—everybody knew that !'

Nevertheless, as the idea itself was very agreeable to him, he seemed inclined, for a moment, to make due allowance for the susceptibilities of Poland and grant her Feodor. But the

very next day he sent for the envoy and reset the question in
its real terms : No effectual union of the two countries could
be insured save under his own sceptre, and it was only right
the mutual advantages should be fairly balanced.   Poland,
therefore, should have Polotsk and Courland, but she must give
up her claim to Livonia and cede Kiev,   And, further, the
title of ' Tsar of all the Russias ' must take precedence of
the title of ' King.'

He was asking too much this time, perhaps, but his cunning
intelligence and sure instinct may have guessed the nature of
the Polish magnates' game, and also the consequences of his
own succession to the throne for which he bargained after this
fashion.   These petty rulers, who cared for nothing but their
own privileges, were only trying to fool him, and prevent
his reopening hostilities during the interregnum ; and what
figure would he cut, once he had passed those Caudine
Forks, their pride and their pretensions ?   His last word, as
he dismissed Haraburda, seems to betray the existence of
such an inner thought.   ' After weighing it all well, he thought
the best thing the Poles could do was to elect the Emperor's
son ; and so long as their choice did not fall on a French Prince,
the Sultan's friend, he should declare himself quite satisfied.'
On his way home the envoy was overtaken by a courier,
bearing still less acceptable conditions.   Whereas the idea at
Warsaw had been that Ivan would turn Catholic, he announced
his intention of being crowned there by his own Metropolitan,
in the absence of the Polish Bishops, who were to be excluded
from the ceremony ; he reserved his right to build as many
Orthodox churches as he chose in the country, and himself
retire into a monastery when he grew old !

Thus was the way prepared for the success of Henri de
Valois.   Yet on the very eve of the election, as is proved by
divers witnesses belonging to the hostile camp, Ivan's name
continued popular, (see the ' Memoirs ' of Montluc's secretary, Choisnin, *coll. Michaud et Poujoulat*, p. 429 ; Lippomano's narrative in the *Hist. Russiæ Monumenta*,' Tur-
géniév's edition, i. 270 ; and another Italian narrative in
the Manuscripts of the *Bibliothèque Nationale*, 15,967, fol. 21).
The lesser nobles stood by their candidate, and they swayed
the poll.   But a speech from the Tsar's envoy, which further
accentuated his master's haughty and unyielding attitude,
spoilt everything, and, the wind veering suddenly round, the
French candidate obtained the advantage.   ' Decidedly,'
thought everybody, ' Ivan was nothing but the barbarian he
had been reported to be.'

Would he have been wiser to be more conciliatory at the
time, and to have shown, later, what sort of a King he must

needs be in Poland if he was to continue to be Tsar of Muscovy? Batory was very soon to prove himself more pliable, but Batory had no boïars to govern, nor had he to support the principle of absolute power in his own country, nor uphold his claim to the Empire of all the Russias in the face of these very Poles. In spite of certain incoherences peculiar to his mental constitution and his natural temperament, the conduct of the conqueror of Polotsk and the head of the *Opritchniki* is easily understood—and justified.

None the less, the election of Henri de Valois was a sharp blow to him. Apart from that friendship with the Porte, the nature and consequences of which he was apt to exaggerate, this event upset the political chess-board, on which his moves were already difficult enough, and on which fresh complications were soon to arise. John III., isolated by the rupture of the family bonds which had insured him the Polish alliance, but released, at the same time, from the considerations they had imposed on him, was seeking an agreement with Spain, while France, which dreamt of checking this latter Power by the help of Denmark, of establishing her own protectorate over Livonia, and cutting off the trade of the Low Countries with the Eastern markets, showed herself inclined to support Frederick II. in stronger measures yet. When this hope failed her, she was to endeavour to find the same support and make the same bargain in Stockholm, through the marriage of one of the Valois Princes to a Swedish Princess (Forsten, 'The Baltic Question,' i. 624, from the Copenhagen Archives).

Ivan's judgment of the situation and the way he faced it prove his possession of close insight and all the qualities of a great politician. At that moment Poland did not count. The new King had work enough to do in getting settled on his throne, and the commander of his troops in Livonia could not muster 200 horses, and was waiting in vain for the payment of a draught for 3,000 florins (*Mittheilungen aus dem Gebiete der Geschichte Livlands*, Riga, 1847-1858, iv. 178, etc.). The Tsar, thoroughly well-informed and quite collected, hurried on, choosing as his first task that of ,crushing the ,Swedes in Esthonia. The Poles' turn was to come later, and meanwhile, though he did not fail to move his troops about threateningly on the disputed frontier, he agreed to prolong his truce with the new King, and was playing the kindly friend, when the flight of Henri de Valois once more destroyed all his plans.

Everything had to be begun over again. Ivan could not turn his back on the new election, all the more so as Poland and Lithuania were sure to play the game which had already answered their purpose so well with him. And the business

14

now promised still better.   Both in Lithuania and in all the
Russian provinces under Polish rule the Muscovite current,
fed by the twofold influence of the Catholic propaganda, which
exasperated the population, and the before-mentioned military
demonstrations, which alarmed it, appeared to be growing
stronger.   Magnus himself had done his share, in Livonia,
towards terrorizing the unhappy country, groaning in the
throes of King-birth.   The Tsar's treatment of the Danish
adventurer had not been over good-natured.   He had married
him, indeed, to one of his nieces, Maria Vladimorovna, sister
of that Euphemia whom he had intended for him, and who
had died.   Her father, the Tsar's first cousin, had just been
put to death by him !   At the nuptial ceremony, which was
of the most pompous description, Ivan himself had led the
chants, taking up his position at the choir-desk, leading the
orchestra with his iron-shod stick, and now and then beating
time on the performers' heads.   Peter the Great's feats of
imperial virtuosity at a later period were a mere imitation.
But the promised dowry—the five hogsheads of gold—remained a promise and no more.   Magnus, reduced to a very
modest appariage in his little town of Karkhus, must earn
the money and the royal state for which he was still waiting.
He did his best, with a body of Tartars added to his German
troops, left the Swedish possessions, which were better defended,
alone, and turned all his efforts to those of Poland, striving to
obtain the capitulation of the Castle of Salis, and threatening
Pernau and Riga.   The great Polish and Lithuanian lords
took this to be a further reason for persevering in their stratagem, and ' amusing ' their terrible Russian neighbour with the
bait of a crown they intended ultimately to refuse him.   But
the lesser nobles made a rhyme, ' *By byl Fiodor jak Jagiello—
Dobrze by nam bylo*' (' With Feodor as with Jagellon—We should
be happy ').   The reports of the Nuncio, Vincenzo Laureo, confirmed by the testimony of the Dantzig agents, very reliable
as a rule, leave us in no doubt as to the feeling thus manifested
(Vierjboiski, *Vincenzo Laureo*, 1888, pp. 69, 238, 257 ; and
Forsten, ' The Baltic Question,' i. 627).

But Ivan's knowledge of the ground on which he had to
manœuvre was not sufficient to enable him to turn this feeling
to account.   The enormous difference between the political
life of the two countries escaped him.   Deceived by appearances,
and interpreting the wishes expressed in his favour and the
messages which seemed to summon him to Lithuania and
Poland, and place both countries at his disposal, by the light
of his half-Asiatic ideas of sovereignty, the Tsar, instead of
sending an embassy to receive the votes of these electors,
already won over to his side, expected them to send an embassy

to him. Great was the surprise of the preparatory Diet of Stezyça (May, 1575) to behold nothing but a mere courier from the Tsar—a courier, too, who had nothing to offer, nor even a promise to make. Better things were hoped for at the Diet of Election in November. The Primate Uchanski, head of the temporary Government, who had been so won over to the Russian candidature that he had furnished Ivan with copies of letters to be addressed by him to the chief magnates, was quite sure the Tsar was going to announce himself a convert to Catholicism. Deputies and senators were scanning the horizon, and sending out couriers to meet the Muscovite mission and the brilliant proposals and splendid *largesse* it was certain to bring with it. A bitter disappointment! With the decisive hour came a solitary letter from Ivan, couched in haughty terms, and announcing *for a later date* an embassy *of moderate rank,* as was befitting, seeing there was no monarch to whom it could be accredited.

What had been happening at Moscow? The embassy in question, which had been despatched in the month of August, 1575, under the leadership of Lucas Zakhariévitch Novossiltsov, had orders to appear before the Diet. Its instructions were to press Feodor's candidature, and support it by promises of money and honours to be distributed among the chief nobles. But it had halted on its way, delayed by the Tsar's order. It had occurred to Ivan, at the same time, to send a confidential man, Skobeltsyne, to Vienna, and commission him to sound the Emperor as to an agreement between the two Powers concerning the Polish-Lithuanian inheritance. As the conditions of the Tsar's candidature for the vacant throne were not such as he would have desired, as neither the Lithuanians nor the Poles seemed to be bringing him the crown on a golden charger, Ivan made as though he would let them have their way, but fell back meanwhile on another idea, already discussed several times and in various quarters—that of a partition of the escheated inheritance. The Emperor's son Ernest was one of the candidates; let him take Poland, and the Tsar would withdraw his own candidature and take Lithuania. Skobeltsyne came back empty-handed : the Vienna authorities believed their cause in Poland safe. But Ivan had since heard that the Emperor regretted his reception of the Russian envoy, and that an Imperial mission was on its way to Moscow. It was for the issue of this negotiation that Novossiltsov must wait.

And this time, by too easily concluding that things really unaffected by his absolute power would bow to his will, Ivan thoroughly missed his calculation. The Diet did not wait. In September, 1575, the Sultan pronounced against any Mus-

covite candidate, and in favour of Batory, and supported
his view by marching out an army of 120,000 Tartars.   There
was a panic at Warsaw, and on December 12, Batory
was elected, together with the Emperor Maximilian himself,
on whom part of the votes fell, to the exclusion of his son
Ernest.

This division evidently left some margin for the arrangement already suggested by Ivan ; but the conferences begun
at Mojaïsk in January, 1576, with the Imperial envoys Cobenzl
and Printz von Buchau, bore no fruit whatever.   Maximilian,
instead of forestalling Batory in Poland, as he should have
done, insisted on sending his son there, and requesting the
Tsar's support for his candidature.   He further claimed the
evacuation of Livonia and an alliance against the Turks, and,
in exchange, he offered Ivan Constantinople and the Empire of
the East !

The game had been played—and lost.

V.—THE ELECTION OF BATORY.

Ivan tried to cut into the game again, and this time rather
awkwardly. At that moment the *Opritchnina* had set his head
in a whirl. He wrote separate letters to the Polish and Lithuanian lords, recommending Ernest to some, with the most
terrible threats of reprisals if they gave the preference to the
Sultan's candidate (Batory), and proposing himself to the
others, either as King of Poland or as Sovereign of Lithuania
apart from Poland. Unfortunately, Novossiltsov, whom he
had at last allowed to proceed, strengthened him in his mistaken
course. Chodkiewicz and Radziwill told the envoy that nothing
would induce them to accept *Obatura* (*sic*). They had only
voted for Maximilian in despair, when they saw the Tsar made
no sign. Ivan fancied he was still master of the day and the
morrow. Any man, indeed, might have been deceived. As
late as in April, 1576, the Nuncio Laureo wrote to Rome that
if a fresh election was rendered necessary by the division of the
vote, the Russian candidate would certainly win the day,
because Ernest was so hated. But both Maximilian and Ivan
should have made haste. For while they were each wasting
precious time, the Emperor parleying with the Poles, and the
Tsar sending Prince Zakhar Ivanovitch Sougorski to Vienna
to reopen the negotiations begun at Mojaïsk, *Obatura* hurried
to Warsaw, and had himself crowned there.

Even then Ivan did not despair, and invited the Emperor to
join him in common action against ' the usurper.'   But when
anybody spoke the word ' Poland ' to Maximilian, he answered
with the word ' Livonia,' and after his death, which occurred

during that same year, his successor, Rudolph, followed in his footsteps. So that, the election being a settled thing, the Tsar was brought back to the Livonian problem, the solution of which to his own advantage, he might imagine would now present fewer difficulties. Batory was King indeed, but, like Henri de Valois, his kingdom kept him very busy. A revolt at Dantzig, which refused to recognise him, brought him a heavy extra task, and the check the French influence had received at Warsaw had been reflected at Stockholm. Turning his back on all his past fancies, and resuming possession of his brilliant powers, Ivan set himself at last to turn circumstances to his own profit. The previous year, in his desire to have free play in the Polish business, he had loosened his hold on Sweden, and agreed to a curious truce, which put a stop to hostilities in Finland and in the province of Novgorod, only. Immediately after this, concentrating all his forces in Livonia, he besieged Pernau, an important strategic point which Sigismund-Augustus had made a stronghold for his privateers. Here the Tsar lost 7,000 men ; but the town was taken, and one after the other, Helmet, Ermes, Rujen, and Purkel shared the same fate. Then, leaving the Poles, and going back to his old plan, which consisted, as my readers will recollect, in settling his account with the Swedes first of all, Ivan made his way into Esthonia. Within a few weeks, in the course of the spring of 1576, Leal and Lode, Fikel and Hapsal, fell without a struggle. At Hapsal, on the day of the capitulation, the inhabitants gave banquets and dances. 'Strange folk, these Germans,' said the Russians ; 'if we had given up such a town, without any reason at all, we should not have dared to look any man in the face, and the Tsar would not have been able to devise a torture sharp enough to punish us !' . . . Oesel was abandoned ; Padis surrendered after a month's siege, and the Swedes made an ineffectual attempt to recover the town.

But these triumphs came to an end. In 1577, the Russians, commanded by Prince M. F. Mstislavski and by I. V. Chérémétiev, appeared at Revel, but were fain to retire, after a six weeks' siege, before the heroic resistance offered by the Swedes. Chérémétiev had sworn to take the town or perish, and he was killed. This Swedish nut was decidedly a hard one to crack ! It broke Ivan's teeth, and he thought it wiser not to be too obstinate. If needful, he could go shares with these competitors who refused to be driven off the field. So, rallying all his forces at Novgorod, the Tsar took the field in person, and, instead of renewing his unsuccessful attempt on Revel, as everyone expected, fell suddenly on Polish Livonia. This was as easy as cutting cheese. In the course of a few days the whole country, except for Riga, was in the invaders' hands.

And it was abominably handled. Ivan, between his last humiliation at Revel and his former one at Warsaw, was in a fury. At Lenewarden he had the eyes of the aged Marshal, Gaspard von Münster, torn out, and then had him whipped to death (Karamzine, 'History of Russia,' ix. 465, note). Other men who had commanded fortified towns were impaled, quartered, hacked to pieces. At Ascheraden the screams of forty virgins, violated all at once in a garden, rang across the Dvina, from one bank to the other, for four hours (Forsten, 'The Baltic Question,' i. 667). The new feats of arms performed by Magnus served to exasperate the Tsar. He suspected his partner of having made terms with the Poles. This was going rather far. The 'King of Livonia' had not reached this point yet ; but between the Tsar and him, the Livonians unhesitatingly chose the lesser evil, and Magnus took advantage of their feeling to act as if he were master, and make his shadowy kingdom a reality. Without orders to that effect, he occupied Kokenhausen, Ascheraden, Lenewarden, Ronneburg, and Wolmar, on his own account, took possession of Derpt, and went so far as to claim that the Russians were not to molest his 'faithful lieges' there. This was but another dream, and the awakening was bitter. Ivan hurried to Kokenhausen, had fifty of the 'King's' Germans put to death, and ordered him to appear before him. 'Obey, or go back whence you came ! We are not far from each other, and I have soldiers and biscuit !' The wretched man tried to negotiate a reconciliation. Ivan had his emissaries whipped, and repeated his order. The next morning Magnus cast himself at his feet. 'Idiot !' shouted the Tsar. 'Beggar, whom I received into my family and fed and shod ! Do you think you can hold out against me ?' He had him shut up in a hut, and kept him there, lying on straw, for several days. Then, from Ascheraden, where his soldiery behaved in the manner I have already described, he dragged him to Wenden. The town surrendered, and the garrison blew itself up with the fortress. Ivan had one of the notable inhabitants, George Wicke, impaled in presence of his fellow-townsmen, and then proceeded to Derpt with his prisoner, who expected the same fate.

Contrary to all expectations, he was pardoned. The Tsar, who now thought his final victory assured, was inclined to mercy. But Magnus, though obliged to content himself with a few small towns, had to undertake to pay a sum of 40,000 gold florins, and he had not a crown to his name ! Very soon Oberpalen, the last bulwark of his ephemeral royalty, fell into the hands of the Swedes, and that was the end of his strange adventure. He fled, reached Pilten, and offered himself, with all his possessions beyond the Dvina—his in name only, indeed

—to Batory, who refused to enter into any definite arrangement with him.   Until 1583, when he died, the ex-King led a miserable life, reduced sometimes to the extremest poverty, assisted at others by his brother, by the Elector of Saxony, and the King of Poland, who all tried to make use of him in their turn.   His widow, a poor creature, of whom Frederick II. used to say that anybody who gave her a little sugar and an apple could make her quite happy, went back to Moscow with her two-year-old girl, and mother and daughter both died in the Monastery of the Trinity during the reign of Ivan's successor.

But Ivan was soon to perceive he had made a terrible mistake.   He thought he had finished with the Poles, and that all he had to do now was to treat with the Swedes.   He should have followed the contrary course, and his first plan had been the best.   Batory would probably have agreed to an arrangement ; at the time of his election to the throne of Poland a powerful conspiracy was promising him that of Hungary (Szadeczky, *Batory Istwan*, in the *Szazadok* of December 15, 1886, and in the *Ungarische Revue*, April-May, 1887).   To a Transylvanian, Hungary was worth more than any Livonia. But Ivan, in a way, had bereft him of his freedom of choice by forcing him to turn his back on this hope, and face an aggression which no King of Poland could leave unpunished without shutting himself out from all possibility of remaining at Warsaw.   Thus war with Muscovy was forced on Maximilian's lucky rival, and when, in 1577, the submission of Dantzig insured him quietness in that quarter, he prepared to cast his sword, his genius, and his fortunes—the fortunes of a crowned parvenu —into the balance.

As an excuse for Ivan, it may be urged that nothing, either in the past history of Poland or in the former career of her new ruler, furnished any reason for anticipating the tremendous impetus with which she and he were to fall, like a hurricane, on the Tsar and his Empire, at a moment when both were still suffering from the effects of the painful internal crisis through which they had lately passed.   This crisis certainly had a considerable effect on the incidents of the struggle now nearing its end, and on its final solution.   Therefore, before I come to this closing episode, I must show how Ivan had come to be weakened and half-disarmed within the borders of his own country.

PART III

THE CRISIS

CHAPTER I

THE POLITICAL AND INTELLECTUAL EVOLUTION

I.—THE CONFLICT OF IDEAS AND PRINCIPLES. II.—THE DIS-
GRACE OF SYLVESTER AND ADACHEV. III.—THE FLIGHT OF
KOURBSKI.

I.—THE CONFLICT OF IDEAS AND PRINCIPLES.

' AFTER the Battle of Montlhéry (1465), the Bishop of Paris,
with councillors and Churchmen, waited on Louis XI. at Tour-
nelles, and besought him in all gentleness to allow his affairs
to be directed, for the future, by *good counsel*. This counsel
was to be given him by six burghers, six Parliamentary councillors, and six clerks of the University. . . . Sixteen years later,
in 1481, the Comte du Perche was arrested, by Louis XI.'s
orders, and shut up in the narrowest cage that had yet been
constructed—a cage only a pace and a half long—all because
he had tried to get out of France. . . .' (Michelet, *Histoire de
France*, vii. 301 ; viii. 343).

Between the years 1551 and 1571, a somewhat similar
drama was played out at Moscow, amidst circumstances which,
though certainly different, possessed many points of analogy.
I have already referred to the current of ideas which marked
the opening period of Ivan's personal government. The
Livonian war, with the diplomatic complications which accompanied it, brought in a draught of European air, which only
increased the strength of this current and the complexity of
the problems tossed on its eddies. Ivan's father had already
presided over the establishment of a foreign quarter in his
capital, and under his own particular protection. The Poles
and Lithuanians settled there were soon absorbed into the

rest of the population, but Ivan's victorious campaigns shortly
brought in a fresh contingent of foreign neighbours, prisoners
of war, or involuntary immigrants, gathered on the battlefields
and in the towns and country places of Livonia.   The suburb
on the right bank of the Iaouza to which they were confined
long preserved a certain autonomy, for it became a centre of
Western culture, and a nursery for men destined to play a considerable part in the national history.   We have already
noted the careers of Taube and Kruse.   Other Livonians,
who belonged, like them, to this German *sloboda*—such men as
Kloss and Beckmann—figured in the Sovereign's immediate
circle, and were actively employed in his diplomacy.

The disembarkation of the English navigators on the
northern coasts of the Empire in 1554 opened a new era of
European dealings with Russia, and another current began to
flow in the opposite direction—from Muscovy to Europe.
Ivan IV. sent Michael Matviéiévitch Lykov, *voiévode* of Narva,
whose father had blown himself up rather than surrender that
town, to travel in Germany, for purposes of study and observation.

And the eastward journeys taken by Russians, which had
hitherto been made for pious objects only, began to alter their
character.   Vassili Pozniakov, a merchant, sent in 1560 to
carry pecuniary assistance to the Patriarch of Alexandria and
the Archbishop of Mount Sinai, was also commissioned to
describe the habits of the countries through which he passed,
and his narrative of this journey attained the extraordinary
good fortune of being handed down to posterity, and gaining
huge publicity, under a false name, and thanks to a misunderstanding.

The fifteenth century had already bequeathed a variety of
pilgrims' narratives, quite as interesting, according to the
testimony of Sreznièvski the linguist, as that of Vasco di Gama,
to the national literature.   Of these the general public knew
nothing, and twenty years after his return to Moscow, Pozniakov's report was equally ignored.   But now another traveller,
Tryphonius Korobéinikov, attracted general attention.   The
story of his adventures, reproduced in over 200 known
copies, and which ran through forty successive editions, is
generally read, even nowadays.   It has been accepted in chrono-
graphic works, and even by hagiographic writers.   Now,
Pozniakov and Korobéinikov were one and the same person,
or, rather, the second man's story was a simple transcription
of his predecessor's.   Korobéinikov had been to Constantinople, indeed, twice over, in 1582 and 1593, but he never got
as far as the Holy Places.

This confusion, unjust as it is to the memory of the more

enterprising of the two travellers, testifies to the progress made in this particular in a very short space of time.   True, Pozniakov's narrative owed its principal interest to the religious element which formed its chief basis, and also to the picture it drew of the sufferings of the Christian populations under the Moslem yoke.   None the less, the curiosity and sympathy it stirred are proof of an enlargement of the minds of its numerous readers.   Muscovy was issuing from the lair in which she had crouched for so many years.   She was venturing outside, and from without, others were beckoning and calling to her.   That adventure of Hans Schlitte which I have already mentioned had another side, puzzling enough, it is true, but which seems to show that this servant, employed by the Tsar to recruit European workmen and artisans, considerably widened the scope of his own mission (Pierling, *La Russie et le Saint-Siège*, i. 324, etc.).   He imposed both on Charles V. and Pope Julius III., and put himself forward as an Ambassador deputed to treat for the reunion of the two Churches.   Ivan was probably quite unaware of this attempt, but the Hanoverian adventurer, well recommended by the Emperor and warmly welcomed at Rome, made so much stir about it, that interest was awakened both in Germany and in Italy, and that Poland was somewhat disturbed.   Thus the episode may be included in that series of gropings which were to result in the final *rapprochement* between modernized Russia and Europe.

Schlitte, as we know, failed even as to that portion of his mission in which he was quite straightforward, but his very failure had indirect results which served the cause.   Ivan, when he heard of the treatment inflicted on his agent by the Livonians, published a ukase at and round Novgorod which forbade the sale of German prisoners in Germany or Poland ; they were all to be sent to the Muscovite markets.   And at the same time the Tsar commanded that all captives appearing well versed in mining operations and the working of metals should be sent to him at Moscow.

Veit Zenge, the Bavarian agent already known to us, dwells, in one of his curious reports, dated 1567, on the Russians' extraordinary facility for assimilating every element of foreign culture—industry, commerce, and art.   After the taking of Narva they had at once entered into relations with the Low Countries and even with France.   Once a thing was shown them, they copied it immediately, and with singular ease. Ivan did not choose this receptivity should be limited to *things* only.   The beginning of printing—that mighty weapon of intellectual growth which the preceding century had bequeathed to the modern world—dated, on Slav territory, from

the year 1491, and amongst the craftsmen Schlitte was to
have sent him, the Tsar had asked for printers. There had
been printers at Wilna since 1525. In 1550 Ivan applied to
the King of Denmark, who sent him, two years later, a man,
half printer and half apostle, Hans Missenheim by name,
who brought with him a Protestant Bible and some books
concerning religious polemics. We have no clear knowledge of
the result of this last attempt. The apostle has left no trace;
but the printer certainly had pupils, for in 1553, we note the
presence of two Russian typographers, Ivan Fédorov and
Peter Timofiéviev, and in 1556, that of a typefounder, Vassili
Nikiforov, at Moscow and Novgorod. In 1564, the printing
of the first book produced by the native presses was completed. It consisted of the Acts of the Apostles and the
Epistles of St. Paul. The edition, though faulty as to spelling,
is of handsome appearance. But the work of the printers
was interrupted, unhappily, by a popular disturbance (p. 72).
My readers will be reminded here of Louis XI., who had to
defend the first printers he brought in from Nüremberg against
accusations of sorcery. Fédorov and Nikiforov were driven
to seek refuge in Poland, but in 1568, Andronik Niéviéja, one
of their disciples, took up their work at Moscow, and printed
a Psalter, of which a later edition appeared in 1578, at the
Sloboda of Alexandrov

Church books still ! Church books indeed ; but in such
works as these their readers—even their Western readers—
found many things we have forgotten how to seek in them. It
was literature, at all events ; it was intellectual food, and, with
the writings of Ivan and Kourbski, of which I shall soon have
to speak, and the travellers' narratives, to which I have already
referred, this same epoch witnessed the beginnings in Russia
of a secular literature which even reached the borders of
romantic fiction.

Thus set in motion, the national mind began by transforming
certain stories of exotic birth—part of the literary inheritance
of the preceding century—which it amplified and adapted to
current events. Thus, in the legend of Drakoul, Prince of
Wallachia, the incident of the nailing of the foreign envoys'
caps to their heads by the *voiévode's* order was applied to
Ivan. In Ivachka Peresviétov's famous epistle to the Tsar,
he speaks of two other little books which, he says, he has
handed to the Sovereign. One of these is still unknown to us.
The other is a sort of novel, half political and half historical,
in which the sayings of Peter, Palatine of Wallachia—which
are reproduced, indeed, in the epistle—and the chastisement
inflicted by Sultan Mahmet on unjust judges and pettifoggers
are used to justify the reign of terror inaugurated by Ivan.

This story was published in the 'Memoirs of the University of Kazan' in 1863.

The external influences thus entering the Muscovite world of the sixteenth century by all these various paths evoked reactions of divers kinds. In the upper classes of society, among those lettered boïars of whom Kourbski was the most eminent representative, they naturally gave birth to leanings such as those Louis XI. had had to put down in the preceding century. They brought with them a breath of liberty, a germ of independent development, and incited to a direct conflict with that autocratic system which, by virtue of the national atavisms, was gaining continuous and increasing strength. Very different was the impression produced on the mind of the representative of that system. All Ivan perceived in the lessons that came to him from the West was their practical teaching as to the reorganization of his Government on a more modern, but a by no means more liberal, basis. Forced into an expensive war, he realized all that he lacked, from the military, financial, and administrative point of view, to enable him to cope successfully with his European adversaries, so much better equipped than he, and when he tried to provide himself with their war machinery the whole of that bygone world of ancient rights and hereditary privilege and family precedence rose up in his path, and interfered, even on the battlefield, frustrating the movements of his troops, thinning their numbers, and disorganizing the highest commands.

Ivan was certainly no opponent of the family principle, to which he owed his own titles, to say nothing of his excessive pretensions. He was disposed to choose assistants of humble birth, because he needed men who would serve him and obey him. But when one of them fell into the hands of the Tartars and besought his help, he did not fail, when he sent the money demanded for his ransom—2,000 roubles—to write : 'Your likes were not worth more than fifty in the old days !' To serve, to obey, this is what the great boïars, now enrolled in the class of the *sloojilyié loodi*, knew not how to do, and did not care to learn.

The war in Livonia, with the general mobilization of all available forces it entailed, and the maintenance of that cumbersome organization its continuance involved, made a conflict —the continuation, under a new form, of the old struggle between Muscovite Russia and the Russia of the appanages— quite inevitable. The ancient Russia of the appanages was a confused agglomeration of principalities, large and small, within which the directing principle of politics was the contract between the Prince and the free man who took service with him, as and when he chose ; hence no constraint, nothing

fixed, nothing eternal.   Muscovite Russia was a centralized
State, based on universal and obligatory service, on the division of the population into classes bound to perform definite
tasks—forced labour in the lower ranks, employed in commerce
or in manual toil, and all feeding the State treasury ; 'men who
served ' in the upper ranks, employed in the State army or
in administrative service, and obliged, from childhood till
they drew their last breath, to give the State their whole life's
labour.   All of these, whether descended from the free comrades or the free peasants of the old days, were now turned
into the living straps and wheels of the Government machine
—*voiévodes*, *starosts*, for criminal or land affairs—set like so
many suction pumps over the very springs of the national
life.   Wherefore, at every step, liberty was strangled utterly,
and duty, regulation, slavery, reigned supreme.

Already, towards the middle of the preceding century, Ivan's
grandfather had found himself obliged to crush two of the great
families, the Riapolovski and the Patrikiév.   This blow only
strengthened the resistance which had its focus in the cell of
Maximus the Greek.   The twofold current, religious and intellectual, of that period corresponded, indeed, with the
antagonism in politics.   While Joseph Volotski and his
followers, the *Iosiflianié*, were popularizing the Byzantine
doctrine of absolute power, the partisans of the old system
of freedom found sympathizers among the monks 'from
beyond the Volga.'   The two oppositions, political and religious, joined hands on the question of the division of power
and the legitimate influence to be exercised over the Sovereign.
One claimed the boïar's right to sit on the council, and the
other that of the Church to intercede.

Ivan's attitude with regard to the problems thus put forward strikes us as being partly in close conformity with his
historical precedents, and, as to another part, quite peculiar
to himself.   He cannot be taken to be the first autocrat, nor
even the first terrorist, Russia had ever known.   From the
fifteenth century onwards, terrorism had become an habitual
weapon of government in the hands of the Russian monarchs.

Was Ivan the Terrible the representative and champion
of a powerful and strongly-centralized monarchy, which he
had received with all its ancient traditions, but which he
sought to renovate ; the disappointed idealist imagined by some
Slavophils, who in his despair, so they assert, struck with his
own hand at what he had failed to transform, grew wilder and
wilder as the ruins thickened round his feet, and ended at
last in a very madness of murder and destruction ? This seems
a somewhat hasty conclusion, which must not be unquestioningly accepted.

In the Tsar's case, as I have already admitted, there was some admixture of intoxication and even of frenzy ; but both the person and the policy of Ivan have their admirers, and his work has been by no means doomed to come to nought. Some of his reforms even yet impart their special and recognised character to Russia, and to her political and social organization.

We have quite as much difficulty in recognising him in the tragic actor, for ever seeking picturesque poses and dramatic effects, depicted by Constantine Akssakov ('Works,' 2nd edition, i. 114, etc.), as in the base and vulgar despot stigmatized by Kostomarov, or the mere maniac ranked by Mikhaïlovski ('Critical Essays,' 1895, p. 112) as a common lunatic. From his ancestors, Ivan inherited a State the archaic basis of which was in process of transformation. Certain principles of the old appanage system he sought to eliminate, but others he sought to maintain, subject to their being brought into harmony with the necessities of modern existence. From his intellectual masters, from Joseph Volotski and Vassiane Toporkov, he learnt that his power, divine in its essence, could not be circumscribed, nor divided, nor controlled ; and Nature, to conclude, had endowed him with a headstrong temperament, violent and irritable, a fiery and disordered imagination, and a mind, quick, subtle, penetrating, and ingenious, but ill-balanced, most unsettled, and prone to exaggeration and excess.

The peculiar way in which he understood his part and played it was the outcome of all these things. He felt it to be very great, and concluded that everything else must be subordinated to it. When he met resistance he broke it down, as his fathers had done before him ; but his effort was greater, because the resistance was more powerful, and his violence was greater, too, because he was violent by temperament.

He did not admit, any more than his ancestors had done, any encroachment on his will in the form of unsolicited advice ; but the practice of his own will and pleasure, which he followed like them, was mingled with a certain roughness and extravagance, because he was rough by nature, and of a most fanciful mind. Yet his fancies, as I shall endeavour to show, never went so far as to lead him out of his path, and though he persevered in it—if not in everybody's teeth, in the teeth of the majority at all events—he claimed to be no despot at all. In this particular, realist as he was in practice, he had built himself up a theory borrowed from the most transcendental ideology. What was it all about, and for what reason was the Tsar imposing this severe law, or that effort, on his subjects, who were trying, some of them, to escape it ? Was it to create a great Empire for himself, to conquer Livonia as he had conquered Kazan and Astrakan, to win triumphs, cover himself with glory ? No indeed ! His one and only aim was to bring his people to a knowledge of Divine truth ! Vainly, then, and falsely, did they attack his person and rebel against his rule. For this rule, properly understood, far from being despotic, had nothing personal about it. The powers that really directed it were : the Divine mercy, the grace of the Mother of Christ, the prayers of all the saints, and the benediction of the ancient Sovereigns ! The reigning Tsar only intervened as the living expression of all these hypostases, amongst which the boïars, importunate and perfidious counsellors, muddlers or traitors, ' barking dogs who strove to bite their master,' had no place at all. The Tsar, when he listened to none save whom he would, and punished as he saw fit, was only insuring the existence within his own Empire of—the kingdom of God !

It is clear that with a man who claimed such authority and such a mission, discussion was impossible, and no division of power practicable. Let us pass on to the history of the struggle.

II.—THE DISGRACE OF SYLVESTER AND ADACHEV.

There has been a dispute, and it still continues, as to the character and performances of the men to whose influence Ivan was pleased to submit, and whose advice he condescended to take, for a certain time. The most probable solution of the question, taking into consideration the many apparent contradictions in their actions and opinions, is that they began by halting between the two parties which stood face to face. At a later period, following the natural bent of their origin, their intellectual associations, and their political connections, they brought over a portion of the opposition to their side, and ended by attempting to form a special group, a select centre, of which they themselves would have been the leaders. Kourbski's passionate apology leaves us in very little doubt on this head.

After the year 1551, the great council of the Empire, the *boïarskaïa douma,* only sat in the most intermittent fashion, for it had been relegated to a secondary position by the ' private council,' the inception of which at this period I have already mentioned (p. 37), and which is easily recognised as a reproduction of analogous institutions belonging to the history of the Western monarchies : the *consistorium principis* or *consilium aulicum* of Germany, the *commune consilium* of the Norman Kings in England, or the *consilium regium* of France.

On this council Adachev and Sylvester sat with Kourbski and some other boïars and Churchmen, amongst whom Kourbski mentions the Metropolitan Macarius and three Morozovs, Michael, Vladimir, and Leo, while other documents give us the names of Princes Dmitri Kourliatev and Simon Rostovski. Until the period of the war in Livonia, Sylvester's influence seems to have been preponderating, at all events, if not undivided. His position as an ecclesiastic, his masterful temperament, and his meticulous pedantry, together with the qualities of a supple and wily courtier, revealed in the *Domostroï*, naturally gave him a strong hold over the mind of the young Sovereign, who was profoundly religious, and not over sure of himself, as yet. But in 1553, the first difficulty between the mentor and his pupil arose. In the course of a somewhat serious illness, Ivan was led to occupy himself with the matter of his succession. The hereditary succession to the throne by primogeniture had only recently been established, and the Tsar thought it prudent to make the nobles swear allegiance to his son Dmitri. Suddenly, Prince Vladimir Andréiévitch, the Sovereign's uncle, put forward his own claim. This was a return to the old appanage system, according to which uncles took precedence of their nephews, and the rage and agitation of the sick man may be imagined, when he saw most of his boïars side with this claimant, and support his pretensions. What were their motives ? A certain regard for the old custom, no doubt, but, above all things, a feeling of jealous pride as to the maternal relatives of the young Prince to whom they were expected to pay homage. The government of such a child should certainly have suited them—it would have insured them years of oligarchy. But for whose benefit ? When the Chouïski and the Biélski fought for power, in Helen's days, it had been a struggle between the descendants of the ancient Sovereigns, at all events ; now it would be a fight between mere parvenus. And round the bed on which Ivan lay, expecting death, the *viélmoji* obstinately clung to their *non possumus*. ' We will not kiss the cross for the Zakharine.' To ' kiss the cross ' meant to take the oath. Already Vladimir and his mother were doing all in their power to stimulate their supporters' zeal, opening their treasuries, showering promises, while the Zakharine themselves had taken fright, and seemed inclined to bow their heads.

At this crisis, Ivan's failing eyes sought Sylvester and Adachev. They were certain to support the few defenders of the legitimate heir with all their strength ! Disappointment ! The only men who proved energetic and faithful, and succeeded in rallying a few boïars to the cause, were Prince Vladimir Vorotynski and the *diak* Ivan Mikhaïlovitch Viskovatyï.

Neither Sylvester nor Adachev lifted a finger. They did not refuse to take the oath themselves, but they observed the most cautious neutrality, and carefully abstained from taking any part in the passionate discussions which disturbed the quiet of the very chamber in which the dying man lay, and increased his suffering. The favourite's own father, the *Okolnitchyï* Feodor Adachev, went so far as to declare himself openly in Vladimir's favour. Thus a whole day dragged out. The next morning the Tsar was better, and Dmitri's partisans increased in number. In a fright, Vladimir hurried to the sick-chamber, in which hitherto he had not deigned to set his foot. Those who had been faithful from the outset stopped him on the threshold, and one voice—one only—was raised to beg admittance for him—the voice of Sylvester, bound to the monarch by old ties of friendship !

Ivan recovered, and he did not forget. In performance of a vow made during his illness, he departed on pilgrimage to the monastery of St Cyril at Biélooziéro, taking his wife and son with him. If Kourbski is to be believed, Maximus the Greek endeavoured to prevent the accomplishment of this pious undertaking. The monks of Biélooziéro were the disciples of Joseph Volotski, and on his way thither, at the monastery of Piésnoché, on the Iakhroma, the Tsar was to meet an illustrious disciple of the same school, Vassiane Toporkhov, who had been exiled by the boïars in 1542. The Albanian monk is even said to have warned Ivan that his boy would die on the journey, and, whether as the result of the exposure of a delicate child to the winter weather, or of an accident—for, according to some versions, Dmitri was drowned—the prophecy came true. The Tsar brought home a corpse. But he saw Toporkov, and, according to Kourbski, again, asked his advice. What was he to do to keep his boïars in order ? ' Never have anybody about you except people who are less intelligent than yourself,' was the reply. It is not very likely that the answer, which is very nearly impertinent, took this form exactly, although the story, introduced into one of the letters written by Kourbski to him, was never contradicted by the Sovereign. We may, therefore, conclude there is some truth in it. But what is still more certain is the state of reciprocal irritation and distrust which reigned between the Tsar and his boïars from the very morrow of the experience through which they had just passed. The refractory nobles' refusal to take the oath was nothing, clearly, but yet another form of their incessant protest against that new order of things of which Dmitri's succession would have been a perpetuation.

In the course of the following years the opposition grew stronger. Some historians, relying on the absence of active resistance or armed rebellion, have gone so far, indeed, as to deny the existence of any struggle at all. They have confused the Muscovy of the earliest Tsars with the France of Louis XI. Owing to the absence of strongly-constituted classes in Russia, the resistance, in her case, could not assume the same character, become collective in its nature, oppose violence with violence. But the men who, like Biélski, offered their services to the enemy, and besought that enemy's assistance to enforce their abolished privileges, or who, like Mstislavski, showed the Tartars the road to the capital—such fugitives and traitors were insurgents, neither more nor less !

Now, just in the year 1554, this flow of emigrants to foreign parts increased to an alarming extent. In July, Prince Nikita Dmitriévitch Rostovski was stopped and arrested on one of the roads leading to Lithuania. It was then discovered that all his family and his numerous relations, the Lobanov, the Priïmkov, had been in treaty with the King of Poland. From the point of view of the old appanages, there was nothing criminal in all this. It was no more than a putting into practice of the ' right of departure,' and so strong were the ancient ideas and habits, still, that the Tsar did not dare to use too much severity. Rostovski, on the intercession of a great number of influential persons, was merely interned at Biéloo-ziéro. But the Tsar was none the better pleased with those who interceded for him, and amongst these, again, was Sylvester.

From that time forward, probably, the pope's position and that of Adachev were very much undermined. The two comrades' behaviour when the Livonian war began did nothing to restore their credit. They loudly espoused the cause of the boïars, who, in their dislike of the effort the war necessitated and of the disturbance it caused in the traditional trend of the Muscovite policy, condemned the whole enterprise. Yet up to July, 1560, Adachev seems to have been actively employed in diplomatic work. It was not till this period that, being sent into a kind of honourable exile far from Court, he re-entered the ranks of the army, then in Livonia, as third *Voiévode* of the first regiment. At the same time, Sylvester went into voluntary retirement at the monastery of Biélooziéro, the common refuge of all fallen grandeurs. In his ' History of Ivan' Kourbski has confused events and dates, and connected these disgraces with the illness and death of the Tsarina Anastasia. According to him, the ex-favourites were accused of having poisoned her. The Tsarina fell ill in November, 1559, and died ten months later, after the departure of Adachev and Sylvester, and the very duration of her sufferings would seem to preclude any suspicion of foul play, which, indeed, would have been punished after quite a different fashion. After that event Sylvester and Adachev underwent a trial. Disgrace is in itself a downward slope, and no doubt some sentiment of caution or some remnant of consideration prevented Ivan from at first revealing the full depth of his resentment. But even now the accused men escaped. One received a sentence of still more distant banishment, to the monastery of Solovki on the Frozen Sea, while the other, after a short stay at Fellin, in Livonia, where he had been appointed *voiévode*, and where, in all probability, he did not keep himself quiet, was sent to prison. No attempt on the Tsarina's life was recognised, evidently, nor, most likely, discussed by the judges; for as to proof people were not over particular in those days. In later years Ivan, in fits of fury, and with the angry clamour of some wild aurochs bellowing in the forest for his mate, reproached his faithless friends with having parted him from ' his doe.' But even then, though he called Sylvester before the ' judgment-seat of the Divine Lamb,' he would not, he said, ' seek judgment against him' here below. And in his very charges he contradicted himself. At one time he accused the two *parvenus* of having sought to place their aristocratic supporters on a par with the Tsar, at another he asserted their intention of dragging their followers down to their own level. He blamed them for having carried out some of the reforms he cared for most, and which he was still pursuing, such as the conversion of the freeholds into fiefs. The grievances pleaded in the Tsar's correspondence with Kourbski are nothing but arguments for the purposes of his controversy, and when he came to polemics, Ivan was never overnice as to correctness or good faith. To demonstrate the interference of third parties in the affairs of his Government, he did not hesitate to exaggerate and alter facts. Sylvester and Adachev, according to his story, had brought him into such a state of tutelage that they even measured out his hours of sleep to him. ' I was like a child; I had no will at all!' And this argument was also used as a retort when Kourbski complained that his own strength had been overtaxed. ' By whom? Was he not master, then, with the pope,' and ' Adachev, that dog taken off a dung-heap ?'

The war in Livonia, undertaken and carried through against the advice of the whole of the ' little council,' in itself suffices to dispose of all these allegations. After the Siege of Kazan, ' all the wise men,' as Kourbski testifies, advised the Tsar to remain in the town for some time. We know he did nothing of the sort. Later, in 1555, the same counsellors met with better success when they begged the Tsar not to flee before the Tartars. A consideration of these facts will enable us to gauge their undoubted influence. Some information as to Sylvester's personal share in it is furnished by one of his letters to the Metropolitan Macarius, concerning the appointment of a prior. It proves that the Tsar commissioned the pope to look into the merits of the candidates brought to his notice. But he had to embody his conclusions in a report, and in the Sovereign's absence, the whole business remained unsettled.

From the day on which they refused to stand by Dmitri, Sylvester and Adachev ceased to be Anastasia's friends. Their destiny may have been affected by her premature end, and it is probable, likewise, that their fall was hastened by some other event, of which we know nothing. All this period of the reign is wrapped in obscurity.

The close of Sylvester's life, too, slips out of the historian's ken. Adachev died in prison at the end of two years. ' If they had not parted me from my doe,' Ivan kept saying, ' Saturn would not have had so many victims !' The confession is worth remembering. Kourbski mentions a widow of Polish origin, Mary Magdalen by name, accused of guilty relations with Adachev, and executed, with five of her sons. At the same time, several of the ex-favourite's relations—his brother Daniel, with his twelve-year-old boy, and his father-in-law, Tourov, three brothers of the name of Satine, whose sister had married Alexis Adachev, and others—are said to have been put to death. A great deal of blood was certainly spilt. Ivan was then beginning a system of wholesale executions, by families at a time, and it was to be long before the red stream was dried up. To the ferocity which marked the habits of that period—my readers will not have forgotten the bloody hecatombs of Henry VIII. and Elizabeth, of Philip II. and Charles XI.—he added the fierceness of his violent nature, and the caprice of a half-Oriental despot. Kourbski mentions, at this time, a Prince Michael Repnine, invited to one of the Tsar's banquets, who refused to take his share in the general merriment, and, pulling off a mask the company had tried to force upon him, trampled it underfoot. A few days later, Ivan had him killed in church, while the Gospel was being read. A similar adventure is said to have befallen Prince George Kachine. The monarch, though he did not disclaim all the facts, denied that he had ever profaned the sacred edifices. According to Guagnino, another member of the upper aristocracy, a young Prince Dmitri Obolenski-Ovtchinine, likewise perished, about this time, in consequence of a quarrel with the Tsar's new favourite, Feodor Basmanov, whom he had offended by an insulting remark—' My ancestors and I, we have served our Sovereign like honest men. You serve him like the men of Sodom !' But on this point Kourbski contradicts the Italian chronicler, and here is another and an instructive proof of the degree of confidence of which Kourbski himself is worthy. Amongst the friends of Sylvester and Adachev involved in their disgrace he mentions, together with Prince Dmitri Kourliatev and other less prominent members of the group, dozens of whom were massacred or exiled, a certain Prince Michael Vorotynski. This gentleman, a valiant soldier, who had won glory on many a battlefield, was sent to Biélooziéro for the first time in 1559, sent back there soon after his recall from exile in 1564, and passed on this second occasion through the torture-chamber, we are assured. After being roasted over a slow fire in the presence of Ivan, who himself raked the hot cinders under his body with his staff, he is said to have died on his return journey. Now, as to this person's first exile, we have official and documentary evidence, and it proves him to have enjoyed a considerable amount of comfort. He complains that he has not been sent the Rhenish and French wines to which he has a right, and asks for various supplies —fresh fish, dried raisins, lemons, prunes—for himself, his family, and his twelve servants, all kept at the Tsar's expense in a prison which would seem to have been by no means a Gehenna. Can it be that people so well treated within the prison walls were thus cruelly handled before being sent there ? (' Historical Documents,' 1841, i., No. 174).

The only absolutely convincing documents we find among the records of the many trials connected with that of Sylvester and Adachev contain no reference either to torture or to execution. These prosecutions generally arose out of some plan to go abroad, imputed to one boïar or another, and invariably ended in mere precautionary measures ; the culprits, whether acquitted or pardoned, had to undertake not to leave the country, and to find security to that effect. This occurred in the case of Prince Vassili Mikhaïlovitch Glinski in 1561, and in that of Prince Ivan Dmitriévitch Biélski in the following year ; on this last occasion, nine-and-twenty prominent men, for whom 120 others went security, gave their signatures.

It will be noticed that this form of procedure implied an acknowledgment of the right claimed by the interested parties. Theoretically, indeed, this right remained unaffected. It had formerly been exercised as between one appanage and another, and the reason of its existence had passed away now Russia was a unified whole ; yet it still subsisted as the counterpart of that freedom claimed, without the smallest regard for frontier lines, by the nomad peasants themselves. But since the fifteenth century, a twofold current of emigration, affecting every class, had been flowing with increasing strength between Muscovy and Poland.

Guedymin's descendants swarmed at the Tsar's Court, and at that of Warsaw, the descendants of Rurik were legion. Through a Princess of Tver, who married Olguerd, many Polish families descended from that Lithuanian Prince were related to Russian houses. The ancestors of the Odoiévski, the Biélski, and the Vorotynski had lived partly in one country and partly in the other ; some of them had served Casimir, and some had served Ivan the Third. The Mstislavski had only left Lithuania in 1526, when they made way for the Czartoryski, a member of which family had once been Governor of Pskov. In 1521, the last Duke of Riazan had sought refuge in Lithuania, and with him representatives of some of the greatest of the Muscovite families—a Biélski, a Liatski, a Vichnioviétski, a Chérémétiév.

Still the stream flowed on, and the Terrible himself hesitated, at first, to check it effectually. Prince Ivan Dmitriévitch Biélski, in spite of the heavy security already mentioned, soon made a fresh attempt, and was once more pardoned. Ivan Vassiliévitch Chérémétiév's turn came in 1564. Kourbski declares he was tortured, loaded with chains, and punished, in the person of his brother Nikita, whom the Tsar had strangled. Concerning Nikita we know nothing, but very shortly after this, we find Ivan Vassilévitch in possession of all his posts, and it was not till long afterwards that he was exiled to Biélooziéro, where he seems to have provided himself with a fairly comfortable retreat.

These details are indispensable to the understanding of an episode identical in its nature with all those we have just reviewed, but which the unrivalled personality of its hero lifts out of the ordinary category.

III.—THE FLIGHT OF KOURBSKI.

Born towards the year 1528, descended, through the ancient Dukes of Smolensk and Jaroslavl, from Vladimir Monomachus, and belonging, like them, to the elder branch of the Rurikovitchy, Prince Andrew Mikhaïlovitch Kourbski was naturally involved in the disgrace that fell upon his friends. After his failure under the walls of Nevel, and the subsequent unsuccessful and suspicious negotiations with the Swedes for the cession of Helmet, he had special reasons for meditating escape. In 1564, declaring, as all who did like him declared, that nothing but pressing danger had driven him to such a course, he took the plunge. If he had stayed, so he averred, his head would have been in danger. Well received by the King of Poland—he had probably taken his precautions to insure this—he was assigned an establishment worthy of his rank, and did not hesitate to bear arms against his fatherland in his new master's service. He spent nineteen years in his adopted country, and did not make himself beloved there. His wanderings have passed into a legend. My readers may know the story of Vaska Chibanov, the bearer of the first letter addressed to Ivan by the refugee, 'From my master to Your traitor.' They may have seen a picture of the scene. Ivan, having received the message, leans, as he reads the letter, on his hunting-spear, and drives it into the messenger's foot. . . . A Moscow bookseller, who bears the name thus glorified by the heroic henchman, takes a pride, nowadays, in adorning his publications and circulars with this picture, which has no historical foundation. Chibanov did not go to Poland with Kourbski. It was on the scaffold, on which he suffered after being arrested with all the fugitive's other servants, that he proved his fidelity by refusing to deny, and by defending, his master. Kourbski's letters, like Ivan's replies, were probably not sent to their destination in this fashion at all. Messengers for such a purpose would doubtless not have been easy to find. These missives were open letters, intended for publication, and reached the persons to whom they were addressed by means of their publicity. One of the Tsar's lucubrations covers sixty pages, and the monarch would certainly not have gone to so much trouble for Kourbski alone. The fact that this argument was carried on *coram publico* lifts the incident above the dulness of everyday life, and constitutes its chief interest for us, now.

In that lazy land of Poland, where he had found shelter, Kourbski must have had a great deal of time on his hands. He turned it to account by writing a ' History of Ivan,' to which I have already referred, and in which he has done his utmost to condemn his former master's personal government, and extol the ' little council ' and its members. To this end he divides the reign into two parts—the period of glory, previous to the disgrace of Sylvester, Adachev, and Kourbski ; and the disastrous, criminal, and shameful period which followed on that event. In the service of his cause, he has drawn largely on his imagination, and has composed a list of Ivan's misdeeds, in which, as we have seen, many errors may be detected. Yet part of his accusation has been accepted, tacitly or explicitly, by the accused person, and part has been verified by other authorities. The historian also turned his attention to ecclesiastical history, and that, considering his own antecedents, in a somewhat unexpected spirit. In Russia he had been the friend, not only of Maximus the Greek, but of that Artemi who was accused of heresy before the *conciliable* of 1531. In Poland, where he was face to face with a Catholic propaganda which threatened his coreligionists, he suddenly discovered, in

some dark corner of his mind and heart, a spirit of fierce and
suspicious Orthodoxy.

And at the same time, the patriotic instinct stirred in the
voluntary exile's heart. As a Polish poet once said in ex-
quisite verse, ' A man's country is like his health : it is not till
he has lost it that he knows its worth.' Kourbski, sending
Prince Constantine Ostroski his Slav translation of one of
St. John Chrysostom's homilies, indignantly exclaims against
the idea that this magnate, who, though a subject of the Polish
King, belonged to the Orthodox faith, should have thought of
translating it into that ' barbarous language '—Polish ! And
he plunged into violent disputes with the Lithuanian partisans
of Theodore Kossoï and other Muscovite heresiarchs, once his
own friends. And he warred against the Jesuits, those ' wolves
brought into the fold,' even though he turned their zeal to
account against the Protestants. And, not to howl with the
wolves, but to be better able to fight them, he began to learn
Latin in his old age, and advised one of his comrades in exile,
young Prince Michael Obolenski, to leave his wife and children
and put himself to school, at Cracow first of all, and then in
Italy—a precursor of the troops of students, male and female,
who now besiege the doors of our teaching centres. Some
of the fruits of this busy effort—fragmentary translations of
St. John Chrysostom and Eusebius, and a preface written for
the ' New Pearl ' (*Novyĭ Margarit*)—have been preserved to us.

But, above all other things, Kourbski mended his best pen
with a view to his explanation with Ivan. In his pleadings
we find more rhetoric than truth, less reason than passion. He
enumerates his services and the ill-treatment he has endured ;
he vents imprecations on the Tsar's crimes and his abuse of
power, on his dissolute life and the unworthiness of his new
favourites—such men as Basmanov and Maliouta-Skouratov,
debauchees or bloody ruffians. Copiously and laboriously, he
exhausts all these facile themes, yet never lays a finger on the
heart of the question, the complex and deep-seated causes of
the disagreement between the Sovereign and the portion of
society which refused to accept the master's will.

This fact diminishes the historical value of the document.
But that its author should have been able to sting the Tsar
of all the Russias into taking up the gauntlet and entering
on a literary duel ; that he should thus have made his own
disgrace and rancour echo far and wide, and drawn the ancient
struggle between past and future, between the partisans of the
old and new system, between the two rival branches of the
house of Rurik, into these narrow lists, is in itself a great
matter, and marks an epoch of capital importance in the
national history. It is an eloquent affirmation of the entrance

of the great Northern Empire upon the track of modern
life.

By his rank, Ivan might have scorned the offered provocation, and his overweening pride would have seemed to
make such a course most probable. But his own temperament, and, added to that, his modern instinct, gained the day,
and to this circumstance we owe, not only a most precious
historical document, but a remarkable writer. I do not refer
to Kourbski. His style is diffuse, confused, and dull. Ivan's
is more prolix still; he sheds no light on the dispute, and
shows no more anxiety than his opponent to bring it back
to its proper limits. His pleading, like Kourbski's, is all one-
sided, and he limits his replies and his own attacks to facts
and interests of quite secondary importance. Did he have
such a boïar killed in church or in his dungeon? Did he or
did he not attempt Kourbski's life? All this is not really
important. But, still, the Tsar invests his arguments, in part
at all events, with that which the other never succeeded in
putting into his. Not style indeed—Kourbski's style is bad,
but Ivan has no style at all—but spirit, vehemence, sustained
energy, words that tell, phrases that hit the mark like an
arrow from the bow. ' You who call yourself just and pious,
how came you to fear death so much that you sold your soul
to save your body?' And he proves his learning, too—gives
us bits of Scriptural exegesis. This is a controversy between
two learned men! Kourbski has quoted Scripture to prove
that a monarch ought to listen to his counsellors. Has he
forgotten Moses, then? He has denounced the executions
ordered by Ivan as crimes. And how about King David?
As to the right of departure, put into practice by the noble
fugitive, as to the other privileges claimed by him and his adherents, not a word. The sole political theory the meaning
and formula of which the Tsar condescends to evoke and set
forth, is that of the absolute power. ' We are free to punish
and to reward as it seems good to us, and no Russian Sovereign
has ever given an account of his actions to anyone on earth.'

I have already pointed out, and shall again have to show,
in the political history of the Moscow of that period, a sort of
tacit agreement whereby realities were concealed under appearances, and which sometimes ended by completely disguising facts
and persons, and the parts these persons played. These two
adversaries, though they crossed pens in public, as I have
said, were to observe an agreement of this kind, and, to the
very end, to avoid tearing the veil asunder, though under its
shadow they dealt each other mighty blows. To defend
himself against the mass of quotations with which the Tsar
sought to crush him, Kourbski appealed to the superiority

of his own literary education. ' You ought to be ashamed
to write like an old mad woman, and send so ill-composed
an epistle into a country full of people who know grammar
and rhetoric, dialectics and philosophy !'   The allusion to
the publicity of the controversy is clear enough here.   But
both parties continued to shirk the pith of the question.

The dates of the first three letters thus exchanged are unknown.   Ivan dates the fourth from Wolmar, the day after
he took that town, in 1577.   The victor does not fail to draw
arguments from his late triumph.   He has won it without the
help of Kourbski and his friends.   Kourbski's reply appeals
to Cicero ; but this time his opponent swerves.   He writes
again, but no answer comes.   Batory has appeared upon the
scene, and given the Tsar other things to think of.

In his own country, Ivan's great antagonist has found
apologists and detractors, all equally convinced.   The first
seem at present to be carrying all before them, and while they
await the statue which will no doubt stand, some day, on
one of the Moscow squares, they are erecting a literary monument which is not devoid of value to the glory of the nation.
In the eyes of the learned author of the ' History of Russian
Literature ' (Pypine, ii. 171, 172), as in those of an older
biographer (P . . . ski, Kazan, 1873), Kourbski, with all his
faults, and in spite of them, is the most eminent representative of the civilizing ideas assimilated by the Russia of the
sixteenth century.   He marks the comparatively high level
to which a Russian of that period, far from the Western
centres of information, hampered in his search after knowledge, choked by Government terrorism, might yet raise
himself.   Kourbski was a man of science, too, who strove to
widen the field of knowledge which had satisfied most of his
fellow-citizens.   He was also the first public writer his country
possessed, and, to crown it all, he was its first citizen, in the
true sense of the word, the first who fell in love with the idea
of progress, and was capable of lifting his voice against a brutal
despotism.

These are noble titles, but they need verification.   Kourbski's Moscow career is still veiled in great obscurity.   The
details of his residence in Poland are better known, for life
there was more open.   These details do not reflect much
honour on the wanderer.   Though sufficiently well provided
with money and land by the country of his exile, he was an
odious master, a hateful neighbour, and the most detestable
and unruly of subjects.   While he was translating St. John
Chrysostom and calling out against despotism, he committed,
or allowed his stewards to commit, abuses of his own power
quite as monstrous as any of which Ivan may have been guilty

—such as shutting up Jews in dungeons full of water . . . and leeches. At war with everybody, beginning with the King, who was certainly anything but a tyrant ; in perpetual rebellion against every authority, even in such matters as the taxes payable on his new properties, or the recruits he was bound to furnish from them, he made himself generally hated.

What he would seem to have especially represented and personified is that class of men with whom Ivan found himself forced to struggle—men whose intelligence was open to certain elements of civilization and certain ideas of freedom, but who interpreted them all in a narrow sense, to suit their own caste or clan interests. Some people have gone so far as to deny that he was one of the group of boïars who clung obstinately to their superannuated privileges ; but did he not put forward his claims to the Duchy of Jaroslavl ? The fact of his poverty has been alleged. If that is so, he was nothing, when he passed over into Poland, but a vulgar fortune-hunter, for in addition to the *Starosty* of Krev, to ten villages and 4,000 *diéssiatines* of land in Lithuania, the town and castle of Kovel, and twenty-eight villages in Volhynia, a very liberal sum of money was bestowed upon him. And this would have involved an abominable deceit practised on Sigismund-Augustus, who, as his letters granting the concession prove, believed himself to be giving an equivalent for the wealth left behind in Muscovy.

All these advantages Kourbski gained in his newly-chosen fatherland, after having dreamed at Moscow, if not of recovering the appanage of his ancestors—and yet one of his peers, Chouïski, when he ascended the throne soon afterwards, was to claim exactly similar rights—at all events of protecting what remained of his inheritance against the encroachments of the State, and increasing it at the State's expense ; of defending his right to sit on his master's councils, too, and make himself heard there, as well as his claim to yield him just so much obedience as might suit his own convenience. Thus, partisan of progress though he may have been, he remained a laggard, dallying behind his time, amidst the formal traditions of bygone centuries. He had an ideal, no doubt — the political ideal, though he did not dream it, perhaps, of the hospitable country he despised and detested, even though he had come to break bread at her board. But this ideal, anarchical enough in its own birthplace, dangerous and even fatal, was not susceptible of transportation to Muscovite soil. Once across the frontier, it collided with different conceptions and habits, it was transformed into a mere negation—refusal of service, desertion, treachery. And thus it comes about that in the popular legend, and in spite of all the exile's pains to endue him with that appearance, Kourbski's crowned adversary is not, and never has been, the persecutor of innocence oppressed. He is, and always has been, ' the destroyer of treason on Russian soil.' That is the one thing the Russian people has perceived and understood in the drama in which itself played the part of the ancient chorus, together with the fact that when the Tsar massacred or ill-used his boïars he did it in defence of the humble and the weak.

This needs explanation, and for that purpose, Kourbski's career may serve. Most of Ivan's historians have refused to admit that the people sided with the despot. What did he offer the mass of the peasants, husbandmen yesterday, half-serfs to-day, and soon to be utterly enslaved—to these beings whose backs were bent in never-ending labour, bound to the soil, and more and more ground down, more mercilessly cheated, as the needs of the State increased ? Yet the facts speak for themselves. Ivan has been sung, lauded, extolled, by the population of helots whose slavery and misery he deepened. When suffering has reached a certain pitch, any change, even if it should increase the torture, is a benefit. In 1582, the peasants of one of the Polish properties bestowed on Kourbski made a complaint against their new master. They had known others, who had not made their life any too easy, but this one they could not endure ! The complaint was admitted to be well founded, and my readers may imagine in what fashion Kourbski had been in the habit of treating the unhappy *moujiks* on his Russian *vottchina*. There were thousands of Kourbskis in Russia, and this one was a liberal, a man of progress ! The hatred all these men inspired built up Ivan's popularity.

The exile died at Kovel in 1583. His family, which had embraced Catholicism in Poland, returned to Russia and to the Orthodox faith, and died out in 1777. In the struggle between the old régime and the new order of things, Kourbski, the most illustrious of the champions of the past, was, taking him all in all, neither a hero nor a martyr. And for this reason, before we plunge into the heart of that battle, where the bloody phantom of the *Opritchnina* awaits them, I have desired to show him to my readers, as an example of the kind of adversaries with whom Ivan had to deal.

CHAPTER II

THE OPRITCHNINA

I.—THE FICTIONS AND REALITIES OF THE DRAMA.   II.—THE TERROR.
III.—THE TSAR SIMEON.   IV.—THE OPRITCHNINA AT THE BAR
OF HISTORY.

I.—The Fictions and Realities of the Drama.

Most of my Russian readers and some of my French ones
have read the adventures of Prince Serebrianyï, as related by
Alexis Tolstoï. The hero of the tale, returning to Russia
after an embassy to a foreign Power, meets a troop of armed
men, whom he takes, by their appearance and behaviour, for
lawless bandits. He sees them sack a village and murder or
violate the inhabitants. He acts according to the dictates of
his brave heart, and then only, when the law has laid its hand
on his collar, does he discover he has been guilty of treason.
The men he had taken for brigands are the Tsar's servants,
and their performances a perfectly regular specimen of the
new order of things imposed on the country. The culprit is
conducted to the monarch's new residence, the *Sloboda* of
Alexandrov, and passes from one surprise and horror to
another—from the courtyard where roving bears bar the way
of suspicious-looking visitors, to the banqueting-hall, the road
to which is fringed with torture-chambers and dungeons,
and where the Tsar, surrounded by guests disguised in
monkish attire, distributes gloomy smiles and cups of poisoned
liquor. Everywhere his foot slips in blood : an evil smell of
carnage hangs in the air, the joyous yells of the drunken feasters
mingle with the shrieks of pain wrung from prisoners who
are being tortured close by. The whole palace is a Gehenna,
a charnel-house. And wherefore ? No man knows, or rather
all men guess : the Tsar is amusing himself, and these are his
pleasures.

The novelist has not relied wholly and solely on his imagination. He has sought to write history, and history, in the
person of her most illustrious exponents in his own country,
has furnished him with the elements of his picture, with his
outline and his pigments. This is the *Opritchnina*, as the story
is told by Karamzine, by Soloviov, by Kostomarov, and in
our own days by Klioutchevski and Mikhaïlovski—a hideous
tale of massacre, ordered, without reason, without object,
by a Sovereign who treated himself to this bloody play, perpetrated, shamelessly and remorselessly, by men who rode up
and down the country with their insignia, a dog's head and a

broom, hung at their saddle-bow, and whose watchword was
murder and pillage.   Soaked with blood, laden with plunder,
they made their way home, donned a monk's frock, to add
profanation to their other crimes, and with their master, himself disguised as a prior, plunged into the vilest orgies. These
were the *Opritchniki*.

But other and later historians have applied themselves to
the same task, and their inquiry into the same facts, and
scrutiny of the same individuals, has led them to a different
view of the same drama, and another interpretation of the
strange riddle it presents. - Behind that terrifying scene and
its horrible surroundings they have discovered an idea ; under
the deceptive appearances of a sanguinary madness they have
thought they perceived a carefully-digested plan, carried out
with as much tenacity as vigour : they have discerned the
existence of huge projects of reform, political, social, and
economic, put into action by means that were reprehensible,
indeed, but which may have been necessary to some extent.
The riddle has not been entirely solved.   It still holds out
against its interpreters' efforts.   But one fact is certain : in
their manner of interpreting and representing the *Opritchnina*, the historians of the old school have fallen into a three-
fold error.   They have mistaken appearances for realities,
accessories for essentials, and a part for the whole.

I shall explain myself better by taking one example.
Imagine a history of the French Revolution—and this, perhaps,
is not an entirely gratuitous supposition—cut down to the
evocation of a few scenes and characters culled from the
Jacobin Club, the Temple prison, and the *Place de la Nation*.
This would be the equivalent of what was given us for a lengthened period as the foundation and essence of ten years of
the political existence of the reign of Ivan the Terrible.   And
this cannot be wondered at, when we consider that the document most indispensable to an understanding of the episode,
the decree which constitutes the *Opritchnina*, though preserved
in the archives, has remained unpublished, and continues
inaccessible, even in our own day.   Other documents have
either been lost or have also remained unknown.   I now
proceed to the facts we do possess.

Kourbski's flight, which was preceded and followed by
similar attempts, some successful and others continually
threatening to become so, had placed Ivan in a position calculated to render his future most perplexing and uncertain.
To accomplish the tasks he had set himself, at home and
abroad, one necessitated by the other—for his internal reforms
supplied the necessary instruments for his external enterprises—many men and large sums of money were needful.

Where was he to find them ?   Except when, more concerned about their own privileges than the common weal, they were losing battles through fighting over their respective places, or making compacts with the enemy, the men melted into space. As to money, the same men, either as heads of the administration or holders of the soil, chief wealth of the country, disposed of that, keeping its use or control in their own hands. Whether as *voiévodes*, lieutenants, judges, members of the Supreme Court, chiefs of the various offices, they were everywhere, held everything, except when, on the ancient *vottchiny*, where each had his own court and his own soldiery, exercised a jurisdiction which was almost without appeal, and refused to pay taxes, almost without exception, they were putting on kingly airs, or else claiming theoretically superior titles, and putting forward pretensions against those of the ' *younger branch* ' at Moscow, which, empty and void as they were for all future purposes, were worrying enough, nevertheless.

As to breaking up the system of his administrative and military organization, Ivan could not dream of such a thing. The life of sixteenth-century Moscow resided in her traditions. Over individuals, the Tsar's power was unlimited ; but it failed in face of an order of things of which he himself, his rank, his prestige, and his authority, were integral parts. While the Princes and boïars, accustomed to look on the government of the country as their own property, a sphere belonging to them by prescriptive right, regarded their functions as independent of any investiture on his part, and considered the *Miéstnitchestvo* a guarantee for this hereditary privilege, the Sovereign found it difficult to say them nay, seeing his own power had the same origin, and was founded on the same title.   All these descendants of Rurik or Guedymin, boïars and Tsar alike, had ruled in Russia in the old days— each man apart, on his own appanage.   The Government was collective now—one man on the throne, the others at the head of an office or a province.   But none the less were they all members of the same company, of the same faimly, and no man of them had any right to say, ' This house is mine, you must go out of it !'   And as far as the individuals were concerned, how would Ivan have filled their places ?   The dozen of men, such as Skouratov and Griaznoï, whom he succeeded in pushing into the foremost rank, after Sylvester and Adachev had disappeared, ' taking them out of the mud,' as he said himself, and generally out of that class of the *Popovitchy* (sons of popes) which still plays so prominent a part in what is called ' intelligence ' in Russia, could not furnish him with the capital, material and moral, represented by the others.   Outside the ranks of that aristocracy with which his policy had

brought him into conflict he had no resources at all—everything was a blank.   Between those two products of history,
the *boïarstvo* and the *samodiérjavié*, no divorce was possible.
A compromise was the thing needful, and it was on a compromise that Ivan decided at this tragic moment.   But he
took good care not to say what he meant to do.   The Russia of
the sixteenth century, as we have already seen, was a country
of mysteries.   There was a mask on every face, and everything
was hidden under some disguise.

On December 3, 1564, a Sunday, Ivan had all his treasures,
his money, his plate, his gems, his furniture, and his ikons,
packed on to waggons, and, followed by a huge train, many
boïars chosen out of various towns, and his whole Court and
household, he left his capital with his second wife, Maria
Temrioukovna, a half-savage Circassian, as violent and passionate as himself.   For some time, nobody in Moscow heard
anything of him, and no man knew whither he had betaken
himself, or wherefore he had departed.   He went first of all
to the village of Kolomenskoié, where bad weather detained
him for a fortnight.   He then spent some days at Taïninskoié,
another village in the neighbourhood of Moscow, and near
the Troïtsa, and finally took up his quarters in a suburb of
the little town of Alexandrov, north of Vladimir.   There he
revealed the motives and object of his unwonted exodus.
On January 3, a courier reached Moscow with a letter
from the Tsar to the Metropolitan.   In it the monarch, after
dwelling at length on the misdeeds of the *voiévodes* and officials
of every degree, and the clergy, upper and lower, declared he
had 'laid his anger' on them all, from the greatest to the
least.   This was what was called the *Opala*, a sort of ban,
which placed all those affected by it in a state of disgrace
and incapacity to perform any active function, whether about
the Court or in the service of the State.   At the same time
Ivan announced his determination to leave the Empire and
establish himself 'wherever God should counsel him to go.'
There was something contradictory in the terms of the message.
The Tsar was abdicating, then ?   And yet he used his authority
to punish his subjects.   But this message, again, was accompanied by another, addressed to the merchants and 'the
whole Christian population of Moscow,' and its contents
were to the effect that, as far as they were concerned, the Tsar
had no cause of complaint, nor any feeling of displeasure.

What was the meaning of it all ?   Probably people knew
that as partially then as they do now.   But so accustomed
were the Russians of that day to riddles, that they did not
hesitate as to the course they should pursue.   The Tsar,
displeased with a certain section of his subjects, was medi-

tating some dark design against them, the nature of which
would not be revealed till its effects made themselves felt.
What was apparent at the present moment was merely the
usual setting of the scene.   Obediently all men prepared to
bear their part in the coming comedy.   The boïars betrayed
the correct amount of emotion, the populace rose up, shouted
aloud, and was much affected.   The merchants offered money,
the most eloquent fashion of proving their share in the general
feeling, and the Metropolitan was called upon to intercede with
the Sovereign.   Ivan was entreated not to forsake his people,
but to rule as best pleased him, and mete out such treatment
as he deemed fit to those of whom he thought he had reason
to complain.   A deputation took its way to Alexandrov, and
the Tsar allowed himself to be mollified, but he made his own
conditions ; he intended to keep all traitors and rebels in
disgrace, to put some to death, and confiscate their fortunes,
and he would not go back to Moscow till he had organized his
Opritchnina.

This, in the common parlance of that day, was the name
applied to the dowry paid to the wives of the great Princes.
At banquets, certain special dishes which the amphitryon kept
in front of himself, and the contents of which he divided
amongst his chief guests, were called *Opritchnyié*.   And a particular class of peasants settled on the lands belonging to certain
monasteries were known as *Opritchniki* (from *opritch*, a part).
Let my readers now cast their minds back to the ukase of
October 10, 1550 (see p. 148), which gave the district of Moscow
a territorial and political constitution of its own, and settled
a selection of *sloojilyié lioodi*, taken from every rank of the
nobility and every province of the Empire, within its borders.
Without any essential modification of the existing order of
things, solely by virtue of this transplanting process and of a
change in the nature of the tenure, Ivan had summoned the
men just transplanted to form the nucleus of a court, an
administration, and an army, all reorganized on a new basis.
The *Opritchnina* of 1565, in its fundamental idea, was neither
more nor less than the extension and wider application of this
original plan.

Ivan now divided his Empire into two parts.   One of these
was to preserve its ancient organization and its ancient government — in other words, the *voiévodes*, lieutenants, bailiffs,
and *kormlenchtchiki* of every kind were to carry on the administration as it had been carried on hitherto, a college presided
over by two boïars taking the place of the Supreme Council
as the centre of the various services.   The other part, which
comprised various portions of the country, a certain number
of towns, and several quarters of the capital city, was converted

16

into a sort of dowry or appanage, which the Tsar kept for
himself, and on which, with a thousand boïars or boïars' sons,
chosen by himself, he was about to follow up the experiment
of 1550.

I must insist here on the scope of this experiment, which
may be summed up in two principal features : the transformation of the freehold properties into fiefs, and the removal
of owners from one holding to another. To take the proprietor of an hereditary freehold, subject to no charges of any
kind, to tear him out of the corner of the soil on which, for
centuries past, his fortune and importance had sprouted,
grown, and struck their roots ; to part him from his natural
adherents, break off all his natural connections, and, having
thus uprooted him, isolated him, and removed him from his
own sphere, to set him down elsewhere, as far as possible
from his native place, to give him another property, but on
a life interest, and on terms exacting service, and the payment of the usual taxes from him, and thus to make a new man
of him, a man without a past, without backing, defenceless—
this was the constitution of the system. So, at least, we may
suppose, for Ivan never revealed his secret. But, though
the fact has hitherto passed unnoticed, the evident connection
between the two decrees, that of 1550 and that of 1565, does
indicate a *system*, and all we know of the two measures, of
their character and their application, is in favour of the correctness of the conjecture I have adopted, after the example
of Monsieur Platonov, who seems to me to have approached
nearest to the truth (' Essays on the History of the Political
Disturbances of the Sixteenth and Seventeenth Centuries,'
St. Petersburg, 1899, i. 137, etc.), and Monsieur Milioukov,
whom I am inclined to think a little further removed from it
(' Essays on the History of Russian Culture,' 1896, i. 147, etc.),
by his determination to see nothing, either in Ivan's reforms
or in Peter the Great's, except financial expedients.

Ivan's horizon was certainly wider than this. During his
lifetime, and even after his death, silence has been kept, by
superior order, concerning all this undertaking. Questions
on the subject must have been foreseen when an embassy from
the Tsar went into Poland in 1565. Muscovite diplomacy
was in the habit of providing against possible indiscretions
by foreseeing such inquiries, and dictating the replies beforehand. Thus, if the envoys were asked what the *Opritchnina*
was, they were to answer, ' We do not know what you mean.
There is no *Opritchnina*. The Tsar is living in the place of
residence he has been pleased to choose, and such of his servants as have given him cause for satisfaction are there with
him, or are settled close by ; the others are a little farther

off—that is all. If peasants, who know nothing about anything, talk about an *Opritchnina*, people should not listen to them.' The same orders were given to other embassies, in 1567 and 1571 (' Collections of the Imperial Society of Russian History,' vol. lxxi., pp. 461, 777).

But facts began to speak in their turn. The part of the Empire originally given up to the *Opritchnina* was gradually increased till it comprised a good half of the Tsar's dominions, and till the *Opritchniki* numbered 5,000, instead of 1,000, men. In 1565, the provinces of Vologda, Oustioug, Kargopol, Mojaïsk, and Viazma were added; in 1566, all the Stroganov properties; in 1571, part of the province of Novgorod. Each fresh extension was accompanied by a distribution of freehold lands or fiefs, taken from their original possessors. These received territorial compensation in other provinces, where they replaced, by a process of exchange, the *Opritchniki* who had been substituted for themselves on their old holdings—unless, indeed, they had the good luck to be received into the *Opritchnina* without undergoing expropriation or exile. And the districts claimed by the *Opritchnina* in the central provinces were just those in which the remnants of the old appanage system were largest and strongest. It laid its hand, thus, on the hereditary patrimonies of the Dukes of Rostov, Starodoub, Souzdal, and Tchernigov. It swallowed up, too, the territories ' beyond the Oka,' the ancient inheritance of yet another group of appanaged Princes—the Odoiévski, the Vorotynski, and the Troubetskoï. Some of these, Prince Feodor Mikhaïlovitch Troubetskoï, Prince Nikita Ivanovitch Odoiévski, allowed themselves to be enrolled under the banners of the new system, and proved its zealous servants. The rest were forced to migrate. Thus, in exchange for Odoiév, Prince Michael Ivanovitch Vorotynski received Starodoub-Riapolovski, some hundred miles further west. Other landowners in that country were given lands in the districts near Moscow, round Kolomna, Dmitrov, and Zvenigorod.

One instance will suffice to show the practical consequences of this moving to and fro. Out of 272 freehold domains in the district of Tver, the proprietors of 53 gave the State no service of any sort or kind; some of these were the lieges of Prince Vladimir Andreiévitch, the Tsar's cousin, the others owed service to descendants of the old appanaged Princes, one to an Obolenski, another to a Mikoulinski, or a Mstislavski, a Galitzine, a Kourliatev, or even to some plain boïar. The *Opritchnina* altered all this. It brought about a general devolution of everything that was owed on the one and only master who had set himself in the

16—2

place of all the others.   At the same time it suppressed the
local military bodies, thanks to which the Tsar's unruly vassals
frequently made themselves more dangerous to him than to
his foes ; it proclaimed the law of individual service, and over
all the country its rule affected it established a system of
direct and indirect taxation levied for the benefit of the
Treasury.

Swayed, too, by economic and financial considerations
which I do not dream of denying, it most particularly sought
to obtain possession of the towns along the great trade routes
of the Empire, and to this change of system—this is worth
observing—the traders affected were by no means opposed.
The representatives of the English company craved admission
to it as a favour.   The Stroganovs followed the same course.
The only roads between the capital and the frontier which
escaped the *Opritchnina's* attention were those running south-
ward, through Toula and Riazan, and these were probably
omitted because no apparent advantage was to be derived
from their inclusion.

It is only with the greatest difficulty that any full inventory
of the territories annexed by the *Opritchnina* has been drawn
up, for documents precise enough to serve as a foundation for
the calculation do not exist.   It seems to have ended by
comprising a great slice of the central and northern provinces,
bailiwicks, and towns, and of the coast as well (*pomorié*),
all the districts of the *Zamoskovié* (Moscow region), all the
regions ' beyond the Oka,' and two districts (*piatiny*) out of
the five which constituted the province of Novgorod—those
of Obonéjé and Biéjetsk.   The *Opritchnina*, the northern
boundaries of which thus rested on the ' great ocean-sea,' as
it was called in those days, cut cornerwise into the territory
handed over to the old system, the *Ziémchtchina* (*ziémia*,
land), as it was called, while it ran southward as far as the
Oka, eastward towards Viatka, and westward up to the Lithu-
anian-German frontier.   The provinces of Perm, Viatka, and
Riazan on the east, and the dependencies of Pskov and Novgorod, with the frontier towns, Vielikié-Louki, Smolensk, and
Siéviérsk, on the west, were not included in the new organization.   Southwards the two zones of the *Ziémchtchina* were
connected by the Ukraine and by wild steppes (*dikoié
pole*).

In the centre of the country, as I have just said, the *Opritchnina* only affected certain localities, and the bailiwicks, towns,
and town quarters under its jurisdiction were mingled in un-
imaginable and indescribable confusion with those of the
Ziémchtchina.   But of the important towns, the old system
only kept Tver, Vladimir, and Kalouga, and it may be said,

generally speaking, to have been pushed back towards the far ends of the Empire. This was a reversal of the history of Rome, which assumed immediate authority over her most distant provinces, so as to draw the steel-clad circle of her legions round the heart of the Empire.

Towards the year 1572, the *Opritchnina* lost its original name. It was then called the Court (*dvor*). At that moment it already possessed all the characteristics of a regularly constituted State organization, and in its working, indeed, it preserved all the administrative forms of the old system, so much so that it is not easy to discover, from any document of that period, which of the two branches thus wedded together has issued it. In principle the *Opritchnina* did not even suppress the *Miéstnitchestvo:* it simply forbade the application of that system within its own borders. Its action and that of the *Ziémchtchina* ran on parallel and concerted lines, and both possessed a common centre in the Offices of War and Finance. *Diaks* attached to these two branches of the Government overlooked the distribution of the business connected with each. It seems probable, at least, that affairs followed this course, for the coexistence and concerted labours of the two sets of officials are an established fact, which suffices to destroy the legend of an *Opritchnina* confined to the duties of a mere political police force. In 1570, authentic documents show us the *Opritchnina* and the *Ziémchtchina* summoned to deliberate, through their respective representatives—all of them boïars— on questions connected with the Lithuanian frontier. The discussions were held separately, but an agreement was reached. There is no trace of any enmity or conflict. That very same year, and the next, detachments furnished by both organizations went campaigning together against the Tartars, and perfect harmony appears to have reigned between them.

The solution of the problem confronting Ivan furnished by the *Opritchnina* was certainly not wholly satisfactory. What was needed was something which would have annulled the twofold contradiction which afflicted his whole Empire : a contradiction in politics arising out of the fact that the historical march of events had endued the Sovereign with an absolute power founded on a democratic basis, which he was obliged to exercise through an aristocracy ; a social contradiction resulting from the fact that this same Sovereign, in his quest of fresh food for the growing ambitions of his Empire, and to insure it, was forced into making over his productive class, bound hand and foot, to the arbitrary will of his nonproducers, his ' men who serve,' his soldiers, and his tax collectors.

As far as the destruction of the aristocratic element is con-

cerned, the *Opritchnina* proved a failure. But it shook
it sorely, and Ivan's plan probably did not go beyond this
result. Apart from the great and mighty lords it enrolled,
and by enrolling disarmed them, only an elect few of the
aristocratic class escaped, such as Prince Ivan Feodorovitch
Mstislavski and Prince Ivan Dmitriévitch Biélski, both of
them placed at the head of the *Ziémchtchina*—two inoffensive
utility actors. It destroyed all the political importance of
the class, and the effect of this was to be manifest, even after
Ivan's death, in the preponderating part played by parvenus
created by him, such as Zakharine and Godounov. Others
of his subjects, of yet humbler extraction, peasants, Cossacks,
Tartars, recruited in increasing numbers to fill the gaps caused
by his confiscations and wholesale executions, not to mention
his *transplantings*, ended by forming a comparatively numerous
body, and a powerful weapon for levelling and democratic
purposes. ' My father's boïars and my own have learnt to
be traitors,' wrote Ivan to Vassiouchka Griaznoï, ' so we have
resolved to call on you, vile varlets, and from you we expect
fidelity and truth !' And Vassiouchka replied : ' You are
like unto God ! You make a little man into a great man !'

This revolution—for a revolution it certainly was—could not
be accomplished without some kind of struggle. Everywhere,
in the lowest classes, where it broke bonds that were centuries
old, in the towns and country places, into which it introduced strange elements, on the great landed properties which
it divided up, calling a new agricultural and industrial
proletariat into existence, it wounded innumerable feelings
and interests. I have already shown how, by destroying
the ancient administrative autonomy of the peasants, now
made subject to their new proprietors in all those matters
as to which they had hitherto dealt directly with the State, it
contributed, indirectly, to the establishment of serfdom. It
had a more immediate effect in quickening the current of
emigration amongst the elements thus disaggregated, and
hastening, through the increase of the calls made on them, the
exhaustion of the resources dependent on those elements.
From this point of view, Ivan's undertaking is open to much
blame, and his conflict with Poland was soon to demonstrate
the weak side of a work in other respects useful, and no
doubt even necessary.

Its execution was attended by excesses of various sorts,
which cannot fail to attract severe judgment. This is the
common law of all great crises of this kind, and few which
have escaped it are known to history. But the historian cannot
regard the *Opritchnina* from one point of view only, and he
must allow for some undoubted exaggeration in all the various

reports of the violence which certainly soiled and jeopardized it at the time, and which in the eyes of posterity, has veiled and warped its real character and genuine aims. These reports, generally emanating from interested witnesses, like Kourbski, or deliberately hostile ones, such as most foreigners were, cannot be unquestioningly accepted. Means of verification are, unhappily, almost entirely non-existent. I will endeavour, however, to get as near the truth as possible, even if I fail to reach it altogether.

II.—THE TERROR.

Ivan had reserved himself the right of chastising certain of his boïars ; nobody could imagine he would relinquish it. Kourbski having escaped him, the Tsar fell on the fugitive's accomplices, real or supposed. Under this accusation, Prince Alexander Borissovitch Chouïski, with his young son Peter and several of his kinsmen, including two members of the Khovryne family—Prince Ivan Soukhoï Kachine, Prince Dmitri Chevirev, and others—were put to death. Other poor wretches— Prince Ivan Kourakine, and Prince Dmitri Niémogo—paid with their heads for misdeeds as to which we have no information. Sentences of banishment and confiscation followed, and it was not till the Terrible had thus satisfied his rage and begun his dreaded work that he consented to return to his captial. One chronicler tells us the inhabitants could hardly recognise their Sovereign ; his face was distorted, and he had lost all his hair. This feature may be noted as a premonitory symptom of what a lively imagination has been able to add to the realities of the drama, already sufficiently gloomy. As the Tsar, like all the men of his period, was in the habit of shaving his head, his sudden baldness can hardly have struck his observers, and soon, indeed, he was to give only too certain proofs of his health and strength.

My readers will recollect the episode of the Polish letters intercepted by Ivan. Some of the persons for whom these missives had been intended, and on whom suspicion now fell— old Ivan Petrovitch Tcheliadnine and his wife, Prince Ivan Kourakine-Boulgakov, three Princes Rostovski, and others— were whirled into the tempest, handed over to the executioner, tortured horribly, and put to death. Even the Church had her turn. Apart from the solidarity of interest which bound her to the victims of the new system, she here found a more pressing opportunity than ever for claiming that right of intercession which was her most precious privilege and her noblest claim to glory. In the person of one of Macarius's successors as Metropolitan of Moscow, she was to draw down the thunder-

bolt on her own head. Macarius himself had already come
forward, very cautiously, but not unmeritoriously, in favour of
several of the attainted adherents of the Church. He had
pleaded for Vorontsov, and probably for Sylvester himself.
His immediate successor, a monk from the monastery of
Tchoudov, Athanasius by name, was more timid, and remained
an impassive spectator of the first violent episodes of the
Opritchnina. Falling ill, he resigned his see, in 1566, to the
Archbishop of Kazan, Herman, who only held it for a very short
time.   Ivan's new favourites plotted his removal, and suggested
a successor, the choice of whom would be quite inexplicable if,
owing to the lack of any other information, we were to accept
that reputation for savage brutality attributed to them.

Philip, abbot of the monastery of Solovki, a member of the
illustrious Kolytchev family, who had been driven from Court
by the disgrace into which his kinsfolk had fallen, and forced to
become a monk, was noted for his great virtues and his remarkable powers of government : Ivan, it is said, had known
and loved him in his youth.   The metropolitan see was offered
to him.   He began by refusing to accept it unless the *Opritchnina* was done away with.   Finally he yielded, and gave a
written undertaking not to interfere in politics, nor in the Tsar's
private life.   This last, which was growing more and more
irregular and dissolute, was beginning to cause general dis-
satisfaction.   But at the same time, Ivan recognised the new
pontiff's right of intercession : ' Your duty is not to go against
the Sovereign's will, but to endeavour to turn his wrath aside.'
In the result, the Tsar soon began to avoid seeing the Metropolitan.   But they lived too near each other.   Even when
he was at the *Sloboda* at Alexandrov, Ivan was obliged to pay
occasional visits to his capital, and put in an appearance
in the churches there.   On such occasions, meetings were
inevitable.

One Sunday—it was on May 31, 1568—the Tsar entered the
Cathedral of the Assumption, attended by his *Opritchniki* disguised as monks, and asked, as usual, for the Metropolitan's
blessing.   Philip held his peace.   Three times Ivan returned
to the charge, each time in vain.   At last, when the boïars
reproached him, the pontiff broke the silence, and before
the astounded company a tragic dialogue between the two
men ensued.   In a long discourse Philip enumerated all the
Sovereign's crimes and all his debauchery, the monarch
vainly striving to interrupt him.

' If the *living souls* were to hold their peace,' said the priest,
' the very stones of this church would speak, and cry out against
thee !'

' Hold thy peace !' said the Tsar over and over again—

' that's all I say to thee ! Hold thy peace, and give us thy
blessing !'

' My silence lays a sin upon thy soul, and calls down thy
death. . . .'

' Hold thy peace ! . . . My subjects, my kinsmen, rose
against me, and plotted my ruin. . . . Rebel no more, along
with them, or quit thy see !'

' I never asked to be put into this see. I used neither money
nor intrigue to obtain it. Why didst thou call me from my
hermitage ? . . .'

Ivan controlled himself, and even made as though he would
return to a more humane state of mind. But the very next
day he had Prince Vassili Pronski put to death with frightful
torments, and in the following month of June, another
dispute at the monastery of the Holy Virgin settled the Metropolitan's fate. The Bishops of Novgorod, Souzdal, and Riazan
lent themselves, like cowards, to a sham trial, in which Philip's
successor at the monastery of Solovki—Paisiï—appeared as a
hostile witness. Without waiting for sentence, and the moment
he was summoned before this court, the Metropolitan attempted
to resign his insignia of office. But Ivan stopped him.

' Wait,' he said ; ' thou hast no right to judge thyself !'
And he ordered him to say Mass the next morning, just as usual.
It was St. Michael's Day. Meanwhile the sentence condemning
the accused man to perpetual imprisonment in a monastery
was to be pronounced, and the Tsar, faithful to his love of
theatrical effect, was preparing a *coup de théâtre*. When Mass
began, the *Opritchniki* entered the cathedral, stripped the
Metropolitan of his vestments, cast a tattered monk's frock about
him, threw him on to a sledge, and drove him off, sweeping up
the ground behind him and beating him with their brooms.
He was shut up at Tver, and thither, the next year, Ivan, then
on his way to Novgorod, sent him the fiercest of his myrmidons,
Maliouta-Skouratov. The Tsar actually dared to claim the
prisoner's blessing ! Some narratives assure us that Skouratov
brought a violent scene to a close by strangling the ex-Metro-
politan. But, according to other witnesses, he was taken to
the *Sloboda* at Alexandrov, and there burnt alive. The corpse
of the holy man, which was brought back to the monastery of
Solovki after Ivan's death, became an object of general venera-
tion. In 1652, under the reign of Alexis, he was canonized,
and his relics still attract crowds of faithful believers to that
Cathedral of the Assumption in which his martyrdom began.

Ivan, more and more resolved to strike hard and spare nobody, could not permit anyone to interpose between himself
and those he thought it necessary to remove out of his path.
He was about to deliver blows just as terrible within his own

family. When, in his altercation with Philip, he spoke of the
kinsfolk who had rebelled against him, he was thinking, no
doubt, of his first cousin, Vladimir Andréiévitch. As early as
in 1563 he had suspected him of being concerned in a plot,
publicly reprimanded him, and obliged him to break with all
his associates, and even with his mother Euphrosyne, who had
been forced to take the veil. In 1566, he deprived him of his
appanage, and only gave him very poor compensation—two
small towns, Dmitrov and Zvenigorod, to replace Staritsa !
In 1569, the unhappy Prince, who, according to a foreign
chronicler, had offered to pass over into the King of Poland's
service, disappeared, either murdered or beheaded, or poisoned,
with all his family, with a poison he himself was said to have
prepared for the Tsar ! All the witnesses on this subject disagree. Taube and Krause, who are responsible for the last
version, declare Ivan was present at the death agony of the
whole family, and diverted himself, when that was over, by the
sight of all the womenservants of the household, who were
stripped of their garments, driven naked through the streets,
beaten with whips, and finally shot or cut down, and their
corpses left to be devoured by birds of prey. This story must
be received with caution. Vladimir's eldest son was still
alive in 1572, for Ivan mentions him in his will, which bears
that date. As for Euphrosyne, Kourbski reports, and Ivan
has not contradicted him, that, whether at that moment or
later, she was taken out of her convent and drowned.

All these terrors are governed by a law of progression. The
passions they excited and the sensations they dulled, united
in a cry for constantly stronger and more startling effects.
Vladimir may have given Ivan cause to suspect him of a certain
guilty connivance with Poland. In the following year a whole
town was to answer for a similar suspicion. A certain Peter,
called *Volyniéts*, who came from Volhynia—a vagabond who
had a crow to pick with the Novgorod authorities—denounced
the inhabitants of that town, declaring they were inclined to go
over to Sigismund-Augustus, and that a written agreement to
that effect would be found behind the picture of the Blessed
Virgin in the monastery of St. Sophia. In Russia, till far into
the eighteenth century, such hiding-places remained in constant
use. Peter *Volyniéts* was an utter miscreant, but previous
events gave some colour to his accusations. Novgorod, a free
town, had already gravitated in the Lithuanian-Polish orbit,
and, when her independence had been threatened, had placed
herself, by a formal deed, under the protection of King Casimir,
and that as his dependent. The document the informer had
described was found in the place he had mentioned, and bore
the signatures, apparently authentic, of the Archbishop,

Pimenius, and many important persons in the city. An
inquiry, the papers connected with which are mentioned by
Karamzine ('History of Russia,' vol. ix., p. 299, note), brought
out facts as to complicity, in which some of the Tsar's new
favourites—Basmanov, Founikov, his Treasurer, and Viskovatyi, his Chancellor—seemed to be involved. No less a thing
had been contemplated than the giving over of Novgorod and
Pskov to Lithuania, and the substitution, on the throne of
Moscow, of Vladimir for Ivan, to be achieved with the help of
Poland. The illustrious historian cannot really have studied
the papers referred to, for all that remained of them in his day
was a memorandum in the lists of the archives, and their disappearance must be taken for granted. Thus we find ourselves
face to face with a fresh riddle. This time Ivan was to make
fearful reprisals, exceeding everything of the sort that had
ever been seen even at Moscow, and under his rule. That they
were prompted by some motive, even if they were not fully
justified, is more than likely. But to what extent ?

The Tsar had paid frequent visits to Novgorod, and his
relations with the Archbishop and his clergy had hitherto been
most excellent. Pimenius had just spent fifteen weeks at
Moscow, and departed bearing a large sum of money given
by the Sovereign to restore a church. The storm that broke
over the town in January, 1570, was therefore quite unexpected.
At that inclement season of the year, Ivan started forth
with his *Opritchniki* and a whole army corps, as if he were going
forth to war. A military execution it was to be, indeed, and one
before which the memories of the first Livonian campaign,
hideous as they had been, were destined to pale. The punishment began on the frontier of the province of Tver, and involved the systematic destruction of the whole country. All
along his road from Klin to Novgorod the Tsar left nothing but a
desert behind him. On January 2, his outposts made their
appearance under the walls of the town, and hemmed it in
completely. The monasteries in the suburbs were sacked, and
the monks, 500 of them, taken away. The next morning, when
the *Opritchniki* entered the town, they carried off the priests
and deacons from every church, and all these men, whether
priests or monks, were sent to the *praviéje*. They were
bastinadoed every morning and every night, and ordered to pay
twenty roubles each. The records lead us to believe that some
were so fortunate as to be able to pay the money, and thus
obtain their freedom. A hideous fate awaited the rest. The
Tsar's myrmidons had meanwhile been busily engaged in
emptying all the houses, and collecting the inhabitants within
a military cordon. On January 6, a Friday, Ivan arrived,
accompanied by his son and 1,500 *Striéltsy*, and his first order

was that every monk who remained in the *praviéje* was to be
flogged to death.   Then the corpses were to be taken back to
the monasteries and buried there.

Now the secular clergy was to have its turn.   On the Sunday,
when the Tsar went to Mass, he was met on the bridge, according to custom, by the clergy, headed by the Archbishop, who,
as usual, offered him his blessing.   Ivan refused it, calling him
a 'ravening wolf,' but nevertheless commanded Pimenius to
officiate as usual in the Church of St. Sophia.   He was preparing him a course of treatment which was to be a repetition
of the story of his dispute with Philip.   According to custom,
again, he accepted an invitation to dine at the Archbishop's
table.   He seemed merry enough, and was eating with a hearty
appetite, when a shrill cry was heard.   At that signal the
Opritchniki flew to perform the task assigned them beforehand.
In a moment the Archbishop's house was given over to pillage,
and he himself stripped of his insignia and cast into prison with
all his servants.   During the days that followed, the terror
attained colossal proportions.   On the great square of the
town, where, in a parody of judicial procedure, the usual
apparatus of implements of torture was displayed, the Tsar
proceeded to mete out summary justice.   The townsfolk, led
before him by 100 at a time, were put to the question,
roasted over a slow fire by some new and, as it would appear,
particularly ingenious process (*podjar*), and then condemned, for
the most part, to death, and sent out to be drowned.   Covered
with blood, and gasping, they were bound on sledges,
driven rapidly down a steep incline to a place where, owing
to the great rapidity of the current, the river never freezes,
and there cast into the abyss.   The children were tied to
their mothers, so that they might drown with them ; and
Opritchniki armed with pikes, who moved about in boats on the
surface of the river, took good care no victim should escape.

These massacres, according to the 'Third Chronicle of
Novgorod,' lasted five weeks, and the days on which the
number of persons of both sexes who suffered did not exceed
500 or 600 were few and far between.   On some the tale of
victims reached 1,500.   The 'First Chronicle of Pskov'
reckons the total at 60,000.   These figures seem improbable.
As to the general statistics of the executions ordered by
Ivan, we possess a document left us by the monarch himself,
and the information he supplies agrees, in many cases, with
that supplied by Kourbski and the various chroniclers.   My
Russian readers will have guessed that I refer to the *Sinodiki*,
a kind of obituary list the Sovereign was in the habit of
sending to the monasteries, to request the monks' prayers
for the persons he himself had sent out of life into death.   His

cruelty, like that of Louis IX., was always, even when it affected Churchmen, attended by pious scruples and devout practices. As regards Novgorod, the list preserved at the monastery of St. Cyril only contains 1,500 names ; but another *Sinodik*, belonging to the monastery of the Blessed Saviour at Prilouki, proves that the names thus enshrined were those of the more prominent victims only. Guagnino and Oderborn speak, in the same category, of 2,770 persons as having been killed at Novgorod, without reckoning the humbler folk.

Be that as it may, the slaughter was immense and abominable, and when there were no more human beings for him to strike, Ivan turned his fury against inanimate things. As he had shown peculiar ferocity in his dealings with the monasteries, which he had taken to be the chief centre of the spirit of revolt, he strove, and for the same reason no doubt, to destroy the trade and industry of the great city. All the shops within the town, and the very dwelling-houses in the suburbs, the chief home of its commercial and industrial life, were first systematically stripped, and then razed to the ground, the Tsar personally superintending the process, while his *Opritchniki* scoured the whole of the neighbouring country within a radius of from 200 to 250 versts, if we may believe the chroniclers, and ravaged every place impartially.

At last, on January 13, 1570, when nothing was left him to destroy, Ivan commanded the chief of the townsmen who had been spared, so many for each street, to be brought into his presence. The poor wretches, already more dead than alive, were asking themselves what yet more hideous fate could be reserved for them. Contrary to all their expectations, the monarch, pacified, turned a gracious eye upon them, and made them a most friendly speech, advising them to cast off all fear, and live peaceful lives, praying God to preserve the Tsar and his Empire from all such traitors as Pimenius.

This was the Terrible's farewell. That very day he departed, taking with him the Archbishop, and his priests and deacons, who, though they had not ransomed themselves from the *praviéje*, had not shared the monks' cruel fate.

Novgorod drew a breath of relief ; but the town had received a blow from which it was never to recover. Together with the flower of its inhabitants, the prosperity of the city had received its deathblow ; and even if Ivan had a thousand reasons for his pitiless treatment, he had carried it too far. But while we make some allowance for the inevitable exaggeration of every witness who deals with this gloomy episode, we must not fail likewise to remember similar events belonging to a not distant epoch of the history of Western Europe. Taking it all

in all, and if we only look, among ten similar scenes, at the story
of the sacking of Liège by Charles the Bold in 1468—an operation performed with the friendly help of his cousin of France—
we shall perceive Ivan to have been nothing but a plagiarist.
Turn to your Michelet : ' The horror of this destruction of a
whole people lies in the fact that it was not a bloody assault,
the rage and fury of a victorious foe, but a long-drawn execution. The persons found in the houses were guarded, kept
back, and then thrown into the Meuse in an orderly and
methodical manner. Three months later the drownings were
still going on. . . . The burning of the town was also conducted in the most orderly fashion ' (*Histoire de France*,
viii. 148). And Henri Martin, writing on lines supplied by
Commines, Jean de Troyes, and Olivier de la Marche, says :
' Women, nuns, were *violated*, and then killed, priests' throats
were cut on the altar-steps. . . . All the prisoners the soldiers
had spared were hung or drowned in the Meuse ' (*Histoire de
France*, vii. 44, etc.).

The copy follows the original in every particular, the
number of victims, in this case, being reckoned at 50,000 and
more. The very setting of the scene is the same ; the carnage
in both cases took place in winter-time, in November and
December.

From Novgorod, Ivan went on to Pskov. All through one
night, while he was encamped in one of the suburbs of the town,
the bells kept ringing. A dreary watch ! But the punishment was here confined to a general pillage ; and, in the popular
mind, this unhoped-for clemency was attributed to the intervention of one of those visionaries who then swarmed all over
the Muscovite Empire from one end to the other. This *iouro-
divyï*, Nicholas Salos, took it upon himself to offer the
Sovereign a slice of meat. ' Lent !' cried Ivan. ' Lent !' came
the reply; 'and thou art making thyself ready to devour human
flesh ?' It is more probable that the satiety which was the
result of all his carnage, and the humble demeanour of the
inhabitants, who had been well drilled by their *voiévode*, disarmed the monarch's wrath. But at Pskov, even as at Novgorod, many families were removed, and taken away into the
interior ; and in this matter, too, Ivan was only following an
illustrious example. ' Louis XI. swore there should be no
more town of Arras—that all the dwellers in it should be driven
out, without even taking their furniture with them, and that
he would take families and craftsmen out of other provinces,
even out of Languedoc, and bring them to repopulate the
fortress.' I quote Michelet once more (*Histoire de France*,
viii. 322).

I should add that shortly afterwards, when Pskov was be-

sieged by the Poles, the townsfolk offered a most heroic resistance. Would they have stood so firm without their terrifying
lesson in fidelity ? We may be permitted to doubt it. The
two cities, whose forcible annexation to the Empire had disturbed their habits and damaged their interests, could hardly
have been forced into the observance of their new duties by
any incentive less strong than fear.

Going back to Moscow, Ivan treated himself to a triumphal
entry, as if he had been returning from a successful campaign,
and to an entertainment in the form of one of those mas-
querading processions in which, at a later period, Peter the
Great was to take so much delight. Preceded by one of his
jesters, mounted on an ox, he was seen parading along at the
head of his *Opritchniki*, and displaying, like them, the insignia
of that dreaded confraternity—a broom and a dog's head.
This over, he applied himself to his preparations for trying the
numerous accomplices of the crime he had just been punishing
at Novgorod and Pskov. This occupation filled many months,
and it was not till June 25, 1570, that the Tsar summoned his
subjects to attend the execution of the culprits who had been
declared guilty. There were three hundred of them, and all
issued, mutilated and worn out, from the torture-chambers
which had already robbed them of everything but the faintest
breath of life. To Ivan's astonishment, the great square was
empty. The instruments of torture that stood ready—the
stoves, and red-hot pincers, and iron claws, and needles, the
cords which were to rub human bodies into two halves, the
great coppers full of boiling water—had failed to attract, this
time. Whether at St. Petersburg or at Moscow, even down to
the middle of the eighteenth century, no other sight could stir
curiosity to such a point, and the audience was almost always
very numerous. But there had been too much of this sort of
thing lately, and the executioners were growing too long-armed.
Every man sought to hide deeper than his neighbour. The
Tsar had to send reassuring messages all over the town. ' Come
along ! Don't be afraid ! Nobody will be hurt ! . . .' At last, out
of cellars and garrets, the necessary spectators were tempted
forth, and forthwith Ivan, inexhaustible and quite unabashed,
began a lengthy speech. ' Could he do less than punish the
traitors ? . . . But he had promised to be merciful, and
he would keep his word ! Out of the three hundred who had
been sentenced, a hundred and eighty should have their
lives !'

But to make up for it, those who were not spared were to pay
for all the rest. Ivan the Terrible certainly was a perfect
virtuoso in the art of inflicting suffering and causing death.
Yet in this matter, too, he was only following an inclination

common to the men of his time, whose imagination was probably inspired and excited in this direction by the very books of
piety they read. \ In this respect some of these menologies,
full of highly-coloured imagery—a curious specimen of which
has been lately published under the name of St. Basil by the
brothers Ouspiénski (1902)—were singularly and cruelly suggestive. Guagnino dwells complacently on the tortures inflicted, in the course of this hideous day, on Viskovatyi the
Chancellor, who was hung up by his feet and cut into pieces
like a butcher's carcass ; and Founikov the Treasurer, who was
sprinkled, turn about, with ice-cold and with boiling water,
' till his skin came off him like an eel's.'

Before he went home to the new palace in which he was now
living—the Kremlin had been given up to the *Ziémchtchina*—
Ivan is said to have gone to Founikov's house, and carried off
the Treasurer's wife, a young and beautiful woman, sister of
Prince Athanasius Viaziémski. As she either could not or
would not tell where her husband had hidden his treasures, the
Tsar had her stripped in the presence of her daughter, a girl of
fifteen, set astride on a cord stretched between two walls, and
dragged backwards and forwards from one end to the other.
The unhappy woman was then thrown into a convent, where
she soon died of the hideous treatment she had received.
For some years her brother had been one of the Tsar's confidential men, and the Sovereign would never take medicine
from any other hand. He, too, was handed over to the executioner. Basmanov, the prime favourite, met the same fate.
He was killed by the Tsar's order, and, according to some
witnesses, by the hand of the heir to the throne, Feodor.
Pimenius was taken to the *Sloboda* at Alexandrov, was the butt
of the *Opritchniki* there for some time, and was finally sent into
exile at Venev, in the province of Riazan.

Guagnino, an Italian and a Catholic, who collected the
materials for his gossiping chronicle in Poland, is an altogether
unreliable witness ; but Horsey, an Englishman, gives quite as
hideous details of the executions he claims to have seen. He
saw one man—Prince Boris Telepniév, whom he calls *Teloupa*—
impaled, and lingering on the stake for fifteen hours, while
his own mother was violated before his eyes by a hundred
Striéltsy, until she died. But this same Horsey speaks of
700,000 men as having been massacred at Novgorod! I
shall have something to say, later, about these foreign witnesses
whose testimony we are forced to turn to account, seeing we
possess no other. Believing these people too easily, most
historians have ended by admitting that Nero and Caligula
were both surpassed at Moscow, and by supposing Ivan to have
lived, at this period, in a state of mental disorder which, if it

did not actually reach madness, was very close to it. I have
already explained my view as to this point. I will now add
that the Tsar himself has left us the most conclusive information as to his state of mind at this time. I have referred to
his will, dated 1571. This instrument must be recognised,
without any contradiction, as the work of a man whose feelings
had been deeply and painfully wounded, but who had preserved
all his faculties intact. No doubt his habitual striving after
poetic effect, his inherent exaggeration of view, and of the
manner in which he puts things forward, forbid our accepting
what he says literally. But the very pains he takes and the
artifices he employs exclude any idea of madness, at that time,
at least. He certainly bewails himself, makes his complaint,
pleads his own cause, too cleverly for any madman. He
feels himself unsteady on his throne, and the future of his family
strikes him as being no better insured than his own present.
He is an exile within his own Empire, waging a struggle, the
end of which he cannot foresee, with most dangerous enemies.
His strength is worn out, his mind sick. He bears wounds
innumerable on his body and his heart, and not a soul has he
found to heal them, nor sympathize with his sufferings ! His
good has been returned with evil—for love he has been given
hate ! He admits, indeed, that his trials are the well-
merited result of the Divine wrath, which has thus punished the
many infractions of its law of which he has been guilty, and
condemns him to live a wandering life, far from his capital, out
of which ' *his selfish boïars have driven him.*' His sons, more
happy than himself, may succeed in weathering the storm.
And he desires, in the will he is now drawing up, to give them
certain counsels to that end. Is he, then, making himself ready
to die ? Not that exactly ! Death would be sweet to him
indeed, and very welcome ; but even this benefit, he concludes,
will be refused him for a time yet, by reason of his sins, which
he must expiate by leading a miserable life. Is his mind wandering ? Not at all ! For the advice he gives is excellent,
full of the strongest and most luminous good sense, though
still, it may be, marked by an excess of suspicion. Ivan is
inclined to see enemies in every corner ; but when, while he
warns his sons against the snares that will be set for them, he
counsels them to inquire personally into every business, and
never to depend on others with regard to anything, unless they
wish those others to obtain the real power and leave them
nothing but its shadow, it is a master in the art of government
who speaks, and no madman ! (This will was published in the
' Historical Documents,' Supplement, i. 222.)

And here is another and a still more conclusive proof of the
complete lucidity, and, further, of the extraordinary versatility

17

of mind, preserved by this man at a moment when the strongest
of mental temperaments might very well have betrayed some
symptoms, however fleeting, of weakness and confusion. On
the very morrow of the Moscow executions, which had followed
on those at Novgorod—hideous scenes, all of them, however
exaggerated we must suppose the accounts of them to have
been—we behold him accepting, even provoking, and prose-
cuting, untiringly and without any visible difficulty, a theo-
logical discussion such as might well have disconcerted a layman
like himself at any time.

It was at this moment that his famous public conversation
with John Rokita, a member of the Confraternity of the Bohemian and Moravian Brothers, took place.

At that time Protestants enjoyed a comparatively privileged position in Russia. They were looked on as allies
against the Latinism every Russian loathed. Lutherans and
Calvinists alike had obtained permission to build churches in
the capital, and Ivan bestowed the most gracious welcome on
the English and German representatives of the Reform who came
to his Court either as visitors, or to enter his service. He was
even fond of listening to Magnus' chaplain, Christian Bockhorn,
and went so far as to speak highly of his teachings. If, he said,
Luther, when he attacked the Papacy, had not also attacked the
ancient ecclesiastical hierarchy, and soiled his interpretation of
Scripture by a shameful renunciation of the monastic rule and
habit, his doctrine would have been exceedingly acceptable.
And, indeed, Bockhorn and his co-religionists—all of them taken
up with their careers and their trade—did not push the advantage they had thus acquired over far. Missenheim's apostulate
seems to have been quite an isolated instance, and one of the
Danish missionary's disciples, Gaspard Eberfeld, said to have
made an attempt to convert the Tsar, would appear to be one
and the same person with a certain Gaspard von Wittemberg
who himself, if we are to believe Oderborn, became a convert
to the Orthodox faith, and the determined detractor of his
former religion. In the provinces bordering on Sweden and
Livonia a certain current of Protestant missionary feeling
was tolerated for political reasons. Elsewhere, this tolerance
was the mere outcome of the scornful indifference of the
general mind.

Quite as an exception, Rokita, who had gone to Moscow with
an embassy from the King of Poland, attempted to follow in
the footsteps of Missenheim. This reformer, a Tchek by birth,
was considered one of the most active members of the community of Bohemian Brothers established in Sigismund's
dominions, and his correspondence goes to prove him to have
been charged with a mission on which he and his party had

founded somewhat ambitious hopes. The embassy, which arrived in February, 1570, just at the tragic moment when Ivan was engaged in the manner we have been describing, was forced to wait the Tsar's return, until the 4th of the following May. On the 7th, the envoys were given their audience, and three days later, Rokita had been invited to speak in public, and Ivan had himself undertaken to reply.

The controversy took place at the Kremlin, in the presence of a numerous audience, ecclesiastical and lay, and it then became evident that the only result of the Sovereign's amicable conversations with Bockhorn and other representatives of the Reform party had been to supply him with weapons against them. Ivan spoke first, and his vigorous attack on the fundamental principles of the new doctrine and its application proved his knowledge of the subject to be deep, though his views, as usual in his case, were not unmixed with passion, and even with strong language. ' To judge by their actions, the disciples of the evangelical faith were nothing but pigs !' After such a preamble, the discussion might have been expected to take an unpleasant turn. Nothing of the kind occurred. Ivan, who had promised not to interrupt his adversary, kept his word. But in vain did Rokita, speaking in the Slav tongue, answer in the most moderate and supremely skilful fashion, deliberately confining his indictment to the weaknesses of the Roman Church. The Tsar heard him patiently, praised his eloquence, expressed a wish to see his speech written down, and announced his own intention of replying in the same way. A few weeks later, on taking leave of his foreign guest, he caused the said reply to be handed to him, richly bound, and there the matter ended.

A perusal of this reply—the original text has lately been discovered and published—was sufficient to convince Rokita he had been wasting his time. From the literary point of view, indeed, the rejoinder does the monarch no particular honour. In the taste of that period, Ivan plays, pointlessly enough, on the word Luther, which he calls *lioutyi* (cruel, in Russian), just as Müntzer, in Germany, had called the Reformer *luegner* (liar) ; and he does not shrink from applying other injurious titles to Rokita himself and his co-religionists. The document is not distinguished either by clearness of thought, solidity of reasoning, or logic. But to atone for this, the fulness of knowledge, sure memory, quickness of mind, and dialectic power therein displayed prove the Sovereign to have been in full possession of his well-known powers. His tricks of expression—we can hardly call them his style—are the same as in his altercation with Kourbski. ' You invoke the prophets ? Well, we will bring you face to face with

Moses.' . . . It is the production of a self-taught man and a strong one, who has received no systematic education, and does not possess a glimmer of artistic feeling; but it is by no means devoid of intelligence and thinking power.

In the obscure history of the *Opritchnina* another episode occurs—one less easily reconciled, apparently, with that certainty as to Ivan's mental health which may be deduced from the facts I have just been describing. This is the most enigmatic point in the drama, and we must pause to consider it. In 1574 or 1575—the date itself is not quite clear—while Ivan was still in life, Russia had a new Tsar.

III.—THE TSAR SIMEON.

The Sovereign had confided the headship of the *Ziémchtchina* to Mstislavski and Biélski. In 1571, the first-named nobleman acknowledged himself guilty of a criminal understanding with the Tartars. He was pardoned, thanks to the intercession of the Metropolitan, Cyril; three prominent boïars went surety for him, and these again found 285 guarantors for the then enormous sum of 20,000 roubles. But within a few years Mstislavski was obliged to confess to another misdeed of the same nature, in which two of his sons were also involved. Once more he escaped death, but a number of executions, which took place in 1574, and as to which a chronicler reports that the victims' heads were ordered to be 'thrown down in front of Mstislavski's windows,' seem to have been caused by this fresh act of treachery. Meanwhile, a Tsarevitch of Kazan, established as Tsar of Kassimov, under the name of Simeon Bekboulatovitch, was proclaimed 'Tsar of all the Russias,' while the real Tsar, putting off all his titles, and renouncing all the honours due to his rank, had himself called plain 'Ivan of Moscow,' and took his way, in the most modest style, 'on litters,' like the humblest boïar in his Empire, to pay his court to the new Sovereign.

What was the meaning of this comedy?

It was part of the practice of the Muscovite system of policy to assign the ancient Tartar Sovereigns new establishments and territories, within which they kept the title of Tsar, and over which they exercised a shadowy sovereignty. By this means Russia succeeded in attaching turbulent Princes to her own side, she avoided difficult dealings with the easily offended hierarchy of the 'men who serve,' and the consideration thus shown to the Moslem world was a useful argument in her intercourse with the Crimean Khans. Another Tsarevitch of Kazan—Kaïboul—was reigning on the same terms at Iouriév (Derpt), and the former Tsar of Astrakan, Derbych-Ali, was at Zvenigorod. Simeon Bekboulatovitch would probably have ended his days at Kassimov, if his conversion to Christianity and his marriage with this same Mstislavski's daughter had not made his continuance in that tsarate a matter of impossibility. The majority of the population was Mahometan, and claimed that its ruler should profess the same faith. But there was no room at Moscow for a Tartar Tsar, even a dethroned one. Ivan cut the difficulty short by giving up his throne and his title to Mstislavski's son-in-law. How? Why? It is a mystery! The one thing we are quite sure of is the fact. From 1575 onward we possess a great number of documents in which Simeon Bekboulatovitch officially assumes the title of 'Tsar of all the Russias,' and others show us Ivan lavishing marks of the deepest respect on this counterpart of himself, addressing petitions to him, like any of his subjects, and leaving his own carriage when he approaches the precincts of the palace he has given up to the new master. Simeon would even appear to have been crowned, although Ivan, after having admitted the fact in one of his conversations with the English agent, Daniel Sylvester, attempted, later, to withdraw his acknowledgment. 'There was nothing final about that,' he then remarked, and exhibited seven crowns and other insignia of sovereignty which he still preserved. None the less, one of his eight crowns had been set on Simeon's head.

This comedy was carried on till 1576, and we need hardly say that never for one instant, during that space of time, did the son of Vassili contemplate ceding anything more than the semblance of sovereignty to his substitute. This period, as my readers will remember, was that of the negotiations as to the succession to the Polish throne ; in these negotiations Simeon Bekboulatovitch was never mentioned. In 1576, when the Emperor's envoys, Cobenzl and Printz von Buchau, arrived, Ivan behaved as if the new Tsar had not existed, and shortly afterwards he dismissed him, having enriched him with the Duchy of Tver, which, as my readers may know, had lately been laid waste, was now reduced to the two towns of Tver and Torjok, with their dependencies, and was only thankful to recover its autonomy to some extent. Here Simeon was very far from likening himself to an independent Sovereign, after the fashion of the old appanaged Dukes. His letters to Ivan are signed ' your slave' (*kholop*). He commanded an army corps during the Livonian campaigns and the Polish wars, cut rather a poor figure, and only outlived Ivan to experience cruel changes of fortune under his successors. Stripped of his duchy by Feodor, deprived of his sight by Boris Godounov, who looked on him as a possible rival, he ended his existence in 1611, at the monastery of Solovki, or, according to other

witnesses, at Moscow, whither he had been recalled by Michael
Feodorovitch in 1616.

But why was the farce played ?

Horsey has ascribed it to financial reasons. Ivan, he thinks,
devised this expedient to bring about a sort of bankruptcy,
by casting certain engagements he himself was unable to
meet on Simeon. Fletcher has referred, in a similar sense,
to a general confiscation of ecclesiastical properties to which
Simeon is said to have proceeded, and after which Ivan, taking
up the reins of power once more, hastened to reinstate the
churches and monasteries in possession of their wealth,
retaining a portion, however, and exacting a heavy sum of
money in return for the favour of his restoration of the rest.
But, according to the same authority, the Tsar's object was
to combat the existing evil opinion of his government by the
substitution of something worse !

These are mere fanciful conjectures, partly contradicted by
the facts. Simeon, indeed, never ruled Russia, either well or
ill. He never ruled at all. He probably replaced Mstislavski
and Biélski at the head of the *Ziémchtchina*, and Ivan, when
he adorned him with the title of which he pretended to strip
himself, may have endeavoured to make this selection more
generally acceptable. But some other secret motives may
also have existed, as, for instance, the idea of imparting a
semblance of reality to the exile which, as he declared, his
' selfish boïars ' had forced upon him, and of thus better
justifying his own anger and the punishment he inflicted.
And, further, let my readers think of Peter the Great, who
withdrew to his little wooden house and left all the cares and
show connected with his official position to Menschikov in his
palace hard by, and who, the day after Poltava, handed in
his ' colonel's ' report to Romodanovski, set upon a throne
and dressed up to represent Cæsar. The generally accepted
opinion is that the great man desired thus to give his subjects
a striking example of the obedience due to the universal law
of service. Now, was not Ivan the first to impose this law ?
And this fashion of enduing the Sovereign with two personalities, in a way, by subjecting him to the general rule of discipline, was not unexampled, even in Western countries.
Look at Louis XV. on the eve of Fontenoy. Of course, the
similarity between the young King who placed himself under
the orders of his own General, and the improbable mas-
querade in which it pleased Ivan to figure with his Tartar
Prince, is not quite absolute, and in any other country such
a game, carried to so extreme a point, would have been too
risky, whatever the secret intention that inspired it. But the
ancestor of Peter the Great seems to have been predestined to

take the measure of the absolute power, as it were, and try it on a people to whom years of tyranny, foreign and domestic, had taught an endless patience and a boundless resignation.

And this farce, as some persons have supposed, may have been connected with the negotiations Ivan was then carrying on with England. As I shall soon have to show, the Terrible, in his great desire for an alliance with Elizabeth, was ready to cross the seas if so he might insure it. At certain moments he seems to have thought of asking the Queen to grant him temporary shelter as well. For the interim government which would then have become a necessity, Simeon's personality offered a valuable guarantee. Ivan would not have run any risk of finding his place permanently filled when he returned. The Tsar was a nobody : he had no connections, and nobody cared for him. In 1576, when Ivan's hopes as to Elizabeth faded and the arrival of Maximilian's envoys calmed his anxieties, he probably came to the conclusion that the farce had lasted long enough.

On the throne, Simeon had been nothing but a puppet. As the chief of an administration, he had no time to prove his capacity, and, indeed, the documents in which his name appears only refer to matters of quite secondary importance. Once he departed, things seem to have returned to their ordinary course, except that during the eight years of the reign subsequent to this episode there were only occasional repetitions, at more and more distant intervals, of the Tsar's bloody chastisements. Did the *Opritchnina* outlive the farce ? We know not. The Terror had spoken its last word.

But the last word of history concerning the *Opritchnina* has not yet been spoken, and the duty of reviewing the testimonies and opinions connected with this confused and confusing chapter of a dim past still lies before me.

IV.—THE *OPRITCHNINA* AT THE BAR OF HISTORY.

Though Soloviov adopted Karamzine's general point of view, he made an attempt to discover some political meaning in the series of events which his fellow-historian had taken to be nothing but a succession of horrors and acts of insanity. In the closing pages of the sixth volume of his ' History of Russia,' at all events, the leader of the *Opritchnina* appears under the guise of a reformer. Kaveline (' Works,' i., ' Sketch of the Judicial Conditions of Ancient Russia ') made the same endeavour. But Pogodine (' Fragmentary Studies, Historical and Critical,' Moscow, 1846), George Samarine (' Works,' v. 203), and even C. Akssakov himself (' Works,' i.), though in more measured fashion, have followed Karamzine's lead, and represented the *Opritchnina* as the work of a capricious despot, the Neronian fancy of an artist in crime. When, at a more recent period, Bestoujev-Rioumine followed Soloviov's lead in the second volume of his ' History of Russia,' he fell under the bitter criticism of Kostomarov (*Messager de l'Europe*, 1871, No. 10) and Ilovaïski (' Russian Archives,' 1889, p. 363), both of them strong supporters of Karamzine's view. Even in Kourbski's business, the last-named critic only perceived a consequence, not a cause, of Ivan's sanguinary excesses, and far less an excuse for them.

These verdicts, pronounced at various times, and all of them too sweepingly severe, have evoked a reaction, which, being excessive, as most reactions are, has swept the authors affected by it into attempts at apology not less sweeping, and by no means easy to accept. Biélov, in a study published in the *Review of the Ministry of Public Instruction*, (1886), has drawn his inspiration from an argument lately much in vogue among German theorists on political law. He has asserted that the Novgorod butcheries were justified, *objectively*, by a certain general excitement of men's minds, and that Philip's martyrdom was rendered legitimate by that prelate's interference in political matters. This road, once entered on, may lead the traveller far, and one of Kourbski's biographers, Gorski (Kazan, 1858), has gone the length of supporting the pronouncing of sentence on Sylvester and Adachev without hearing the accused persons' plea—' They certainly would not have confessed their misdeeds !' With regard to that Prince Pronski whose execution I have already mentioned— he was drowned, according to Kourbski's report, and cut in pieces, according to Taube and Kruse—Gorski draws the following conclusion : that he died in his bed ! Concerning Leonidas, Archbishop of Novgorod, he has to admit that he was thrown to the dogs after having been sewn up in a bearskin. But as he was guilty, Ivan only acted ' in conformity with fair justice.' These inversions of judgment and failures of moral consciousness are sad to witness. The Terrible's apologists and his detractors would have spared them us, no doubt, if they had made a really *objective* study of the great subject, submitted all its elements to a more exact process of analysis, and more thoroughly realized the historical conditions of the phenomenon under discussion.

They would have noted, in the first place, that even Ivan's foreign contemporaries were far from regarding him indiscriminately as a monster of cruelty, or even as a merely cruel Prince. I do not here refer to the friendly testimony brought by Forsten (' The Baltic Question,' i. 467) from Lubeck—accommodating witnesses, indeed, if such there ever were—which lauds Ivan's humanity and guarantees his good intentions as to the reunion of the two Churches! This was a mere matter of trade, and when Lippoman, who was Venetian envoy in 1775, converted Ivan into a righteous judge (*Hist. Russiæ Monumenta*,' i. 271), he was probably inspired by similar considerations. But the Polish electors of 1572 and 1575, who were so ready to welcome the Tsar's candidature, furnish us with a far more valuable guarantee!

As a rule, the chroniclers and foreign historians of that period have drawn a terrifying and repulsive picture of the *Opritchnina* and its founder. But ought we to grant full belief to the stories of Taube and Kruse, who, describing the Novgorod massacres, which they claim to have witnessed, place that town on the banks of the Volga? Henning, a Livonian chronicler, tells us of a baby taken out of its cradle by the *Opritchniki* and carried by them to Ivan, who began by kissing and caressing it, and then cut its throat with his dagger and threw the little corpse out of the window! It is a hideous tale, but Henning had it from Magnus, and from the Palatine of Vilna, Radizwill, both of them very poor authorities. Oderborn (*Joannis Basilidis vita*, Vitebsk, 1585, reproduced by Sartchevski, ii. 228) has accused the Terrible of yet more frightful acts of cruelty, with a tincture of the unnatural about them. He talks of women torn from their homes to gratify the passions of the Sovereign and his minions, then murdered, and their corpses brought back to their husbands' houses, where, for whole weeks, they were hung over the dining-room tables, at which the widowers were forced to eat their food; others, matrons and maids, met by chance in town or country, were first violated, and then stripped naked in the bitter cold and exposed on the snow to the eyes and insults of the passers by. Oderborn was a Protestant pastor whose work was composed and printed on Polish soil, at a moment when the reformed religion had lost the privileges it had once possessed in Russia, and when Poland, fitting every arrow to her bow, by no means scorned a well-informed and skilfully-handled Press as an instrument towards that conquest of Muscovy for which she was preparing. The work of Guagnino, no less strong in its leanings, had figured, a few years previously, amongst Batory's munitions of war.

But as to Oderborn's book we have a criterion which may be applied to all such writings. The Pomeranian historian has devoted one of his most truculent pages to a description of the sacking and carnage which—either in 1578 or in 1580—put an end to the prosperity of the German suburb of Moscow. Young girls, we are told, were violated and then put to death under the very eyes of the Tsar, who took his share in the

massacre, thrusting the victims through with his hunting-
spear and throwing them into the river.   The Sovereign's
two sons, summoned to witness the sight, were so sickened
by it that the youngest braved his father's wrath and took to
flight.   Not a detail is lacking.   Some rich merchants offered
a ransom for their children.   When Ivan refused it they up-
braided him, and the Tsar, mad with rage, inflicted the most
hideous tortures on the unhappy German women.   They
were flogged till the blood came, their nails were torn out, and
when, even in the midst of their tortures, they continued to
pray and call on the name of Jesus, their tongues were torn out
too.   At last they were killed with lance-heads, heated white-
hot and thrust into their bodies, and their corpses were burnt.
Other narratives of this same episode have come down to us.
That of Horsey may possibly apply to some other scene of
the same sort, for at the date given by Oderborn (1578) the
English writer was not in Russia.   But it seems unlikely that
the suburb can have been destroyed twice over, and a French
author, Margeret, like the Englishman, gives the date of the
incident as 1580.   Now, as to the horror and odiousness of
the details given, these two last versions do not approach that
of Oderborn.   Margeret only mentions the destruction of
two Protestant churches and the pillage of the German dwelling-houses, while all their inhabitants, ' without respect for
age or sex,' and regardless of the winter season, were stripped
' as naked as children just out of their mothers' wombs.'   Horsey
speaks of women and young girls violated on the spot or carried
off by the *Opritchniki*, some of whom sought refuge, after
they had been stripped of their clothing, in the house of one
of his fellow-countrymen.   Margeret, indeed, does not dream
of pitying the victims.   ' They could not lay the blame of
this on anyone but themselves, for, forgetting all their past
sufferings, their behaviour had been so arrogant, their ways so
haughty, and their dress so sumptuous, that they might all
have been taken for princes and princesses.'   The inhabitants
of the suburb drew their wealth from the sale of strong drinks ;
they had levied excessive profits in their trade, and thus abused
their monopoly.

But the most authoritative witness of all has yet to be
summoned.   In a Latin pamphlet, entitled *Psalmorum
Davidis Parodia Heroica*, a native of Lubeck, bearing the
name of Boch or Bochius, has inserted notes relative to a stay
he made at Moscow in the year 1578.   His presence there may
have been connected with the negotiations then pending
between Rome and Moscow.   He was on the spot, in any case,
when the events related by Oderborn took place ; he bore his
share in them, and, seeing he himself was a sufferer by them,

he cannot be accused of favouring Ivan. He had been hos-
pitably received by a countryman of his own who lived in a
house near the suburb. One day, when everybody was at
dinner, the quarter was invaded by a troop of warriors, all
dressed in black. They were headed by the Tsar, with his
son and several important men. In a moment every house
was being sacked and the inhabitants turned out of doors,
stripped of their clothing. Men, women, and children, all
stark naked, fled to seek shelter from the bitter cold.

The order was that the houses were to be sacked, but that
nobody was to be hurt, yet they were pursued and struck
without mercy. Several men dealt Boch blows in the face
with their fists, and he was whipped all over his body and
quite disfigured. He had been stripped of his clothes like
the rest, was dragged out of the hiding-place he had found,
flogged several times over in the course of the night, and
tormented in every kind of way, till, when the day broke, a
Livonian nobleman interfered, took him out of his tor-
turers' hands, and got a surgeon to attend to him.

The scene thus described is revolting enough, but my
readers will perceive a difference. There are no violations of
women, no massacres ; all we have is a police operation rather
roughly carried out, after the fashion of those times. Boch
asserts it to have been caused by the Metropolitan, who had
declared the foreigners were debauching the Tsar's soldiery
in their drinking-shops. Oderborn and Horsey have evidently
embroidered on a web which stood in no need of any such over-
ornamentation, and taking them thus in the very act of in-
venting their slanders, we attain a certainty as to the truth-
fulness of other testimony of similar origin.

Summary and violent, excessive and extravagant, was the
chastisement administered by Ivan the Terrible, and we cannot justify it. The *Sinodik* of the Monastery of St. Cyril
alone enumerates 3,470 of the Tsar's victims, and many
names are followed by the words, which make one shiver :
' With his wife '; ' with his wife and children '; ' with his
daughters '; ' with his sons.' We find, too, such sentences
as these : ' Kazarine Doubrovski and his two sons, with ten
men who had come to his help '; ' twenty men belonging to
the village of Kolomenskoié '; ' eighty belonging to Mat-
viéiché. . . .' And under the head of Novgorod we read :
' Remember, Lord, the souls of Thy servants, inhabitants of
this town, to the number of fifteen hundred and five
persons ' ! Thus did Louis XI. pray for his brother, the
Duc de Berry !

In other documents Ivan leaves the exact number of souls
to the Divine knowledge, and simply recommends ' the dead,

men, women, and children, whose names are known to God,'
to His mercy.   In the obituary lists at the monastery of
Sviajsk we find the names of ' the Princess-nun Eudoxia, the
nun Maria, and the nun Alexandra,' all three of them drowned
in the Cheksna, which flowed into the White Lake (Biélooziéro).
Princess Eudoxia was Ivan's ' Welsh aunt,' Alexandra had
been betrothed to him, and Maria was one of Vladimir's sisters.
The Terrible did not spare his own kinsfolk, and if any caprice
or calculation moved him to spare a particular individual, he
struck at those nearest to him.   ' Why should I wreak my
vengeance on a monk ?' he wrote, of Chérémétiév, to the abbot
of the Monastery of St. Cyril.   ' Have I not all his relations
under my hand ?'

The *Opritchnina* was all this—or all this, at all events, was
part of the *Opritchnina*.   But according to one of the King of
Poland's agents (Schlichting, *Scriptores rer. pol.*, i. 145-147),
Ivan could not have maintained himself upon the throne
unless he had employed these terrorizing methods.   When he
struck Ivan Petrovitch Chouïski—with a dagger-thrust dealt,
so Schlichting asserts, by his own hand—the Tsar had a document in his possession according to which this boïar, with
many others, undertook to give his master's person up to the
King of Poland as soon as that monarch had set his foot within
the Muscovite borders.   Some people have denied the existence of any struggle between the Tsar and the defenders of
the old system.   But if the preparation of such attempts does
not constitute a struggle, there is no meaning in words !   The
struggle—a fierce and obstinate one—was carried to extremes
by both parties : all feeling of duty and honour was forgotten
on one side, all pity on the other.

Yet all the eagerness and violence of the fray did not eradi-
cate that resignation to accomplished facts and submission
to superior strength which are an unalterable feature in the
national character.   When Prince Sougorski, whom Ivan had
despatched to the Emperor Maximilian, was stopped on his
way by a serious illness, he bewailed himself : ' If only I was
able to get up !   My life is nothing so long as the Tsar is well. . . .'
' How can you show so much zeal for so great a tyrant ?'
inquired the Duke of Courland.   And Sougorski answered :
' We Russians are devoted to our Sovereigns whether they
are cruel or kind.'   And he added, to prove the fact, that a
boïar who had been impaled by the Tsar's orders some time
previously, for some comparatively trifling fault, had endured
his hideous torments for four and twenty hours, and never
ceased talking to his wife and children, constantly repeating,
' Great God, protect the Tsar !'   This fact is chronicled by
Karamzine (ix., chap. iv.).

Ivan's foes aimed at his heart in front and struck at him from behind, and he did not always content himself with giving back blow for blow. Even in the popular poetry, which treats him with so much indulgence, the feeling that the Tsar, ' after he had punished for injustice and rewarded for justice,' grew more cruel, and ceased to assign favour and chastisement in proportion to the faults and virtues with which he had to deal, becomes evident (Kiriéiévski, ' Collection of Songs,' Moscow, 1860-1862, part vi., p. 2015). But Ivan, hovering like a spectre over a heap of corpses against a red background of aurora borealis, is no isolated phenomenon, either in his country or his century. In his own country, even as the renewer of the methods of Nineveh and Babylon, the brutal proscriber of whole populations dragged from Novgorod to Moscow, or from Pskov to Riazan, he was only carrying on a tradition. Vassili, before him, had done the same thing with hundreds of families— taken them out of the same provinces, sent them into the interior of the country, and filled their places with others brought from the basin of the Volga. Thirty years before the *Opritch-nina* came into existence, Maximus the Greek speaks of imaginary crimes imputed to innocent persons, and visited on them. When the Tsar's agents wanted a culprit they introduced a corpse or a stolen object into the house indicated, and the justice of the Sovereign took its course.

Ivan, in the course of his own century, had examples and imitators in a score of European countries, and the opinion of his time was his accomplice. Look at Italy. Read Chaplain Burckhard's notes, written in cold blood as he sat between Alexander VI. and the Borgias ; or the ironic, easy-going despatches of Giustiniani, the Venetian Ambassador ; or the cynical memoirs of such a man as Cellini. Make your way to Ferrara, the most refined Court of the period : you may happen on Cardinal Hyppolite d'Este, his own brother Giulio's rival in a love affair, having that brother's eyes torn out in his own presence. Look through the records of the *giustizie* of that time, and you will find the horrors of the Red Square equalled, if not surpassed—men burnt and hanged at the same moment, bleeding limbs crushed betwixt two pulleys. . . . All these things were done in broad daylight, and nobody was surprised, nobody was horrified, nobody rose up in indignation against them.

Now go to the other end of the continent—to Sweden. Eric XIV.—a great King till madness overtook him—awaits you there, with a Maliouta-Skouratov of his own, Persson, his favourite, both of them just out of the famous bath of blood of the year 1520—ninety-four bishops, senators, and patricians, all executed at Stockholm in one day. Next, John III. appears.

Persson has gone too far, wherefore, on the new King's command, he is first of all hung, but so as not to strangle him completely, then his arms and legs are broken, and, as he still continues to breathe, his chest is riddled with knife-thrusts. You must not overlook the Low Countries. The sacking of Liège, which I have already mentioned, took place a century earlier, I know ; but was not Ivan taking lessons in civilization from Europe ? Even at that distance he may well have drawn his inspiration from the lord of Hagenbach, that Governor of Alsace after the style of Charles the Bold, whose exploits are already known to you. He may, perhaps, have heard the story of the celebrated entertainment at which, by the Governor's order, each male guest was expected to recognise the person of his own wife, every lady having previously been stripped perfectly naked, except for the veil which hid her face. Those who made mistakes were thrown from the top of the staircase. But I might just as well have evoked the memory of the capitulation of Mons, violated in 1572 by Alva's lieutenant, Noir-carmes, and followed by eleven months of bloody excess, in the course of which the 20,000 citizens of Haarlem were all put to the sword by the Duke in person, while Philip II., in an official letter, offered a reward to anybody who would murder William of Orange ! And, seeing we are on Spanish ground, you will not forget the Inquisition and the forty Protestants burnt alive at Valladolid on March 12, 1559. Then, if you leave the hot cinders of the *auto-da-fé* and pass over into France, your foot will slip in the blood of the massacre of St. Bartholomew. Cross the sea, and you come on Henry VIII., the dungeons of Charterhouse and Sion, the gibbets of Tyburn and Newgate ; the head of Fisher, Bishop of Rochester, rots in the pillory on London Bridge, and behold the gay sight presented by the King, all dressed in white silk, leading Jane Seymour to the altar on the very morrow of the day which has seen Anne Boleyn's head fall at his command !

On the scene of history whereon it thus performs, the spectre becomes a living body, and, due allowance being made for distances and for difference of culture, its flesh and blood do not appear far removed from those of the Christian, civilized, European world of the period.

I have spoken of a moral complicity. If Europe's has been proved, that of Russia is no less certain. Kourbski, who gave the tone to the Tsar's detractors, was a party to this suit ; and he represented a refractory minority. The Russian masses expressed their feelings in their popular poetry, and the sense of that is already known to my readers. The Russian people not only submitted to Ivan—it admired, applauded, loved him. Of all the crowd of comrades about him, it has retained two

names and two faces only : one of these figures is that of a
parvenu, the other that of an executioner—Nikita Romanovitch Zakharine and Maliouta-Skouratov.   Of the first-named
history knows but little.   He was the Tsarina Anastasia's
brother, and, like a certain witness of the French Terror in
the eighteenth century, he was a man of breeding.   The legend
has turned him into a hero.   It shows him refusing the Tsar's
favours, and content to beg new laws, ' more tender to the
people,' for the lands he already holds.   But the popular preference is given to Maliouta-Skouratov, the legendary bully of
Prince and boïar alike.

This democratic instinct, so strongly marked in every per-
sonification of the popular idea, explains the secret of the
Opritchnina and its original·conception, and also of the comparative facility with which Ivan was able to force it on certain
persons, and induce a still larger number to accept it.   The
scenes evoked by the popular muse, which show us peasants and
boïars set face to face, always assign the shabby part to the
boïars.   They are either rogues or fools.   If the story concerns
a riddle which the Sovereign has to guess, and on which his
fate depends, it is a peasant who supplies the solution, after all
the great lords called into council have failed to find it.   One
legend, indeed, asserts the Tsar to be descended from a humble
stock, and attributes an equally modest origin to his power.
A certain Tsar having died, his late subjects all betake themselves to the river bank, bearing lighted torches, which they
plunge into the water.   The first who can relight his torch is
to have the crown.   ' Let us go to the river,' says a *barine* to
Ivan ; ' if I become Tsar, I'll set thee free !'   ' Come, then,'
Ivan replies ; ' if I am made Tsar, I'll have thy head cut off !'
He wins the crown, and keeps his word.

Herein lies the whole philosophy of the populace.   It seems
to have forgotten all about Ivan's wars, and all it remembers
of the administrative reforms simultaneously effected is their
levelling action.

> ' All the masters and princes,
> I will flay them alive. . . .'

sings the Tsar *Groznyï*, Ivan Vassilovitch.
   Or, again :

> ' I will have you cooked, every one,
> Boïars and princes, in a caldron !'

The *Groznyï* is a pious man, and the poets admire this quality
of his, but,

> ' As soon as he has heard Mass,
> He'll cut their little heads
> Off princes and boïars. . . .'

This is the essential part of the business.   It may be, too, that
what we see here is the unconscious expression of another
feeling besides those of hatred and vengeance.   If Ivan, when
he fought against the boïars, was not defending the fundamental
principles of Russian life—the absolute power, Orthodoxy,
nationality—as some writers have asserted, he was certainly
protecting the integrity of the common fatherland after a more
general fashion.   Kourbski, as we have seen, was no less
orthodox and no less Russian than the most fanatical of his
peasants, and devotion to the absolute power can hardly, at
that period at all events, be taken to be a feature in the popular
psychology of a country in which the memory of the ancient
viétchié had not entirely died out.   But when Kourbski and
his likes entered into secret intercourse with Poland they were
betraying their Sovereign and their country.   They were
conspiring with the foreigner, and treason in every form,
dogging Ivan's steps, crushed twenty times over in its own
blood, and perpetually raising its head afresh, is the *leitmotiv*
of all the poems which take the Terrible for their hero.

As to the origin of this universal treason, which in itself
justifies all the *Groznyï's* violence, the legend gives an oddly
suggestive hint, in connection with which the popular logic
would seem to be at fault.   This is an accident which not
infrequently occurs.   Ivan, who numbers all the Kings of the
earth among his vassals, as the Tsar of a legend should, calls
on them to send him the tribute they owe.   They reply :
' We will send thee the tribute, and we will add twelve hogsheads of gold to it, if thou canst guess these three riddles.'   In
such matters, as we have already seen, all the wisdom of the
Sovereign's ordinary counsellors, whether boïars or Princes,
is of no avail.   The man to help the Tsar out of his difficulty
is a poor carpenter, who is promised one of the hogsheads of
gold as his reward.   But the Sovereign mixes the gold with
sand, and the *moujik*, guessing the imposture as he has guessed
the riddles, thus addresses him : ' Thou shalt be punished even
as thou hast sinned ; thou hast brought treachery into this
land, and from treachery thou shalt suffer, more than any other
man !' (Rybnikov, ' Collection of Popular Songs,' ii. 232-236).

The populace is an *enfant terrible !*   One more witness must
be quoted, and a weighty one.   Chancellor, an English traveller
who was a spectator of the sanguinary executions ordered by
Ivan, is moved by them to the following reflection, which, from
a purely practical point of view indeed, expresses the opinion of
the enlightened and polished men of his period : ' Would to
God our own stiff-necked rebels could be taught their duty to
their Prince after the same fashion !' (' Hakluyt Collection,'
i. 240).

So far, I have deliberately neglected Ivan's relations with England. They would not have been intelligible until the facts contained in this chapter had been clearly set forth. But the place they occupy in the Tsar's own life and in the history of his reign is an important one. I shall now turn to them.

CHAPTER III

THE ANGLOMANIA OF IVAN THE TERRIBLE: IVAN AND ELIZABETH

I.—THE FIRST ENGLISHMEN IN RUSSIA. II.—PROJECTS OF ALLI-
ANCE. III.—A PROJECTED MARRIAGE. IV.—MARY HASTINGS.
V.—THE DUTCH COMPETITION AND THE RUPTURE.

I.—THE FIRST ENGLISHMEN IN RUSSIA.

JUST when Ivan was seeking to enter into contact with Europe by the way of Livonia and the Baltic, other peoples, dwelling in other countries, were much disposed, as we have seen, to move forward and meet him. The epoch of the heroic voyages of discovery had not come to a close. From Spain and Portugal a great current of adventurous navigation was flowing round the Channel coasts, carrying the French to Brazil with Jean de Léry, to Canada with Joseph Cartier, and to Florida with the first Protestant colonists of that country, while a whole army of English sailors was following in the wake of Columbus, Cortez, and Gama. Eager to open England's road to India, or increase her colonial dominions, such men as Cabot, Raleigh, Drake, Dawes, and Frobisher explored Labrador, discovered Louisiana, imitated Magellan's wonderful journey round the world, and plunged into the snowbound plains of North America.

In all these bold enterprises England was more deeply engaged than any other country. Then, as now, the conquest of fresh outlets for her trammelled trade was a question of life and death. In the year 1552, parleys were opened in London between a number of merchants on one side, and the famous Venetian navigator, Sebastian Cabot, on the other. They culminated, the following year, in a plan for an expedition to discover new territories in the North-East. The necessary funds, amounting to £6,000, were obtained by subscription, and on May 23, 1553, three ships sailed from Harwich—the *Bona Esperanza*, commanded by Sir Hugh Willoughby; the *Bona Fortuna*, by Richard Chancellor; and the *Bona Confidentia*, under Cornelius Durforth. Cabot was a distinguished cosmographer, and as

the greatest dignitaries in the country—the Marquis of Winchester, Lord Treasurer ; the Earl of Arundel, Comptroller of
the Court ; the Earl of Pembroke, Lord Privy Seal—had shares
in the undertaking, it probably possessed a scientific as well
as a commercial character.   And probably, too, though chance
was to play so great a part in the incidents of the voyage, a
pretty clear idea of its object existed ; for when one of the
vessels reached the shores of Russia, interpreters were all ready
on board her.

Martens ('Collection of Treaties,' ix. [x.], Introd., p. 6)
mentions documents which go to prove that diplomatic relations between Ivan and Edward VI. had subsisted previously.
The object of these is quite unknown to us.   They had not
served to propagate conceptions as to the great northern Empire
that even approached reason and probability.   Herberstein
was to speak of it, twenty years later, as a legendary country,
and gravely reproduce absurd tales of a huge idol called the
Zlataïa Baba (an old woman modelled in gold), before which
brazen trumpets stuck into the ground kept up a perpetual
braying ; of tribes who habitually died in the autumn and
returned to life the following spring ; and a great river in which
fish were caught 'which had the head, eyes, nose, mouth,
hands, and feet of a man, but which could not talk, and were
very good to eat. . . .'

Trials of a more tangible kind than any meeting with monsters
such as these awaited Willoughby and his bold comrades.
A storm dispersed the little squadron, and Chancellor, with
the *Bona Fortuna*, lost sight of his two consorts.   Vainly he
waited for them at Vardôhus, the port appointed for that
purpose on the Norwegian coast, started forth again alone, and
found himself, on August 28, in a bay, from which, on his arrival,
several boats manned by fishermen took to flight.   Pursued
and brought back, these strangers informed the voyager that
he had reached the shores of Muscovy.   The authorities at
Kholmogory hastened to warn Ivan, who invited the foreigners
to Moscow, but gave them leave to dispense with this journey,
and trade freely with his subjects, if that was the object of their
coming.   Chancellor, without even waiting for the Tsar's
message, made his way to the capital, spent thirteen days there,
saw the Tsar, and departed again to England, bearing the
monarch's friendly reply to the circular letter of introduction
with which the leaders of the expedition had been provided.

During the following winter, news reached Moscow that two
ships laden with merchandise, and with the corpses of dead men
on board, had been discovered on the shores of the White Sea.
These were the *Bona Esperanza* and the *Bona Confidentia*, with
their crews—83 out of the 125 men who had sailed from

Harwich. The storm had carried them into the gulf formed by the mouth of the Arrina, and there Willoughby had seen his comrades die off, one by one, of cold and hunger. The notes his splendid courage enabled him to keep prove that he himself survived till January, 1554.

When Chancellor got back to England he found Edward VI. dead; but Philip and Mary, on the report he submitted to them, sent him back to Moscow as the representative of a new company, the ' Fellowship of English Merchants for the Discovery of New Trades,' which was to take the place of the old ' Society for the Discovery of Unknown Lands,' which had organized the first expedition. For practical purposes, this company was always called the Russian or the Muscovite Company. Two special agents, Richard Grey and George Killingworth, were associated with the leader of the new mission, and provided with instructions which betoken a marvellous insight as to the interests concerned. The agents were desired to study the character and habits of the Russian nation, and the taxes, coinage, weights and measures of the country. They were to take care that all their fellow-countrymen carefully obeyed the Russian laws; they were to open counting-houses and shops in Moscow and the other principal towns; they were to notice the kinds and qualities of merchandise likely to find a good market, and they were to look out, at the same time, for the best means of making their way into the Far East, and more particularly into China. The instructions also enumerated those Russian products—wax, tallow, tar, hemp, flax, and furs —which it would be well to import into England; and asked for samples of the minerals the company might undertake to bring to the surface in the Tsar's dominions, and details as to the German or Polish woven stuffs which might be replaced, on the Russian markets, by others of English make. They contemplated the possibility of monopolizing certain branches of the external trade of Russia, and drew up a complete programme, in the execution of which Chancellor, Grey, Killingworth, and their successors were to prove fully equal to their task.

Chancellor re-embarked on the *Bona Fortuna*, reached Moscow without a hitch, opened negotiations with Viskovatyï, the Chancellor, and succeeded in obtaining a charter which granted his company the most precious favours—complete freedom of trade, a special jurisdiction for all Englishmen settled in Russia, autonomy as regarded differences between English subjects, and the Tsar himself to decide all causes involving litigation between subjects of the two countries. At first the profits of the Company were enormous. According to one of its agents, a piece of cloth, which cost, transport

18—2

included, no more than six pounds, was sold for seventeen roubles, equalling as many pounds in the reckoning of those days. But this prosperity was soon to attract formidable competition. Norwegian and possibly even Danish ships (see Monsieur Kordt's preface to the papers published by him in the 116th volume of the ' Collections of the Imperial Society of Russian History,' 1902, p. xviii) were already sailing in the wake of the English navigators. The monopoly these last thought they possessed was threatened. Disputes broke out, and thus Ivan was led to send a negotiator of his own to England, and charge him with the duty of bringing these complications to an end.

On July 21, 1556, Joseph Grigoriévitch Nepiéia, *Namiéstnik* (lieutenant) of Vologda, sailed with a whole fleet of ships laden with merchandise, and commanded by Chancellor. The *Bona Fortuna* was one of these, and with her sailed Willoughby's two vessels, which the Russians had returned to their owners, and the *Philip and Mary*, which had lately come from England. Alas ! within a year it became necessary to despatch an English expedition, led by Stephen Burrough, in search of three of these ships, which were never seen again ('The Voyage of Mr. Stephen Burrough, An. 1557, from Colmogro to Wardhouse, which was sent to seeke the *Bona Esperanza*, the *Bona Confidentia* and the *Philip and Mary*,' Hakluyt, ' Travels,' i. 328). After three months of stormy seas, the *Bona Fortuna* reached the end of her journey alone, only to be wrecked on the Scottish coast ! Chancellor, who, with Nepiéia, was on board the vessel, was drowned, with his son and part of the crew, in an heroic attempt to save the Russian envoy's life. Seven of his Russian companions likewise perished, and £7,000 worth of merchandise —the whole of Nepiéia's private fortune—was lost or pillaged by the natives of the coast, from whom, thanks to an inquiry ordered by Queen Mary, some few remnants were painfully recovered. The envoy escaped with his life, but, owing to the delay imposed by the above-mentioned inquiry, he did not reach the gates of the English capital till February, 1557. A splendid reception had been prepared him, as some sort of compensation. A hundred and forty merchants, with all their servingmen, attended him. He was presented with a richly-caparisoned horse for his solemn entry, and the Lord Mayor came to meet him. When Philip returned from Flanders in the following March, he gave the envoy audience, and in May, Nepiéia, a novice in diplomacy, flattered himself he had brought his mission to a happy conclusion, after all the horrors of the outset. He had obtained a certain reciprocity of privileges for his country—free trade with England, a special jurisdiction, that of the Chancellor himself, over Russian subjects sojourning on British soil, and leave to engage artisans, engineers, and physicians for the Tsar's service. He had not settled the essential question of the commercial competition in Russia itself, but Philip and Mary relied, as to that matter, on the man in command of the English ship on which he was to sail from Gravesend—a man destined, indeed, to play a leading part in the agreement arranged between the two countries.

His name was Anthony Jenkinson, and he served the Russian company for a wage of £40 a year. He was worth more. Since 1546, he had travelled all round Europe, and all the coast of Asia and of Africa. He had landed on Russian soil in July, 1557, made a long stay, for purposes of study, at Kholmogory and Vologda, and had not reached Moscow till December in that year. Well received by Ivan, he soon proved himself so thoroughly 'the right man in the right place' that once the Sovereign knew this particular Englishman he refused to have any other about him. He seems to have been a finished specimen of that race of *business men* to whom Great Britain owes her present position in the world—an extraordinary business mind, a broadness of view, a spirit of adventure, which no risk could alarm, a heart of steel, and an iron temperament. In April of the following year, we find him at Astrakan, after a whole winter season spent at Moscow. In August, first of all English sailors, he hoisted the red-crossed ensign on the waters of the Caspian. With only two of his fellow-countrymen to keep him company, he sailed away with a huge cargo of merchandise, enough to load a thousand camels, which he hoped shortly to hire from the Turkomans, and so make his way to Bokhara, across the steppes of Turkestan, and to more distant countries yet, if that might be. Why not to China ? But at Bokhara war was to overtake him ; the master of Samarkand was threatening the town. Jenkinson, as cautious as he was bold, beat a timely retreat, avoided the siege and the scenes of pillage that followed on it, and reappeared at Moscow in September, 1559, with a Bokharian embassy and five-and-twenty Russian prisoners rescued from the Turkomans. He offered the Tsar gifts, which the monarch graciously received—the tail of a white buffalo and a Tartar drum—and returned to England with a young Asiatic, the Sultana Aura, whom he proposed to present to the new Queen, Elizabeth. He also carried back the conviction that, from the commercial point of view, the Far Eastern countries through which he had just travelled were quite valueless. But he contemplated opening up relations with Persia, and, starting forth again in 1561, he received a friendly welcome at Kazbin, the capital of the Shah Tamas, and won the personal regard of Abdul-Khan, ruler of the Chirvan.

While he busied himself about acquiring these new markets

and ensuring in them the privileges already given to his own country in Moscow, he was fighting a stiff battle with his Italian and Flemish competitors.   Raphael Barberini, an Italian agent, contrived to overreach Queen Elizabeth, and induce her to give him a patent, which he used to spread a belief that the English were mere middlemen, bringing Dutch and French merchandise into the Russian markets.   Jenkinson's rejoinder took the form of a new charter, granted to the Russian company by the Tsar, which confirmed it in all its monopolies, and extended them from the mouths of the Northern Dvina to the banks of the Ob, including Kholmogory, Kola, Mezen, Petchora, and Soloviétsk ; gave it the sole right to a trading-house (*dvor*) at Moscow, and depots on the Dvina, at Vologda, Iaroslavl, Kostroma, Nijni-Novgorod, Pskov, Narva, and Iouriév, and granted free passage to all its merchandise sent to Bokhara and Samarkand.

These concessions—unhoped for, no doubt, and undeniably excessive, from the Muscovite point of view—were probably connected with overtures of a different order, which were being made to Jenkinson at this time, and which mark a new phase in Anglo-Russian relations.

II.—Projects of Alliance.

Ivan could not fail to be deeply impressed by all his English guests had shown him, or allowed him to guess, in the course of several years, concerning the genius and the greatness of their nation.   And the struggle in which the Sovereign was engaged, both within and without the borders of his own country, had inspired him with a painful sense of his own isolation.   In his eager, masterful, and obstinate mind, this twofold impression naturally became a fixed idea, which he was to carry with him to his grave.   Against his external foes, their armies, their fleets, and their treasuries, he would make an alliance with a Power whose fleet, whose commerce, whose credit, were beginning to rule the whole world ; against his foes at home he would thus ensure himself a support, perchance a refuge, that nothing would be able to shake.   A glorious dream !   Thanks to his imaginative powers, Ivan no doubt saw himself really driven into exile, and, backed by his formidable ally, able to return in triumph at his own time.   Perhaps, indeed, but this point is less clear, he mingled a more romantic project with this plan.   Elizabeth was fated to be the object of perpetual proposals of a more or less flattering nature, in which politics and gallantry both had their share.   In spite of the fact that his youth had faded, in spite of his infirmities, which he exaggerated, but which were genuine, of his unsociable nature, and his four or five previous wives, living or dead, Ivan may possibly have thought of trying his own chance. On the other hand, as we know, Elizabeth was a mistress, from an early age, in the art of evading matrimonial proposals without offending or disheartening her suitors, and the conduct of Jenkinson, himself a good diplomatist, may have been inspired, in this particular, by his knowledge of the ideas and habits of his royal mistress. The one undoubted fact is that, when he came back from England in 1567, he was the bearer of a secret message, the contents of which are unknown to us, but the subject of which must have been exceedingly puzzling, seeing that for a long time the answer tarried.

So long did it tarry, indeed, that English trade in Russia suffered by the delay. The opening of the port of Narva to foreigners in general, followed by the establishment at Antwerp, and even in England, of several rival associations, threatened the monopoly of the great company whose interests Jenkinson had so firmly established. In 1568, Elizabeth recognised the necessity of repairing the damage, and, as Jenkinson's services were not available at that moment, she made up her mind to send an Ambassador of mark—Thomas Randolph, the head of her postal arrangements—in his stead. The instructions she gave him enlighten us—to some extent, at all events—as to Ivan's secret proposals. Randolph, whose official mission was to ' re-establish order in the English trade,' was desired to evade these proposals as much as possible, but to assure the Tsar that, in case of any misfortune, the Queen would not refuse him her hospitality. Ivan was seriously thinking, then, of passing over into England ! But the difficulty was that he would only accept shelter on the basis of a reciprocal arrangement. His pride forbade him to receive more than he was able to offer, and he demanded that the Queen, who also had rebels to deal with and risks to run, should formally accept the Kremlin as a refuge officially placed at her disposal ! My readers will imagine that Henry VIII.'s daughter could not very well agree to such a bargain.

Randolph reached Moscow in October, at an unpropitious season. It was just at that moment, as my readers will recollect, that the dispute between the Metropolitan Philip and Ivan was going on. The Tsar was out of temper. There is some reason to believe that the agents of the Russian company, who, in the course of their disagreements with their rivals or with the monarch himself, had been guilty of a certain amount of rough dealing, made no effort to obtain a friendly welcome for a mission which rather disquieted them. Elizabeth's long silence had ended by wounding and irritating the irascible Sovereign. The result was that in February, 1569, the Ambas-

sador, according to a method of diplomatic procedure not
uncommon in the history of the Moscow of that period, found
himself a prisoner in the house assigned as his residence,
isolated there, and quite unable to perform his functions.
When, after three months' waiting, he at last succeeded in
obtaining an audience, the usual honours were not paid him,
and the Tsar omitted to invite him to his own table, which was
the established custom. What transpired in the course of that
first interview ? We know not ; but it seems to have altered
the monarch's views, for some days afterwards Ivan invited
Randolph to take his way to the palace once more, this time
in the greatest mystery, at dead of night, and wearing a
disguise. This conversation lasted three hours, and as to
what may have passed at it we are reduced to conjecture. The
next morning the Tsar departed for his *Sloboda*, and did not
come back till the following April. But when he did return,
a sudden and total alteration in his attitude became apparent.
Not only did he agree to restore the Russian company to the
enjoyment of its former privileges, but he granted it fresh and
greater advantages—free trade with Persia, power to mine for
iron at Vytchegda, and to recoin money for its own benefit at
Moscow, Novgorod, and Pskov, and the closing of the port of
Narva to the newly-formed English company, while the old
one was authorized to drive away the ships of any other nation
that ventured into the White Sea.

Randolph had evidently flattered the Sovereign with some
new hope, the performance of which was to be claimed by
another Russian embassy to London.

Nepiéia's successor bore the name of Savine. Alas ! all he
brought back, after ten months spent on the banks of the
Thames, was a letter from Elizabeth couched in somewhat
vague and anything but satisfactory language. To a promise
of help, on which it would not have been very easy to reckon,
the Queen merely added a fresh assurance of the pleasure it
would give her to welcome the Tsar, with all the honours due
to his rank, whenever it suited him to become her guest, and
to undertake all the charges connected with his entertainment.
Instead of the coveted alliance, she offered him alms !

Ivan's behaviour, indeed, proved he had been wakened out
of a beautiful dream, and when disturbed he was habitually
bad-tempered. As usual, he lost all self-control, and sent
Elizabeth an answer quite in the style of the epistles with which
he was obliging the King of Sweden just at that time. He
would not admit that the Queen herself would have treated a
Sovereign who traced his descent from the Cæsars in so cavalier
a fashion, and wrote to her as follows : ' I had thought thee
mistress in thine own house, and free to follow thine own will.

I see now that thou art ruled by men. And what men ! Mere
moujiks ! Thyself thou art nothing but a vulgar wench
(*pochlaïa diévitsa*), and thou behavest like one ! I give up all
intercourse with thee. Moscow can do without the English
moujiks.'

The abuse was a mere nothing ; it was a change from the
madrigals usually served up to Elizabeth, and was only calculated to make her laugh. But before there had been time for
the Tsar's message to get to London, news reached the capital
that he had stripped the Russian company of all its privileges,
old and new, confiscated its merchandise, and forbidden its
trading operations. This was far more serious. The openings
obtained by dint of so much effort were lost ! The hope of
snatching the Eastern markets from the Venetians and Portu-
guese had faded ! The disaster must be remedied, and but one
man in the world seemed capable of doing that. Elizabeth,
when she confided the leadership of her solemn embassy to
Robert Best, associated Jenkinson with him in the business.

But the bold explorer, who was to act as the head of an
independent mission, was to begin by himself suffering cruelly
from the altered circumstances. He landed in July, 1571, on an
island in St. Nicholas' Bay, called ' Rose Island ' by the British
sailors, because of the wild roses they had found growing there,
and sent a former interpreter of Savine's, Daniel Sylvester,
to announce his arrival at Moscow. Sylvester could neither
get there himself nor send back news, because of the plague,
which had been laying the country waste ever since the Tartar
invasion, and which had necessitated quarantines and barriers
on every road. Another messenger, who tried to force his way
through, barely escaped being burnt alive. Besides this, Ivan
was campaigning against the Swedes, and the Russian authorities declared nobody must think of approaching him. They
further asserted that Jenkinson would have risked his own
life by so doing, for the Tsar held him responsible for the failure
of his proposals, and had declared he would cut off his head
if he showed his face in his dominions.

Quite unmoved — though the Governor of Kholmogory,
influenced by existing circumstances, refused him shelter,
food, or protection, and left him exposed to the hostility of
the townsfolk—the Englishman waited on wearily in the
inhospitable town till January, 1572, and then, putting on a
bold face, contrived to force his way through, and ventured
to beard the monarch in his den at Alexandrov. He had
managed, no doubt, to justify himself in the meantime, for
the Sovereign gave him a most gracious reception. Ivan
hurried through the necessary ceremonial of the public audience, and eagerly broached a private conversation, at which

he only allowed two of his most intimate associates to be present. After his usual custom, he mixed up a dozen other subjects with the one business he really cared for. He talked long and loud about certain English merchants on whose persons injurious letters concerning himself and his Government had been found, and, after endless circumlocutions, came to the real fact : what about the ' secret business ' of which he had spoken to Jenkinson, and in regard to which Randolph had given a positive undertaking ? This was Jenkinson's reply : ' I informed Her Majesty, word for word, of the proposals addressed to her through me, and Her Majesty, having accepted them, commanded Randolph to treat concerning them, but Randolph denies having given any undertaking about them. There must have been a misunderstanding, attributable, no doubt, to some interpreter's blunder.' In support of his assertion the envoy produced a letter from Elizabeth.

Ivan was agreeably surprised, no doubt, to find it contained no reply to his own insolent remarks. The Queen contented herself with saying, in very dignified fashion, that her own subjects gave her no reason for such displeasure or alarm as would lead her to seek refuge in any foreign country whatever. But for all that, she continued to have the most friendly feelings for the Tsar, and, provided he would consent to forget his *legitimate* complaints against the British merchants, and restore them their privileges, she declared herself ready to afford him the most convincing proofs of her regard. Thanks to Jenkinson's cleverness, doubtless, Ivan took what was really a proof of scorn for a mark of deference ; as Elizabeth's reply contained no strong language, he considered his honour satisfied, and was mollified. After hesitating for awhile, he gave Jenkinson another audience at Staritsa, and appeared inclined to restore the company and its principal member, William Garret, to unconditional favour. He would give up all idea of a secret understanding for the time being, and when Jenkinson asked for the names of the British subjects of whom he had had reason to complain, he replied, with a dignity that equalled Elizabeth's, ' What matter ? If I pardon them, it is not so that you may have them punished by their Queen !'

What secret thought he had in his mind at this moment we cannot tell, but Jenkinson's success was certainly as fleeting as it had been personal. In July, 1572, the gifted diplomatist quitted the shores of Russia for the last time, and in the following year Sylvester, sent back by the Russian company, bore evil tidings to London. Ivan, on the score of relations with the Polish King, of which the English merchants were accused, had imposed fines on them in the shape of taxes—

not half as heavy, indeed, as those other foreigners had to pay, but an infringement, none the less, of the privileges granted to them. And the ci-devant interpreter was convinced that this recrudescence of hostility arose from the Tsar's disappointment concerning the alliance he had planned. Elizabeth then made up her mind to entrust a fresh mission to Sylvester himself. She agreed to treat with Ivan as secretly as the Russian Sovereign desired ; but she could not allow her subjects to think she was in any danger among them without placing herself in a really perilous position. Sylvester must try to make the Tsar understand this fact.

He found him, in November, 1575, in the new dwelling he had built for himself in the Kremlin, and which he claimed to inhabit as a private individual, having given up the Kremlin itself and the throne to Simeon. ' You see,' said he to the English envoy, ' I was right when I appealed to your mistress, and she did not act wisely when she refused my proposals !' Sylvester was still pondering over the meaning of this new state of things, which had not been foreseen in London, and considering how he could best accommodate himself to it, when Ivan, leaving him to his own reflections, quitted his capital to meet the Ambassadors of the Emperor, then just about to arrive. When the Sovereign returned, his language had completely altered. ' If Elizabeth did not give him full and complete satisfaction, the whole commerce of his Empire should be made over to the Venetians and the Germans.'

The envoy was fain to carry this ultimatum back to London. We know nothing of the reply Elizabeth charged him to deliver, for he was killed by lightning at Kholmogory on his return journey, and all his papers were burnt in the house in which he had been living. Did Elizabeth yield ? The fact is admitted by the Russian historian who has devoted the most profound study to this chapter of history (Tolstoï, ' The Relations between England and Russia,' p. 31). Yet such a fact seems very improbable, for during the three following years, diplomatic intercourse between the two countries appears to have been entirely broken off. Before it could be renewed, Ivan was to allow himself to be bewitched by another chimera, inspired, as it would seem, by one of the foreigners who had formed part of the Tsar's personal circle since the period of Savine's mission to England.

III.—A Projected Marriage.

His name was Elysius Bomel or Bomelius. Born at Wesel, in Westphalia, he had studied medicine at Cambridge, but his chief interest was in astrology, and his reputation as to this particular science had earned him a prison cell, in which he was lying, at the time of Savine's arrival in London, by the Bishop of London's orders. As the only terms on which he could obtain his liberty were an undertaking to leave England, he made up his mind to follow the fortunes of the Muscovite envoy, and take service with the Tsar. At Moscow he promptly amassed a large fortune and a very evil reputation, and was believed to be the person employed in the preparation of the poisons used by the Tsar upon his victims. He was also accused of corrupting Ivan's mind by his offensive remarks about religion, and by advising him to seek refuge in a foreign country.

The Tsar, as we have seen, had not waited the arrival of this adventurer before he turned his mind to England, and, it may be, even to Elizabeth. But we possess various indications of the fact that Bomel endeavoured to direct the current of his ambitions into a new channel. He was not himself destined, indeed, to play any part in the development of the intrigue he had thus prepared. Implicated in a plot discovered in 1579, the hatred and jealousy of which he was the object no doubt contributed to ensure a recognition of his guilt, and his life ended under frightful tortures. His wife, an English-woman of the name of Anne Richards, remained in Russia, and was only sent back, with a few of her fellow-countrymen—a physician named Richard Elmes and an apothecary named Richard Frensham—after Ivan was dead, and at a moment when all foreigners in Russia were proscribed.

It was more as a German than as an Englishman that Bomel had been hated and denounced, and though Ivan ordered the unhappy astrologer to be executed, he proved himself very ready to reopen intercourse with England.

In 1580, Jeremy Horsey, one of the Russian company's agents, was commissioned by the Tsar to induce Elizabeth to send him a certain supply of military stores—lead, copper, saltpetre, sulphur, and gunpowder. Ivan was then engaged in measuring his strength against Batory's. But Horsey's instructions, which were hidden in a flask of brandy, were not confined to this request. The Tsar, influenced by Bomel, was more than ever set on seeking something else in England. If Elizabeth persisted in refusing her own hand to all her suitors, she had kinswomen of a marriageable age.

In the spring of 1581, Horsey brought back thirteen ships laden with the supplies for which the Tsar had asked, together with a party of surgeons and apothecaries, and, to fill Bomel's place, a physician, whom Elizabeth declared she valued highly —so highly that she made a sacrifice in sending him to the Tsar. This practitioner, better known in Russia under the name of Roman Elizariév, but who was really called James Roberts, had undertaken to make up Ivan's mind for him by pointing out the kinswoman of the Queen on whom he would do well to fix his choice.

In the course of that same year, a Muscovite Ambassador, Feodor Ivanovitch Pissemski, set sail for England, charged with the official conclusion of a treaty of alliance, and with the unofficial duty of opening negotiations for a marriage between his master and one of the Queen's nieces—the daughter of ' Prince Titounski ' (sic). The lady in question was Mary Hastings, daughter of Lord Huntingdon. Her grandmother had been Elizabeth's first cousin.

IV.—MARY HASTINGS.

Ivan had then just married for the sixth time. His bride was Maria Nagaïa, the daughter of one of his Court councillors (doumnyï dvorianine). But that was a matter of little consequence—so little, indeed, that the lady's own father, Athanasius Nagoï, had been one of the members of the Commission which had questioned Roberts concerning this other prospective bride. Previous to Pissemski's departure, in July, 1581, a representative of the English merchants trading with Russia landed at Arkhangel. He was the bearer of a letter from Elizabeth, dated from Westminster on January 23, 1581, which contained complaints about the King of Denmark, who was putting obstacles in the way of British trade. As Sovereign of Norway and Iceland, he claimed the right of collecting dues on all ships plying between the two countries. The Ambassador was therefore deputed to carry the Tsar's reply on this special point. Ivan suggested that the Queen should have all vessels carrying merchandise to Russian ports under the British flag convoyed by ships of war. But above all other things, Pissemski was to obtain the Queen's leave to see ' the Princess Titounski.' He was to look at her most carefully, to note her face, her complexion, her figure, her proportions ; he was to collect information as to her age and her family relations, and he was to try to bring back her picture, as well as exact measurements of her person, ' set down on paper.' If any objection was taken to the Sovereign's recent marriage, he was to reply that as the lady in that case was a mere boïar's daughter, the union possessed no importance whatever. It would not prevent the new bride from assuming the position of Tsarina. As to the children born of the projected marriage, the throne was reserved for Feodor, the Tsarevitch, but they would be given suitable appanages. Of course, the future Tsarina, like all persons in attendance on her whom she desired to retain about her person, would be expected to change her religion. And, to conclude, the betrothal must be preceded by the conclusion of an alliance, well made and duly signed. Ivan asked no favours : he offered his own person in exchange for a political advantage. If Mary Hastings was to have the happiness of becoming the rival of Maria Nagaïa, England must send her armies and her fleets to help the Tsar against Batory.

As to the outstanding commercial questions, one of the Russian company's agents, Egidius Crew, was associated with Pissemski, who was also accompanied, as his interpreter, by Roberts the physician. He was charged with a special mission of his own, to inform Elizabeth of the Tsar's intention of proceeding secretly to England. Ivan, as my readers will perceive, was planning a regular assault, which, he felt sure, would this time turn his stubborn dream into a reality.

Pissemski reached England in September, 1582, and did not have his first audience at Windsor till the 11th of the following December. At that moment, apparently, the object of one portion of his mission no longer existed. Vanquished in his struggle with Batory, Ivan had made peace. The Muscovite Ambassador made as though he had been unaware of this event. Probably he had received fresh instructions, according to which he was to carry the projected alliance to a conclusion, and thus pave the way to a recommencement of hostilities against the victorious Poles. But this he would not admit, and his position was rendered all the more difficult by the fact that an envoy from Batory had reached London, and was not wasting his time there. Both the Polish and the English archives are dumb on this subject—unless, indeed, they have never been searched in connection with it—and all we have to go on is the attitude of the English Cabinet with regard to the Muscovite Ambassador. This seems to indicate that by the time he arrived Elizabeth had already made up her mind, or was on the point of making it up, as to diplomatic arrangements, and that Poland was victorious once again. When Pissemski showed himself eager to enter on his business, the opening of negotiations was put off from week to week, and on various pretexts. First of all on account of Court festivities, then because of the plague. ' The plague doesn't prevent you from treating with the Poles,' grumbled the Russian. But he had to wait till the Poles had departed, and even then, if he had been more experienced, he would have perceived the Government was doing its best to get rid of him civilly. Solemnly introduced into the Queen's presence by the Earl of Leicester, Lord Howard, Sir Christopher Hatton, and the Earl of Huntingdon himself, he handed Elizabeth the presents sent by the Tsar, his own gifts, and those of his principal associate, who bore an unlucky name—Niéoudatcha (meaning ' failure '). These presents consisted, as usual, of dozens of sable furs. Elizabeth, according to the Ambassador's report, was very gracious. ' She began to be gay,' inquired after the Tsar, saying she loved him like a brother, and that she would be rejoiced to see him and make an alliance with him. But, the audience once over, there was less talk than ever of the negotiations. All Pissemski had attained by the end of the month was an invitation to a stag hunt. Rather roughly, he replied that he had no time to waste over such amusements, and, further, that he and his comrades never ate game at that season—it was in Lent. Having consented at last, with a very bad grace, to take his share in the proposed entertainment, he heard, on December 13, that the Earl of Leicester, Lord Hunsdon, Sir Christopher Hatton, and Secretary Francis Walsingham, had been appointed to treat with him. The conferences were to take place at Greenwich, and the representatives of the Russian merchants who had interests in Muscovy were to be present at them.

There was a disagreement from the very outset as to the basis of the negotiations. Pissemski offered England complete freedom from taxation on all the Russian merchandise she exported, and demanded, in return, her alliance against the King of Poland, ' who was being assisted by the Pope, the Emperor, and other Sovereigns.' ' But,' replied the English, ' your master has just been reconciled with Poland by the good offices of the Pope.' The Russian clung obstinately to his clumsy pretence. ' The Pope can say what he likes behind people's backs ! In the Tsar's letter to the Queen he calls Batory his enemy, so that must be.' Under such conditions there was scant hope of any understanding. Elizabeth's great object, for the moment, was to save her trade in the White Sea from Danish interference. To this end she consented, in January, 1583, to humour the Tsar and his Ambassador by giving Pissemski a secret audience. Pissemski, on his side, was anxious to open the question of the marriage. But the Russian, reaching Richmond at the appointed hour, was not a little astonished to find the palace in full festivity, music and dancing going on. The same thing happened every day, he was assured, and the Queen, indeed, forsook the merry throng to receive the Ambassador apart, without any witness save Roberts, the indispensable interpreter. Niéoudatcha was not summoned for another hour, and Elizabeth, excusing herself, told him she had ' been carried away by the conversation.'

This conversation, we may conclude, was principally concerned with Mary Hastings. When Pissemski pressed his

request to be allowed to see the young lady and have her
portrait painted, the Queen seemed very much put out. She
would have been heartily glad to enter into family relations
with the Tsar, but she had heard he cared very much for
beauty, and Mary Hastings was not a beautiful woman.
Besides, she had only just got over the small-pox, and the idea
of having her picture painted at the present moment was not
to be dreamt of. Nevertheless, the wily Sovereign pretended
to discuss the conditions for the marriage. She expressed
special anxiety about any daughters her niece might have.
' Our Sovereigns,' answered Pissemski proudly, ' always marry
their daughters to foreign potentates !' And he quoted the
case—unique, indeed, in the course of several centuries—of the
Princess Helena, married in 1495 to Alexander of Poland.
But before any marriage could be settled, the alliance must be
arranged. The Ambassador had handed in a memorandum
on this subject, and was waiting for his answer. Elizabeth
promised to hasten it, and that was all.

Thus two more months slipped by, and when the envoy,
whose patience was very nearly worn out, received his answer,
what disappointment was his ! The Queen agreed to make
an alliance with the Tsar, and give him armed help against
all his enemies, but in return she demanded a monopoly of all
the external trade of Russia for England ! Pissemski proved
his simplicity once more, for he did not realize that Elizabeth
was making a mock of his master and himself. He quibbled
and argued over the terms of the document, as if its substance
did not suffice to make it utterly unacceptable. It described
his overtures as ' requests,' and called the Tsar the Queen's
' nephew.' The English negotiators offered to alter the terms
of the agreement, but they refused to change their conditions.
In April they invited the Ambassador to a banquet, to which
seventeen great dignitaries of the State—Edward Clinton,
Earl of Lincoln ; George Talbot, Earl of Shrewsbury ; Thomas
Radclyffe, Earl of Sussex ; Ambrose Dudley, Earl of Warwick ;
Francis Russell, Earl of Bedford ; and others—sat down with
him, and at which the Queen drank to the Tsar's health.
When the feast was over they informed the importunate diplomatist that the Queen was about to give him his farewell
audience. For as he assured them he had no instructions to
accept the English counter proposals, would not his best course
be to go back to his own country, and there obtain fresh powers ?

Loudly the poor fellow objected, ' But what about the
marriage ?' In reply, the Englishmen showed him gazettes,
which announced that Maria Nagaïa had borne the Tsar a son.
Once more Pissemski feigned ignorance, and the ignorance of
the man who has no desire to be enlightened. ' Wicked

people were putting about stories to prevent a good understanding between his master and the Queen.' So angry was
he, and such a coil did he raise, that Elizabeth, after due
reflection, made up her mind to lend herself to a farce—for
a farce it certainly was—well calculated, indeed, to deceive
the envoy and keep Ivan's illusions alive. On May 17,
Pissemski was invited to proceed, with no attendant save
Roberts, to a country house belonging to the Chancellor, Lord
Bromley. The Chancellor, having ceremoniously received him
at the entrance of his dwelling, conducted him to the garden,
where refreshments were prepared. Very soon a party of ladies
appeared in one of the garden alleys. At the head of the
group, between Lady Bromley and Lady Huntingdon, walked
the person the envoy already delighted to call 'the Tsar's
betrothed.' The gentlemen saluted from a distance, and
the Chancellor told Pissemski the Queen had given orders
that he was to be shown her niece—'not in a chamber, but in
broad daylight, so that he might see her better.' The Russian
stared with all his might. A turn in the park was suggested,
and arranged so that he might meet the object of his curiosity
several times over. After this, Bromley said to him, 'Have
you looked at her well?' 'I have obeyed my instructions,'
was the reply; and in his report Pissemski wrote: 'The Princess
of Hountinsk, Mary Hantis (*sic*), is tall, slight, and white-
skinned; she has blue eyes, fair hair, a straight nose, and her
fingers are long and taper.'

Horsey has left us his own account of this scene, which may
very well have been touched up a little in Pissemski's narrative,
the essential features of which I have just reproduced. The
English chronicler declares that when he saw the 'betrothed'
the envoy was so overcome with emotion that he retired backwards, saying he must be content with a single glance at the
angel he believed destined to become his Sovereign's wife.
But Horsey was not present, and the angel had very nearly
reached her thirtieth year!

Elizabeth was determined to give herself the amusement of
carrying on the farce to the very end. Once more she sent for
Pissemski, told him how much she regretted her niece was not
sufficiently beautiful to please the Tsar's taste, and said, 'I
think you did not think her very fair yourself!' But the
Russian held his ground.

'I think her fair: the rest is in God's hands.' And he
pressed the Queen to make her intentions on the subject clear.
But Elizabeth had already invented a new means of delay.
She would send a confidential man of her own to Russia
with Pissemski, and this Ambassador should receive all her
instructions and be invested with all the necessary powers.

19

The farewell audience soon took place. Pissemski was the recipient of another volley of compliments and empty protestations of friendship, and was assured the Queen would give free passage through her territories to all the Tsar's envoys to any foreign Power, the Pope alone excepted. ' Your master must not betray me to the Pope !' Elizabeth is reported to have said. Here, again, we may suppose, Roberts proved himself a faithless interpreter. By the middle of June, Mary Hastings' portrait was finished, and after witnessing a review of the British fleet —eighty ships of seventy or eighty guns, and crews of a thousand men or more apiece—Pissemski and Niéoudatcha embarked with Jeremy Bowes, Her Majesty's chosen Ambassador. Her choice, though it had fallen on a professional diplomat, was not a happy one.

V.—THE DUTCH COMPETITION AND THE RUPTURE.

Bowes had a difficult task before him. He was to talk of trade, and of nothing but trade, to a man who did not want to listen to anything but projected alliances, political and matrimonial. And these same commercial relations were passing through a very trying crisis. The English merchants, whose privileges were nominally maintained—they only had to pay half other people's taxes, at all events—found themselves forced to pay extra imposts, arbitrarily demanded and perpetually increased. These were the result of the hostile operations the Tsar dreamt of reopening with England's help, and which had already reduced his resources to a most exhausted condition. Meanwhile, other foreign competitors were gaining ground. The Russian Treasury, hard pressed for money, was selling fresh privileges to the highest bidder, and the liberal gifts cunningly distributed by the Dutch were bribing precious support among the persons nearest to the Sovereign. Three of Ivan's chief councillors—Nikita Romanovitch Zakharine, the incorruptible hero of the popular legend, Bogdan Biélski, and Andrew Chtchelkalov—had been completely bought over. The Tsar probably recognised the competition to be a means of forcing Elizabeth's hand, and rendering her more obedient to his desires. Since the year 1575, as a matter of fact, Antwerp ships had been making regular voyages to the White Sea, and Captain Carlile, who reckoned the money sunk by the English Company in the monopolies now endangered at £80,000, had presented his Queen with a memorandum in which he proposed to turn efforts apparently likely to be wasted, for the future, in Russia, to the continent of America (' A Briefe and Summary Discourse upon the Intended Voyage to the Hithermost Parts of America,' April, 1583, Hakluyt, 'Collection of Early Voyages, iii. 228).

Bowes was not the least like Jenkinson. Haughty and abrupt in his address, brusque and unmannerly, he was a fair sample of the worst side of that national character of which his predecessor had exemplified the best aspect. He began with a tolerably ill-natured dispute about a horse offered him for his entry into the capital, and which did not measure a sufficient number of hands to please him. The instructions with which he was provided did not help him to wipe out the memory of this bad beginning. Elizabeth not only maintained her demand for an exclusive monopoly, but claimed to impart a somewhat peculiar form to the alliance which was to depend on this *sine quâ non*. She would not proceed to assist Ivan actively against his enemies until she had exhausted every attempt at reconciliation between him and them. This was as much as to say to the Tsar, ' You desire my help to enable you to take vengeance on Batory—very good ! But I shall begin by warning the King of your intention !'

We have two sources of information as to the negotiations thus begun—Bowes' own report (Hakluyt, i. 458, etc.) and the records of the Muscovite Chancery. These documents constantly contradict each other. The British envoy, while admitting certain misunderstandings and unavoidable annoyances, flatters himself he has won all along the line. Ivan, according to his testimony, is disposed to give the Queen's subjects back all their privileges, and even to increase them. At the same time, his desire for an English wife—some other relative of the Queen's, if Mary Hastings was not inclined to accept his suit—was stronger than ever, and he was ready to go to London for this purpose. He even went so far as to ask the ' preacher' of the English Embassy to furnish him with a memorandum as to the chief points of the Protestant faith, had it read aloud before a numerous audience, and liberally rewarded its author. He inflicted severe punishment on those of his councillors who betrayed any hostility to Bowes, and advised them to alter their behaviour. And the fruit of all these successes, couched in writing, and duly signed and sealed, was on the point of being delivered to the envoy, when the Tsar's sudden death destroyed the work so successfully performed, transformed triumph into disaster, and cast the victory into the hands of the hostile party.

The Russian version is very different. Ivan's reply to the British ultimatum is said to have been embodied in the following counter-propositions : As the King of Poland, in contravention of all treaties, had taken Polotsk and Livonia from the Tsar, the Queen must invite him to restore the conquered territories and pay an indemnity, or, in the event of his refusal, she must join hands with the Tsar and make him do it by force. In exchange, she was to receive the monopoly of certain ports —the Flemish and French merchants had standing rights in certain others. The King of France had just sent several ships to the port of Kola. He was desirous of the Tsar's friendship, and had begged Ivan to send him an Ambassador. This was simply a way of telling Bowes, ' We are by no means bereft of powerful friends.'

All the Englishman could do was to take refuge behind his instructions. But then the Russian delegates, Zakharine, Biélski, Chtchelkalov, and Frolov, approached the matter of the ' secret business.' ' Could not Bowes tell them anything about that ?' Yes; but it was for the Tsar's ear alone. They promised a private audience, and went on splitting hairs about the projected alliance. When Elizabeth had granted the Tsar's Ambassadors free passage through her dominions, she had claimed her right to exclude the representatives of hostile Powers. There must be some understanding as to this. As far as Rome was concerned, there was no question of a difference. ' The Tsar would not betray the Queen to the Pope.' And he also included the Kings of Poland, Sweden, and Denmark among his enemies. Now it was Bowes' turn to specify, and a disagreement at once arose. ' The Emperor,' said the British envoy, ' is the Queen's enemy, and the King of Spain such a friend as anyone might buy for a dienga.' But Elizabeth had just sent the King of Denmark the Order of the Garter, which marked him in the front rank of her friends, and as much might be said of the King of Sweden. The negotiators fell back on the monopolies question. As a final concession, Russia granted England five ports on the White Sea, not including Kola, which was to be left to the French, and Poudojersk, at the mouth of the Northern Dvina, at which place a Nimeguen merchant named Johann von Valle, known in Russia as *Biélobrod* (White-beard) had set up his trading establishments.

Bowes protested. What was to become of the solemn charters previously bestowed on the Russian Company ? The reply given him was that ' the English merchants, Thomas Glover and Rudolph Ritter, have misused the Tsar's favour, plotted with his enemies, and acted as their spies.' To which Bowes answered : ' Glover is a rogue, but England is a free country, in which every man can hire himself out to serve whatever master he chooses. And neither your Frenchmen nor your Flemings give you first-rate merchandise, as we do. . . .' Then the Russians raised a clamour. The English cloths were just what they did complain of. They brought patterns. ' I know nothing about cloths,' quoth Bowes, with an air of offended dignity.

I have summed up the pith of a score of meetings, the result of which was *nil*.

The private audience took place on December 13, 1583. Bowes had to present himself unarmed and unattended, for the Tsar was going to receive him *tête-à-tête* to discuss the ' secret business '—in other words, the marriage. This *tête-à-tête* did not exclude the presence of a dozen persons, amongst whom was the reigning favourite, Boris Godounov, shortly to be Tsar himself. In presence of this company the whole of the farce arranged by Elizabeth was played again. Ivan desired to be informed of the Queen's intentions as to Mary Hastings, and Bowes declared the Queen had sent him to find out the Tsar's. But the envoy, now he had his back against the wall, entangled himself in a series of miserable shifts and excuses. ' The Queen's niece was ill—very ill indeed ; and besides, he did not think she could agree to change her religion. . . . And, further, she was one of Her Majesty's most distant relations. There were a dozen other ladies whom the Tsar might very well prefer . . . .' Ivan broke in sharply :

' Who are these ladies ? Are they the daughters of appanaged Princes or subjects of the Queen ? . . . Speak ! Explain thyself ! . . .'

' I have no instructions.'

This time the Tsar could not control his rage. According to his usual tactics, he executed a flank movement, so as to have his opponent more completely in his hands. Several times Bowes had fallen out with the Russian negotiators, and in the course of their altercations he had dropped various offensive expressions. With these Ivan now taxed him, and when the envoy denied them, he flew into a rage, as was his wont. The Russian record omits this episode, but Bowes gives a full account of it. Certain persons have objected to the dialogues I have introduced into my narratives of a less remote past, believing they may be an alteration of the original texts on which my story is based. If my critics will be good enough to consult the documents of which the sense is here reproduced, they will acknowledge that if I have been guilty of any alteration at all, it has been in my avoidance of the conversational form, infinitely more frequent in documents of this kind than they will imagine. In Bowes' report he gives the dialogue as follows :

The Tsar (to Bowes) : ' . . . You have assumed airs of superiority over my plenipotentiaries which cannot be endured ; for I know Sovereigns among my own equals who take precedence of your mistress !'

Bowes : ' My mistress is as great a Princess as any in Christendom, equal to those who think themselves the greatest, and able to make head against them all !'

The Tsar : ' You mean the Kings of France and Spain ?'

Bowes : ' Certainly. I believe my Queen is worthy to be their peer. . . .'

The Tsar : ' And the Emperor's ? . . .'

Bowes : ' When the King, my mistress's father, was warring against France, he once had the Emperor in his pay. . . .'

These words, if we may believe the Ambassador, put Ivan into such a fury that he went so far as to threaten to throw his guest out of the window, to which menace Bowes replied that the Tsar could do as he chose, but that the Queen of England knew how to avenge insults laid on her representatives. Whereupon Ivan hastily dismissed his bold opponent, and spoke of him, once his back was turned, in terms of praise, saying he would himself be thankful to have such men to serve him.

As to all this episode the Russian authorities are dumb. According to them there was a dispute about the insolence, which Bowes denied and the Russian delegates asserted, to which the Tsar put an end by making a long speech on the origin of the British trade in Russia, the causes of the partial abolition of the excessive privileges primarily granted, and the reasons which forbade their restitution. The Queen's subjects were very far from supplying the Russian markets in any sufficient or satisfactory manner. Drawing a ring off his finger, Ivan declared Von Valle had only made him pay 60 roubles for it, and 1,000 for the big emerald in his cap. The English merchants brought no gems at all, and charged exorbitant prices for all the merchandise they did bring. The ring was worth 300 roubles, and the emerald 40,000, if not more ; Bowes was obliged to admit the fact. Further, the Tsar had asked, through Pissemski, for cloths, silks of good quality, and laces. He was still waiting for the laces, and the cloths, like the silks, were very highly priced, and worth nothing at all. Those sent from Poland looked much better. At a sign from the Sovereign various stuffs were brought in, and while he fingered them and made comparisons, to which Bowes replied by a fresh assertion of his own incompetence in such matters, Ivan continued to hold forth. What was the meaning of this friendship the Queen offered him, if it was to be confined to his custom, and to an alliance which had no existence save a verbal one ?

All the Ambassador could do was to appeal to his instructions, and the result of another and still more confidential interview, which took place five days later, on December 18, and at which the only members of the council present were Troubetskoi, Zakharine, Biélski, Chtchelkalov, and Frolov—and even these were sent off to the other end of the room, ' close to the stove '—was not any more satisfactory. Meanwhile Ivan had heard, through James Roberts, who probably interpreted at all these meetings, that Bowes was desirous of seeing him quite alone. The envoy denied the fact. All he had said was that when he had been on other missions, to the King of France and other Sovereigns, he had never been expected to deal with a third party with regard to important negotiations.

' The Court of France is no rule for ours,' grumbled Ivan. ' Tell me what thou hast to say about our marriage.'

' I know from the Queen, my mistress, that she desired your friendship above that of all other Sovereigns, and I have on other personal desire, save that of pleasing and serving you.'

' Give me the list of all the nieces of the Queen of whom you speak, with their names and titles. I will send an Ambassador to England with you, and he shall look at them all, and send me their portraits.'

' I offer you my own services for that purpose.'

All this I quote from the Russian version. According to it, Bowes now retracted his former assertions, and denied he had ever been heard to mention any other female relatives of Elizabeth's whom the Tsar might have preferred to Mary Hastings. When he stood convicted as a liar, he once more took refuge behind his instructions, or gave it to be understood, with a mysterious air, that he would shortly be in a position to give the monarch satisfaction, ' but his time was not yet come.' He asked leave to send a courier overland to England to bring him back fuller powers ; raised trivial questions about the quantity and quality of the supplies sent him, demanding as much as 10 pouds (320 pounds) of butter a day ; requested the Tsar to administer severe chastisement, *manu propriâ*, to Chtchelkalov, whom the envoy held responsible for the grievances of which he complained, but got nothing for his pains except a discourse from the Sovereign, under five heads, which wound up in the following fashion : ' You are an ignorant man, and you have no idea of how an envoy ought to behave !'

After that one would have fancied there was no more to be said. But Ivan was too much set on his own idea. With the obstinacy of a lunatic, he strove to lay his hand on the dream which perpetually eluded his grasp. He summoned Bowes to more private interviews, and over and over again he repeated his same monotonous argument : ' Thou hast told us of a score or two of young girls of thy country amongst

whom we might choose a wife, and thou wilt not give us
their names. Yet how can we take any steps on such
vague information as this ? It appears there are more than
a thousand marriageable girls in England, several of them
kitchen wenches ; would you have us pay our addresses to
them all ?'

These interviews, which constantly recurred during the
two first months of the year 1584, culminated, on February
14, according to the Russian records, in another and most
violent altercation. Bowes, after having undertaken to give
the Tsar's Ambassador to the King of France a passage on
board his ship, backed out of his promise, saying the Queen
had ordered him to go back to England overland.

'So as to sell me to my enemies !' cried Ivan, beside himself
with rage. 'I'll not permit it !'

Since Russia had lost Livonia, the overland route ran through
Poland. Recovering his self-control, though still furious,
Ivan continued : 'As thou didst not come here to treat
seriously, thou hast my leave to go, and take away all thou
broughtest in with thee ! This very hour we will dismiss
thee !'

Bowes was well accustomed to such angry outbreaks, and
this one, as the Russian records admit, by no means overwhelmed him. He was not dismissed, and three days later the
envoy was summoned to listen to the reading of a suggested
treaty, in which the Tsar had caused the minimum of his
wishes and demands to be embodied. All our knowledge of
the sense of this document is gathered from the objections
made to it by Bowes. Substantially, what Ivan demanded
was an offensive alliance for the reconquest of Livonia. As
always, the Ambassador gave prevaricating answers. His
mistress, a very pious lady, had a horror of conquests. The
Low Countries had vainly besought her to take them under
her protection, and even France would have been thankful to
pass under her rule. . . .

'But this is not a matter of conquest,' replied the Tsar ;
'Livonia is our ancient patrimony !'

'Are you quite sure of that ?'

Ivan was furious.

'We do not ask your Queen to judge between us and Poland !'

And this time the farewell audience was fixed for February 20. It was put off on account of the monarch's illness,
and on March 18, Chtchelkalov had Bowes informed that
'his English Tsar was dead.' Like Randolph, in former
days, the envoy was kept a prisoner in his own house, and exposed to every kind of ill-treatment, until the month of May,
when Ivan's son sent him back to Elizabeth with a letter which

contained no reference to an alliance nor any special favours to be granted to the British merchants.

According to Horsey's report, Chtchelkalov and the Ambassador's other foes went so far as to plot his death, and it was only his fellow-countryman's intervention that averted this catastrophe. But this was probably a mere boast on Horsey's part. Boris Godounov was the real master at that moment, and we know—though he did it secretly, indeed—that he sent Bowes a present, and coupled his gift with assurances of his devotion. But, in spite of all Bowes' blustering talk, a town was rising up and a port was being dug on a site chosen by the Dutch, hard by an ancient monastery, on the right bank of the Dvina. This they had promised to make into a second Narva for Russia, and with their help, and no other, in the beginning, it was to become the centre of the maritime trade of the Empire, snatched, once and for all, from the hands of the British monopolists. This town was Arkhangel, where the English were only to put in an appearance at a much later date, and in quite a secondary position. In this apparently unequal struggle the victory remained with Holland, and its effects are manifest in the history of Peter the Great.

In 1838, Count Wielhorski, happening to visit Italy to collect antique works for a museum then in process of formation in Russia, believed himself to have discovered a well-executed and well-preserved portrait of Ivan, said to have been sent to London in 1570 (' Russian Archives,' 1888, i. 123). This canvas, a unique specimen of the Russian art of the sixteenth century, was then in the possession of the Russian Consul at Genoa, Monsieur Smirnov, who had bought it from a London curiosity dealer. To my great regret, I have failed in my endeavour to discover the present whereabouts of this picture, which, if authentic, would be of priceless value, both as to the history of artistic development in Russia and as to that of the curious diplomatic episode which I have just related to my readers. No authority, whether Russian or English, mentions any picture of the Tsar as having been despatched to England.

Ivan, as my readers have seen, was led to seek the English alliance, and desire it with a passionate longing, in the first place by the pressure of the internal crisis, and in the second, by that of the external one which was affecting and imperilling both his fortunes and his policy. I now pass on to the history of that closing phase of his reign.

PART IV

THE END

CHAPTER I

THE POLISH INVASION : BATORY

I.—BATORY. II.—THE STRUGGLE. III.—THE POLISH ARMY. IV.
—THE RUSSIAN ARMY. V.—THE CAPTURE OF POLOTSK. VI.
—THE POLES IN MUSCOVY. VII.—THE DIPLOMATIC INTER-
LUDE. VIII.—THE SIEGE OF PSKOV.

I.—BATORY.

AFTER the year 1572, when the election to the Polish monarchy became genuine instead of fictitious, as it had hitherto been, the electoral meetings on the field of Wola developed into what was neither more nor less than a gambling hell. The whole continent of Europe played there, and once only in the course of two centuries did the players cut a King. He was an unknown man. A pure-blooded Hungarian, through his father, Stephen Batory of Somlyo, and his mother, Katherine Telegda, he was of a good family, and nothing more, had seen honourable service with the Imperial armies, and manœuvred in still more successful fashion behind the diplomatic scenes at Vienna and Constantinople—so successfully, indeed, that, thanks to the united goodwill of the Sultan and the Emperor, he found himself *Voiévode* of Transylvania in 1571, when he was only thirty-eight. In Poland this foreigner was very little known. He was reported to have ruled a small territory exceedingly well, and was said, at a later period, to have studied at the Academy of Padua, at which place, in 1789, the last of his successors on the throne of the Jagellons was to erect a second-rate work by Carlo or Ferrari as a monument to his memory. He learnt no Polish there. When he was elected King, he either talked Latin to his new subjects or held his tongue—the best plan in a

298

country where everybody talked too much. At the election of
1575, he was the Sultan's candidate, in opposition to the
Emperor's; for Ivan, as we have seen, had retired, and Maximilian's son based his claim on the Austrian alliance against
the Turks. Whether to make war against the Turks, backed by
Austria, or to make war against the Muscovites, backed by the
neutrality, at all events, if not the assistance, of the Porte—
there lay the dilemma! But the Polish electors, wrapped up
in their own concerns, were moved and divided by other
considerations. The aristocracy leant towards Maximilian,
because he offered it titles and money; the lesser nobles went
over in a body to the Hungarian, because they were convinced
so modest a personage would be their King and their slave too,
and that either he would govern through them or they would
govern without him, against the oligarchy of the great lords.

The stranger, as it turned out, wanted to be everybody's
King, and he knew how to get what he wanted. He began
by outstripping his rival at Warsaw. That was easy enough,
for haste, on Maximilian's part, meant considerable risk—the
Turk had his eye upon him. The Emperor's death, which took
place in October, 1576, left Batory alone. All he had to do
now was to unravel the difficulties of a position in which Henry
of Valois had not even tried to see his way. The ex-*voiévode*
proved himself the possessor of an unexpectedly clear insight,
and an unrivalled knowledge of the art of government. Physically, as we see him in a portrait painted in 1583 by an unknown
artist, and now preserved in the Church of the Missionary
Fathers at Cracow, he was a typical Magyar—short and thick-
set, with prominent cheek-bones, a long nose, and a low forehead. The countenance is massive, energetic, rugged. We see
no regard for effect, no elegance; he looks fierce and uncouth.
The new King, who, both from necessity and because it suited
his tastes, had lived in a most simple way, never dreamt for
a moment of changing his habits, nor imagined he had been
given a crown so that he might lead an easy life. It was
noticed that he never wore gloves, and the story goes that,
though he was shod with Polish boots, he scorned the stockings
then coming into general use. His health was anything
but good. He had been suffering, for a considerable time, from
a mysterious complaint which seems to have hastened his
end. He had an open sore on his left leg, and a belief grew up,
when this trouble grew worse, that, in spite of all his appearance
of strength, he had suffered, during his residence at the Emperor's Court, from attacks of epilepsy or apoplexy. The
doctors of that period were not over clear-sighted. But the
new King showed no sign of anything of this sort when he
arrived in Poland. He worked his secretaries to death, spent

whole days on horseback, and, whenever he had a moment's
leisure, proved himself the boldest of sportsmen.

Mentally he was a curious mixture of stiffness and pliability,
of masterfulness and liberalism, of violence and gentleness.
When one of the deputies to the Diet raised his voice, he clapped
his hand upon his sword, and shouted ' *Tace nebulo !*'   When
the King of Sweden put forward claims that displeased him, he
repeated the same gesture, and grumbled the words, ' *Docebo
istum regulum !*'   Contrary to all precedent, he had a turbulent
nobleman belonging to one of the most powerful families in
the country condemned and executed.   Supplications and
threats were all equally vain.   ' *Canis mortuus non mordet !*'
was his imperturbable reply.   *Plectatur !*

He treated the rebellious Cossacks after the Tsar's own
fashion, had them put to death by dozens, and, so some people
asserted, caused their bodies to be cut into pieces.   And when,
in the course of an audience he was giving a foreigner, a dog
ran in and disturbed him, he sent the beast flying to the other
end of the room with a blow from his spurred boot.   But he
knew how to employ more gentle methods with the turbaned
suzerain of his former days.   In Transylvania he had been half
a Protestant, but he was a zealous Catholic once he was in
Poland.   At the Diet of Election he had been represented by
an Arian, Blandrata ; his election once ensured, his counsellors
were Jesuits.

He intended to be master in his own kingdom, but in the
sixteenth century he refused to make a difference between a
starost and a Jew.   He thought of reducing forced service,
and substituting fines for flogging.   More than once, on the
battlefield, he turned peasants into noblemen ; and, hard as he
was to others and to himself, this same man was tender-
hearted—nay, sentimental—to such a point that his grief for
the loss of a friend brought on a serious illness.

At a Court which the last Jagellons had Italianized, and in
a country into which the intellectual currents of the day had
penetrated freely, he was at first looked on as a peasant.   But
hardly had be been brought into contact with his new surroundings, before — though he repudiated refinements unsuitable to his character and temperament—he placed himself in the forefront of the most enlightened Princes of his
time.   He founded the Academy of Wilna ; he was the partisan
and initiator of the reform of the calendar, the organizer of
the postal and financial administrations, the creator of a new
judicial system. . . .

And, above all, he governed.   He brought the machine,
which was beginning to go astray, back into order, and thus,
though a foreigner by birth, habits, and language, he was a fine

representative of the living forces of the Poland of the sixteenth century, which was, and still remains—I believe I may say it without offence—the highest historical expression of the Slav race the world has ever seen, a country already sapped by anarchy, but capable, materially speaking, as he was to prove, of a mighty and formidable effort, and prepared, morally speaking, for the noblest conquests of the modern intellect ; a land of sublime warriors and inspired poets, of fluent political writers and orators, whose eloquence, sacred or profane, reaches the very heights ; where Frycz Modrzewski, with his programme of social reform, claiming universal rights for all, outstripped all the writers of his day, where Kochanowski's grace and feeling made him Ronsard's worthy compeer, and where Skarga was the forerunner of Bossuet.

Foreign and uncouth as were his extraction and appearance, Batory brought all this about by the grace of his own genius. And this being so, he prepared the struggle with Moscow—for Livonia, in the first place, and after that for the very existence of Poland. He saw, in fact, that Poland as he realized her, civilized, well governed, liberal, turbulent, Catholic, must either absorb her great neighbour, and impose her own culture and political system on her, or be herself absorbed and brought into subjection by her.

The coexistence of these two great Slav States, each moving in its own orbit and developing after its own independent, if not contrary, fashion, might not have been so utterly impossible, indeed. But to that end the Poland of the Piasts and the Jagellons should have moved in the direction naturally indicated by her own origin—that is to say, westward—and drawn the Slavs of the west and south after her. Whereas, driven backward by the German *Drang nach Osten*, Poland had been forced eastward, and had founded a great State, half Polish, half Russian or Ruthenian, half Catholic and half Orthodox, at once a republic and a monarchy, a compound of civilization and barbarism.

There was but one orbit, and a planet too many—two Sovereigns of all the Russias, and only one empire for them to rule.

No sooner had Batory seated himself firmly on his throne than he had to put down a revolt at Dantzig. Though he had had some experience of siege-work, his success on this occasion was not conspicuous. His Poles were not well in hand as yet. And, indeed, his right to be numbered among the great military leaders of his epoch has been disputed. Those who have taken him to be the inventor of the red-hot bullets, which, as a matter of fact, produced little or no effect at the Siege of Dantzig, are certainly mistaken. The use of these engines, according to

Meinert (*Geschichte des Kriegwesens*, i. 370), dates from the beginning of the fifteenth century, at least. It may be, as one of the King's biographers—Albertrandi—asserts, that the Polish army owed him improvements in heavy ordnance, and in its cavalry armament and equipment. More certain titles to fame are the remodelling of the Cossack military system, undertaken during his reign, the raising of a Royal Guard in 1576, and the embodiment, in 1578, of a regular infantry, recruited on the King's own lands. To these local forces Batory added a strong contingent of foreign troops—Hungarian infantry and German cavalry—and thus effected, in the land of his adoption, the revolution which had already modified the bases of military power and the very art of war in Western countries. He endowed Poland with a standing army, equipped and drilled after the European model. And specialists consider the three campaigns, in the course of which he penetrated into the very heart of Muscovy, both well conceived and skilfully carried through, in spite of some failures and weaknesses of detail. Those who have endeavoured to minimize his personal share in them have not been particularly successful. He may not have proved himself a commander of overwhelming talents, and the tactics Ivan adopted may not have given him any opportunity of proving himself one. His real merit lies in the fact that he was a man who knew how to lead, who had the gift, the instinct, the genius of command ; and the method he employed to ensure himself every possible advantage in the duel he foresaw to be inevitable between Poland and her Muscovite neighbour may be considered a masterpiece.

II.—THE STRUGGLE.

Both opponents showed equal resolution in the combat. Up till the moment of Maximilian's death, Ivan clung obstinately to the plan sketched out at Mojaïsk, and sent courier after courier to Vienna. When that event took place, the Tsar dismissed the two Ambassadors Batory had despatched to his Court, one after the other, in his endeavour to gain time, cut short all negotiations by putting forward impossible demands, claimed Kiev, after he had asked for Vitebsk, and would shortly have claimed Warsaw, and turned his mind exclusively to the pursuit of the advantages he had already gained in Livonia.

In March, 1578, he agreed to another three years' truce ; but this suspension of hostilities did not extend, of course, to territories on which either party was at home, and both believed themselves to be at home in Livonia. Further, Ivan arbitrarily inserted a clause forbidding the Poles to interfere in Livonian affairs, into the Rùssian text of the treaty.

The result was a fight, in the spring of that same year, for the possession of Wenden. Ivan had sent out an army of 18,000 men—more than enough, he had reason to think, to make head against the troops commanded by Chodkiewicz and Sapiéha, which were not nearly so numerous, and had hitherto, as we know, been destitute of every kind of necessary. Batory despatched a fresh embassy, and the Tsar told it to wait ; ' there would soon be news from Livonia !' The news came, and Ivan learnt that matters at Warsaw had quite altered.

At the very beginning of his reign, Batory had sent the castellan of Sanok, John Herburt, to Stockholm, whence he had returned with a treaty of alliance, offensive and defensive, for the recovery of Livonia. The course of the Narova was to mark the dividing-line between the possessions acquired, or to be acquired, by the two allies. Now, the Poles, under Andrew Sapiéha, had joined forces with the Swedes, under Boë, had forced the Russians to fight in the open, and had once more proved their own superiority in conflicts of this kind. Four *voiévodes* had been killed, four more taken prisoners, 6,000 men slaughtered in the Russian camp, Ivan's gunners had strangled themselves across their own guns—this was the news the Tsar received. His Tartar cavalry alone had escaped the disaster, with his Commander-in-Chief Galitzine, who, according to the Polish authorities, hastened the Russian defeat by taking to flight, and carrying several of his more prominent comrades with him—a seasoned warrior, the *okolnytchyi* Feodor Chérémétiev, and one of the Sovereign's most trusted men, Bowes' enemy, the *diak* Chtchelkalov.

This put a stop to all thought of truces and negotiations. Ivan dismissed Haraburda, the Polish envoy, but not until he had taken a characteristic revenge. Ever since Batory's accession he had refused to call the King of Poland his ' brother.' ' Did you not try to elect John Kostka ?' he said to the Poles. ' Would you have me call him my brother, too ?' Kostka was a private nobleman. ' And what is this Transylvanian Prince of yours ?' he went on. ' Nobody ever heard of that principality till now !' Haraburda was obliged to listen to a good deal of talk of this kind. But the Tsar's two Ambassadors, Karpov and Golovine, were still at Warsaw, and Batory treated them accordingly. When he received them on December 3, 1578, he did not rise to his feet, as the protocol demanded, to inquire after their master. So the envoys at once declared themselves unable to discharge their mission. And, indeed, the whole country about them was in a ferment. The Diet, which had been called together on January 19, 1578, had voted an extra war subsidy for the next two years. This was reckoned at 800,000, or even at 1,200,000, florins—no very large sum, indeed,

for the annual expenses of keeping up the Spanish army in the
Low Countries at that time reached 7,000,000 florins ! (Philippson, *loc. cit.*, p. 240). Yet the Republic had never made such an
effort before, and if the money paid in had reached the amount
calculated on, it would have been amply sufficient. But it was
far from doing that. Nevertheless, Batory, who had bent
the Diet to his will, managed to find money. He had no personal expenses, and was thus able to pass all the income from
his own lands into his war-chest. He obtained credit abroad,
and once he had the money, he was able to get the men.

III.—THE POLISH ARMY.

The Polish nobles provided him with a splendid body of
cavalry, which had lately proved its prowess at Wenden. But
the Muscovites seemed more than likely to profit by their late
experience, and await the Polish attack under the shelter of
their fortress walls. The historian Dlugosz gives us reason to
conclude that Poland had possessed infantry troops as early as
in the beginning of the fifteenth century, but this body of men
—a small one, numbering not more than 2,000—was only armed
with pikes. Batory provided a more modern armament—
muskets, swords, and battle-axes—and trebled the strength of
his infantry by calling out the peasants on the crown lands.
Those who enlisted of their own freewill were forgiven all they
owed. The volunteers were many, and distinguished themselves by their bravery : some of them performed prodigies of
valour. Besides these men, the King had a body of Hungarian
infantry, some 5,000 strong, another of Polish infantry equipped
in the Hungarian style, and consisting of the serving-men
attached to the army, and a third recruited among the nobility.
These he reinforced by divers bodies of auxiliaries belonging to
the same arm of the service—Germans, who formed themselves
into huge squares, Scotsmen, and Cossacks. Into his cavalry
he introduced German and Polish arquebus-men.

The total number of troops, including the Lithuanian contingent, does not seem to have exceeded 20,000 men. It is
worth remarking that in this war, certain separatist tendencies
notwithstanding, Lithuania, or at all events the nobility of the
country, which was still half Russian and half Orthodox, was
heart and soul with Batory. This fact is acknowledged by
the Russian historians themselves (Lappo, ' The Grand Duchy
of Lithuania,' 1569-1586, St. Petersburg, 1901, p. 179). The
sister nation gave all she could—a few thousand horsemen, who
proved most invaluable, during the winter season especially,
when, better able to endure the terrible climate and less distant
from their own homes, they made up, to some extent, for the

dispersal of the main army. This consisted of a mere handful of men, but it was the first, as to composition and quality, in any Slav country. The proportion of foreigners it contained was very large, but in the sixteenth century this was by no means an exceptional case. At the Battle of Dreux (December 19, 1562) Guise had over 12,000 Germans, Swiss, and Spaniards in his army, as against 6,000 Frenchmen, and in his enemy's camp the state of things was similar.

The Poles' weak point, in this and all the succeeding campaigns, was to be their enemy's strong one—artillery. In vain did Batory engage cannon-founders in Germany and even in Italy, and beg the Elector of Saxony to send him siege-guns and ammunition; he never could get enough ordnance together, and his artillerymen, of whom he only had seventy-three in 1580, shrank, in the following year, to twenty.

Taking it altogether, the King must have been a very brave man to face the struggle before him with the resources at his command. For this was no matter of fighting the Battle of Wenden over again, and carrying on deceptive hostilities within the borders of Livonia. In that country, worn out by fifteen years of incessant warfare, the ground crumbled beneath the feet of those who fought for it. It was a struggle between phantom armies for shadowy conquests. There was no possibility of winning any definite future advantage, nor even, in the long-run, of keeping up any campaign at all, in a desert sprinkled with ruins. As early as in 1562, Sigismund-Augustus had arrived at the conclusion that the key of the province must be sought elsewhere, and would only be found by attacking the chief competitor on his own hearthstone at Moscow. He had not succeeded in finding means to enable him to take these bold, offensive measures, but Batory had made up his mind to attempt them; and what he meditated was an invasion, a decisive struggle, a desperate game, in which the stakes were far to exceed the original object of the quarrel. This fight for Livonia was really a battle for the empire of the north-west, in which the hegemony of the Slav nations was to be lost or won.

Now for this enterprise, Poland could only reckon on her own efforts. Sweden had allied herself with her, but solely as far as Livonia was concerned, and within Livonian borders. All Sweden saw in Batory's new plan of campaign was an excuse for keeping herself free. She appealed to the letter of her treaty, and claimed to act independently. When Denmark was sounded, she declined; her relations with Ivan were growing pacific. The Khan offered his support, promised to have his Tartars on the move by the month of August, 1578, and ended by doing nothing at all. And when Batory confided his plans to the Grand Vizier, Mehemet-Sokolli, that illustrious warrior gave him a discouraging reply : ' The Tsar was a formidable foe, and nobody in the whole world, except the Sultan, was fit to measure swords with him.' For the Sultan, too, proposed to observe a strict neutrality. But the King, we may be sure, had foreseen all these disappointments, and made his calculations accordingly.

The point of attack had yet to be selected. The Lithuanians wanted to march on Pskov. Once there, the only road that connected the Russia of those days with the Baltic coast was cut. The way was barred, northward, by a series of lakes, and south-ward by marshes, rivers, and pathless forests. But before the army could get to Pskov it must either march right through Livonia, and thus deal the final blow to a country it had better spare, or make its way through Russian territory, leaving a ring of fortified places in its rear, and Lithuania without any protection at all. Batory decided to strike first at Polotsk. This town, on the banks of the Dvina, commanded, to some extent, the roads into Livonia and Lithuania. The place had been quite lately snatched from Poland, and thus might fairly lay claim to the King's first attention. He could go on to Pskov afterwards.

This point once settled, the great Hungarian worked wonders, as will be proved by the choice of Svir as his starting-point, which enabled him to conceal the object of his expedition till the very last moment ; by his skilful division of his forces on the roads leading to this trysting-place ; by his equally skilful flank movement from Svir to Disna, while continuing to screen Wilna and the parks of artillery with the main army ; and his ingenious utilization of rivers and boat bridges for his heavy transport. Specialists have objected that this method of acting on the enemy's lines of communication was not known in Europe till towards the close of the seventeenth century. That may be. But inventors of methods are frequently fore-stalled by men of action.

Yet Batory was not able to carry out his plan according to his original idea. The tryst at Svir had been fixed for May 4, 1579. But, in spite of all the King's energy, there were delays—money, supplies, troops, all fell short. And for this reason, too, the Russian envoys, who had been dragged from town to town and from one audience to another, were not dismissed till June, and not till then did a Polish courier carry the formal declaration of war to Moscow. A few days later Batory had opened his campaign. The army which crossed the Disna with him, on a bridge of boats put together in the space of three hours, numbered, as to the Polish contingent, 6,517 horsemen, 1,338 of whom were Germans or Hungarians ; 4,830 foot soldiers, 3,431 of these also being Germans or Hungarians ; and 4,000 Lithuanian cavalry, or thereabouts. Among the foreign officers was one George Farensbach, formerly a Colonel in the Danish service, and more recently a General in the Tsar's. His advice was probably most valuable. No more than 15,000 men in all, without reckoning for garrisons and reserves, proposed to invade the huge Empire of Muscovy and make it sue for mercy !

In the Polish camp the opening of the campaign partook of all the peculiarities of the European habits of that day. Before any powder was burnt, a very great deal of ink—even printers' ink—was spilt. Batory's declaration of war was preceded by a long historical exposition, crammed with dates, diplomatic texts, and epigrams. It did not forget Prous, the famous brother of Cæsar-Augustus, from whom Ivan claimed descent. A pamphlet published at Nuremberg in 1580, and of which very few copies now exist, contains, together with a very incorrect reproduction of this document, a vignette which shows Venceslas Lopacinski, the bearer of the message, in the act of performing his mission. The nobleman, a naked sword at his side, holds out the letter to the Tsar with a gesture of defiance. This picture is as unreliable as the letterpress accompanying it, which has lately been corrected by the Abbé Polkowski (*Acta Historica*, Cracow, 1887, xi. 162). Ivan never admitted Lopacinski to his presence, and Batory chiefly reckoned for the effect to be produced by his declaration on the publicity he ensured by having it printed in Polish, Hungarian, and German, in the presses he carried about with him during the whole course of his campaign. At Svir, where he arrived on July 15, 1579, the King issued another manifesto, no doubt intended, in his mind, to justify his undertaking, and conciliate public opinion both within and without the borders of the country.

Never, indeed, in any document of the kind, had the leader of an army given proof of such generous feeling. Batory promised to respect the persons, property, and privileges of non-belligerents ; he undertook to forbid and put down, as far as he himself was concerned, violence of every kind; nothing was lacking to the formula now grown so commonplace—as commonplace, alas ! as it is deceptive. At this period it was a novelty, one of which the Poland of the sixteenth century may well be proud. Never did the leader of an expedition betray greater eagerness to keep himself in mental touch with a sensitive and easily offended public. All future incidents of the campaign were to become the subjects of similar publications. The bibliography of that period contains a mass of pamphlets and printed matter, official or semi-official, dilating or commenting on the most insignificant episodes in the struggle. These literary efforts, which were sent into Poland and Germany, and even as far as Rome, where the King's envoy, Peter Dunin Wolski, Bishop of Polotsk, had them reprinted, were not remarkable for any very scrupulous adherence to historical accuracy. But it was essential to make head somehow or other against the German press, which was exceedingly eager to provide information for a public that was excessively greedy of news. One broadsheet (*Zeitung*), containing a report of one of Batory's victories, soon ran into four editions. To the paper warfare he so largely employed, the King added, after 1580, all the severities of a rigorous censure, and a German historian (Hausmann, *Studien zur Geschichte des König's Stephan*, Derpt, 1880, p. 34, etc.) has admitted that an edict then issued pronounced sentence of death on the authors and publishers of hostile works. This may well be, for even in 1576 the publication of a pamphlet at Cracow had been punished in this fashion, and in Germany the laws of the period were no more merciful.

I note these details because they seem to me indispensable to any faithful picture of the struggle under our consideration. It involved a conflict between two peoples which, though of the same race, nevertheless represented two different worlds set in opposition to each other, and the vari-coloured horde of soldiers from many lands, with its scribes and printers in attendance on it, was, in good sooth, the Latin West, working backwards, under the Slav banner, along the path of the great Oriental invasions. This victorious war may be looked on as Poland's last will and testament, and the story of it, for that reason, must present a certain interest.

In the present day the manifestoes of invading armies do not impose on our credulity. Batory was to be faithful to his. 'Never was any war conducted with greater moderation and more humanity as to labouring men and peaceful citizens.' This testimony in the King's favour is borne by the Russian historian Karamzine ('History of Russia,' ix., chap. v.). It is further proved by two other documents : by a circular addressed by Batory on May 4, 1580, to the nobility of the territory of Polotsk ; and, more especially, by the military regulations in force during the campaign. The circular amounted to a charter, ensuring the most precious immunity to the persons affected by it ; the regulations forbade the killing of children, old men, and Churchmen, the violating of women, and any destruction of, or damage to, crops, even for the purpose of feeding horses !

In spite of Russian excesses and of provocations acknowledged by Russian authorities, these regulations were faithfully observed. Karamzine speaks of a number of Polish prisoners who were put to death during the early days of the siege of Polotsk by the defenders of that town, and whose bodies were sent floating down the Dvina under the besiegers' very eyes ; but the Polish army set the world an example which might well have been a lesson to the most civilized nations of that period, and hardly ever indulged in reprisals. Provost-Marshals, endowed with far-reaching powers, kept up severe discipline in every rank. The King himself did not spare his own person, and set the best of examples in every way. He forbade all dissipation and all unnecessary luxury, frequently slept on a heap of dry leaves, ate his meals on a wooden trestle ' without a cloth,' and showed no mercy to marauders. At the same time, he strove to raise and keep up moral feeling among his men by appealing to the religious sentiment which was so strong in most of them. Even the passwords he gave them served this purpose. One day it would be ' Lord, forgive us our sins !' and another, ' God punishes the evil-doer !'

All this did not put a stop to certain practices usual, and considered indispensable, in those days, such as that of torturing prisoners to extract information from them. The extreme ardour of the Polish warriors, gentlemen and peasants alike, resulted, especially at the beginning of the war, in some excesses which nobody was able to prevent. Private troopers, riding their horses full gallop, would smash their lances against the walls of a besieged town. Such madmen were not always easy to restrain. The Hungarian infantry, skilled as it was in all siege work, and always first, not only on the breach, but when a chance of pillage offered, was often insubordinate. And between one battle and the next, the turbulent spirit of the *szlachta* often claimed its rights, and the army discussed the scope of the advantages already gained, and the conditions of the fresh effort demanded of it. But, on the whole, and considering the inherent cruelty of such sanguinary sports as these, at every period and in every country, the war, on the Polish side, was a noble war, and the annals of the sixteenth century have not registered its like in any other country.

Though the courage of the opposing forces was quite as great, the other features apparent in the hostile camp were very different.

IV.—The Russian Army.

If Batory's attempt to get help for his campaign from Sweden had failed, Ivan's at Vienna had met with no better success. Vainly had Kvachnine, whom he had despatched to Rudolph in 1578, striven to obtain the conclusion of the alliance

previously suggested to Maximilian. As a preliminary condition, the Emperor insisted on the acknowledgment of his
own suzerainty over Livonia! A similar failure awaited the
Tsar at the Court of the Khan, who demanded Astrakan and
a great deal of money into the bargain. At one moment Ivan
had reason to fear he was really going to have the Tartars on
his hands, as Batory would have desired. One of the King of
Poland's envoys, John Drohojowski, did his utmost, indeed, to
negotiate an alliance, in which the Khan would have been included, at Constantinople, but the Porte needed the Tartars
to keep the Persians down, and the Tsar and the King were left
face to face at last, alone and unallied. Still Ivan had not to
beg subsidies from a recalcitrant Diet, or appeal to the goodwill of his subjects to recruit his army. His Empire was his
own, with every soul and all the wealth within its borders.
When he heard the Poles had marched against him, he threw
garrisons into eighty towns on the Oka, the Volga, the Don,
and the Dnieper, and ordered the bulk of his forces to concen-
trate at Novgorod and Pskov.

As to the strength of these forces, the information at our disposal is contradictory in the extreme. Karamzine's reckoning,
notoriously exaggerated as to the Polish troops, concerning
which we are better informed, would appear to be equally
unreliable as to the strength of the Russians. With reference
to these, Fletcher, who is generally well posted, has accepted
a total of 300,000 men. But some writers, and amongst them
Biélaiév, have raised this figure to a million, and Karamzine's
view, according to which Ivan might have drowned the Polish
army at a word under the wave of Russians, loosed in resistless
flood upon Vilna and Warsaw, has thus acquired a new lease
of authority. Students of a later date, however, have shed
light on the great historian's blunder. According to the calculations of Monsieur Pavloff-Silvanski (' The Men who Served,'
p. 117, etc.), after the garrisons already mentioned had been
deducted, something like 10,000 warriors out of the 23,000
boïars, boïars' sons, and men belonging to the Court, on whom
he could originally reckon, remained at Ivan's disposal. Each
of these gentlemen was attended, on an average, by two armed
men on horseback, making 30,000 horsemen in all—or 31,596,
to give the author's exact figure; and there were 15,119
striéltsy and Cossacks, horse and foot, 6,461 Tartars, and 4,513
men of various arms, comprising a certain number of foreigners
—Dutchmen, Scots, Danes, and Greeks—57,689 men out of
the total of 110,000 which represented the whole fighting force
of the Empire. Forced labour, recruited in varying quantities
according to the necessities of each campaign, swelled the ranks
of the army very considerably. But these men were only avail-

able for camp and fortress duty, or for digging earthworks, and the Polish army was likewise attended by a very numerous train of similar auxiliaries. The proportion between the two sides, to sum it up, was as four to one, or very near it.

This left Ivan with a numerical superiority large enough to impart an appearance of recklessness to Batory's undertaking. But it was an appearance and nothing more. Some historians, swayed by Kourbski's assertions, have supposed the Tsar to have suffered painfully, at this juncture, from the lack of the better military leaders, of whom the *Opritchnina* had deprived him. The consequences of the great political, social, and economic crisis through which the country had just passed are clearly recognisable in the incidents and the issue of this decisive struggle, but this particular interpretation of them cannot be accepted. The best leader Ivan had employed since his accession was Peter Chouïski, and he did not make a very brilliant show under the walls of Orcha. The country, worn out and sore, was to prove itself incapable of any prolonged effort, but as far as the preliminaries of a campaign were concerned, the *Opritchnina* left the machinery of war intact. Yet here we see, save for the artillery and a few hundreds of foreign soldiers and officers, face to face with Batory's *European* army the ancient fighting-machine of Muscovy, the insufficiency of which Ivan had already proved against the Swedes, and against the Poles themselves, indeed—an agglomeration of armed men whose personal valour, and powers of endurance and of heroic devotion, in officers and men alike, could not make up for its inferior equipment, its want of discipline—or of drill, at all events—and the shortcomings of its leaders.

Ivan's very clear realization of the causes of this weakness influenced his decision at this critical moment as much as his own natural temperament. I have already shown that he was no soldier. Whatever the condition of affairs, the idea of checking the invasion by facing Batory at the head of his boïars cannot have occurred to him. Such a thing had never been seen in Muscovy since the far-distant and legendary days of Dmitri Donskoï ; and when another horde of Tartars had threatened the capital, the son of the national hero himself had fled to Kostroma. This was the traditional line of conduct, and on this particular occasion especially, the Tsar was bound to follow it faithfully ; the *Opritchnina* had not robbed him of his army, but if he led out that army to meet Batory and his Poles and Hungarians in the open, he might make up his mind beforehand to a beating.

And, further, Ivan was completely taken in, at first, as to his adversary's plans ; he thought his blow would be struck, as in past days, at Livonia. Thus, when he reached Novgorod in

July, 1579, he detached a few thousand of his Asiatic cavalry, with orders to receive the enemy's first attack, and these troops, encountering no resistance whatsoever, contented themselves with a repetition of Schah-Ali's exploits; while Batory, leaving the wretched province to its fate, and contenting himself with some mere precautionary measures for the protection of his army on that side, marched straight on Polotsk. By the time the real state of affairs was known in the Russian camp it was too late to provide for the defence of the town. As for barring the Poles' onward progress, such a notion never entered Ivan's head at all. In the most deliberate manner he dispersed his forces, sent one army corps to fight the Swedes under Fellin, another under the walls of Ostrov, ordered Princes Lykov and Paletski to succour Polotsk—though he foresaw they would have to content themselves with harrying the enemy and intercepting food convoys—and made up his mind to a system of flabby defence, interspersed with attempts at diplomacy. And to this system he was to adhere. He hoped, no doubt, to wear the Poles down by a war of sieges, in which Russian obstinacy and the Russian artillery were both likely to serve him well.

And it was a war of sieges, indeed, that Batory had to face, as he had foreseen. But his genius and his luck were to bring the Tsar's strategy and diplomacy to nought.

V.—THE CAPTURE OF POLOTSK.

The siege of Polotsk began early in August, 1579. The garrison behaved with great bravery ; the artillery, 107 guns, kept the Poles at bay for a considerable time. But after three weeks, when no succour came, the town was forced to surrender. The Bishop, Cyprian, refused to acknowledge the capitulation, shut himself up, with a certain number of boïars, in the Church of St. Sophia, and it became necessary to reduce them by force. This incident proves how desperate the resistance was. The booty found in this church, believed to be full of treasure, and all over the town, fell far short of the victors' hopes and expectations. The most precious thing they found was a library containing great numbers of chronicles and Slav translations of the Fathers of the Church, and this was burnt. Nevertheless, the capture of the place was a great success for the Poles, and Batory at once proceeded further on his way. He took Sokol, where a terrible massacre occurred, and occupied several forts in the neighbourhood, while Prince Constantine Ostrogski ravaged the province of Siéviéia right up to Starodoub, and Kmita, *Starost* of Orcha, treated the province of Smolensk in similar fashion. Ivan left them to do their will.

The Tsar took to flight. Hastily leaving Novgorod, he betook himself to Pskov, and from that place, like a true Oriental, to save his own face, and decoy the opposite side into negotiating, he opened a correspondence with the chief Lithuanian nobles —Radziwill, Palatine of Vilna, and Wolowicz, Chancellor of Lithuania. He had been prevented, he said, from sending succour to Polotsk, and was still prevented from retaking the town by force of arms, by the entreaties of his boïars, who were bent on putting a stop to the effusion of Christian blood ; wherefore he trusted Radziwill and Wolowicz, inspired by the same feelings, would use their best endeavours to have peace restored.

The reception these overtures obtained may be easily imagined. But the year was drawing to a close, and Batory was not disinclined to accept the semblance of a diplomatic interlude, until the opening of the next campaign, for which he had to make fresh preparations. Lopacinski, the bearer of his declaration of war, had been detained at Moscow ; the King demanded his liberation, and Ivan received the victor's messenger, a mere courier, with the greatest civility, and invited him to his own table. Lopacinski was set free, of course ; but the Tsar, who did not quite relinquish all his pretensions, expressed a wish to receive a Polish embassy to discuss conditions of peace. The nature of Batory's reply may be easily conceived. He was not the person, now, who could be expected to send ambassadors.

Disconcerted, Ivan fell back on Vienna, whither he sent Athanasius Rezanov with a fresh and more pressing appeal. But he did not show any touch of humility, as yet, in that quarter ; for his envoy was told that if the Emperor invited him to his own table he was to refuse any place except the foremost, even if he found himself in the company of the representatives of the French King or the Sultan ! And if anybody asked him how the King of Poland had been able to take Polotsk, he was to reply, ' By a surprise, and by violating a three years' truce which he had signed.' Rezanov reached his destination in March, 1580, and was dismissed, as all his predecessors had been. Batory was so well able to stir up revolution in Hungary that the Emperor did not care to disoblige him. And, besides, he swayed Vienna through Rome, and Rome through the Jesuits. After the capture of Polotsk, the Pope had sent the King a sword and lance, which he had solemnly blessed at Mass on Christmas Day, and which were to be ceremoniously presented to him. All Rezanov could get was civil talk. The Viennese authorities thought Batory's money would soon begin to fail. ' He won't be able to feed his soldiers with his Hungarian lice !' said Count Kinski scornfully.

Ivan realized he must lower his tone to Poland. He sent one courier after another to Warsaw, and appeared disposed, at last, to take the initiative, in order to prevent a second campaign, if Batory really intended to undertake another. His couriers were actually told they need not remonstrate if the King did not stand up when he inquired after the Tsar's health! Batory gave the messengers of peace a friendly reception, but continued to hurry forward his preparations. When June came, he gave the Tsar five weeks in which to send him an embassy; otherwise, he said, 'he would mount his horse'; and Ivan, 'noting his neighbour's condescension in satisfying his demands,' as he put it in his instructions, despatched the embassy forthwith. Before it had got halfway, with its huge suite of 500 persons, its leaders learnt there was nothing more for them to do at Warsaw. The King of Poland had 'mounted his horse,' and, followed by his troops, had just started forth from Vilna.

VI.—The Poles in Muscovy.

The capture of Polotsk had made no real breach in the Muscovite Empire. That was a mere taking back of what had once been a Polish possession. It was only now that Batory and his army were really to plunge into the heart of the enemy's country. In the Polish camp opinion was divided, as it had been at the opening of the previous campaign. Some wanted to march from Czasniki, the new point of concentration, half-way between Smolensk and Viélikié-Louki, straight on Smolensk, while others desired to move on Pskov. Batory decided to strike at Viélikié-Louki, a fortress standing in the midst of a rich and populous country, used by the Russians as a storehouse for their war material, and the usual base of their operations against Lithuania.

The invading army, reinforced by the infantry recruited on the royal properties, the organization of which had been somewhat delayed, was a little stronger, numerically speaking, than it had been in the previous year. Its effective strength now amounted to about 17,500 men, 8,321 of whom were Polish or Hungarian infantry, and a Lithuanian contingent which may be reckoned at about 10,000 men. The march to Viélikié-Louki was a severe one. To avoid crossing the Dvina under the guns of Viélije, another fortress in the same region, the Poles cut their way through thick forests, and split up their forces to such an extent that one corps of 6,000 men completely lost contact with the main body of the troops. The foolhardiness of this operation has been criticised, but its boldness would seem justified by the remoteness of the Muscovite

forces, which were concentrated at Novgorod, Pskov, and
Smolensk, far from the theatre of war, while the body of troops
which adventured itself alone was commanded by the new
leader of the Polish contingent, in whose person Batory had
unexpectedly discovered the best of all his lieutenants. This
leader's name was John Zamoyski, and he had succeeded a man
of the old school, Nicholas Mieleçki, who, during the previous
campaign, had been more distinguished by his bravery than by
his military talent. Zamoyski, who was more of the statesman
than the warrior, and a former warden of Padua, did not at first
appear destined to eclipse him. His conduct was a revelation.
While the King carried Ousviat, as he marched along, Zamoyski, by a skilful manœuvre, turned the defences of Viélije, took
possession of that town, and joined the main army close to
Viélikié-Louki.

Here the Poles found a surprise awaiting them. The Muscovite embassy had arrived. For awhile, Ivan had hesitated as
to the course he should pursue. To send it marching after the
invading army was a cruel humiliation. After the fall of
Viélije, the Tsar summoned one of those assemblies, the story
of which I have already told (p. 133, etc.); and as it decided in
favour of a desperate resistance, he commanded his Ambassadors, Prince Ivan Sitski, Roman Mikhaïlovitch Pivov, and
Thomas Palentiélev, to retrace their steps. But very soon the
emissaries sent out to reconnoitre brought back alarming news.
'The Poles were as thick as plant-lice.' And again Ivan made
up his mind to treat, though he gave his envoys fresh instructions, which proved him more ready to defend himself on the
field of diplomacy than on the battlefield. He offered
Batory Courland, which had never belonged to Russia, and
sixty-five Livonian towns, skilfully chosen, thirty-five others
to remain in his own hands. Sitski and Pivov began by demanding that the siege of Viélikié-Louki should be instantly
raised, and they themselves received *on Polish ground :* for
no Tsar had ever consented to treat on his own territory.
They received a rather rough reply, and consented to enter
on their business without further preliminary. But Batory
demanded the whole of Livonia, with Viélikié-Louki and
Smolensk as well. The negotiations hung fire, and while the
Russian envoys were referring back to the Tsar, Zamoyski
was pressing the town hard. Its ramparts, like those of most
Muscovite fortresses, were only built of wood—a double range
of heavy boards, filled in with soil, which resisted the red-hot
balls. And the Polish artillery, weak and badly handled, was
quite unable to silence the heavy fire kept up by the besieged.
But one fine day a Mazovian peasant set fire to one of the
towers at the risk of his own life, and the garrison offered to

capitulate. Conditions were actually under discussion, but the Hungarians could not wait. They and their leader, Gaspard Bekiesz, an old political rival of Batory's, always showed an impetuosity as exaggerated as their want of discipline was excessive. Fancying the booty on which they had been reckoning was about to slip through their fingers, or that the lion's share would go to the Poles, they threw themselves upon the town, and in the wild mêlée that ensued nothing was spared. Even monks carrying crosses and ikons in procession were murdered, though Zamoyski vainly strove to restore order. He only succeeded in saving two *voiévodes*.

As a consequence, the whole of that country lay at the victor's mercy. Prince Khilkov, who had been holding it with a strong detachment of troops, was beaten by the Polish, Hungarian, and German cavalry, under Prince Zbaraski. The town of Nevel was set on fire, and capitulated, and the Poles did not prove over-scrupulous in their observation of the conditions they themselves had granted. In the European warfare of that period this was a pretty general rule. On most occasions, pretexts for neglecting engagements were discovered. Oziérichtche fell almost without a struggle. Zavolotché, better protected by the fact that the waters of the Lake of Podsoch very nearly transformed it into a fortified island, withstood the first assault. A bridge broke down under the besiegers' feet, and the *szlachta* had already begun to talk of beating a retreat, for its members wanted to get home for Christmas. But Zamoyski, proving himself as cunning a diplomatist as he was a capable leader of troops, induced his Poles and Hungarians to vie with each other on the two bridges he built to replace the broken one. Religious feeling entered into this. Volunteers who had just received the Holy Communion and listened to an appropriate sermon, offered their services to lead the attack, and on October 23, 1580, the town was taken. According to a Polish chronicler, the Muscovite *voiévodes*, who had been obstinately determined to hold out, were forced into capitulation by a mutiny amongst the garrison.

A single success achieved by one of the Tsar's lieutenants, Ivan Mikhaïlovitch Boutourline, did not compensate for all these disasters. This Muscovite leader surprised the titular Khan of Smolensk, Filon Kmita, on the Lithuanian frontier, surrounded him with a superior force, killed 700 of his men, and took all his artillery—ten guns. But, notwithstanding this, the whole of one large province of Russia was in the hands of the Poles, and when these returned to their winter quarters the Lithuanians carried on the campaign, seized Kholm, burnt Staraïa-Roussa, and even forced their way into Livonia, where they took possession of the castle of Smilten, and, with Magnus' help, ravaged the province of Derpt right up to the Muscovite frontier.

The Swedes, on their side, did not stand idle. In November, 1580, Pontus de la Gardie had made a raid into Carelia, and taken Kexholm, at which place, so the Livonian chroniclers declare, 2,000 Russians met their death. Another body of Swedish troops besieged Padis, some six leagues from Revel, and after thirteen weeks of the most desperate resistance, in the course of which the besieged, commanded by their *voiévode* Tchikhatchev, devoured hides, straw, and even, as it has been believed, human flesh, the town was carried by assault. Then came the turn of Livonia, where Pontus de la Gardie suddenly appeared in the spring of 1581, and shortly captured Wesemberg. Thus was a third robber making himself ready to snatch the conquest which had already brought his foes halfway on their victorious road to his capital, from the Tsar's grasp.

And meanwhile Batory, to whom, in February, 1581, the Diet had granted fresh subsidies for another two years, was preparing for his third campaign. With the prestige he had now acquired, with the experience he had gained, and his seasoned army, hot with the glory of so many triumphs—whither would he not go ? And on his heels another army followed : the Jesuits, who were carrying on a religious campaign, of which the effects were already felt in the Russo-Lithuanian countries, and even in Livonia. Since 1576, Batory, who favoured these efforts, had been hoping, thus aided, to break the links that bound these countries to Orthodox Russia or Protestant Germany, and at Vilna the Fathers had been able to celebrate the conversion of eighty Lutherans and fifty catechumens of the Greek rite (Lubkovitch, ' Contributions to the History of the Jesuits in the Russo-Lithuanian Countries,' Warsaw, 1888 ; in Russian).

The aims of this endeavour were far distant, and its nature was most wide-embracing. The triumphant current of Catholicism was to flow across Livonia and so reach Sweden, where, thanks to Catherine Jagellon, Rome had once more gained a footing. When the ground lost there had been recovered, the Reformation was to be shut up and stifled within a hostile circle, and Muscovy, once vanquished, was to undergo recapture by victorious Rome. And thus, under the hero she had chosen to be her leader, and by the victories which contemporary nations already took to be *a sign from God*, the foremost of the Slav races of that day was to solve the twofold problem, political and religious, on which the future of the North-West of Europe hung, and there was to be an end of the ' third Rome ' and all the ambitious hopes therewith connected.

Ivan must have felt all this, no doubt, and must have felt

also how powerless he was to avert the danger by force of arms. The ring of fortresses within which he had fancied himself safe was broken. Slowly but surely the tide of invasion was advancing. After Viélikié-Louki, Novgorod and Pskov would open their gates. And the Tsar was less than ever able to think of pitting his ill-equipped, badly-drilled, armed bands, so utterly deficient in cohesion, against these formidable troops, before whom even fortresses could make no stand. The only refuge left him was diplomacy.

VII.—THE DIPLOMATIC INTERLUDE.

By the month of September, 1580, without even waiting for Rezanov's return, Ivan made up his mind to appeal from Vienna to Rome. His new envoy, Istoma Chevriguine, was ordered to solicit the Pope's intervention, and to represent ' Batoura ' —Ivan, a little out of ignorance and a little out of scorn, continued to deform the King's name after this fashion—as being the Sultan's ally. But this effort could not take effect as rapidly as the necessity of the case demanded ; wherefore the Tsar's Ambassadors, multiplying their concessions and swallowing the most painful insults in the process, continued to allow the victor to drag them in his train. They had been ordered, in January, 1581, to Warsaw, where, having added a fresh list of Livonian towns to those they had already offered Poland, they flattered themselves they were about to obtain a truce and the preliminaries of a peace. But the answer they were given was, ' The whole of Livonia, or war !' In their report they note the fact of their having been forced by threats and abuse to kiss the hand of the King, who, this time again, when the Tsar's name was pronounced in his presence, had not risen to his feet, nor even desired them to greet the Sovereign in his name, and they had been obliged to depart empty-handed.

Ivan realized that he must give in. He was to bow before Fate, and to bend his back lower and lower. He wrote a mighty humble letter to ' Batoura,' in which—and for the first time—he addressed the King as ' brother,' and announced the departure of another embassy. The envoys, Evstafii Mikhaïlovitch Pouchkine, Feodor Andréiévitch Pissemski, and Andrew Trofinov, were ordered to endure every kind of ill-treatment, and even blows, without complaint. The Tsar had come to that ! And he now offered Poland the whole of Livonia, except four towns. He would even give up his title ; but he could not refrain from mingling some bitter with all this sweet, and seasoning his final concession with an epigram. The Ambassadors were further to say that, in spite of all, their

Sovereign was 'not a Sovereign of yesterday.' If they were
asked what they meant, they were to reply, ' The Sovereign
who is that knows himself !'

Ivan's cleverness was one of the most dangerous factors in
his character, and he was quite capable of sacrificing a province
to a sally, and then patching up the damage by some fresh
sacrifice of his dignity, which he always fancied himself to be
protecting after this fashion.

So eagerly did he hurry forward his envoys' departure that
they reached Vilna, where Batory had desired them to meet
him, long before the appointed date. In spite of all apparent
probabilities, the Tsar still hoped to prevent any resumption
of hostilities. But, in the King of Poland's mind, Vilna was
but one stage on the road of the new conquests he was meditating. When he reached that town, in May, the Russian
Ambassadors heard him demand, not Livonia only, but Novgorod, Pskov, Smolensk, the whole of Siév#ria, and a war
indemnity of 400,000 ducats ! When Pouchkine and his
comrades sent a messenger to Moscow to ask for orders,
Batory had him accompanied by a courier of his own, Dzierzek by name, who conveyed an ultimatum which reduced his
claims to some extent, but still insisted on Livonia and the
indemnity, though he limited his further demands to the
razing of certain frontier fortresses. And the Polish King
would only wait for his answer till June 4.

At that moment Chévriguine's mission was already producing
some preliminary effect. I shall show, a little further on, how
the Pope had yielded to the charm of the idea of a mediation,
which, even if completely successful, could not have made up,
from the Catholic point of view, for the advantages likely to
accrue from Poland's decisive triumph. The appointed
mediator, a Jesuit named Possevino, was actually at Vilna,
and the fact of his presence there was infinitely useful to Ivan.
Roma locuta erat. If the Holy See pronounced against the
continuance of the war, Poland's onward progress would
be checked, and stopped outright, if she persevered, by the
thunders of the Vatican. The Tsar fancied so, at all events,
and, recovering himself at once, he treated Dzierzek much
as Batory· had treated his own Ambassadors, and sent his
courier back with a letter for the King beginning thus :
' We, Ivan Vassilévitch, the humble, Tsar and Grand-Duke of
Russia . . . by the grace of God, and not by the turbulent will
of man. . . .' This opening phrase will enable my readers to
guess the rest for themselves. In Kojalowicz's edition the
document covers three-and-twenty printed pages. After para-
phrasing the Psalms of David after a fashion of his own, calling Batory an Amalek, a Sennacherib, a Maxentius, greedy of

bloodshed, and declaring that unless peace was made forthwith
he would send no Ambassador into Poland, nor receive any from
that country, for the next thirty or forty years, Ivan rejected
the ultimatum in every particular. And more : he retracted
his previous concessions, and refused to be satisfied with only
four Livonian towns. He must keep six-and-thirty—Narva
and Derpt among the number—and would only give up
Viélikié-Louki and twenty-four small fortified places in the
neighbourhood. This was his ' final calculation.'

He was labouring under some illusion as to Possevino's
power. When his letter, and the instructions he sent with it,
arrived at Vilna, Batory was not there. The King had
already reached Polotsk, and was preparing to march out his
army. The Jesuit and the Muscovite envoys followed him,
and the Papal envoy did his best to mediate. But Pouchkine
and Pissemski were as intractable now as they had lately been
docile and conciliatory. When Possevino inquired why the
Tsar had altered his proposals, ' The New Testament wipes out
the Old,' was Pouchkine's scornful answer ; ' the King of
Poland had refused the Tsar's first offers, and the Tsar was now
making others, and would add nothing more—not that !' he
added, and twisted a bit of straw in his fingers as he spoke.
Batory, on his side, was in no humour for more negotiations.
He must, no doubt, show some consideration for the Papal
mediation ; so he undertook to tell Possevino he would give
up the indemnity and the destruction of the strong places.
But he certainly never expected the Russians to take him at
his word. As a matter of fact, Ivan's Ambassadors turned a
deaf ear, and the King, hurrying forward the date of their farewell audience, told them he was going to set forth without
more delay, and make war—' not to take Livonia, but everything their master owned.' The Jesuit perceived he would gain
nothing here by insistence. He announced his intention of
proceeding to the Tsar's Court, in the hope of bringing him
back to a better state of mind, and Batory wished him a
pleasant journey. But the Polish army was already on its
march.

Batory would even have left Ivan's last letter unanswered
altogether, but the King's counsellors did not wish the German
and Polish gazettes to remain under the impression produced
by the insults it had contained. The effusion of ink and blood
had been simultaneous up to this, and the same course must be
pursued. The royal Chancery was set desperately to work,
and evolved an epistle numbering forty pages—so that the
insulter might have full measure—which reminded him that
his mother had been the daughter of a mere Lithuanian
deserter, and attacked his own public and private life,

denouncing both his debauchery and his bloodshed. The Tsar had reproached the King with seeking to ally himself with the Sultan. To this Batory triumphantly opposed Ivan's marriage with a Moslem woman—the Temrioukovna Tsarina— and the customs of his ancestors, ' who licked the mares' milk off the Tartar horses' manes.' His reluctance to making any personal appearance on the battlefield was not forgotten, and that was a fair hit. ' A hen defends her chicks against the hawk and the eagle, but thou, a two-headed eagle, hidest thy head !' This last apostrophe was followed by a challenge to single combat, which my readers may think ridiculous ; but such a proposal is quite within the precedents of that period. In 1561, Erik XIV. sent a similar challenge to Dudley, whom he regarded as his rival with Queen Elizabeth. And nobody expected the Tsar to take up the glove.

He never thought of it for an instant, and was more than ever driven to ' hide himself.' His treasury was empty, his country worn out, his boïars demoralized, and all his resources exhausted. At one moment, so the chroniclers assure us, there were not more than 300 men with him at Staritsa. Yet, convinced that Batory's next blow would be struck at Pskov, he contrived to throw a strong garrison, the flower of his troops, into that town. It was well provisioned and supplied with powerful artillery. The Tsar could rely on its keeping back the Poles for a considerable time, and under the walls of the town, even if no relieving army was there to confront him, Batory would meet Moscow's most formidable ally in every one of her wars of defence : winter was close at hand. Possevino had not been in time to stop the King's departure, but the King's campaign had been begun too late.

VIII.—The Siege of Pskov.

He had been obliged to spend the whole spring parleying with his Diet. ' The King has given all he can out of his own pocket,' cried Zamoyski to the deputies. ' What more do you expect of him ? Would you have him flay himself alive ? He would do it readily enough, if any alchemist had discovered the secret of making gold out of human skin !' When he had contrived to squeeze out subsidies for another year, and that only on condition that the war was brought to an end, the collection of the taxes voted was very much delayed. The King pawned the crown jewels, got 50,000 crowns from the Duke of Anspach, and as much from the Elector of Brandenburg, and started. But at Disna a fresh hitch occurred. The troops were as slow about coming in as the taxes had been.

21

And meanwhile the King was informed that a body of Russian troops which had been collected at Mojaïsk had made a raid into Lithuania towards Smolensk, burnt two thousand villages, laid a whole province waste from Orcha to Mohylev, and carried away the entire population, peasants and nobles alike, to the further bank of the Dnieper. It was not till July 15, and then by travelling sixteen leagues a day, that Batory reached Polotsk, where he reviewed his army ; and on the 29th he arrived at Zavolotché, and there held a council. So far was the season advanced that it was difficult to know what course should be pursued. There had been an idea of attacking Novgorod. But, as Ivan had foreseen, the choice fell on Pskov, which was nearer. And even so, it was clear the town would not surrender before the cold weather came. Batory's correspondence proves him to have resolutely accepted the contingency of a winter campaign, in the course of which either Pskov would be taken or Ivan forced to make peace. To retain possession of Pskov, the Tsar would give up Livonia, and, owing to the intervention of Rome and the attitude taken up by the Diet, the King was fain to ask no more, and go no further, for the present.

On August 25 the Poles, who had carried the town of Ostrov as they marched along, arrived under the walls of Pskov. They were struck by the size of the town and its imposing appearance. ' It is like another Paris,' wrote the Secretary of the King's Chancery, Piotrowski, in his diary, which has come down to us. This observation is repeated, word for word, in the ' Memoirs ' of Müller, another eye-witness. Pskov, which had been in a state of defence, and kept constantly fortified, for hundreds of years, on account of the proximity of the Germans, possessed stone ramparts, to which a strong surrounding palisade had recently been added. Within the walls two Princes of the Chouïski family, Vassili Feodorovitch and Ivan Petrovitch—the last-named a grandson of the Regent, with whom we made acquaintance during Ivan's minority— both of them brave and experienced men, commanded 30,000 troops, according to Russian authorities, or 40,000, according to the Poles. Both calculations are certainly excessive as regards the effective force available, and properly so-called, and as certainly below the mark. if we reckon the ' eaters of bread,' as Rodolfini, a Venetian who served as a Colonel in the Polish army, denominated the serving-men and labourers who followed in its train, and some of whom, at all events, were capable of using firearms in a moment of need. He reckoned the total of these at 170,000 men. A considerable number of these must also have been attached to the garrison of Pskov, but the information we possess as to that period is quite devoid

of the accuracy of our modern statistics. As to the Polish
army, more exact data can be had from the Treasury accounts,
which I have already consulted. They give us 21,102 men,
about half of them infantry—or only 18,940, according to
another calculation—as having been under Batory's orders,
together with some 10,000 Lithuanians.

It was a small army to undertake the siege of a town 'like
Paris.' Heidenstein, the official historian of the campaign (on
the Polish side) does mention the 24,000 splendid horses that
defiled before the astonished eyes of the natives of the town.
But he must have seen double, just as Ivan saw triple, and
more, when he complained that ' Batoura ' had armed ' all
Italy against him.' At the date mentioned by Heidenstein
there were only 6,469 Polish and 674 Hungarian cavalry in
Batory's camp, and all Italy had sent him was a few engineers,
just as France had sent him one or two officers, like that
Captain Garon of whom Piotrowski tells us, ' a little man, a
good musician, and very brave,' who went, ' dear frog !' and
measured the town ditches with his sword. A Gascon this, no
doubt—a valiant soldier, we may be sure !

But he could not suffice to capture a first-class fortress
which seemed resolved on a desperate resistance. We may
even doubt, considering the means Batory had at his disposal,
whether he really proposed to lay a regular siege. His artillery
did not reach a total of more than twenty guns, and his
supply of powder was to fail after the very first week. The
King probably reckoned on his cavalry to enable him to cut the
town off, and so reduce it by hunger. But he himself was no
better prepared for a winter before the walls of Pskov. He
had been obliged to spare the nerves of his army, which would
have taken fright at the sight of the necessary supplies, the
tents and the provisions. And lack of money had combined
with the lateness of the date on which he had begun his campaign to upset his plans and throw his calculations out. The
game in which he had risked his stake was a most dangerous
one, indeed. But his own genius and the forward impulse
imparted by his previous successes were strong chances in his
favour, and were destined, in fact, to decide the issue of the
struggle.

It is not easy to reconstitute the history of this struggle, even,
and perhaps especially, from that *moral* point of view in which
its chief interest resides. The Russian and Polish authorities,
though they agree as to its details, are in perpetual disagreement as to its essence, as to the attitude of the combatant
parties, and the general features of their battles. While one
side declares a most important part was played by the sorties
made by the besieged, the other asserts that the garrison was

not nearly so enterprising, and always hung nervously back under the cover of its own guns. On the other hand, Polish documents lay stress on the constant and effectual work performed by small detachments of Russian troops, which scoured the whole country, worried the besiegers, and interfered with their convoy service. On the Russian side, we are told the population of Pskov was as enthusiastic as its defenders were brave, that it backed them up in all their endeavours, and agreed with them that the town must resist to the bitter end. Another version comes to us from Polish authorities. Nothing but the energy displayed by the Chouïski prevented the *tchern* (common people) from bringing about a comparatively early capitulation.

As to this last point, we have what would appear decisive testimony from a Russian source. When the two Chouïski were appointed to their joint command, the Tsar made them accompany him to the Church of the Assumption, and there take an oath to defend the town to the last extremity. Several times over they were obliged to make the inhabitants of Pskov take the same oath. This proves the population was not of itself very strongly inclined to hold out. It must be added that the most important Polish document dealing with this episode in our possession, the Abbé Piotrowski's journal, is the production of a malcontent, embittered by the length of the war and the weariness of a winter campaign. Even at Polotsk he had thought Batory was asking too much, and that the war ought to have ended then, without further parley. ' Everybody was tired of it.' At Pskov, naturally, everything was wrong, in his eyes, and as the siege dragged on he grew more and more inclined to exaggerate the suffering on both sides.

The undoubted fact is that the Poles' first attack, on September 8, 1581, was valiantly repulsed by the Russians, who inflicted cruel loss upon their adversaries. Gabriel Bekiesz, brother of the intrepid leader of the Hungarian cavalry, who had himself succumbed to the fatigue endured in the course of the previous campaign, lost his life on this occasion. And it was long before the attempt could be renewed. The Poles' supply of ammunition was already insufficient, and now a powder magazine at Susza exploded. More powder had to be fetched from Riga, and Batory had ample time to study the art of war as expounded in the book by Count Reinhardt von Solms, sent him by the grandson of Charles V.'s illustrious Marshal, while the besieged rained insults on the besiegers: ' Why don't you shoot ? There is no common-sense in trying to take a town when you can't make your guns talk ! You'll gain nothing if you sit looking at our ramparts for the next two years !'

When the end of October came, cold and fever were deci-
mating the ranks of the Polish army. There were not more
than forty horses in any squadron, so Piotrowski tells us, and
the Lithuanians were beginning to talk of taking their departure. Batory had to call their leaders together and harangue
them. Things grew worse when the King thought it his
duty to proceed to Warsaw to persuade the Diet to make
another effort. A fresh assault, delivered on November 3,
after the expected convoy from Riga had arrived, was no more
successful than the first ; the guns were dismounted from the
batteries, and peace awaited more confidently than ever. The
chief command was now in the hands of Zamoyski, and the
most recent Polish historians have delighted to exalt his merits
to the detriment of the 'Maygar King.' But would he have
succeeded in keeping his army together, and inducing it to
face the cruel trials of this siege, if he had not been backed by
a Sovereign whose temperament and grip were known to all ?
It is more than doubtful. Without Davout and Lannes,
Masséna and Ney, Napoleon would probably have failed to win
most of his battles, and it was when he was left with Grouchy
that the end came at Waterloo. And all Zamoyski did was to
carry out a plan which nobody ascribes to anyone but Batory,
and which, in the long-run, was to prove the best possible under
the circumstances. The men of Pskov were to be convinced,
at last, that a town may be taken 'by looking at it'! The
Poles did not fire their guns, but they kept their lines intact,
and stopped all communication between the fortress and the
outer world, and the supply of provisions Ivan had brought
together was not inexhaustible.

Meanwhile, in Livonia, into which country Ivan was now
powerless to send a single man, the Swedes were pursuing their
victorious career. Poland had now more reason to fear these
too independent allies of hers than to hope much from their
help. Yet they struck hard blows at the common foe. In the
course of the summer Horn and Pontus, at first acting independently, and then in unison, carried Lode, Fickel, and Hapsal,
and in September they laid siege to Narva. The German town
capitulated, after a siege which, according to the Livonian
chroniclers, cost 7,000 lives, and ,the Russian town was
surrendered by Athanasius Biélski. By the end of November all the coasts of the Gulf of Finland were in the hands of
the Swedes, who succeeded in capturing the English ships that
were bringing war supplies to Ivan. De la Gardie threatened
Pernau, Derpt, and Fellin, and was on the point of taking
possession of the last ramparts of the Muscovite conquest in
that country.

These triumphs produced their natural effect at Pskov, by

strengthening the pacific inclinations to which both sides were beginning to lean. At the close of November the besiegers' courage was warmed by an intercepted message from Chouïski to the Tsar. According to its tenor, the town, which was starving, could not hold out much longer unless help was sent. A few days later, indeed, two boïars of the garrison, who had been captured by the Poles, told quite a different tale. The besieged, they said, had plenty of bread and of everything else, except meat. But at that moment Batory's plenipotentiaries were actually starting to meet Ivan's envoys at Iam-Zapolski, and there, under Possevino's mediation, to treat for peace.

The part played by the Pope's Legate in this business has been viewed in various ways. To shed light on the controversy, I must go back to the origin of a mission which, from a more general point of view, marks an epoch in the diplomatic relations between Rome and Moscow.

CHAPTER II

THE LOSS OF LIVONIA—ROME AND MOSCOW

I.—CHÉVRIGUINE'S MISSION.   II.—THE PAPAL MEDIATION.   III. —THE TRUCE OF IAM-ZAPOLSKI.   IV.—POSSEVINO AT MOSCOW. V.—THE DAY AFTER THE TRUCE.

I.—CHÉVRIGUINE'S MISSION.

THE despatch of Chévriguine to Rome was an unprecedented event. Advances, up to that time, had always come from the Papal Court, and Poland had always interposed, and brought every attempt to nought, while Venice, to whose interest it was that commercial relations with Muscovy should be opened, vainly strove against the opposition of a watchful and suspicious diplomatic system. Batory's predecessor had stopped Pius IV.'s emissaries—Canobio, Giraldi, and Bonifaccio—on their way.

In 1570, Pope Pius V.'s Nuncio in Poland, Vincenzo del Portico, had endeavoured to mediate between Ivan and Sigismund-Augustus, with a view to forming a league against the Turks. But Ivan's envoy at Constantinople was at that very moment representing his master as exceedingly well disposed towards the Sultan. This fact became known at Rome, and the perusal of a memorandum drawn up by Albert Schlichting, a soldier of Prussian origin, who had escaped from a Moscow prison after a detention lasting seven years, still further contributed to chill the Sovereign Pontiff's ardour. In 1576 a fresh attempt was made. The Pope's Nuncio, Laureo, driven out of Poland by the double election of Batory and Maximilian, conferred on German soil with the two Russian envoys, Sougorski and Artsybachev. The new Legate at the Emperor's Court, Cardinal Morone, had a hand in this negotiation, and, duly authorized by Gregory XIII., chose Rudolph Clenke, a man of learning, gifted with a strong constitution and an adventurous spirit, to bring about the long-wished-for agreement. But Poland was on the watch, and at the very last moment Maximilian objected to the departure of the chosen representative. In 1575, too, during Batory's first campaign, Laureo's successor, Caligari, renewed Portico's attempt, but with no better success.

Now it was the Tsar who took the first step. He deputed Leonti Istoma Chévriguine, known to foreigners as Thomas Severingen, to propose that very league against the Turks on which the Roman calculations, half political, half religious, were all based, and to set forth the preliminary condition he demanded. This condition was that the King of Poland should be advised, and if necessary forced, to make peace. On his way through Prague, where the Emperor gave him a somewhat chilly reception, Chévriguine entered into relations with the Papal Nuncio and the Venetian envoy. Doubt has been expressed as to whether he had any mission to the Republic at all. He certainly was not even acquainted with the Doge's titles, and believed Venice to be part of the Papal States. But on his way to Prague he had taken him two companions—a Livonian German, named Wilhelm Popler, and a Milanese Italian, Francese Pallavicini. These two men were better informed than he, and possessed a lively imagination as well. Attended by these acolytes, he proceeded to Venice, and presented the Doge with a letter from the Tsar, forged by himself, as Father Pierling believes ('Russia and the Holy See,' ii. 14, etc.), to constitute a claim on the liberality of the Signory, or fabricated at Rome, as Monsieur Ouspiénski supposes ('Relations of Rome with Moscow,' *Journal of the Min. of Public Instruction*, August, 1885), so as to ensure the association of the Republic with the missionary undertaking the Roman authorities were now hoping to initiate.

This improvised Ambassador does not seem to have made any very great effort, diplomatically speaking. He enjoyed the civilities heaped upon him, spoke in a general way of commercial relations which might be established, with a somewhat vague reference to the route by the Caspian and the

Volga ; talked too freely, and so revealed the difficulties of his master's position ; and hurried off to Rome, where he arrived on February 24, 1581.

He was made welcome at first, and better treated than his rank—that of a mere courier (*goniéts*)—warranted. But the perusal of the letter—genuine this time—he had brought from his master cast a chill over things. It expressed the Tsar's wish that the Pope should *order* Batory to ' renounce the Moslem alliance and the war he was making against the Christians.' But as to the religious question his message breathed never a word. Ivan was asking a great deal, and offering nothing at all, and the Roman authorities were well informed as to the extent of the Porte's share in the war that was being carried on. Yet the temptation to open intercourse by hook or by crook was too great, and the Pope decided to send an emissary to Moscow, charged with the duty of presenting the terms of the problem in their proper order : the religious union first of all, and after that the political understanding. Polish influences may, as some have supposed, have had something to do with the adoption of this plan. In any case, and from every point of view, it was the wisest.

But once the emissary had been chosen, matters, under his personal influence, went further still. Possevino was a diplomat by profession. He had been employed, twice over, in 1578 and 1580, on a somewhat similar mission to the Court of Sweden. He had been appointed Vicar Apostolic for all the North of Europe, had acquired a certain reputation for cleverness, and betrayed a strong inclination to suppress the spiritual in favour of the temporal side of his mission, and even to sacrifice the former to the latter. At Stockholm, where he had appeared dressed as a nobleman, sword on hip and bonnet in hand, he had not achieved any union with Rome, but he had been an active agent in the negotiations between Sweden and Poland for that alliance against Moscow which had turned out so ill. In 1579, he waited on Batory at Vilna, and with the same object. So well did he now play his cards that the Court of Rome, swayed by his influence, allowed itself to be led, unconsciously, to set politics before religion.

The idea of a league against Islam was a chimera. Portugal, Philip's new conquest, gave him too much trouble, and Venice had too many new-found interests in the Levantine seaports. But at Rome, as at Moscow, this same league—perpetually put forward, though Rome knew right well there was nothing and nobody behind it—was a sort of decorative façade, which concealed other and more practical arrange-

ments. The Papacy, even if its attempt to induce the
European Powers to arm for a fresh crusade resulted in failure,
perceived a means, if so much as a mutual concert could be
organized under its own auspices for such a purpose, of recovering some portion, at all events, of its ancient supremacy.
At several points, already, Protestantism seemed to be shrink-
ing backwards. Alexander Farnese was gaining ground in
the Low Countries. The Guises were lifting their heads in
France. In Sweden, the Queen, whose husband had already
been secretly won over, was bringing up her son a fervent
Catholic. In Poland the dissidents had no existence save as
a political party ; and Livonia, once lost to Germany, would
be lost, likewise, to the Reformers. Very soon, according to
the Roman view, the Reform would have nothing left save
England, a portion of the Empire, and little Denmark. If,
Muscovy and Poland once reconciled, it became possible,
under pretext of common action against the Turks, to induce
the House of Hapsburg and Venice to form a coalition of
which Rome would be the natural president, she might yet
rule the whole world once more !

The Papacy was approaching that phase of mind in which,
realities being non-existent, appearances themselves become
very precious things.

The Pope's brief to Ivan, in response to his letter, was
inspired by all these considerations. His Holiness accepted
the League, and the condition on which the Tsar made it
contingent. He would intervene between the Tsar and the
King of Poland. But on his side he burdened his mediation
with conditions. Peace must be ensured by a bond—a bond
only to be found in the bosom of the true Church. It was a
bold move, but in Possevino's secret instructions, which he
himself had helped to draw up, the sense of this reply was
greatly attenuated. According to these, the union of the two
Churches continued to be the higher end to which the Jesuit's
mission was to tend ; but his duties were reduced, practically
speaking, to the attainment of two essentially secular objects
—the establishment of commercial relations with Venice, and
the re-establishment of peace between Poland and the Tsar.
For the rest, His Holiness would be content with a minimum
result. If Ivan should refuse to consent to the building of a
church, or to allowing the Jesuits to settle in his capital,
Possevino was to be content, for the present, with opening
up regular intercourse with him.

Taking it all in all, Chévriguine had succeeded far better
than his master could have expected. This barbarian, whom
Rome could not dazzle, either with her works of art or her
ecclesiastical pomp, and who, though he did show more

interest in the Pope's presents—a magnificent *Agnus Dei*, a gold chain, and a purse of 600 ducats—would not say he was satisfied with them—this boor had not only succeeded in bringing about the reconciliation which Poland had so laboriously opposed—he had done it in spite of her. For while Batory had been going from triumph to triumph, and from conquest to conquest, Rome and Moscow had agreed to snatch the fruits of his victory out of his hands. And that although the Tsar's envoy had in no wise flattered the hopes of the Papal Court as to the religious advantages it might ultimately attain. This is proved by the correspondence of the Cardinal of Como, who drew up the greater part of the instructions Possevino took with him. Writing to Caligari, he expresses, in the clearest language, his conviction that Ivan's step had been dictated, not by any good intentions such as might give Rome reason to rejoice, but by the hard knocks which had been dealt him : ' *Non nasce de buone intezione, ma solo delle buone battiture.*'

Chévriguine left Rome on March 27, 1581, carrying a living testimony to his success with him ; Possevino was his fellow-traveller. Together, on the road Ivan's envoy had already trodden at Venice and the Imperial Court, they were to carry out their preconcerted plan. The Pope's Legate expounded the common proposals before the Council of Ten. The Signory divided them up at once, and without any hesitation, in the manner most convenient to itself. Enter into commercial relations with Moscow ? Good ; that was a long-wished-for event. Reconcile the Tsar with the King of Poland ? Good again ; peace was indispensable to trade. As to the rest, they left it all to Rome. The Doge, Nicola da Ponte, expressly asserted, in the course of a confidential conversation with Possevino, that since Lepanto his faith in leagues was utterly broken. Both at Vienna and at Prague the idea of the League was entirely put aside. The Emperor, indeed, would not show himself at all, and the Legate only saw the Archduke Ernest, who, having been a candidate for the Polish Crown, viewed Muscovite affairs solely from that particular point of view. The Austrian diplomats probably found it easy to see through the quibble on which this new understanding between Moscow and Rome, the expenses of which were to be borne by Poland, was based. ' The King of Poland's whip,' wrote Possevino to the Cardinal of Como, ' is, perhaps, our best means of introducing the catechism into Muscovy.' Chévriguine, emboldened by the advantages he had gained, flattered himself he would be able, when he returned from Vienna, to carry his master the title of Emperor of the East. All he got for himself was a

purse of 100 florins, and then the comrades parted—the
Russian proceeding to Lubeck, while the Jesuit took his way
to Vilna, there to begin his duties as a mediator.

II.—THE PAPAL MEDIATION.

The Papal Nuncio, Caligari, had already informed the King
of Poland of the Legate's approaching arrival, and requested
passports for him. His reception had been cool in the extreme. The Rector of the College of Wilna, Skarga, himself
a Jesuit, considered the mission most inopportune. Batory,
in addition to the general reasons which made him share this
opinion, had others of a more private nature, which led him
to suspect the present policy of the Holy See. For some
time the Pope had been holding him out hopes of a conquest
of Wallachia, then just about to change masters, and it was a
well-known fact at Warsaw that Gregory XIII. was secretly
assisting the candidature of Peter Czerczel, who was supported
by the French. Advices from Rome also made it evident that
Cardinal Madrucci, a former Papal Nuncio in Germany, had
been present at the Congregation which had decided on the
appointment of Possevino, and the conferences between the
Legate and the Archduke Ernest could not fail to stir suspicion in the King of Poland's mind.

The passports were granted, nevertheless, and Possevino
found Batory in a more friendly frame of mind. The delay
about opening his campaign had something to do with this,
we may be sure. In the Sovereign's immediate circle there
was open talk of putting an end to the business by a peace of
some sort or kind. When, towards the close of July, 1581,
the Pope's envoy started for Ivan's residence, and the King
marched away to Pskov, the best wishes of many Poles attended the Jesuit's progress. On August 20, after some
misadventures, one at Smolensk especially, when, believing
he was going to a dinner (*obiéd*), he very nearly attended an
obiédnia (Orthodox Mass), Possevino reached Staritsa, and
was permitted to ' contemplate the calm eyes of the Tsar.'

Nothing that could have ensured the Roman representative
a favourable reception had been overlooked by the Papal
Court. To his brief for the Tsar the Pope had added a letter
addressed to the Tsarina Anastasia, whom the Pontiff, unaware that she had been dead for years, and her place filled
several times over, addressed as his ' well-beloved daughter.'
The Sovereign Pontiff's gifts—a crucifix carved in rock crystal,
enriched with gold ; a copy, in the Greek language, of the
records of the Council of Florence, splendidly bound ; a
rosary of precious stones mounted in gold ; and a crystal

cup, also gold-mounted—were rendered more precious by the
addition of a morsel of the True Cross, enclosed in the crucifix,
and Ivan declared them worthy of the giver. At the very
last moment Possevino decided to withdraw a picture of the
Holy Family, in which a perfectly nude figure of St. John the
Baptist might have offended eyes accustomed to a more
modest style of art.

The Jesuit employed tactics which had already served him
well elsewhere, in the most skilful manner, and made the great
object of a common faith the foundation of his speech, though
he still contrived to keep it in the background. He was
supple and insinuating, eloquent and crafty, all at once, and
proved himself worthy of his mission. But his task was a
hard one. The answer to the pacific overtures of the Roman
envoy is a curious monument of Muscovite diplomacy. Six
men of the Court were deputed to reply to the Legate, and
given special instructions, so that each might treat one particular point of the whole problem—the League against the
Turks, the state of the negotiations already entered into with
Batory, the relations with Rome, etc. But when this first
work was accomplished, the Tsar's Chancery began it all over
again, in a fresh series of inquiries, superadded to the first,
and which were followed by several more. In the end there
was a total of six-and-thirty documents, which Possevino had
to peruse. At the head of each was inscribed an invocation
of the Holy Trinity, and a complete list of the Sovereign's
titles, and this whole collection was only to serve as the basis
of a controversy destined to drag on for weeks and weeks,
diversified with personal discussions, exchanges of notes, perpetual interventions on the part of the Tsar himself, and misunderstandings as to meanings, such as arise between people
who do not speak the same language—a Tower of Babel in a
Labyrinth.

From the very outset, besides, it was clear that the two
parties were not agreed as to the starting-point of the negotiations. The Legate represented Batory as having been led
by the Papal influence to consent to large concessions, and
requested Ivan to take some similar step on his side. Now,
the very fact of the Pope's intervention made the Tsar exceedingly grasping. Instead of coming forward, he went
backward, withdrew what he had previously offered, and
demanded that the siege of Pskov should be raised at once,
and a Polish embassy sent to him. Was it not for that he
had applied to the Pope? Batory's letter challenging him
to fight a duel was not calculated to inspire him with more
conciliatory feelings. At first he affected to speak of it more
in sorrow than in anger, and when Possevino asked to be

allowed to see the document, the Tsar decided he should only be given a summary containing the political matter, and leaving out the abuse. But very soon after this he was unable to refrain from drawing up and exhibiting a reply, in which, to facilitate his retorts, he reproduced, one after the other, the most offensive passages in the letter, and employed the most unexpected arguments. If, as Batory asserted, he had not flown to the assistance of the besieged towns, it was because he felt himself prevented from so doing by the truce he had made with his adversaries. And how could the King deny the Roman descent of the reigning house of Moscow ? If *Prous* had never existed, where did the name *Prussia* come from ?

At the end of a whole month, in fact, the mediator was no further advanced than on the day of his arrival. As to the religious question, he had gained something—no churches, indeed, and no establishment for the Jesuits, but the Tsar was most willing to keep up constant intercourse with Rome, and offered free passage through his dominions to any envoys the Pope might desire to send into Persia. This was a beginning, and the civilities in which every refusal was enwrapped, the understandings coupled with every concession, gave the Pope's representative reason to hope for still better things once peace was established. The Jesuit was always being brought back to that primordial postulate, though what the Tsar called his ' final calculation '—which Batory had already refused—was steadily maintained. Possevino had hoped to kill two birds with one stone by reconciling Russia with his former clients, the Swedes, likewise. Out of respect for the Pope, the Tsar agreed to depart from the rule according to which negotiations with Sweden must take place at Novgorod, and consented to receive King John's Ambassadors at the Kremlin. But the Swedish King, instead of despatching an embassy, was carrying his career of personal conquest along the Baltic coast, and it was quite clear that Ivan was resolved to make him pay for them dearly, once he himself was clear of Batory, and likewise that, for getting rid of Batory, he relied on the winter season and the Pope. Very skilfully, pitting his own tactics against his adversary's, he applied himself to keeping the Legate in good humour, by pointing him to a far-distant mirage of religious union, while Bogdan Biélski, who, with Nicholas Zakharine, was employed to direct the negotiations, ventured an attempt—an unsuccessful one indeed—at corruption of a more brutal kind.

By the middle of September the Jesuit had realized he was losing his time in this quarter, and made up his mind to fall back on the Polish camp. This was just what suited

Ivan best. ' Go to King Stephen,' he said, when he dismissed the Legate, ' salute him in our name, and when thou hast arranged peace according to the Pope's orders come back to us, for thy presence will always be welcome here, because of the Court which sends thee, and because of thine own faithfulness in our affairs !' He was taking the Jesuit into his service, and would gladly have paid him wages. And as the Pope had ordered peace should be made, according to the Tsar's desire, it must be made to suit the Muscovite Sovereign's convenience. Ivan would not hear of anything else. This is the one clear impression produced by this diplomatic episode.

Possevino arrived at the camp before Pskov in the early days of October, and this time played the part of the honest broker in most conscientious fashion. He informed the Poles as to the opinions he had arrived at during his stay at Staritsa, and endeavoured to combat those they had formed from the pamphlets written by Guagnino and Kruse. In his letters to Moscow he applied himself to representing military matters in the sense most favourable to the besiegers. The Poles, he said, were making great preparations. Supplies were coming in from Riga. Reinforcements were expected. Pskov was in a very bad way. The campaign would certainly be carried on all through the winter, and once the spring-time came there would be no possibility of stopping Batory.

All this was true enough at bottom, and proof of it may be found in those very reports, drawn up on the spot, which have produced such a contrary impression on the minds of the Polish historians. I have already quoted the Abbé Piotrowski's testimony as to the effective strength of the Polish cavalry, which he represents as having been reduced almost to nothing, even by the month of October. Further on, the same witness refers to a review held on December 4, in which 7,000 horses figured. And ' the horses are good.' Losses cannot have been so great, then, or the Poles had been able to make them good, at all events. Possevino's own narrative falls into another mistake. The Jesuit mentions the enthusiastic welcome which greeted him in the Polish camp. This trait, if we take it to be correct at all, can only be ascribed to the turbulent and unruly element, the existence of which I have already noted, in Batory's army—an element which both he and Żamoyski knew how to control and bend to the necessities of war. Into this the intervention of the Papal Legate certainly introduced an additional ferment, and incited some minds to a cowardly abandonment of duty. But as far as the chief command was concerned, the Abbé Piotrowski is the first to strike a very different note.

' The great General '—he refers to Zamoyski—' has never met a more odious man '—the epithet is applied to Possevino— ' and he means to drive him out with a stick as soon as peace is made.' Will my readers kindly imagine the appearance as a mediator, under the walls of Paris, while the Germans were besieging that city, of the representative of any of the European Powers? Possevino, being the Pope's emissary, seemed the natural ally of the Polish cause, the triumph of which, even in Livonia, involved the victory of Catholicism and of the Papacy. Yet the very essence of all mediation is that it should be used *against the strongest*, and the strongest in this case was most incontestably Poland. As a matter of fact, the siege of Pskov was destined to last till January 15, 1582, and by that time the most difficult period would be past, the terrible trials of the winter safely faced, the besiegers over the Christmas and New Year festivals without having yielded to the tempting summons of their own hearths, and the approach of spring would be bringing all the chances of success over to their side. Surrender was inevitable, and with that, Ivan's submission to the victor's demands. Even if Possevino hastened the issue of the conflict, all he could do was to make it rather less disadvantageous to *the weakest side*.

Ivan did not need the Jesuit to inform him as to the state of things at Pskov, and the condition of the Polish army, but no doubt the Legate's letters, which confirmed his other information, convinced him he had reckoned too surely on the result of his intervention. And very soon he changed his tone, and, ' recognising the power of Batory and his Swedish ally,' bowed his head once more. He was ready, now, to send Ambassadors to treat directly for peace, and he reduced his pretensions. On the twofold condition that the valley of the Viélikaïa and a point of territory running up to Louki should remain Russian, and that Sweden should not be included in the treaty with him, he was willing to give up the whole of Livonia. Part of this country was already in the hands of the Swedes, and, he thought, might ultimately become the object of victorious reprisals on his part, while the valley of the Viélikaïa would ensure him a sufficient line of defence on the north-west frontier, in rear of which he might lay the foundations of a not far distant revenge. A fresh effort in the direction of the sea-coast would be attended by more favourable circumstances.

Well conceived as this retreat was from the strategical point of view, a retreat it was, nevertheless. Some Russian historians, in their anxiety to spare the national pride, have gone so far as to take it to be quite the contrary. According to them, the Polish army, which was almost entirely destroyed by this time, was obliged to accept peace. The Russia of the present day can very well dispense with these travesties of the realities of history, the last and most pitiable refuge of the vanquished. In a war the result of which hangs on a siege, negotiations begun under the guns of the besieging army are simply capitulation in another form. There is only one way in which the besieged can bring the struggle to a victorious conclusion—that employed by Peter the Great under the walls of Poltava ; and the valley of the Viélikaïa notwithstanding, the abandonment of Livonia threw the political, military, and social development of Russia back more than a hundred years.

Once Ivan gave up Livonia, the object of Batory's campaign was attained. The King, though he, too, might make reservations as to the future, could not refuse to treat, nor could he, Possevino being present, decline a mediator accepted by the Tsar. His opinion of this mediation is evidenced by the following fact. The Jesuit, on his own showing, had to deliver a regular assault before he could induce his Polish clients to inform him as to their intentions with regard to the peace in connection with which he himself was to act as arbiter.

Towards the middle of November, Iam-Zapolski, on the road to Novgorod, between Zavolotché and Porkhov, was unanimously chosen as the meeting-place for the plenipotentiaries. Prince Eletski—who, as Zamoyski remarked, lacked nothing save a principality to make him a Prince—Roman Olferiev Verechtchaguine, and Sviazev, a secretary, were the somewhat shabby representatives of the Tsar of all the Russias. In the persons of Prince Zbaraski, Palatine of Braclaw, Prince Albert Radziwill, Marshal of the Court, and Secretary Haraburda, the King of Poland brought a more capable set of diplomatists into action. Batory's envoys were the bearers of carefully-prepared instructions. What did these embody ? Possevino, who arrived at the same time, knew nothing about them, and wherefore, a message sent him by the King, just at this time, pretty plainly shows us. Distrust rings in every line of it. The Sovereign, not without bitterness, contrasts the devotion of Poland to the Holy See, which had stood firm for hundreds of years, with the Papal Legate's sudden zeal for the interests of a third party, which had no evident claim to such a favour.

The quibble which lay at the foundation of the Jesuit's mission inevitably doomed him to this disgrace. Thanks to it, even when he disappointed the hopes of one party, he was suspected by the other, and to the very end the part he played suffered from this fact. All through the Iam-Zapolski negotiations, which lasted from December 13, 1581, to January 15, 1582, while the Russians were accusing him of making common cause with the Poles, Zamoyski was to call him a sycophant and a traitor, cast doubt even on the sincerity of his religious zeal, and declare him 'more interested in political arrangements than in the hierarchy of heaven.'

III.—THE TRUCE OF IAM-ZAPOLSKI.

I will spare my readers the details of these negotiations, and refer them to Father Pierling's deep and learned study ('Russia and the Holy See,' ii., 115, etc.), in which I shall only have to notice a few errors of judgment quite explicable in the case of that eminent historian. Iam-Zapolski, an almost ruined village in a country which had been laid waste, could scarcely provide sufficient accommodation for the Polish envoys and their numerous suite. The Russians therefore sought shelter close by—at Kiverova-Gora—and as the mediator also established himself in a smoky cabin at the same place, the sittings of the Congress were practically removed to that locality. Under this humble roof, between a temporary altar and a *brasero*, the smoke of which, there being no other exit for it, had to find its way out of the windows, so that by the end of each sitting the negotiators looked like so many chimney-sweeps, the fate of two great Empires was discussed and settled.

Both sides, according to the tradition, which had grown into a sort of protocol between the two countries, began by formulating the most extravagant demands. This deceived Possevino at first, and for some considerable time. When he sounded the Muscovites, he became convinced that the surrender of certain Livonian towns by Poland was a *sine quâ non* if peace was to be established. He at once concentrated all his endeavours on this point, and thus played for one party, while he fancied he was serving the other. As a matter of fact, neither side gave him their full confidence, and he was really playing a game of blindman's-buff. It was not till the second half of December had been reached, indeed, that the Poles, after the inevitable preliminary hesitations and gropings, resolved on what their last word should be, and spoke it. Father Pierling is certainly wrong when he accuses Zamoyski of duplicity in this particular, as also when he concludes there was a disagreement between the King of Poland and his Chancellor, or between the Chancellor and the Polish plenipotentiaries. The learned historian seems to have depended, in this particular, on the Russian summary, frequently very incorrect, of the Polish documents published by Kojalowicz. Zamoyski was the King's own man, and from his twofold position as General-in-Chief and Chancellor we may argue that the persons he selected to treat were personally devoted to him. By the middle of December, a letter from Zamoyski, which embodied an absolute refusal to give up anything, of any sort, in Livonia, had reached Possevino's hands. A few days later, the Chancellor sent a courier to the Polish plenipotentiaries, authorizing them to give up three Livonian towns, which the Russians had previously claimed. The Jesuit was much astonished and sorely puzzled. But the incident was natural enough. Between the first date and the second, Zamoyski had changed his mind. His letter to Possevino was written on December 13, 1581, and he wrote to the King the same day and in the same sense —no concessions to be made in Livonia. But on December 16 bad news arrived. The Swedes were making steady progress in Livonia, and the arrival of a much-desired supply of powder had been delayed. The next morning the Chancellor decided to modify his last instructions ; he suggested three fresh bases of agreement to his plenipotentiaries, and one of the three included the concession to which we have just referred. The trifling importance of the towns mentioned permitted the making of the sacrifice, to which Batory had agreed. Zamoyski adverts to the fact in his letter to the King, dated December 26, 1581. As regards this matter, therefore, there was no disagreement at all. As for the objections, and even reproaches, Father Pierling has imagined on the part of the Polish plenipotentiaries, the modern historian has suffered from the misunderstanding to which the mediator of the year 1581 likewise fell a victim. The Chancellor certainly ought to have kept Possevino informed, but the general watchword among the Poles was to keep the arbiter, whom they endured out of respect for the Pope, but whom they would far rather have done without, at a distance. Further, Zbaraski and Radziwill thought it wise to make more difficulties than their superior had made. They considered his concessions too liberal, declared they would not act on his letter until they had fresh orders, and wrote him—the letter, dated December 21, is still in existence—that ' it was only to deceive the Legate.' The proceeding was not altogether correct, but the three Livonian towns were not to be given up except in the very last resort, and only if the two other schemes utterly failed. Thus the whole thing was a diplomatic secret, and to have confided it to Possevino would, in the eyes of the Polish negotiators, have been to make it over to the Muscovites. This was Zamoyski's own view of the matter, for, in a letter dated December 27, he expressed his approbation of his subordinates' conduct; and though his correspondence with Batory contains most uncomplimentary references to ' the good shepherd of the Muscovites, who is striving to turn wolves into sheep,' he had no need to advise the King, as Father Pierling has imagined him to have done, not to let the Legate into the secrets of the negotiations then being carried on—such advice would have been quite superfluous (Kojalowicz's ' Collections,' 1867, p. 396, etc.).

But the negotiations still threatened to drag on. The Russian plenipotentiaries were in no hurry at all. They found their rustic accommodation less trying than the Poles did; they knew better how to obtain the necessary supplies, and, with the ingeniousness of their race, they turned the position to account, transformed their camp into a fair-ground, and carried on a profitable trade in the intervals of the sittings. They still hoped, too, that the severity of the winter season would make their opponents more tractable. Zamoyski set about undeceiving them, and Polish swords were in the end to do more to overcome the final resistance than Possevino's eloquent tongue.

The General-in-Chief, who exhausted every means in his endeavour to worst the heroic defenders of Pskov, hit on some rather blameworthy devices. The story of a certain infernal machine introduced into the town is a somewhat obscure one. Zamoyski is said to have permitted the construction of a box filled with powder and projectiles, which a Russian prisoner undertook to deliver to Chouïski. In connection with this incident the Polish historians mention a violation of the law of nations, by which the besieged had fired on a flag of truce, and also to a trap into which Chouïski tempted Zamoyski by challenging him to single combat. The excuse is insufficient, and the provocation alluded to seems to have been given at a period subsequent to that at which the infernal machine, which indeed did no damage whatever, was sent into the town. The General-in-Chief, whose idea on this occasion was certainly a very bad one, was better inspired shortly afterwards. He resorted, on January 4, 1582, to a more legitimate trick, pretended to relax his guard, succeeded in tempting the garrison into a general sortie, and gave it a most terrible reception. In vain did he write the Polish plenipotentiaries, soon afterwards, that his army could not hold out for more than another week, and that they must make a speedy end of the business. He had just given clear proof to the contrary, and the Muscovite plenipotentiaries were not deceived. When Ivan heard the news, he sent them instructions of the most conciliatory nature, which included the total cession of Livonia, and any further difficulties they made solely concerned questions of detail.

Possevino raised one by his obstinate endeavour to have
Sweden, which desired neither mediation nor peace, brought
into the treaty. He was obliged to relinquish all hope of
satisfaction on this point, but the Swedish conquests in
Livonia were another source of complication. The Muscovites pointed out, not unfairly, that they could not be asked
to give up places which had passed out of their possession.
After a great deal of further discussion, the Poles agreed to
reserve their rights with regard to the third belligerent party,
and it was settled that a detailed list of the places given up
by the Russians should be prepared. On the north-western
frontier of the country a system of partition was resorted to
—Viélije, which stood on the left bank of the Dvina, and belonged to the group of towns that were to pass under Polish
rule, was handed over to that country ; but Siebiéje, the out-
post of the Muscovite provinces at the entrance to the valley
of the Viélikaïa, was restored to its former owners. The
question of titles remained. Ivan was not satisfied with
being described in the text of the treaty as *Tsar ;* he was
anxious to continue the nominal Sovereign of Livonia, at all
events. There is no sense in giving with one hand and taking
back with the other, said the Poles, and what did this new
title of *Tsar* mean ? *Tsar*, after the fashion of the ancient
Tartar Sovereigns of Kazan and Astrakan, was too small a
thing for the master of Moscow, and if the word *Tsar* was to
be translated into *Cæsar*, it was too much. The real Cæsar,
the only one recognised by modern Europe, the Emperor,
might fairly object. This last quarrel was an old one, as we
know, and Zamoyski attached no importance to it. He
spoke, indeed, in this connection, of a facetious nobleman of
Warsaw, who had dubbed himself ' King of Zakharansk,'
without raising anything beyond a laugh. The two parties
could always fall back on the expedient, already so frequently
employed, of drawing up double copies of the same treaty.
There was no real difficulty in the matter, but Possevino, in
his ignorance of precedents, made a mountain out of the mole-
hill. Setting himself to rectify the historical facts on which
the Russian plenipotentiaries based their claim, he strove to
convince them that the Emperors Arcadius and Honorius,
who had both died five centuries previously, could not have
conferred the Imperial title on the great *Kniaz* Vladimir, took
good care to hint that Rome was the fountain-head of all
such honours, and reminded them that Charlemagne had
been crowned by one of Gregory XIII.'s predecessors. A
great deal of time was lost before the usual compromise was
arrived at. And even then the Jesuit himself raised a fresh
and final subject of debate.

Though the Poles had nothing to do with it—Father Pierling has certainly been completely misled, probably by a
mistranslation, as to this matter—the Legate claimed that
his signature should be appended to the treaty, or at all events
that it should contain some mention of his share in it. The
Russian envoys, who had received no instructions to this
effect, absolutely refused to agree to his request. The Jesuit's
patience was exhausted, and he lost his temper thoroughly.
To conceal the real cause of his wrath, he fell back on a trick
in the drawing up of the treaty, whereby Eletski and Olfériev
desired, contrary to the principle adopted, to include Riga
and Courland amongst the towns and territories ceded by
the Tsar, thinking they would thus create a future title for
their master. Whereupon the mediator threatened to break
off everything. ' You have come here to steal, not to treat !'
he shouted to the Muscovites. ' Be off ! Away with you !'
The plenipotentiaries did not move a muscle, and the Legate
grew still angrier. Olfériev had the manuscript of the treaty
in his hand. Possevino snatched it from him, threw it out
of the window, and, taking hold of the astounded diplomatist
by the buttons of his pelisse, shook him roughly, pushed
him outside the door, and thrust his companions out after
him.

His will carried the day, and on January 15, 1582, the signatures were duly exchanged. Not without some help on Possevino's part, the advantage, from the purely diplomatic point of
view, lay with the Russians. Their final position was very
much that they had taken up at the opening of the Congress,
and they only surrendered what the Tsar himself had sacrificed
some three months previously. The sacrifice was a heavy one,
nevertheless. After twenty years of a struggle which had
apparently been crowned with success, Russia was once more
cut off from Europe and the Baltic. Yet a twofold result, of
which the country may scarcely have been aware, had been
gained in that very country of Livonia, possession of which she
was forced to relinquish for a time. The Teutonic order of
knighthood was extinct, and that meant the destruction of the
German garrison in the province. And a conflict between
Poland and Sweden had been prepared—a storm-laden future
—in the course of which the two countries, wearing out their
own strength in a fierce struggle, were to ensure their common
foe a double and most profitable revenge.

The Russian occupation of Livonia, shortlived as it had been,
had left a durable mark on the Russian nation, and strongly influenced its ultimate development, by introducing a number of
foreign elements into the country, which ultimately incorporated
and absorbed them—the nucleus of that German colony

destined to play so important a part in the Empire of the Tsars, and the civilizing influence of which cannot be denied.

After all, what had just been signed was not a peace—it was only a ten years' truce. According to precedent, certain disputed points which had been kept out of the discussion—such as the theoretical claim to the disputed possession of all the Russo-Lithuanian countries—prevented any final agreement. When the victors occupied the town and province of Derpt, now made over to Poland, they were struck by the proofs left by their beaten foes of a power—a gift of organization and a military superiority, at all events—which would have been turned to better account, no doubt, in the hands of such a genius as Batory. ' We were all astonished,' writes the Abbé Piotrowski, ' to find in every fort a quantity of guns and an amount of powder and ball such as we should not have been able to get together in the whole of our country.' And he adds : ' We have won something like a little kingdom ; I doubt whether we shall know what to do with it !' In spite of the fault-finding quality so constantly apparent in the Abbé's diary, these impressions of his reproduce a certain amount of truth, the consequences of which were to be evidenced by history.

Latin inscriptions on the restored walls of the castle of Riga and on the doorway of the church at Wenden thus expressed the meaning of the event which was taking place.

> ' *Devicto Moscho* . . . .
>
> *Prisca religio Rigam renovato vigere*
> *Cœperat in templo. . . .*'

And again :

> ' *Hæresis et Moschi postquam devicta potestas*
> *Livonidum primus pastor ovile rego.*'

All this was a proof, in the eyes of the Livonians, that Batory's triumph was above all things the triumph of Catholicism and of the Jesuits, who came close on the victor's heels, wherever he went. The new Polish Government was to feel the consequences of this conviction.

As far as Possevino was concerned, the important matter was the form the treaty took. It openly asserted the Pope's authority, ' so that everything appeared to have been carried out in his name.' Thus the Legate boasted in his letters to the Cardinal of Como, and, in spite of his disagreement with the Muscovite envoys, he was eager to pursue the advantage he had gained at the Kremlin itself. To put forward the anti-Ottoman league once more, seeing it would serve as a pretext for the intervention of the Holy See ; to open the question of the reunion of the two Churches, seeing it had been agreed that should be discussed when peace had been arranged, but, above all, without indulging in any great illusion as to the success of these two items in his programme ; to carry on his mediatorial functions ; to intervene as to the difficulties arising out of the treaty of Iam-Zapolski ; to make a fresh attempt to take Swedish affairs in hand ; and in every case to *appear*, or make the Pope *appear*, the final arbiter accepted by both sides— such, seemingly, was the Jesuit's plan of action. Circumstances so fell out that this plan agreed fairly well with the state of mind then dominant at Moscow. Disappointed as the Tsar was with the power of the Pope's *authority*, he might still make use of it to mask the humiliation of his defeat to some extent ; and it was well, for the sake of appearances, that the Pope's emissary should *seem* to have transacted the Tsar's business, and should continue to employ himself in the same fashion. Wherefore Possevino was to be made welcome at the Court of Ivan the Terrible.

IV.—POSSEVINO AT MOSCOW.

The historical terms of the religious problem, the solution of which was to be the ostensible and principal object of this journey, are well known. The separation of the two Churches, prepared as early as in the seventh century by John the Faster, Patriarch of Constantinople, who had assumed the title of ' Bishop Universal,' and then by the *conciliable* called *in Trullo*, or *Quinisext* (690), which authorized the marriage of priests, had been accomplished in the course of the ninth century. At that moment the Greek Church, during and after her war with the iconoclasts, reached the height of her glory and external development, gave birth to a pleiad of doctors, saints, and poets, and was called to the great work of evangelizing the Slav races. Photius, who carried the principle laid down by his predecessors, that the fall of the Roman Empire had involved the ruin of the spiritual sovereignty connected with it, to its extreme point, converted the schism into an actual fact. The union of the two Churches, re-established afterwards for a very short time, and in the most precarious manner, was finally severed by Michael Cerularius in 1054. Attempts to restore it were numerous, from the thirteenth century onwards. The Council of Florence (1439) only renewed the endeavour made at the Council of Lyons (1274). In 1518, Poland, contrary to her usual policy, seems to have favoured a fresh attempt (Fiedler, *Ein Versuch der Vereinigung . . . Sitzungsberichte der K.K. Akademie in Wien*, vol. xl., 1862). But the idea of a third Rome, already well rooted and constantly strengthening at Moscow, was an unexpected obstacle to all such undertakings. In vain did a physician in attendance on the Grand Duke Vassili, one Nicholas Boulew, or Lueo, commonly called Niémtchine, carry on an active campaign in support of union at the Sovereign's own Court, and hold controversy on the subject with Maximus the Greek and Filofeï, a monk of Pskov. The only proselytes he is known to have won were a boïar named Feodor Karpov, and one prior whose name has not been handed down to us.

The Pontificate of Gregory XIII. did not appear likely to win much more success for the claims of the Roman Church. Though the Pope's skilful efforts had succeeded in making the King of Spain arm against the heretic Queen of England, and in supporting the struggle for restoration carried on by the Bavarian House of Wittelsbach—the Guises of Germany—they could not wipe out the stigma laid on the Catholic religion, in the eyes of the whole world, by Alva's rule in the Low Countries, by St. Bartholomew, by the horrors of the Inquisition, and, above all, by those scandals within the Papacy itself, which had been the direct cause of the Reform. It was to the political, and not to the religious, power in Rome that Ivan had first addressed himself through his Ambassador, and it was the representative of this same secular power, the diplomat, not the apostle, whom he prepared himself to welcome in Possevino's person.

The Jesuit reached Moscow on February 14, 1582. He found the Court in mourning, and the Tsar himself plunged into deep sorrow, by a tragic event, which, if the question they had to discuss had been one of moral interest only, should in itself have sufficed to exclude any possible communion of thought or feeling between the priest and his royal host. The Tsar, in a fit of rage, had just killed his own son. I shall have to return to this gloomy episode. But there was no question of moral interests here ! The anti-Ottoman league itself was very soon to be put aside. Ivan, to enable him to hold his own against Batory, had been obliged to make a truce with the Khan of the Crimea ; he now avowed himself ready to break it, and take up arms against the Turk, but not until the Pope had made arrangements with the Holy Empire, France, Spain, Venice, England, Denmark, and Sweden, and requested all these powers to send embassies to Moscow, to concert a final arrangement ! The Tsar was evidently joking, though he did offer to send an important Ambassador of his own to Rome, instead of a mere courier. He was anxious to preserve the useful friendship he had made.

The agreement with Sweden fell through likewise. It was not for the sake of treating with King John that the Tsar had yielded up Livonia to Batory. Gently but firmly Ivan cleared the ground, limiting Possevino's good offices to the only matters still to be settled with Poland—frontier delimitations and exchanges of prisoners. At the same time, fond as he was of a controversy, he endeavoured to slip out of any discussion of a religious nature. He constantly affirmed that such a debate might become offensive to the Pope. When, on February 21, in the course of an audience devoted to secular interests, Possevino requested a private conversation to discuss 'the great business,' the Tsar devised another excuse. He was quite incompetent, personally, to carry on a controversy of this kind. But when the Jesuit pressed him, and begged to be allowed to communicate his views in writing, Ivan probably concluded he had better end the matter. And his love of polemics may have overcome his other objections.

By a literary artifice which has no doubt deceived himself, Father Pierling has imagined the existence of a dialogue prepared beforehand, as in Rokita's case, and graced with appropriate surroundings. The very dates and words quoted by the learned historian prove that nothing of the kind can have occurred. It was quite unexpectedly—this detail is somewhat important—at this very sitting, devoted, in the first place, to quite different subjects, and in the absence of those representatives of the clergy whose presence would have been indispensable if the discussion was to be of a really serious character, that the Tsar made up his mind to settle the question, or, rather, to cut short the importunities in connection with it, which were a constant worry to him. He did not fail, indeed, to lay stress on the uselessness of a controversy carried on under such circumstances. But, after all, as the Jesuit seemed so anxious about it, he should have an immédiate explanation ('Diplomatic Documents,' 1851-1871, x. 247, etc.).

Possevino forthwith laid himself out to offer the most tempting arguments, with the most cunning precautions as to the language he employed. This was no question of a break with the Greek Church, the ancient and venerable Church of St. Athanasius, St. Chrysostom, and St. Basil, to which the Church of Rome felt herself bound by indissoluble ties, but that of restoring a unity which had only been disturbed by the abandonment of certain ancient traditions. It was a work of restoration, which would also inevitably lead to the creation of a new Empire of the East, whereof the Tsar, crowned by the Pope, like a second Charlemagne, might be the head. This proved the Jesuit little knew the formidable antagonist with whom he had to deal. Ivan, with his self-possession, his quickness, and his wealth of fantastic erudition, made short work of the brilliant display on which the Roman orator had reckoned to dazzle him. ' What was this talk of Byzantium and the Greeks ? The Greek religion bore that name because King David, long before the birth of Christ, had foretold that Ethiopia should enjoy the first-fruits of the Divine mercy ; now Ethiopia was Byzantium ! But he, Ivan, cared neither for the Greeks nor for Byzantium ! His religion was not that of the Greeks, but that of Christ—the only true religion ! And what was this talk, again, of a traditional union with people who shaved their beards off, contrary to every tradition ?'

Possevino fancied he had found a crushing answer : Gregory XIII.'s chin was adorned with a magnificent beard.

' And thou thyself ?' rejoined the Tsar, pointing to the Legate's shaven countenance.

According to the record of the sitting drawn up at Moscow, Possevino, whose own report is dumb as to this incident, ascribed his hairless condition to a physical cause : he did not cut his beard, and neither did he shave. But already Ivan was growing hot over the game, and, carried away by his natural temperament, he was to deliver yet harder blows, and crush his adversary altogether. Very cunningly he turned the discussion to a question where all the advantage would be on his side, and which, indeed, was the crux of the disagreements between East and West—that of the Pope's primacy. The Popes of the earlier centuries—Clement, Sylvester, and so forth—had always been revered as saints by the Muscovite Church. But their successors, who had cast off the poverty and austerity of the primitive Christians ; who lived in a pomp which had astonished Chévriguine ; who had mounted a throne, and wore the holy symbol of the Cross upon their *boots ;* who, forgetting every feeling of decency, publicly indulged in the most shameful debauchery—this new order of Pontiffs must be considered to have fallen from their ancient dignity ! In vain did Possevino make signals of distress and strive to check the flood of invective. He had had his warning. If the dispute turned out ill, now, for his master and himself, so much the worse for them ! Like all orators of his kidney, Ivan lost control of his own tongue, and when the Jesuit tried to put in a timid apology, the Tsar cried out, ' Your Roman Pontiff is not a shepherd at all : he is a wolf !'

' If the Pope is a wolf, I have nothing more to say !'

This reply, and the outrage which called it forth, both of them reproduced in the Russian version, do not appear in Possevino's published narrative (*Moscovia*). But the original manuscript, it would appear, does mention the incident (Pierling, as above, ii. 169). According to the Russian version, it ended the discussion, and Ivan dismissed the Jesuit with more kindly words, and immediately afterwards sent him

dishes from his own table. But Possevino asserts that the
dispute went on, and even grew more lively, so much so that the
Tsar at one moment came very near striking his opponent with
the terrible spear of which we have already heard, while the
Russians present talked of ducking the Jesuit in the water.

In any case, the parties separated on tolerably cool terms,
and a few days later, on February 23, when Possevino received
another summons to the Palace, he betrayed no desire to reopen the conversation. This time the Tsar, on his own initiative, and as though to make up somewhat for his previous
sharpness, suggested he should send him a memorandum
dealing with the differences between the two Churches. But
the Jesuit had convinced himself, no doubt, that this would be
mere waste of time. He contented himself with offering the
Sovereign a Latin copy of Gennadius' book on the Council
of Florence, and fancied he had got rid of this far too dangerous
subject. But he was reckoning without the great despot's
capricious and masterful nature. A surprise was in store for him.

As to this final episode, again, the witnesses are at variance.
Possevino, according to the Russian version, expressed a wish
to see one of the churches in the capital, and the Tsar suggested
his accompanying him to a service to be performed for his
special benefit with all the pomp of the Orthodox rite. Whereupon the Jesuit, who had eagerly accepted the invitation, took
it into his head to enter the precincts of the church before the
Sovereign had arrived. A dispute ensued, and, to cut the
matter short, the Tsar sent orders that the Legate was to be
brought back to the Palace, there to continue the discussion
of the political business still to be settled. The invitation,
Possevino declares, was quite unexpected, and he simply declined it, and slipped away when the boïars tried to drag him
towards the church. Most likely there is an equal amount
of truth and invention in both stories. The Jesuit, in all
probability, did betray a very natural curiosity, and also most
probably refused to take part in a function which would certainly have compromised him. The one undoubted fact,
amidst all the contradictions and obscurity which still hang
round this chapter of history, is that the attempt to which
Rome thought fit to sacrifice the interests of her Polish
adherents utterly failed. On May 11, 1582, Possevino took
farewell of the Tsar, and Ivan's Ambassador, Iakov Molvianinov, who was sent with him to Rome, went there empty-
handed, save for civil speeches and sable skins. The Pope's
representative had made an *appearance* in the agreement
brought about between Russia and Poland, and might even
claim to have played a leading part therein ; but the work he
had done, being purely secular, and in opposition, as I have

shown, to those real interests which the Holy See should have striven to protect, was threatened, like all the rest, with early and complete extinction.

V.—THE DAY AFTER THE TRUCE.

Very soon—and this time Rome never even dreamt of any interference—the relations between the two countries were to culminate in a fresh and most violent rupture. The difficulties connected with the execution of the treaty of Iam-Zapolski were not very important in themselves, and on both sides the inclination was to solve them in the broadest and most conciliatory spirit. There was a dispute over the possession of a small fort in the province of Viélije, at the mouth of the Méja, on a very important line of river communication between Smolensk and Louki. When the Palatine of Witebsk, Paç, seized this place in a somewhat high-handed fashion, Ivan ordered his envoy to give up the whole province rather than risk any reopening of hostilities, and Batory, for his part, had the fort destroyed. But though both parties were bent, for the present, on avoiding any immediate conflict, we know that Ivan meditated a fresh appeal to arms, at a more or less distant period, and was soliciting England's help for the purpose. And the whole history of the closing years of Batory's reign proves that he himself looked on the truce of 1582 as a mere halt on that victorious march whereby, his turbulent Poles once thoroughly tamed and subjugated, he hoped to lead his armies on triumphant, far beyond Pskov. I have already made my readers aware of this vaster military undertaking meditated by the King, supported by the assistance. swiftly obtained, of Rome, and the hoped-for help of Florence and Venice, and which he began to put into execution in the course of the years next following. Under the charm of the great warrior's bold spirit, Gregory XIII.'s successor, Sixtus V., was to turn his back on fancies, and enter the sphere of practical realities, themselves splendid enough. The anti-Turkish league, in which Ivan proposed to wed Elizabeth with the Emperor, never advanced beyond the condition of a theme for the Tsar's bitter jests. But Batory, having proved the road from Moscow to Constantinople ran through Warsaw, was resolved, now, to pass through Moscow on his own way to Constantinople, and to make others furnish him with the means of doing it. In former conversations with Possevino at Wilna he had outstripped Peter the Great, and mentioned Azov as the indispensable base of any decisive action against the Ottoman power. To obtain a hold on Azov he must have a Moscow won over to the common cause behind him—and this had just proved impossible ; or else a Moscow conquered—and this Batory was prepared to do.

That the plan was feasible was to be proved by Dmitri's easy triumph, and the victorious though useless campaigns of his Polish protectors under Sigismund III., and only the premature death of the victor of Polotsk, in 1586, wiped out a project so worthy of his powers. Ivan himself was not to live long enough to feel the direct threat it involved. But we may be quite sure he had an alarming inkling of it. The phantom thus rising up before him certainly darkened the Sovereign's closing days, and affected his last decisions. Even before the King of Poland, having resolved to relinquish his views on Hungary and end the consideration he had hitherto shown the Porte, fully revealed his idea to the Papal Nuncio Bolognetti, in a conversation lasting four hours (1584) (Boratynski, 'Stephen Batory and his Plans for a League against Turkey,' Reports of the Cracow Academy, May, 1902), Ivan, moved by his sense of approaching peril, had made up his mind to treat with the Swedes. After appealing to England, he appealed once more, and as vainly, to Germany. The Empire was wrapped up in its religious quarrels, and the Emperor in his artistic and scientific studies. By a truce made in August, 1583, all the Russian towns taken by the Swedes—Iam, Ivangorod, and Koporié—were made over to them altogether. And after this, as Vienna still turned him a deaf ear, Ivan fell back again on London, clinging to this last plank with the gestures of a drowning man.

In the hour of his supreme effort, death overtook him. But Fortune, who does not love old men, and who had steadily failed her former favourite, showed greater kindness, at that very moment, to the interests of the Empire he was leaving behind him. Batory was not to outlive his adversary long, and at the other end of the huge dominions, scarce nibbled at, as yet, by Poland, an unforeseen and mighty compensation for the loss of Polotsk and Livonia was beginning to appear. Siberia, distant, mysterious, far extending, was opening her arms, not, as has been so generally supposed, to the bold attack of a handful of Cossack raiders, but to the long and patient efforts of a peaceful army of toiling colonists.

CHAPTER III

THE CONQUEST OF SIBERIA : ERMAK

I.—CONQUEST AND COLONIZATION.   II.—THE STROGANOVS.
III.—THE COSSACKS.   IV.—ERMAK IN SIBERIA.

I.—CONQUEST AND COLONIZATION.

THE word ' Siberia ' does not appear in any Russian document until towards the latter half of the fifteenth century, and it was only applied at that time to a portion of the present Government of Tobolsk, occupied, till the sixteenth century, by Tartar Khans. But long before that period the Russians had discovered the road to the highlands of the Ural, and, crossing that chain of mountains, had slowly made their way from the basin of the Piétchora to the basin of the Ob. Even in the eleventh century, the servant of a Novgorod nobleman, called Giouriata Rogovitch, had reached the mountains, and in 1364 an expedition sent out by that enterprising republic got as far as the river. In the following century the Novgorodians were keeping up regular political and commercial intercourse with the *Iougra*, as the countries west of the Ural were called from the twelfth to the fourteenth centuries ; and the name was extended, in the fifteenth, to the western slopes of the Ural Mountains. The *Iougritchy* paid the republic a regular tribute in furs, and even in silver. The metal was probably taken out of some primitive workings, now known as the Finnish mines (*Tchoudskiié Kopi*), which have quite lately served as a guide to modern prospectors.

After the annexation of Novgorod, the Grand-Dukes of Moscow carried on the work, but impressed it with the military character inherent in their own traditions. In 1472, Perm was conquered ; in 1483, an army commanded by Prince Feodor Kourbski, ' the Black,' and by Ivan Ivanovitch Saltyk-Pravine, crossed the Ural, followed the course of the river Tavda, which falls into the Tobol, an affluent of the Irtych, and then that of the Irtych itself, reached Siberia, and penetrated into the basin of the Ob. The Princes of the *Iougra* and the *Vogoula*, and the Siberian Prince Latyk, all made their submission, went to Moscow, and agreed to pay tribute to the Grand-Duke, who added the name of Sovereign of the *Iougra* to his other titles, but was obliged, in the year 1499, though as successfully as on the first occasion, to re-establish himself in possession by force of arms.

The advantages thus gained were by no means commensurate

with the object it was necessary to attain. After the capture of Kazan and Astrakan, numbers of other Princes offered to pay tribute, and among them Iadiger, a Siberian Prince, who held a Tartar *iourt* in the middle of the present province of Tobolsk, and reigned over some 30,000 subjects. But few of the engagements taken were kept. In 1556 Iadiger only sent in 700 out of the 30,000 marten-skins he had promised—one for each inhabitant. He excused himself on the score of the violence and exactions he had been forced to endure on the part of his neighbours, against whom the Tsar had promised him assistance and protection. But the Tartar Princes, who were perpetually fighting amongst themselves, were not easily put down, or even reached. When hard pressed they fled into the steppes, and ensured themselves impunity by accepting the sovereignty of Moscow, coupled with similar obligations, quite as unfaithfully fulfilled.

When Ivan's attention became quite absorbed by his Livonian enterprise everything went thoroughly astray, and the Tsar's last envoy, a sort of half ambassador, half tax-collector, was killed. No effectual and lasting result was attainable in such a country, save by a conquest on quite different lines, of the necessary elements for which the Muscovite Empire was by no means destitute.

Even nowadays, mobility is one of the most characteristic features of the race which has peopled the huge tracts of the European east and the Asiatic west, and I have already pointed out the reasons which account for this (p. 23). ' The fish seeks the deepest water, and man the place where he can live best.' This proverb reproduces, in most expressive fashion, a tendency which is the secret of the great work of colonization accomplished by the subjects of Ivan the Terrible and Peter the Great.

For this work the resources supplied by the basin of the Piétchora—the base of perpetual military enterprises up till the sixteenth century—were insufficient. Only an industrial population could have turned them to account, and the Muscovite nomads were a race of husbandmen. It was on a private family that the honour devolved of imparting a more useful character and a more favourable direction to the national expansion, by appealing to the powerful current of emigration which constituted its real strength, and directing that current towards the basin of the river Kama.

II.—THE STROGANOVS.

At a very early date the Stroganov family had been given special privileges, with a view to populating the uninhabited tracts in the district of Oustoug, north of Viatka. The social and judicial position of this family is still under discussion. Tradition connects its members with the patrician stock of the Dobrynine. But, historically speaking, it seems to have been included in the class of the merchants or husbandmen, between whom no distinction existed in the Muscovite law of the sixteenth century (Serguiéiévitch, 'Lessons on the History of Russian Law,' St. Petersburg, 1883, p. 622; and Tyjnov, 'Siberian Collections,' 1887, p. 119). '*Illi vivunt sua negotiatione*,' says the unknown author of the *Historia de Siberia* (1681), when referring to the Stroganovs. They were neither boïars nor '.men who served.' Yet, on the huge domains which constituted their patrimony in the sixteenth century, they enjoyed very exceptional privileges. They had power to exercise justice of every kind, and themselves answered to nobody but the Tsar. They built towns and fortresses—it is true they had to get the Sovereign's leave each time—they had an army and a cannon foundry of their own, they made war on the Siberian Princes, and traded, untaxed, with the Asiatic races. They were merchants and husbandmen indeed, but of a special kind ; For though, in Alexis' Code, we see them assimilated to the *gosti*, or merchants of the first rank, it is a matter of assimilation, and not of confusion. In the chapter devoted to the fines due for certain offences, the same scale is applied to the *gosti* and to the Stroganovs, but these last are mentioned by name. It has therefore been claimed, and with some show of reason, that this family constituted a social class in itself.

In 1558, Gregory Anikiév Stroganov applied to Ivan for a concession of 106 square versts of land on both banks of the Kama, above Perm ; he proposed to build a fort to defend this tract against the Tartars, to break up the soil, lay down pasture lands, and establish salt-works. His request was granted, and the Tsar released the concession from all taxes for a period of twenty years, only reserving any silver, tin, or copper mines that might be discovered on the ground. This was the usual condition on which such favours were granted, and the Sovereigns of Moscow were habitually open-handed in this respect, save as regards the right of keeping up an armed force. In this matter their political system was opposed to any division of power. But on the Siberian frontier necessity became a law unto itself. Stroganov built his fort on the Piskorka River, and called it Kankor. In 1564 he solicited and obtained permission to build another, about 20 versts away, on the Orel, and this was Kergedan. In 1566, at the powerful family's own request, all its establishments were included in the *Opritchnina*, and in 1568, these were still further and considerably increased. But these wide tracts of land had to endure perpetual attack on the part of the Tcheremisses, Bachkirs, and other wild tribes of the neighbourhood. Ivan, informed of this, advised the colonizers to arm a sufficient number of Cossacks and Ostiaks to enable them to put a stop to these aggressions. The Cossacks, in their pursuit of the aggressors, soon found their way across the Ural, and thus the legendary series of brilliant exploits began.

Just at that time a Tartar Khanate had risen up in Siberia, founded, it is believed, by the Taïbougi family, which, having quarrelled with the reigning house, had separated from it, and was labouring to bring the neighbouring countries, held by Bachkirs and Ostiaks, under its own rule. The capital of this State was called Sibir, or Isker. Here a Khan of Kirghiz-Khaïsiac origin, named Koutchoum, had reigned since 1556, when he had dethroned Ivan's former vassal, Iadiger. Alarmed by the progress made by the Stroganovs, and anxious to preserve his own independence, Koutchoum despatched his son or nephew, the Tsarevitch Makhmetkoul, to attack the new Russian settlements. Hostilities continued till 1582, and Ivan was thus led to increase the concessions and powers granted to the brothers James and Gregory Stroganov. The banks of the Tobol and its affluents beyond the Ural were made over to them. Between 1574 and 1579, the inheritance of this immense power and the burdens connected with it passed, by the death of its holders, to a third brother, Simon Anikiév, and to his two nephews, Maximus Iakovlevitch and Nikita Grigoriévitch, who, to save a perilous position, had recourse to a most dangerous expedient. The Cossack encampments (*stanitzy*) on the banks of the Don were the refuge and meeting-place, as I have already remarked, of a population of outlaws, drawn from every corner of the Russian Empire—men who were half-robbers and half-soldiers, most of whom had slipped through the hangman's fingers, and in whom that recollection served to wipe out all fear of Tsar, or God, or devil. Proposals for enlistment sent to these places, and coupled with liberal largesse, attracted to the banks of the river Kama, with a whole troop of bold companions, the man who is taken, even nowadays, to have been the conqueror of Siberia, but who was only the hero (his special glory was the result of a mere accident) of one out of a thousand episodes in which brute force, serving the steadier and surer progress of civilization, has insured the Muscovite domination in the Far East of Asia. Legend will indulge in such whims as these.

23

III.—The Cossacks.

All over the Empire, the Cossacks formed an integral portion of the Muscovite population. In the northern provinces, they were nomad labourers, agricultural or industrial. In the southern zone, the perpetual state of warfare generally converted them into soldiers. Commonly speaking, however, the generic title of Cossack was applied to vagabonds of every description, whether husbandmen or warriors—peaceful labourers when the occasion served, robbers in convenient seasons. The word, of Tartar origin, originally meant a peasant who had no local or personal connections, but more particularly, a soldier recruited from this nomad class. These men, in whom the quality of submission was lacking, to all eternity, went whither their fancy led them—some fled into the farthest steppes, and there formed military brotherhoods ; others stayed in their birthplace, and there organized armed bands, employed, for the most part, in robbery by violent means. For these last the official name was ' Cossack robbers ' (*vorovskiié*).

The constitution, geographical and ethnographical, of ancient Russia, her lack of strictly-defined limits, and provinces possessing historical boundary-lines, resulted in the fact that this mobile element, nominally dependent on the State, but practically almost completely independent of it, became the vanguard of the great colonizing movement. Thus, under Vassili, the Riazan Cossacks had sought, and found, the road to the Don ; under his successor they were settled on both banks of that river, and were soon a bugbear to the Tartars of the Crimea and of Azov, and the Nogaïs. The northern Ukraine was the first to send them a contingent of intrepid comrades, recruited among the Siévrouki, whose courage was proverbial ; but the attractions of the settlement were soon felt on every side. Town Cossacks and country Cossacks, all of them, the moment they were guilty of any crime, hurried to the same city of refuge. It gave Ivan considerable trouble. The Tartars, who were perpetually harried, made complaints, and the Tsar was fain to plead his own powerlessness in the matter. He could not contrive to keep all the ' brigands ' in order. Now and then, in the interval between two incursions into Tartar territory, the said ' brigands ' would take to the Volga, turn themselves into pirates, and, manning their swift *tchaïki*, fall on the Russian merchants. Then the Tsar's troops took action, and regular campaigns were made against them.

Yet it was with the Sovereign's permission that the Stroganovs enlisted a body of these miscreants, 640 men, commanded by two principal chiefs. One of these, Ivan Koltso, had already been sentenced to death, and the other appears to have possessed a heavily-laden conscience and a tolerably black judicial history—his name was Ermak Timofiéiévitch.

Historians do not agree as to the origin of the name which has attained such extraordinary popularity. Some guess it to be a corruption of Ermolaï or Hermann ; others take it to be a nickname, recalling the humble duties performed by the hero in connection with the preparation of the *kacha* in some *stanitsa*. *Ermak*, in the speech of the Volga country, means a handmill. Yet Monsieur Nikitski has found the name and its diminutive, Ermachko, in the lists of the inhabitants of Novgorod, where they seem to have been common.

On September 1, 1581, a little body of these Cossacks, strengthened by a detachment of soldiers drawn by the Stroganovs from the garrisons of their different forts—Russians and Lithuanians, Tartars and Germans—which swelled its numbers to some 840 men, all under Ermak's command, started forth to cross the Ural, following the path of twenty previous expeditions in the same direction, and attack Koutchoum on his own ground. That very day, a band of savage warriors, gathered by the Tartar Prince of Pelym, raided the province of Perm, and the *voiévode* of that province found himself overmatched. He applied to the Stroganovs for reinforcements, and they were obliged to decline on the score of the weak state in which the departure of Ermak and his men had left them. The *voiévode* made a complaint to Moscow, and so little was the Tsar disposed to look on this new trans-Uralian campaign as anything decisive or even exceptional, that he taxed the Stroganovs with treason, and sent orders to Perm that Ermak and his followers were to be brought back without the smallest delay. This order could not be carried out. Ermak was far away already.

IV.—Ermak in Siberia.

Makhmetkoul, who had been sent to meet the invaders, came upon them on the banks of the Tobol, and was terrified —he had never seen firearms before—by the ' bow that smokes and thunders.' He was completely routed. Arrived at the Irtych, Ermak defeated Koutchoum himself, and, in October, took possession of the capital, from which the Khan had fled. In the spring his Cossacks captured Makhmetkoul, and they spent the summer in occupying and subduing the little towns and Tartar *ouloussy* on the Irtych and the Ob. This done, Ermak bethought him of sending news of his doings to the Stroganovs, and even to the Tsar, actually venturing to send Koltso, the sentenced man for whom the executioner was still waiting on the scaffold, to the Sovereign.

He was not mistaken in thinking Ivan would be disarmed. Koltso was not even questioned as to his past, and, with the Tsar's congratulations, Ermak received a considerable sum of money, to which, so the legend assures us, Ivan added splendid gifts—two richly-adorned cuirasses, a silver goblet, and a pelisse taken off his own shoulders. At the same time the Tsar despatched two of his *voiévodes*, Prince Simon Bolkhovski and Ivan Gloukhov, to take possession, in his name, of the territories wrested from Koutchoum. This was the usual course of events. The Cossacks were sent on in front : when they were beaten they were disowned and called ' brigands '; when they won, the fruits of their victories were forthwith absorbed.

Ivan the Terrible did not live to hear of the fate which overtook his envoys, nor the tragic close of the enterprise in which Ermak had just won immortal renown. In the month of August, 1584, the valiant leader lost his life, on the banks of the Irtych, in a night surprise, the details of which have never been known. According to the legend, he tried to swim the river, and was dragged down by the weight of his cuirass, the Tsar's fatal gift. The Tartars recognised his corpse by the armour, which bore a gilded eagle, set his body on a scaffold, and used it for a target for the space of six weeks. Meanwhile, the huge clouds of birds of prey that hovered over the brave man's corpse did not dare to settle on it ; terrifying visions appeared around it, and so alarmed did the Tartars become that they resolved to give the hero magnificent burial, and killed and ate thirty oxen in the course of the ceremony. But fresh wonders occurred, even over the ashes of the heroic warrior, and at last the Moslem priests resorted to the expedient of burying the remains, and so thoroughly hiding the place of sepulture that it has never been discovered.

The only fact known to history is that Bolkhovski had already been carried off by sickness, and that after Ermak's death the second envoy was fain to beat a retreat in the direction of the Piétchora. As to its immediate results, therefore, this expedition was very much on a par with its predecessors. And yet a new thing had happened. The popular imagination had been stirred—by a more resounding name, it may be, or a bolder gesture—and out of the long series of efforts, repeated year by year, out of the crowd of unknown heroes in whose steps Ermak had followed, the popular legend had chosen its own. The bandit of those far-off days, whose glories the *bylines* have sung, whose monument stands at Tobolsk, whom the very Church venerates almost as a saint, was to be lifted up, in posthumous apotheosis, as high as Cortez or Christopher Columbus.

Legend is a power, for it commands, in a certain measure, those moral forces which play so decisive a part in the destinies of every race. It was inevitable that Ermak, magnified after this fashion, should have imitators and avengers. Dying, as he did, when his task was but half accomplished, he might well have said, ' *Non omnis morior !*' He had been no more than an instrument, and behind him, ready to begin again, to send forth more warriors, and push forward the never-ending progress of their peaceful toil under cover of the ' bows that smoked and thundered,' stood the real conquerors of Siberia—the Stroganovs, and their industrious army of colonists.

When the news of the catastrophe on the banks of the Irtych which had momentarily checked the Cossacks' onward march reached Moscow, Ivan was no more. Before I relate the story of the Sovereign's end—as tragic, though in a different way, as Ermak's—I will endeavour to evoke, in its splendour, its singularity, its horror, the picture of the strange surroundings, both of the Court and the home circle, in which he lived.

CHAPTER IV

THE COURT OF IVAN THE TERRIBLE—HIS PRIVATE LIFE

I.—THE COURT.   II.—THE SLOBODA OF ALEXANDROV.   III.—IVAN'S DOMESTIC LIFE.   IV.—THE TSAR'S FAMILY.

I.—THE COURT.

CHANCELLOR'S first impression, when he arrived at Moscow, was a mixture of admiring astonishment and disappointment. The town struck him as being larger than London—city and suburbs together—but he looked in vain for the splendour of which he had heard at Kholmogory. The only way in which the Kremlin surprised him was by its lack of everything he had expected to find there. He was conducted into an edifice which he had heard described as a ' palace of gold,' and it was not much more than a hut.

The celebrated enclosure already presented that appearance of an agglomeration of small things forming one huge whole which endues it, in our day, with such a peculiar type of its own. The great hall of the Palace, with its low vault resting on a single pillar, was ill-suited to the splendour of which it was destined to be the scene. And Ambassadors and distinguished travellers were generally received in another building, of still more modest proportions. Here and there, the furniture stood sparse and rustic—benches and stools of unpainted wood ; no trace of comfort of any sort, except a certain quantity of fine carpets and, if we may believe Mas-kiévitch, whose Memoirs were written in 1594, a *calorifère* which heated the great hall, and possibly some of the rooms nearest it.

In the sixteenth century, as now, the Kremlin was above all things a little town of churches—the Church of the Annuncia-tion, nearest the Palace, where the Tsar went to Mass every day ; the Church of the Assumption, the Metropolitan's cathedral, where the Sovereigns were crowned, and whither they went to hear Mass on great feast-days ; the Church of the Archangel Michael, which contained the tombs of the reigning family, and where in those days, as now, wax tapers dropped oily stains on the black palls that covered the wooden coff.ns ; the Church of St. John, with its tall tower full of a multitude of very heavy bells, never rung, for the building would have fallen down, but sounded by moving the clappers to and fro—some score of churches altogether, crammed into a comparatively narrow space, nestling one against the other, and rubbing shoulders with monasteries ; dwelling-houses reserved for the use of persons belonging to the Court, shops and workshops.

But Chancellor's first impression was to be altered when he was brought into the presence of the Tsar and his Court. He had seen the royal pomp of the Tudors and the Valois, but none the less was he astonished and delighted. The Sovereign, first of all. . . . Was that a mere Sovereign he beheld, seated on the famed throne, borne by four creatures modelled on the fantastic monsters of the Apocalypse ? Some twenty years later, when Possevino thus saw the Tsar, robed in a long tunic-shaped garment, a tiara on his head and a crozier in his hand, he fancied himself face to face with another Pope, a Pontiff-King, a *rex sacrorum*. A picture of the Virgin above the throne, one of the Saviour on its right, and Biblical scenes painted on all the surrounding walls, framed the monarch in a religious setting, like a god in a temple. Young warriors, with axes on their shoulders, stood on either side of him, indeed, but the Roman Pontiff had his halberdiers. And the most striking point of all, in these sacerdotal surroundings, was the attitude preserved by every person present—motionless, as though stricken with a kind of stupor. At a slightly later date, Margeret and Fletcher were to be equally struck by this detail. When the Tsar made his entry, the silence over that crowd of officials of every rank, and the serried lines of guards, in long white velvet or satin gowns, and tall white fur caps, half soldiers and half Levites, their gold chains crossed over their breasts, their gleaming axes lifted as though to strike, was so intense that an onlooker, closing his eyes, might have fancied the Palace utterly deserted.

Certainly, if the Sovereign's dwelling struck the traveller as being unworthy of its owner, his courtiers, both as to numbers and splendour, exceeded any to be seen in other countries. A perfect swarm of gentlemen, all glittering with gold and gems, crowded each other to suffocation within the narrow limits of the presence-chamber, overflowed on to the outer landing and the staircase, and filled all the approaches to the building.

Let us consider the elements which composed this gorgeous Court. In the Russian of the sixteenth century the word Court (*dvor*) had two meanings. It was used to designate the Sovereign's residence, and also to describe the various services centralized in it, and connected alike with the monarch's person and with the necessities of the State. The Sovereign lived in the upper story (*vierkh*) of the Palace ; the rest of the edifice and the buildings connected with it were occupied by various officials who worked in different offices or departments (*prikazes*), and were employed either in the business of keeping up the Court or in administering the affairs of the country. A century later, Kotochikhine counted forty of these *prikazes*, divided into chambers (*palaty*), and forming as many independent ministries—the town *prikaze*, the Customs *prikaze*, the Chief Court *prikaze*, which last fulfilled the functions of the present Court Minister. Yet the service of the Court was in the hands of a number of special departments—the *prikaze* for supplies, or *jiteïnyï dvor*, for the Court table ; the *kormovoï dvor* for bread ; the *khlebnyï dvor* for the cellars, the wardrobe, the stables. The wardrobe department, which had to clothe, not the Sovereign only, but, on certain occasions, the whole of the Court, both great dignitaries and ordinary officials, had its own workshop, the *masterskaïa palata*, and huge warehouses, and its work was no sinecure.

The posts connected with the Court were very numerous. Some were very ancient, others of quite modern growth. Nestor mentions the *stolniki* (*dapiferi*), whose duty it was to offer the dishes, afterwards cut up and distributed by the *kraïtchyï* and the *okolnitchyï* (carving equerry and Great Officer of the Crown), to the Sovereign and his guests at the State banquets. In very ancient times, too, the *stolniki* were employed in other ways, as envoys to foreign Courts and as provincial governors. The number of these dignitaries reached 500. In the second rank came the *spalniki* (from *spat*, to sleep) and the *postiélniki* (from *postiél*, bedtime), whose duties were to dress or undress the Sovereign and look after his bedchamber. Besides this, the *spalnik* was a member of the Privy Council, and the *postiélnik* was Keeper of the Seals for all secret business. Both these officials slept in the Tsar's room.

The *okolnitchyié* (from *okolo*, around—*qui circa principem versabantur*, as Du Cange says) make their first appearance in 1356, and their duties, likewise exceedingly varied, were generally of a judicial nature. For current affairs the Sovereign also had his *striaptchyié* (from *striapat*, to fulfil a duty), who, on great ceremonial occasions, bore the sceptre before him, held up his train, and looked after his arms. These were officers of an inferior rank, but not the lowest in the official hierarchy. After them came the *diaki* and the *podiatchyié*, clerks, learned men, who knew how to read and write. Their original function had been to sing in church, and hence their name—*diak* stands for deacon. They were employed at a later period as clerks in the offices, and by the sixteenth century these *diaki* were doing very much the work of the modern French *référendaire*. Some of them had seats on the Council, and were called *doumnyié diaki*. The *podiatchyié* were their assistants. At the very bottom of the ladder, and occupying a post which in other countries, and especially in Poland, carried much more prestige with it, came the *dvoretskii*, or *dvornik*, originally a sort of Court Marshal, but from the sixteenth century onwards a financial official, more especially—Keeper of the Privy Purse—a reproduction of the Eastern *curialis*, who underwent the same transformations.

The Tsarina's Court, with the exception of a few pages, none of them over ten years of age, who passed, as they grew up, into the Tsar's household, consisted of ladies only. The chief post was held by a *boïarinia*, who was responsible for the Privy Purse and the Bedchamber. Next to her a *kraïtchinia*, whose duty it was to look after all the *personnel* of the household, ruled a little world of *maïsterytsé*, dressmakers and embroideresses, gave orders to the *postiélnitsé*, and shared with them the honour of sleeping, turn about, in the Sovereign's room, and attending her on the rare occasions when she went abroad. When this occurred, the *postiélnitsé* turned themselves into amazons, mounted horses, and surrounded the Tsarina's coach

The largest and best-lighted apartment in the portion of the Palace reserved for the Consort's use was a workroom, out of which opened a suite of other chambers—*sviétlitsy* (from *sviétlyi*, light)—occupied by some fifty women, all employed either in 'white sewing,' otherwise the making of linen garments, or 'gold sewing,' embroidery in gold or silver thread or silks. These last rooms formed a sort of school of art, just as the *Ikonopisnaïa palata*, on the other side of the Palace, was at once a studio for producing ikons and an academy of painting. In the *sviétlitsy*, ikons were also embroidered with a delicacy which still stirs the wonder of modern archæologists.

Ivan, as we have already perceived, was the very wealthy Sovereign of an exceedingly poor country. When Fletcher paid a visit to the Tsar's treasury, he thought he must be dreaming. Great heaps of pearls, emeralds, and rubies lay amongst piles of gold plate and hundreds of gold cups enriched with gems and precious stones of every kind. These riches, which had been constantly amassed from reign to reign, were generally kept hidden away. They were only shown on rare occasions, and then chiefly for the benefit of foreigners. Chancellor, on the occasion of the departure of an embassy to Poland, saw 500 horsemen dressed with a magnificence exceeding anything he had ever imagined. Their garments were of gold and silver tissue, their saddle-housings of pearl-embroidered velvet. All these splendours had come from the Grand Duke's treasury. The boïars composing the guard of honour in attendance on Maximilian's embassy undressed before the envoys to show off the splendour of their undergarments; but all their clothes, upper or under, were the Sovereign's property, and, the display over, everything had to be returned to the place whence it came, 'untorn and unstained,' on pain of fine.

And all this splendour was combined with strange omissions. Jenkinson, when invited to the Tsar's table, was served on gold plate, and reckoned the value of the goblets handed about among the guests at an average of £400 sterling. Fletcher, on a similar occasion, counted 300 officials in gold and silver brocade, who waited at the repast. The Sovereign himself sat at a massive gold table. One hundred dishes, gold, silver-gilt, or silver, were brought in at the same time. But the guests were given neither plates nor knives and forks, much less napkins. The Muscovites habitually carried a knife and spoon in their belts, and the lack of any other convenience was supplied by little cakes, round and flat. In 1576, the Emperor's envoys noticed that the guests, numbering some 200, at the banquet given in their honour, were themselves supplied before the repast with gold brocade gowns from the Sovereign's wardrobe, and these were replaced, as soon as everyone was seated at table, by white mantles trimmed with ermine.

All these features have an importance of their own with regard to the history of the country and the formation of the national ideas and habits ; for they inculcated the conviction that the Russian people, in itself, was nothing, and had nothing. Everything was summed up in the Sovereign's person, and to him everything belonged. The ceremonial observed at these banquets contributed to this belief. The Tsar, having first crossed himself devoutly, helped himself to a slice of meat carved by the equerry carver, offered morsels of it to some of the great personages present, and overlooked the distribution of the dishes amongst the other guests, the bearers of the portions saying to each person, ' The Tsar sends you this,' whereupon the recipient rose in his place and thanked the donor. The same ceremony attended the pouring out of the various beverages. The quality of these last was generally praised by foreigners, but the saffron used in seasoning the dishes, the sauces made of sour milk, and the condiments, cucumber and vinegar, introduced into many of them, were unpleasant to their palates ; while the necessity of remaining at table for five or six hours, and drinking every cup of wine sent them, was a trial to the toughest. Further, there was a custom whereby the Sovereign, after the banquet, sent his chief guests, at their own houses, a further supply of victuals and drink, which they were expected to share, then and there, with the Tsar's officers who had brought it. On one occasion one of the Emperor's Ambassadors thus received seven goblets of Burgundy, as many each of Rhine wine, Muscat, French white wine, Canary, Alicant, and Malmsey, twelve measures of the best hydromel, seven hundred jars of an inferior quality, eight dishes of roast swan, as many of spiced crane, several dishes of cocks dressed with ginger, boned fowls, black-cock cooked in saffron, hazel-grouse cooked in cream, ducks with cucumber, geese with rice, hares with dumplings and turnips, elks' brains, innumerable cakes and pies made with meat, cheese, or sugar, besides pancakes, fritters, jellies, creams, and preserved walnuts. And the poor man had just risen from table !

In that country, truly, Gargantua dwelt in flesh and blood.

At Court, as in all private houses, feasts, immoderate and excessive eating and drinking, were the indispensable accompaniment of every merry-making, and the greatest entertainment that could be offered. And, in spite of the Church's anathemas, other pleasures were by no means banished. One special chamber, the *potiéchnaïa palata*, had charge of these, in fact. Games were much played in the Tsar's immediate circle—

chess, draughts, and cards. There was much hunting with hounds and greyhounds, hawks and falcons. There was bear-hunting, too, and in his earlier years Ivan appears to have been passionately addicted to this sport. Later, when the cares of government absorbed him, the hunting department suffered from his neglect, and when, after the truce of Iam-Zapolski, Batory expressed a desire to have red falcons, such as he had heard the Tsar possessed, Ivan sent the King back a message to the effect that the breed was extinct ; the Tsar, owing to his sorrows, had long since given up hawking. Batory, on his side, inquired what present from himself would be most agreeable to the Sovereign. The reply was ' Good horses, iron helmets, and light, straight-carrying muskets.'

All the vanquished foeman of Polotsk and Viélikié-Louki asked of the victor was arms !

Yet even at that moment he kept a certain number of jesters about him, those *douraki* or *chouty* who, even as late as towards the middle of the eighteenth century, were to form an integral part of the Court circle. The jokes perpetrated by these official entertainers may have been more or less witty, but they were almost always obscene. Poverty of intellectual culture favoured an excessive coarseness of imagination, and the extreme moral pressure imposed by the ascetic doctrines which prevailed drove men, by a sort of natural reaction, into the most cynical license. Further, the jester, with the freedom of speech permitted him within certain limits, supplied that need of critical and satirical expression which exists in every society, and which, having no literary vent, here found some measure of satisfaction. The *choute*, with his jeers at the precepts of the *Domostroï* and the rules of an Oriental etiquette, stirred the heavy atmosphere of prison and cloister combined, which hung stagnant in every Russian household ; he opened doors and broke window-panes, and let a little fresh air into these smothering stoves. In those days every house of any importance sheltered one or two such persons. Ivan had dozens of them, and some paid with their lives for the honour of rubbing elbows familiarly with their Sovereign. There was one called Gvozdev—a Prince, like the man who afterwards became the Empress Anne's *dourak*—who held an important Court appointment ; such pluralism was quite a usual and recognised thing. On a certain day, Ivan, for a joke, turned a bowl of boiling soup (*chtchi*) over Gvozdev's head. When the poor fellow cried out, the Sovereign, who was drunk, replied by a dagger-thrust, and the jester fell, covered with blood. A physician was summoned. ' Cure my faithful servant,' said the Tsar, quite sobered now ; ' I have played with him imprudently.' ' So imprudently,' replied the leech, ' that neither

God nor your Majesty will ever make him play again in this world !'

Gvozdev was dead !

Like Peter the Great in later days, Ivan gave his jesters a place and a part even in the most solemn ceremonies, and hence the religious emotion felt by those present on these serious occasions, and shared by foreign witnesses, was now and then replaced by very different impressions. Ivan the Terrible, being what we know him to have been, was not capable of keeping up that hieratic attitude in which he would first reveal himself on his throne to his admiring spectators. One day he snatched the cap off a Polish Ambassador's head, put it on that of a *choute*, and ordered him to bow in the Polish manner. When the man demurred, on the score of ignorance, the Tsar himself mimicked the gesture, went into fits of merriment, and raised a laugh all through the assembled gathering at the foreigner's expense. Or, again, like Napoleon I., he would startle another envoy by an outbreak of rage, a flood of abuse and threats. And it was terror, then, that bowed the backs of the courtiers gathered under the low-vaulted roof of the Kremlin.

But at the *Sloboda* of Alexandrov, most especially, the various aspects of the Court life, thus adapted to the character and habits of the Sovereign of that particular period, made up one of the strangest pictures ever bequeathed by history to a wondering posterity.

II.—THE SLOBODA OF ALEXANDROV.

After the conflagration of 1547, by which the Kremlin was almost entirely destroyed, Ivan lived for some time in the village of Vorobiévo, while a wooden residence was being hastily constructed for his use at Moscow, and the brick-built Palace, which had been ravaged by the flames, was being restored. In 1565, when he founded the *Opritchnina*, the Sovereign thought for a moment of building himself another palace within the Kremlin. On consideration, however, he concluded it would be better to remove his new dwelling-place to some distance from that he was giving up to the Tsar Simeon, and he chose a site outside, on the Vozdvijenka, and close to the present Gate of the Holy Trinity. Here he took up his quarters in 1567, but his stay was not a long one. Moscow was always as hateful a residence to him as it was to be to Peter the Great. He preferred Kolomenskoié, his father's favourite home, where he himself went every year to keep his fête-day. In spite of its wild and forbidding landscape, Vologda, on the river of the same name, also had its charms for him. Here, by his orders, a huge wooden palace was raised on an eminence on which the present Government offices now stand. Here, too, he built a cathedral on the model of that of the Assumption. But before long the *Sloboda* of Alexandrov took the gloomy despot's fancy, and held it.

This famous suburb was Ivan the Terrible's Plessis-les-Tours, just as Maliouta-Skouratov was his Tristan-l'Ermite. A. Tolstoï has given us a picturesque but purely imaginary description of the dwelling. The buildings of the present Monastery of the Assumption at Alexandrov are said to contain part of the ancient Palace, which has disappeared and left no visible trace behind. This monastery, like the Palace at Vologda, stands on an eminence over the river. The cathedral within its walls does appear to be of Ivan's date. We can still recognise a door brought from Novgorod after the sacking of that town, and the whole edifice looks like a reconstruction, into the composition of which elements originally intended for a quite different purpose have entered ; the doors and windows are dotted about with no apparent meaning, and there are recesses in the walls which are quite unsuitable to modern requirements. The same peculiarities are noticeable in the Monastery of the Child Jesus at Tver, where St. Philip's cell has been turned into a chapel. At Alexandrov, apart from the cathedral, a block of masonry which certainly belonged to some other building still exists. Some persons have thought they recognised in this the site of the rooms once tenanted by Ivan and his associates. This conjecture would seem to be confirmed by the huge basements, with their mysterious recesses and subterranean passages plunging into unknown depths, out of which the visitor expects to see bloody phantoms rise.

But these walls, which may have seen and heard so many things, are dumb now, and local tradition is as dumb. To reconstitute the history of all that happened there—all that stood for so much in the life of a most remarkable man, and the story of a great country, we are fain to fall back on legends and on a few unreliable chroniclers. This suburb, the seat of a government, the centre of an administration, has slipped, as to both these memories, through the fingers of posterity, even that nearest to it ; and those contemporaries who mention it at all consider it little better than a resort of brigands. Yet a verification of their narratives by comparison with some few more reliable documents and certain established facts may enable us to form some idea of what the dwelling, and the lives of those who dwelt in it, may have been.

I have already given my opinion as to the accusations brought against the *Opritchnina*. It was a revolutionary undertaking, and its natural consequence was a reign of terror, attended by inevitable excesses. The fellow-workers to whom Ivan found himself obliged to appeal, some of them drawn from the lowest strata of society, and all incapable of understanding the nature and real object of his enterprise, were even more inclined than he himself to confuse violence with energy. And, docile instruments and complaisant courtiers as they were, they flattered and increased the taste for coarse debauchery which the Sovereign owed to his education, and to certain cruel instincts, inherent, no doubt, in his temperament. The chroniclers have preserved the names of these fellow-workers to us. First of all, and in the front rank, came the boïar Alexis Basmanov and his son Feodor ; Prince Athanasius Viazemski ; Vassili Griaznoï, Archimandrite of the Monastery of Tchoudov ; Levkiï ; and, fiercest and most illustrious of them all, Gregory Loukianovitch Maliouta-Skouratov. At a later period, Bogdan Biélski, who, with Basmanov and several others, was reported to be the Tsar's *mignon*, and Boris Goudounov, Skouratov's son-in-law, and himself to be Tsar one day, were paramount in the Sovereign's favour and confidence.

In this inner circle, legend assigns the highest place to Anastasia's brother, Nikita Romanovitch Zakharine, a personage with whom we have already made acquaintance. Relying on I know not what or which appearances or realities, it has endued him with virtues — a generous and loyal heart, and a pure and upright mind—which strike one as being somewhat incompatible with such surroundings. Taking it all together, I am inclined to think Ivan, in that particular phase of his life, at all events, could not have put up with a comrade of this sort, and that Zakharine has reaped the benefit of a deliberate process of idealization applied to the historical origin of the whole of his family, once it had become the ancestor of an Imperial house.

In principle, indeed, the *Sloboda* of Alexandrov was anything but a home of debauchery. Ivan, as we know, always affected a great inclination towards the monastic life, and certain monastic tendencies were frequently allied, in his case, with a looseness of morals really by no means foreign to the cloistered rule of those days. We have seen, too, that he was anxious to work a reform which would have brought back the monastic world to a stricter observance of the rules, all too often broken, of the religious life. The idea of setting a personal example in this respect certainly swayed the conception of the system he adopted, and applied, for many years, to the internal arrangements of his Court at Alexandrov. The chief features of the constitution of the *Opritchnina* already endued it with certain of the characteristics of a brotherhood. Each of the *Opritchniki* took a special oath which bore some resemblance to vows. He renounced the world, after a fashion, and gave up all his former relations. The *Sloboda* bore all the outward appearance of a hermitage. Within its walls 300 comrades, more specially attached to the Sovereign's person, lived according to a most severe rule. Over their gold-embroidered kaftans they had to wear black gowns, and take their part in most complicated religious observances. The Tsar was the prior, Viaziémski cellarer, Skouratov sacristan. The Sovereign himself, with his sons, rang the bells for service. At midnight everybody was on foot for the first prayers. At four o'clock in the morning all were in church again for matins, which lasted till seven. At eight everyone heard Mass, and Ivan took pains to edify his comrades by prostrating himself over and over again, till his forehead was covered with bumps. At twelve o'clock dinner was served in the refectory, the Tsar reading aloud from some pious book, and, as in the best-managed monasteries, all the food that remained over was given to the poor. The Sovereign, as prior of the community, ate his meals alone, but everybody sat down together afterwards to drink. Some of the *Opritchniki* made these entertainments as lively as if they had been qualified jesters, and ladies were admitted to them. . . .

To Ivan, as to most of his contemporaries, this constituted the ideal of the religious life—excess of devotion redeeming excess of debauch, external practices and material austerity atoning for lack of internal piety, and excusing the worst moral failings. And in that sense, the *Sloboda* of Alexandrov was a place of stern discipline. There is no doubt Ivan took his parody in the most serious way. I see a proof of this in the celebrated epistle he addressed, in 1575, to the Archimandrite and monks of the Monastery of St. Cyril at Biélooziéro. The man who indited this missive was certainly imbued with the conviction that he himself was a monk called to hold converse with other monks on a subject peculiarly interesting to men of the same vocation. The correspondence took its rise out of the following circumstances. The powerful family of the Chérémétiév was one of those which had been most sorely tried by the persecution under which the upper aristocracy had suffered subsequent to Ivan's accession to the throne. One of the three brothers who were its chief members, Nikita Vassilivitch, had been put to death ; another, Ivan, a renowned warrior, had made acquaintance with prison and the torture-chamber. To escape worse treatment, he had retired to the Monastery of Biélooziéro, and there become a monk, under the name of Iona. According to the custom of those days, such an entrance into the religious life, imposed by sheer necessity, admitted of a very liberal amount of compromise. Brother Iona gave up part of his fortune to the community, but he still retained a very large amount, and led an independent life in a house close to the monastery, where he was attended by numerous servants, and kept a liberal kitchen, and everything else to match. He was exceedingly hospitable, and the monks, who took advantage of this, returned the compliment by showing him every kind of civility, sending him presents and dainties of various kinds. The monastery itself was not addicted to privation. The establishment was an enormous one. Round the chief building stood eleven others, which sheltered the kitchens, the bakeries, the storehouses, and in one part of the edifice, still intact, there are 700 rooms, supposed to have been occupied by servants. Chérémétiév was not the only monk of noble birth in the establishment. The community could likewise boast the presence of Vassili Stepanovitch Sobakine, known in religion as Varlaam ; Ivan Ivanovitch Khabarov, son of the famous Khabar Simskii ; and other *viêlmoji*, sent there in disgrace by Ivan. There were frequent disputes between these guests, some of whom, less rich, and consequently less well treated than Chérémétiév, looked on the favours of which he was the recipient with a jealous eye. In this way a complaint reached Ivan, who could not fail to be displeased at hearing that men whom he had disgraced were still enjoying so many privileges in their exile. And the Sovereign at once set about calling the monks to order. Chérémétiév must take his meals at the common table. When the monks excused themselves by saying that their brother's health had rendered the concession necessary, the Tsar thought it well to press the matter further, and wrote the epistle, which, from the literary point of view, is probably his masterpiece.

He begins by a confession which would seem to justify the worst of the accusations brought against his private and his public life. With his usual bluntness, he calls himself a ' stinking dog,' living in ' drunkenness, adultery, murder, brigandage,' and other mortal sins. Are we to take him literally ? One might fancy there was no reason why he should slander himself. But still less do we see any reason why he should declare, immediately afterwards, that the few truths he proposes to tell his brothers ' come out of his foolishness.' The real meaning of this preamble is very soon apparent. The Prior of Alexandrov is talking the language habitually used by the monks of his period. He accuses himself and humbles himself, he bows his head and strikes at himself by a sort of irony, which is to make the blows he is

about to deal others mightier still.   His conscience is a heavy
one indeed.   But the repentance of which he makes such a
show is as sincere as his claim to be a member of the Biélooziéro community, and thus to a right to interfere in its inner
workings, is serious.   Some years ago, when paying a visit to
the monastery, he remembers having expressed a desire to
enter the Order at some future date, and now, turning that
intention into accomplished fact, for his own convenience,
he arrives, taking this ingenious by-way, at the object
of his endeavour, in other words, to lash his contradictors
with the spiritual rods which, for the moment, are the chosen
weapons of his fancy.   And after this fashion he addresses
them, sprinkling his discourse, as usual, with quotations and
examples culled from the Fathers of the Church and from
Scripture   history,   from   Roman   annals   and   Byzantine
chronicles.

' Under your roof you have Haman and Caiaphas—Chérémétiév and Khabarov.   You have Pilate—Varlaam Sobakine—and you have the Christ, nailed once more upon His
Cross. . . .   It is no longer Chérémétiév, it is no longer
Khabarov, who have taken the monkish habit in your house
—it is you who are their guests.   They are a law to you.
Go on !   To-day some boïar will introduce one piece of license
into your midst.   To-morrow another will make you accept
some fresh concession to your common weaknesses, and thus,
little by little, the whole rule of the monastery will be broken
down, and your way of life will become exactly the same as
that of the rest of the world. . . .   You began by giving
Jehosaphat (Kolytchev) a pewter service, and allowing him
to be served in his own cell. . . .   Now Chérémétiév has his
own table and his own kitchen.   And the consequences are
beginning to be manifest : all the monks live just as they
please. . . .   Tumult, disorder, noise, rebellion, frivolity !
. . . Wherefore ?   For whom ?   For that rogue, that dog
whose name is Sobakine ' (a play on the word *sobaka*, dog), ' or
for that son of the devil whose name is Chérémétiév, or for
that idiot whose name is Khabarov ! . . .'

This epistle has been published in the ' Historical Documents ' (i., No. 204).   Karamzine (' History of Russia,' ix.,
p. 37, note) believes it was written about 1578.   But A. Bars-
soukov seems to me nearer the truth when he gives the date
as having been somewhere between the spring of 1574 and
that of 1575 (' The Chérémétiév Family,' i. 324).   I must add
that all Ivan did was to take and rearrange, to suit his own
purpose, texts borrowed from old works on religious contro-
versial subjects, current diatribes against the dissolute habits
of the religious communities, with which the monks of Biéloo-

ziéro were already well acquainted, as the copies found in
their own library prove. As for the spirit which inspired his
intervention, it is made evident by the following detail :
With the epistle he sent a gold *bratina* adorned with *figures
of naked women, in relief*, as a present from the Tsar to the
community he desired to recall to a sense of its duties !
Here we have the true spirit of the *Sloboda* of Alexandrov !

Ivan lived there, as Louis XI. had lived at Plessis-les-Tours
a century previously, between the monks whose pious exercises he shared, the locksmiths who laboured on the famous
fillettes du roi—heavy chains fastened on the legs of the
prisoners shut up in the iron cages,—and those other servants
of his, whose accounts appear in His Majesty's books under
the head of ' *Voluptés* '—so much one day for having brought
a lady who pleased the King's fancy from Dijon to Tours,
and so much another for purchasing two dozen of canary-
birds ! (Henri Martin, *Histoire de France*, vii. 145). Though
Louis did not turn Plessis - les - Tours into a monastery,
we know he built one, close by, for the Calabrian monk
Francesco di Paulo. He, too, surrounded himself with ' evil
folk of low condition,' while at the same time, to drive away
the ennui which devoured him, or still the terrors that haunted
him, he collected ' players of the bass viol and of sweet instruments ' from all parts of the world. But, so the chronicle of
St. Denis tells us, ' nothing could amuse him.'

After evening prayers at the *Sloboda* of Alexandrov, Ivan
betook himself to his bedchamber, where three blind old men
awaited his coming. Their duty was to send him to sleep by
telling him stories, and no doubt to save him, by their company, from the horrors of loneliness and darkness. In the
daytime the Sovereign had other amusements. Is it true,
as we have been told, that, when dinner was over, he went
round the torture-chambers to enjoy the sight of the anguish
inflicted at his command ? Did he even act as executioner
himself from time to time ? Can it be that, morose and
gloomy as he was everywhere else, his face changed and he
grew merry in the midst of all these horrors, mingling his
shouts of laughter with the shrieks of his victims ? It may
be so. But the Tsar also found pleasure in the less sanguinary
sport afforded him by *skomorokhy*—tumblers, jugglers, and
bear-leaders. Search was made for these all over the country,
and those who chose them out were not over-particular. The
Novgorod chronicle tells us the story of a certain Soubota
Osiétr, who, after abusing and striking a *diak* named Danilo
Barténiev, turned a bear loose on the unlucky official's heels,
and let it hunt him into his office, where it spread terror among

a knot of employés, some of whom were knocked down by the infuriated creature's paws. After this exhibition of prowess, the beast and its owner were deemed fair game for the Tsar's entertainment, and were at once sent off to Alexandrov with a troop of *skomorokhy*.

Bears, whether wild or tame, played a leading part in the life of the suburb. They were made to perform grotesque pantomimes. They were used to startle and mystify visitors. Often, too, they were set to fight pitched battles, not with dogs only, but with human beings. Horsey's story of the terrible experience of six fat monks who were accused of rebellion and forced to fight for their lives with six huge bears, which ate up five of them, though the sixth beast's adversary was strong enough to overcome him, may not be worthy of credence. Guagnino declares that in winter, as soon as the ice-bound river became, as usual, the common haunt of the whole population, which crowded to amuse itself by staring at the shops, the Tsar *habitually* let some of his domestic planti-grades loose on the peaceable inhabitants. One isolated fact of this nature may have taken place, but its *habitual* recur-rence would no doubt have prevented people from coming back to the river. On this point, as on so many others, the chronicle has probably exaggerated features belonging to some extent, as we have seen, to the history of the general habits of a country and a period in which bear-baiting con-stituted one of the favourite and most ordinary entertainments of every class of society.

All legends apart, the *Sloboda* of Alexandrov has left memories most offensive both to morality and decency. The banquets that followed on the pious exercises already referred to were absolute orgies. Women played an im-portant part in the life of Ivan the Terrible, and the *Opritchniki*, it may be, did what they could to ensure the satisfaction of tastes and needs which neither age nor sick-ness seem ever to have diminished, in this passionate and most immoderate nature. It is quite probable that this daily debauch may have been marked by odious and occa-sionally cruel refinements of detail, even if we conclude the chroniclers to have been drawing on their imaginations when they describe Skouratov and Basmanov and their peers as indulging in a delirium of monstrous wickedness with the young peasant women they had stripped and forced to run naked after flying poultry, while they shot at them with arrows. . . . At a time when genuine monasteries only too often took on the appearance of houses of ill fame, we may easily guess what went on in this one, which was a mere imitation. Adultery throned it there, with the Tsar-Prior, the husband of three or four cast-off wives ; and after Anastasia died there was certainly nothing edifying about the life Ivan led.   Yet the very fact of his otherwise inexplicable obstinacy in seeking to enter into fresh bonds of matrimony would seem—so far as the Sovereign himself is concerned, at all events—to weaken the authority of the legend concerning the troops of women conveyed into the suburb, and the harem said to have accompanied the Tsar wherever he went.   Ivan was a man addicted to women, but his religious scruples made him a man addicted to wives, and who cared so much about marrying them that he would play at being honestly wedded just as he played at living in a monastery.

III.—IVAN'S DOMESTIC LIFE.

The Tsar's second wife, the wild Circassian called Temrioukovna, baptized under the name of Maria, whom he married in 1561, and who died in 1569, bears the reputation of having possessed morals as loose as her instincts were fierce.   Two years after her death, Ivan's choice fell on the daughter of a plain Novgorod merchant, called Marfa Vasiliévna Sobakine. She only lived a fortnight after her wedding-day, and the Tsar declared she had been poisoned before she had really become his wife, and died a maid.   Thus, at least, he strove to justify the fourth union, to which he at once turned his mind, and which the rules of his Church forbade.   He pleaded necessity, pointed out that three of his wives had been poisoned, one after the other ; that when the second died he had felt a strong inclination to enter a monastery; that the cares of his children's education and of his Empire—his exact words were ' of the defence of the Christian faith '— had kept him in the world, and still retained him there, and that therefore, ' to avoid falling into sin,' he must take him a wife.   The Church gave in, though she imposed a penance on this obstinate espouser of wives, and in 1572 he led the daughter of one of his *dvorniks*, Anne Koltovski, to the altar. Three years afterwards he sent her to a monastery, accused, so it seems, of being mixed up in a plot, and in the massacres consequent on this accusation the whole of the wretched woman's family appears to have perished.   Under the name of Daria, this ex-Tsarina lived on at Tihkvine till the year 1626.
The Tsar then took two mistresses, one after the other, named Anne Vassiltchikov and Vassilissa Meletiév.   They passed as his wives, though the Sovereign never went beyond asking his confessor's leave to live with them, and no doubt this dignitary felt the confessional must not deal too strictly with a man of Ivan's kidney.   About both these favourites a

crop of legends has sprung up, and the work of many a poet
and novelist has been inspired by them. Ostrovski, in a
famous play which puts both heroines on the scene, and sets
one against the other, gives us a striking picture of a rivalry
which may be imaginary, but which is wonderfully representative of the historical surroundings amidst which the two
women lived and suffered. He makes Anne Vassiltchikov,
who realizes that she is on the brink of being supplanted by
Vassilissa, whom the author turns into her serving-woman,
speak as follows :

> ' I am terrified here, I cannot breathe ; my heart
> Is not at rest : the Tsar has ceased to be kind to me :
> The servants look at me askance. From far away
> I hear the echoes of the master's pleasures,
> The noise of his gaiety. . . . This dreary palace, for an instant,
> Is full of singing and laughter,
> Then the silence of the grave falls on it again, as though
> Death were everywhere. Only in the recesses
> Of the *terem* I hear low whispers—of executions.!
> Nothing to warm my heart ! I am the Tsar's wife in the flesh,
> But in my heart I am a stranger to him ! He frightens me. . . .
> He terrifies me when he is angry, and quite as much when he is
> merry.
> I do not know his love. . . .
> . . . Like a beast
> He seeks my caresses. . . . Never a tender word!
> And as to what I feel in my heart he never asks !'

Ostrovski has probably written true history, again, when
he shows us Ivan alone with Vassilissa, now his acknowledged
favourite. The Tsar wants to leave his new companion, of
whom he is beginning to tire, and she keeps him because she
is afraid. She speaks of the dead folk that lie between them,
and makes him tremble too. She bids him amuse her, and
in vain he answers roughly that he is not where he is for her
amusement ! She feels cold, and at a sign from her, and
after drawing his dagger to strike her, he takes off his kaftan
and throws it over her feet. She asks him to call her Tsarina.
He answers indignantly, ' What kind of a Tsarina are you ?
Did I lead you to the altar ? Did I have you crowned ?'
But she replies, ' How can you argue with a silly woman ?
Spit on her, and then do as she chooses !' And the Tsar
obeys once more. She falls asleep, and then, when he is sure
she cannot hear him, he speaks to her of love. He, who
dares everything, had not dared to do it before !

As to the causes which brought about the disgrace of these
two favourites we have no information. Ostrovski may have
guessed them rightly when he puts these words, addressed
to Anne Vassiltchikov, into Ivan's mouth: ' You are growing
thin. . . . I do not like thin women ! . . .'

According to one of the current legends, a third mistress succeeded these two in 1573, Maria Dolgorouki by name, who was sent away after the very first night—either because the Tsar suspected her affections were engaged elsewhere, or because he had discovered she was not a maid—and drowned in a carriage dragged by runaway horses into the river Siéra. But this story has been told of several of the Tsar's temporary companions, and Anne Vassiltchikov, according to several chroniclers, whose testimony is confirmed by that of Printz von Buchau, was still in favour three years later than this, and finally died a violent death, as it would seem. Vassilissa, after a much shorter career, was shut up, while still young and beautiful, if we may believe the chroniclers, in a cloister at Novgorod, Ivan having perceived that she cast a too friendly eye on Prince Ivan Devtelev, whom he caused to be executed at the same time.

In September, 1580, just when Batory was preparing for his second victorious campaign, the Tsar contracted a seventh or eighth union, more or less legitimate, with Maria Nagoï, daughter of Feodor Feodorovitch, one of his boïars, and this lady soon became the mother of the Tsarevitch Dmitri. At the same time he married his son Feodor to Irene, sister of Boris Godounov, and thus provided himself with a fresh family circle, on which he seems to have concentrated all the affections of his later years. This, however, did not prevent him, as we have already seen, from pursuing his plan for a marriage with Mary Hastings.

My readers will imagine what were the conditions, under such circumstances, of the family life still further disturbed and darkened, in 1581, by a catastrophe to which I have already referred.

IV.—THE TSAR'S FAMILY.

By his first wife Ivan had two sons. Of these, the second, Feodor, sickly in body and weak in mind, was a person of small importance. The eldest, Ivan, seems to have borne a considerable resemblance, both physically and morally, to his father, and he shared all his occupations and amusements. Like his progenitor, he had literary tastes, and composed a Life of St. Anthony, the manuscript of which is preserved amongst the papers of Count A. Tolstoï. And by the time he was thirty he had married his third wife. Oderborn declares the father and son were in the habit of exchanging their mistresses. When one of these, living at that moment with the Tsarevitch, complained of the language used about her by other ladies, the Tsar is said to have had the culprits seized and laid naked on the snow, so that all the passers-by might see them and jeer at them. I merely mention this story to give some idea of the general opinion as to the relations existing between the Sovereign and his heir.

The Tsarevitch's first wife was called Eudoxia Sabourov ; the name of the second was Praxevna Solov. Both were cast off, and forced to take the veil. The third wife, Helena Chérémétiév, was pregnant when the Tsar killed her husband in a fit of rage. There are various versions of what happened in connection with this murder. Some chroniclers have invented a scene in the course of which the Tsarevitch reproached his father for his cowardice in face of Batory's successes, and demanded the command of an army to make an effort to drive out the invader. Others have supposed he interfered in favour of some Livonian prisoners who were being ill-treated by the *Opritchniki*. Considering the agreement of feeling and thought which, according to most witnesses, admittedly existed between father and son, these stories strike one as highly improbable. Possevino, who was at Moscow three months after the catastrophe, suggests another, and a much more plausible cause. Ivan seems to have met his daughter-in-law within the precincts of the Palace, and noticed a lack of modesty in her attire. She may, owing to her condition, have omitted putting on a girdle over her *sorotchka*. In his displeasure, the Tsar Prior struck the poor woman, and so roughly that she miscarried in the course of the following night. As an inevitable consequence, the Tsarevitch reproached his father, who at once flew into a rage, raised his cruel spear again, and this time his son was struck on the temple.

The crime, unintentional though it was, was beyond what even Ivan had accustomed his contemporaries to expect, and the Sovereign, Possevino tells us, was in despair. He spent his nights weeping, yelling aloud in his grief, and every morning he called his boïars together and told them he felt unworthy to continue to be their ruler. But at the same time, basing his request on Feodor's incapacity, he requested them to choose some other successor, and the courtiers, suspecting a trap, besought him to remain in power.

Of all the events which crammed the reign of Ivan the Terrible, this one has taken the strongest hold on the popular imagination. From Arkhangel to Vladimir, from Olonetz to Nijni-Novgorod, over all the wide expanse of the Russian Empire, songs inspired by the hideous drama have been gathered. Rybnikov has published five of them, Bezsonov twelve, and Hilferding eleven. In one of these *by-lines* the victim is not Ivan, but Feodor, whom Maliouta-

Skouratov has denounced as a traitor to the Tsar. 'Treason is in thine Imperial Palace ; it sits beside thee : it eats out of the same dish with thee ; it wears the same garments as thou.' The poet evidently had a passage out of St. Matthew in his mind (chap. xxvi. 23) : 'He that dippeth his hand with Me in the dish, the same shall betray Me.' And then, careless of chronology, he brings in the Tsarina Anastasia and her brother Nikita Romanovitch, who save the innocent Tsarevitch just when he is about to suffer final execution. In others of the poetic versions of the story the Tsar commands that his son's head shall be cut off and set up in front of his Palace ; his heart and liver torn out and brought to him ; the dagger dripping with his blood shown him, at the very least—and Nikita Romanovitch, the darling hero of the popular poet, deceives the Sovereign by killing a slave, and thus renews the story of Cyrus saved by the envoys of Astyages, or that of Geneviève de Brabant, or of the Sleeping Beauty.

In spite of his resemblance to his father, or because of it, rather, the elder Tsarevitch himself enjoyed considerable popularity. His death was regarded as a national calamity, and all the more so because the future of the country seemed to be threatened by it. Feodor was half an idiot, Dmitri was a little child. The Tsar had had several sons by his numerous concubines—Feodor Basmanov, a brave but cruel man, was believed to be one of these—but none of them had been acknowledged by him. More than ever did Ivan cling to his adopted family, for this man, who did not know what pity meant, had a great need of tenderness. Speaking of Boris Godounov and his sister, he was heard to say they 'were like the two fingers of his hand.' But more than ever, too, he sought to drown his sorrows, and, it may be, his remorse, in an excess of debauchery which was completing the ruin of his already sorely-tried health. Did those gloomy suburb walls hide a mixture of Sodom and Cythera, as most chroniclers have admitted, and as Sylvester's former warnings to his unruly pupil might well lead us to suppose ? The authenticity of Sylvester's epistle is doubtful, and a passage from Possevino's narrative has certainly been quite wrongly interpreted in this sense. The Latin words, *Qui gratissimus tredecim annos apud Principem fuerat, atque in ejus cubiculo dormiebat*, simply imply that Bogdan Biélski, to whom they refer, performed the duties of a *spalnik* about the Sovereign's person (see *ante*, p. 360). Many items of the accusation brought against the mysterious Sovereign by chroniclers and historians are no better founded, doubtless, than this one. But the disorders of his life cannot be denied, and they certainly hastened the close of a career which, with

Ivan's robust temperament, should have been a very long
one.

After Anastasia's death, the Tsar sent 1,000 roubles to the
Monastery of the Troïtsa, just twice the amount of the offering
he had given for 'the repose of his father's soul.' In the
Tsarina Marfa's case, he reduced his gift to 700 roubles. In
that of his son, and moved by feelings which are easy to divine,
he sent five times as much, and added an equal sum for himself. He was taking his precautions, and he was not mistaken.
His days were numbered.

CHAPTER V

THE MAN AND HIS WORK

I.—HIS DEATH.   II.—CHARACTER AND TEMPERAMENT.   III.—
KNOWLEDGE AND INTELLIGENCE.   IV.—IDEAS AND FEELINGS.
V.—THE RESULTS OF HIS REIGN.

I.—HIS DEATH.

IN August, 1582, Possevino, delivering his report of his
mission to the Signory of Venice, expressed an opinion that
the Tsar would not live long. Early in 1584, alarming
symptoms began to disturb the minds of the persons composing his immediate circle. His body began to swell, and the
odour became almost unendurable. The physicians recognised
signs of approaching mortification, and, according to Horsey,
Bogdan Biélski consulted the astrologers, who announced that
death would ensue on a certain date. The favourite did not
care to tell his master of this gloomy forecast, but he warned
the prophets that they would be burnt alive if it did not come
true. This amounted to putting a price on murder, and hence
the suspicion as to poison cast, after the event, on Boris
Godounov, and the accomplices he is said to have secured for
his ambitious plans.

Horsey further tells the story of an extraordinary scene
witnessed by him in the treasure-chamber, where the dying Tsar
was fond of lingering amidst all the riches he was soon to quit for
ever. One day he desired the Englishman to attend him there.
He had a number of precious stones exhibited, and explained
their quality and value to the persons about him. Suddenly
he took up some turquoises, and said to Horsey, ' See how they
change their colour! they are turning paler. That is because
I have been poisoned : they foretell my death !' Immediately
afterwards he asked for his sceptre, ' made of a unicorn's horn.'

My readers are aware that until Ambroise Paré's days, and even later, the ivory of the narwhale was believed to exercise certain curative properties. The Tsar's physician, armed with this instrument of magic, was made to draw a circle on a table, and within the line some spiders were put down. These died at once, while others, placed outside the circle, ran away. 'Too late!' said Ivan; 'the unicorn's horn cannot save me now!' And he went back to his gems. 'Look at this diamond,' said he to Horsey again : ' it is the finest and most precious of all the Eastern stones. I have never cared for it. It curbs fury and lust ; it instils abstinence and chastity. . . . I feel ill. . . . Take me away. . . . We will come back another time. . . .'

On the day the astrologers had fixed—March 18, 1584—the Sovereign, according to Horsey's account, felt rather better. Biélski reminded the diviners of the fate that awaited them. ' The day will not be over till the sun sets,' was their answer. Ivan, having taken a bath, asked for a chess-board. On the preceding days circulars had been sent to all the monasteries asking their prayers for the ' sick man who repented,' and who likewise besought the Divine mercy—on the faults of which the monks had been guilty with respect to himself ! These documents, still in existence, prove that the Sovereign, even yet, was striving to combine his care for the safety of his own soul with that of his political interests. The legend assures us, too, that, though he treated all those about him with a most unaccustomed gentleness, and enjoined his son to follow this example, to avoid wars with Christian Princes, to reduce taxes, and set prisoners free, he never ceased indulging in every kind of physical excess, even going so far as to make an abominable attempt, so Oderborn affirms, on his daughter-in-law Irene, whom he had treated with paternal fondness.

The only points quite free from uncertainty are the date of Ivan's death and a few trifling details connected with it. He had sent for Boris Godounov to play with him, and was setting up the pieces on the chess-board when he turned faint. A few moments later the death-rattle was in his throat, and the astrologers' presage was realized. The last sacraments were administered, and at his own request the usual ceremony of putting on the monkish habit was performed upon the Tsar's person ; so that it was the monk Iona who relinquished the crown into Feodor's hands, and the power into those of Boris Godounov.

I have endeavoured to show what the first Tsar of all the Russias was. I must now close by defining some features of a physiognomy by no means easy to reconstitute, athwart all the uncertainty which hangs round so obscure a past.

II.—CHARACTER AND TEMPERAMENT.

This uncertainty defies any attempt beyond a general approximation, even as to the external appearance of the man. According to Russian authorities, he was tall and thin. He struck foreigners, on the contrary, as being stout and fat. This, probably, is a mere question of *standard*. The Russians of that period, as we know, were most of them corpulent to an extent rare in other countries. As to Ivan's stature, everybody is agreed. He was very tall and strongly built, high-shouldered and broad - chested. Yet in the Treasury of the Laura of St. Sergius at the Troïtsa there is a kaftan which belonged, so tradition asserts, to the Sovereign, though Monsieur Glagoliév, who has lately taken and published its measurements (Russian Archives, July, 1902), seems to have been led by them to a different conclusion. As to the Tsar's face, his portraits, all of them of most doubtful authenticity, are no guide at all. Contemporary witness is fairly agreed in describing his nose as long and flattened, or turned up ; his eyes as blue, small, but very quick and keen-looking ; his moustache long, his auburn beard thick, and grizzled towards the close of his reign. He shaved his head : *Capillos capitis utque plerique Rutheni novacula radit*, says Printz von Buchau.

During the second half of the Sovereign's life, as to which we possess most information, his habitual expression struck the majority of witnesses as being threatening and gloomy, though he often burst into roars of laughter. But here we come to the moral aspect of his physiognomy, which even now remains a riddle, in spite of the innumerable attempts made to solve it, and we find ourselves face to face with contradictions resulting not so much in a divergence of opinion among observers, as in a division of the subject they observe.

Ivan was energetic to the point of violence, and yet timid to downright cowardice ; his pride amounted to positive madness, and his humility occasionally descended to baseness.) He was intelligent, and yet capable of saying and doing the most foolish things. Why did he insult Erik just when he desired his alliance ? How did he come to call himself a ' stinking dog,' and yet persevere in the behaviour which led him to apply this epithet ? To such questions, which might be multiplied without end, some people have thought an answer had been found in the recent discoveries of a science at present enjoying what may prove to be an ephemeral favour. Ivan's father and grandfather appear to have possessed well-balanced minds, but his great-grandfather, Vassili the Blind, was a man whose intellect and will were both equally weak. His mother, Helen Glinski,

was a sickly creature, and his father was over fifty when the
boy, whose childish health was most frail, was born. His
grandmother Sophia may have brought the vitiated blood
of the Paleologi, with all that predisposition to nervous complaints which was so strongly marked among them, into her
husband's family. Ivan's brother George became an idiot ;
he himself had three times as many wives as he had children.
His eldest boy died an infant ; his second, a man of cruel and
sanguinary tastes, died by his own father's hand ; another,
Feodor, was half-imbecile ; Dmitri is said to have suffered from
epileptic fits.

My readers will guess the conclusion : Ivan the Terrible was
probably a ' degenerate,' one of those ' paranoics ' to whose
psychology Lombroso has devoted so much attention.

The most evident weakness of this explanation is that it
does not explain anything at all. Before the days of the
Italian psychiater, Reveillé-Parise (1834) and Schilling (1863)
had already made an attempt to establish the fact that genius
is always a form of neurosis, and very often of madness ; and
this theory may be traced back to far more ancient authorities,
from Aristotle down to Pascal. More recently Monsieur Méjja
(*Nevrosis de los Hombres Célèbres*, Buenos Ayres, 1885) has
told us that almost all the great men of the Argentine Republic
have been drunkards, neuropathic subjects, or madmen.
What of that ? It is an established fact, in the eyes of Lombroso and his disciples, that Napoleon's genius was a phenomenon produced by epileptic neurosis. Does that take us
any further ? Epileptic neurosis is a label—it is not an explanation. The fact still remains that between such a degenerate as Napoleon and such a degenerate as Ivan a huge
difference exists : that the acts and behaviour of one present
a logical sequence, a harmony, entirely absent from those of
the second ; that the first, though he may be mad, if that
please you, acts like a reasonable being, and that the other
betrays, or seems to betray, frequent symptoms of mania ;
that it is the reason for these differences which has to be discovered, and that the hypothesis of malady of the brain in
both cases may alter the conditions of the problem, but does
not solve it.

The interpretations laid on the character and temperament of Ivan the Terrible seem to me based, in the first
place, on a general error, which I am inclined to consider
an anachronism. The subject under examination has been
treated as though he had lived in our own day, and an analysis
correct enough in itself falls to the ground because it has
been arrived at without any regard for historical surroundings,
which ought to have been taken into account. Take such

a man as Louis XI., with the faculties everyone recognises him
to have possessed. Put him down into the nineteenth or
twentieth century, and ask yourself whether he would be
capable, *now*, with his inherent caution, of falling into the snare
laid for him by Péronne, and letting himself, with all his
cunning, be conducted right up to the walls of Liège, there to
witness the destruction of a town that was under his own protection. Surely not ! Then, why was he guilty *then* of this
twofold piece of folly, aggravated, in the second case, by downright infamy ? Because he was the man of his own time, of
a half-barbarous period during which we see, even at the very
top of the intellectual ladder, a lack of that arrangement and
discipline of the mental faculties which years of hereditary
intellectual culture have now made a common thing, even in
a much lower order of intelligence. Louis XI. was a man of
impulse, like most of his contemporaries, and like certain eccentric persons of our own day, who owe the quality to certain
atavisms which make them ' throw back ' to former generations.
Apply this elementary clue to the person and career of Ivan
the Terrible, and you will have gone a long way, in my opinion,
towards finding the desired solution.

Even oftener than in Louis XI.'s case, Ivan obeyed his
impulses. Some of these came from without—the result of
impressions produced by the men or the events about him ;
others came from within, and these he owed to his birth and
education. Combined with his grandfather's intelligence—
though his own was broader—and his energy—though his was
weaker—the Tsar, whose father's influence on him was *nil*,
possessed his mother's passionate and violent heart. His
action was often taken with a jerk, in most irregular fashion.
But the man who conceived the idea of the *Opritchnina* and
put it into execution cannot be said to have been lacking
either in will or in sequence of ideas. I have already shown
the value of the theory according to which he always made
over his power to other people, because he did not know how
to use it himself. But Adachev and Sylvester were no more
the masters of Russia between 1548 and 1560 than the Tsar
Simeon was from 1575 to 1576, though the Sovereign was
pleased, in the first case, to give himself out as the victim of
his favourites, and in the second, to play a farce with his
phantom Sovereign for the world's benefit.

Ivan, according to Printz von Buchau—a really reliable
witness, the most faithful of them all—was violent-tempered
to such an extent that the smallest annoyance made him ' foam
like a horse.' Often he quite failed to restrain and master his
rage. But often, too, as during his struggle with Batory,
he showed himself extraordinarily pliant. In this case, when

he had given up everything, or very nearly, on the battlefield, he disputed the victory, foot by foot, in that of diplomacy, never neglecting any expedient nor the smallest chance of success.

I have already spoken of his education. It is not surprising, considering the lack of affection, and even of kindness, he experienced, and the perpetual terrors he had to endure, that he should have contracted a timidity which sometimes took the form of want of confidence in himself, and sometimes that of physical collapse in the face of danger. But the man who held his own for twenty years against all the Kourbskis in his Empire was no coward. From the same source, thanks to those who brought him up with an equal care to flatter his worst instincts and offend his best feelings, he drew that scorn of men in general which accident transformed into downright hatred. Taube and Kruse both speak, as men who know, of his *listiges krokodilisch Herz*. Cunning he was, indeed, and cruel. He had been ill-treated and scoffed at in his youth, and all his life long he seems to have sought impossible revenges. He seems to have felt a passionate need of jeering at men, when he could not or did not desire to make them suffer otherwise ; a bitter pleasure in putting them in the wrong, and taking advantage of it ; an utter and absolute lack of sympathy and pity. This last feature he possessed in common with Peter the Great, and it had its roots in the same cause. Read these lines addressed to Kourbski after a victorious campaign : ' You have complained that I sent you to distant towns, as though you were in disgrace ! With God's help, we ourselves are now much farther off. . . . And where did you expect to find repose after such great fatigues ? At Wolmar ? We are there now, and you have had to flee whither you did not expect to go !' . . . And remember the story of the favourite *Opritchnik* Vassili Griaznoï, who was taken prisoner by the Tartars. Did his master pity him, and take compassion on his fate ? No, indeed ! ' You should not have gone into the infidels' camp for no reason at all, Vassiouchka, or, having gone there, you should not have slept like a top according to your usual habit ! You thought you were out hunting with your hounds, and would have caught your hare, and instead of that the Tartars have caught you in your form, and tied you up to their saddle-bow ! . . . These Crimean fellows do not snore, like all of you, and they understand how to humble you, pack of women that you are ! . . . I wish they were like you ! Then I should be sure they would not dare to cross the river, and still less should I have to fear I should see them appear at Moscow ! . . .'

Yet after he had thus made merry at the captive's expense, Ivan paid his ransom, just as, after he had torn his beard out in the presence of Devlet-Ghireï's envoy, he consented to treat with the Khan. This is a true picture of the man. For if there was no method in his madness, he had constant recurrences, at all events, of the most perfectly lucid reason, and the very same irascible despot who raised his staff to strike the Protestant pastor who dared to compare Luther to St. Paul in his presence was soon to be seen calmly arguing with Rokita.

Judging by his constant fits of rage, one might fancy him imbued with that insensate fury which afflicted the Norsemen, according to the Sagas, and under the influence of which they would spend their strength against trees and rocks, when there was no living adversary within their reach. But this passionate being did not war with mountains, nor yet with windmills. He was no Norseman—he was a Mongol, rather, cold in his anger, and as perfidious as he was cruel, full of artifice and hypocrisy, but knowing what he wanted, and only wanting reasonable things, or which seemed so to him, considering the circumstances, subtle, refined, full of a universal curiosity.

If he sometimes overshot his mark, it was because he did not know how to control his temperament ; and if he made more victims than he had enemies, it was because, as Lombroso remarks, and very truly this time, ' Once the horrible delight of shedding blood has been tasted, the necessity for slaughter becomes so imperious that no man can master it.' And he adds, ' It almost seems as if physical love were often connected with this phenomenon, and as if the sight of blood imparted a special stimulant to this passion. . . . These sanguinary scenes are almost always followed by shameful fits of debauchery ' (L' Uomo Delinquente, i. 389).

This explains the Sloboda of Alexandrov.

And here, too, the historical surroundings must not be allowed to slip out of sight. Soloviov was certainly wrong when he quoted the example of St. Philip as a rehabilitation of the habits of his period. Saints have always been the exceptions everywhere. Was Ivan an exception in the opposite sense ? The docility with which the massacres he ordered were endured would seem a proof to the contrary. There is no doubt that by their means he aggravated the savage atrocity of the instincts and habits of those about him, and sowed the Russian soil with a seed of blood, whereof the murder of his younger son at Ouglitch, the reign of the false Dmitri, and the horrors of the ' troublous times ' were the harvest. But the Chouïskis and the Kourbskis only reaped what they themselves had sown by teaching him who was to become their executioner to disdain human dignity and human life, and scorn all justice and every law.

And Ivan's education bore a much closer resemblance than

has been commonly imagined to that of all the European
Princes of his time. We all know what the childhood and youth
of Don Carlos—that cruel tormentor of the men and beasts
about him, that hideous monster who had the birds brought
in from his hunting excursions roasted alive, and delighted in
mutilating the horses in his stables—were, before the fictions
of poets and romance-writers cast a glamour over them.

Some people have regarded Ivan's propensity to confess
his crimes, and even exaggerate them, to which I have already
referred, as a sign of mania or neurosis. This, as it seems
to me, is merely a symptom of the actor's temperament,
frequent in the case of men who, having every other passion
likewise, have that for showing themselves off, attracting
onlookers' attention, even to their own disadvantage. Look
at Luther, amongst the Tsar's own illustrious contemporaries.
He carried his mania for this sort of thing beyond all the limits
of decency. And, in this matter, Ivan proved how modern he
was. None of the Sovereigns of ancient Russia had felt his
need or possessed his gift of speaking, discussing, either *vivâ
voce* or in writing, on the public square or between four walls,
with a fugitive boïar or a foreign envoy, ceaselessly, unrestingly,
without decency, too ; for on these occasions he undresses his
soul as he might undress his body ; he strips it naked, he shows
all his sores and all his warts, and cries, ' See how ugly I am !'
He exaggerates them, writing to Kourbski, ' Though I am still
alive, I am nothing in God's eyes, thanks to my vile actions,
but a corpse, unclean and hideous. I have done worse than
Cain, the first murderer ; I have imitated Esau's shameful
excesses ; I have been like Reuben, who soiled his father's
bed !' Which does not prevent him from thinking and saying
that the man to whom he confesses himself guilty of so many
shameful acts is quite in the wrong as to the disagreement
between them. But if he cannot make himself admired, he
is quite willing to inspire horror, so long as people notice him
and pay attention to him. Jean Jacques Rousseau must
surely have been trained in the self-same school.

Though he generally appears in tragic parts, Ivan, as I have
shown, does not object to play chief buffoon at his own Court.
Any part will do for him, so long as he can be upon the stage.
Now and then he mingles the two styles together. The aged
Tchiéliadnine falls under suspicion of being a conspirator.
The Tsar is not content with handing the traitor over to the
executioner. He steps down from his throne, seats the astonished boïar upon it, bows to the ground, salutes him by the
title of Tsar, and then thrusts his dagger into his heart. ' You
were able to think of taking my place, but I am able to kill
you !' Printz von Buchau recognises features of resemblance

between Ivan the Terrible and a certain cardinal celebrated
for his jovial gestures and talk.   He is also struck by the extreme mobility of the Sovereign's countenance and attitudes ;
the very expression of his eyes and his voice changing from
one minute to the next.   The Tsar would be talking with some
of the gentlemen about him, his language might be gentle and
his gestures kindly ; but 'supposing one of the persons with
whom he was conversing was slow to understand his meaning,
his words instantly became rough and his manner threatening,
and everybody was in expectation of some outburst.   And
with all that, so the same witness tells us, there was something
about him which would have marked him out as a great personage, at all events, if he had been put in the middle of four
hundred peasants, and dressed exactly as they were dressed.

In him, as in most men, the mania for putting himself forward
was a form of pride—a pride which in his case was overweening,
though by no means so extravagant as it has been taken to
have been.   Acquainted as he was with both history and
geography, he may very naturally have believed himself
superior to, all the other European Princes—to the Emperor
himself, who was only an elective Sovereign, or to the Sultan,
who could not trace his family and titles back to the Romans.
Did not a Pharaoh of the twentieth dynasty claim to be
master of the whole world ?   And do not certain Sovereigns in
the Far East still betray symptoms of a similar infatuation ?

This pride, too, had something to do with Ivan's dislike of
risking his own person in the tumult of battle, which might
have placed his hierarchic Majesty in too dangerous a position.
And in this, as I have already observed, he was only obeying the
traditions of his race.   Ivan, like his grandfather, was no hero
in the commonly accepted meaning of that word. -Such men
as Alexander, Hannibal, Gustavus-Adolphus, Charles XII.,
Napoleon, come and go like meteors.   For labour which is to
endure, men like the *Rurikovitchy* are far more reliable.   It is
true that Louis XI., though he had nothing in common either
with Alexander the Great or with Napoleon, exposed his own
person bravely at Montlhéry, but then Louis XI. was not a
semi-Oriental Sovereign.

Ivan was Oriental, too, in the ease with which he would pass
from the heights of insolence, in prosperity, to· the depths of
humility when evil fortune overtook him.   And yet he is not
broken down by adversity.   He bends his back, he crawls,
but he is always ready to rise up again.   The qualities of the
European and the man of culture reappear in some other
features.   He does not like coarse flattery.   The following
anecdote, reported by Guagnino, the probability of which is
strengthened by several others of the same nature, would

25

appear authentic. Two *voiévodes*, Joseph Chtcherbatyi and George Bariatinski by name, who had been taken prisoners by Batory, were ransomed by the Tsar. He plied them with eager questions. The first spoke honestly as to the King of Poland's power; the second, thinking to please his master, contradicted his comrade's assertions, declaring Batory had neither men nor forts, and that the Tsar's very name made him tremble. 'Poor King!' quoth Ivan, 'how I pity him!' And then, grasping his spear, he dealt the impudent courtier a sudden blow. 'Here are your wages, impostor!'

After his own fashion, Ivan was more cultivated than the majority of his Russian contemporaries, and quite as much so as the most enlightened European Princes of his period—if not as to what he knew, as to his desire of knowledge, at all events. In this he differs essentially from Louis XI., 'who had a mortal hatred of literature,' and said 'learning made him melancholy.' He was more like Francis I. But to what did his knowledge really amount?

III.—KNOWLEDGE AND INTELLIGENCE.

He knew many things, drawn from his wide reading, but he was incapable of understanding them thoroughly, or setting them in clear order in his mind. During the first years of his reign, when, the government being in the hands of the boïars, he had long hours of leisure, and was driven to commune with himself in savage loneliness, he read everything that fell into his hands and roused his curiosity—sacred history, Roman history, Russian and Byzantine chronicles, the works of the holy Fathers, and menologies. His memory retained many passages, and by preference he chose those that seemed to him applicable to his own person, his position in the world, and the part he desired to play in it. His correspondence with Kourbski gives us a sort of inventory of the knowledge he thus acquired, and also some idea of the use to which he knew how to put it. It constitutes a pamphlet in two parts against the boïars, combined with a treatise on the absolute power, both of them elaborated by means of quotations which are certainly from memory. In most cases, indeed, the words are not exactly quoted, though there is nothing to indicate any intentional alteration. Gregory of Nazianzus and St. John Chrysostom, Moses and Isaiah, the Bible and the Greek mythology, the 'Iliad' and the legends of the Siege of Troy, which have been incorporated into the ancient literature of Russia, have all been laid under contribution, and present us with an extraordinary mixture, in which we come on names which must be astounded to find themselves in such close proximity—Zeus and Dionysius

along with Abimelech and Gideon, Æneas beside Genseric,
King of the *Sauromates* (*sic*)—Ivan writes his name *Zinzirikh*—
swarming with the most improbable anachronisms, and in which
the boldest political aphorisms rub shoulders with the most
unexpected philosophical considerations. And yet, in spite
of Kourbski, who calls all this literature 'old woman's talk,'
this confused tumult of memories and impressions, this chaos
of imagery and confusion of ideas, forms a solid whole, bound
together, evidently, when we look at it closely, by a thin bu-
always visible thread, which connects it all with one sole and
only object, the theory of sovereign power as the author con-
ceives it—supreme and absolute, Divine in its origin and
superior in its essence. And little does it matter, in all truth,
that the self-taught writer confuses dates and events, talks of
the division of the Empire under Leo the Armenian, makes a
mistake of two centuries as to the period of the conquest of
Persia by the Arabs. His trumpery barbarian's learning is a
thing of nought. It is the ideas and feelings that live in it and
use it which are important, and when we see the fiery despot
juggling with things of which his father and grandfather knew
nothing at all, and turning them into arguments in favour of a
theory of which they never dreamt, or to which, at all events,
they never gave a thought, we realize that a new world has come
into being, and that to have been conscious of that fact is in
itself sufficient to make the glory of the extraordinary man
who, in spite of his lack of modern science, was the first, in his
own country, to acquire the instinct, the taste, the passion,
for modern progress.

On this impressionable nature, indeed, memories acted like
events. To such an extent did they take hold of Ivan's thought
and rule his speech that the erudition he had gathered up so
confusedly in his mind was a law to him as much as it was his
servant; it dragged him perpetually from one subject to
another; it suggested the most unforeseen digressions to him,
and at the same time the eagerness he threw into everything, like
the rage that almost always shook him when he was writing,
rendered him incapable of using his knowledge with discernment, weighing the elements he drew from it, and considering
how he should employ them.

And though he may be fond of showing off what he knows,
or fancies he knows, he is, speaking from the literary point of
view, above all things a controversialist, wordy and prolix to
excess, but skilled, amidst all his digressions and circuitous
ways, in finding out his opponents' strong and weak points,
and bent, most especially, on striking home. Kourbski,
according to the fashion of those times, was a learned man—
in other words, a man of wide reading—and the Tsar breaks

him down with his own booklore, convinced, and rightly so,
no doubt, that the other will be quite incapable of verifying
the accuracy of his quotations. But, knowing him as religious as he is lettered, he does not forget to address himself
to this weak point, and we find him calling up a picture of the
fugitive boïar helping the Poles to destroy the Orthodox
churches, trampling the holy ikons underfoot, and presiding,
like a second Herod, over massacres of innocent children. . . .
He weeps over the victims and their executioner, for he
loves the lyric, and by no means despises the pathetic.
Kourbski has said something about the blood he has shed in
the Tsar's service. ' And I,' replies Ivan, ' have I not shed
my blood too ? If not from wounds made on my body, at all
events in the tears of blood your treacheries have drawn from
my eyes ! . . .'

We may agree with Monsieur Klioutchevski ('Course of
History,' i.) that this rhetoric betrays more artifice than conviction, more phosphorescent brilliance than heat ; but it is
an anachronism to seek in the sixteenth century, close to the
Scholastics, all the sincerity and emotion the modern soul has
learnt, since those days, to put into its external manifestations.
As for taking the Tsar's letters to be a collective work in which
his favourites were his collaborators, this conjecture, borrowed
by Monsieur Mikhaïlovski, an acute but biassed critic, from
the author of an inferior novel ('Prince Kourbski,' by Fédorov,
1843), will not bear even a superficial examination of the document, in which Monsieur Mikhaïlovski himself recognises the
existence of a perfect unity of style and composition, and in
every line of which the author's hall-mark, his personal touch,
is evident.

Ivan certainly does not hold the first place in the intellectual
movement of the period, and the part he played in the struggle
then going on between the moral idea elaborated in the hermitages of the north, and the coarse corruption prevalent among
the great majority of Russians, was neither the best nor the
worst. This conflict had brought two eccentric types face to
face and into bitter conflict. There were solitary ascetics on
one side and heroic bandits on the other, and both classes
lived on the outer margin of society. Ivan remained in the
middle. Highly gifted as he was, his mind was not sufficiently
ripened by study, nor, above all, was his soul so filled with
generous impulses, as to enable him to represent the noblest
tendencies of a chosen few. He went to the *Stoglav* firmly
intending to support the reform party, and he failed to adhere
to his intention, less from lack of energy than from want of
conviction. In religious matters he continued, at heart, to
belong to the old school, in which the wearing of the full beard

and of the *odnoriadka*—a garment recently recalled to honour—
were matters of doctrine. Nil Sorski's teachings glided over
his intelligence, but never reached his conscience. And, on the
other hand, he possessed no means of initiating himself into the
wider intellectual currents of Europe, whether in the domain of
science or in that of art. Europe was still too far away, and
Russia too far behind the West. Ivan turned his mind to
the most pressing matters, and those easiest of accomplishment. What he asked his neighbours to give him was
results—engineers, artisans, printers. This is the course
generally pursued by backward peoples anxious to make up for
lost time. Look at Japan. In this fashion, too, artificial and
superficial civilizations are attained. Modern Russia is an
example of this even in the present day.

The detractors of Ivan the Terrible have gone the length of
refusing him any originality at all, declaring all he did was to
walk, and rather clumsily at that, in the rut his grandfather
had cut for him, defend old theories against literary attack
on the part of the opposition party, and turn over ideas drawn
from the books he had read. The historic prerogatives of the
Boïarchtchina were already broken down, the appeal to the
new strata of society had begun, the attempts to reorganize
the communes on the autonomic principle were nothing but a
return to the older form of these institutions, and Ivan, even
in his conception of the part he was personally called to play,
simply drew his inspiration from the teachings of Holy Writ.
These over-severe judges seem to me to forget that it takes
something to make anything, and that Napoleon did not find
the elements of his Code in his own brain. Besides, they
graciously grant the great value of the reforms carried out in
the early years of Ivan's reign, though they give all the credit
for them to the men who were about the Sovereign. Have
they taken the trouble of reading the thirty-seven proposals
as to the reorganization of the Church, and the ten proposals
or rough drafts of laws, for the organization of the State ?
If so, they should have realized that the man who wrote these
pages was the man who corresponded with Kourbski at a period
when Adachev and Sylvester were both far away. In both
cases the spirit and style are identical, and that style is most
personal in its nature. Adachev, Sylvester, and Kourbski
certainly had no hand in the *Opritchnina*, and yet the *Opritchnina* and the reforms of the year 1551 together form one
complete whole. I have demonstrated this already. And it
is because Ivan's biographers could not understand what the
Opritchnina was that they have refused to grant him what they
have granted to his fellow-workers. Peter the Great was
never deceived in this matter.

Ivan was the first of the Russian Tsars, not only because he was the first to assume the title, but also and especially because he was the first to comprehend the realities corresponding with it. The theory was there, no doubt, and had been worked out, ever since the fifteenth century, in the literature of the country. But neither to Vassili nor to Ivan III.—the Great—had it occurred to lay hold of the concrete meaning of that theory—the idea of a Sovereign whose power came to him from God, and who was responsible to God alone for the way in which he used it, unaided, as the sole representative of the Divine will and the Divine wisdom, on whom no human assistance could be imposed, and who could not accept any control whatever.

To this theory Ivan added a personal commentary of his own of which none of his predecessors had thought, and which none of his successors were to adopt. Peter the Great was to regard himself merely as the first servant of the State ; Ivan regarded the Sovereign's person as a kind of Divine essence, and boldly set it far above the State. ' We know,' he writes, after pouring abuse on Batory, ' what is due to the majesty of Princes. But the Empire is majesty, and above that majesty stands the Sovereign in his Empire, and the Sovereign is above the Empire !' (Note handed to Possevino in September, 1581, ' Historical Documents,' x. 223). Poland had won the day, and Muscovy was forced into submission. But the Tsar set himself above this necessity — he hovered in higher space, where no such outrage could reach him. The idea is a subtle one, but it is a feeling rather than an idea. Ivan's ideas and feelings have often been confused together, and a short analysis must be devoted to them.

IV.—IDEAS AND FEELINGS.

Ivan the Terrible went through a great deal of suffering, and these sufferings, which he exaggerated as he exaggerated everything, have been rightly ascribed to a twofold moral cause—to his very lively consciousness of all the faults and vices of the political and social organization over which he had been called to rule, and an equally painful consciousness of his powerlessness to apply any efficacious remedy to them. This painful sensation was repeated in his own consciousness, in the midst of the personal weaknesses of which he recognised the shamefulness, and the useless acknowledgment of which he was perpetually multiplying. But it is a mistake, in the first place, to take all this for an exceptional case of self-distrust. It is the eternal history of the human race before Medea's *video meliora proboque*, and after it, for ever and ever. Historians of the school of George Samarine are certainly mistaken when they take Ivan to be a man who lived lonely and misunderstood. He alone, according to their theory, recognised that the habits of his period were full of terrifying symptoms of decomposition and awful omens for the future, and, finding nobody would share his scorn and hate of all these things, he grew so bitter in his loneliness that he struck out blindly at everything around him, because he did not know how to separate the evil from the good, either in himself or his surroundings, and also because his will was not so strong as his intellectual superiority was great. This judgment wrongs the Sovereign and his period. Ivan knew and frequented the company of men far more capable than himself of conceiving the necessity, and also the conditions, for a renovation of morals. In this particular the disciples of Nil Sorski aimed at a much higher ideal than his. On the other hand, the Tsar, in his struggle with his boïars, knew right well what he was doing, and the objects at which his blows were struck. To represent him, as Bestoujev-Rioumine has represented him, as a sort of Hamlet, constitutionally inclined to abstract reflection, and stumbling hither and thither at every step the moment he entered the world of realities, is an historical absurdity. The *Opritchnina* was not an abstract idea, and Hamlet would certainly have been quite incapable of playing the most delicate of games with the most finished diplomatists of his time.

Ivan had a will of his own. Some people have thought they perceived a proof of the weakness of his will in the instruments he chose to carry out his plans—instruments which he constantly destroyed because he could not find suitable ones, and which he nevertheless replaced, because, being himself unable to give form to his own ideas, he could not do without them—a man of meditation, not of action, a theorist, an artist too, who could conceive what was good and beautiful, but had not the skill to pass from conception to realities ; and a man, also, who sought sensation and picturesque effect even in the horrors of the torture-chamber. . . . This is the theory put forward by Constantine Akssakov. It seems to admit the possibility, for the head of a State, of doing everything himself. In this even Peter the Great could not succeed, and he has been blamed, with some show of justice, for having lost himself in details. The great man could not find enough helpers. Ivan's helpers were inadequate, like Biélski, or vile, like Skouratov ; but he set to work in his own person, and put his own hand to the task, oftener, indeed, than he should have done.

Like Peter the Great, again, he was a carrier on of a previous work. He followed in his grandfather's footsteps, and was, like him, the champion of similar interests—moral, intellectual, social, and more especially political—in the struggle between the future and the past. He brought in a few new ideas, but more particularly some new weapons, of his own. Ivan III. had fought in silence, with an axe. Ivan IV., true to his own period, did not, indeed, put the axe back into its bear-skin sheath, but he supplemented the labours of the executioner by the action of his economic reforms and of the power of speech. Was he not bound to speak, since men's tongues were wagging all round him ? Silence was to fall once more, when the theory of the absolute and despotic power had triumphed, and the Empire was subject to its rule ; and no faint echo of Kourbski's bold clamour was to rise till Europe witnessed the coming of another epoch of revolutionary disturbance, and heard the voice of Radichtchev. But Ivan, in the sixteenth century, could do no less than follow the impulse which prompted every intellectual being, even in Russia, to discourse.

Yet, contrary to the general opinion, he proved himself much stronger in practice than in theory ; for though within the borders of his own country he maintained his adopted programme against every Kourbski of them, and carried it to its logical conclusion, and though, outside them, he yielded to nothing but Batory's genius and the good fortune which attended it, his ideas, both as to politics and religion, frequently strike us as vague, confused, and unsettled, and his powers of reflection by no means correspond with the power of his instinct, which is extraordinarily sure, as a rule. He is instinctively inclined to depend on the masses of the population, and yet he gives over his peasants to be squeezed by his ' men who serve.' Devout as he is—a fortnight after his marriage in 1547 he makes a pilgrimage to the Troïtsa, and goes the whole way on foot, in spite of the bitter cold—and deeply convinced of the excellence of his form of religion, as his discussions with Possevino and Rokita prove, he frequently gives vent to sallies savouring strongly of free-thought. On other occasions he shows a tolerance which does not seem to be founded on any principle, for it is intermittent and opportunist. The Protestants had an experience of this when they were first permitted to build two churches at Moscow, and then vilely maltreated after they were built. After the taking of Polotsk in 1563, the Tsar was present at a general drowning of the Jews in the river Dvina. Just at that moment there was an interdict on all Jewish trading in Muscovy ; but Ivan gave a very singular explanation to the Polish envoys when they complained of this edict. ' The Jews,' he said, ' were turning his subjects away from the Christian faith, and, further, they were addicted to guilty attempts to kill with poisoned herbs.'

The Tsar was here alluding to a most extraordinary story. Giovanni Tetaldi, a Florentine agent, who lived in Russia from 1551 to 1565, and whose recollections have been published by Monsieur Chmourlo (St. Petersburg, 1891), speaks of certain mummies, the introduction of which into the country would seem to have resulted in a smuggling trial, complicated by aggravating circumstances. These embalmed corpses, imported from Africa viâ Constantinople, were, it appears, much sought after in Russia, and there was a considerable traffic in them, which, like that of all kinds of spices, was in the hands of the Jews. To play a trick on some of these, a Polish merchant sent them, as though it had been a mummy, the body of a recently executed criminal, which he had previously stuffed with aromatic herbs. Mummies paid no entrance duty, and the Jews were accused of habitually and fraudulently introducing, under this name, products liable to a very heavy tax. To this sin the popular imagination had added homicidal intentions. Ivan does not seem, however, to have taken any pains to clear the matter up, being quite satisfied with the repugnance with which the Jews inspired him personally. This man of impulse was, after his own fashion, likewise a man of sentiment.

No one can deny that there was a great deal of sentiment in the fixed idea of going to England which he nursed until he died. That was the romance of his life, and though he did not overlook the practical side of the adventure, he put a great deal of fancy into it. The alliance against Batory and the marriage with Mary Hastings were part of the same dream.

Ivan's exceedingly personal conception of his part and way of playing it, his impetuous vigour of action, his exuberant mimicry, his fulness of gesture and redundance of language, have built up the illusion as to his having been a sort of *hero-Cossack*, out of the cycle of Ilia of Mourom. It must be admitted, indeed, that this cycle was only definitely closed in Russia by the reforms of the eighteenth century, and that up till that date the existence of the race ruled by Peter the Great was spent in a series of exploits, and lulled by the harmonious chantings of its rustic bards. Ivan shares with Ilia of Mourom that quality of humour which still exists in the national temperament, and his fits of furious rage. But the Tsar's psychology is far the more complicated of the two. Behind the external mask which imparts a family resemblance to these figures, and in spite of the dreamy quality common to both, we note, in Ivan's case, a great depth of realism. After he passed away, leaving his iron sceptre in feeble hands, and carrying the secret of his all-powerfulness with him into his grave, his people was to sing on, and dream on, for another century. But he had shaken it rudely once, and his life had narrowed the space available for heroes who would not wake out of their dreams and take their place amongst realities, in the hierarchy, under discipline. Such as they had better flee to the Ukraine.

Imagination held a great place in the moral existence of the man we are now studying, and in this there is an essential difference between Ivan and Peter the Great, one of the most positive intelligences the world has ever known. He is also distinguished from his great successor by his very high opinion of his own powers, which is most curiously mingled with that distrust of himself and others of which he was never to rid himself. Peter, like that builder up of a colossal American fortune whom a reporter lately questioned as to the talents to which he owed his success, would have readily affirmed, ' Talents ? I have none at all ! I work—I work myself to death, and that is all !' Ivan thought he had a great many talents, if not every one. He represented a race of foreign conquerors, and in this very fact of his origin he recognised an element of personal superiority. In Peter the Great we see the consciousness and pride of a *common* nationality strongly developed. As to certain sides of his temperament, the Reformer was of the populace, and was proud of it, and he would never have said, when handing over some ingots of gold to a foreign workman, ' See well to the weight, for all Russians are thieves !' Ivan frequently made speeches of this kind. He was always talking about his ' German ancestors.' Do the Viennese archives contain a last will, according to which the son of Vassili left his Empire to the House of Hapsburg ? I have not been able to verify this fact, which has been advanced by Kostomarov (' Monographies,' xiii., p. 304, note), and I think it most improbable. But the clumsiest fables often have some foundation in truth, and Veit Venge was no doubt merely echoing some remark that had fallen from the lips of the Sovereign—who was fond, it seems, of tracing back the derivation of the word boïar to *Baiern* (Karamzine, ix., note to p. 166)—when he speaks of the *Bavarian* descent of Ivan the Terrible. Ivan's real last will, and the best expression of his being, is to be found in his work, to which I must now return for the last time, so as to sum up its nature and point out its results.

V.—THE RESULTS OF HIS REIGN.

The massacres ordered by Ivan have been notoriously exaggerated by his enemies and his detractors, the first egging on the second. Kourbski mentions the *entire destruction* of families—such as the Kolytchev, the Zabolotski, the Odiévski, the Vorotynski—all of which appear in the inventories of the following century. The gaps created in the ranks of the aristocracy by emigration were certainly much larger, and even so they were not entirely emptied. Ivan's conduct in this particular was not dictated by any fixed principle, and he himself endeavoured to ensure the future of three great houses —the Mstislavski, the Glinski, and the Romanov—whose fidelity seemed guaranteed by lack of connections in the country, by a material state of dependence, or by family relationships. The two first-named families had just arrived from Lithuania, and the last was related to the Sovereign's own house.

The principal factors in the weakening of the aristocratic element were economic causes and political measures. In the course of the sixteenth century, as a result of the condition of debt to which everybody had been reduced, landed property began to crumble away of itself in the boïars' hands. In the registers kept by a moneylender of that period, named Proto-popov, is a list of noble names, and the archives of the Monas-tery of St. Cyril afford proof of the continuance of this state of things. In 1557 Prince D. D. Oukhtomski, whose credit with such persons as Protopopov had probably become exhausted, sold the monks a village, with twenty-six hamlets round it, for 350 roubles ; three years later he received 150 roubles, and gave up possession of four more outlying places. At about the same time the community acquired a large property, also belonging to this family, and in 1575 it received another lot of meadows, ' for Masses ' ; so that, in one way or another, the whole of the Oukhtomski properties passed into the same hands (see Rojkov, ' Agriculture . . . in the Sixteenth Century,' 1899, p. 396).

Now, this financial distress amongst the great families was the direct consequence of the new political system, and the obliga-tions it had cast upon them. Universal service implied resi-dence at Court, or near it, even if it did not imply active military service or the performance of some official function or other. When the nobles had lived on their family properties they had found it hard enough to draw a scanty income from them. Once they left them, they were very soon ruined. Thereupon came the *Opritchnina*—that is to say, wholesale dispossession under the conditions I have already described—and this dealt the position, economic and political, of the persons concerned its death-blow. Ivan's system of guarantees increased the effect of emigration twofold—nay, a hundredfold, seeing that for every fugitive there were from ten to a hundred persons who had to pay for him. Except for the Stroganovs, you will not find a single instance of a large fortune in the aristocratic class which escaped this other form of massacre. If in the present day some few authentic descendants of Rurik and

Guédymine, such as the Troubetzkoïs, the Galitzines, the Kourakines, the Soltykovs, the Boutourlines, still possess some worldly wealth, their opulence only dates from the eighteenth century, and from the favours of some Empress.

And thus a class which already differed from the Western aristocracies, in that the feudal principle was entirely absent from it, was completely and democratically levelled. The hierarchy of the service did indeed create new titles and fresh prerogatives, guaranteed by the *miéstnitchestvo*, but these were not corporative elements in the Western signification of the term. They rather tended to break up the family and reduce it to atoms, on which the hold of the absolute power continued, and grew perpetually stronger.

This revolution, which had seemed destined to benefit the popular element, brought it nothing but the bitterest fruit. The new system was a house of two stories, both built on the same plan. The officials were upstairs, the serfs below, and slavery everywhere. But in this matter all Ivan the Terrible did was to complete or carry on that which had been the Moscow programme for two centuries past, and the *Opritchnina* itself was no more than an extension of the policy applied by the Tsar's predecessors to all their conquered towns and territories. It was a sort of colonization backwards. As to colonization in the normal direction, it continued to depend on private enterprise ; but Ivan opened a wider field for it.

Westwards his expansive policy failed. It would not be just to cast all the responsibility for this on him. If Peter the Great, when he took the same road 150 years later, had found his way barred by a man like Batory, instead of by a madman like Charles XII., the result of the Battle of Poltava might have been very different. Eastward, Kazan, Astrakan, and Siberia make up a noble score in Ivan's favour.

From the economic point of view, the conquest of Kazan did not result in the immediate advantages that might have been expected from it. The trade of that place, which the Tartars had exaggerated in their desire to induce the Sultan to retake possession of the town, was a disappointment to the English merchants. Ivan did not fail to seek compensation elsewhere. When he offered the Swedish traders a free passage through his dominions, even for going to India, he stipulated for a similar privilege for his own subjects, in their enterprises, existing or to be undertaken, with Lübeck and even with Spain. In 1567 the chroniclers mention the departure of Russian merchants for Antwerp and London, and in 1568 English authorities mention the presence on the banks of the Thames of two such Muscovites, Tviérdikov and Pogoriélov, who were taken to be Ambassadors. They performed both offices, no doubt, and devoted their endeavours partly to diplomacy and partly to mercantile affairs.

The development of industry in Ivan's time was rather superficial ; the field was widened by the annexation of the eastern provinces. The acquisition of the Lower Volga favoured the development of fisheries. There were ninety-nine establishments of this kind at Péréiaslavl in 1562. After the occupation of the banks of the Kama by the Stroganovs, and the discovery of salt-mines near Astrakan, the salt-works there attained great importance.

Ivan's financial policy does not call for praise. It may be summed up as a series of expedients, all savouring more or less of robbery. Fletcher mentions several of these. Governors of provinces were treated with the utmost tolerance till they had gorged themselves with plunder, when they were forced to give up the spoil. The same system was applied to monasteries, which were allowed to heap up wealth in the same way. There were temporary seizures or monopolies of certain forms of produce or merchandise, thus made to bring in very large profits. Fines were imposed on officials for imaginary offences. The English diplomat tells an almost incredible story about a capful of *live flies* demanded in this way from the Moscow municipality.

The taxes themselves were managed in the most senseless manner that could have been devised. Generally speaking, every fresh need resulted in the imposition of a fresh tax, and there never was the smallest care as to fitting the burdens to the means of those who had to bear them, nor the slightest prudence as to killing the goose that laid the golden eggs. By the time the end of the reign was reached, the bird's laying-powers were very nearly exhausted.

The interests best served by the conquest of Kazan and Astrakan were those of the Church, whose borders were thus enlarged. Gourii, first Archbishop of Kazan, made a good many converts among the Tartars ; but this triumph of orthodox proselytism was counterbalanced, till the close of Ivan's reign, by the prolonged resistance of the paganism still existing in the interior of his dominions, and especially in certain districts in the province of Novgorod. As to the Tsar's attempts at religious reform, which he soon abandoned or only carried on in a most perfunctory fashion, they produced no appreciable result at all, and the intellectual and moral condition of the clergy was in no way altered by them.

Yet, from a more general point of view, there was a visible increase in the intellectual life of the country. Though the schools planned in 1551 never were anything but plans, though printing did not get beyond the stage of rudimentary attempt, the author of the letters to Kourbski did none the less witness a certain upward trend of ideas, which took their flight out of the narrow walls of the cloister and the confined circle of religious discussion into the world of secular thought. This beginning of the secularizing process was one of the great conquests of Ivan's reign.

On the other hand, Ivan, even in his international dealings, could not or would not break with certain barbarous traditions which harmonized but ill with progress such as this. Just as in past times, envoys sent to his Court were often treated as if they had been prisoners of war, and the fate of his genuine prisoners of war continued to be lamentable. The happiest thing they could expect was to be sold or given to the monasteries as serfs. Occasionally they were simply thrown into the water. In 1581, Ivan gave orders that when the Swedish ' tongues '—in other words, the persons, belligerents or. non-belligerents, taken with a view to obtaining information—had served their purpose, they were all to be killed. Polish and Swedish captives were used as current coin in the exchanges arranged by Tartar merchants on the Constantinople markets.

But as he stood, with all his faults and vices, his errors and his crimes, his weaknesses and his failures, Ivan was popular, and his was a genuine popularity, which has stood the twofold test of time and of misfortune. This, too, is a result. In the cycle of the historic songs of Russia, the Tsar holds the place of honour, and is shown in by no means repulsive colours ; he is open to every feeling of humanity—severe, but just, and even generous. True, indeed, his sacerdotal majesty lifts him up so high and surrounds him with such an aureole of glory that no critic would dare to lay his hand upon him. But we feel that, in spite of that, all the popular sympathies are with him. When he indulges in savage orgies over the corpses of the vanquished Tartars, or hands one of his boïars over to the executioner on the merest hint of suspicion, the masses are on his side ; they applaud the carnage, and rejoice in their master's joy. Even when they cannot applaud, they shut their eyes respectfully, religiously, and cast a mantle of decent fiction over that which makes their consciences revolt. The populace will not admit that the Tsar killed his own son. The Tsar of the *bylines* bestows a noble reward on Nikita Romanovitch, who, at the peril of his own life, saves that of the victim ; for the moment the order was given the Sovereign had repented. This Tsar has some weaknesses, indeed ; he is apt to be choleric, and his first instinct is not always his best. Under the walls of Kazan, whither the intentional anachronism of the poets has already brought Ermak and even Stenka Razine, Ivan taxes his artificers, who have been too slow about blowing up a mine, with treason, and threatens them with the gallows. The chiefs, cowards in this case, as always, according to the popular historians, shelter themselves behind their subordinates. But one young soldier speaks boldly in defence of his fellows, the mine blows up, and the Tsar acknowledges his own mistake and the merit of the humble hero. Passing into the conquered town, Ivan spares the Tsarina Helen, who comes out to meet him bearing bread and salt, and is content with having her baptized by force and thrust into a convent. But he has the eyes of the Tsar Simeon, who shows less goodwill and greater dignity, torn out of his head ; and here, again, the populace applauds the victor.

This is the theory of morals peculiar to the period to which Ivan's name is attached. The ideal it evolves is one of material greatness and brute force—a twofold postulate to which the Russian race has proved itself ready to sacrifice everything else, though it has endeavoured to delude itself as to the value of the end pursued, and the extent of the sacrifice it has entailed. In this other dream, Tsar and people both had their part, and they were to make it a living reality on the day when Peter took Ivan's place, and completed the incarnation which gave birth to modern Russia. But when Ivan died, this work was in the embryonic stage. His labour had been one of destruction, more especially, and he had no time to build up again. Still less had he ensured the continuity of his effort. The legacy left his country by the luckless adversary of Batory, the murderer of the Tsarevitch, his own heir, was a war with Poland and a state of anarchy. The germ was there, too, of a fresh inroad by the rivals of the Slavonic West, destined, under the shelter of the false Dmitri, to reach Moscow itself, and of a triumphant return of the aristocratic oligarchy, which, favoured by the general crumbling of the unfinished edifice, was to recover its old advantages. This was to be the history of the seventeenth century. But Peter the Great was not to guard his inheritance any better against future risks ; and yet, after a fresh eclipse, Catherine was to come, even as he had come. The strength was there still, increased materially and tempered morally—the imperishable pledge of a mighty future.

BIBLIOGRAPHY

AFANASSIEV (V.) : *The Campaign of Kazan* (K 350 liétiou pokorénia Kazani . . .). Moscow, 1902 (pamphlet).
AKSSAKOV (C.) : *Works.* Moscow, 1889, vol. i., second edition.
Akty arkeogr. Ekspedytsyi. See Documents.
ALBERTRANDI : *The Reigns of Henry of Valois and Batory* (Panowania Henryke Walezyuska i . . .). Warsaw, 1823. 1 vol.
Alexandrovskaia Liétopis. See Chronicles.
AMMAN (JOST) : *Gyneceum seu Theatrum mulierum.* Frankfort, 1586. 1 vol.
Ancient Russian Library (Drevnaïa Rousskaïa Vivliofika, 1787–1791). Second edition, vols. xii.-xx, and new edition, 1891. 5 vols.
ANNERSTADT (C.) : *Die Begründung der Schwedischen Herrschaft in Livland.* Stockholm, 1868. 1 vol.
Archiv Nachrichten von Unterhandlungen zwischen Rüss. und Dän. Höfe. (Busching's Magazin, vii.).
Archives of the Sapieha Family. Lemberg, 1892, vol. i.
Archives of the Radziwill Family. Cracow, 1885. 1 vol.
ARTSYBACHEV : *Study of Russian History.* Messager de l'Europe (Viéstnik Evropy), 1821.

BAGALIÉÏ (D.) : *Essays on the History of the Colonization of the Steppes* (Otcherki iz istorii kolonizatsii . . . Okrainy). Moscow, 1887. 1 vol.
BANTYCH-KAMIENSKI : *Diplomatic Correspondence between Russia and Poland* (Piériépiska miédjou Rossiéï Polcheï . . .). Readings of the Antiquarian and Historical Society (Tchténia), 1860.
View of the External Relations of Russia (Obzor Vniéchnykh Snochenii . . .). Moscow, 1894, vol. i.
BARROW : *A Chronological History of Voyages.* London, 1818. 1 vol.
BARSSOV (N.) : *On the Author of the Epistle to the Tsar Ivan Vassilié-vitch* (K voprossou ob avtorié poslania k tsariou I. V.). Collections of the Archæological Institute (Sbornik arkheolog. Inst.), Book IV.
Two Epistles by Pope Sylvester. Christian Readings (Christianskiié Tchténia), 1871.
BARTOSZEWICZ : *Anne Jagellon* (Anna Jagiellonka). Cracow, 1882. 1 vol.
BAUER : *The Relations of Russia with Germany.* Review of the Ministry of Public Instruction (Journal Ministerstva narodnavo prosviéchtchénia), 1870.
Beiträge zur Kenntniss Russlands und seiner Geschichte. Evers and Engelhardt. Derpt, 1816. 10 vols.
Beiträge zur Kunde Ehst. Liv. und Kurlands. Pabst., Revel., 1868–1887. 4 vols.

BESTOUJEV-RIOUMINE (C.) : *History of Russia*, Istoria Rossii, 1885 vol. ii.
Diverse Tendencies of the Study of the Popular Element in Russia. Annals of the Fatherland (Otiétchestviénnyié Zapiski), 1860.
The Slavophil Teachings (same collection), 1862.
Study of the Character of Ivan. Dawn (Zaria), 1871.
The Diplomatic Relations between Russia and England (Pamiatniki diplomatitcheskikh snochenyii). Collection of the Imp. Historical Society of Russia (Sbornik . . . Istoritcheskavo Obchchestva), xxxviii.
Bibliotheca Livoniæ Historica. See Winkelmann.
Library of Foreign Writers on Russia. St. Petersburg, 1847, vol. i.
BIÉLAIÉV (A. M.) : *The Protective Service on the Polish Frontier* (O storojévoi . . . sloujbié na polskoï okraïnié). Moscow, 1848. 1 vol.
BIÉLAIÉV (J. D.) : *Lessons on the History of Russian Law* (Lektsyi po istorii rousskavo zakonodatiélstva). Moscow, 1888. 1 vol.
The Peasants in Russia (Khréstianié na Roussi). Moscow, 1891. 1 vol.
BIÉLOKOUROV : *Library of the Muscovite Sovereigns* (O Bibliotékié moskovskikh gossoudareï). Moscow, 1898. 1 vol.
BIÉLOV (E. A.) : *On the Historical Importance of the Boïar Class* (Ob istoritcheskom znatchenii rousskavo boïarstva). Review of the Ministry of Public Instruction, 1886.
History of Russia down to the Reform of Peter the Great (Rousskaïa istoria do reformy Piétra Viélikavo). St. Petersburg, 1895.
Introductory Notes to the History of Ivan the Terrible (Predvaritiélnyïa zamiétchania k istorii Ivana . . . groznavo). Review of the Ministry of Public Instruction, 1887.
BIÉLSKI (M). : *Polish Chronicle* (Kronika Polska). Collection of Polish Writers, xvii.
BIENEMANN (FR.) : *Aus Baltischer Vorzeit.* Leipzig, 1870. 1 vol.
Briefe und Urkunden zur Geschichte Livlands in den J. 1558–1562. Riga, 1865–1879. 6 vols.
Riga's Stellung bei der Auflosung der livlandischen Ordenstaates. Russische Revue, 1877.
Biéssiéda Vlaamskikh Tsoudotvortsev. See Conversation.
BLUMENFELD : *On the Forms of Landed Property in Ancient Russia* (O formakh ziémliévladiénia v drevniéï Rossii). Odessa, 1885. 1 vol.
BOCH or BOCHIUS : *Psalmorum Davidis parodia heroica.* Antwerp, 1608. 1 vol.
BORATYNSKI (LOUIS) : *Stephen Batory and his Plans for a League against Turkey* (Stefan Batory i jego plan ligi przeciw Turkom). Reports of the Academy of Sciences at Cracow, 1902.
BOUSLAIÉV (F. I.) : *General Ideas on Russian Iconography.* Collections of the Society of Ancient Art, 1866.
Sketches of Literature and Art (Istoritcheskiié otcherki rousskoï narodnoï sloviésnosti i iskoustava). St. Petersburg, 1861, vol. ii.
A Study of Russian Art. Critical Review (Krititcheskoié Obozriénié). Moscow, 1879.
BOUTOVSKI (V. DE) : *History of Russian Decoration from the Eleventh to the Sixteenth Century.* Paris, 1872. 1 vol.
BREDENBACH (TIELEMANN) : *Belli livonici Historia.* Startchevski, vol. i.
BROEL-PLATER (VLADIMIR) : *Collection of Memoirs for the History of Poland* (Zbiòr Pamiétnikòw . . .). Warsaw, 1858, vol. iii.
BRUTTO (J. M.) : *De rebus gestis Stephani I. narratio.* Rome, 1852. 1 vol.

BUCHAU (DANIEL PRINTZ VON): *Moscoviæ artes et progressus*. Scriptores rerum livonicarum, ii. See that title.
BUNGE (F. G.). See Archiv für die Geschichte Liv. Ehst. und Kurland. *Der Orden der Schwertbruder*. Riga, 1875. 1 vol.
Busching's Magazin. Hamburg, 1767-1793, vol. vii.
BUSSE (K. H. V.): *Herzog Magnus, König von Livland*. Leipzig, 1871. *Zur Geschichte Livland's in den Jahren, 1581-1582, Mittheilungen aus dem Gebiete der Geschichte Liv. Ehst. und Kurland's*. See this title (Journal of the Abbé Piotrowski. See that name).
BUTTNER : *Die Vereinigung d. Liv. Schwertbruder Orden mit d. deutschen Orden*. Leipzig, 1865. 1 vol.

CAHUN (L.): *Introduction to the History of Asia*, 1896. 1 vol.
CALIGARI. See Kallenbach.
CAMPANI. See Pierling.
CAWSTON and KEANE : *The Early Chartered Companies*. London, 1896.
CELSIUS (O. v.): *History of Eric XIV.*, a French translation by Genest. Paris, 1777. 2 vols.
CHANCELLOR : *Travels*. Hakluyt, i.
CHAUDOIR (BARON V. DE), *Aperçu sur les monnaies Russes*. St. Petersburg, 1836. 1 vol.
CHEVIREV : *Journey to the Monastery of St. Cyril* (Poiézdka v. Kirillo-Biéloziérski monastyr). Moscow, 1850, vol. ii.
CHIJAKOV (N. V.): *Ermak in 1581*. St. Petersburg, 1901 (pamphlet).
CHMOURLO (E.): *The East and the West in Russian History* (Vostok i Zapad v rousskoï istorii). Derpt, 1895. 1 vol.
Essay on the Life and Labours of C. I. Bestoujev-Rioumine (Otcherk jizni . . . K. I. B. R.). Derpt, 1899. 1 vol.
CHNOURLO (E.): *The Russian Narratives of Giovanni Tetaldi* (Izviéstia G. T. o Rossii). St. Petersburg, 1891 (pamphlet).
CHOISNIN (J.): *Memoirs*. Michaud and Poujoulat Collection, xi.
CHRISTIANI: *Die Gegenreformation in Lifland*. Baltische Monatsschrift, 1889.
Chronicle of the Reign of Ivan IV. (Tsarstviénnaïa Kniga ou Liétopissiéts Tsartsvovania Tsaria I. V.). St. Petersburg, 1769. 1 vol.
The Russian Chronicle of Lvov (Lvovskaïa Liétopis). St. Petersburg, 1792. 1 vol.
The Russian Chronicle of Niconius (Nikonovskaïa Liétopis). Complete Collection of the Russian Chronicles, ix. and x. See this title.
The Siberian Chronicle of Essipov (Essipovskaïa Liétopis), Spaski's edition. St. Petersburg, 1823. 1 vol.
The Siberian Chronicle of Stroganov (Stroganovskaïa Liétopis), Spaski. St. Petersburg, 1821. 1 vol.
The Siberian Chronicle, Remezov (Remezovskaïa or Koungourskaïa Liétopis). St. Petersburg, 1880, published by the Archæographical Commission. 1 vol.
Chronicle, Alexander Nevski's (Alexandrovskaïa Liétopis). Bibliog. Hist. of Russia, iii., 1876.
Chronicles, Novgorod (Novgorodskiié Liétopisy). Complete Collection of the Russian Chronicles, iii. and iv.
Chronicles, Pskov (Pskovskiié Liétopisy). Complete Collection of the Russian Chronicles, vols iv. and v.
Chronicle, Moscow (Moskovskaïa Liétopis), Lébédiev, Readings of the Moscow Society, Historical and Antiquarian (Tchténia), 1895.
Chronicle, Normantski (Normantskaïa Liétopis). Annals of the Imperial Society, Historical and Antiquarian (Vrémiennik Imperatorskavo Obch. 1st i Drev), 1850.

Chronicle, Tver (Tverskaïa Liétopis). Complete Collection of Russian Chronicles, xv.
Chronographers, Russian. See Popov.
CHTCHERBATOV (M. M.): *History of Russia* (Istoria Rossii). St. Petersburg, 1777, vol. v.
CHYTRÆUS (D.): *Chronico Saxoniæ.* Leipzig, 1593. 1 vol.
CIAMPI: *Bibliographia Critica.* Florence, 1838-1842. 3 vols.
Code of Ivan IV. (*Soudiebnik*), with the Commentaries of Tatichtchev. Moscow, 1786. 1 vol. Text of the Code, and additional laws. Historical Documents, vol. i., 1841.
Collection of Polish Historians (Zbiór dziejopisów polskich). Warsaw, 1766, vol. ii.
Collection of the Russian Imperial Historical Society (Sbornik 1st Obchtestva), vols. xxxviii., liii., lix., lxxi., cxvi.
Collection of State Papers and Treaties (Sbranié goussoudarstviénnykh gramot i dogovorov. Roumiantsov, St. Petersburg, 1819, vol. i.
Collection of Travels in the North. Amsterdam, 1727, vol. viii.
Complete Collection of Russian Chronicles (Poinoié Sobranié Rouskikh Liétopissov). Moscow, 1846 (in course of publication).
CONTARINI: *Diplomatic Reports.* Library of Foreign Historians of Russia.
Conversation of the Wonder-workers of Valaam (Biéssiéda Valaam. Tsoud.). V. G. Droujinine and M. A. Diakonov. St. Petersburg, 1890 (pamphlet).
CUSTINE (M. DE): *La Russie.* Paris, 1855. 1 vol.
CZERMAK (V.): *Lithuanian Parliamentarianism previous to the Union of Lublin* (Parlamentaryzm litewski . . .). Lemberg, 1891. 1 vol.
CZUCZYNSKI, editor of Piotrowski. See that name.

DAHLMANN (A.): *Dissertatio de Occasione Fœderum Regis Erici XIV. cum Russiâ.* Upsala, 1783. 1 vol.
DARCEL: *L'Art Russe.* Gazette des Beaux Arts, 1878.
DEBOLSKI (N. N.): *Judicial Capacities in Russian Law up to the End of the Eighteenth Century* (Grajdanskaïa diéiésposobnost po rousskomou pravou). St. Petersburg, 1903. 1 vol.
An Examination into the Literature of History affecting the Question of Serfdom. Review of the Ministry of Public Instruction, 1895.
DELMAR-MORGAN: *Early Voyages . . . to Russia.* London, 1886. 1 vol.
De rebus gestis Stephani I. . . . contra Magnum Moschorum Ducem. Rome, 1852. Pamphlet (Manifesto of Stephen Batory to his army in 1579).
DIAKONOV (M. A.): *Enquiries into the History of the Serfdom of the Russian Peasantry* (Razzyskania po istorii prikriépliénia vladiéltcheskikh Krestiane v Moskovskom gossoudarstvié). St. Petersburg, 1901. 1 vol.
General View of the History of the Rural Population in Russia (Otcherki po istorii ssiélskavo nassiéliénia Moskovskavo gossoudarstva. St. Petersburg, 1898.
The Power of the Muscovite Sovereigns (Vlast Moskovskikh Gossoudareï). St. Petersburg, 1889. 1 vol.
Documents connected with the History of the Qualified Population (Akty otnossiachtchyiésia k istorii tiaglavo nassiéliénia v Moskovskom gossoudarstvié). Derpt, 1895-1897. 2 vols.

DITIATINE (J.) : *Organization and Administration of the Russian Towns* (Oustroistvo i Oupravliénié gorodov v Rossii). St. Petersburg, 1875, vol i.

DMITRIÉV (F. M.) : *Works*. Moscow, 1899, vol. i.
Dniévnik posliédnavo pokhoda Stefana Batoria (Journal of Batory's last campaign), Kojalowicz's edition. See that name.
Documents, Diplomatic. See Papers.
Documents of the Archæographical Society (Akty Arkhéogr. Ekspedytsyï). St. Petersburg, 1836, vols. i. and ii.

DOGIEL : *Codex Diplomaticus Regni Poloniæ et Magni Ducatus Lithuaniæ.* Vilna, 1758, vol. v.

Domostroï, The, Golokhvastov's editions. Readings of the Historical and Antiquarian Society of Moscow, 1849. Iakovlev's edition, St. Petersburg, 1867 ; and Zabiéline's edition, Moscow, 1882, etc.

Drevnaia Rousskaia Vivliofika. See Ancient Library.

Essipovskaïa Liétopis. See Siberian Chronicle.

EVERS. See Beiträge.

EVFIMENKO (MME. A. I.) : *Studies of the National Life* (Izsliédovania narodnoï jizni). Moscow, 1884. 1 vol.
Peasant Property in Land in the Far North (Khréstianskiié ziémliévladiénié . . .). Russian Thought, 1882–1883.

FAHNE (A.) : *Livland, ein Beitrag zur Kirchen und Sittensgeschichte.* Dusseldorf, 1875. 1 vol.

FECHNER (A. G.) : *Chronik der Evangelischen Gemeinden in Moskau.* Moscow, 1876. 1 vol.

FIEDLER : *Ein Versuch der Vereinigung der russischen mit der römischen Kirche* (Sitzungsberichte der K.K. Akademie der Wissenschaften). Vienna, 1862, vol. xl.

FISCHER (I. E.) : *History of Siberia* (Sibirskaïa Istoria). St. Petersburg, 1774. 1 vol.

FLETCHER (G.) : *The Treatise of the Russian Commonwealth*, published by the Hakluyt Society in ' Russia at the close of the sixteenth century.' Bond, London, 1856. 1 vol. Translated into French by Du Bouzet, ' La Russie au Seizième Siècle.' Leipzig and Paris, 1864. 1 vol.

FORSTEN (G. V.) : *The Struggle for the Empire of the Baltic* (Borba iz za Gospodstva Balitiiskavo moria). St. Petersburg, 1884. 1 vol.
The Baltic Question (Baltiiskii vopros), vol. i. The Struggle for Livonia (Borba iz za Livonii). St. Petersburg, 1893. 1 vol.
Documents connected with the History of the Baltic Question (Akty i pisma k istorii b. v.). St. Petersburg, 1889–1893. 2 vols.

FORSTER : *Geschichte der Entdeckungen im Norden.* Frankfort, 1784.

FOSCARINI : *Narratio Historica de Moscovitico Imperio* (Historica Russiæ Monumenta). See that title.

GOLOKHVASTOV (D. P.), continued by Monsignor LEONIDAS : *Silvester and his Writings* (Blagoviéchtchenskii iereï Silvester i ievo pisania). Readings of the Historical and Antiquarian Society, 1874.

GOLOUBINSKI (E.) : *History of the Canonization of the Saints of the Russian Church* (Istoria kanonizatskii sviatykh v rousskoï tserkvi). Sergiévskii Posad, 1894. 1 vol.

GORSKI (C.): *Life . . . of Prince Kourbski* (Jizn i istoritcheskoié znatchénié Kniazia A. M. Kourbskavo). Kazan, 1858. 1 vol.
History of the Polish Infantry (Historya piechoty polskiej). Cracow, 1893. 1 vol.

GORSKI (C.): *History of the Polish Cavalry* (Historya jazdy polskiej). Cracow, 1894. 1 vol.
History of the Polish Artillery (Historya artyleryi polskiej). Warsaw, 1902. 1 vol.
The Wars of the Polish Republic with Moscow under Batory (Wojny Rzeczypospolitej z Wielkiem Ksiestwem Moskiewskiem za Batorego). Warsaw Library (Bibljoteka Warszawska), 1892.
GOUMILEVSKI (MONSIGNOR PH.): *History of the Russian Church* (Istoria Rousskoï Tserkvi). Moscow, 1888, Part III.
GRADOVSKI (A. D.): *History of Local Administration* (Istoria miéstnavo oupravliénia). St. Petersburg, 1868, vol. i.
Principles of the Common Law in Russia (Natchala rousskavo gossoud, prava). St. Petersburg, 1883, vol. iii.
Study of the Peasantry. Review of the Ministry of Public Instruction, 1868.
GREFENTHAL: *Livonian Chronicle* (Monumenta Livoniæ, vol. v.). See that title.
GUAGNINO (A.): *Omnium Regionum Moscoviæ descriptio* (Startchevski, i.). See that title.
GUÉPIN (DOM): *Vie de St. Josaphat.* Paris, 1874, vol. i.
GYULAY: *Commentarium rerum a Stephano R. P. . . . gestarum,* anno 1580. Claudiopolio, 1581. 1 vol. (No author given.)

HAKLUYT (R.): *Collection of Early Voyages.* London, 1599, vol. i.
HAMEL (J.): *Tradescant der æltere,* 1618, *in Russland.* St. Petersburg, 1847. 1 vol. English translation by J. S. Leigh, ' England and Russia.' London, 1854. 1 vol.
HANSEN (H. I.): *Geschichte der Stadt Narva.* Derpt, 1858. 1 vol.
HAUSMANN (R.): *Studien zur Geschichte des Koenig's Stephan von Polen* (Verhandlungen der gelehrten etnischen Gesellschaft in Dorpat, 1880).
HEIDENSTEIN (R.): *De bello Moscovitico . . . commentariorum, libri vi.* Bâle, 1588, and Startchevski, vol. ii.
Rerum Polonicarum, libri xii. Frankfort, 1672. 1 vol.
HENNING (SALOMON): *Liflendische und Churlendische Chronica* (Scriptores rerum Livonicarum), vol. ii.
HERBERSTEIN (S.): *Rerum Moscoviticarum commentarii.* Bâle, 1571, and Startchevski, i.
HEWINS: *English Trade and Finance.* London, 1892. 1 vol.
HIAERN (TH.): *Ehst. Lyf. und Letlaendische Geschichte* (Monumenta Livoniæ Antiquæ, i.). See that title.
Historical Papers (Akty Istoritcheskiié). Published by the Archæographical Commission. St. Petersburg, 1841, vol. i., and Supplement, 1845, vol. i.
Historical Documents connected with the History of Western Russia (Akty otnosiachtchyiésia k Istorii zapadnoi Rossii). St. Petersburg, 1846–1853, vols. i., ii., and iv.
Historical Documents connected with the History of South-western Russia (Akty otnosiachtchyiésia k Istorii iougo-zapadnoi Rossii). St. Petersburg, 1862–1869. 6 vols.
Historical Documents connected with the Reign of Stephen Batory (Akty historyczne do panowania S. Batorego), Ianicki. Warsaw, 1881. 1 vol.
Historical Documents (Akty historyczne). Published by the Academy of Sciences at Cracow, 1887, vol. xi.
Historia rerum a Poloniæ rege in Moscovia . . . gestarum. Place of publication not mentioned (ascribed to Heidenstein).
Historiæ Ruthenicæ Scriptores Exteri. See Startchevski.

Historicæ Russiæ Monumenta. Published by A. I. Tourguéniév. St. Petersburg, 1841, 1 vol., and Supplement, 1 vol. (The Russian sub-title, Akty Istoritcheskiié, has led to some confusion.)

HORSEY (J. J.): *Travels.* Published by the Hakluyt Society (' Russia at the Close of the Sixteenth Century '), 1856. 1 vol. Extracts in the Purchas Collection.

HÜPEL (A. W.): *Nordische Miscellaneen and Neue Nordischen Miscellaneen.* Riga, 1781–1798. 5 vols.

HÜPPE (S.): *De Poloniæ post Henricum Interregno.* Breslau, 1866. 1 vol.

IANICKI. See Historical Documents.

IANNAU (H. VON): *Geschichte von Lief und Ehstland* (Hüpel's Neue Nordische Miscellaneen, iii.). See that title.

IAROCH (C.): *Psychological Parallel between Ivan the Terrible and Peter the Great* (Psikhologitcheskaïa parallel). Kharkov, 1898 (pamphlet).

IASINSKI (A. N.): *Works of Prince Kourbski* (Sotchiniénia Kniazia Kourbskavo). St. Petersburg, 1889. 1 vol.

IKONNIKOV (V.): *Essay on the Byzantine Influence on the History of Russia* (Izliédovania o glavnykh napravleniakh v naoukié rousskoï istorii, Vlianié Vizantiïskoi i joujno-rousskoï obrazovannosti). Kiev, 1869. 1 vol.
  Biography of the Metropolitan Macarius (Review of the Ministry of Public Instruction, 1881).

ILINSKI (A. K.): *The Town Population of the Province of Novgorod in the Sixteenth Century* (Gorodskoïé nassiéliénié Novgorodskoï oblasti v XVI. viékié). Same collection, 1876.

ILOVAÏSKI (D.): *History of Russia.* Moscow, 1890, vol. iii.
  Critical Notes on Ivan the Terrible. Russian Archives (Rousskii Arkhiv), 1889.

IVAN IV.: *Two Epistles addressed to the Monastery of Souzdal.* Russian Archives, 1888.

IVANICHEV (N. D.): *The Life of Prince Kourbski in Lithuania* (Jizn Kn. A. M. Kourbskavo v Litvié). Kiév, 1849. 2 vols.

JDANOV: *Materials for a History of the Conciliable of 1551* (Materialy dla istorii Stoglavnavo Sobora), Review of the Ministry of Public Instruction, 1876.

JENKINSON (A.): *Voyages to Russia and Persia.* Hakluyt, i.

JEWLASZEWSKI (TH.): Memoirs, edited by Prince Lubomirski. Warsaw, 1860. 1 vol.

JMAKINE (V.): *The Mental Struggle in Russia during the First Half of the Sixteenth Century* (Borba idéi v Rossii v piérvoï polovinié XVI. viéka). Review of the Ministry of Public Instruction, 1882.
  A Document dealing with the History of the Anti-Catholic Controversy in Russia in the Sixteenth Century (Pamiatnik rousskoï protivkatolitcheskoï polémiki). Same Review, 1880.

Journals of the Polish Embassies. See State Papers.

JOVE (PAUL): *De Legatione Basilii magni Principis Moscoviæ ad Clementem VII. pontificem maximum* (Rerum Moscovitarum auctores varii).

JUUSTEN (PAUL): *Narratives concerning Muscovy* (Beiträge zur Kentniss Russlands, iii.).

KALLENBACH: *Extracts from the Reports of Caligari, Papal Nuncio in Poland, as to Stephen Batory.* Weekly Illustrated Review (Tygodnik illustrowany). Warsaw, 1887, No. 206.

KAPTEREV (E.) : *Nature of the Relations between Russia and the Orthodox East in the Sixteenth and Seventeenth Centuries* (Kharakter otno chenii Rossii k pravoslavnomou Vostokou . . .). Moscow, 1885. 1 vol.

KARAMZINE : *History of Russia*. St. Petersburg, 1818–1829 (French translation by St. Thomas and Jauffret, Paris, 1820), vols. viii. and ix

KHARPOV (G. F.) : *Diplomatic Relations between the Empire of Moscow and the Polish-Lithuanian State*, 1487–1571 (Pamiatniki diplomatitcheskikh snochenii . . .). Collection of the Imperial Russian Historical Society (Sbornik), vols. xxxv., lxi., and lxxi.

KARWOWSKI : *De Livonia Imperio Sigismondi Augusti regis Poloniæ subjecta*. Halle, 1870. 1 vol.

KATYREV-ROSTOVSKI (PRINCE I. M.) : *Chrestomathy* (Izbornik). Also ascribed to Koubassov, A. N. Popov, Moscow, 1869. 1 vol. see Popov.

KAVELINE (C. D.) : *Works*. Moscow, 1859, vols. i. and ii. *Notes on the History of Russia*. Messager de l'Europe, 1866.

KELCH (CH.) : *Lieflaendische Historia*. Revel, 1695. 1 vol.

KHLIÉBNIKOV (N.) : *On the Influence of Society on the Organization of the State during the Tsarian Period of Russian History* (O vlianii obchtchestva na organizasion Gossoudarstva v tsarskii périod rousskoï istorii). St. Petersburg, 1869. 1 vol.

KHOMIAKOV (A. S.) : *Thirteen Years of the Reign of Ivan Vassiliévitch* (Trinadtsat liét tsarstvoviania Ivana Vassiliévitcha). Educational Library (Bibliotéka dla vospitania). Valouiév, 1845.

KHROUCHTCHOV : *Book of Degrees, or Genealogy* (Stiépiénnaïa Kniga). MS. the property of A. F. Khrouchtchov, drawn up about 1690 by S. S. Koltovski (see Platonov's Notes on Russian History, 1903), and now in the Archives of the Moscow Foreign Office.

KIPRIANOFF (V.) : *Picturesque History of Russian Architecture*. St. Petersburg, 1864. 1 vol.

KIRIÉIÉVSKI (P. V.) : *Collection of Songs* (Piésni sobrannyïa). Moscow, 1860–1862. 1 vol.

KISEWETTER (A. A.) : *Ivan the Terrible and his Foes* (Ivan Groznyï iévo oponenty). Moscow, 1898 (pamphlet).

KLIOUTCHEVSKI (V.) : *Course of Russian History* (lithographed). *The Council of the Boïars in Ancient Russia* (Boïarskaïa douma drevneï Rossii). Moscow, 1883. 1 vol., second edition. *Internal Economy of the Monastery of Solovki on the Shores of the White Sea* (Khoziaïastviénnaïa diéiatiélnost Soloviétskavo monastyra v Biélomorskom kraié). Annals of the University of Moscow, 1867. *Summary of Russian History* (Kratkoié posobié po rousskoï istorii). Moscow, 1883. 1 vol. Second edition. *The Russian Rouble in the Sixteenth and Seventeenth Centuries* (Rousskii Roubl xvi i xvii v). Moscow, 1884. 1 vol. *The Origin of Serfdom in Russia* (Proïskhojdiénié Kriepostnavo prava v Rossii). Russian Thought (Rousskaïa Mysl). 1885. *The Composition of Representative Assemblies in Ancient Russia* (Sostav predstavitiélstva na Ziémskikh sobovakh drevneï Roussi). Same publication, 1890.

KLOSSIUS (FR.) : *The Library of the Grand Duke Vassili Ivanovitch and of the Tsar Ivan Vassiliévitch*. In Russian, Review of the Ministry of Public Instruction, 1834, and in German in the Dorpater Jahrbücher für Literatur und Kunst, same year.

Kniga Possolskaïa metryki. See State Papers.

KOÏALOVITCH (M. O.) : *Journal of the last Campaign of Stephen Batory against Russia, and Diplomatic Correspondence of that Time* (Dniév-

nik posliédniavo pokhoda Stefana Batoria i diplomatitcheska
piériépiska tavo vremieni). St. Petersburg, 1867. 1 vol. (from a
manuscript in the Imperial Library at St. Petersburg). The
original, utilized by Polkovski (see that name), is in the Library
at Dzików (Grand Duchy of Posen). The journal is composed of
the Abbé Piotrowski's letters (see that name).

KORDT : Documents bearing on the Commercial Relations between Russia
and Foreign Countries. Collection of the Imperial Society of
Russian History, cxvi.

KORKOUNOV : Map of the War Operations between the Russians and the
Poles. In Russian, St. Petersburg, 1837, and in Polish, Breslau,
1840.

KORZON (T.): Criticism of C. Gorski's Work on the Wars of Batory.
Quarterly Historical Review (Kwartalnik Historyczny) of Lemberg, x.

KOSTOMAROV (N. I.): Sketch of the History of the Commerce of the
Russian Empire during the Sixteenth and Seventeenth Centuries.
(Otcherki Torgovli moskovskavo gossoudarstva . . .). St. Peters-
burg, 1889. 1 vol.

Monographies and Enquiries. St. Petersburg, 1868, vols. vii.,
viii., xiii., xix., and xx.

The History of Russia in Biographies (Rousskaïa istoria v
jizniéopisaniakh iéia glavniéichykh diéiatiéleï). St. Petersburg,
1896, fourth edition, vol. i.

Study of the External Policy of Ivan IV. Messager de l'Europe
(Viéstnik Evropy), 1871.

Study of the Origin of Serfdom. Collection of Historical and
Practical Science (Arkiv istoritcheskikh i praktitcheskikh sviédiénii), 1859.

Study of the Assemblies of the Sixteenth and Seventeenth Centuries
(Novoié Vrémia), 1880. No. 1485.

KOUBASSOV. See Katyrev.

KOULICH : History of the Reunification of Russia (Istoria vozsoiéjdin-
iénia Roussi). St. Petersburg, 1874. 2 vols.

KOURBSKI (PRINCE A. M.): Narratives (Skazania), Oustrialov. St.
Petersburg, 1868. 1 vol.

KOUZNIÉTSOV : Information . . . as to the Construction of the Church
of the Intercession of the Blessed Virgin at Moscow (Novyïa liétopis-
nyïa dannyïa . . .). Readings (Tchténia), 1896.

KOVALEVSKI (M.): Modern Customs and Ancient Laws of Russia.
London, 1891. 1 vol.

KOVALEVSKI (P. I.): Attempts at the Psychiatry of some Historical
Personages (Psikiatritcheskiié otcherki . . .). St. Petersburg,
1893, vol. iii.

KRAUSHAAR (A.): Magic at the Court of Batory (Czary na dworze
Batorego). Cracow, 1888. 1 vol.

The True History of the Unhappy Fate of John, Duke of Finland,
and of Catherine, Princess Royal (Historya prawdziwa . . .).
Cracow, 1892 (pamphlet).

KROUTCHTCHOV (I.) : Enquiry into the Works of Joseph Sanine (Izliédovania o sotchiniéniakh I. S.). St. Petersburg, 1868. 1 vol.

KRUSE (ELERT): Wahrhaftige Gegenbericht auf die anno 1578, einge-
gangene lieflendische Chronica B. Russow's. Riga, 1861 (pamphlet).

LAMPRECHT (K.): Deutsche Geschichte. Berlin, 1891–1895, vols. iii.
and iv.

LANGUET (HUBERT) : Arcana Sæculi decimi sexti. Halle, 1699. 1 vol.

LAPPO (I. I.) : *The Grand Duchy of Lithuania in* 1569–1581 (Viélikoié Kniajestvo Litovskoié v. 1569–1581 godakh). St. Petersburg, 1901. 1 vol.
LAPPO-DANILEVSKI (A. S.) : *Narrative of the History of Peasant Serfdom in the Muscovite Empire in the Sixteenth and Seventeenth Centuries* (Razskazania po istorii prikriépliénia vladiéltcheskikh krestiane). St. Petersburg, 1901. 1 vol.
LASICIUS (JOHN-LASIÇKI) : *De Russorum, Moscovitarum et Tartarorum religione.* Spire, 1582. 1 vol.
LATKINE (V.) : *Lessons on the External History of Russian Law* (Lektsii po vniéchniéi istorii rousskavo prava). St. Petersburg, 1890. 1 vol.
The Assemblies of Ancient Russia (Ziémskiié sobory drevneï Roussi). St. Petersburg, 1855. 1 vol.
LAUREO (VINCENZO). See Wierzbowski.
LÉBÉDIEV (N.) : *The Conciliable of* 1551 (Stoglavnyï Sobor). Moscow, 1882. 1 vol.
The Metropolitan Macarius (Makarii, métropolit vssiérossiiskii). Moscow, 1881. 1 vol.
LÉGER : *Russes et Slaves.* Paris, 1890. 1 vol.
LEONIDAS. See Golokhvastov.
LEONIDAS (MONS.) : *Biography of St. Philip.* Moscow, 1861.
LÉONTOVITCH (F. I.) : *Study of the Work of Sainokvassov.* Collections of Political Science, ii., 1875.
LERPIGNY (M.) : *Un Arbitrage Pontifical au Seizième Siècle.* Brussels (undated). 1 vol.
LEVENCLAVIUS (J.) : *De Moscovitarum bellis adversus finitiones gestis.* Startchevski, i.
LIKHATCHEV (N. P.) : *The Origin of Alexis Adachev* (Istoritcheskii Viéstnik), 1890.
The Library and Archives of the Moscow Sovereigns in the Sixteenth Century (Bibliotéka i Arkhiv Moskovskikh gossoudareï). St. Petersburg, 1894. 1 vol.
LILIÉIÉV (N. V.) : *Simeon Dekboulatovitch, Tsar of Kassimov.* Tver, 1891. 1 vol.
LIPPOMANO : *Narrative* (Hist. Russiæ Monumenta, i.)
LISCH (G.) : *Study of the Livonian War* (Jahrbücher für Mecklem. Geschichte), 1857.
Book of Degrees (Stiépiennaïa Kniga). Moscow, 1775. 1 vol.
LOSSIUS. See Urkunden.
Lvovskaïa Liétopis. See Russian Chronicle.

MACARIUS (MONS.) : *History of the Russian Church* (Istoria Rousskoï Tserkvi). St. Petersburg, 1877, vol. viii.
MACIEJOWSKI (W. A.) : *History of Slav Legislation* (Historya prawodawstw slawianskich). Warsaw, 1856–1858. 6 vols.
MAÏKOV (L.) : *Chronological Notes on the Union of Siberia with Russia* (Kronologitcheskiié spravki . . .). Review of the Ministry of Public Instruction, 1881.
MALINOVSKI : *Historical Proof of the Ancient Desire of the Polish Nation for Union with Russia.* Readings (Tchténia), vi.
MARGERET (JACQUES): *État présent de l'Empire de Russie.* Paris, 1669. New edition, Paris, 1854. 1 vol.
MARKIÉVITCH (A. I.) : *History of the Miéstnitchestvo* (Istoria Miéstnitchestva). Odessa, 1888. 1 vol.
MARTENS : *Collection of Treaties and Conventions between Russia and Foreign Powers.* St. Petersburg, 1874–1892. 9 vols.
MARTYNOV (A.) : *Ancient Monuments in the Neighbourhood of Moscow.* St. Petersburg, 1889. 1 vol.

MARTÝNOV (FATHER) : *Russian Art.* Arras, 1878 (pamphlet).
MASKIEWICZ (S.) : *Memoirs.* Vilna, 1838. 1 vol.
MASSA (ISAAC) : *Chronicon Moscoviticum* (Rerum Rossicarum scriptores exteri, ii.).
  Relatio de Siberica. Collection of Northern Travels. Amsterdam, 1727, vol. viii.
MAYERBERG : *Travels in Muscovy.* Russian and Polish Library, vols. i. and ii.
Memorabilis et perinde stupenda de crudeli Moscovitarum expeditione narratio, ex germanico in latinum conversa. Douai, 1563. Facsimile published at Paris, 1858. 1 vol.*
MICHALON (THE LITHUANIAN) : *De Moribus Tartarorum Lithunaorum et Moschorum.* Bâle, 1615. 1 vol.
MIECHOWSKI (MATTHEW, also called MATHIAS A MICHOVIA) : *De Moscovia.* Startchevski, i.
MIKHAÏLOV (A.) : *Study of the ' Domostroï.'* Review of the the Ministry of Public Instruction, 1889.
MIKHAÏLOVSKI (N. K.) : *Critical Studies* (Krititcheskiié opyty). St. Petersburg, 1895.
MIKLACHEVSKI (I. N.) : *Contribution to the Economic History of the Russian Empire* (K Istorii Khoziaïstviénnavo byta rousskavo gossoudarstva). Moscow, 1894. 1 vol.
MILIOUKOV (P.) : *Essays on the History of Russian Culture* (Otcherki po istorii rousskoï Koultoury). St. Petersburg, 1896–1901. 3 vols.
  Disputed Historical Problems (Spornyié Voprossy). St. Petersburg, 1902. 1 vol.
MILLER (G. FR.) : *Description of Siberia* (Opissanié rousskavo tsarstva). St. Petersburg, 1750. 1 vol.
Mittheilungen aus dem Gebiete der Geschichte Liv. Ehst. und Kurlands. Riga, 1847–1858. 8 vols.
Moskovskaïa Liétopis. See Moscow Chronicle.
MOUKHANOV : *Collection* (Sbornik). Moscow, 1836. 1 vol.
MÜLLER (LAURENZ) : *Polnische Lifl. Mosc. und andere Historien.* Leipzig, 1585, and various other editions and translations.
MÜNSTER (SEB.) : *Cosmographei.* Bâle, 1550. 1 vol. (French translation by François de Belle-Forest, Paris, 1575. 1 vol.).

NAPIERSKY (K. E.) : *Russisch-livlandische Urkunden.* St. Petersburg, 1868. 1 vol.
Narrative of the Siege of Pskov by Batory (Poviést o prikhojdenii Litovskavo Korola Stepana na . . . Pskov). Readings of the Moscow Historical and Antiquarian Society, 1847, and separately under another title (Poviést preslavna . . .). Pskov, 1878. 1 vol.
Narratives of the Apostolic Nuncios and other Persons with regard to Poland (Relacye Nuncyuszów), Ryaczewski. Berlin, 1864. 2 vols.
NEHRING : *The Polish Historians of the Sixteenth Century* (O Historykach Polskich, XVI. w.). Posen, 1862. 1 vol.
NEKRASSOV (N.) : *Attempt at an Enquiry, Historical and Literary, into the Origin of the ' Domostroï ')* Opyt . . . izsliédovania o proïskhojdienii . . . Domostroïa). Moscow, 1872. 1 vol.
NIÉBOLSINE : *The Conquest of Siberia* (Pokorénié Sibiri). St. Petersburg, 1849. 1 vol.
NIEMCEWICZ (I. U.) : *Collection of Memoirs* (Zbiór Pamietników). Warsaw, 1822, vol. ii.
NIÉVOLINE (K. A.) : *Complete Works.* St. Petersburg, 1857. 3 vols.
  * One of the best-known pamphlets of the period, and quoted for that reason.

NIKITSKI (A.): *Sketch of the Internal History of Pskov* (Otcherki vnoutrennoï istorii Psokva). St. Petersburg, 1873. 1 vol.
  Origin of the Name of Ermak. Review of the Ministry of Public Instruction, 1882.
NIKOLAIÉVSKI (P.): *Russian Sermons in the Fifteenth and Sixteenth Centuries.* Same Review, 1868.
Nikonovskaïa Liétopis. See Chronicle of Niconius.
NOAILLES (MARQUIS DE): *Henri de Valois et la Pologne en 1572.* Paris, 1867. 3 vols.
Normantskaïa Liétopis. See Chronicle of Normantski.
Novgorodskiié Liétopisy. See Chronicles of Novgorod.
NYENSTAEDT (F.): *Chronicle* (Monumenta Livoniæ Antiquæ, ii.).

ODERBORN (P.): *Joannis Basilidis vita.* Vitebsk, 1585, and Startchevski, ii.
OKSENOV: *Ermak in Historical Poetry.* Siberian Collection (Sibirskii Sbornik), 1886.
  The Relations between Novgorod and the Iougra. Literary Collections, 1885.
OLMEN (P.): *Chronicle.* Startchevski, i.
OPOKOV (Z.): *Prince Kourbski* (Kniaz A. M. Kourbskii). Kiév, 1872. 1 vol.
ORIGNY (D'): *The Life of Father A. Possevino.* Paris, 1712. 1 vol.
OUMANIÉTS (F. M.): *The Russo-Lithuanian Party in Poland* (Rousskolitevskaïa partia v Polché). Review of the Ministry of Public Instruction, 1875.
  Degenerate Poland (Vyrojdiénié Polchi). St. Petersburg, 1872. 1 vol.
  Study of St. Philip (New and Old Russia, 1877).
OUSPIÉNSKI (F.): *The Relations between Rome and Moscow.* Review of the Ministry of Public Instruction, 1884, 1885.
  Negotiations for Peace between Muscovy and Poland (Peregovory o mirié). Odessa, 1887. 1 vol.
  Origin of the Eastern Question (Kak voznik . . . Vostotchnyi vopros). St. Petersburg, 1887 (pamphlet).
OUSPIÉNSKI (BROTHERS): *Menology of the Emperor Basil* (Litsevoï Miéssiatsoslov . . . Imperatora Vassilia). St. Petersburg, 1902. 1 vol.
OUSTRIALOV (N. G.): *The Stroganov Family* (Imiénityié lioudi Stroganovy). St. Petersburg, 1842. 1 vol.

P . . . SKI: *Prince Kourbski* (Kniaz A. M. Kourbskii). Kazan, 1873. 1 vol.
PABST (E.): *Die Anfange der Deutschen Herrschaft in Livland* (Archiv zur Geschichte Liv. Ehst. und Kurlands), vols. iii. and iv.
Pamiatniki Diplomatitcheskikh Snochenii. See Papers.
Pamiatniki drevneï pismiennosti i isskoustva. See Papers.
PAVLINOV (A. M.): *History of Russian Architecture* (Istoria rousskoï arkhitektoury). Moscow, 1894. 1 vol.
PAVLOV (A. S.): *History of the Secularization of the Ecclesiastical Properties in Russia* (Istoritcheskii otcherk sekouliaryzatsii tserkovnykh ziémiél). Odessa, 1871. 1 vol.
  Of Certain Assemblies. . . . Annals of the Fatherland. 1859.
PAVLOV-SILVANSKI (N.): *The Men who Serve* (Gossoudarevy sloujilyié lioudi). St. Petersburg, 1898. 1 vol.
PAWINSKI (A.): *State Papers.* See that title.
  The Early Years of the Reign of Stephen Batory (Poczatki panowania . . .). Historical Authorities, iv. See that title.

PAWINSKI (A.): *The Financial History of the Reign of Batory* (Skarbowosc i jej dzieje . . .). Historical Authorities, vii.
   Treasury Accounts during the Reign of Batory (Ksiegi Podskarbinskie . . .). Historical Authorities, ix.
PERESVIÉTOV (IVAN): *Narratives* (Skazania). Reports of the University of Kazan, 1865.
   Epistle and other Writings, published by the Imperial Historical Society. Moscow, 1902 (pamphlet).
PETREUS (P.), or PEER PERSSON: *Narrative concerning Russia* (Rerum Rossicarum scriptores exteri, i.).
PETROV (I. N.): *Influence of the Literature of Western Europe on the Literature of Ancient Russia* (O vlianii zapadno-evropeïskoï litiératoury . . .). Published by the Ecclesiastical Academy at Kiév, 1872.
PHILIP (ST.): *Sketch of a Biography* (Natchertanié Jitia . . .). Moscow, 1860. 1 vol.
   Contemporary Biography, annexed to the preceding work.
PHILIPPSON (M.): *Westeuropa im Zeitalter von Philipp II*. Berlin, 1882. 1 vol.
PIERLING (FATHER): *La Russie et le Saint-Siége*. Paris, 1901, vol. ii.
   Bathory et Possevino, documents inédits. Paris, 1887. 1 vol.
PILINSXKI (T.): *Das Polnische Interregnum*, 1572–1573. Heidelberg, 1861. 1 vol.
PIOTROWSKI (ABBÉ JOHN): *Journal of Batory's Pskov Campaign* (Dziennik wyprawy . . .), Czuczynski. Cracow, 1894.
PISSEMSKI (F.): *Extracts from his Diplomatic Correspondence*. Siéviérnyï Arkhiv, 1822.
PLATER. See Broël.
PLATONOV (J. F.): *Lessons on Russian History* (Lektsii po rousskoï istorii). St. Petersburg, 1901. 1 vol.
   Historical Studies (Stati po rousskoï istorii). St. Petersburg, 1903. 1 vol.
   Sketch of the History of the Disturbances in the Muscovite Empire during the Sixteenth and Seventeenth Centuries (Otcherki pi istorii smouty . . .). St. Petersburg, 1899. 1 vol.
POGODINE (M.): *Fragmentary Studies, Historical and Critical* (Istoricocrititcheskiié otryvki). Moscow, 1846. 1 vol.
   Study of the Origin of Serfdom in Russia. Russian Conversations (Rousskaïa Biéssiéda), 1859.
   The Tsar Ivan Vassiliévitch. Archives of Historical and Practical Science (Arkhiv istor, i prakt, sviédiénii), 1859.
POLEVOÏ (N.): *History of the Russian People* (Istoria rousskavo naroda). Moscow, 1833, vol. vi.
POLKOVSKI (ABBÉ): *Documents Bearing on the Wars of Batory* (Historical Documents published by the Academy of Cracow, xi.). See that title.
Polnoié sobranié rousskikh Liétopissov. See Complete Collection.
POPOV (A. N.): *Sketch of Russian Chronographers* (Obzor khronografov). Moscow, 1866. 1 vol.
   Collection of Russian and Slav Writings inserted in the Russian Chronographers (Isbornik). Moscow, 1869. 1 vol.
POSSEVINO (A.): *Moscovia et alia opera*. Vilna, 1587. New edition, edited by Father Pierling. Paris, 1882.
Poviest o prikhojdenii Litovckavo Korola Stepana (Story of the Siege of Pskov by Batory). See that title.
Pskovskaïa Liétopis. See Chronicle of Pskov.
PRIJOV (I.): *History of Russian Taverns* (Istoria kabakov). St. Petersburg, 1868. 1 vol.

PRIJOV (I.) : *Reports of the Assembly of* 1551 (Stoglav), Khojantchikov. St. Petersburg, 1868. 1 vol.

PRZEZDZIECKI (A.) : *The Polish Princesses of the House of Jagellon* (Iagiellonki polskie). Cracow, 1868–1878, vols. iii., iv., and v.

PURCHAS (SAMUEL) : *The Pilgrims.* London, 1625–1626. 4 vols.

PYPINE (A. N.) : *History of Russian Literature* (Istoria rousskoï litiératoury). St. Petersburg, 1898, vols. i. and ii.

RACZYNSKI (COUNT E.) : *Memoirs connected with the Reign of Stephen Batory* (Pamietniki do historyi Stefana króla). Warsaw, 1830. 1 vol., 8vo.

RAMBAUD (A.) : *La Russie Épique.* Paris, 1876. 1 vol.

REGEL : *Analecta Byzantino-Rossica.* St. Petersburg, 1891. 1 vol.

REIMANN : *Das Verhalten des Reiches gegen Livland in den Jahren,* 1559–1561. Historische Zeitschrift, 1870.
Die Pölnische Konigswahl von 1573. Same publication, 1864.

Reimchronik (*Die*). Scriptores Rerum Livonicarum, i.

Relations des Nonces Apostoliques et d'autres personnes sur la Pologne (Relacye Nuncyuszów), Rykaczewski. Berlin, 1864. 2 vols.

Remizovskaea Liétopiś. See Siberian Chronicle.

RENNER (J.) : *Livlandische Historien.* Gottingen, 1876. 1 vol.

Rerum Moscovitarum auctores varii. Frankfort, 1600. 1 vol.

Rerum Rossicarum scriptores exteri. St. Petersburg, 1851. 2 vols.

RICHTER (A. v.) : *Geschichte der Ostsee Provinzen.* Riga, 1857–1858. 3 vols.

RIDOLFINI (DOMINIC) : *Correspondence.* Scientific and Literary Collection (Przewodnik Naukowy). Lemberg, 1878, vol. ii.

ROJKOV (N.) : *Agriculture in Muscovite Russia* (Ssiélskoïé Khaziaïstvo v Mosskovskoï Roussii). Moscow, 1899. 1 vol.

ROSTOVSKI (ST.) : *Lithuanicarum Societatis Jesu Historiarum librii decem.* P. Martynov, Paris, 1877. 1 vol.

ROVINSKI (D.) : *History of the Russian Schools of Iconography* (Istoria rousskikh chkol ikonopissania). Memoranda of the Archæological Society, vol. viii., and separately. St. Petersburg, 1856. 1 vol.

Russia at the Close of the Sixteenth Century. London, 1856. 1 vol. See Fletcher and Horsey.

RUSSOW (B.) : *Chronicle.* Script. rerum livon, ii.

RUTENBERG (O.) : *Geschichte der Ostsee Provinzen.* Leipzig, 1859. 2 vols.

RYDBERG (O. S.) : *Swedish Treaties.* Stockholm, 1877, and following years.

RYTCHKOV : *Attempt at a History of Kazan* (Otcherk istorii . . .). St. Petersburg, 1867. 1 vol.

SAMARINE (G.) : *Works.* Moscow, 1880, vol. v.
Under the pseudonym of M. Z. K., *Study of Ivan the Terrible in the ' Muscovite '* (Moskvitanine), 1847. (Reply to Kaveline.)

SCHIEMANN (CH.) : *Russland, Polen, und Livland, bis ins XVII. Jahrhundert.* Berlin, 1887, vol. ii.

SCHIEMANN (TH.) : *Charakterköpfe und Sittenbilder aus der Balticher Geschichte der XVI. Jahrb.* Mittau, 1877. 1 vol.

SCHIRREN : *Quellen zur Geschichte des Untergangs der Livländischer Selbstandigkeit.* Revel, 1880–1881. 8 vols. And *Neue Quellen,* etc. Revel, 1883–1885. 3 vols. Archiv für die Geschichte Liv. Ehst. und Kurland. See that title.

SCHLICHTING (A.) : *Nova ex Moscovia . . . de principis Ioanni vita et tyrannide . . . narratio* (Scriptores rerum polonicarum, i.). See that title.

SCHWARTZ (P.) : *Chronologic der Ordenmeister ueber Livland.* Riga, 1879. 1 vol. (From the papers of Baron von Toll.)
Scriptores rerum Livonicarum. Riga and Leipzig, 1853–1854. 2 vols.
Scriptores rerum Polonicarum. Cracow, 1872, vols. i. and vii.
SENIGOV (J.) : *The Work of Ivan the Great as Judged by Popular Opinion* (Narodnoié vozzrenié na diéiatiélnost Ioanna Groznavo). St. Petersburg, 1902 (pamphlet).
SERGUIÉIÉVITCH (V.) : *Judicial Antiquities* (Drevnosti rousskavo prava). St. Petersburg, 1890–1903. 3 vols.
Lessons on the History of Russian Law (Letksii po istorii rousskavo prava). St. Petersburg, 1883.
The Assemblies under the Muscovite Empire (Ziémskiié ssobory v moskovskom gossoudarstviénnykh znanii). V. P. Bezobrazov, vol. ii.
Landed Property in Ancient Russia. Review of the Ministry of Public Instruction, 1901.
Historical Study, in the *Observer* (Nablioudatiél), 1881.
Sibirskaïa Liétopis. See Siberian Chronicle.
Epistles. Barssov, Christian Readings (Khristianskiié Ichténia), 1871.
Simbirskii Sbornik (Simbirsk Collection). Published by Iazykov, Khomiakov, and Valiouév). Moscow, 1845, vol. i.
SOKOLOV (M. I.) : *Summary of Ten Years of Labour by the Archæological Commission* (Otcherk diéssiatiliétnieï naoutchnoï diéiatielnosti . . .). Moscow, 1902.
SOKOLOVSKI (G. P.) : *The Economic Existence of the Agricultural Population in Russia* (Ekonomitcheskii byt ziémliédiétiéltcheskavo nassiélenia v Rossii). Historical Library (Ist. Bibi.), 1878.
Sketch of the History of the Rural Commune in the North of Russia (Otcherk istorii ssiélskoï obchtchiny na siéviérié Rossii). St. Petersburg, 1877. 1 vol., 8vo.
SOLOVIOV (S.) : *History of Russia*, numerous editions, vols. vi. and vii.
Study of the Assemblies of the Fifteenth and Sixteenth Centuries. Messager Russe (Viéstnik Evropy), 1857.
History of the Relations between the Russian Princes of the House of Rurik (Istoria otnochenii miédjou rousskimii Kniaziami . . .). Moscow, 1847. 1 vol.
Soudiébnik gossoudaria Tsaria Ivana. See Code.
Sprawy wojenne Króla S. Batorego. See Wars.
STARTCHEVSKI (A. VON) : *Historiæ Ruthenicæ scriptores exteri sæculi XVI.* Berlin and St. Petersburg, 1841. 2 vols.
State Papers of the Polish Kingdom relating to the Reign of Batory (Akta Metryki Korronej . . .), Pawinski. Warsaw, 1884. 1 vol.
State Papers of the Grand Duchy of Lithuania dealing with the Diplomatic Relations of that Country during the Reign of Batory (Kniga possolskaïa Metryki viélikavo Kniajestva Litovskavo). Pogodine and Doubiénski, Moscow, 1843. 1 vol.
STEIN (FR.) : *Geschichte des Russischen Heeres.* Leipzig, 1895. 1 vol.
Stépiénnaïa Kniga. See Book.
Stoglav. See Report.
Stroganovskaïa liétopis. See Siberian Chronicle.
STRYJKOWSKI : *Chronicle.* (Collection of Polish Historians.) See that title.
SULICOVIUS (I. D. SOLIKOWSKI) : *Commentarius brevis rerum polonicarum.* Dantzig, 1647. 1 vol.
SYLVESTER : *Epistles.* Barssov, Christian Readings (Khristianskiié Tchténia), 1871.

SzADECZKY (LAJOS) : *Bathory Istvan.* Budapest, 1887. I vol.
SZLACHTOWSKI : *Ten Years of the Reign of Stephen Batory* (Dziesiec lat panowania S. B.). Cracow, 1850, unfinished.
SZUJSKI (J.) : *Works,* second series. Cracow, 1894, vol. ii.

TATICHTCHEV. See Code of Ivan IV.
TAUBE (J.) and KRUSE (E). : *Zar Ivan der Grausame, Sendschreiben an Gotthard Kettler* (1579), (Beiträge zur Kenntniss Russlands.) See that title.
TCHETCHOULINE (N. D.) : *The Towns of the Empire of Moscow in the Sixteenth Century* (Goroda moskovskavo gossoudarstvo). St. Petersburg, 1889. I vol.
TCHITCHERINE (B. N.) : *Essays on the History of Russian Law* (Opyty po istorii rousskavo prava). Moscow, 1858. I vol.
Popular Representation (O narodnom predstavitiélstvié). Moscow, 1866. I vol.
THEINER : *Annales ecclesiastici.* Rome, 1856. 3 vols.
TIÉPOLO : *Narratio Historica de Moscovitico Imperio,* 1559. Hist. Russiæ Monumenta, i.
TOLSTOÏ (G.) : *Relations between Russia and England from* 1553–1593 (Piérvyi ssorok liét snochenii miédjou R. i A.). St. Petersburg, 1875. I vol.
TOLSTOÏ (I.) and KONDAKOV (N.) : *Monuments of Ancient Art in Russia* (Rousskaïa drevnosti v pamiatnikakh isskoustva). St. Petersburg, 1897–1899, vols. iv., v., and vi.
TRATCHEVSKI : *The Interregnum in Poland after the Extinction of the Jagellon Dynasty* (Polskoié bezkorolévié po prckrachtchenii dinastii Iagiéllonov). Moscow, 1869. I vol.
Tsarstviennaïa Kniga. See Chronicle of the Reign of Ivan.
TSVIÉTAIEV (D.) : *Protestantism and Protestants in Moscow* (Protestanstvo i Protestanty v Rossii). Moscow, 1890. I vol.
Tverskaïa Liétopis. See Chronicle of Tver.
TYJNOV : *View of the Information collected by Foreigners as to Siberia.* Siberian Collection (Sibirskii Sbornik), 1887.

ULEFELD (J.) : *Legatio Moscovitica sive Hodœporicon Ruthenicum.* Startchevski, i.
Urkunden der Grafen de la Gardie. J. Lossius, Derpt, 1882. I vol.

VALIOUÉV (D. A.) : *Study of St. Philip.* Educational Library (Biblioteka dla Vospitania), 1845.
VASILIÉVSKI : *The German and Polish Press on the War between Batory and Ivan IV.* Review of the Ministry of Public Instruction, 1889.
VÉLIAMINOV-ZIÉRNOV (V. N.) : *Study of the Tsars of Kassimov* (Izsliédovania o Kassimovskikh tsariakh). St. Petersburg, 1870. I vol.
VIGENÈRE (BLAISE DE) : *Poloigne.* Paris, 1573. I vol.
VIOLLET-LE-DUC (E.) : *L'Art Russe.* Paris, 1877. I vol.
VLADIMIRSKI - BOUDANOV (F.) : *Chrestomathy of Russian Law* (Kristomatia po istorii r.p.). Moscow, 1887. I vol.
Sketch of the History of Russian Law (Obzor istorii rousskavo prava). Moscow, 1890. I vol.

WARSZEWICKI : *Vita . . . Stephani, regis Poloniæ.* Bâle, 1612. I vol.
WIELEWICKI (ABBÉ JOHN) : *Journal,* 1579–1599. Scriptores rerum polonicarum, vii.
WIERZBOWSKI (F.) : *Vincenzo Laureo, Bishop of Mondovi, Nuncio . . . in Poland,* 1574–1578. Warsaw, 1888. I vol.

WIERZBOWSKI (F.): *Two Candidatures for the Throne of Poland*, 1574–1575 (Dvié Kandidatoury na polskoii prestol). Warsaw, 1889. 1 vol.
WINKELMANN (E.): *Bibliotheca Livoniæ Historica*. Berlin, 1878. 1 vol.
WITTSEN: *North-Western Tartary*. Collection of Northern Travels, viii.

ZABIÉLINE (I.): *Private Life of the Tsars*, and *Private Life of the Tsarinas of Russia* (Domachnii byt tsarov and Domachnii byt tsarits). Moscow, 1872 and 1895, third edition. 2 vols.
History of Moscow (Istoria Moskvy). Moscow, 1902. 1 vol.
Characteristics of the Knowledge of Ancient Russia. Annals of the Fatherland, 1856.
Original Features of Ancient Architecture. Archives of Russian Art, 1894.
View of the History of the Development of the Muscovite Autocracy. Historical Messenger (Istoritcheskii Viéstnik), 1881.
ZAGOSKINE (G.): *History of Political Law in the Muscovite Empire* (Istoria prava Moskovskavo gossoudarstva). Kazan, 1877. 1 vol.
ZAKRZEWSKI (V.): *After the Flight of Henri de Valois* (Dzieje Bezkrólewia . . . 1574–1575). Cracow, 1878. 1 vol.
Relations between the Holy See and Ivan the Terrible (Stosunki miedzy Stolica Apostolska a Iwanem Grozny). Cracow, 1874. 1 vol.
ZALESKI (ABBÉ): *The Jesuits in Poland* (Jezuici w Polcse). Lemberg, 1900, vol. i.
ZAMYSLOVSKI (E.): *Herberstein's Data, Historical and Geographical*. Review of the Ministry of Public Instruction, 1882.
The Conquest of Siberia. Same publication, 1882.
Study of Sylvester. Political Science Collection (Sbornik Gossoudarstviénnykh Znanii). St. Petersburg, 1875, vol. ii.
ZAOUSTINSKI (C.): *The Metropolitan Macarius*. Review of the Ministry of Public Instruction, 1881.
ZARINSKI (FATHER P.): *Sketch of the Ancient History of Kazan* (Otcherk drevnieï Kazani). Kazan, 1877. 1 vol.

INDEX

ABDUL-KHAN, Jenkinson, relations with, 277
Absolutism, Ivan IV., growth under, 12-16
    origin of, 10-12, 37
Academy of Wilna, 300
Adachev, Alexis, birth of, 123
    Council, member of, 224
    Dmitri's succession, attitude towards, 225
    exile and disgrace of, 226-228
    Livonian deputation, reception of, 179
    Okolnitchyï, raised to rank of, 133
    Sylvester and, work of, 132
    Daniel, commander of Muscovite forces, 170
    Feodor, Dmitri's succession, attitude towards, 225
Adams, Clement, traveller, 161, 162
Agraféna, sister to Obolenski, 120
Agricultural classes, depression among, 22-24
Akssakov, Constantine, reference to, 222, 263, 391
    Ivan, 78
Alatyr, forts at, 149
Albert, Bishop, founder of Riga, 173, 174
Albert of Brandenburg, 175
    of Prussia, 202
Alevisio, 80
Alexander of Bulgaria, 118, 124
Alexandrov, Sloboda of, flight of Ivan to, 199 ; retirement to, 240 ; life at, 256, 364-372 ; Russo-Swedish treaty signed at, 195, 196
Alexis, Bishop of Rostov, 154
Amman, Jost, 94
Anastasia, wife of Ivan the Terrible, 127 ; death of, 189, 226
Andréiévitch, Prince Vladimir, 130, 224, 243 ; punishment and death of, 250
Anikiév, Simon, 353
Arcudius, Peter, 66

Aristocracy, the, condition of, 7-10, 13-16
Arkhangel, exports from, 50, 53
    rise of, as a port, 297
Arkhangelsk, 3
Army, the Polish, 304-309, 314
    the Russian :
    artillery, development of, 162, 163
    cavalry methods of, 161, 162
    composition and strength of, 159-161, 309-312
    Foscarini's description of, 172
    Possokha, division of the, 160, 161
    Striéltsy, division of the, 159, 160
Art, 78-85, 297 ; Byzantine style in, 80, 81
Artemi, prior of Troïtsa, 89, 151
Artsybachev, envoy, 327
Arundel, Earl of, 274
Arzamas, position of, 5
Ascheraden, atrocities at, 214
Assanids of Bulgaria, 125
Assemblies : of 1566, 148, 149 ; of 1551, 149
Astrakan, capture of, 168, 169
    fisheries of, 53
    Tartar claims on, 199, 200
Augsburg Reichstag, the, 183
Aura, Sultana, 277
Azov, 348

Bachkirs tribe, 167, 352
Bantieh-Kamiénski, 123
Barberini, Francesco, 77
Barma, artist, 83
Barsoukov, A., 369
Barténiev, Danilo, 370
Basmanov, Alexis, Alexandrov, at, 366 .
    Feodor, Alexandrov, at, 366, 376
    death of, 256

Basmanov, Feodor, Kourbski's opinion of, 232
Obolenski-Ovtchinine, quarrel with, 228
Batory, character of, 299-301
Cossack military system remodelled by, 302
election of, 188, 298, 299 ; supported by the Sultan, 212
funds, scarcity of, 321
Iam-Zapolski, truce of, 337-343
Ivan the Terrible, struggles with, 171, 285, 286 ; campaigns against, 306-343 ; diplomatic relations with, 318-321
Magnus and, relations between, 214, 215
moderation of, 308, 309
Stephen, of Somlyo, 298
Batou, 62
Bear-baiting, 113, 114, 370, 371
Bearskins, white, export of, 53
Beckmann, 217
' Bee,' the, reference to, 65, 67, 73
Bekboulatovitch, Simeon, 260-263
Bekiesz, Gabriel, 324
Gaspard, 316
Berthold, Bishop, 173
Best, Robert, envoy to Russia, 281, 282
Romanus, commercial agent, 48, 49
Bestoujev family, the, 49
Bestoujev-Rioumine, 264, 391
Bezsonov, 375
Biéjets, district of, 4
Biela River, 3
Biélaiév, 310
Biélooziéro, fisheries of, 53
monastery at, 27, 104 ; Vassiane Kossoï in, 88, 89
Biélov, reference to, 264
Biélski, Athanasius, 325
Bogdan, councillor to Ivan the Terrible, 290, 292, 295, 333 ; favourite of, 366, 376 ; death of Ivan, connection with, 377, 378
family, 224, 230
Prince Ivan Dmitriévitch, pretensions of, 120 ; Biélooziéro, at, 121 ; Sigismund-Augustus and, 194 ; death of, 199 ; prosecution of, 229, 230 ; Ziémchtchina, at head of, 246
Simon, at Kazan, 157
Birds, export of, 54
Black Cross Knights, 174-177
Blajennyié, the, 114, 115
Blandrata, 300
Bobyli, class, 19, 20
Boch or Bochius, Opritchniki, account by, 266

Bockhorn, Christian, 258
Boë, 303
Bohemian and Moravian brothers, the, 258
Boïars, aristocracy of Russia, the, 7-10
Council of the, 35
dress and manners of, 109-111
first assembly of, 133-135
government of the, 120-123
Ivan, opposition to, 225
literature among the, 220
Boïarskaïa Douma, the, 36, 223
Bolkhovski, Prince Simon, 356
Bolognetti, Papal Nuncio, 349
Bomel or Bomelïus, Elysius, 110, 283, 284
' Book of the Hundred Chapters,' 152, 155
Boratynski, reference to, 349
Borovski, Paphnucius, monk, 119
Botvid, John, 64
Boudomirovitch, legend of, 25
Boulat, Tartar warrior, 157
Boulew or Lueo, Nicholas (Niemtchine), 344
Boutourline, Ivan Mikhaïlovitch, 316
Bowes, Jeremy, embassy of, 290-297
Brakel, Tilman, preacher, 176
Brattchiny, 110, 111
Bribery, prevalence of, 50
Bromley, Lord and Lady, 289
Brothers of the Sword, order of the, 174
Buchau, 95
Buckwheat, culture of, 50
Budget, the Muscovite, 61
Burckhard, chaplain, 269
Burrough, Mr. Stephen, 276
Byzantine chronicles, reference to, 10

Cabot, Sebastian, 273
Cahun, Monsieur Léon, 62
Caligari, Papal Nuncio, 327, 330, 331
Calvinism in Moscow, 258
Cannon, first use of, 162
Carelia, iron and mica found in, 54 ; Batory's fight in, 317
Cartier, Joseph, 273
Casimir of Poland, 63, 117, 250
Castiglione, Baldassare, 78
Catherine, Queen of Sweden, 189, 190, 199
Cellini, 269
Cerularius, Michael, 343
Chamane, the, 69
Chancellor, Richard, expedition to Russia, 273, 274, 275 ; return to England, 275 ; death of, 276
impressions of Russia, 357
reference to, 162, 272, 361
Charles the Bold, 1
Chaudoir, reference to, 60

Chérémétiev, Feodor, flight of, 303
  Helena, 375
  Ivan Vassiliévitch, Russian commander, 213 ; punishment of, 230, 367 ; monastery of St. Cyril, in, 268
  Nikita Vassiliévitch, 367
Chevirev, Prince Dmitri, death of, 247
Chévriguine, Leonti Istoma (Thos. Severingen), Russian envoy to Rome, 318, 319, 326-331
Chmourlo, Monsieur, 393
Chodkiewicz, Gregory, Grand Hetman of Lithuania, 194, 212, 303
Choisnin, reference to, 208
Chouïski, Andrew, 120, 122
  Ivan, 120
  Ivan Petrovitch, death of, 268
  party, the, 120, 121, 224
  Peter, 311 ; death of, 247
  Prince Alexander Borissovitch, death of, 247
  Vassili Vassilévitch, 120
Christian II. of Denmark, 185, 186
Chronicle of Khrouchtchov,' 134
Chtchelkalov, Andrew, Russian councillor, 290, 292, 295, 296, 297, 303
Church, the, despotic influence of, 10 ; lands held by, 17, 18 ; wealth of, 27-29 ; power of, 26, 27; primacy, struggle for, 29 ; Greek element in, 31; Government, cooperation with, 33, 34 ; usury of the, 59, 60 ; effect of, on the people, 62 ; learning, effect on, 62-67 ; characteristics of the national, 64 ; ritual, importance attached to, 68 ; Finnish element in, 69 ; art in, 85 ; heresy in, 86-90
Clenke, Rudolph, Papal envoy, 327
Clinton, Edward, Earl of Lincoln, 288
Coalitions, Russo-Swedish, 194, 195 ; Polish-Danish, 195
Coast fisheries, 53, 54
Cobenzl, Russian envoy, 261
Code, 1497, of, 8, 20, 37, 47, 48, 97, 147 ; Soudiébnik, the, 8, 47 ; 1550 and 1551, of, 142 et seq.
Collo, Francesco da, reference to, 126
Colonization, monasteries, influence on, 29
Colonna, Egidio, 77
Combat, trial by, 48, 49
Commune, the, 43-46
Communities, Zadrouga, the, 107, 108; brattchiny, 110, 111
Company, the Russian or Muscovite, 275-290
Conciliable of the Hundred Chapters,' 150-156
Conrad, Duke of Mazovia and Cujavia, 174

Constantine the Great, 47
Constantinople, fall of, 11 ; offered to Ivan by Maximilian, 212
Copronymus, Constantine, 47
Corn, export of, and price of, 50-52
Cortez, 273
Cossacks, depredations of, 58
  origin of, 169, 170
  Riazan, the, 354
  Stroganovs and the, 354, 355
Coulanges, Fustel de, 22
Council of Boïars, 35
  of Florence, 343
  of Lyons, 343
  of war, scope of, 36-38
Courland, Duke of, 268
Court customs, 362, 363
  jesters, 363, 364
  of Ivan IV., description of, 357-364
Crimea, Ivan IV., attitude towards, 170-172
  Tartars, dominated by, 157
Crimes, fines and penalties for, 47 et seq.
Crops, Northern Russia, of, 50 ; rotation of, 52
Currency : coinage, scarcity of, 60
  monetary system, 51, 52
Customs, Court, 362, 363
Cyprian the Bulgarian, Metropolitan, 124
Cyril, the Metropolitan, 33
Czartoryski family, 230
Czasniki, 314
Czerczel, Peter, 331

da Collo, Francesco, reference to, 126
Dahlman, reference to, 195
Dantzig, 193, 194
Darcel, 81
de Coulanges, Fustel, 22
de la Gardie, Pontus, 317, 325
de Léry, Jean, 273
de Mornay, Philip, 191
de Ponte, Nicola, doge, 330
de Valois, Henri, candidature of, 207, 208
  elected King of Poland, 209
  flight of, 209
del Portico, Vincenzo, Papal envoy, 326
Denmark : Livonia, encroachments in, 198, 199
  Poland, attitude towards, 305 ; negotiations with, 191
  Sweden and, treaty relations, 198
Deputationstag of Spire, the, 183
Derbych-Ali, Tsar of Astrakan, 168, 260
Dereviénskiié, class, 19
Derpt, 178, 185, 187, 192, 214

27—2

Devlet-Ghireï, Khan of Kazan, 163
Devtelev, Prince Ivan, 374
di Paulo, Francesco, 370
Diakhonov, Monsieur, historian, 19, 24
Diakovo, 84
Disna, 306
Dithmar, reference to, 10
Dlugosz, historian, 304
Dmitri, Tsarevitch, question of succession, 224 ; childhood of, 374, 376
Dmitrov, *Opritchniki* in, 243
Dnieper, the Lower, 2, 3, 6
Dokladnyie, class, 20, 22
Dolgorouki, George, 2
    Maria, 374
Domestic life, description of, 100-109
' Domostroï,' the, 52, 72, 74-78
Don Carlos, 384
Dorokhobouje, exports of, 54
Douchan, the Servian, 118
Douma, the, Lay Council, 33
Doumnyi Dvorianine, office of, 36, 37
Dress, men's, 92 ; women's, 92, 93
Dreux, Battle of, 305
Drohojowski, John, envoy of Batory, 310
Droysen, reference to, 177, 183
Drujen, town of, 184
du Perche, Comte, arrest of, 216
Dubiélov, Professor, 66
Dudley, Ambrose, Earl of Warwick, 288
Dues, trading, 56, 57
Dunaburg, town of, 184
Durforth, Cornelius, 273
Dvina, Northern, colonization in valley of, 4 ; mica found on banks of, 54
Dvinsk, 54
Dzierzek, Polish envoy, 319

Economic System, the, 50-60
Edward VI. of England, Ivan IV., relations with, 274, 275
Eletski, Prince, Russian envoy in truce of Iam-Zapolski, 336, 341
Elizabeth of England, Ivan IV., trading relations with, 277, 278 ; diplomatic relations, 279-290
Elizariév, Roman, physician, 285
Elk-skins, export of, 53
Elmes, Richard, 110, 284·
England : embassies to Russia, 277, 279-290
    monopolies question, 292
    trading relations with Ivan IV., 274-278 ; diplomatic relations, 279-290
Eric XIV., King of Sweden, dethronement of, 188
    Ivan, relations with, 191, 192

Eric XIV., King of Sweden, madness of, 197
    Russian nobles, intrigues with, 194, 195
Ermak (Ermak Timofiéiévitch), exploits of, 169, 355-357 ; Koutchoum defeated by, 355
Ermes, Siege of, 213
Ermine, export of, 53
Ernest, Archduke, 330, 331
    Czarevitch, candidate for Polish throne, 211, 212
Esthonia, Denmark's claim to, 182, 186, 192
    Ivan's conquests in, 213
Eudoxia, Princess, death of, 268
Euphemia, daughter of Ivan IV., 203
Europe, Russian trade with, 54
Exports, 53, 54

Fairs, 54-56
Farensbach, George, 307
Fédorov, Ivan, typographer, 219
Fellin, Swedish leader, 312
    town, 182
Feodor, Czarevitch, Polish throne, candidate for, 205, 206, 208 ; Tsar Simeon stripped of his duchy by, 261
Feodorovitch, Feodor, 374
    Michael, 262
    Vassili, Pskov defended by, 322
Ferdinand I., Emperor, 183
Fickel, fall of, 325
Fiedler, reference to, 343
Fikel, conquest of, 213
Finance, 61
Finns, religion of the, 30, 69, 70
Fioraventi, Aristote, 80
Fires, frequency of, 57 ; in Moscow, 128
Fish, export of, 53, 54
Flax, export of, 54
Fletcher, traveller, reference to, 31, 51, 53, 59, 61, 92, 95, 163, 310, 361, 397
Florentine Union, the, 11, 29, 64, 67
Foreign Affairs, Office of, 35, 134
Forsten, reference to, 209, 214, 264
Foscarini, Venetian envoy, 172
Founikov, treasurer, 256
Frederic II. of Denmark, 186
Frensham, Richard, apothecary, 110, 284
Friasini, Italian architect, 121
Frolov, Russian councillor, 292, 295
Furs, export of, 53
Fürstenberg, governorship of Livonia refused by, 203
    prisoner at Moscow, 182
    successor to Von Plettenberg, 176

Galitzine, 169, 303
Gama, 273
Garon, Captain, 323
Garret, William, of the Russian Company, 282
Gdov, 4
Germany, Livonia, struggles for, 173,
Ghireï, Outémich, 157, 158
  Safa, Khan of Kazan, 157
Giustiniani, 269
Glagoliév, Monsieur, 379
Glastonbury Library, the, 65
Glinski, Helen, 118-120
  Prince George Vassilévitch, 128
  Prince Michael Vassilévitch, 128, 129, 179
  Prince Vassili Mikhaïlovitch, 229
Gloukhov, Ivan, 356
Glover, Thomas, 292
Godounov, Boris, Bowes, attitude towards, 297
  favourite of Ivan IV., 246, 293, 366
  Ivan's death attributed to, 377
  Tsar Simeon and, 261
Golovine, Russian Ambassador, 303
Golovoiou, punishment, 49
Goobnyié starosty, 145
Gooby, districts, 143, 144
Gorbatyï, Prince Alexander Borissovitch, made Governor of Kazan, 166
Gorski, biographer, 264
Goundorov, Prince, 114
Gourii, Archbishop of Kazan, 397
Government: absolutism, origin of, 37
  Boïars, of the, 120-123
  central power, 35-38
  commune, the, 43-46
  economic system, the, 50-60
  finance, 61
  judicial organization and legislation, 46-50
  Miéstnitchestvo, the, 41, 42
  Parliament, see that head
  provincial organization, 38-40
  Vodskaïa-Piatina, the, 70
Gregory XIII., Pope, policy of, 331, 344
Grey, Richard, English agent, 275
Griaznoï, Vassili, 366, 382
  Vassiouchka, 239, 246
Grigoriévitch, Nikita, 353
Grünwald, fight at, 175
Guagnino, reference to, 60, 112, 228, 253, 256, 371 ; work of, 265
Guédymin, 7, 89, 120
Gyllenstjerna, envoy of Eric XIV., 195

Hakluyt Collection, reference to, 49, 59, 272, 276, 291
Hansa, the, 172, 178, 184, 185

Hanseatic League, the, 195
Hapsal, fall of, 213, 325
Haraburda, Michael, Polish envoy, 207, 303, 336
Harrien, 174, 185, 187
Hastings, Mary, proposed marriage to Ivan IV., 285-290
Hatton, Sir Christopher, 287
Hausmann, reference to, 308
Haxthausen, Baron von, 43
Heidenstein, reference to, 323
Helmet, Siege of, 213
Hemp, export of, 54
Henning, reference to, 265
Henry the Lion, 173
Henry I. of France, 63
Henry VIII. of England, 61, 270
Herberstein, reference to, 15, 50, 51, 56, 87, 112, 119, 126, 274
Herburt, John, 303
Heresies in the Church, 86-90
Herzen, 84
Hilferding, 375
Horsey, reference to, 256, 262, 266, 267, 289, 297, 371, 377
Hungarian Infantry, 309
Hunsdon, Lord, 287
Huntingdon, Lord, 285

Iadiger, 353
Iagiello, military leader, 175
Iakhroma River, the, 225
Iakovlevitch, Maximus, 353
Iam-Zapolski, negotiations at, 336
  truce of, 337-343
Iaouza River, the, 217
Iaroslav, founder of Iouriév, 182
Iaroslavitch, Michael, 29
Iconography, 81, 82
Ierwen territory, 185
Ikonnikov, Monsieur, 28
Ilovaïski, reference to, 264
Imports, 53, 54
Indiger-Mohammed, 163
Iouriév, town of, 173, 182
Iron, Carelia, found in, 54
Isoiflianié sect, the, 89, 151, 221
Iousouf, head of Tartar-Nogaïs tribe, 168
Ismaïl, of Tartar-Nogaïs tribe, 168
Ivan III. (the Great), Church, attitude towards, 34
  conquests of, 3
  death of, 118
  land laws under, 18
  Rome, attitude towards, 117
Ivan IV. (the Terrible), Batory, campaigns against, 285, 286, 310-326 ; diplomatic relations with, 315, 318-321
  Boïars, treatment under, 7-10 ; opposition to, 225 ; punishment of, 247

Ivan IV. (the Terrible), Bowes, negotiations with, 293-297
Catherine of Sweden, claim for,
201
character of, 12, 221-223, 379-
386; motives of, 223; mo-
nastic tendencies of, 368-
370; knowledge and intelligence of, 386-390; ideas and
feelings of, 390-394
Codes of, see Codes
Elysius Bomel, relations with,
283, 284
England, relations with, under
Edward VI., 274, 275; Philip
and Mary, 275-277; Elizabeth,
277-290
Eric XIV., King of Sweden, correspondence with, 194, 195;
treaty with, 188, 192, 195;
Sweden, claims on, 196, 197;
Swedish envoys, treatment of,
199
Esthonia, conquests in, 213
favourites of, 366
financial policy of, 397
flight to Alexandrov and Rostov, before Tartar invasion,
199
Iam-Zapolski, truce of, 337-343
letters of, on monastic life, 86,
87; to Sweden, 201, 202;
Kourbski, to, 232-234
Livonia, conquests in, 213;
abandonment of, 335-337
Magnus, negotiations with, 203;
treatment of, 210
Moscow, secret departure from,
240; cruelties in, 255, 256
Novgorod, pillaging of, 251-254;
Pskov, 254
Opritchniki, organization of, 237-
273; cruelties of, 265, 266
Poland, and (see also Batory),
proposed alliance with, 188;
candidate for Polish throne,
188, 205-209; Feodor's election, attitude towards, 206-
209; Polish crown claimed for
Ernest, 211; Polish missionaries, reception of, 258, 259
popularity of, 236, 270, 271, 398
results of reign of, 394-399
revenue of, 61
Rome, diplomatic relations with,
326 et seq.; Papal mediation
between Poland and Russia,
331-337
Russia, state of, on accession, 3
Sigismund-Augustus, and, relations between, 189-191
Swedes, Magnus supported
against the, 198

Ivan IV. (the Terrible), Tsar Simeon,
260-263
Tsarevitch, murder of, 375
Vienna, relations with, 313
will of, 257
youth of, 116-123; marriage
and coronation of, 123-128;
family of, 374-377; death of,
291, 349,.377, 378
Ivangorod, 175
Ivanovitch, Michael, 149
Prince Peter, death of, 190
Vassili, 1, 30

Jacob, Emmanuel Ben, astronomical
tables of, 153
Jagellon, Alexander, 206
Catherine, 317
Jaroslav the Great, 173
Jaroslav, early government of, 3;
agriculture in, 50; fish, honey, and
tallow, exported from, 53; salt-
petre prepared at, 54
Jehosaphat of Troïtsa, conciliable of
1551, in, 154; advice of, regarding
Ivan's stay in Moscow, 157, 158
Jenkinson, Anthony, reference to, 5,
59, 92, 95, 112, 163, 172, 361;
Russia, trading adventures in, 277-
279
Jesuits, religious campaign in Russia
and Livonia, 317 et seq.
'Joachim's Thaler,' 60
John, Duke of Finland, afterwards
King of Poland, 190, 197, 209
the Faster, patriarch of Constantinople, 343
Judicial organization, legislation and,
46-51
Junsten, Paul, 201

Kabalnyié, class, 20, 22
Kachine, Prince George, death of,
228
Prince Ivan Soukhoï, death of,
247
Kaïboul, Tsarevitch of Kazan, 260
Kalita, 28, 29
Kalka, disaster of the, 3
Kalouga, town of, 53, 244
Kaluga, 3
Kama River, 3, 6, 352
Karamzine, reference to, 83, 106, 237,
263, 268, 308, 309, 310, 369, 394
Kargopol, iron-mines of, 54; Opritch-
niki, in, 243
Karkhus, 192
Karpov, Russian Ambassador, 303
Kashira, 6
Kassiane, Bishop of Riazan, 151
Kassimov, khanate of, 2c0
Kaveline, reference to, 21, 263

Kazan, conquest of, 6, 163-166, 396 ;
  results of, 166-168
  expeditions against, 158
  'office of,' 35
  Tartar claim on, 199, 200
Keppen's map, reference to, 69
Kettler, Gotthard, successor to
  Fürstenberg, 182 ; Sigismund-
  Augustus, relations with, 184-187;
  governorship of Livonia refused by,
  203
Kexholm, fall of, 317
Kezholm, 191
Khabarov, Ivan Ivanovitch, 368
Khilkov, Prince, 316
Kholm, fall of, 316
Kholmogory, 53, 274,
Kholopii gorodok, fair of, 54
Khoperski polk, Cossack regiment, 149
Khortitsa Island, 170
Kiev, early government of, 2, 9 ;
  democratic institutions of, 11 ;
  claimed by Ivan, 302
  period, influence of Eastern
  Church under, 10 ; literature
  of, 71
Killingworth, George, English agent,
  275
Kinski, Count, 313
Kiriéiévski, 269
Kiverova-Gora, 337
Klioutchevski, Monsieur, 35, 237, 388
Kloss, 217
Klossius, savant, 66
Kmita, Filon, Khan of Smolensk,
  312, 316
Knijniki, 87, 88
Kobyla, Andrew, 127
Kojalowicz, reference to, 319, 338
Kokenhausen, town of, 184, 214
Kola Peninsula, furs from, 53 ; port
  of, 292
Kolomenskoié village, 240, 364
Kolomna, 6 ; Ivan IV. at, 168 ;
  Opritchniki in, 243
Koltovski, Anne, 372
Koltso, Ivan, 355, 356
Koltychev, the, 127
Kondakov, 85
Kordt, Monsieur, 276
Kormlenchtchiki, the, 144
Kormlénié, class, 40, 144
Kormtchaïa Kniga, the, 74
Korobéinikov, Tryphonius, 217, 218
Korvinus, Matthius, 60
Kosmodiémiansk, 53
Kossoï, Theodore, 232
  Vassiane (Prince Vassili Ivano-
    vitch Patrikiev-Kossoï), 32,
    88-90
Kostka, John, 303
Kostomarov, reference to, 10, 222,
  237, 264, 394

Kotochikhine, 359
Kourakine, Prince Ivan, death of,
  247
Kourakine-Boulgakov, Prince Ivan,
  death of, 247
Kourbski, Prince Andrew Mikhaïlo-
  vitch, writings of, 78, 129,
  130, 132 ; reference to, 165,
  227-230, 250-252, 270, 311 ;
  Livonia, conquests in, 182 ;
  Nevel, defeat at, 194 ; council,
  member of, 224 ; flight of, to
  Poland, 230 ; Poland, in, 231-
  236 ; Ivan, correspondence
  with, 231-234, 382, 384, 388 ;
  possessions of, 235 ; character
  of, 235, 236
  Prince Feodor, 350
  Simon, councillor, 118
Kourliatev, Prince Dmitri, coun-
  cillor, 224, 229
Koustar, 53
Koutchoum, Khan, 353 ; defeat by
  Ermak, 355
Koutia, the, 70
Kremlin, the, collection of classics
  in, 66 ; architecture of, 81 ; fall
  of bell of, 128 ; fire in, 128 ;
  paintings in, 153 ; description of,
  357, 358
Kriepostnoïé pravo, law, 24
Kruse, intrigues of, 202, 203 ; Derpt,
  flight to, and death of, 204
Kursk, 3
Kvachnine, 309

Labour, price of, 52
Ladoga, land service in, 39
Lampojnia, fair at, 5, 55
Land, possession, modes of, 17, 38 ;
  Church's acquisition of, checked,
  151, 152
Lands, 'black' and 'white,' 17,
  18, 46, 47, 52
Lane, Henry, commercial agent, 48, 49
Lantag of Wolmar, the, 175
Lappo, reference to, 304
Lapps, conversion of, 30
Lasicius, reference to, 87
Latyk, Siberian Prince, 350
Laureo, Vincenzo, Papal Nuncio, 210,
  212, 327
Lavisse, reference to, 56
Leal, conquest of, 213
Learning, character of, 64-67
Legislation, judicial organization and,
  46-50
Leicester, Earl of, 287
Lenewarden, 214
Leo, Emperor, 124
  the Grammarian, 63
  the Isaurian, 47
  the Philosopher, 47

Leon, Emperor, 10
Leonidas, Archbishop of Novgorod,
    death of, 264
Liatski family, 230
Liège, 1
Lippoman, Venetian envoy, 265
Lippomano, reference to, 208
Literature, beginnings of secular,
    219-220
    nature of, in sixteenth century,
    71-78
    poverty of, 153
    reform in, proposed, 153, 154
Lithuania, Ivan's candidature, atti-
    tude towards, 206
    Livonia and, union of, 186, 187
    Poland and, union of, 177, 194
Livonia, Batory's conquests in, 317
    et seq.
    Catholicism in, 317
    Denmark's encroachments in,
    198, 199
    German colony in, 173
    Ivan IV., conquests in, 170, 178-
    182 ; cession of, to Batory,
    339
    Lithuania and, union between,
    186, 187
    Poland's help for, 184 ; demands
    on, 186
    struggle for, the, 302-305
    Swedish fighting in, 325
Lobanov family, 226
Lode, conquest of, 213, 325
Lombroso, quoted, 383
Lopacinski, Venceslas, 307
Lopasna, the, 200
Louis le Débonnaire, 48
Louis XI., barons, struggles with, 2
    character of, 381, 385, 386
    cruelties of, 216, 254
    Plessis-les-Tours, life at, 370
    posting system established by,
    58
    printing under, 219
    XV., 262
Louki, plague at, 59
Lubeck, founding of, 173
Lubkovitch, reference to, 317
Lucidarius, 66
Lutheranism in Moscow, 258
Lvovitch, Vassili, 119
Lykov, Michael Matviéiévitch, 217
    Prince, 312

Macarius, Metropolitan, accident to,
    128
    attainted Churchmen, interces-
    sion for, 248
    council, member of, 224
    conciliable, at the, 151
    reference to, 62, 71-74, 89, 130
    reform, attitude towards, 155, 156

Macarius, Metropolitan, Sylvester
    and, 132
Maciejowski, 97
Madrucci, Cardinal, Papal Nuncio,
    331
Magnus, Batory's campaign, help in,
    316
    Ivan IV., relations with, 188,
    198, 203, 210
    Livonia, pretensions to, 186, 187,
    193
    Poland, conquests in, 214
    Revel besieged by, 203
Maïkov family, the, 88
Makhmetkoul, Tsarevitch, 353 ; cap-
    tured by Ermak, 355
Maliouta-Skouratov, Gregory Lou-
    kianovitch, 232, 249, 271, 366
Maltsev, Simon, envoy, 199
Manuce, Alde, 66
Manufactures for home consumption,
    54
Margeret, French author, 266
Mario, 80
Marriage, mode of, 100-104
Martens, reference to, 175, 274
Martin, Henri, 370
Martynax, Father, 81
Martynov, Father, 83
Maskiévitch, 358
Maximus the Greek, monk, reference
    to, 32, 65, 66, 89, 118, 130, 225,
    269
Mecha River, 168
Mehemed-Ghireï, Khan, 200
Mehemet-Sokolli, Grand Vizier, 306
Meinert, reference to, 302
Meinhard, Canon, 173
Méja, 348
Méjja, Monsieur, 380
Meletiév, Vassilissa, 372-374
Mengou-Timour, 33
Merseburg, reference to, 10
Metayage system of holding land, 17
Metropolitans, number of Greeks
    among, 31
Mica, 54
Michalon, reference to, 95, 112
Michelet, reference to, 130, 216, 254
Miechovski, Matthew, 53
Miéleçki, Nicholas, military leader,
    315
Miéstnitchestvo, the, 41, 42, 148 ;
    Opritchnina and, 245
Mikhaïlovski, reference to, 222, 237,
    388
Mikoulinski, Prince Simon, Khan of
    Kazan, 158
Milioukov, Monsieur, 43, 118, 125,
    242
Military service, 13-16
Mir, the, 45
Missenheim, Hans, 219

Missionaries in Livonia, German,
  173, 174
Mojaïsk, architecture in, 83
  Opritchniki in, 243
  plague in, 59
  Russo-Danish treaty signed at,
    192
Mokhilev, 2
Molvianinov, Iakov, Ambassador, 347
Monasteries, labour, employers of,
    52
  learning in, 64-67
  rule of, 31, 32
  wealth of, 30
Monastyrskïé dietienychy, class, 20
Monetary system, 51, 52
Monks and clergy, ignorance among,
    153
Monomachus, Vladimir, 2, 77, 124
Monopolies, State, effect on trade,
    50, 51
Montluc, envoy of Henri de Valois,
    207, 208
Mordvians, tribe, 167
Morone, Cardinal, Papal legate, 327
Morozov, Leo, councillor, 224
  Michael Iakovlevitch, 192, 224
  Vladimir, councillor, 224
Moscow, absolutism in, 13
  destroyed by fire, 128
  founding of, and description of,
    2, 9, 10
  defences of, 5
  plague in, 59
  Possevino at, 343-348
  Saïp-Ghireï, attacked by, 157,
    158
  Tartar invasion of, 199, 200
  trade, centre of, 54
Mount Athos, monastery of, 88
Mourachkine, 169
Mourom, 5, 53
Mstislavski family, 230
  Prince Ivan Feodorovitch, 201,
    246, 260
  Prince M. F., 213
Müller, 322
Münnich, 169
Münster, Sebastian, 176
Muscovite Chancery, records of the,
    291

Nagaïa, Maria, wife of Ivan IV., 285,
    288
Nagoï, Athanasius, envoy, 199, 200,
    285
  Maria, 374
Narova River, navigation of, 171,
    183, 198
Narva, exports from, 50 ; trade of,
    178 ; blockade of port, 205 ; open-
    ing of, 279 ; Siege of, 325
Nemanitch, 125

Nepiéia, Joseph Grigoriévitch, expe-
    dition to England, 276
Nestor, 10, 339
Neuhausen, town of, 178
Nevel, capture of, 194, 316
Nevski, Alexander, 120, 174
Niémogo, Prince Dmitri, death of,
    247
Niéoudatcha, envoy, 287 *et seq.*
Niesloojilyié, class, 8
Niestiajatiéli, the, 139
Niéviéja, Andronik, 219
Nihilism, beginnings of, 140
Nijni - Novgorod, position of, 5 ;
  fisheries of, 53 ; fort at, 149
Nikiforov, Vassili, type-founder, 219
Nikitski, Monsieur, 355
Noircarmes, 270
Novgorod, early government and
  laws of, 3, 47 ; absolutism in,
    11, 13 ; democratic institu-
    tions in, 11 ; archbishops of,
    27 ; land service in, 39 ; ex-
    ports of, 53 ; plague in, 59 ;
  art in, 81 ; *Opritchniki* in,
    243 ; Peter Volyniéts, betrayed
    by, 250, 251 ; sacking of, by
    Ivan IV., 251-254
  Siéverskii, 3
Novomoskovsk, 84
Novossiltsov, Lucas Zakhariévitch,
    169, 211, 212
Nyenstaedt, chronicler, 66

Oats, culture of, 50, 52
Obdorsk, 53
Oberpalen, 214
Obolenski, Prince Michael, 232
Obolenski-Ovtchinine, Prince Dmitri,
  death of, 228
Oderborn, reference to, 253, 265, 266,
    267
Odoiévski family, 230
  Prince Nikita Ivanovitch, 243
Oesel, island, 187, 192, 213
Oka River, 6, 50
Oléarius, reference to, 106, 112
Olguerd, 230
Olonetz, 3, 4
Onega, 4
Opritchnina, the, action of, 237, 238,
    245-247
  districts comprised in, 244, 245
  historians, criticised by, 263
    et seq.
  organization of the, 148, 194,
    195, 241-243
  results of, 243, 244
Orcha, *starost* of, 42, 190, 311, 312
Ordnance possessed by Ivan IV., 163
Orel, district of, 3 ; River, 352
Oriéchek, land service in, 39
Osiétr, Soubota, 370

Ostrogski, Prince Constantine, 232, 312
Ostrov, fall of, 322
Ostrovka, punishment of Pskov inhabitants at, 127, 128
Ostrovski, dramatist, 42, 373
Otchakov, 169
Ouglitch, exports of, 53, 54
Oukhtomski, Prince D. D., 395
Oula River, 190
Oulong-Beg, astronomical tables of, 62
Oumaniéts, 205
Ouspiénski brothers, 256
Monsieur, 327
Oustiou ·, 54, 243
Oustioujna, iron mines of, 54
Oustoug, 351
Ousviat, captured by Batory, 315
Oxen, 53
Oziérichtche, fall of, 316

Padis, Siege of, 191, 213, 317
Pakhatnyié class, 19
Pakhomii the Servian, 124
Palatine of Vilna, 265
Palentiélev, Thomas, envoy, 315
Paleologus, Andrew, 117
Emperor John, 124
Sophia, wife of Ivan III., 110
Paletski, Polotsk defended by, 312
Pallavicini, Francese, 327
Parliament, first assembly, 133-136
second assembly, 136-138
Patrikiév family, the, 221
Vassiane, divorce of Vassili, attitude towards, 118
reforms, attitude towards, 89, 90, 139
Pavloff, Monsieur Silvanski, 310
Peasantry, classification of, 19
condition of, 16-18
privileges of, 18, 19
Pelym, 355
Pèmbroke, Earl of, 274
Penalties, 47
Penza, 3
People, character of, 23
dress and appearance of, 92-97
family, habits and customs of the, 100-109
moral aspect of, 95-97
physical aspect of, 91-95
poverty of, 59, 60
society, 109-115
woman, position of, 97-100
Péréiaslavl, 397
Peresviélov, Ivachka, epistle of, to Ivan IV., 219
pamphlet by, 139-142
Perm, elk in forests of, 53 ; conquest of, 350 ; Tartar raid on, 355
Pernau, town of, 191, 192, 213

Persia, English trading attempts in, 277
Persson, Peer, reference to, 91, 95, 196, 269, 270
Peter the Great, 172, 262
Peter, Metropolitan, 29
Petrovitch, Ivan, Pskov defended by, 322
Phéodonite, monk, 30, 32
Philip and Mary of England, Ivan's relations with, 275-277
Philip, Metropolitan, 248, 249
Philip II., 183, 270
Photius, 63, 343
Pielten, 187
Pierling, Father, 125, 218, 327, 337, 338, 341
Piésnoché, monastery of, 225
Piétchora, 53
Pilten, 192, 214
Pimenius, Archbishop, betrayal of, 250-252 ; exile of, 256
Piotrkow, town of, 184
Piotrowski, Abbé, reference to, 322-325, 334, 342
Piskorka, the, 352
Pissemski, Feodor Andréiévitch, envoy, 318-320
Feodor Ivanovitch, 285, 286
Pius V., Pope, 326
Pivov, Roman Mikhaïlovitch, envoy, 315
Plague, visitations of, 59
Platonov, Monsieur, 134, 242
Plettenberg, Walter von, 176
Podsoch, Lake of, 316
Pogodine, 41, 263
Pogoriélov, 396
Poland, army of, 302, 304-309, 314, 334
Black Cross Knights, opposition to, 174, 175
Denmark and, negotiations between, 191 ; Polish - Danish alliance, 195
Henri de Valois elected King, 209
Ivan's candidature, 205-209, 211 ; wars with, 170 ; relations with, 188, 189, 198
literature of, 72
Lithuanian union, 194
Livonia and, relations between, 177, 184, 186
Possevino's attempt to reconcile, with Ivan, 331-337
Sweden and, relations between, 305, 341
throne of, candidates for, 205-209
Polkowski, Abbé, 307
Polnyié, class, 20
Polotsk, capture of, by Batory, 312-314 ; by Ivan, 190

Polotsk, democratic institutions in, 11
effects of capture, 314
plague in, 59
Pomiéchtchiki, class, 22, 23, 38, 141
Pomiéstia, class, 38, 39, 148
Popler Wilhelm, 327
Populations, early Russian, 6
Possevino, Moscow, at, 343-348
Papal envoy between Poland and Russia, 319, 321, 326, 330-337
peace of Iam-Zapolski, negotiator in, 337-343
policy of, 328
Possokha, 160, 161
Posting system, 58
Postnikov, artist, 83
Pouchkine, Evstafii Mikhaïlovitch, envoy, 318-320
Poudojersk, port of, 292
Poutivl, fort at, 149
Povalnyï obysk, trial by, 49
Pozniakov, Vassili, 217, 218
Pozwol, 176
Praviéji, punishment, 49, 50
Priïmkov family, 226
Prijov, Monsieur, 32
Printing, absence of, 72 ; introduction of, 218, 219
Procopius, reference to, 10
Pronsk, 170
Pronski, Prince George Ivanovitch, 168
Prince Vassili, 249, 264
Protestantism in Russia, 258
Protopopov, moneylender, 395
Prussia, religious Orders in, 174
Pskov, absolutism in, 11
early government of, 1, 3, 4, 47
exports of, 53, 54
pillage of, by Ivan IV., 254
plague in, 59
siege of, by Batory, 321-326
Punishments : Golovoïou, 49
Praviéje, 49, 50
Purkel, Siege of, 213
Pypine, Monsieur, 78

Radclyffe, Thomas, Earl of Sussex, 288
Radziwill, Nicholas, cession of Livonia demanded by, 186 ; successes of, 190
Palatine of Vilna, 313
Prince Albert, envoy, 336-343
Rafli, 70
Rambaud, 56
Randolph, Thomas, mission to Russia, 279
Razine, Stenka, 398
Reforms, religious, 150-156
'service' in, 148, 149

Reforms, the first, 138 et seq.
Rej, Polish writer, 72
Religion (see also Church), superstition in, 69-71 ; reform in, 150-156
Repnine, Prince Michael, death of, 228
Reveillé-Parise, 380
Revel, ceded to Denmark, 174 ; held by Sweden, 187, 192 ; nobility of, appeal to Swedish King, 185 ; Ivan's claim to, 194 ; defended by John, King of Sweden, 197 ; besieged by Magnus, 203, 204 ; Russian repulse at, 213
Revenue, amount of, 61
Revski, envoy, 199
Rezanov, Athanasius, envoy, 313
Rhode, Kersten, 198
Riapolovski family, the, 221
Riazan, early government of, 3 ; absolutism in, 11 ; exports of, 53
Richards, Anne, 284
Richter, reference to, 178
Riga, 173, 178, 184, 187, 194, 341
Ritter, Rudolph, 292
Rjev, 6
Rjevski,169
Roads, condition of, 57, 58
Roberts, James, interpreter, 290, 295
Rod, the, 70
Rodolfini, 322
Roeskilde, 197
Rojanitsy, the, 70
Rojkov, Monsieur, 18, 51, 395
Rokita, John, 258, 259
Rome, Ivan's appeal to, 318, 319
mediation between Batory and Ivan, 331-337
policy of, 328, 329, 342-344
Ronneburg, 214
Rostov, early government of, 3 ; forests of, elk in, 53 ; flight of Ivan to, 199
Duke of, 243
Rostovski, Prince Nikita Dmitriévitch, 226
Prince Simon, councillor, 224
Rouskaïa pravda, 47, 142
Rovinski, 131
Rudolph of Vienna, 213, 309
Rujen, Siege of, 213
Runnafer, 194
Rurik, 7, 120
Russell, Francis, Earl of Bedford, 288
Russian Company, the, 277-292
Russo-Swedish alliance, 194, 195
Rybnikov, 272, 375
Rye, culture of, 50, 52

Sables, export of, 53
Sabourov, Eudoxia, 375
Salomelouriévna, 118
Sadko, legend of, 25

St. Cyril, monastery of, 27, 30, 86, 225, 267, 395
St. Nicholas, port of, 57
St. Philip, martyrdom of, 34
Saïp-Ghireï, Moscow, attack on, 157, 158
Salt, export of, 54 ; works at Solovki, 4 ; at Astrakan, 397
Saltyk-Pravine, Ivan Ivanovitch, 350
Salza, Hermann von, 174
Samara, sulphur from, 54
Samarine, George, 263
San Giorgio, Cardinal, 66
Sanine, Ivan, Josoph Volotski, 87, 88, 90
Sapiéha, Andrew, 303
Sartchevski, 265
Savine, England, embassy to, 280-284
Schah-Ali, or Schig-Aleï, 157, 158 ; punitive expedition to Livonia, 179
Schilling, 380
Schlichting, Albert, 268, 326
Schlitte, Hans, 177, 178, 218
Schnaase, 79
Seal-oil, export of, 53
Seal-skins, export of, 53
Secreta Secretorum, the, 153
Selim II., 199
Serebrianiki, class, 22
Serebrianyï, Vassili Siémiénovitch, 166
Serguiéïévitch, Monsieur, 19, 24, 35, 37, 44, 352
Serpoukhov, 6
Servants, treatment of, 76
Service, land, 38
    reorganization of the, 148, 149
Sforza, Bona, 184
Siabry, class, 44
Siberia, conquest of, 350, 351
Sibir, or Isker, 353
Siéra, 374
Siestra River, 171
Siéviéia province, 312
Sigismund-Augustus, King of Poland, alliance with Frederic II., 188
    character of, 184, 204
    Ivan and relations between, 176, 189-191
    Livonia, relations with, 184, 185 ; campaign against, 193
Silver, mining of, 350
Simbirsk, 3
Simon the Superb, 28
Simskii, Khabar, 368
Sinodik of the monastery of St. Cyril, 267
Sitski, Prince Ivan, 315
Sixtus IV., Pope, 117
Sixtus V., Pope, 348
Skarga, Rector of the College of Wilna, 72, 331

Skladniki, class, 44
Skobeltsyne, 211
Skomorokhy, 113
Skouratov, favourite, 239, 367, 371
Slavery, classes of slaves, 20
    laws for slaves, 24
    origin of, 21-23
Sloojilyié, class, 8, 22, 38, 41, 141
Smirnov, Monsieur, Consul, 297
Smolensk, democratic institutions at, 11
    early government of, 3
    exports of, 53, 54
    fortress of, 4
    plague at, 59
    Russian capture of, 190
Snitzpanner, 125
Sobakine, Marfa Vasiliévna, 372
Sobakine, Vassili Stepanovitch, 368
Social classes : despotic classification, 7-10
    peasants, the, 16-20
    serfs, 20-24
    the Church, 26-34
    townsfolk, the, 24-26
Sokol, taking of, 312
Solario, Pietro, 80
Solov, Praxevna, 375
Soloviéï, legend of, 25
Soloviov, 237, 263
Solovki, saltworks and fisheries of, 4, 5 ; monastery of, 248
Sorski, Nil, 32, 88, 89, 90, 139, 389
Sossiédy, class, 44
Soubatoï, 62, 63
Soudiébnik, the, of 1497, 8, 47, 142
Sougorski, Prince Zakhar Ivanovitch, 212, 268, 327
Soukine, Feodor Ivanovitch, envoy, 123, 189
Souzdal, absolutism in, 11
    Armenian workers employed at, 80
    art in, 81
Squirrel-skins used as currency, 60
Sreznievski, linguist, 217
Standish, Doctor, 110
Staraïa-Roussa, burning of, 316
    exports of, 54
    plague at, 59
Staritsa, 6, 250
Starodoub, 312
    Duke of, 243
Stassov, Monsieur, 79
State, Church and, 59, 60
Stengler, Fr., 77
Stettin, 192, 198
Stezyça, Diet of, 211
Stiépiénnaïa-Kniga, the, 71, 124, 134
Stoglav, the, 155, 156
Stoglavnyi-sobor, 150-156
Stoianov, Istoma, 123
Striéltsy, the, 159, 160

Strigolniki sect, the, 85, 86
Stroganov family, the, 59, 169, 243, 351, 352 ; charter granted to, 24 ; Cossacks enlisted by, 354, 355
Gregory Anikiév, 352, 353
James, 353
Sulphur, 54
Superstition, 69-71
Susza, magazine explosion at, 324
Sviajsk, 158, 163, 166 ; monastery of, 268
Sviazev, envoy, 336
Svir, 306
Sweden, Batory helped by, 316, 317
coalition against, 192
Denmark, treaty relations with, 198
Ivan IV., claims on, 196, 197 ; Swedish Ambassadors, treatment of, 199, 201 ; treaty relations with, 188, 195, 198 ; wars with, 170
Maximilian, manifesto against, 193
Livonia, possessions in, 191 ; successes in, 325, 328
Poland, treaty with, 305
Sylvester, Alexis Adachev, and, 132
council, member of, 224
Dmitri's succession, attitude towards, 225
'Domostroï,' author of, *see that title*
Ivan, relations with, 128-132
retirement and disgrace of, 226-228
Rostovski, intercession for, 226
work of, 131
Daniel, of Russian Company, 281, 282, 283
Sytine, Feodor, 114
Szadeczky, 215

Taïbougi family, the, 353
Taïninskoié, 240
Talbot, George, Earl of Shrewsbury, 288
Tallow, export of, 54
Tamas, Shah, 277
Tambov, 3
Tar, export of, 54
Tartar conquest, effects of, 156, 157
Tartar-Nogaïs tribe, 168
Tartary, trade with, 54 ; depredations of, 58 ; Tartar influences, 91 *et seq.*
Tatichtchev, 78
Taube, 202-204, 217
Taxes : land tax, 17
methods of imposing, 25, 39, 40
toll-bars and river dues, 56, 57

Tchadaiév, 84
Tcheliadnine, Ivan Petrovitch, death of, 247
Tchelobitnyi prikaz, 38
Tcheremisses tribe, 167, 352
Tchernigov, 3, 243
Tchetï-Minei, the, 72, 73, 100
Tchiéliadnine, 384
Tchikhatchev, 317
Tchine, the, origin, of, 36
Tchitcherine, Monsieur, 43
Tchoudov, monastery of, 248
Tchouvaches, tribe, 167
Telegda, Katherine, mother of Batory, 298
Telepniév, Prince Boris, death of, 256
Telepniév-Obolenski, Prince, 119, 120
Temnikov, fort at, 149
Temrioukovna, Maria, wife of Ivan IV., 240, 372
Terem, the, 97, 99, 104, 105, 111
Terpigorev, envoy, 178
Tetaldi, Giovanni, 112, 393
Theodore, Archbishop (Santabaren), 63
Thorn, town of, 175
Tiaglyié, class, 19
Tihkvine monastery, 372
Timofiéviev, Peter, typographer, 219
Tobolsk, government of, 350
Tolokno, drink, 112
Tolstoï, Alexis, 84, 237
Toporkov, Vassiane, 222, 225
Toropiéts, plague at, 59
Toula, 170
Trade, dues, effect on, 56, 57
Dutch competition, 297
Early English, in the East, 277-290
Europe, with, 54
exports and imports, 53, 54
fairs, 54-56
free, between England and Russia, established, 275-277 ; scope of, 278 ; fluctuations in, 279-290
routes, *Opritchniki*, effect on, 244
Tartary, with, 54
Traders, foreign, 55, 56
Trades, cause of non-development, 52 ; *Koustar*, 53
Travelling, posting system, 58
Treitchke, 175
Tremer, savant, 66
Trials, combat, by, 48, 49
Povalnyi obysk, the, 49
Triphonius, monk, 30
Trofinov, Andrew, envoy, 318
Troïtsa, monastery of, 27, 28, 44 ; library of, 64, 65 ; Ivan's offering to, 377
Troubetskoï, Prince Feodor M., 243, 295

Tsar, first use of title, 123-125
Tshoussova River, 3
Tsylma, silver formed on banks of, 60
Tula, 3
Tver, Duchy of, given to Tsar
    Simeon, 261
    early government of, 3, 6
    exports from, 53
    Opritchniki in, 244
Tviérdikov, 396
Tyjnov, 352
Tyrnov, 118

Uexkull, 173, 184
Ulfeld, 95

Valladolid, 270
Valouiév, historian, 42
Vardôhus, port of, 274
Varegians, enterprise of, 25
Vaśa, Gustavus, 185
Vaska Bouslaiév, legend of, 25
Vassili Blajennoï, the, 84
Vassili, bribery, attitude towards, 50
    conquests of, 3
    divorce of, 118 ; death of, 119
Vassiltchikov, Anne, 372-374
Venge, Veit, 394
Venice, Russian envoy at, 327
Verechtchaguine, Roman Olferiev,
    Russian envoy, 336, 341
Viatki, bribery, 50
Viaziémski, Prince Athanasius, 256,
    366, 367
Viazma, 53, 54, 243
Vichmoviétski family, 230
Vielije, town of, 340
Viélikaïa, valley of, 335, 340
Viélikié-Louki, 4 ; Batory's attack
    on, 314-316
Vienna, Ivan's relations with, 313
Viétchie, popular gatherings, 11,
    136
Vigenerius, reference to, 91
Viollet-le-Duc, 79, 81
Viskovatyi, Ivan Mikhaïlovitch,
    chancellor at Moscow, 275
    death of, 256
    Dmitri's succession, supporter
    of, 224
Vitebsk claimed by Ivan, 302
Vladimir, town of, 244
Vodskaïa-Piatina, the, 70
Volhynia, Prince of, 9
Vologda, early government of, 3
    exports from, 53
    Ivan's home at, 276, 364, 365
    Opritchniki in, 243
Volok-Lamskoii, monastery of, 30,
    87, 89
Volost, privileges of, 44

Volotski, Joseph, 87, 88, 90, 221,
    222
Volyniéts, Peter, 250, 251
von Bell, Philip Schal, 182
    Werner Schal, 182
von Buchau, Printz, Ivan's envoy,
    261, 381, 384
von Galen, Heinrich, 182
von Münchausen, Christopher, 186
    Johann, Bishop of Oesel, 186
von Münster, Marshal Gaspard,
    death of, 214
von Solms, Count Remhardt, 324
Von Turn, 117
von Valle, Johann, 292, 294
Vorobiévo, village of, 128, 129, 364
Vorotynski family, 230
    Prince Michael Ivanovitch, 164,
    200, 243 ; death of, 229
    Prince Vladimir, Dmitri's suc-
    cession, supporter of, 224
Vorontsov, Feodor Siémiénovitch,
    121-123
Voropaï, F., Polish-Lithuanian envoy
    to Ivan, 205-207
Votisks tribe, 167
Vottchiny, class, 22, 23, 38-40

Walrus teeth, export of, 54
Walsingham, Sir Francis, 287
War, council of, scope of, 36-38
    Office, character of, 35
Warsaw, 194
Wax, export of, 53
Wenden, town of, 191, 197, 214, 303
Wesemberg, 317
White Sea, fisheries of, 53, 54
Wicke, George, death of, 214
Wiek, 187
Wielhorski, Count, 297
Willoughby, Sir Hugh, 273-275
Wilna, printers at, 219 ; Academy
    of, 300
Winchester, Marquis of, 274
Wirland, 174, 185, 187
Wisniowiecki, Prince Dmitri, 170
Witold, military leader, 175
Wittenstein, 191, 192
Wolmar, 191, 214
Wolowicz, Chancellor, 313
Wolski, Peter Dunin, Bishop of
    Polotsk, 308
Woman, position of, 97-100 ; re-
    strictions of, 75

Zabiéline, Monsieur, 10, 131
Zadrouga, the, 107
Zakharine, Daniel Romanovitch, 179
    Nicholas, 333
    Nikita Romanovitch, 271, 290,
    292, 295, 366

Zakharine - Kochkine, Iouriévitch, 127
Zakharov, Vassili, 122
Zamoyski, 315, 316, 325, 337-343
Zamyslovski, Monsieur, 54
Zavolojskiié startsy, sect, 90
Zavolotché, 316

Zbaraski, Prince, Palatine of Braclaw, 316, 336, 337, 343
Zenge, Veit, 193, 218
Ziémchtchina, 245
Ziémskiié sobory, 136, 137
Zoubstov, 6
Zvenigorod, fort at, 149, 243

THE END